Major General Robert E. Rodes
of the Army of Northern Virginia

A Biography

Darrell L. Collins

SB
Savas Beatie
California

Cataloging-in-Publication Data is available from the Library of Congress.

ISBN-13: 978-1-61121-420-8 - CIP 2008298031

05 04 03 02 01 5 4 3 2 1
First trade paperback edition, first printing

SB

Savas Beatie
989 Governor Drive, Suite 102
El Dorado Hills, CA 95762
916-941-6896 / sales@savasbeatie.com
www.savasbeatie.com

Savas Beatie titles are available at special discounts for bulk purchases in the United States by corporations, institutions, and other organizations. For more details, please contact Savas Beatie, 989 Governor Drive, Suite 102, El Dorado Hills, CA 95762, or by email at sales@savasbeatie.com, or visit our website at www.savasbeatie.com.

Proudly printed in the United States of America.

To the loving and cherished
memory of Dad and Mama

Maj. Gen. Robert E. Rodes, Army of Northern Virginia

Virginia Military Institute

Contents

Contents (continued)

Maps

Photos and Illustrations

Photos and illustrations have been placed throughout
the book for the convenience of the readers.

In life, Robert E. Rodes was held in the highest regard by his contemporaries. Many went so far as to compare him favorably with Thomas "Stonewall" Jackson. "The sight of him," one proudly proclaimed, "was sure to extort a cheer which was rarely given to any besides Gen. Jackson." In death, Rodes' reputation rose to even greater heights among those who had known or served with him. "We have never suffered a greater loss save in the Great Jackson," declared Jedediah Hotchkiss, Jackson's renowned mapmaker. "Rodes was the best Division Commander in the Army of N. Va. & was worthy of & capable for any position in it."

But as time passed and memories faded, succeeding generations found it increasingly difficult to appreciate Rodes and his impact upon the era in which he lived. It was not until the beginning of the 21st Century, in 2000, that a full length biographical treatment of the increasingly obscure Civil War general appeared.[1] The paucity of biographical studies is explained at least in part by the behavior of Hortense, the young widow Rodes left behind when he fell at Third Winchester. "His private correspondence save a (precious) few letters," she confessed late in life, "I burned many years ago, and also his correspondence with brother officers. I kept a few momentos [sic] only."[2]

Many personal items, thankfully, escaped the grasp of Rodes' well-meaning wife and are preserved by institutions scattered across the country. Though perhaps not as revealing, or even as interesting, as confidential letters to a beloved spouse or "brother officers," these items nonetheless help construct a meaningful portrait of their primary subject. Surviving items include letters from Rodes to his father, friends, colleagues, and associates, as well as many of Rodes' official reports, both civilian and military. Of no less importance are the extant letters written to Rodes from many of these same sources. Finally, there are the letters, diary entries, reminiscences, memoirs, and testimonials written about Rodes by people who, in one way or another, knew him and what it was like to work with him, to break bread with him, to share their feelings with him, to serve under him, and to entrust their lives to him.

Pieced together, these sources present a man of remarkable intelligence, courage, and sensitivity. Yet he also was a surprisingly simple man. In both civilian and military life he lived by one word—discipline, a creed that earned him his fair share of detractors. "The stern military precision of Gen. Rodes," declared one observer, "were not such as to render him a favorite with a citizen soldiery." Though he might be "stern in the discharge of duty and in exacting it of others," as one contemporary described him, Rodes also was known as a man of "firmness tempered with kindness." With a reserved but "generous, cordial and lovable disposition" that was "soft and genial in his hours of ease and relaxation," Rodes knew how to draw the line between business and pleasure, duty and off-duty. Combined with the advantage of a striking personal appearance, these characteristics won him great loyalty, admiration and respect.[3]

As a commander on the defensive, Rodes proved extremely reliable, steady, persistent, and rock solid. On the offensive he was often cautious, and sometimes exceedingly so. Unlike the impetuous A. P. Hill, who was always ready to launch a devil-may-care assault, Rodes preferred not to strike until he had deployed his entire force. But when he unleashed his legions, Rodes did so with unrivaled ferocity, always leading, encouraging, and spurring on his men at great risk to his own personal safety. Rodes was in the thick of every combat and played a major role in nearly every battle fought by the Army of Northern Virginia, from the Peninsula Campaign in the spring of 1862 through Third Winchester in the fall of 1864.

If he could, Rodes might object to being the subject of a biography. It is even possible that he would not have agreed to be interviewed for one. In life, he had craved recognition, even glory, but he despised those who tried to promote themselves by anything other than their own achievements. The reputation of a man, the Lynchburg, Virginia, native firmly believed, should be formed more by his deeds than by his words.

Perhaps Hortense, who knew Robert Rodes better than anyone, may have realized the same thing when she cast most of her love's letters into the flames.

| Acknowledgments

It has taken many years to produce this book, and many people and institutions provided tremendous assistance along the way. Almost certainly I have forgotten to list someone who helped me, so if your name is not found here, please accept my apology and know that I will also appreciate your kindness and assistance, great or small, that helped me write this book.

I want to thank the very helpful staffs at the following institutions: Alabama Dept. of Archives & History, Birmingham Public Library, Auburn University Library, University of Alabama Libraries, Georgia Dept. of Archives & History, Maryland Historical Society, Duke University Libraries, North Carolina Dept. of Archives & History, University of North Carolina Libraries, U.S. Army Heritage Center, University of Virginia Libraries, Museum of the Confederacy, James Madison University Library, The Handley Regional Library in Winchester, Virginia Historical Society, Preston Library at the Virginia Military Institute, and the Virginia Tech. Libraries.

My publisher Savas Beatie is a first-class organization, and I want to thank everyone there for believing in this project. Managing Director Theodore "Ted" Savas in particular provided invaluable help and insights as this project developed. His editor Terry Johnston, formerly of *North and South Magazine*, did a superb job editing my work. I also wish to extend a hearty thanks to Lee Meredith for indexing my book.

Thanks also to Tim Reese for producing the excellent maps.

A very special thanks to Mary Rodes Dell, the great-great granddaughter of the subject of this book, for her very significant last-minute contributions in obtaining some very special photographs.

And of course, all is meaningless without Judith Ann.

Chapter 1

From Childhood to Manhood

After crossing the English Channel from Normandy in 1066 and successfully making his claim upon the English throne, William the Conqueror set out to measure the exploitable wealth of his hard-won domain. By means of a pervasive grand survey, he sought to identify every landowner within his new realm, as well as the value and extent of all their property. Completed in 1086, this remarkable record became known as the Domesday Book, so named because, like the Biblical Final Reckoning, it purported to judge all men impartially.

The Great Book included the names of Hugh and Wilmus, two Norman warriors upon whom the Conqueror had gratefully bestowed a land grant known as the "Moiety of Rode," which in time became the modern village of Rode, located near Macclesfield in the present County of Cheshire. In the centuries following the Conquest, the Rodes name and family spread from this area to flourish across the counties of Nottingham, Lincoln, York, and Derby, during which time one line gradually ascended into the lower ranks of English nobility.

The ascent began with Francis Rodes (1534-1591), whose rise to prominence included service as a Justice of the Court of Common Pleas and as a judge at the 1586 trial at Fotheringay of Mary, Queen of Scots. Such prominence enabled Francis to build in Derbyshire a fine estate he named Barlborough Hall, which eventually claimed "the unique fame of being equidistant from all places where English speaking children dwell." Upon Francis's death, Barlborough Hall went to his eldest son, John (1562-1639), one of seventeen children sired by two wives.

John Rodes married three times, served as the High Sheriff of Derbyshire, and in 1603 was knighted at the Tower of London. He left Barlborough Hall to his second son, Francis (1588-1645), who in 1641 was created a baronet. With the family estate having gone to an older brother, Sir Francis's son John (1620-?) slid into such an undistinguished and probably poor existence that his third son, Charles (1661-1719), decided to try for a better life across the sea in Virginia. Though it remains uncertain when exactly he arrived in the New World, we know that in 1695 he married in New Kent County.

In keeping with the early American tradition of moving westward when denied an inheritance, Charles's son John (1697-1775), born in the lower end of what is now Hanover County, acquired four hundred acres on the north fork of the Rockfish in Albemarle County, Virginia, in 1749, and established there a plantation he called "Midway." In 1756, John's son David (1731-1793), in turn, received from King George II a grant of several hundred acres on Moorman's River in Albemarle about ten miles northwest of Charlottesville. In addition to building up a fine plantation in this beautiful mountain setting, which he called "Walnut Grove," the ambitious David owned and operated a store and a mill, held the office of magistrate, and served as county sheriff.[1]

In late 1774, amid growing tensions with Great Britain, the citizens of Albemarle chose David to serve with ten others, including Thomas Jefferson, on a general committee originally set up to enforce local trade restrictions with the mother country. This group eventually became a quasi form of government that provided the county with order and stability during the ensuing turmoil of the American Revolution.

David Rodes, however, initially showed little enthusiasm for the new American cause. His local militia company drummed him out of its service for being one of only two cooler heads to advise against the prevailing rebellious sentiment, much of which was fueled by the recent outbreak of fighting at Lexington and Concord. The ardor of the day called for a march on Williamsburg to rescue the colony's powder and munitions that the appointed royal governor, Lord Dunmore, had seized and stored on a British naval vessel during the night of April 20-21, 1775. This disgrace, however, did not prevent David from continuing to prosper. By the end of the Revolution, the 1782 county tax records list him as the owner of seventeen slaves, twenty-five cattle, and eleven sheep.[2]

In 1793, David bequeathed his beloved "Walnut Grove" to his twenty-eight-year-old son Matthew (1765-1834). Had he lived, the father would have been proud to see Matthew appointed a magistrate in 1816. Had he lived a few years longer, the elder Rodes would have been very displeased with his son, who amassed a large debt that could be lifted with the humiliating sacrifice of selling "Walnut Grove" at public auction. However, David would have derived much satisfaction from seeing the family pride and heritage restored by his grandson and namesake.[3]

*   *   *

David Rodes was born at "Walnut Grove" on February 27, 1795, the oldest of ten children belonging to Matthew and Ann Blackwell Rodes (1774-1853). As indicated by his letters and the business he conducted in later life, David received a good education, probably from tutors and local private schools, as well as from the experience gained while a boy working in his grandfather's store. Though he saw no service in the conflict, David joined a local militia company during the War of 1812, rising at age nineteen to the rank of ensign. Having no taste for farm life, he left "Walnut Grove" in 1816 to take a position in Charlottesville as the deputy court clerk of Albemarle County. A few years later he moved farther away, some sixty miles south to become deputy clerk at the District Courthouse in Lynchburg.[4]

By the time of this move, David's father had come under extreme financial difficulties, resulting mainly from his using "Walnut Grove" as security against a number of unwise loans he allowed to go into default. In the spring of 1822, creditors brought a suit against Matthew that required, "for the benefit of the Commonwealth," the submission of the plantation to public sale. The auction took place on May 17 after having been delayed more than two weeks by the county sheriff "under the hope," he wrote David, "that, by such time, you will be enabled to interpose successfully in behalf of one who, I assure you, has, upon this melancholy occasion, the full tide of my sympathy." With his younger brother Robert, who continued to live on the plantation, David somehow managed, then and over the ensuing years, to keep "Walnut Grove" in the Rodes family and also to provide for their parents. "Whereas my sons David and Robert have for some years been purchasing my Estate at public sale made under execution at the suit of the Commonwealth," Matthew gratefully acknowledged in his will dated September 30, 1833, "and taken possession thereof & afforded me and family support based upon mutual agreements . . . I give them my land to be divided equally."[5]

Though he and his brother managed to make "Walnut Grove" sustainable by renting out portions of the vast estate, David seems to have considered the whole matter a great drain and annoyance. He broke with the then near-sacred tradition of honoring a paternal grandfather by refusing to name one of his sons

Matthew—a strong indication he was ashamed of his father for shoving the Rodes family to the edge of financial ruin. [6]

On November 21, 1822, David married eighteen-year-old Martha Ann Yancey, the belle of "Rothsay" plantation, located across the county line in Bedford. Martha was the daughter of Major Joel Yancey (1773-1838), a distinguished veteran of the War of 1812, and Nancy "Peggy" Burton, the daughter of Jesse Burton and Ann Hudson. [7]

Martha's American roots ran slightly deeper than those of her new husband. Her great-great-grandfather, Charles Yancey, arrived in Virginia from England about 1674. The Yanceys eventually settled in Louisa County, where Martha's father was born in 1773, nearly one year after the death of his own father, Joel Sr. When still a young man, Joel Jr. accepted from friends a commission to buy land in the Campbell/Bedford County area. While fulfilling that obligation, he demonstrated an enterprising streak by acquiring a sizable piece of land from Thomas Jefferson. In a grove of oaks near the roadside, he built an impressive brick home called "Rothsay." In this beautiful mountain setting Martha was born in December 1803. [8]

On January 5, 1824, Martha gave birth to her first child, Virginius Hudson (1824-1879), whom family and friends called "Gin." David soon realized that his new and growing family could not comfortably survive on the meager income of a court clerk. Over the next several years, he resourcefully supplemented his earnings by speculating in local real estate and by acquiring in Lynchburg a number of rental houses, efforts that, though somewhat risky and certainly troublesome, generally met with moderate success. Moreover, by drawing on the experience gained in his grandfather's store, David in the early 1830s opened his own establishment in partnership with Edward Burton, one of Martha's cousins. "Burton and Rodes" (later changed to "Rodes and Burton") sold cotton yarn, leather goods, and other dry goods. The two men took turns managing the store and traveling, Burton sometimes riding as far as Philadelphia and New York to acquire inventory. After a few years of modest success, the partners considered opening a second branch store in Martinsburg, but wisely decided against doing so when they determined they had little chance of effectively cutting into the competition there. Indeed, they had enough competition at home. Faced with as many as seventeen local competitors, their small enterprise in Lynchburg eventually began draining their resources. In 1843, they sold off their inventory to pay more than $2,000 to creditors and gave up the business for good. [9]

During this time David remained active in the local state militia, which met for drill on a regular (usually monthly) basis. By 1825, he had risen to the rank of captain of the 2nd Battalion of the 53rd Virginia Regiment. In that capacity on July 20, 1826, he served as one of seven marshals in a Lynchburg memorial procession honoring former presidents Thomas Jefferson and John Adams, both of whom had died on the fourth day of that month. On August 7, David became one of four men appointed to appraise Jefferson's Campbell County properties, a job that took nearly four months to complete. By the end of the decade, David had received command of the entire 53rd Regiment. The promotion earned him the right to be addressed, in both correspondence and polite conversation, as "Colonel Rodes." In 1834, Governor John Floyd appointed David a brigadier general, largely a position of honor, in command of the Twelfth Brigade. The organization consisted of the 53rd, 117th, and 131st regiments of Virginia militia. Then as "Captain Rodes" had done for Thomas Jefferson and John Adams in 1826, "General Rodes" on July 15, 1834, performed a similar duty by serving as marshal of a memorial service honoring the recently deceased (May 20) Marquis de Lafayette, for whom the "General" later would name a son.[10]

David's community involvement also included a brief tenure in 1827 as clerk on the town council. His term of service saw the successful passage, after much debate and controversy, of a bill authorizing the borrowing of $50,000 to build a dam at nearby Little River in order to create a 250-foot deep reservoir of fresh water, a project that consumed two years.[11]

Meanwhile, on April 4, 1827, Martha gave birth to the couple's second child, Ann Maria (1827-1847). Nearly two years later, on March 29, 1829, the Rodes family expanded yet again. The proud parents named the infant after David's brother Robert, who lived at "Walnut Grove," and Martha's brother Robert Yancey, who eventually settled in Missouri, about four miles from the Mississippi River, where he scratched out a hard life as a farmer. Though most sources agree that Robert Emmett Rodes was born in Lynchburg, at least one lists his birthplace near Liberty in Bedford County. If true, this might be explained by a desire of Martha, for whatever reason, to have this child at "Rothsay." One other minor discrepancy concerns the actual date of birth. A seemingly reliable source, Rodes' gravestone, declares he was born on March 30. However, the stone was erected quite some time after his death, and the marker conflicts with other documents that give the date as the 29th.[12]

Though it remains uncertain where exactly in Lynchburg the Rodes' lived at the time of Robert's birth, it is known that when the boy was four years old his father moved the family to a house on Harrison Street atop Federal Hill, overlooking the growing town. On October 21, 1833, David paid $900 for a beautiful five-bay facade, forty-five foot long, three-story house that would remain in the family for the next forty-six years. David apparently took advantage of a depressed local housing market. In 1816, the original owner, William B. Roane, paid $1,000 to city founder John Lynch for just the two-lot building site.[13]

That hilltop site marked the beginning of an elevated plain that rose dramatically a few hundred feet from the town below. The slope of the site left the lowest, or basement, level of the house fully above ground on one side, which added to the overall grand appearance of the place. The front boasted a strikingly elegant but simple main doorway approached by a double stairway rising from opposite ends. The door opened onto a central hallway flanked by a large room on either side. Throughout, the inside displayed impressive and elegant woodwork of the period. David later gave the house a three-story L-shaped addition and a back porch for each of the two top levels. Clearly, David Rodes was doing quite well.[14]

The porches built onto the house afforded a magnificent view of Lynchburg, which was founded in 1786 when the Virginia General Assembly granted John Lynch forty-five acres along the rocky, tree-lined banks of the James River. By the time of Robert's birth, the "City of Hills" had grown into a bustling and prosperous community.

In 1830, the town contained 4,628 people numbering 2,492 whites, 1,751 slaves, and 385 free blacks. And though it did not have its own opera house, that year the city proudly welcomed at the Masonic Lodge a performance by the New Orleans Opera Troupe. The Rodes family received a special invitation to attend from the company manager.[15]

By 1830, the fertile soil of the vast surrounding Virginia countryside had turned Lynchburg—"Tobacco Town"—into the nation's tobacco capital. Demand for the crop was so great that in 1832, the Virginia General Assembly authorized the construction of a canal stretching from Lynchburg to Richmond. The bureaucrats hoped to expedite the shipment east of massive quantities of the weed to satisfy growing demand. The completion in 1840 of the 147-mile waterway with its fifty- two locks, and the subsequent arrival of the Southside Railroad twelve years later, brought significant wealth to Lynchburg. By 1860, the town had one of the highest per capita incomes of any city in the United States. How much any of this may have interested young Robert Rodes is unclear, but one day the canal and the railroad would play important roles in the development of his life and career.[16]

Robert was fortunate enough to be born into a close and loving family. While traveling in the spring of 1833 through Virginia's northern counties buying goods for the store, his father David penned a revealing letter. "The pleasure a husband and father feels upon receiving the outpourings of a faithful heart," he tenderly told Martha, "when at a distance from all that is dear to him, can only be justly appreciated by one similarly situated." The "outpourings," however, included pangs of despair at having to run the house without David while pregnant with their fourth child, Sarah (Sally) Harrison (1833-1886), who would be born that August. "My dear Martha," David added by way of trying to comfort her, "keep your spirits up, be firm under your afflictions & household concerns. I have got on so far very well—no accidents—in good health—little gloomy at times when I think of my wife & children." While thinking of his children, he closed with, "adieu my dear Martha—kiss Ann Maria & <u>Sam Crack</u> [Robert]—not forgetting papas Scholar [Virginius]."[17]

Four-year-old Robert seems to have earned the nickname "Sam Crack" when he amused his father by mispronouncing Sam McCackle, a neighbor of the Rodes' and a family business associate. Another early childhood pet name, which remained with Robert far longer than he wanted, grew out of his unusual fondness for certain baked goods. "Oh how is Bob the Bread Eater," his uncle Joel Yancey teasingly wrote from New Orleans in April 1837. "[G]ive my love to him and tell him he had better come here, that we eat English bread here altogether[,] black and white."[18]

Virginius's nickname, "papas Scholar," is indicative of the value his father placed on education and learning. In 1839, Washington Macon College at Washington, Virginia, elected David an honorary member of its Literary Society. David and Martha saw to it that the Rodes children received a good education, primarily from local private schools in Lynchburg. A five-month semester at one of the many institutions on what became known by 1830 as School Street typically cost each student fifteen dollars. Robert is known to have attended one of the best of these institutions, a school for boys located in the basement of a Baptist church run by a Mr. John Cary, whose impressive credentials included a university degree.[19]

Robert's education also included unavoidable exposure to the system of negro slavery and the Southern code of race relations. Unlike most white children growing up in the region at the time, Robert had the "advantage" of being intimately involved with that system and code, for Lynchburg's slave owners included David Rodes. He inherited a few slaves when Martha's father died in 1838, but most he acquired with his own earnings. Being town dwellers, however, the Rodes family did not require many slaves. David usually owned a few household servants, but others he treated as commodities to be used for financial gain. In 1831, for example, he paid $62 "and one negro girl named Matilda" for a lot on "10th Street and 2nd Alley." In 1860, when the census showed that he owned seven slaves, David freed his fifty-five-year-old slave George when the man's wife paid him $300. How she managed to raise the incredible sum is unknown. Robert grew up in an environment that accepted slavery as the natural order of things. There is nothing in the historical record to suggest that he raised any moral questions regarding the institution.[20]

By every objective indicator, Robert was an active, healthy youth who enjoyed playing outside. One of his best childhood friends was Kirkwood Otey, who lived nearby in a fine house on Federal Street on a block adjoining Harrison. The two boys remained fast friends well into adulthood, and went away together to school.[21]

* * *

In the late 1820s, "Colonel" Rodes used his influence, presumably through his congressman, to secure the appointment of Robert Burton (possibly the son of business partner Edward) to the United States Military Academy at West Point. How much more influence would his honorary rank of "General" have in securing an appointment to the academy for his own son, Virginius?[22]

David Rodes held the highest regard for West Point, not only because it provided an excellent and free education, but because his own long and active service in the state militia had convinced him of the great benefits to be derived from military discipline. The law, however, allowed but one annual appointment per congressional district. By the time David submitted an application on behalf of Virginius, the opening in his district had gone to another boy. Disappointed but not disheartened, David turned to a second option, which promised Virginius not only a quality education in a disciplined setting, but the added benefit of keeping the young man fairly close to home.[23]

In February 1816, the Virginia General Assembly authorized the construction of three new arsenals for the purpose of providing a convenient supply of arms to militia companies located in Richmond and in some of the state's remoter western counties. That year the state paid $278.62 for a seven-acre building site located on a ridge above Jordan's Point near Lexington in the upper Shenandoah Valley. It erected there a four-story, sixty-foot square structure that resembled a fortress, complete with two-foot thick brick walls, narrow window embrasures, and a ten- foot high surrounding brick wall. In 1818, the site began receiving weapons and powder transferred in from Richmond. The new arsenal held up to 20,000 stand of arms, all guarded by a militia captain, one sergeant, two or three corporals, and ten to thirteen privates. In time, however, the garrison, "having nothing to do beyond a little guard duty," wrote a future cadet, "fell into bad habits, committed petty depredations, and became drunken and worthless." By 1834, the exasperated citizens of Lexington had had enough. Late that year they launched a movement to have the arsenal replaced by "a military and scientific school" modeled upon the academy at West Point.[24]

Recognizing the problems rampant at the arsenal, the General Assembly responded quickly. In early 1835 it created a five-man Board of Directors presided over by Claudius Crozet, a veteran of Napoleon's 1812 Russian Campaign and a renowned engineer. It was left to Crozet to develop the Lexington site into a military academy. In doing so, legislators hoped to gain the additional advantage of acquiring for Virginia a core of well-trained militia who, by being utilized while cadets to guard the armory, would also save the state money that could be used to help financially strapped families send qualified boys to the institute. After two years spent modifying the arsenal to accommodate classrooms, and constructing an eighteen-room dormitory just outside the lower 153-foot long east-west portion of the surrounding wall, the Virginia Military Institute opened its doors. Its first cadets numbered all of twenty-eight, and they began their studies on November 11, 1839.[25]

VMI's superintendent position carried with it the rank of colonel of state militia. The first to hold this position was a twenty-seven-year-old named Francis Henney Smith. A Virginia native, Smith ranked fifth in the West Point graduating class of 1833 and had most recently served as a professor of mathematics at Hampden-Sydney College. With great distinction, Smith held the superintendent job for the next fifty years, during which time he shaped the character, development, and destiny of VMI.[26]

Though a great admirer of his West Point alma mater, Smith considered VMI's military training and discipline as subordinate to the school's primary mission of preparing men to be teachers of science and mathematics. Convinced that students must learn to be efficient and useful, he daringly broke with the traditional acceptance of classical and metaphysical subjects. He took pride in the fact that, unlike most other institutions of higher learning, VMI did not have Greek classes. With its heaviest emphasis on math, the curricula included sciences, languages, military tactics, and drill. As far as Smith was concerned, the institute's mandate was to promote the development of proper character and moral values, which he strongly believed could not be accomplished without the inspiration of an abiding religious faith. At VMI he made Sunday church attendance compulsory, encouraged frequent prayer meetings, conducted informal Bible classes in his office, and established the VMI tradition of presenting each graduate with a diploma and a Bible.

Smith's belief in the importance of religion and discipline in an educational setting harmonized perfectly with the VMI Board of Visitors first annual report to the governor: "At an age when passions are yet unmitigated by the lessons of experience, it is generally imprudent to trust to the self-government of a young man. Habits of unrestrained indulgence have frequently laid the foundation of ruin of youths . . . . The wise and prudent parent will choose for his son that education which will import to him habits of order and regularity."[27]

In the summer of 1840, sixteen-year-old Virginius and fifty-five other boys entered this demanding setting to begin the first of a three-year program at the new institute. Virginius did well in his studies, and he seems generally to have liked the cadet life, particularly the camp outs and field trips taken each summer between semesters. He greatly missed his family, however, especially his little brother. "I have been waiting with impatience," the young student wrote home on May 8, 1841, "for an answer to my letter to Bob."[28]

That summer, the boys' mother Martha fell ill. Exactly how ill is unclear, but she may have been unwell for some time. Back in October 1837, for example, her brother Joel Yancey wrote from New Orleans to express concern about her health. He encouraged her not to "give up to low spirits." And nearly two years later, Martha's cousin in Bedford did the same. "The last accounts I had of your health," she wrote in July 1841, "you were not well."[29]

Virginius wished he somehow could help. "I should like Mama to try what good this side of [the] Va mountains could do for her by means of its splendid scenery its limestone waters and its pure mountain breezes," he wrote home from "Camp Rutherford" on August 14, 1841.

In the same letter, the homesick young cadet gave his twelve-year- old brother some playful scolding, even going so far as to call him by his detested childhood pet name. "However I had like to have forgotten [to] rate Bob soundly for treating me as shamefully as he did in writing me a few lines and then throwing down his pen and going out to play with Kirk Otey: so that as a punishment to his pride tell [him] I say he is a real <u>bread eater</u> and that I hold myself responsible to him for applying to him this ignoble epithet. Tell him if he does not write me immediately that I will make it my business to pull his nose for him."[30]

That winter, an opening at West Point suddenly became available when a boy from Amherst County, within the Rodes' congressional district, unexpectedly gave up his appointment. On January 20, 1842, Virginius excitedly wrote home to ask his father to reapply for him. Because many other boys also were interested, he begged his father to hurry, "if it still meets with your approbation that I go to West Pt." He added in closing, "We have commenced study today, and you can depend we _have_ all of us pretty long faces after having been enjoying ourselves so long eating pound cakes to have to return to old Mathematicks dry bread and _beef beef beef_."[31]

Despite whatever favorable opinion the elder Rodes held of VMI, he obviously preferred West Point for his son. He did indeed hurry an application to Congressman Walter Coles, who proved equally prompt in his reply. "This business of nominating cadets for West Point," the representative complained in a February 5 letter to David, "has been a matter for which I have received perhaps fewer thanks, and more complaints then for any thing else I have to do." Then Coles went on to explain why he refused to nominate Virginius. "Lynchburg & Campbell have furnished all the young men who have been at the Institution [West Point] for more than twelve years, this has been a subject of just complaint, and I regret to have to say to you (what I have said to several other applicants from the same quarter) that I do not feel myself at liberty longer to defer the claims of the other two counties of the District."[32]

His West Point dream shattered a second time, Virginius buckled down for the long haul at VMI. He graduated with distinction, ranking eighth in the class of 1843. The July 4 graduation ceremony, however, was not the happy occasion he had expected it would be, for but a few weeks earlier his mother Martha had died at the age of forty. She was buried in the Presbyterian Cemetery on the edge of town. The loss devastated the family.[33]

After graduation, Virginius—who would remain a life-long bachelor, apparently having cared in his youth for but one young lady— left almost immediately for New Orleans. He took a job there for $1,000 a year working for his uncle Charles Yancey, a tobacco broker. Still, Virginius craved letters from home; his younger brother, however, continued to neglect him. "Bob is in arrears to me," he complained to his father in August 1847. "[P]lease remind him in your letter that I am waiting patiently for an answer to my letter."[34]

With Virginius now a VMI graduate and working in Louisiana, the time had come for David to consider Robert's future education. Having been twice turned down in applying for Virginius to West Point, the second time by an irate congressman who made it clear that Lynchburg and Campbell County had supplied more than their fair share of boys from his district, David decided to pursue a different option. Following in the footsteps of his brother, sixteen-year-old Robert entered VMI in July 1845.

Like so many children away from home for the first time, young Robert experienced a difficult period of adjustment. The strict regimen at VMI, however, allowed little time for the luxury of brooding about one's change of circumstances. The routine for cadets called for reveille at 5:30 a.m. (6:00 a.m. Nov. 1 to March 1), breakfast at 7:00 a.m., classes from 8:00 a.m. till dinner at 1:00 p.m., classes again from 2:00 p.m. to 4:00 p.m., followed by drill, parade thirty minutes before sundown, then supper followed by call to quarters thirty minutes after return from supper. Tattoo was played at 9:30 p.m. sharp, with taps following one-half hour later. Moreover, a strict code of conduct required cadets to keep themselves and their dorm rooms neat and orderly at all times, and forbade them, among other things, from having waiters or slaves, or horses or dogs. They were also forbidden from using tobacco, playing cards or dueling. The boys lived in an eighteen-room barracks, heated by wood stoves and illuminated by oil-burning lamps. The cadets cut and drew the wood from a huge supply behind the barracks, which local merchants delivered at prices generally costing VMI $2.20 a cord for oak to $2.40 for hickory. Oil for lamps the boys drew from a storeroom every Saturday.[35]

Based on the views expressed by those who knew him later in life, it is safe to conclude that Robert already possessed the personality traits he would carry for the rest of his life. He was somewhat reserved, unpretentious but extremely proud, very loyal, and generally quite pleasant in manner. His fellow cadets considered him a good, fun-loving companion who never neglected his military duties and studies. Robert easily made friends at VMI; many remained in contact with him throughout the remainder of his life. His classmates that first year included several young men who later worked with him on railroads and/or who served with him in the army, including James M. Corry, Charles V. Winfree, George W. Robertson, Briscoe G. Baldwin, R. Ross, Charles A. Derby, and boyhood friend Kirk Otey.[36]

In his light-gray uniform, complete with a single-breasted coatee of eight gilded buttons, a standard collar and four-inch cuffs, a tall cylinder- shaped hat with a pompon on top and the engineer plate in front, Robert adjusted reasonably well to VMI's strict regimen and military-style discipline. He met the institute's difficult intellectual challenges, though without exceptional distinction. He finished the 1845-46 academic year twentieth in a class of thirty, nine of the original thirty- nine boys having dropped out along the way. In Mathematics, which that first year included Algebra and Geometry, Rodes ranked thirteenth. In French he ranked eighth, in Drawing, which clearly was his best subject, Robert sat at the top of his class. He owed his relatively low overall standing to 110 demerits, resulting mostly from the improper care of his uniforms, which placed him twenty-fourth in Conduct. "He has not been extravagant," Colonel Smith explained to David Rodes, "his expenses having heretofore been kept within the estimate, but he is harder on clothes than Virginius, not as careful of them and hence, consumes more." However, Smith went on to reassure David, "I think he is gradually improving in his studies and standing and will in the end make a fine soldier and scholar."[37]

The thirty-five-year-old, gold-spectacled, tall, lithe, and by now prematurely gray Smith, knew what he was talking about. His attention to the progress of each cadet had become renowned for proving so thorough and personal as to have the effect of being "at once a warning and stimulus to the boy."[38]

Through the severe winter of 1846-47, the increased difficulty of the second-year course studies accounted in large measure for the reduction of the class from thirty to twenty-five young men. Of these, Robert placed sixteenth, having been also promoted sergeant in the corps of cadets. Once again, demerits kept him from placing higher. In Mathematics, which included geometry and calculus, he ranked fourth, in French sixth, Latin fourteenth, Drawing third, and Conduct twenty- second.[39]

With classes over, Rodes and his fellow cadets went into the traditional, and generally well-liked, summer camp, which that year went by the name of Camp Braxton in honor of the president of the Board of Visitors. The purpose of these camps was to provide a military-like experience of "being in the field." As such, a professor with the rank of captain or higher ran them under a fairly strict regimen, complete with drill and inspections. This summer, however, the boys lost no time in taking advantage of "the inability of Captain Richardson to handle the disciplinary features of camp life." Their mischievous behavior included "pillaging Colonel Caruther's corn field," and "killing and taking Sam'l Moore's and others chickens." Moreover, the upperclassmen took great delight in subjecting the new plebes to "quizzing," which involved such high jinks as blanket stealing and being dragged from a tent when asleep. A favorite prank was called "Marching on Orderly," whereby new cadets were told to put on their best clothes to begin their duties as orderlies the following Sunday. After marching around camp for some time, usually in groups of five or six, the boys were brought to a halt in front of a specific tent, whereupon older cadets sprang out and drenched them with buckets of water.

"The screws have gotten loose,"wrote professor and board member Major Dorman with some alarm to the vacationing Superintendent Smith. "[C]ome quick and tighten them." It is not known if Rodes participated in any of what Dorman labeled "Depredations, affecting seriously the reputation of the corps," but the number of conduct demerits he had earned the previous semester suggest he may well have been involved. It also is possible the conduct and fate of Captain Richardson, who left VMI a few months later, taught him a great lesson regarding the value of discipline.[40]

Rodes also witnessed the growth of VMI during that summer of 1847, including the completion of the superintendent's house and the L- shaped, ten-room extension of the barracks. Almost certainly he could not have escaped participating in some of the many campus discussions concerning the war raging with Mexico.[41]

In his third, final, and toughest year, Rodes rose to the rank of lieutenant, a high honor among cadets. He graduated a respectable tenth in a class of twenty-four. In Mathematics he placed fourth, in French sixth, Latin thirteenth, Drawing third, Natural Philosophy (physics) third, Chemistry third, Engineering (Civil and Military) fourth, English fourth, and Tactics second. He received 159 demerits. On Tuesday, July 4, 1848, a moving ceremony took place in the Presbyterian Church in Lexington. Colonel Smith handed a diploma and a Bible to Rodes, who by this time was a handsome six-foot tall, blond haired, blue eyed, athletic-looking nineteen-year-old. The young man would always cherish his three years spent at VMI.[42]

Back home, meanwhile, Robert's family underwent significant changes. On May 12, 1846, his fifty-one-year-old father remarried, to twenty-eight-year-old Francis (Fannie) Louisa Penn (1818-1888). Their first child, Lucy Steptoe (1847-1894), arrived a year later, followed the year after that by Lafayette Penn (1848-1894). In 1847, Robert's oldest sister, twenty-year-old Ann Maria, died suddenly of fever after three- and-a-half years of marriage to Maurice Langhorne of Lynchburg. They had two children, Maurice Jr. and Allen Rodes, the latter of whom died before reaching his second birthday.[43]

With VMI behind him, Rodes faced the difficult question of what to do with the rest of his life. Much as it had before he went to VMI, the answer remained largely in the hands of his still-domineering father. David was satisfied by what he perceived as Smith's molding of his son into a man. "I am highly pleased to learn from your letter that my boy is getting on well and I ought to be proud of him," he wrote Colonel Smith that May. "You have my grateful heartfelt thanks for your individual personal attention to him whilst under your rule."

Though David indeed was proud of his son, he remained concerned about his future, having no idea what Robert should do, nor professing to know what he was qualified to do. The course finally chosen proved somewhat unorthodox. Despite having failed to get his sons into the U.S. Military Academy at West Point, David in February supported Robert's decision—indeed he may have been the main inspiration of it—to apply for a commission in the U.S. Army. With the war in Mexico still underway, David and Robert perhaps believed the Army was in need of officers. Robert, too, probably hoped to see action before it ended.[44]

The elder Rodes turned to Colonel Smith for a letter of recommendation. The answer probably was not what David expected to hear. "While I hope if it be your desire he may succeed," Smith replied, "I always feel reluctant to see a young man of talent enter the Service. For, if he seeks promotion, he must get it through political influence, and if a mere livelihood, there are a thousand pursuits which are more agreeable. I speak, General, as an old soldier, and from the lessons which experience has taught me." Smith then added, "I can recommend Robert very highly, and indeed so much do I esteem his qualities as an officer that I should be pleased to retain him here as an assistant after he graduates."[45]

Despite his reservations, that same day Smith wrote to Congressman Thomas S. Bocock:

> I am requested to write to you on behalf of Robert E. Rodes, a son of Genl. David Rodes of Lynchburg, who is desirous of obtaining a commission in the U.S. A[rmy]. I do so with great pleasure. Young Rodes graduates here in July, and had maintained a position near the top of his class. As an officer, I have rarely seen his equal, and I consider him qualified in a preeminent degree for the post which he so desires. So highly do I value his service, that I should esteem this Institute fortunate, if we can secure him as an assistant after he graduates."[46]

A week later, Bocock received a second letter of recommendation from Robert's uncle, William Yancey of Lynchburg: "Mr. Rodes is a young man of unsurpassed moral worth and fine talent and if successful in his application I doubt not will prove an ornament to the service. He has a peculiar aptitude for military life, has devoted the last two or three years to the study of the profession at the Virginia Mil. Institute."[47]

Despite these glowing recommendations, the swift and successful conclusion of the Mexican War in the spring of 1848 brought with it the predictable denial of Robert's application. The few officers the small peacetime Army needed would come from the graduates of West Point.

David explored other possibilities. Through personal connections, he secured for Robert an appointment as a clerk, like himself, in a Richmond court. That option, possibly at Robert's insistence, fell through. David next wrote Martha's brother, Robert Yancey, to inquire if Missouri might hold any opportunities for Robert as a teacher, a surveyor, or even as a preacher. "I should rejoice to see your son Bob here," Yancey's reply began with deceptive encouragement. "We need teachers, but are too poor to pay much, and as for surveyors is he woodsman enough? As for preaching, such as we occasionally have among us wear good clothes and get their share of 'corn bread and common doings' and sometimes of 'flour . . . and chicken fixins.' I am afraid [however] he would . . . not hold the candle, or as a hunter once told [me], that a Virginia gentleman was of no more use here than a dog at a fishing place."[48]

With Missouri holding little appeal to the "Virginia gentleman," attention turned to Colonel Smith's "attempt to gain him as an assistant upon graduation." For Robert, this proved the most desirable option and one he never abandoned, his greatest hope: to become a professor at VMI. "If you can give Robert an office or place in the Institute when he graduates," David wrote the colonel,

> suited to his Capacity and talents, & will be sufficient to support him, & at the same time, so situated as to be improving his education, I shall be very thankful for it. I had intended if I was able to give him a year or two at the University [of Virginia], but my resources have been so crippled by the failure of my Judge to do business in my court, for a year or two, I am forced to give up the pretention [sic]. I feel deep solicitude for his future success, & would have more confidence in his ability to command his future fortune with success, were he a year or two older."[49]

Smith was sincere in his wish to "gain him as an assistant." With the expansion of the course studies to a four-year program, beginning in the fall of 1848, VMI needed additional instructors. On graduation day, July 4, 1848, Smith issued Order #42: "Mr. R. E. Rodes, a recent graduate of the Institute having been appointed assistant professor with the rank of Lieutenant will be obeyed and respected accordingly. He is assigned to duty in the departments of Tactics, Phil. and Mathematics." The following day, Smith issued Order #43, which appointed Rodes adjutant of the institute. These orders are a strong testament to Rodes' obviously impressive potential as a scholar; Colonel Smith knew him as well as anyone, and did not hesitate to hire him on the day of his graduation.[50]

Before going into summer recess at "Camp Scott," named in honor of Mexican War hero General Winfield Scott, Rodes proudly traded in his cadet grays (in summer the cadets wore white trousers) for the blue uniform worn by the institute's professors and instructors which, except for the buttons bearing the Virginia seal, was modeled on the uniforms worn by officers in the U.S. Army Corps of Engineers.[51]

Rodes' first duty as a VMI adjutant included the fairly pleasant task of helping organize that summer's field trip. Each August, the corps marched to a nearby town, which helped the cadets gain valuable military field experience while promoting the image of the institute. On August 28, "Lieutenant" Rodes rode ahead to make arrangements for the corps to camp at Alum Springs the next day. After starting out early that morning, the cadets endured a hot and humid but generally enjoyable march over the mountains and arrived about 3:00 p.m. on the 29th. Rodes had a number of wagons filled with tents and rations waiting for them. The next day, the cadets performed inspection and drill, then went out to relax and enjoy the town for three or four days. On September 2, they received an invitation to visit Warm Springs, the Bath County seat, some thirty miles northwest of Lexington. Setting out at midnight so as to avoid the heat, the spirited boys, with much laughing, joking, and fife playing, greatly enjoyed the enchanting moonlit march. At Warm Springs they were allowed to take the baths free of charge. The night they left the town, Judge John W. Brockenbrough gave a ball in their honor, which, to the delight of the cadets, included many pretty local girls.[52]

Later that fall of 1848, Rodes sat in on VMI's first court-martial. One of the reasons for his presence was to acquaint faculty and staff with court procedure. Rodes listened attentively to charges brought against a cadet who, as a bystander to a fight between two other cadets, had picked up a stick and struck one of the combatants. The court unanimously voted for dismissal and recommended that the sentence be remitted, all of which was approved.[53]

For Rodes, 1848 ended on a peculiar note. In the December 19 issue of the Richmond *Whig and Public Advertiser*, and in the December 22 issue of the Richmond *Examiner*, appeared notices of his December 12 marriage to a Mary Jones of Lexington. No other record of this union exits. Rodes never mentioned it, and neither did his family or friends. A second marriage notice, under equally mysterious circumstances, was published nearly one year later in the October 13, 1849, issue of the Rockingham *Register and Village Advertiser*: "Rhodes: On the 2nd inst., in Lexington, Va., by the Rev. Mr. Willis, Lieut. R. Rhodes, assistant professor of Tactics in the Virginia Military Institute, to Miss Jane F. Baxter, all of that place." There is no record of such a marriage. No one mentions it in any correspondence, and a "Jane Baxter" does not appear in the census. This raises the possibility that Rodes may have been the victim of a pair of practical jokes perpetrated by some of VMI's more mischievous cadets.[54]

Meanwhile, the yet unmarried Rodes thoroughly enjoyed his first semester of teaching, which included assisting that year's forty-seven new cadets with math instruction. He gradually assumed the responsibilities of teaching chemistry and tactics to upperclassmen. The Board, in turn, was so pleased with Rodes that for the fall semester of 1849, it promoted the twenty-year-old to the rank of captain, with a small increase in salary, and assigned him as the Assistant Professor of Chemistry and Assistant Instructor of Tactics.[55]

The following semester did not go as smoothly. During a chemistry lab session Rodes suffered a severe mishap. The details of the accident are unclear, and the only known record of the event is a vague reference in a letter penned by Colonel Smith. The situation seems to have posed significant danger to Rodes and, for Smith at least temporarily, brought into question the young instructor's capacity to teach chemistry. The incident was the likely catalyst that prompted Rodes to gain approval to revise the manner of conducting lab sessions. The improvements that followed enhanced Rodes' reputation as a promising young teacher.[56]

The completion of the 1849-50 semester marked the eleventh year of VMI's existence. Applications increased every year, which inevitably led to overcrowding. Hoping to enhance the image of the institute by favorably impressing state officials—who were considering a pending piece of legislation to appropriate $46,000 for a new barracks to house the growing student body—Colonel Smith arranged to take the corps to Richmond to participate in the ceremonial laying of the cornerstone of the Washington Monument. Smith selected Major William Gilham, assisted by Captain Rodes and Lieutenant Massie, to lead the expedition.[57]

To many of the diversion-starved cadets, the coming journey seemed like the adventure of a lifetime. When the February 14th day of departure finally arrived, the boys eagerly arose at 3:00 a.m. to the sound of a driving rain and hailstorm. They packed their gear and took it down to the river by 5:00 a.m.. After a quick breakfast, they shoved off on four canal boats (Rodes was in charge of boat number two) and began their free passage up the James River and Kanawha Canal to Balcony Falls (Glasgow), and then down the North River to Lynchburg. Despite the beautiful mountain scenery, the forty-five-mile trip proved agonizingly slow. After passing Balcony Falls and stopping "somewhere in the Blue Ridge" to sleep, the cadets arrived in Lynchburg about 11:00 a.m. on the 15th. They leisurely spent the day in the city before transferring to the canal boats, where they spent that night in dock. Although the record is silent on this score, Rodes almost certainly would have taken the opportunity to spend some time with his family a short distance away on Harrison Street.

Starting out early on the 16th, the cadets slowly continued down the James River and arrived at Richmond about 9:00 a.m. Three days later, Colonel Smith, who had arrived several days earlier to confirm arrangements, met them at the dock and marched the boys to the governor's mansion. After Governor John B. Floyd delivered a brief welcoming speech, the cadets moved to their assigned quarters at Lafayette Hall.

On the evening of the 21st, Rodes and the corps received the special honor of marching up to the railroad station on Broad Street to meet President Zachary Taylor and his staff. With the state guard and other volunteer companies, they escorted the chief executive to the Exchange Hotel.

At 9:00 a.m. the following morning, Washington's birthday, Rodes and the corps marched back to the hotel to escort President Taylor to the great ceremony. "When the General [President Taylor] was ready," a cadet remembered, "we marched down to Main Street, where we formed procession and after marching through all the streets of importance (enough by the way to kill any common man) we at last reached Capitol Square." The president, Governor Floyd, and former president John Tyler each spoke to much applause from a dignitary-studded audience. When the ceremonies ended later that afternoon, the corps returned the president to the Exchange Hotel and continued on to Lafayette Hall, where the cadets arrived about 5:00 p.m.

Colonel Smith, however, had more public relations work in store for his students. Early the next morning they boarded the steamer "Curtis Peck" and sailed down the James to Norfolk. Several groups of well-wishers gathered along the riverbank delighted the boys with their applause as they slipped past. To the sound of salutary cannon fire, the cadets arrived in Norfolk about dusk. After leaving their gear at a place called Gray's Gunhouse, the boys dispersed throughout town to stay with citizens who had volunteered to take them in. In the ensuing days, the corps performed an impressive drill display, attended the Episcopal Church, and ate dinner at the local armory.

All too soon it was time to return to VMI. After going by steamer over to Petersburg, then by rail up to Richmond, Rodes and the corps began on March 6 the slow trip up the James to Lynchburg. When they arrived there on the 9th, the cadets were released from duty with instructions to make their own way back to Lexington and the institute; free passage by boat, however, had not been arranged. Most of the boys chose the least expensive method and walked forty-five miles alongside the river and canal. After spending some time with his family on Harrison Street, Rodes took charge of a large number of the walking cadets, camping with them overnight along the way back to Lexington.[58]

Soon after Rodes arrived on campus he learned that Colonel Smith's mission had already enjoyed success—the barracks appropriations bill was approved on March 8. On Thursday, July 4, 1850, the corner stone of the new barracks went into place which, in combination with the graduation ceremonies, made for a grand day. Capping the events were several prominent local speakers. Judge John W. Brockenbrough, the same man who two years before had given the cadets a fine ball at Warm Springs, however, cast something of a pall over the happy occasion, when he spoke ominously of "the dark cloud which [had] lowered in the North."[59]

Four days later came the shocking news of the death by illness of President Taylor, with whom the corps felt a special attachment as his escort and body guard in Richmond just five months before. A period of genuine morning began, marked by a day of half-hour gun salutes and the suspension of duty. A few weeks later, further gloom settled on campus when on August 13, George D. Chichester died of apoplexy. He was only the second cadet to die at VMI since it began operation.[60]

Despite whatever news might arrive, Rodes prepared for his third year as an instructor. Though he considered the job highly gratifying, he found it increasingly difficult to survive on its meager wages. To get by, he adopted such cost-saving measures as living on campus with two other assistant professors. This arrangement, however, had its disadvantages; one can endure only so long the annoying idiosyncrasies of three tightly cramped roommates. "We have dissolved our Mess," he told his father in a letter of May 21, 1850, "and are now boarding at the Hotel in town." Initially, Rodes tried to make this appear as though it had been a rational, mature decision. "We were led to this step by the desire to get rid of an immense deal of trouble necessarily encountered in catering & keeping the place & by the necessity which we all three felt for our taking more exercise," he explained. But the real reasons came out in his next, veiled statement: "I might mention another fact, which had possibly some little influence in the decision of ours but inasmuch as it effects each & all of us in the respect of our housekeeping & providing talents, I shall not mention it." The young bachelor closed on a lighter note: "Are any of the Lynchburg girls coming to the Cadet Ball next 4th of July," he asked, adding, "they ought to."[61]

Despite his sincere affection for VMI, Rodes harbored serious doubts about the institute's ability to provide him with a financially rewarding career. He explained as much to his father in the same letter of May 21:

> Since I wrote my last, I have consulted Maj. Gilham or rather got Maj. G[ilham] & Col. Smith to express themselves as to raising my salary next year. Maj. G[ilham] said to me positively that he thought my salary ought to be raised if I staid [sic] & that he thought that Col. S[mith] was in favor of it too. (The Col. wouldn't commit himself by the expression of opinion to me altho he did to the Major). I am in great hopes then from what each of them said that they will both recommend to the Board at its next annual meeting to raise my salary. The Board alone have the power of raising it. I would rather stay here next year with a raise in salary than do anything else. So if it is raised I shall remain here one more year at least. If there is any prospect of my securing a permanent situation year after next, I will remain with my present salary. So you see my inclination is strong toward staying here longer & the reason is that I am hardly fit now for anything except teaching & of course then I ought to follow that as a profession, why I ought to do so with as much advantage to myself as possible.[62]

The approach of Major Gilham about a raise in salary implies that Robert was reluctantly considering leaving VMI. He gave some thought to the possibility of studying mathematics and engineering at the University of Virginia at Charlottesville. He did not have complete confidence in this course of action, however, not only because it meant leaving VMI, but because it required more money than the impoverished teacher possessed. Once again, he turned to "Papa," as he touchingly called his father. "I hurried my last letter without even thinking about asking whether you could send me to the University (in the event of our deciding upon that plan)," he added with some deference, "without inconvenience to yourself & the rest of the family. Unless you could send me with <u>perfect</u> convenience I will not go one step, not even if it could be demonstrated clearly (which cannot be done I believe) that it would be the best plan for me to pursue." He concluded, "Let this then decide the matter—that under no circumstances will I go to the U—unless with entire convenience to yourself & family & not then unless it can be shown that I had better do so."[63]

Robert once again left the matter of his immediate future in the hands of his father. Perhaps he was seeking an excuse not to go to the university. Whatever his thoughts, in the spring of 1850 the twenty-one-year-old realized he was at the crossroads of three career options: If "Papa" could both afford it and "clearly demonstrate" the necessity, he would attend the University of Virginia; if an increase in salary was in the cards, he would remain at VMI for at least another year, or, if no increase in salary was forthcoming, he could remain at VMI if the institution offered him a "permanent position"—in other words, a full professorship—in the near future.

The first two options quickly proved unrealizable. David Rodes decided that, despite owning nine slaves worth several thousand dollars and real estate totaling some $15,000 more, he could not afford to send Robert to the university. Colonel Smith and the Board offered no indication that they intended to raise Robert's salary. And so the third and last, and probably most desirable, option tantalizingly dangled before Robert that fall.[64]

Back in 1848, the Board of Visitors voted to create a new chair for Chemistry, Geology, and Mineralogy. The Board hoped to relieve the overburdened Major William Gilham, who also was commandant of cadets and the instructor of tactics and every science course. When the Virginia General Assembly finally approved financial appropriations for the new chair two years later, the President of the Board, General Corbin Braxton, authorized Colonel Smith to find suitable candidates. Smith strongly preferred a West Point graduate, not only because of the great prestige such a man would bring to the institute, but because he wished to follow the example of the Academy of not making any of its graduates a professor for at least twenty years after the opening of VMI. After visiting both West Point and the War Department, Smith decided to recommend Major John James Peck of the U.S. Army. Except for the fact (at least for some people) that he was a Northerner, Peck possessed excellent qualifications. He graduated from West Point at the head of his class in the subjects to be taught at VMI, and enjoyed the added distinction of having twice been brevetted for bravery in the war with Mexico.[65]

To Smith's great consternation, he returned to VMI to discover that the Board was already considering someone else who did not possess the desired qualifications. "In Colonel Smith's absence," wrote Jennings Wise in his 1915 *Military History of The Virginia Military Institute*, "politics had entered into the matter, and strong pressure was being exerted upon the Board for the appointment of Captain Robert Emmet Rodes . . . who had many influential friends and was a man of exceptional ability."[66]

Despite having received little training in the subjects to be taught, Rodes jumped at the chance to fulfill one of his most cherished dreams, convinced that with hard work and intelligence he could overcome any lack of qualification. "The situation now at the disposal of the Board," he explained in writing to Colonel Smith on September 23, "is one which you will readily suppose would be to me in every way desirable." Rodes continued at length:

> It would be desirable to me in a pecuniary point of view, and especially so in affording me the opportunity & facilities of mental culture & improvement. May I ask then that you will do me the favor to suggest my name to the Board among those who may already have placed their applications in your hands. It may seem presumptuous of me to take this step, but knowing neither the character of those who may be applying nor the standard of qualification the Board may require I have thought it possible that I might by industry and perseverance be able to discharge the duties that may devolve upon me. I bring no recommendations, for the reasons that the Board will doubtless, as they ought, depend upon the character given me by you and the rest of the faculty, men under whose observation that character has been in a measure formed & that the majority of the Board have known me several years. I will not ask you to use your influence in my behalf when my application comes to be considered, for I know you have the interest of the Institute at heart, and

that that influence will be wielded so as best to promote this interest. If however by a review of the names of those who have applied you can conscientiously give me the weight of your influence I should be most happy & feel under obligation of no ordinary character.[67]

Though he very much liked Robert and highly respected his intelligence and moral character, the colonel remained adamantly opposed to giving him the new chair and forthrightly told his former student as much. "I received your note yesterday morning," Smith wrote Rodes on the 24th,

and lost no time in laying it before the Board. In doing so I said to them what I will now say to you—That I consider the Chair of Chemistry, Mineralogy and Geology in the present state of those sciences, as too important to be filled by one of your limited experience. In consequence of the pressure upon his department Maj. Gilham has only partly organized the studies in these branches and as a consequence those who have graduated here hitherto are only partially furnished with the Knowledge which would be required of one expected to teach them. Besides we are as an Institute still in our infancy and are hardly yet prepared to stand alone. If we attempt at so early a day to cut ourselves off from West Point we shall lose esteem with the Army and with the Scientific world and do ourselves irreparable injury. West Point was in existence 20 years before it relied upon its own graduates as Professors.

Smith then alluded to Rodes' chemistry mishap of the year before. "I had another apprehension in your case," he went on, "which I also expressed to the Board, and that was your health. To come up to measurable expectations you would have to busy yourself in the Laboratory. I was afraid from the experience of last year that you would run [great] risk."

Smith admitted to Rodes that he already had recommended another for the job. "With the expression of these views to the Board," Smith declared, "it gives me pleasure to express my confidence in your character and intellectual qualifications and my deep regret that my sense of duty to the Institute impelled me to urge the appt. of Bvt. Maj. J. J. Peck of the Army."

Smith closed with a deceptively reassuring note. "I cannot say what will be the Board's action," he confessed. "The subject came up to day. You have many warm friends in the Board and in the faculty all of whom are interested for you as a Virginian and as one of our own graduates. Should you be appointed we will hail it with pride and pleasure. And should another be preferred you must be satisfied that he was an older soldier if not a better."[68]

In an amazing testament to Rodes' impressive popularity at VMI and in a stunning rebuke to Colonel Smith, the Board brushed aside the superintendent's recommendation. The members cited the fact that Peck was too far away in Santa Fe and that he was not a Virginian. Its members voted four to one in favor of hiring Rodes, with Major Gilham alone voting for Peck.[69]

Contrary to his word to Rodes regarding the appointment, a frantic Smith did not "hail it with pride and pleasure." In fact, he stubbornly refused to accept the vote. If the Board did not like Peck, he argued vehemently, there yet remained other candidates with much stronger qualifications than Rodes. Moreover, the hard-pressed superintendent cleverly persuaded the reluctant Major Gilham to switch his assignment and take the chair of Chemistry, Mineralogy and Geology, hoping to increase the chances of attracting a West Point man to the much more appealing chair of Natural Philosophy. Smith's manipulations ultimately persuaded the Board to rescind its vote for Rodes and in his stead accept Alexander Stewart of the West Point class of 1842. When Stewart refused to leave his position as professor of mathematics and philosophy at Cumberland University, however, pressure resurfaced to hire Rodes.

Again a determined Smith acted swiftly to head off the movement. This time he turned to his friend Daniel Harvey Hill, a professor of mathematics at nearby Washington College who had been brevetted a major for gallantry in the Mexican War. To Smith's great relief, this tactic succeeded—at least in preventing Rodes from assuming the position. In February 1851, the Board accepted Professor Hill's recommendation and appointed Hill's future brother-in-law, Thomas J. Jackson, to the post.[70]

T hough extremely disappointed by the crushing career blow administered by Colonel Smith, Robert Rodes gave no outward indication of bitterness at the unexpected turn of events. He seems maturely and nobly to have accepted Smith's admonition that, with the institute having chosen another candidate, "you must be satisfied that he was an older soldier if not better." He held no grudge against the colonel, and indeed, remained on cordial terms with him for the rest of his life. Regardless of where fortune would lead Rodes, he continued to correspond with Smith, as a protégé to his mentor, as a son to his father, and as friend to friend. Remaining at VMI, however, was no longer a viable alternative. Rodes reluctantly left the beloved institution and accepted a position with the North River Navigation Company.

To provide the farmers and merchants of the central portion of Rockbridge County with a reliable two-way transportation system to and from markets in the east, the Virginia General Assembly in 1841 granted a charter for the construction of a twenty-mile canal stretching along the North (present day Maury) River from its mouth at the James River near Balcony Falls (Glasgow) to Lexington. The project did not get underway, however, until the James River and Kanawha Canal reached Balcony Falls in 1848, which opened the possibility of directly connecting central Rockbridge to Lynchburg and thence on to Richmond. After Rockbridge voters approved a new tax subscription, bonds were issued, the necessary funds were raised, and the North River Navigation Company formed in the summer of 1850.[1]

The company's chief engineer, Major Thomas H. Williamson, had been one of Rodes' instructors at VMI, where the two developed an abiding mutual respect. For seventy dollars a month, Rodes became one of two assistant engineers brought in by Williamson to help survey and mark out the course of the canal, whose plan included ten dams and twenty-three locks designed to raise and lower canal boats 188 vertical feet. Rodes probably intended to take the job as a means of gaining some practical engineering experience while earning extra money between semesters. But when VMI turned him down for the full professorship and Williamson left the project to resume his own post at the institute, Rodes that fall became the company's chief engineer.[2]

Rodes, in turn, took on an assistant and over the ensuing weeks continued working to meet the difficult challenge of surveying—and often re-surveying—an appropriate route for the canal. Work progressed rapidly, and in November Rodes began accepting construction bids, an aspect of the job he found particularly distasteful, mostly because it took him away from pure engineering. One of his "onerous" tasks in this regard included contracting with a Buena Vista, Virginia, company to provide cement at twenty-five cents a bushel.

With surveying finished by year's end, construction upstream from Balcony Falls began the following summer. By that time Rodes had turned his attention elsewhere to seek his fortune.[3]

*   *   *

Frustrated in his cherished ambition to be a VMI professor, and unhappy with the work on the North River Canal, Rodes finally got a break in the late fall of 1850 when he met Charles O. Sanford, the chief engineer of the Southside Railroad. Sanford easily persuaded the aspiring young engineer to come work for him, beginning on the first of the year. Rodes gladly made the leap, wisely reasoning that canals were dying as a form of transportation. "Railroads are now the great improvement of the day," he wrote his father, "and Canals are now unpopular in this Country."

In his eagerness to attach his star to "the great improvement of the day," Rodes did not bother to inquire about his new salary. He guessed it at a mere $500 a year plus expenses. "I could have gotten $900 here at least if I had staid [sic]," he wrote his father in reference to the North River Navigation Company, "but that I would not have done, for $1200 hardly." Extremely dissatisfied with his present job, working for an increasingly behind-the-times industry, Rodes "was fearful I would fail in my duties and thus damn my reputation at once." Ruining his name meant ruining his career. "I know if I wished to make a reputation rapidly or at all I must get on the most popular kind of improvement and that quickly."[4]

Preparations for the exciting new job included the removal of such anticipated encumbrances as his precious "fencing instruments" and his nine-year-old horse, both of which he sent home to Lynchburg under the care of a young slave named George. "He is a boy I have had with me on the N. River," Rodes told his father, without explaining how one so impoverished came into possession of such valuable property, "and who is going with me upon the SSR Rd. He once lived in Lbg [Lynchburg] & belonged to the late Mr. Lancaster." Rodes wanted his father to sell the horse, hopefully for $100. "I should like to have him rest two or three days tho before he is sold," he instructed his father, "as he will be seen to disadvantage unless my boy George is easier on him than Darkies generally are."[5]

Rodes needed that money, and more. After somehow getting stiffed by businessmen who failed to pay the rent on four of his slaves, John B. Lyle of Lexington became destitute, with most of his profits from past transactions having been donated to the church. The situation deeply moved Rodes (notwithstanding his apparent disregard for the slaves). He asked "Papa" for seventy-five dollars, roughly equivalent to a month of his own as-yet unearned salary, in order to help the proud slave owner by buying his watch, with the promise of repayment from his new wages. "Can you do it conveniently?" young Rodes inquired of his father. "If you cannot I beg of you papa to let me know candidly. I know you would if you could." There is no record of "Papa's" response, but it is unlikely he gave in to this whim, however good-hearted it may have been.[6]

Having thus settled his meager affairs in eager anticipation of taking a promising new direction in his career, Rodes in late December 1850 set off for Petersburg, the company headquarters of the Southside Railroad. After forming in 1846, the company three years later began surveying and locating a line stretching from Petersburg 123 miles to a hoped-for connection with the Virginia & Tennessee Railroad at Lynchburg. From there, it would run all the way to Memphis on the Mississippi River. As the fourth railroad to serve Petersburg, but the first to link it through the Piedmont to Lynchburg and other points west, the line was destined to be a major conveyor of trade through all of southern Virginia (In 1851, the Board of Directors voted down a proposal to change the name of the company to the "Petersburg & Lynchburg Railroad.")[7]

Grading began in March 1850 and progressed rapidly. By the time Rodes came on at the beginning of the following year, the line, for the sake of administrative efficiency during construction, had been divided into four "divisions." The First Division ran west fifty-two and-one-half miles, from

Petersburg to a junction with the Richmond & Danville Railroad. The Second Division ran fourteen-and-a-half miles, from the junction to near Farmville. The Third Division ran from near Farmville westward for thirty miles, while the Fourth Division ran from the above point twenty-three miles to Lynchburg.[8]

Under Chief Engineer Charles O. Sanford, who received an impressive annual salary of $3,000, the "Engineer Corps" included nine "Assistant Engineers," whose pay ranged from one making $1,000 a year, through seven others, including Rodes, who received $1,200 annually, to a top assistant who brought down $1,500. Their primary job was to locate, survey, and precisely mark the route and the ground upon which to lay the roadbed, taking into account calculations for proper grades, curvatures, and basic support. When the engineers had done their job, men came in under contract to begin the work of building the line.[9]

After making several trips to company headquarters in Petersburg to negotiate the details of his employment, during which he missed the 1850-51 Christmas-New Year holidays with his family, Rodes went to work with a "locating party" out near Farmville in Prince Edward County with the Second Division. He reassured his family that as his new responsibilities took him closer to Lynchburg, he would try to get home more often. By this time Rodes had so completely accepted the second wife of his father that his letters to him often ended with, "Give my love to Mama."[10]

Rodes quickly fell in awe of his new boss, a man of consummate engineering skill and accomplishment much sought after by other companies. He inevitably looked up to the chief engineer as an inspiring role model, learning much from him through a working relationship that gradually included an element of friendship. As Rodes candidly told his father, "Mr. Sanford is one of the best men I ever saw I believe."[11]

But along with the motivating inspiration came the harsh realities of life as an engineer in the field. Rodes faced grueling and tedious work. He spent his time almost entirely outdoors on the move, often sleeping in tents or some other makeshift accommodation, with little or no social life. "I have just got in from a weeks hard field work," one of his colleagues wrote home, "working in the sun from sunrise to sunset and being bitten by ticks, mosquitoes &c, to whom I gave my body." Weeks later he added, "When I come in in the evening I am so completely tired out that I go to bed as soon as I get any supper."[12]

After working under these trying conditions in the Farmville area through the fall of 1851, Rodes set about finding a more permanent shelter for the winter. The task proved more daunting than he likely expected. "I shall move up on my Division in about a week from now I suppose," he informed his father, "and a hard place it is." He continued:

> I have been all along the line above here making changes in the location, & keeping a watch in for a good stopping or boarding place for we will in all probability be stationed here two years & of course would like to have comfortable quarters. In the first Division commencing below & running 8 miles above Farmville there are several good places & of course the Engineer in charge of it will have his office & headquarters at Farmville, a very hospitable place. But the next division, mine, oh, horrors—I see no chance in the world of avoiding the punishment of living in that garret room over the parlour with two port holes and 1 door for egress & ingress & ventilation—& as for an office, I have found no place yet where I could obtain a room that would not be public to the whole family.[13]

In these rather unpleasant surroundings, Rodes remained extremely busy over the ensuing weeks. In expectation of still getting home for the year-end holidays, he jokingly reassured his father on November 17 that "I will try to spend one Xmas at least in six years with you." He eagerly looked forward to going to Scottsville about the middle of December to pick up his sister Sally, who was staying with friends, and bring her home to Lynchburg for a happy holiday family reunion. But it was not to be. "I find now that I shall be out in the field then," he regretfully informed his father on December 7, "& moreover shall be busy all the holidays— getting my division ready for work by the 1st January."[14]

In addition to being deprived for so long of the pleasures of seeing his family, Rodes at this time also suffered from the inability to satisfy fully an indulgence forbidden to him at VMI. "I wish you would get me about 10 lbs of chewing tobacco of the very finest quality," he pleaded with his father. "I desire them immediately from the fact that I am chewing the meanest compound under the sun tho called tobacco, now I can't get any other kind. . . . Do not neglect this if you please Papa. I will settle with you fair when I come to L[ynchburg] which will be I hope next February. My whole stock in cash is a 3 cent piece." Rodes' tobacco addiction extended beyond the chew, for he is known at least once to have joined a friend in buying several boxes of cigars just off a boat from Havana.[15]

Meanwhile, on November 12, 1851, Chief Engineer Sanford delivered his annual report to the company directors. In it, he optimistically predicted a finished bridge over the Appomattox River by the following October. Elsewhere, he reported, work was progressing rapidly. Twenty-five miles of track had been laid in the First Division, fifteen more were expected by the end of the year, and the final twelve- and-a-half miles would be completed by the following March. Grading in the Second (Rodes') Division was to be completed by spring of the following year and in the Third Division by the following winter, while the Fourth Division had been surveyed only, with no contracts yet awarded.[16]

As Sanford predicted, the last rail of the First Division was laid at the end of February 1852. A few weeks later, all fifty-two-and- one-half miles of that section of the line opened to a quickly booming business that brought the company much needed revenue. To its many investors, the finances of the Southside Railroad seemed reassuringly sound.[17]

The same no longer could be said of David Rodes, at least ostensibly. His seemingly deteriorating situation resulted from having taken the unpopular side of a controversial issue in state politics. The new Virginia state constitution, adopted in 1850, made subject to public election various positions in state government that formerly had been filled by appointment, including that of Clerk of the District Court at Lynchburg. Strongly opposed to what he called this "so-called democracy," where important government positions might be filled by the unqualified, he made no secret of his disapproval. The elder Rodes voted against adoption of the new constitution. Its passage forced him to accept the bitter pill of having to stand for election for a job that had been his for more than twenty years. Despite the advantage of all this experience, he found himself at the mercy of an electorate that had not forgotten his unpopular stance. Running as a Whig Party candidate, he lost his post to a Democrat in the spring of 1852.[18]

"I wish to say how much I regretted that democrats & rowdies, in the plenitudes of the lately acquired privileges, had thought proper to cast their votes against you & eject you from the office you lately filled," wrote a sympathetic friend. "Doubtless you were defeated on acct. of your having voted against the new Constitution. But you were right, for its adoption has brought on us a horrible state of things, & in many instances filled the offices with persons entirely destitute of any necessary qualifications. Democracy is in the ascendant," he continued, "and may be expected hereafter to carry every thing before it."[19]

The potentially disastrous news was a hard blow for Robert to swallow. "I too am very mortified that you should have been beaten for the Clerkship, but I am much more astonished," he confessed in a tender letter to his father. "I was astounded to hear the result." Then he added some consolation and sympathy in a manner that indicated a growing maturity in the young man. "It is too late & useless to talk about it now. All that can be done is to preserve our spirits. This I am glad to see from your letter you have done—it lessened my sorrow very much to see you bear up against the misfortune so well." The younger Rodes took the unusual, almost unthinkable, step of offering his father advice, which he based upon his own growing appreciation of discipline and self-control. "I hope you will say nothing to anyone about the result but keep your disappointment in your own family and above all don't give the successful candidate the advantage of you by shouting your feelings to him. Nothing would please him more than for you to treat him otherwise than with perfect politeness." As he suddenly remembered himself, Robert quickly added, "I beg of you to pardon the liberty I have just taken in presuming to advise you. I was led into it by the anxiety I always feel for your fortune & good repute among men. Not because I believed you stood in need of any advice." Still, the son offered a bit more of the same. "Have you determined what to do yet [?]" he asked. "The salary of the Clerkship of [the] District Court is only $150 I thought—is it so? Have you no chance of filling an office in that new bank[?] Just now you stand a better chance of getting a post in it than ever, just as you stand now in need of it."[20]

Having recently become a father again at age fifty-seven when Fannie bore a son named David Jr. (the boy would die three years later on June 25, 1855), the senior Rodes now found himself out of a job. This so upset Robert that, in addition to the almost blasphemous act of offering advice, he for the first time made the astonishing offer to send money home. "I hope you will not be pinched so much as to be compelled to alter any of your Customs &c.," he wrote in the same letter, dropping the familiar "Papa" perhaps in response to the perceived gravity of the situation. "If so father than know that you may command all my means. I am getting about square now. I will be economical till you get out of this." The younger Rodes had not finished with his astounding proposals. He offered to take care of his nineteen-year-old sister, even so far as to have her come live with him. "I can lay by enough to support Sally," he went on. "I will do it with great pleasure, & after that as long as I am on this road I will have more than enough to support Sally & myself & can assist you."[21]

Rather than live in a hovel with her brother near Farmville, however, Sally went to stay in much more pleasant accommodations provided by family friends in Charlottesville, where the lovely, intelligent nineteen- year-old quickly became very popular. "She has since been invited to several parties & attended one, where she was the star of the gay young circle," Sally's new host reported to her father in June. "She has been kept quite busy in receiving the calls of the crowds of visitors who have thronged every day to see & become acquainted with her. Several companions of ladies have come from the university & town to pay their respects & great numbers in pairs & single. They are eager to be near her & to converse with her, and she shines brilliantly in every circle. We are truly delighted to have her with us & sincerely congratulate you on the happiness you must enjoy in the possession of so lovely & interesting a daughter."[22]

Pleased and relieved to have Sally happily situated, David Rodes somehow managed to get by financially. His son probably did not know the full extent of his father's worth. David still possessed a number of valuable assets, including several slaves and a few town properties that could be liquidated if necessary to ensure the continued support of himself and his young second family. Moreover, he still drew a decent income from his rental houses (his 1857 will listed ten such properties) in town as well as from the rent of his inherited Walnut Grove property. At any rate, David's ensuing correspondence with Robert gave no further indication of financial stress. Indeed, in the 1860 census, David listed his occupation as "Gentleman," with an impressive net worth of $32,000.[23]

Meanwhile, work on the rail lines continued. Unlike the swift, relatively trouble-free labors of the First Division, Rodes' Second Division in 1852 came up against two unforeseen challenges that caused serious delay. The first took the form of rampant sickness, which so devastated work crews it pushed back by several months the expected completion date of the Appomattox Bridge and several miles of the line. The second problem required a rerouting through the Blue Ridge through Farmville instead of near it, that added five miles to the line. It also added significant additional expense because of the need to reduce the grade to no more than sixteen feet per mile, which in the long run would eliminate the cost of having to add locomotives to pull trains up and over certain high points.[24]

But as Rodes and his talented fellow engineers inevitably met these difficult challenges, the end of the entire project came into view. By the fall of 1853, sixty-three miles of the line, from Petersburg to High Bridge, were open for business. On October 18, President Pannill reported that High Bridge and the final few miles to Lynchburg would be completed by the following summer. Chief Engineer Sanford added that at a total cost of two million dollars, the entire 123-mile line from Petersburg to Lynchburg (a journey Sanford had estimated the year before would take about twelve hours, including stops) would be completed by the following fall. What this meant to Rodes, if he did not see it already, became clear in the report of the Special Committee. "The salary of the Chief Engineer," it began rather matter-of-factly, "is $3000 per annum [despite Sanford's repeated threats to resign if it were not increased] with 8 assistants at a salary of $1200 per annum. . . . They are informed by the Chief Engineer that two of those assistant Engineers can probably be dispensed with on the 1st of January next, and two more on the 1st of July next, that it will [be] necessary after that time to keep two engaged in Superintending the grading and construction of the road, and two more attending to the laying of the track and constructing buildings and turnouts."[25]

In July 1854, after employing him for three-and one-half years, the Southside Railroad officially "dispensed with" the services of Assistant Engineer Robert E. Rodes.

*   *   *

Though he understood it to be the nature of his work, Rodes must have been somewhat bitter at being rewarded with release for doing a job well and efficiently to its completion. But the nature of his work also meant that the nationwide boom in railroad construction guaranteed a number of employment opportunities. After leaving the Southside Railroad, he lost no time joining a new company with a promising future and an ambitious- sounding title: The Texas Atlantic and Pacific Railroad. For the first time in his life, Rodes left Virginia to begin what he fully expected was going to be an exciting and rewarding career on the "frontier" of Texas.

The company had only recently opened for business in the summer of 1854, when trains began running some twenty miles between company headquarters in Marshall, located in Harrison County in the northeast corner of the state, and the line's eastern terminus near the Louisiana border. Under Chief Engineer Major E. A. Blanch, Rodes went to work that summer at an annual salary of $2,000—$800 more than he had earned at the Southside Railroad. His primary job was to locate the best line of extension toward Trinity River and, hopefully before winter set in, to the Sabine River thirty miles west of Marshall. The intention was to eventually extend the line all the way to Dallas and then points farther west. The project's vision was immense, the work seemingly endless, and the country magnificent.[26]

"Young Engineers have a more brilliant prospect on this road than on any other in this Country," Rodes declared with bright enthusiasm in a September 24, 1854, letter to Alfred Rives. The words were an effort to persuade his friend and former VMI classmate to join him on the frontier. After VMI, Rives went on to the University of Virginia and had just graduated from the prestigious Ecole Polytechnique in Paris when he received Rodes' plea to come to Texas. "[You] cannot fail to rise here as fast as [you] can desire," Rodes went on, "and besides the Country is a very healthy one, the pay liberal and the Corps Composed of gentlemen and <u>Virginians</u>." Rodes confidently expected that before November, the company would have "at least a thousand hands on the road," and that within two years engineers would be working on sixty-six miles of line. "Our prospects are more brilliant here than those of any Corps in the old states," he boasted to Rives, "as the road is the longest in the world[,] more certain of being made[,] requiring more time to build it than any other I know." But Rodes had not forgotten that there was more to life than a career, however superlative it seemed. "The Country is thinly settled—but with people of good character," he observed, "and affords me enough to eat, and as much fun as a surveying party ever has in any Country." After pausing to quickly assure Rives that the "fun" was not of the disreputable type—"We are not troubled in the least with that sort of amusement and glad I am of it"—Rodes continued to sing, somewhat repetitiously, the praises of his current situation. He added that, of the eleven members of the engineer corps, six were VMI alumni. "It is a little singular that without special intention we should have got together in this Corps." Rodes levered additional inducements into the postscript, adding, "If you conclude to come out on the prairie," he admonished, "bring a Sharp Rifle with you—it will be of use in hunting deer, antelope & an occasional Indian."[27]

Despite the tempting offer to work with fellow VMI Virginians while occasionally taking shots at animals and the "occasional Indian," Rives returned to the U.S. to begin an impressive career, first as Secretary of the Interior under President Franklin Pierce, and then as an assistant engineer in the construction of the capitol building in Washington. One day, he would become chief of the Confederate War Department's Engineering Bureau.[28]

As the future would prove, Rives was fortunate that he did not allow Rodes' dramatic letter to throw him into a swoon, for the Texas Atlantic & Pacific Railroad—and Rodes' enthusiastic optimism—collapsed with breathtaking speed. In April 1855, after becoming "financially embarrassed," a common occurrence among railroads that tried to do too much with too little funding, the company filed for bankruptcy.[29]

* * *

After being so high on the new and seemingly exciting career possibilities in Texas, Rodes fell into a state of despondency. Four times in less than five years a career path, for one reason or another, had been pulled out from under him. And now he saw no viable prospects for a fifth. On the forlorn return trip to Virginia he stopped off in New Orleans to visit his brother Virginius and their uncle William Yancey, with whom he briefly considered taking the drastic step of joining in the cotton business. But the railroad mania that currently gripped the nation quickly intervened to save him.[30]

Chartered in 1853, the North East & South West Alabama Railroad received a large government land grant of more than 400,000 acres to build a line from the Mobile and Ohio Railroad at Meridian, Mississippi, through the Alabama counties of DeKalb, Jefferson, Tuscaloosa, Greene, and Sumter, to the Knoxville and Georgia Railroad in the northeast part of the state. The company's first elected president, University of Alabama professor Landon C. Garland, immediately arranged a merger with the Wills Valley Railroad, whose projected route extended through the mountains in northeast Alabama to Chattanooga. The move made the entire line 294 miles long. Moreover, Garland vowed to avoid his contemporaries' mistakes by not beginning work on the new line until the company acquired sufficient funding. "The ground of such assurance," he wrote, "shall not be less than subscriptions in work adequate to grade and prepare the roadbed for the ties and iron in its entire length, including subscriptions in money to the amount of six hundred thousand dollars." With the stipulated amount finally raised, Chief Engineer Edward D. Sanford, nephew of Charles O. Sanford (with whom Rodes had worked on the Southside Railroad), received orders in December 1854 to begin work.[31]

On July 5, 1855, Sanford reported to the Board of Directors that the probable cost of building the line would be six million dollars. "Changes have occurred in the corps since your last meeting," he also reported. "Mr. R. H. Deas of South-Carolina, and Mr. R. E. Rodes, of Virginia—both gentlemen of experience, ability and energy, have joined me."[32]

Going to work with Sanford on the NE & SW Alabama was a major turning point in Rodes' life because it took him, for the first time, to Tuscaloosa,

Alabama. Founded in 1816, the city took its name from the fierce Choctaw leader Tashka Lusha—"Black Warrior"—who in 1539, near the junction of what are now called the Tombigbee and Alabama rivers, suffered defeat by the Spanish conqueror and explorer Hernando De Soto. Growing up on the banks of the Black Warrior River, Tuscaloosa served as the state capital from 1826 to 1846, its oak-lined streets and fine homes making it known as "Druid City." Though a center of the cotton trade and home to the University of Alabama, the city also was a manufacturing town, producing clothing, plows, hats, and paper. As in many communities along the proposed route of the Northeast and Southwest Alabama, news of the approval to begin work on the line gave cause for celebration. The people of Tuscaloosa and the surrounding county made it a day of festivities as politicians, clergy, University of Alabama faculty and students, and ordinary citizens gathered on a bright sunny morning to watch the ceremonial turning of the first spade of earth.[33]

A probable participant in the day's festivities was David Woodruff (1795-1876), a prominent local bookseller and slave owner who had just finished a one-year term as mayor. The son of Eli Woodruff (1776-1818) and Polly Fenn, David was born in the Milford, Connecticut, homestead built in 1640 by his great-great-grandfather Matthew Woodruff of England. Before moving to Tuscaloosa in 1827 or 1828, David lived for a time in Winchester, Virginia, and Shelbyville, Tennessee. In 1829 he married his second wife, Eliza Antoinette Bell, the operator of a female institute in Tuscaloosa who had been born in Norfolk, Virginia, in 1811. Their children included Milford Fenn, who ran a prep school he had set up on the lower floor of the Odd Fellows Hall on Greensboro Avenue. His boys studied Greek, Latin, and Mathematics in preparation for admission to the University of Alabama. Milford still lived at home with his nineteen-year-old brother Daniel Webster, a clerk, fifteen-year-old David Pendleton, ten-year-old Eliza Belle, and eight-year-old Zachary Taylor. Other children had been lost along the way, with the Woodruffs being no stranger to that form of tragedy. Six-year-old Florence died in 1844 when she fell into a well, Horace died in 1852 at age ten, and Plymouth died in 1854 at age twenty-two.[34]

The Woodruff of most interest to Robert Rodes, however, was the beautiful twenty-two-year-old Virginia, who went by her middle name of Hortense. After growing up in an atmosphere of books and learning, she taught school for a year in Selma and was doing the same thing in Tuscaloosa—probably in her mother's "female institute." Bright, attractive, and an accomplished musician, Hortense, as Rodes later claimed, immediately captured the heart of the twenty-six-year-old engineer from Virginia. He probably met her in Tuscaloosa's Presbyterian Church, where she served as leader of the choir. Initially, however, Hortense discouraged his interest in her because she was still in mourning over a previous suitor, who died during a yellow fever epidemic that had recently swept through the area.[35]

Before Rodes could win her heart, circumstances forced him to leave Tuscaloosa. By that fall, "the Condition of the Company," Chief Engineer Sanford reported, "did not warrant an immediate construction of the work." A dramatic, unexpected rise in cotton prices had driven up the cost of labor, making it difficult and prohibitively expensive to contract for slave laborers. Despite President Garland's careful planning, the company fell into financial difficulties and released its entire engineer corps. Once again, Rodes found himself out of work, but once again he landed on his feet, this time in North Carolina.[36]

*   *   *

"Railroad mania" came relatively late to North Carolina. By the mid 1850s, the state could boast of only two main lines: the North Carolina Railroad to Wilmington, and the Atlantic & North Carolina Railroad progressing toward completion at the harbor in Beaufort. On August 30, 1855, the Western North Carolina organized as a company, with R. C. Pearson as president and James C. Turner as chief engineer. The line was designed to be among the first to penetrate the mountains and connect eastern and western North Carolina, the ultimate goal being to reach the Tennessee roads and establish a link to the Mississippi River. Beginning in Salisbury and running through Statesville and Newton to Morganton, the proposed line extended through North Carolina for seventy-seven and three-quarter miles. This distance was divided into two divisions, the first stretching fifty-three miles from Salisbury to the Catawba River, and the second for twenty-four miles from the river to Morganton. In November 1855, Rodes joined the company as "Principal Assistant Engineer." Given his own staff of assistants, he took charge of locating and surveying the Second Division line, with the First Division under the control of R. C. McCalla.[37]

Locating the fifty-three miles of the mostly flat First Division track proved relatively easy. In March 1856, the twenty-five mile section from Salisbury to Statesville was put under contract to be built, and twelve of the next twenty-eight and three-quarter mile section to Newton went under contract in mid-July.

Though it covered less than half the distance of the First Division, the Second Division's task posed a much greater challenge. Beginning his work in extremely cold weather with several heavy snowfalls, Rodes struggled mightily to penetrate the steeply graded mountains. Other major obstacles included Third Creek, whose span required a sixty-five- foot-high viaduct, Back Creek, which needed a thirty-seven-foot-high viaduct and the numerous crossings of Clark's Creek. But as the weather improved progress picked up. Sometime during the mid-summer of 1856, Rodes and his assistants finished their challenging job. This great success, however, brought an end to Rodes' connection with the Western North Carolina. "In conclusion," Chief Engineer Turner gratefully acknowledged in his annual report dated August 27, 1856, "it affords me pleasure to state, that I have been ably and zealously assisted in making the surveys and location by Mr. R. C. McCalla and Mr. R. E. Rodes, as principal assistants, together with the young gentlemen associated with them."[38]

Rodes, however, had at last "made his reputation," something he had been determined to do since leaving the North River Navigation Company more than four years earlier. His successful work in North Carolina, particularly that involving steep mountain grades and the numerous, sometimes deep and wide creek crossings, brought him widespread attention as a first-rate engineer. Several companies were now interested in securing his well-demonstrated talents.

In the summer of 1856, Rodes went to work near Saint Charles, Missouri, as a division chief for the North Missouri Railroad. His soaring reputation, however, provided no guarantees regarding the length of his employment. As he lamented to Colonel Smith on October 8, 1856, "The fates are against me unless they have just taken a favorable turn. The work upon my Div in Missouri was suspended." Once again, financial troubles brought both an end to the railroad company and yet another direction in Rodes' career.[39]

* * *

While Rodes was traveling to Missouri to work for the North Missouri Railroad, the fortunes of the NE & SW Alabama improved dramatically. On June 3, 1856, it received from Washington an additional grant of more than 227,000 acres. Though the company would not take possession of these new lands for four more years, the grant raised the confidence of investors, who

This beautiful cup, from Rodes' railroad days, tells a story of its own. The engraving says: "Presented to R. E. Rodes, Principal Assistant Engineer, W.N.C.R.R., By the members of his corps as a small token of their high regard and esteem. June 8th 1856."

Photo courtesy of Mary Rodes Dell and the Rodes Family

promptly restored the concern to financial health. That same year (1856) the company began construction of the first one hundred miles of the line, from the Mobile and Ohio Railroad at Meridian to Tuscaloosa. The completion date was set for the fall of 1859.[40]

In October 1856, Rodes returned to the NE & SW Alabama, twelve months after it had put him out of work. He secured a meager, simple residence near company headquarters in the small town of Eutaw, the seat of Greene County, thirty-five miles south of Tuscaloosa. Provided with two assistants, he took charge of fifty miles of the road—"the most important part of it," he boasted to Colonel Smith, because it included the bridges over the Black Warrior and Tombigbee rivers. Optimistic over the prospects of his new position, as he always seemed to be with each job despite the ephemeral nature of his work, Rodes gushed with enthusiasm when writing to Smith. "I am located in the finest portion of Alabama," he declared, "in the respect of wealth, improvements & soil."[41]

Despite having been denied the opportunity to teach at VMI, Rodes always maintained a warm, filial loyalty toward "Colonel" Francis Smith. No matter where his work took him, the young engineer always kept in touch with his former mentor. The two exchanged friendly, cordial letters in which Rodes generally kept Smith up to date not only on his own situation but also on other VMI alumni. "[He] is perfectly crazy to try the married life again," Rodes unsympathetically wrote Smith in November 1856 regarding former classmate Charles Derby, an Episcopalian minister who had lost his wife eighteen months before. "He is in love as young widowers are always & is actually so eager that he Can't stand still. He rooms next door to me & annoys me terribly by his incessant noise. He has been out of doors tonight many times notwithstanding it is raining hard, & now as a last resort he is coming in here to bore me about himself, his troubles & his sweetheart, & I must stop & Collect my patience for the trial." With regard to his own love life, the twenty-seven-year-old Rodes confessed, "I am not married yet, but will be one of these days to some poor lady—poor literally, I mean it is my destiny & that of all really honest & proud men."[42]

"I am sorry for poor Derby," Smith replied. "Give my regards to him & tell him his proximity to so incorrigible an Old Bachelor as yourself ought to cure him of all love sickness."[43]

As Rodes, the "incorrigible Old Bachelor," always held Smith in the highest regard, the colonel in turn looked with special favor on his former pupil. As he confessed in one letter to Rodes, "My heart has always turned with peculiar affection and interest [to you]." Smith's pride in Rodes was never more evident than when he gave a speech that fall of 1856 to the Corps of Cadets, wherein he held up his former pupil's character and intelligence as admirable examples the students should seek to follow.[44]

On November 27, the proud but ever outwardly humble Rodes wrote to thank Smith for the flattering remarks made during that speech. There was, however, "One objectionable feature I discovered in said address," he protested in a rare display at attempted humor. "Contained in a marginal note, wherein you mention my name in an agreeable manner but in bad Company. G. Jordan & Vaughn tho Clever fellows were nincompoops at College and are so still." Rodes then returned to the serious nature of the compliment. "Every day of my life," he assured Smith, "I see the tremendous advantage VMI graduates have over all others in our profession."[45]

That engineering profession provided Rodes with the unexpected but very welcome opportunity of returning to Alabama, where he immediately resumed his pursuit of Hortense Woodruff. Grief for her lost beau having waned over the past year, she now allowed herself to become interested in the handsome, young engineer. Rodes fell hopelessly in love with her.[46]

Mainly because of the many uncertainties in his career, Rodes until now had avoided the prospect of marriage, even to the point of perhaps considering himself, like his brother Virginius, a life-long bachelor. In support of that position he adopted a defensive attitude against those who annoyingly professed to know better, judging as overrated matrimony's alleged blissful benefits.

Not unnaturally, this concerned his family and friends, particularly Francis Smith. "Why are you not married?" the colonel scolded in a letter he had written back in November 1856. "Too poor to support a wife? Marry one to support you or at least to know where you are docked." Smith perceptively blamed the situation on Rodes' nomadic lifestyle, especially since several of the colonel's letters had been returned as undeliverable. But the colonel refused to give up. He relentlessly pressed Rodes on the matter. In the December 6 letter regarding Charles Derby, for example, Smith chided Rodes as an "incorrigible Old Bachelor," and three days later reminded the young engineer that by now most of his friends and former classmates had married.[47]

And so it was with some relief and joy that Smith at last received the welcome news. "I am about to announce to you," Rodes wrote to him from Eutaw on August 28, 1857, "that I have at last become in some way a Convert to your theory that we are happier married than single. I am going to test the matter practically merely to see whether you are infallible or not of Course. On the 10 Sept—near two weeks off, I shall be married, DV [Lord willing], to the noblest and poorest woman in Alabama. I have known her since April 55 and since then have been trying to attain the result which the 10th Sept. now promises me."[48]

Despite the nearness of the wedding day, Rodes felt a strange lack of assuredness about the whole idea, well beyond the traditional cold feet of the prospective groom, quite as though he had been banged around once too often by the anxiety-producing circumstances of his career. Many times had he excitedly "wedded" himself to a new direction in that career, only to see the "marriage" collapse. "But you know how uncertain the sea & earthly things are," the often unemployed engineer rather nervously told Smith. "I hope only don't feel Certain. I would not have Mrs. Smith or the future Mrs. R in any way think that I was so little world wise as to believe two weeks before marriage that the marriage was certain. Still I have a better right than usual to think I shall be safely married on the day we timed."[49]

What came next undoubtedly put an I-told-you-so smile on the face of the colonel. "Yes, I know I ought to have been married long ago," Rodes confessed, "because I can see clearly now how much better the man married is than the man singly & how different the steady & holey [sic] happiness I now feel is to the fleeting deceptive thing the bachelor calls happiness. But I have been so long suspicious of praise of matrimony coming from [the] likes of married people," he continued, "that I feel awkward at it myself & will stop."[50]

Perhaps realizing that he had reached a moment in his life that may have only slightly less significance than life's beginning and end, Rodes seemed unusually reflective, even philosophical, in his letter to Smith. His happiness, he lamented, remained cruelly and ironically incomplete. "Everything would be bright in my place," he continued, "but for a cloud that has risen here quite recently in my monetary and business [situation]. It seems probable now that at the next meeting of the Board of Directors of the Road in October next that a difficulty will arise between them & the Engineer Department which will result in the resignation of the whole Engineer Corps[,] Chief and all. I have no prospect anywhere in case of this result."[51]

Clearly growing disgusted with the ever-present threat of being unemployed, as well as with the difficult life of an engineer in the field, Rodes again turned his thoughts to the profession that always had remained dearest to his heart. "But this result," he confided to Smith, "added to the many other instances of bad luck of the same kind I have had in this profession [engineering] & to the great discomfort of the life had determined me to quit this profession for one more congenial & more lucrative & more pleasant, that of teaching. I do aspire & have always done so since & before this life failed, to becoming a professor in some establishment of Engineering or Math or both."[52]

Despite all of his uncertainties, real or otherwise, and after receiving a "Sufficient Warrant" from Tuscaloosa County probate judge, Moses M. McGuire, Robert married Hortense on September 10, 1857, in the Presbyterian Church in Tuscaloosa. The two lived in Robert's humble rented place near company headquarters in Eutaw. "My fiancee is from Tuscaloosa," Rodes explained to Smith in his letter of August 28, "but she is well known down here & has a great many friends here and in the Country at large so that she will be at home."[53]

Like Francis Smith, many others found it difficult to believe that Rodes at last had shed his title as "the incorrigible Old Bachelor." "I suppose by the time you receive this," Rodes' assistant and good friend Peyton Randolph wrote on September 6 a few days before the scheduled wedding, "you will have left the ancient and honorable order of bachelors and have gone over to the enemy, let me congratulate you but at the same time allow me to feel a little envious at your superior good luck while I am still left in the gall of bitterness and the bonds of iniquity." Rodes' marriage made someone else envious, too. "Amagonia or as you call her 'Glum,'" Randolph added, "has been making inquiries after you several times since you left and will I have no doubt feel much disquieted at your being out of her reach. I have just discovered a new & interesting habit of hers she smokes a pipe what do you think of that, horrible is it not to see one so feminine as she with a pipe in her mouth, pity me."[54]

Rodes met Randolph some three months before, with each man immediately forming a favorable opinion of the other. Born in Frederick County, Virginia, in 1833, Randolph graduated from Columbia College (George Washington University) in Washington D.C., and lived in Cincinnati while working as an engineer for the Ohio & Mississippi Railroad. In early June 1857, he arrived in Meridian, Mississippi, to begin his new job with the Northeast & Southwest Alabama, happy at last to be living again below the Mason-Dixon Line. "I have not yet seen the Chief Engineer [Sanford]," Randolph wrote his mother on June 7, "but the Principal Assistant [Rodes] is a very fine fellow, genuine Virginian, is a gentleman, and all the corps whom I have seen I like very much, all Southerners not a foreigner or Yankee on the road."[55]

Though their relationship consisted primarily of long-distance correspondence, Rodes and Randolph quickly developed an abiding friendship. Later that December Rodes invited him to spend Christmas in Eutaw with himself and Hortense, forgetting, however, to make good on a promise to pay Randolph's way from Mississippi. "Why in the name of all that is holy & righteous & the Contrary," Randolph howled in despair on December 22, "have you not sent or brought me funds for my trip? Here I am dead broke and as crusty as a bear with a sore head. I have not heard a word from you about the matter for a fortnight." It is unclear whether Rodes kept his promise to Randolph and brought him up to Eutaw for the holidays.[56]

A month or so after Robert and Hortense were married, the Board of Directors held their annual meeting. Though the anticipated dispute alluded to in his August letter to Colonel Smith did not bring about the resignation of the entire engineer corps, as Rodes had feared it might, it apparently did bring about the resignation of Chief Engineer Edward Sanford. Others saw it differently. "Mr. Sanford (nephew of the Southside man) has resigned," Charles Derby, Rodes' friend and former classmate, wrote his sister. "[He] has married a young wife and she of course needs his presence with her. Hence the resignation."[57]

Regardless of its cause, the resignation made Rodes a prime candidate to replace Sanford. After having been victimized so often in this profession by what he termed "instances of bad luck," Rodes did not allow his hopes to get too high. Ostensibly, he remained determined to seek out a teaching position. Indeed, during the previous fall of 1857, he considered a tempting offer by the College of Lynchburg in his hometown, but he refused it because the math chair included that of philosophy, the pay was well below his current earnings of $2,500 a year, and too many tasks remained unfinished in his present job. It quickly proved a wise decision.[58]

Perhaps a contributing factor to Sanford's resignation was the overwhelming responsibility of supervising the entire nearly three hundred miles of line. Just as VMI nine years before had sought to relieve the overburdened Major Gilham by dividing his chair, the NE & SW Alabama Railroad now did likewise, putting the line under two chief engineers. This time around, however, Rodes would not be denied.

"It will be seen that Col. E. D. Sanford has resigned the office of Chief Engineer," the Tuscaloosa *Independent Monitor* reported on January 28, 1858,

and that Messrs. Rhodes [sic] and Curry have been appointed Assistant Engineers each with the special charge of a subdivision of the Road—Mr.

Curry being assigned to the portion North East of Elyton, and Mr. Rhodes [sic] to the portion South West from Elyton. . . . We are unacquainted with Mr. Curry, but we have been favorably impressed by what we have seen of Mr. Rhodes [sic], and we understand that he is fairly competent to the important task before him. His charge is decidedly the most important part of the work. Indeed, upon the completion and good management of his division the remainder of the Road, and the success of the work itself, is absolutely dependent.[59]

By a resolution of the Executive Committee of the Northeast & Southwest Alabama Railroad, dated February 4, 1858, Rodes received the promotion and took charge of construction over the lower portion of the line, stretching from Elyton, Alabama, to Meridian, Mississippi. The job carried with it a handsome salary of $3,000 per year. Just weeks short of his twenty-ninth birthday, Rodes now stood at the top of his profession. At last he felt fairly secure working in a field that had, for him at least, been a sea of stressful volatility.[60]

The pendulum of anxiety and discontent, however, continued its relentless swing. On the eve of the happy occasion of his marriage, Rodes had fretted over the possibility of losing his job. Now with his career secure with a new and important promotion, his new marriage faced an unusual strain. Hortense suffered from what was described vaguely as a "delicate constitution." The newlyweds barely had had time to get accustomed to each other when she fell gravely ill. The specific nature of the malady remains unclear. Rodes referred to it as "neuralgia," a common mid-nineteenth century general diagnosis for many ailments. The modern definition of this term is "a severe pain along the course of a nerve or in its area of distribution." Whatever Hortense's exact condition, it frequently required Rodes' attention—often at the expense of his career duties. Moreover, the problem persisted with varying intensity for months at a time across a span of many years, with the fear occasionally arising that Hortense might not survive. At times the stress and anxiety seemed almost unbearable, and undoubtedly it contributed to the six-year delay in their having children. But through it all, Robert and Hortense remained fiercely devoted to each other.

The persistence of the problem and its effect upon Rodes is revealed in part by the letters of his friends and fellow workers. They frequently referred to Hortense's suffering when writing to him, and either expressed hope that she would recover or gladness when they learned she had improved. "Hope Mrs. R is better & that you will not be so harassed after a month or so," assistant engineer James A. Corry (who eventually would give up engineering for the less stressful profession of farming wheat and corn in Georgia) wrote on May 25, 1858. "Hope Mrs. R is better," he remarked on June 19.[61]

Fearful of leaving her alone, and hoping that the distraction might provide some benefit, Rodes took Hortense with him on a lengthy business trip through Virginia and on to New York City. Along the way, he consulted with other engineers and arranged various transactions for the company. The trip also gave him the opportunity of presenting his new wife to his family in Lynchburg.[62]

"Hope Mrs. R will profit enough by the trip," Corry wrote Rodes on July 24, "& that you will recuperate so as to go through the fall & winter Campaign in good trim." The journey lasted through that August and much of September. "If it were right to envy, it would be the trip you have taken this summer," Corry wrote Rodes on September 21. "I hope Mrs. R's health is established & that you will go on to prosper."[63]

Apparently, the extended trip produced the desired effect. "Your last news is about Mrs. R's recovery," Corry wrote Rodes on October 11, "& I am very glad to hear she is gaining so fast." Four days later the company president, William Foster, added, "I was glad to learn from Mr. Woodruff yesterday that Mrs. Rodes was much better."[64]

The salutary effect proved fleeting. "I had not heard before of Mrs. Rodes' sickness," Corry wrote Rodes on December 6. "I can truly sympathize with you & do hope that lingering disease Neuralgia may be driven off." Two weeks later, Corry resorted to offering medical advice. "I want you to obtain <u>Some Horseradish</u> & bruise it & apply to the part affected by Neuralgia, hoping it may relieve Mrs. Rodes." The problem persisted. "I hope to hear that Mrs. R's health is better," Corry wrote Rodes on January 23, 1860, "& that you have no cloud of doubt now of Complete success."[65]

Added to the anxieties over the health of his wife was the ongoing concern Rodes felt for his friend and former VMI classmate, Charles Derby. "I lived in Eutaw with Derby two years and more," he wrote October 8, 1859, in response to Colonel Smith's inquiry into rumors that Derby had been drunk while delivering sermons in the Episcopalian church in Eutaw. "When I first met with him it was within a year of the death of his wife, [and] he seemed to be dreadfully distressed and was so in reality doubtless—he never ceased to talk about her death and his troubles & himself generally and really was so horribly and whining a bore that I had to avoid him. He was beginning to 'take notice' some few months after the time alluded to—with his egotism making him disagreeable to men and women, but not enough so apparently for his task he added to his boring capacity a propensity to flatter, and flatter poorly. He flattered me in such a way," continued Rodes, "as to make it necessary for me to Cut him. I began to be confirmed in a suspicion I had at first had that his mind was out of fix."[66]

Rodes became even more convinced of this when he learned that Derby, already failing as a teacher and a preacher, was considering starting up a church newspaper. Then there was the drinking. Back in July 1858, Derby had caused quite a stir when he failed to come out of the vestry to deliver his sermon, whereby churchmen found him inside vomiting and intoxicated. "Really his mind is getting weak and he will be crazy one day," Rodes bluntly concluded. "He confessed to me and all who knew him and treated him kindly after the above occurred that he was drunk that time—that it was an accident &c—And that he was never fit for a preacher (a fact because he cannot preach and ought never to have attempted it)." Rodes assured Smith, however, that for the sake of VMI's reputation, he would speak of this to no one.[67]

Despite all these anxieties and distractions, Rodes managed to put together his first annual report as chief engineer of the First Division, which he delivered to the board at Eutaw on October 11, 1858. Though weighed down in places with what might be called first-year enthusiasm and salesman-like emotional appeals, the document is remarkably detailed, revealing Rodes' thorough grasp of his responsibilities and the situation of the line upon which he worked.

"Since your last meeting," he began, "all the work in Mississippi not then let out, has been let to reliable parties. . . . The Tombigee Bridge was begun with Commendable energy by Mr. J.W. Derby [of Chicago]. . . ." Concerning the future of the company, Rodes expressed glowing optimism. "Several interviews with the President of the Virginia and Tennessee Railroad, with the President of the East Tennessee and Georgia Railroad and with various Railroad and Iron men in the City of New York satisfied me that our Road has the most Commanding position of all in the South and that no man capable of judging of such matters Can say honestly that the Road will not pay upon Completion a very handsome dividend over 12 1/2 per cent." Because of future connections with lines coming in from the northeast and west, "this road is destined to do the largest business in the South and the largest traveling business in the Country. . . ." Rodes predicted that the line would be completed in three-and-a-half years. "It is time," he declared, "that stockholders should realize that they are not throwing away their money on the Road, and that they are making the best investment of the times in building it."

Rodes also made several recommendations: to purchase iron for rails from England, which had the best quality for the price; to immediately begin, at a cost of $250,000, grading the line above Tuscaloosa, for to end the line there would be a tragic mistake; and to maintain the present pace of construction by using temporary track, which he considered superior to some permanent track being used on other lines. He also provided work cost estimates based on current contracts, apparently negotiated by himself, for each section of the line, 89 through 114, as well as estimates for crossties and iron to finish the road from Tuscaloosa up to the Mobile and Ohio Railroad, all to be paid for by using a combination of cash and subscriptions.

"The duties in my office and out of it," Rodes added by way of justifying the hiring of additional personal help, "have become so onerous as to make it a matter of impossibility to get along without assistance at least until I have finished all my office work and drawing relative to the Bridges [Black Warrior and Tombigee] on the road. [Contracts for building the bridges had been awarded to W.M. Derby and James W. Derby of Chicago]. I have therefore employed since the 27th of September Mr. Horace Harding at a salary at the rate of $700 per annum."

Rodes informed the board about his trip to Virginia to consult with his former boss on the Southside Railroad, Charles Sanford, "relative to his bridge plans &c." The consultation proved fruitless, he added, because "it was upon the question of long and short spans the we differed mainly in the whole matter, he is opposed to long spans and I am not."

Rodes' report ended with a stirring finish. "In conclusion," he declared,

> I desire to Congratulate you, Gentlemen, upon being at the head at one of the most important Roads of the day, of the Road upon the most solid basis, of all that I have known except a few in the North West, and of a road which is as certain of being built as that we live.
>
> Neither lukewarmness on the part of its friends or the efforts of its enemies can prevent it from forcing its way through to that Commanding position in respect to location, business and money which Nature has given it.
>
> Let no man think then that by delay he is earning himself of his subscription or that by that Course he is doing more than taking interest and money out of his own pocket.[68]

Justifiably proud of this report, Rodes considered it a measure of hard-won success in a field that had plagued him with "many instances of bad luck . . . & great discomfort." This, in turn, brought to mind the man who, with the North River Navigation Company more than eight years before, helped set him on that path. "Tell Prof. [Thomas] Williamson," Rodes proudly wrote Colonel Smith on January 2, 1859, "I have just published my first report which I ought to dedicate to him, and shall do so secretly—will send him a copy as soon as it is issued in pamphlet form."[69]

Yet even this great success brought with it a certain degree of unpleasantness. At the beginning of his career with the North River Navigation Company, Rodes quickly found distasteful any work that took him away from pure engineering. Those "onerous duties," as he labeled them in his report, seemed at times nearly overwhelming. They included negotiating and enforcing contracts, raising funds, and otherwise promoting the company. Peyton Randolph got a taste of these tasks when he filled in for Rodes during the latter's trip to New York. "I am constantly interrupted by the Contractors coming in and as the Chief Engineer [Rodes] has gone on a trip to the North," Randolph complained in a letter to his sister. "I have to attend to his Correspondence and do the talking with the folks that come in."[70]

In another letter written to a friend on January 9, 1859, Randolph explained how "Rodes had gone up to Tuskaloosa to start the survey toward Elyton." A month later, he was still away. "Rodes is still in Tuskaloosa. Expect he will be down here [Eutaw] sometime this week, he is as busy as he can be raising funds, talking up the road &c. Has a party in the field to complete the location to Elyton."[71]

Contractors often gave Rodes headaches. On August 3, 1859, for example, he declared forfeited a contract made with S. G. Shear and James Coleman for grading sections 45 and 46. Thirty days after its execution, work had not yet begun. This failure forced Rodes to improvise. In a desperate search of workers, he placed ads for three weeks in the Sumter, Greene, and Tuscaloosa newspapers.[72]

To solve the seemingly ever-present problem of worker shortages, Rodes often resorted to another strategy commonly used by railroads in the South. Throughout 1859, he signed several company vouchers to pay for slaves to work on various sections of the line. A typical agreement was that of "Bill, George and Charles," hired out from owner Thomas Giles at $200 per annum each. This was something of a bargain over hiring a free white man. In January of that year, for example, Rodes' twenty-two-year-old brother-in-law Daniel W.

Woodruff went to work on the line for the standard pay of $20 per month, or $240 per year (though later that year Rodes extended him a personal loan of $20).[73]

Usually, the company obtained slaves from owners who lived near the line. Occasionally, however, it became necessary to look farther for the laborers. When bridge builder J. W. Derby needed to add to his forty- man work force, he went to Mobile to make arrangements "to buy [contract] Negroes, as you probably knew," Peyton Randolph informed Rodes. Randolph added that a man named Gould "goes to Charleston next week to purchase [contract] darkies also."[74]

But slaves were not always easy to obtain. In late 1858, slave owners nearly brought the line to a halt when they insisted upon full compensation if any of the men were lost while working on section 89, a dangerously wet, swampy area just south of Tuscaloosa. The company appealed to the mayor and city government of Tuscaloosa, who responded by authorizing a bond issue of $40,000, which allowed work on section 89 to resume.[75]

Rodes' current level of prosperity and solid social standing offered him the opportunity to become a slave owner—and he took it. With a down payment of $1,700 (presumably borrowed from his brother Virginius), and a balance of $1,800 to be paid one year later (which he paid), on January 1, 1859, Rodes entered into a contract with his former boss, E. D. Sanford of Tuscaloosa, to buy a slave named Hannah (about 35 years old) and her three children. Their names were Oscar (about fourteen), Dick (about twelve), and Matilda (about eight). Sanford had bought them two years before from David Woodruff, meaning that Rodes' purchase returned them to the family. He put them to work helping to take care of Hortense and the household. Sentimentality and practicality, however, were not the primary reasons for expending so much money and the concurrent responsibility that went with it of four more mouths to feed. Like many of his peers, Rodes almost certainly sought the prestige that came with the appearance of being a prosperous slave owner.[76]

Even when sufficient in number, line workers, be they free or slave, sometimes presented the company with special problems. For example, in June 1857, while still section chief at Eutaw, Peyton Randolph in Mississippi alerted Rodes to be on the watch for a runaway slave named Ruffin. After a line foreman named Gene threatened to "brush" Ruffin for being insubordinate the slave disappeared, presumably headed for Eutaw. Randolph asked Rodes to "take measures that will assure his apprehension." He went on to add that work on the line was going slowly because "there is considerable sickness among the men and some little insubordination."[77]

Though there may have been little he could do about illness among the men, Chief Engineer Rodes, much like the future General Rodes, did not tolerate insubordination. He insisted that his engineers and foremen in the field demand strict obedience from their workers. To enforce discipline in Corry's section, Rodes suggested using a strict foreman he had worked with on the Texas and Pacific, a man named Ramsey. "I will be glad to have your Texas friend with me," Corry replied, "for my boys are such miserable asses that my field work progresses very slowly, when may I expect him?" Soon after hiring the Texan the following spring, Rodes inquired after his effectiveness. "I have not answered your query about Ramsey's firmness," Corry penned in an overdue reply. "[H]e is firm enough & knows how to make them [the workers] obey."[78]

Firmness to the point of rigidity was proving to be Rodes hallmark. He was strict and exacting with his own subordinate engineers to the point of offending and upsetting his friends. In one instance, Randolph complained bitterly to Rodes over criticisms regarding a copying error of a mere forty cents in a construction account, and for not inspecting a load of timber before accepting an estimate of its cost. The criticism so upset Randolph that he wrote a full page to explain and apologize. "I acted as I thought fair for both parties," he tried to explain, "but as you have expressed yourself against my Course so decidedly I will be very Careful not to err in this way again."

More than one year later, Randolph found himself apologizing for yet another transgression, this time for not responding promptly to recent inquiries and for making another minor copying error. "I regret very much the error in my estimate," he explained. "The sheet was made at night when I was very tired and in Copying off the work which was unchanged since last estimate & the previous payments I must have copied from the wrong estimate. . . . When I came in at night [I] did not think of writing as I might have done." The friendship had clearly suffered, if only temporarily, by Rodes' martinet style of handling simple human mistakes. "[Y]our quasi-satirical manner induces me to think you are dissatisfied about something," added Randolph, his feelings obviously hurt. "[B]e kind enough to let me know what it is and in what respect you suppose I have been delinquent."[79]

Though strained at times, Rodes and Randolph remained lifelong friends. Strict and demanding when "on duty," Rodes was very sociable and charming in an unofficial capacity. When combined, these personality traits would one day earn him the respect, loyalty, and devotion of thousands of men who would serve under him during the Civil War.

A striking example of that respect and devotion in the civilian sphere occurred soon after the arrival of the 1859 new year. "The members of the [Engineer] Corps have it in contemplation to make Mrs. Rodes a New Year's present," Randolph wrote fellow engineer George W. Robertson, "and have selected for that purpose an Etagere, a kind of parlor Sideboard." To raise the $44.50 asked for by the étagere's owner, none other than former chief engineer E. D. Sanford, each of the corps' seven engineers contributed $6.50. That money, however, eventually went back into their own pockets. "Our plans were knocked in the head," Randolph sadly related to Robertson, "by Sanford's selling the article we wanted before [Horace] Harding got to Tuskaloosa [sic] so the prospect falls to the ground."[80]

There are a few rare examples of Rodes mixing on-duty business with off-duty affability. He maintained a running joke with George W. Ross, an engineer (and future member of the Sixth Alabama Infantry) on the Northern Missouri Railroad. The humor centered on their mutually unreadable handwriting (Rodes' being especially atrocious). Rodes highly respected his former VMI classmate. "Ross is your trump card in our profession now," he wrote Colonel Smith back in late 1856. "He is truly the most accomplished Engineer I know." Ross appears to be the only person to write "Dear Bob" when addressing letters to Rodes, and he jokingly referred to Hortense as "Madame." "I send you the plan of the piers as you requested," Ross wrote from Saint Charles, Missouri, "& hope you will have less difficulty in understanding it then you seem to have had with my letters—it is doubtful however, as a man who can't understand plain english can hardly be supposed to understand much about architecture." After describing some business matters, Ross closed with, "Give my respects to Madame, & tell her I hope she will hammer some courtesy into you before you write again."[81]

There is little in the historical record up to this point in his life to mark Rodes as a man of serious religious sensibilities. Despite an upbringing in the Calvinist, predestination faith of Presbyterianism, none of his few pieces of personal prewar correspondence contain any religious themes or references—not even a perfunctory "God bless" or "thank God." He never recommended that anyone seek peace and comfort through prayer. In an effort to console his father for losing the clerk of the court election in 1852, for example, Rodes urged him to rely on his own inner strength. This is not to conclude that Rodes was anti-religious or did not believe in God. No doubt with his son's knowledge, David Rodes had once given consideration, albeit briefly and more in the nature of a business or career choice, to the possibility of Robert becoming a preacher. Soon after marrying Hortense, Robert joined the local lodge of Freemason's, whose sole membership requirement was a belief in a supreme being. Yet even in this, Rodes may have had an additional motive: furthering his social and business connections. Although Rodes probably believed in God, it is fair to conclude that religion did not play a predominating influence on his life at this time.

There is no doubt, however, that by this time in his life Rodes had established a solid social and business network. "I know nothing about such matters," James Corry wrote Rodes regarding an upcoming "Grand Celebration" of many lodges in which he assumed Rodes "will be engaged in some way." In order to contrast himself with his friend, Corry added, "and not being very ambitious, though always needing friends, may not find it necessary to ask for particulars in that way—it seems to be Common to the American mind to desire association in every kind of pursuit & to act with the maxim that 'in Union is strength.'"[82]

A measure of the impressive extent of Rodes' social connections at this time, as well as of the high regard in which important members of the community held him, came in the form of a flattering governing board request for a consultation concerning the possibility of converting the local campus into a military school. Rodes informed Smith about this development at some length shortly after the new year, 1859:

> Some discussion is going on here about the University of Alabama. [P]eople complain of the languishing condition of the whole concern and are rubbing the Faculty and Trustees pretty severely. I saw one unpublished article which handles every member of the faculty severely, mentioning them by name. In truth tho' I think the faculty are with few exceptions efficient men, but their system of teaching is absurd and their discipline more so. The mathematics course is a very inferior one. Pure mathematics is not dignified with a full Chair. But be that as it may parties have sought me privately to enquire about our [VMI] system of teaching, discipline &c—and I think it would be well for them to read your pamphlet on teaching, published a year or two ago.[83]

During the long road to his current impressive success as an engineer, Rodes never lost his interest in teaching and in the field of education. He kept a close eye not only upon developments at VMI and the University of Alabama, but on educational trends in general. "I am truly delighted," he wrote Colonel Smith on May 4, 1859, "that you, my old preceptor and superintendent, and the head of my alma mater, are the first man to recognize and defend in this Country the necessity for the great educational reforms now in progress in the old Country [Europe]—And still more delighted to see and know that our institution has in fact been keeping pace with, if not in advance of the movement." He continued: "I see more clearly than ever before, by reading your last publication ["Report to the Legislature of Virginia on Scientific Education in Europe"] what a glorious destiny awaits our establishment, and how far ahead of all other schools ours is in its capacity to meet the demands of the times and people as to education."[84]

"I recognize too with pleasure a more decided blow than usual at the tendency, which, pardon me for saying so, once I thought had assailed the V.M.I. as it had assailed nearly all schools in the Country—to popularize text books." Rodes' ideas on the matter were crystal clear: "perfect mastery of a subject," he wrote Smith, could be attained only by "hard study and close application with the principles of the subject." Moreover, Rodes strongly objected to curricula that stressed theory over practical application, an unfortunate trend that he saw creeping into American schools, particularly in the South. "German engineers are invariably our superiors in the school of practice," he told Smith. "So with the French, not only superior but infinitely so." Then he offered his assessment of native schools, with the maxim that would earn him both praise and enmity in the coming war. "The only American educated Engineers who can meet them [the Germans and the French] are from New England schools—Where the pupils are <u>drilled</u> drilled drilled in the school of application." In addition to French, which he had studied at VMI, Rodes possessed a reading knowledge of German, and he recommended to Smith "the best treatise on mechanics of the day—Weisbach's—It is German, but it is practical and scientific and greatly superior to Buchalet or any other I have seen."[85]

Then Rodes narrowed his focus to the University of Alabama, revealing an interesting peculiarity in his growing obsession with discipline. No military school could maintain effective discipline, he declared, without the physical presence of walls on its campus. "For heavens sake," he pleaded with Smith regarding the possible transformation of the university into a military school, "do not recommend its Conversion without the use of walls. . . . I did not see your letters to Dr G[arland] but he told me you advocated a plan which did not look to walls as essential to the enforcement of laws &c &c. . . . It can never succeed as a military school without being backed by state authority and good brick walls."[86]

That summer, Rodes gave Smith some indication of why he believed strict discipline so essential on a college campus. "Make all Alabamians," he warned the colonel regarding the admission to VMI of a local boy (possibly Frank Stafford, son of a Mrs. Stafford, a family friend), "or at least young F—join the Temperance Society—sign the pledge. He is not addicted to frolicking that I know of—but most of our College boys out here are apt to frolic under favorable circumstances." One wonders if Smith smiled at least slightly while reading these words, penned by one of VMI's prior good- natured rapscallions who managed to accumulate more than his own fair share of demerits.[87]

Meanwhile, in its search for suitable teaching candidates, the Board of Directors of the Louisiana State Seminary (the future LSU), a new school forming near Alexandria, turned to Smith for recommendations. The colonel immediately thought of Rodes, not only for an engineering professorship but for the superintendency of the entire school. "Mr. Rhodes [sic]," began his reply written to the board on June 12, 1859,

> is a native Virginian & graduate of this Institution and for three years held the office of Principal Assist't Professor. He has been for seven years in the successful prosecution of his profession as a Civil Engineer, & is at this time the Chief Engineer of a large Rail Road in Ala. I know Mr. Rhodes [sic] qualities well, & I do not know an individual better suited than he is for the chair to which he is recommended, especially when that chair is associated with the general Superintendence of the Institution. It is in the latter connection, that I would especially press his claims before your honorable Board. Mr. R. has the talent & the tact for such peculiar duties—He is a gentleman of high tone, holds correct views of discipline & government, & would be an honor & an ornament to the Institution.[88]

Eight days later on June 20, Smith told Rodes about the recommendations. With the professorship and the superintendency paying a combined annual salary of $3,500, the colonel obviously considered this a great opportunity for his former pupil. He also drew his attention to the *National Intelligencer*, a weekly newspaper in which the new school had been advertising for teaching candidates.[89]

Rodes replied on July 4, the eleventh anniversary of his graduation from VMI. "A thousand associations spring up connected with to-day, yourself and the Inst.," he fondly reflected. He then told Smith that he had seen the notices in the *National Intelligencer* and had thoroughly looked into the situation. "It looks very much as if they were trying to set up a cheap school," he scoffed, no doubt to Smith's great surprise, "and therefore that it is to be a humbug. The salary is enough, I don't care about that, but I will not give up any chance for reputation and position in my profession for a place in a 3rd rate College, or for a place in a military school when there is no means of Controlling the pupils. Nothing but walls and bars will suit out here nor indeed anywhere I think."[90]

Perhaps reflecting on his own youthful indiscretions, and/or remembering witnessing those of others, the now thirty-year-old Rodes possessed an almost maniacal insistence on the need to "Control the pupils" by means of a prison-like setting.

There was more. He believed the new school intended to use professors in more than one capacity, a practice to which he strongly objected because it sacrificed proficiency and teaching skill in any one subject. "No one professor of the S[chool] but what has at least twice as much to teach as he can attend to properly." His list of complaints went on. "No place designated clearly as location of the seminary—no information as to source wherein money must come." Then, almost as an afterthought, Rodes remembered to thank the colonel, adding rather dryly, "I feel complimented that you should mention me as suitable for the post."[91]

Smith must have been astonished. After years of hearing Rodes complain about his lot in life and of how much happier he would be teaching, the colonel was reading Rodes' almost angry rejection of what seemed like a golden opportunity. If he read between the lines, however, Smith may have realized that his former pupil now enjoyed a level of success in engineering that set the highest standards for any possible career change. Rodes had worked hard at his profession and was proud of his accomplishments with the NE & SW Alabama. Like an architect working on a grand project, he naturally wanted to see his efforts on the line brought to a successful conclusion. His income of $250 a month was more than ten times that of an average laborer. "The salary is enough," he told Smith regarding the pay at the new school, "I don't care about that." What he did profess to care about was "reputation." Too often in the past he had eagerly joined a new railroad company, hoping there to establish his reputation, only to see that company fold or otherwise put him out of work, forcing him to start all over again somewhere else. That same dreaded fear arose when he contemplated giving up his current, hard- earned reputation to go with a new unestablished (and what he called) "3d rate College."

Whether he read between the lines or not, Smith refused to give up. Convinced that his former pupil was making a serious mistake, he continued to press him on the matter until, surprisingly enough given his adamant earlier rejection, Rodes overcame his fear of risky change and agreed to make the leap. Deep down, he truly wanted to be a teacher.

Then came something worse than fear—humiliation through rejection. By the time Rodes made up his mind to apply, the superintendency of the "humbug" passed to future Union general William T. Sherman. Rodes felt like the suitor who finally expressed his feelings, only to discover that the fair maiden was already betrothed. His hurt pride searched for reasons why it all was for the best. "If I had left here," he explained to Smith, "the inimical influences existing here against me, which are powerless as long as I am here, would have ruined my reputation professionally at least if strenuous effort could have done so. This influence has force enough to appoint my successor unless I could produce a man preeminently qualified to take charge of this road. Of course too, having buckled to this road body and soul almost, I am naturally desirous to see it through."[92]

Here the affable, almost universally liked Rodes had made a rather startling revelation, that in his current work he faced opposition, or "inimical influences," from those who apparently disagreed with some of his decisions, and he feared that once he left the railroad they might reverse or alter those decisions to the detriment of his sacred reputation. But, for the sake of returning to teaching, Rodes had been willing not only to risk all this, but also to leave behind something to which he had "buckled [his] body and soul."

"Nevertheless," he continued, "I was so strongly drawn to the life and position your exertions in my behalf opened to me that I obtained what letters of recommendation I needed. . . . I am bound to confess to you that apart from the mortification of being placed in such a ridiculous position. . . . I do not yet feel much regret at the result of this Louisiana affair."

Despite all this, Rodes remained determined eventually to realize his deepest desire. "I know now as I have always known," he touchingly reassured himself in writing to Smith, "that I would be happier and more useful as a teacher than in my present profession."[93]

To avoid the humiliation of doing it himself, Rodes asked Smith to write Dr. Graham, the president of the Louisiana Seminary Board, and explain the reason for the late application. Smith evidently did so, for Graham contacted

Rodes directly. "He seems to think in his letter to me," Rodes told Smith by way of further easing his own ill feelings over the whole matter, "that I would have been dissatisfied with the state of things I would have found in Louisiana—lodgings board &c. Too late now this."[94]

Any lingering ill feelings over the "Louisiana affair" quickly dissolved with the arrival of the day for which Rodes had been waiting nearly ten years. In 1859, the VMI Board decided to divide the chair of Natural Philosophy, then held by Thomas J. Jackson, and create a chair of Applied Mechanics. With the institute now having been open for twenty years, Smith was at last willing to consider one of its own graduates. Two prime candidates stood out: Rodes, and his good friend and former classmate Alfred L. Rives, the same man who five years earlier Rodes had tried to persuade to come to Texas. Despite his own intense desire for the position, Rodes nobly wrote a letter to the Board praising Rives' qualifications. Unaware of Rodes' actions, Rives did the same on his friend's behalf and then withdrew from the candidacy.[95]

On July 2, 1860, the VMI Board appointed Rodes a Professor of Civil Engineering and Applied Mechanics. Because of the time needed to approve funding, however, the board told him not to assume the new chair until the beginning of the following year's fall semester. That date was September 1, 1861.[96]

The dream finally granted, alas, would never be fulfilled.

Chapter 3

| From Engineer to Brigadier General

On Monday, November 21, 1859, a special meeting took place in the Tuscaloosa City Hall. Various officials and numerous citizens gathered to discuss how to raise funds for the use of forming a new, local militia company. The issue at hand was not whether the company should be raised, but how quickly.[1]

About five weeks earlier, an important event occurred in Harpers Ferry, Virginia, when an abolitionist fanatic named John Brown seized a Federal arsenal in a mad attempt to foment servile insurrection throughout Virginia and ultimately the entire South. Though the fantastic scheme lacked any real chance of success, it did have the effect of spreading terror throughout the slaveholding states at the very thought that it might. The citizens of Tuscaloosa County responded by arming about one hundred men and forming them into a company they called the Warrior Guards.

Though the company was new, the name was not. On April 3, 1820, less than one year after the admission of Alabama to the union, the Warrior Guards dressed ranks for the first time in the narrow, unpaved streets of what was then the small town of Tuscaloosa. Though the company periodically dissolved and revived over the ensuing years as perceived need determined and available funds permitted, the name lived on as a symbol of community pride. This latest incarnation of the "Guards" would be led by a man well known to the community for more than four years, but who only recently had taken up residence in Tuscaloosa. Everyone now recognized him as Captain Robert E. Rodes.[2]

Robert and Hortense moved from Eutaw to Tuscaloosa earlier that fall. The change may have been undertaken as part of a gradual transition toward a return to VMI at Lexington, or it may have been business related. Since the couple moved in with Hortense's parents, it seems likely that Robert sought relief from the sometimes overwhelming burden of caring for his still ailing and childless wife. Whatever the cause, the move took several months to complete, the bad roads that time of year delaying until February the shipment of Rodes' books and tobacco and Hortense's precious geraniums, the pots safely packed in sand.[3]

The circumstances surrounding Rodes' appointment as captain of the Warrior Guards remain unknown. Everyone concerned knew of his qualifications for the highly honored post. The community respected Rodes for his VMI background, his extensive engineering experience, and for his current position as chief engineer of the NE & SW Alabama. Whether Rodes sought the appointment—and how he felt about receiving it—is not known. But he did not take lightly this added responsibility to his already heavily burdened life. As with all serious endeavors, in this too he strove for "perfect mastery of the subject," diligently drilling his new command on a regular, usually monthly, basis. The fortuitous move to Tuscaloosa, therefore, proved to be an important step on the road to his future position as a Confederate major general in command of a combat division in one of the most renowned armies in American history.

*   *   *

Meanwhile, work on the railroad continued. Through the early months of 1860, the line continued its slow march up from Meridian toward Tuscaloosa. In July news arrived of Rodes' appointment as professor at VMI. The news meant he effectively became a lame duck chief engineer with more then one year to go before assuming his new post. Francis Smith wrote Rodes on September 9 to offer advice on how best to use his time. "My own opinion," he explained, "is that your influence and your chair here would be immeasurably promoted if you could go to Paris and spend say one month in the School of Bridges and Roads."[4]

However much he may have wished to do so, Rodes did not take Smith's advice. Personal finances, Hortense's health, the Warrior Guards, and concern about those in the company who might somehow undermine his work contributed to his decision to stay home.[5]

At Eutaw in October 1860, Rodes delivered his second annual report as chief engineer. He optimistically assured the directors that "there now was more confidence in the undertaking than at any time in its history." A mere month later his assessment would change dramatically.[6]

By November, Rodes the perfectionist had elevated the Warrior Guards to such a state of proficiency that at the Fair of West Alabama in Demopolis they won first prize, a banner proclaiming the outfit to be the best drilled company. Both Rodes and Hortense derived deep satisfaction from this award. The former indicated as much in a January letter to his old mentor Smith of VMI in which he momentarily set aside his reserved nature in order to boast of the prize. The latter recalled the memorable occasion in a sad note written to a friend on the fortieth anniversary of Robert's death.[7]

By the time Rodes and the Guards won that banner, however, the "Black Republican" Abraham Lincoln had been elected president. The news soon made it clear to many that militia companies might have to do work of a far more serious nature than competing for prizes at a fair. In anticipation of Alabama's secession, and everything that implied, on November 21 Rodes began drilling the Warrior Guards on a daily basis.[8]

Investors hate nothing more than uncertainty. As the threat of war increased, nervous creditors became more unwilling to risk their capital. This, in turn, made it increasingly difficult for companies to do business. The NE & SW Alabama was no exception. Rodes, however, continued to press on, hoping for the best. "I saw Chiles today about the negroes you wish to hire next year," Peyton Randolph wrote him on December 20. "[H]e says you can get them."[9]

On Christmas Day, however, Rodes confessed in a letter of recommendation written on behalf of a friend and VMI alumnus that "hard times and gloomy political prospects for our country have almost entirely put an end to our operations here—Certainly have Compelled us to discharge many of our Assistant Engineers."[10]

As happened so often to him as an assistant engineer, Rodes now was discharging his own assistants, this time in a "gloomy" atmosphere, not only for the company but also for the entire nation.

With the coming of the new year, the political situation deteriorated rapidly. On Saturday, January 7, 1861, the state secession convention convened at Montgomery. After four days of heated debates, during which Tuscaloosa County's two representatives (Robert Jemison and the leader of the "Cooperationists," William R. Smith) voiced their strong disapproval of secession, the committee, by a vote of sixty-one to thirty- nine, took Alabama out of the Union on January 11.[11]

In anticipation of that dramatic result, Governor Andrew Barry Moore the day before sent orders for Captain Rodes to take the Warrior Guards to Fort Morgan, which guarded the entrance to Mobile Bay on the Gulf of Mexico. "All Alabama is ablaze, the state is out of the union and we are all expecting a brush with the Federal troops at Mobile or Fort Morgan," was how Rodes described the situation to Colonel Smith on January 13.[12]

Rodes, however, probably did not include himself among those who were "ablaze." Though proud to lead his company in defense of his adopted state, he bitterly realized that, for him at least, this national crisis had come at a most inopportune time. He had waited patiently for years for the chance to fulfill his cherished dream of taking a chair at VMI. Now that chance was within his grasp and he had to let it go, at least temporarily. It must have torn him apart. "Under these circumstances and the uncertainty of the future," he sadly informed Smith, "I cannot readily give you any promise in regard to my moving to Virginia and taking service with you—a week ago I should have accepted almost any place you could have offered me at the Inst.—now I must bide the result of the military movements a foot here."

Like many people across the North and South, Rodes did not expect the current crisis to last long. He believed it would be over after a brief but severe lesson had been taught to those unwilling to accept the new situation, whereupon he could resume the pursuit of his personal dream. "This much only I can say," he somewhat apologetically went on to Smith, "that if I come out of the campaign alive and in time, and you are still willing to accept my services at the Institute, I believe that I shall be but too glad to go then. If it be possible to postpone my decision until June, or until this brush is over here in Alabama, I of course would be glad to have that privilege."[13] As he prepared to lead the Guards to Mobile, Rodes realized with no little dread that a prolonged sojourn in the military might thrust his family into abject poverty.

On the cool and crisp Tuesday morning of January 15, Rodes assembled the Guards at the county courthouse and marched the men down to the wharf. The Tuscaloosa Board of Aldermen had appropriated all of $200 to help pay the Guard's expenses, and the townspeople, including Hortense and the Woodruffs, provided a festive if somewhat sad send-off as Rodes boarded his men on the steamer *L. D. Wallace* and set sail down the Black Warrior River for Mobile.[14]

The first leg of the winding sixty-five mile journey took Rodes and his men past the unfinished railroad bridge masonry the engineer had worked three years to create. The *L. D. Wallace* entered the Tombigbee River at Demopolis, where the men began their second leg, a twisting, turning 145-mile ride down to Mobile. When they disembarked, the Guards received a warm welcome and a ceremonial escort from the "Mobile Cadets" (future Company A, Third Alabama Infantry), who first led them over to the armory for supplies and then on to a fine banquet dinner at "Battle House." The next day the Guards left on another thirty- mile ride out to Fort Morgan.[15]

Zealous state secessionists already had seized the place back on the 5th, six days before the vote that formally severed Alabama from the Union. Completed in 1834 after sixteen years of construction, and named for Revolutionary War hero Daniel Morgan, the imposing five-sided structure (replacing old Fort Bowyer, whose huge smoothbores helped drive off the British nearly fifty years before) stood at the tip of Mobile Point on a long neck of land stretching across the entrance to Mobile Bay. Supported by Fort Gaines three miles to the northwest on Dauphin Island, and by Fort Powell four miles farther on at Grant's Pass, Fort Morgan appeared nearly impregnable. The land behind it had been cleared for some distance, and the main ramparts looked down over a series of dark thick red brick walls protected by smooth, sloping, double-tiered embankments. After filing into the "citadel," a large ten-sided brick structure capable of billeting about four hundred soldiers and their supplies, Rodes and his men were instructed on working and defending the fort's forty heavy guns located in barbette and casemates.[16]

To the surprise of some, the days and weeks passed quietly with no sign of an impending "brush" with the enemy. "It is a very healthy location and so far a very pleasant one," wrote a member of another militia company stationed in the fort. His description helps illuminate what Rodes and his men were also experiencing:

> [I]f it were not for the irksome garrison duty I should enjoy myself very much. My duties are very onerous Commencing at day light and ending at ten o'clock at night and then we are frequently turned out by green sentinels firing at bushes, cans +c and causing the whole garrison to run to their posts on the wall. The Companies are required to drill about seven times a day and by the time the tattoo had sounded at night we are all willing to go to bed. Our quarters in the fort are very good and the food as good as any one Can require, we get all the substantials from the government and can get an abundance of fine fish and oysters from the fishing smacks at a very small price.[17]

Under these "irksome" circumstances, Rodes kept his men busy and vigilant, protecting them from the "evils" of inactivity. "From the press and from our citizens who have visited them," reported Tuscaloosa's *The Independent Monitor* on February 1, "we learn, with much satisfaction, that this gallant company sustained its prestige and its morals amidst the trials of garrison duty, at once the most onerous, as it is the most trying and demoralizing to the volunteer soldier. The Guards were justly the pride of our city, and in every situation have sustained themselves in a manner gratifying to their friends and to themselves. May they continue to do so." Bursting with pride for the company that so nobly upheld the honor of the community, Tuscaloosa's citizens "raised a subscription" to send the Guards much needed "pecuniary aid."[18]

Under Colonel J. B. Todd, Rodes and the Warrior Guards remained in state service at Fort Morgan until their term of enlistment expired in mid-March. At that time, a company of Confederate troops relieved them and control of the fort passed to national Confederate authority. Rodes gladly took the Guards back to the welcoming arms of Tuscaloosa.[19]

The happy homecoming quickly turned sour when Rodes discovered that Hortense again was quite ill. Moreover, he learned that his good friend Peyton Randolph had left the rail line to go with his own militia company to the Florida coast opposite the still Federally-held Fort Pickens. Unlike most men in his company, Randolph dreaded going, "not wishing to have a sudden and violent end put to my Career by a grape shot or Minie ball."[20]

These anxieties notwithstanding, Rodes plunged back into his work on the railroad. Racing against the increasing probability of the national crisis exploding into war, he strove to wrap things up by the time of an emergency meeting of the company directors. "If it is at all possible," he anxiously wrote Randolph in Florida on March 19, "I wish you to come up and render final estimates on all Derby's work [on the bridges over the Warrior and Tombigbee rivers] by the 10th of April next when the board meets at Eutaw." Then he added rather ominously, "We are all anxiously awaiting the war news."

As two dedicated engineers are apt to do, Randolph previously had shared with Rodes his observations concerning the design of the local military installations. This prompted the perfectionist chief engineer, quite as if his assistant still worked for him on the railroad, to urge his commanding officer "to construct outworks at that narrow neck of land just up the beach from the Fort, and on the Gulf Shore between that & the fort and moreover and especially to have the embrasures [openings] of the Fort remodeled. As they stand now," admonished Rodes, "a man can plug you without firing into the throat of the embrasure directly." In a postscript, Rodes offered an unusual (for him) boastful reference to the Warrior Guards: "Look out for us if we have a fight."[21]

Ten days later Rodes again appealed strongly to Randolph to try to make the big board meeting in Eutaw, even offering to write his captain to gain permission. By then, the new Confederate States government had formed in Montgomery, with Jefferson Davis as president. The new national authority began accepting troops. Rodes thought hard about joining. Given his ambitious nature, he desired a commission but was yet undecided as to whether the state or the new national service offered the best chance for advancement. "I feel more and more inclined to enter the service," he confided to Randolph in the same letter of March 29, "but I fear to enter the state service, and have not influence enough to get [a] position in either I think." Many of those already sporting a commission did not impress him. "The list of Army Appointments is a sweet and odorous one from the Captain down," he scornfully added with a sarcastic air of superiority.

Rodes closed with reference to a seemingly endless source of stress in his life: Hortense's health. "Mrs. Rodes is improving," he declared hopefully, "and will be glad to hear from you—write again—you can write a readable letter [even] for a sergeant."[22]

For the time being, however, Rodes remained in state service. In late March, the Warrior Guards re-enlisted for another nine months and reorganized. Rodes easily won reelection as captain, the men believing it was in their best interest to continue under his firm guiding hand. The company's other officers included First Lieutenant Henry A. Whiting, Rodes' friend and former VMI classmate and railroad associate. William Fowler (who the following December would become the company's captain upon its reorganization into an artillery battery) was elected second lieutenant. Dr. N. Venable became the company surgeon with the rank of third lieutenant. John Phelan was made orderly sergeant, and the new quartermaster sergeant was Rodes' twenty-nine-year-old brother-in- law, Plymouth "Ben" Woodruff.[23]

When the reorganization was complete Rodes resumed training the company, drilling it daily. The "pecuniary aid" the Guards received from the good people of Tuscaloosa while at Fort Morgan proved inadequate for their needs, and Rodes believed the company to be in such a desperate situation as to require an emotional appeal to a very special group of citizens.

"To The Ladies of Tuscaloosa," began his long open letter that was printed in *The Independent Monitor* on March 29:

> We appeal to you in behalf of the Warrior Guards. They have reflected credit upon our community wherever they have been. They are justly becoming the pride and ornament of our city, and we are already one of its institutions. We appeal to you to make it a permanent one and we will tell you why—Though they have a complete camp equipage, complete uniforms, and excellent arms and accoutrements, they have no place in which to keep these things dry and in good order, they have no house—no armory. Their tents, arms and uniforms are being ruined for want of an armory. They have no drill-room, and unless these wants are supplied the Company must decline.
>
> The "Arsenal" does not supply them in any respect. Its walls are unplastered, its joists destitute of both laths and plaster, its roof leaks, and above all it is too low pitched to allow the men to handle their arms properly. It lacks glass, doors, windows and a roof. To keep up the espirit of the Company, nay, to keep up its organization it is necessary that a comfortable drill-room should be provided for them. The stated drills will not alone keep up the Company in an efficient a state as it was on its return from Fort Morgan, and then it had much to learn.
>
> The Captain of the Company desires to make it the best drilled "Company" in the State and in the South, and he can do this if you will assist him. He and his brother officers desire, in order to insure these results, to fit up at the Arsenal a meeting room, a drill-room, wardrobes for uniforms, tents, &c. They wish to make it a pleasant place of meeting for men and officers, to render it comfortable and attractive, and thus to offer to the members of the Company an inducement to practice constantly at the manual and bayonet exercise, and to become good soldiers, and you who have husbands, sons, brothers and friends in the Company, remember that in doing this you are supplying a want to our young men which has heretofore been supplied by the bar rooms, billiard saloons and other places of like character.

Rodes, continued, making a direct pitch for assistance:

Will you not help them to carry out this laudable design? Already they have begun with their limited means to fit up one room, but they need about Five Hundred Dollars more to carry out their whole design. To help them do this is to help the community and yourselves. Raise the money for them, and in the meantime do not let their muskets suffer for want of covers. Green baize is abundant, get a pattern made (for everything pertaining to soldiers should be uniform) and make by it sixty green covers. The citizens have done much for this Company, but it has done as much in sustaining the character of our city, in the trying ordeal of barrack duty—as citizen soldiers. All admit the high character, soldierly bearing, and gentlemanly demeanor of its officers and privates. The ladies as yet, have done but little, but it was because there was no pressing necessity, we know they will now respond to a call from them, upon whom they will have to depend in the hour of danger. We have made this appeal to them, when we learned the true condition of the Armory &c., because we believed that they too, would like to assist in the equipment of the Volunteer Company in the city, to inspire the heart and nerve the arm of the soldier by its recollection—should the dread battle come.[24]

Before the good ladies of Tuscaloosa could do much to help alleviate problems Rodes only months later would consider embarrassingly trivial, circumstances intervened to pull the Guards away from their hometown. In response to Governor Moore's call for volunteers, on April 1 Rodes formally offered the company for service under the new national government.[25]

The firing on Fort Sumter in Charleston Harbor on April 12, 1861, coupled with President Abraham Lincoln's subsequent call for volunteers to help suppress the rebellion made Rodes' already precarious future even more uncertain. His view of the situation, however, undoubtedly coincided with those of his friend Randolph, who wrote, "I am decidedly warlike in my feelings since reading Lincoln's proclamation which shows that we must fight." After explaining that his own company would soon disband, Randolph begged Rodes to accept him, even as a private, into the Guards. "I had rather see service in your command," he pleaded, "then in any other."[26]

Rodes replied the next day, April 18. "The Warrior Guards are going again to the wars under my Command," he explained. [A]t least we have a reasonable prospect for getting up there 76 men." He then said he would try to get his friend into the company, "but don't let what you have said to me bias you. In these times let every man do his best for himself first of all." He added, "I shall receive you any time with open arms."[27]

Before "going again to the wars," Rodes thoughtfully prepared for the worst by quickly settling his personal affairs. He began by wrapping up his business with the railroad. He justifiably felt quite proud of his work on the line. After operating for nearly eight years, the Northeast & Southwest Alabama had completed twenty-seven miles of track, from Meridian, Mississippi, to York, Alabama. Moreover, much of the gradation had been done between York and Tuscaloosa and the masonry had been set for both the Black Warrior and Tombigbee River bridges. As the national crisis deepened, however, it became increasingly difficult for the company to do business, with credit and building supplies almost impossible to secure. At the special meeting held at Eutaw on April 10, Rodes promised the directors to report "in full all the work done on the [Black Warrior and Tombigbee] Bridge Contracts to this date & render a final estimate of all work done," a promise ensuing events prevented him from keeping. By the end of the month, Rodes paid off all the assistant engineers who either had been let go or who had left to join the service. He even made sure to pay up his Masonic dues.[28]

In addition to all these stressful matters, Hortense's health, as if in reflection of the worsening national situation, took a dramatic turn for the worse. "Mrs. Rodes [sic] illness keeps me confined at her bedside," Rodes sadly wrote Randolph on April 29. "She is not past hope but is so ill." Her plight deepened Rodes' concern that his decision to enter the military might leave her helpless, penniless, and in debt.[29]

This justifiable concern led Rodes the following day, April 30, to sign his new will. Having little to do with bequeathing, the document was more of a directive on how to free Hortense from his own financial obligations.

In truth, Rodes had but little to give away. His beloved books by Francois Rabelais, the sixteenth century satirist and humorist and author of *Gargantua and Pantagruel*, he willed to Norton Whitfield, the president of the NE & SW Alabama. His military and scientific books were to go to "my friends H. A. Whiting and George W. Robertson," both railroad associates. His cherished gold-headed cane to fellow engineer A. P. Hagan. For his executors, Rodes appointed Whitefield and Hagan. His other meager assets included about $1,000 owed him by the railroad, and another $200 owed him by friend and bridge builder, J. W. Derby, all of which he wanted collected for the benefit of Hortense.

Rodes' debts, on the other hand, were substantial. Though his New Orleans-based thirty-seven-year-old brother Virginius, or "Gin" as he was known, had never asked for repayment, he had loaned Rodes three years ago $1,700 to buy Hannah and her children. Rodes wanted to pay it back. For a reason he did not specify but which probably involved a real estate investment, Rodes owed $1,364, which was due the following February to a Mrs. Margaret Gooch. He owed $835 in two remaining yearly payments for his half of a $2,250 home in Tuscaloosa in which he and friend William Foster had invested. Finally, he owed his father-in-law David Woodruff several months of room and board.

In the event of his death, Rodes wanted Hortense to meet these obligations by disposing of, in whole or in part, his most valuable property: five slaves. These included house servant Betsy, and the four slaves he purchased in January 1859. Rodes stipulated that since the value of these slaves amounted to more than the sum of his financial obligations, Hortense should have the option of either selling them all and keeping the remaining money, or of selling off only those necessary to pay his debts.[30]

Having grown up in the midst of slavery and in a slave-owning family Rodes, like most Southerners, accepted the institution as a fact of life. That acceptance argued that slavery existed not only throughout history but also had received the sanction of Holy Scripture because the Old Testament patriarchs owned slaves and Jesus never spoke against slaveholders. As such, many Southerners did not believe slavery inherently sinful or evil, though they generally accepted the notion that slaves should be treated in a decent, Christian manner. Rodes' last option for Hortense ran against the decades-long appeal of clergymen throughout the South, who now were transforming those appeals into dire warnings that God's favor surely would be denied the fledgling Confederacy if slaveholders did not improve their treatment of slaves—particularly with regard to maintaining slave families intact. By allowing his wife to sell some of Hannah's children to pay off a debt, Rodes revealed himself to be rather cold hearted on this issue.[31]

*   *   *

After taking care of personal matters, Rodes prepared to comply with orders to take the Guards to Montgomery. He originally intended to leave Tuscaloosa on May 5 and march the company sixty or so miles down to Newbern, and from there travel by rail to Selma, where transports would complete the trip up the Alabama River to the capital. He abruptly changed that plan when he discovered that the "last remaining steamer" down at the wharf could accomplish the first leg of the trip one day early. Such eagerness impressed many in the community. "This we think is very patriotic," declared an editorial in *The Independent Monitor*, "and will be appreciated by all. . . . We wish them all success."[32]

The change in plans, however, did not alter the festive nature of the occasion. By every available means, including foot, horse, wagon, and buggy, people from the surrounding area came into town to see their boys off to war. At 10:00 a.m. on the beautiful Saturday morning of May 4, the University of Alabama Corps of Cadets escorted the Guards down to the wharf, where the company boarded the steamer *Cherokee*. From ship to shore and back again, cheers and sad farewells rang out as the little boat set off down the Black Warrior River. No doubt with a heavy heart, Rodes spoke what he may have believed to be a last goodbye to his ailing and beloved Hortense.[33]

Moving only slightly faster than a walk, the *Cherokee* turned and twisted down the stream for several hours before finally depositing its cargo at Candy's Landing, north of Demopolis. There, local farmers provided wagons to take Rodes and the Guards about ten miles east over rough roads to Newbern, whose warm welcome included an invitation, gladly accepted, to stay the night. The following morning the Guards took the train about forty miles to Selma, where they boarded the *Southern Republic* for the final twelve-hour leg of the journey up the Alabama River to Montgomery. Crammed into the boat with four other companies, the men shared their limited space with the horses and the slave deck hands. "[F]ortunately," one soldier scribbled in his diary, "the boat arrived before night, so we were not necessitated to sleep with our black and equine companions." Late on Sunday, May 5, Rodes finally put his exhausted men into Camp Jeff Davis, a patch of land on the state fair grounds in Montgomery.[34]

There, Captain Rodes beheld an amazing sight: a city swarming with volunteer companies rapidly joining newly-formed regiments. The Guards' turn came on May 11, when they became Company H of the Fifth Alabama Infantry. The other companies assigned to the Fifth Alabama included Co. A (Grove Hill Guards, Capt. Josephus M. Hall); Co. B (Livingston Rifles, Capt. John Hubbard Dent); Co. C (Pickensville Blues, Capt. Sampson Noland Ferguson); Co D (Monroe Guards, Capt. Giles Goode); Co. E (Talladega Artillery, Capt. Charles Miller Shelley); Co. F (Sumter Rifles, Capt. Robert P. Blount); Co. G (Cahaba Rifles, Capt. John Tyler Morgan); Co. I (Greensboro

Guards, Capt. Allen C. Jones); and Co. K (Mobile Continental State Artillery, Capt. William H. Ketchum.)[35]

As it was with volunteer companies, state law required volunteer regiments to obtain their officers by the process of election. This method followed the rather peculiar nineteenth century American tradition of democracy in the military. With a VMI education and nearly two years experience as a company captain, Rodes faced little competition for the office of colonel. His closest rival was Greene County planter and state legislator Captain Allen Cadwallader Jones of the Greensboro Guards, who became the regiment's lieutenant colonel. The third highest office, that of major, went to attorney John T. Morgan, captain of the Cahaba Rifles. Rodes' friend, Henry Whiting became regimental adjutant. Unfortunately, there is no extant record of how Rodes felt about being made colonel. Judging by his reactions to later promotions, it is safe to assume that, although he did not openly seek out the office, he was highly gratified to receive it. Finally, he had his coveted army commission, making the jump from captain to colonel in a single stroke.[36]

The new colonel enjoyed barely a moment to comprehend his new, daunting responsibilities, let alone get acquainted with his command. Orders quickly arrived to take the Fifth Alabama down to Pensacola, Florida. Near there, on Santa Rosa Island not quite two miles across Pensacola Bay, stood Fort Pickens. The stronghold still was defiantly held by Federal forces. Many observers throughout the North and South believed the war might begin in earnest at Fort Pickens, but after Fort Sumter fell rather easily and the Federals in turn heavily reinforced Pickens, it became clear that seizing the place would require a prolonged effort. The Confederate commander in charge of taking the fort, General Braxton Bragg, decided to put it under siege. He developed a plan to seize the eastern end of Santa Rosa, five miles from Pickens, and from there and the mainland pound the fort with huge siege guns and mortars until it gave up. To protect his newly-arrived batteries, Bragg set up around the bay a six-mile-long semicircular defense perimeter. The Fifth Alabama was one of several regiments sent to help defend those guns.[37]

Around noon on Sunday, May 12, Colonel Rodes, Major Morgan, and seven companies of the Fifth, about 480 men, made a fatiguing march to the depot, where they boarded a special train and left Montgomery. After a rickety 160-mile ride on the recently completed line between the two towns, during which the men had little or nothing to eat and were forced to sleep lying jammed on the floor of their box cars, they arrived in Pensacola about daylight the next morning. The tired men gathered their baggage and followed a guide out to their new campground, about three- quarters of a mile southwest of Pensacola and two hundred yards from the bay. They reached the site in time to face a drenching rain sweeping in from the gulf. As the men struggled to put up their tents, Rodes rode on to meet General Bragg at Fort Barrancas, nine miles west of Pensacola.[38]

The skies cleared the following day and the sun mercilessly beat down on the men as they worked to create a drill ground by clearing the area of trees and burning the logs. While sweating along with his comrades, the Fifth's new quartermaster, Captain James D. Webb, was delighted to receive a visit from Colonel Edward Bullock, an old Barbour College friend and an officer with the Eighteenth Alabama. "I was holding on to the tent as he came up," Webb wrote his wife. What happened next surprised Webb even more. "Col Rodes ordered me to his headquarters & invited Col. B. & myself to join him in a glass of champagne. It was a picture—I had on no coat or vest—in fact nothing but my white flannel shirt & the perspiration rolling off me."[39]

That Rodes offered champagne to fellow officers at this time does not mean that he viewed this encampment as something of a festive occasion. On the contrary, in keeping with his past practice as captain of the Warrior Guards, he now meant to impose upon the Fifth Alabama his version of strict discipline. No man, he firmly believed, could be a good soldier without discipline, and no officer, no matter how brave or intelligent, was complete without the strict implementation of discipline, particularly in wartime.

This was not a recently acquired conviction. It took root in the early years at home under the influence of his militia general father, grew under the guidance of Francis Smith and the strict professors at VMI, and matured with his rise to chief engineer of an important railroad company. In that maturity, Rodes firmly held the belief that one's full potential could be realized only through strict guidance and discipline. That belief may also have been based on a certain measure of contempt for the uneducated, "ungentlemanly" sorts now under his care, with a corresponding sense of his own self-superiority.

Whether teaching students, supervising workers, or training soldiers, Rodes professed the same goal—"to strive for perfect mastery of a subject by hard study and close application with principles of the subject." That goal could not be achieved without discipline backed up by obedience to superiors, strict observance of the rules and of what is right and proper, and appropriate punishment for violating any of the above. As a teacher, as an engineer, and especially as a soldier, he never wavered from this conviction. Many would come to admire him for it, and not a few would come to despise him. As

Alabama historian Willis Brewer accurately wrote after the war ,"The stern and military precision of Gen. Rodes were not such as to render him a favorite with a citizen soldiery."[40]

Yet when the day's work was done and duty fulfilled, Rodes, though somewhat reserved by nature, could relax and be charming, friendly, and sociable. At the appropriate time, he could offer a glass of champagne to a fellow officer and drink to their health and to the success of their cause. "Just, stern in the discharge of duty and in exacting it of others," declared a postwar memorial to Rodes, which added that his military style of command was marked by "firmness tempered with kindness."[41]

It was at Pensacola that the men of the Fifth Alabama began to take the measure of their new colonel. He drilled them several hours every morning, extremely hard work in the sometimes ankle deep sand on the drill ground. He ordered them to clean their camp in the afternoons. He put them through a thirty-minute dress parade at six every evening, which called for inspection of arms and accoutrements, and he sent them to bed every night at nine. Rodes' demanding schedule, declared one soldier, proved to be "about as much as we could stand."[42]

Meanwhile, on the 15th the remaining companies of the Fifth Alabama came in with Lieutenant Colonel Jones, bringing the regiment's strength up to about 1,000 strong. Three days later, General Bragg sent over his aide, Captain John Forney, to swear in the entire regiment for a term of twelve months in the service of the Confederate States, with some soldiers grumbling that they already had served one month before being sworn in.[43]

Like at Fort Morgan two months before, duty at Pensacola was relatively quiet and easy. Throughout the month of May, the overall situation progressed from the expectation that Fort Pickens would be the scene of the first battle of the war, to the conviction that it represented an indefinite standoff.

Though Rodes' men managed to temper somewhat the harshness of their existence by bathing regularly in the bay and buying fresh fish at local markets, they began to despair about the purpose of their mission. Battling heat, fleas, mosquitoes, and boredom, many started to question the wisdom of enlisting. "When we came to Pensacola we were in high spirits at the prospects of a brush with the Yankees, and thought Fort Pickens would be attacked as soon as we arrived," grumbled one soldier to his diary. "We are getting tired of Pensacola and desire to be sent immediately on to Virginia, where it is not so warm, and where we think most of the fighting will take place." The soldier summed up his frustration in lyrical fashion: Just let Col Rodes take the 5th Regt. down And We'll give the Yankees one good round."[44]

No one wanted more than Rodes to go to Virginia, the probable scene of action. There, in Lynchburg, stood his boyhood home, where lived his sixty-six-year-old father David and beloved stepmother Fannie, fourteen-year-old half-sister Lucy and thirteen-year-old half-brother Lafayette. Within this strong desire to go, desperation and optimism became virtually indistinguishable. "We do not know how long we will be here," Captain Webb wrote on May 16 to a friend. "Our Col is under the impression not long."[45]

Before Rodes and the Fifth could stand toe-to-toe with the Yankees, however, they first had to battle another fierce and merciless enemy— illness. Most of the recruits hailed from wide-open farmland, where they had had little opportunity to build immunities to disease. Crammed into tight living conditions with nearly 1,000 men, they became easy prey for aggressive bacteria and viruses. Severe colds and diarrhea attacked first, sweeping through the ranks and striking down men and officers alike, including the commander. "Col Rodes has been quite indisposed for a day or two," a concerned Captain Webb wrote his wife on May 23. "[H]e says he will be on duty tomorrow."[46]

Next came measles, mumps, and pneumonia, which by the end of May rendered unfit for duty some 200 men out of 965, "[with] the number increasing." Before running its course, measles alone would strike two out of every three men in the regiment, killing several.[47]

Despite the heroic efforts of a Mrs. Kerr, who voluntarily came down from Greensboro to run the regimental hospital, a responsibility that won her high praise and appreciation from the men, the Fifth Alabama seemed to be losing this battle. To make matters worse, the regiment received no supplies or medicines, compelling Rodes on more than one occasion to dip into his own meager funds to help buy them in Pensacola. Moreover, once the regimental hospital became full, he unselfishly helped pay the "rent" for private hospital space in town.[48]

Exasperated at the apparent inefficiency of the fledgling Confederate government, Rodes sent Major Morgan to Montgomery to plead for help from Leroy P. Walker, the new secretary of war. The colonel instructed Morgan to argue that the regiment desperately needed tents, decent food, medicines, and such basic supplies as cartridges, cartridge boxes, belts, cap boxes, bayonet scabbards, even musical instruments and regimental colors. Through Morgan, Rodes explained that he now appealed directly to the War Department only because of past failures to achieve anything through normal channels. "I have exhausted all the resources at my Command in obtaining tents &c," he wrote, "and am constantly met with the reply 'none on hand' or 'none allowed' in response to articles that are really needed and are always furnished to troops in service." Rodes then revealed the extent of his own personal involvement. "To store the provisions take care of the advance guard and protect the sick," he informed the secretary, "we have been compelled to spend our money freely and I for one am absolutely ruined by this draft on my resources." The colonel even complained about something the regiment possessed but did not want. "We have been compelled by order of General Bragg to accept as chaplain a man who however clever he may be has not a single voice in the regiment in favor of his appointment and who though assured of this and that nine tenths of my Command desire the appointment of a Chaplain from our midst."[49]

Instead of getting a favorable reply to these requests, Rodes received something he was not expecting. On June 2, orders came through Bragg for the Fifth Alabama to proceed at once to Richmond.[50]

The recent secession of the Old Dominion and the subsequent transfer of the Confederate capital from Montgomery to Richmond made it clear that Virginia would become a major theater of war. That and the continuing standoff with Fort Pickens made excessive Bragg's force of nearly 8,000. He was directed to give up three regiments, about 2,800 men, and send them to Virginia. "Everything seems to tend in that direction," Bragg sadly wrote his wife. "[W]e are considered here as secondary."[51]

Delighted finally to get these orders, Rodes wasted no time implementing them, quite as though he feared they might be rescinded if he did not act quickly. With incredible speed, six companies readied themselves and boarded a special train that took them into Montgomery the next day. They wasted no time in the capital, either. "We will leave here to night with a portion of our Regiment," Captain Webb wrote his wife. "I have to accompany the Col . . . with the first detachment."[52]

By this time Rodes and the twenty-one-year-old Webb, a graduate of the University of Alabama, had developed an abiding mutual respect. Rodes appreciated and often complimented the former attorney for his reliability and intelligence, even going so far as to write Hortense about his fine qualities. "He is exceedingly kind & attentive to me," Webb wrote his wife on June 3. "[H]e has on more than one occasion spoken to me of the regard that his wife expresses for you & for me—says to me that Mrs R will be delighted to know that I am to be his intimate right hand man." Still, Webb added, not every officer in the regiment had Rodes' confidence. "Our Col feels that he has to look to Major Morgan & myself for the assistance he needs—he is disappointed in the Lieut Col [Jones]—this is strictly confidential."[53]

With his men "crowded as they could be packed" into boxcars, while he rode in a separate comfortable passenger car for officers, Rodes and the first detachment of the Fifth Alabama left Montgomery by rail on June 3, a Monday evening, and rode the East Tennessee and Georgia Railroad up to Virginia. Though at night the men "could get no sleep at all scarcely," complained one grumbling soldier, they generally "had a very pleasant time during the day, at the different stations looking at the ladies cheering us on, waving flags, throwing us bouquets, pieces of poetry, &c." At nearly every stop along the way Rodes and his men received warm greetings from large crowds, who gave them fine foods and made requests for speeches. Though there is no known record to indicate whether Rodes spoke to the admiring throngs, it is certain that he left in their care scores of men who were too ill to go on.[54]

About 9:00 p.m. on June 9, the train finally pulled into Richmond. Rodes bedded down his men in and around a church located near the Exchange Hotel, where some eleven years before "Lieutenant" Rodes and his cadets had arrived as an escort for President Taylor. The next morning, Rodes marched the regiment out to its new encampment, a racetrack located more than one mile from the city. The next day, three more companies of the Fifth Alabama arrived, bringing with them a new recruit for Company H, Rodes' twenty-five-year-old brother-in law Daniel Webster Woodruff. On the 12th, the regiment received its new Company K, the Barbour Grays, under Captain Eugene Blackford. The outfit replaced the Mobile Continental Artillery, which had been left behind in Pensacola.[55]

To Rodes' great satisfaction, it was in the new nation's capital that he finally saw his regiment receive adequate supplies and provisions. "My company will be one of the best equipped in the army," Captain Blackford proudly wrote to the home newspaper, the Greensboro *Deacon*. "We have fine knapsacks and really elegant uniforms." Soon, Blackford also might consider his company one of the most proficient in the army. While awaiting orders, the predictable Rodes drilled his men incessantly—sometimes for three hours without stopping—on the sweltering, shadeless grounds of the racetrack.[56]

In compliance with General Order 22, Rodes early on Tuesday the 18th took the Fifth Alabama back to the train depot in the city, a difficult march for some on the hot dusty roads. He put them on the cars around 9:00 a.m. After a twenty-five mile ride up to Hanover Courthouse on the Richmond, Fredericksburg & Potomac Railroad, they bumped and rolled their way forty

Brig. Gen. (later Lt. Gen. Richard S. Ewell.

Generals in Gray

miles to Gordonsville on the Virginia Central and sixty-five more miles north on the Orange & Alexandria before arriving in Manassas Junction at 1:30 a.m. the following morning. Rodes marched his exhausted command through the darkness six miles across rough and broken roads to a new camp on the farm of a man named Van Pelt, "a Pennsylvanian, thoroughly union at heart," near the Stone Bridge over Bull Run. There, the Fifth Alabama was brigaded with the Second Brigade under Brigadier General Richard S. Ewell, who had received his commission just two days earlier. The new brigade included the Sixth Alabama under Colonel John J. Seibel; the Sixth Louisiana under Colonel Isaac Seymour; the Washington Artillery, a howitzer battery under Lieutenant Thomas Rosser; and four companies of cavalry under Lieutenant Colonel Walter Jenifer.[57]

The brigade was one of seven, each with its own artillery, the whole numbering about 20,000 men. This powerful force held the "Manassas Line" under the command of the hero of Fort Sumter, General Pierre G. T. Beauregard. The other six brigades were led by James Longstreet, Milledge Bonham, Philip Cocke, David Jones, Jubal Early, and Nathan Evans.[58]

Beauregard held an ideal position at Manassas. From that location he could guard against a Union movement toward Richmond via either Fredericksburg or Culpeper. With control of the junction he held a rail link with Joseph Johnston's 12,000 men in the Shenandoah Valley. Beauregard placed the brigades under Longstreet, Jones, and Evans in a line behind Bull Run. In advance of the line facing east toward Alexandria he deployed Bonham's brigade at Fairfax Courthouse, with Cocke's command in support at Centerville. Beauregard directed Ewell to move his brigade up to Fairfax Station, five miles south of Bonham's position. Rodes' Fifth Alabama would be posted as an advance picket at Farr's Crossroads on the Old Braddock Road, about half-way between Fairfax Courthouse and Fairfax Station. If they confirmed a Union move in their direction, the advanced brigades were to fall back and rejoin the other four brigades behind Bull Run and form a six-mile-long cordon defense that covered the stream's several crossings. Bonham's orders were to fall back toward Mitchell's Ford, drawing the Federals after him. Ewell was to cover Bonham's right and fall back over a rough road that led to Union Mills Ford, the extreme right of Beauregard's extended line.[59]

At 2:30 p.m. on Saturday, June 22, Rodes received orders to march without delay up the Warrenton Turnpike to Centerville and go out from there on the Braddock Road to Farr's Crossroads. He moved out at 8:30 p.m., and after a difficult all-night march of thirteen miles over rough, rocky roads, guided the Fifth Alabama into Farr's at daybreak. It was "the worst march yet," judged one of his young soldiers. "We however got through it pretty well, but we were well nigh broken down when we stopped." Rodes reported the strength of his regiment as 612 men present for duty. Of the original complement, 146 men were on the sick rolls, and many others had been left behind at nearly every stop along the way up from Pensacola. Measles and diarrhea continued to exact the heaviest toll, with seven men having recently died from the former disease. Despite the illnesses and hardships, discipline in the Fifth remained remarkably good. These men expected a big battle any day, and being the neophytes that they were, looked forward to the approaching spectacle.[60]

Rodes' task was to guard the Braddock Road against an enemy attempt to slip between the brigades of Bonham and Ewell. He immediately had his soldiers prepare rough entrenchments at an advanced position across the road near a branch of Pohick Run, a source of refreshing, cold drinking water slightly more than three miles northeast of his main camp at Farr's. A lack of tools made the job difficult. "I never worked so hard in my life," complained one soldier, "cutting trees and pulling them about." The entire regiment owned but six spades, two picks and five or six axes. The lack of implements limited the effort to the confines of the clearing on the branch, which gave the position a less than ideal command of the surrounding area. Rodes tried to make up for this by sending out scouting parties in several directions. And while all this was transpiring, of course, he drilled the men whenever possible. "We have no place here to drill except an old field full of stumps and ditches," a private confided in his diary, "yet Col. Rodes puts us through. It is amusing to see the boys tumble over the stumps and in the ditches."[61]

Rodes already was attracting attention as an officer of promise. At Farr's, he selected good fortified main and advanced positions and his men appeared well disciplined and in fine spirits. Many in the regiment understood that they were in good hands, and outside the Fifth others looked with increasing envy and admiration at the manner in which he handled his command. "Our Regiment has quite a reputation in the army for its discipline & efficiency," Captain Webb proudly wrote his wife. "Our Col is daily gaining in the estimation of the military men with whom he is brought in contact." Not everyone, however, looked so favorably upon Rodes and his style of command. "I have reason to believe that he is not very popular with some men in the Regt [who] feel it bothersome to be required to discharge diligently & faithfully every duty," admitted Webb. As for himself, he considered Rodes "a prompt & efficient officer [who] knows his duty & requires every one to be prompt & efficient."[62]

Fully expecting in his advanced position to soon clash with the enemy, Rodes wanted his men to be sharp and well prepared. He rotated companies on twenty-four hour picket duty, and for those who remained in camp he intensified the drilling. "We drill now mostly in the double quick," a soldier told his diary on July 1, "which gives us about as much as we can stand up to." Two days later, he added that such drilling "makes a fellow sweat like a horse, but we nevertheless have to jog along. I had to trot over stumps, stones, ditches through briers &c for three hours." When Rodes took pity on the men that hot day and "allowed us to rest twice," the same soldier gratefully concluded that the colonel must have "felt a little lazy."[63]

That night about 9:00 p.m., a shot rang out in the darkness. Drums beat the "long roll," which produced "such hustling about as was never seen," a diarist commented. "We snatched up our guns and accoutrements, ran out in the 'color line,' formed and fixed bayonets." For the first time in its history, the Fifth Alabama formed up to face the enemy. Within a short time, a sentinel walked into camp and reported that he had just shot an old sow. The death of the animal was only the first of what would be several false alarms.[64]

Early in the evening of Thursday, July 11, Rodes held his first known "council of war." He met with his captains to belatedly explain that upon the approach of the enemy in force and the subsequent withdrawal of the Confederates from Fairfax Courthouse, the Fifth Alabama would pull back all the way to a creek called Bull Run. "It amused me very much by the pains [Rodes] took to avoid using the term retreat, substituting always instead the word 'recede,'" wrote Captain Blackford in a letter proudly headlined "Camp of the Advanced Guard, Army of the Potomac.[65]

The meeting proved timely. About 2:00 a.m. the next morning, the stillness in camp broke when the alarm again sounded. "The drums beat to arms and all the Companies formed in order of battle on the color-line," explained Captain Blackford. "Twas done quickly and in good order," he proudly added, "my men responded well; I detected but two cases of alarm [panic], but these recovered very soon. I somehow felt much more composed, and quiet than I could have thought possible." After holding his men in tense readiness for some time, Rodes allowed them to return to their beds when he received word that the Yankees "had gone back to their camp."[66]

The day following the meeting with his captains, Rodes directly addressed his men about the situation confronting them. He told them "it was beyond doubt" they soon would face the enemy. He expected the men to know their place in the line and to obey orders strictly. He stressed the importance of remaining calm and composed, for he fully intended to fight the enemy, no matter how superior their numbers. "He appears to have great confidence in his own ability and in the courage of the regiment," an impressed soldier concluded.[67]

Later that evening a heavy rain blew in, giving comfort to some who believed it might retard the advance of the enemy. "I am rather sorry for it, as it will cause us to be in arms all night," wrote Blackford, who preferred a quick break to the now almost unbearable tension.[68]

The tension lifted somewhat the next day, Saturday July 13, when Rodes cancelled drill in order to allow the men to receive their pay. That afternoon near Springfield, however, the Fifth Alabama suffered its first official field losses when enemy troops captured four Alabama soldiers on patrol from Company E. (The four would escape during the enemy's panicked retreat from the Bull Run battlefield eight days later).[69]

Not only did the Federal toops intercept one of Rodes' patrols, but they also managed to gather excellent information on his position. A recent issue of the Baltimore *Sun*, "formerly a good democratic newspaper," judged one of Rodes' soldiers, "and one of the best published in the South, has been frightened into the service of Lincoln, and comes down 'hot and heavy' on the Rebels." The paper, he continued, offered "a very graphic description of our camp, its strength, the fortifications &c." It even identified Rodes by name, crediting him with "great military skill considering that he is a southern man."[70]

On July 16, Rodes sent Company E, sixty men with rifled muskets under Captain Charles Shelley, a former architect and future brigadier general, to take its turn manning the forward defenses up at the Pohick branch. Around 10:00 p.m. that night Rodes received word from General Beauregard that the enemy was advancing. "Everything for awhile was in a perfect stir," wrote a soldier, "packing knapsacks and preparing rations." Rodes gave orders for the men to sleep on their arms.[71]

Early the following morning Captain Shelley left behind six privates and Second Lieutenant T. M. Riley to act as pickets and started the balance of Company E rearward. His men had not had anything to eat for breakfast and there was no provision for relief, so he marched them back to the main camp. About 7:00 a.m. a courier brought Rodes a Yankee prisoner captured by one of the Fifth's advanced sentinels. The prisoner offered the startling news of an enemy advance in force down the Braddock Road.[72]

*   *   *

Under Brigadier General Irwin McDowell, the Federals had begun the move to take the new Confederate capital at Richmond. McDowell did so against his better judgment, Washington having compelled him to use his inexperienced army before it should dissipate from expirations of terms of service of its ninety-day volunteers. With five divisions embracing about 35,000 men, most of whom could be considered as little better than militia with barely two months of training, McDowell pulled out of his camps around Arlington and Alexandria on July 16 and marched west. His move marked the beginning of the long war's first major campaign. After a short march that day, McDowell started for Fairfax Courthouse early the next morning. He sent a brigade from Samuel Heintzelman's division numbering about 2,000 men on a leftward probe down the Braddock Road—straight toward Rodes' position.[73]

When he received definite word of the enemy's approach, Rodes acted accordingly. Though his heart rate no doubt quickened considerably at the prospect of commanding men in battle for the first time, he maintained a clear and focused mind, coolly issuing orders designed to deal promptly and efficiently with the developing situation. He sped a courier to tell Shelley to return to the advanced works and delay the enemy as long as possible. He then ordered the regiment roused—they were all asleep except for the sentries—and quickly put them in their prepared breastworks three-quarters of a mile east of camp, with one company (Company I, Captain Edwin Hobson) in reserve.

As if to confirm what Captain Webb had confided to his wife two months before, Rodes gave assignments to his two immediate subordinates that obviously reflected his confidence in each man. Along with only one company (Company A, Captain Christopher Pegues) he gave Lieutenant Colonel Jones the less important task of watching the road coming in from Fairfax Station to the south, while to Major Morgan he gave the job of taking another company to reinforce Shelley at the "front line." To complete his flurry of activity, Rodes sent a courier south to Fairfax Station to get instructions from Ewell, and he sent Captain Webb north to find General Bonham and remain with him until that officer began his retreat. When satisfied that he had done all that seemed possible for the time being, Rodes braced himself and his men for the coming onslaught.[74]

Captain Webb promptly sped up to Fairfax Courthouse, only to make the startling discovery that Bonham already had abandoned the place. The captain rode down the road toward Centerville until he caught up with the retreating column. When he found Bonham and explained the situation, Webb received the reply, "Tell Colonel Rodes to commence his retreat immediately, and inform General Ewell of it." Webb put his spurs to his horse and raced back toward what he now undoubtedly realized was Rodes' dangerously exposed position.[75]

In the meantime, Shelley had almost reached the regiment's main works when he received Rodes' orders to turn around and go back into the advanced line. The captain spun his men about and quickly moved forward. The enemy soon marched into view and Shelley ordered his sixty men of Company E to open fire. Return fire came in at once, eventually hitting one Alabamian in the leg and taking off the ear of another. Faced with increasing pressure, Shelley withdrew his men to a nearby woods, where Major Morgan joined them. Slowly falling back, the two outnumbered companies maintained a brisk fire for nearly an hour.[76]

Refusing to retreat without orders, Rodes underwent a test of nerves as he monitored the situation facing his two forward companies. Hoping to buy as much time as possible and yet not jeopardize his position or his regiment, he coolly waited until Morgan and Shelley fell back to within 400 yards of the main breastworks. Only when that occurred did Rodes pull in his men and prepare to make a stand with the entire regiment. The prospect of holding firm, however, looked grim. The enemy was moving through a clearing beyond his right flank, and in front were bringing up at least one piece of artillery.[77]

Finally, however, Rodes received news from both Ewell and Bonham. In accordance with instructions to retreat upon the first sign of the enemy's advance, Bonham was falling back and had sent word of his movement to Ewell. The message did not get through for some time, however, so Ewell could not coordinate his retreat with Bonham. This, in turn, left Rodes in a dangerously exposed position until news from Ewell to pull out arrived.

Moments later, Captain Webb rode on the scene with Bonham's instructions to "retreat immediately." Rodes now could honorably leave the field.[78]

While Ewell marched the rest of the brigade down to Union Mills, and with bullets now occasionally "whistling in over our heads," Rodes quickly and efficiently pulled his own men out of their positions. "We left our breastworks with great reluctance," one soldier confessed, "for there was all our work to be abandoned to the enemy without a fight." Rodes put the men on the Braddock Road and, in accordance with Beauregard's July 8 instructions, marched them down to D. R. Jones's position at McLean's Ford on Bull Run.

Though Rodes stressed in his report the deliberate good order of the withdrawal, others in his command did not quite see it that way. "I have seen something of the realities of war," Captain Blackford wrote his mother. "On Wednesday last we were attacked . . . and after and during the enemy's fire for some time we were forced to retreat at the double quick, owing to the retreat of the South Carolinians at the Court House. We ran and walked 20 miles that day, nowhere stopping one moment even for water." According to Blackford, "My company was the last to leave the trenches & was deployed in the rear to protect our Regiment for more than 13 miles over the roughest country I have ever seen. I can't describe to you the fatigue I felt as I was exceeding heavily [burdened] with guns of men who had broken down." The diary entry of a soldier in Company D concurs with Blackford's account. "The day was intensely warm, but we had to march ahead to avoid being flanked, as the enemy pressed forward with great rapidity. . . . A good many broke down on the march."[79]

Around 3:00 p.m., the Fifth Alabama finally crossed Bull Run. Shortly before sunset Rodes received orders from Beauregard to move one mile on down the run and reunite with Ewell at Union Mills Ford. "I have had nothing to sleep on," Blackford complained to his mother, "nor anything to eat, since Tuesday, except hard bread. We have no baggage."[80]

Despite the rather hurried nature of the withdrawal, the first stand against the enemy had been a splendid little affair for the Fifth Alabama and its colonel. Rodes had done well. His only mistake, which might have proved crucial, was to not provide Captain Shelley with either relief or provisions before the enemy appeared on the morning of the 17th. But he had selected a good position, and he refused to panic by over committing himself when faced with superior numbers, all of which contributed to the safe withdrawal of his regiment. He lost only two men wounded (and a dozen tents and two barrels of crackers, sacrificed to make room in the wagons for the sick and wounded). Moreover,

Rodes' delaying action helped cover the retreat of the brigade to Union Mills. Ewell was gratefully impressed. "Colonel Rodes is an . . . excellent officer," the brigade commander wrote his fiancée several days later. "[H]e behaved very gallantly, but in the blaze of more recent events his little skirmish will be overlooked. He killed or wounded some forty of the enemy [Rodes estimated the enemy's loss at twenty, but both estimates probably are too high], including one captain, and drove them back to wait for their artillery."[81]

Rodes' stature and reputation soared dramatically following the brief but stubborn action at Farr's. Campbell Brown, the son of Ewell's fiancée, recalled shortly after the war that when he joined Ewell's staff on July 19, "Rodes was already prominent, being much commended for his conduct on the retreat from Fairfax station & [Farr]'s X Roads to the present position."[82]

Beauregard, too, was impressed. "It is proper here to state that while from the outset it had been determined on the approach of the enemy in force to fall back and fight him on the line of Bull Run, yet the positions occupied by General Ewell's brigade, if necessary, could have been maintained against a largely superior force," he declared in his official report of the campaign. "This was especially the case with the position of the Fifth Alabama Volunteers, Colonel Rodes, which that excellent officer had made capable of a resolute protracted defense against heavy odds." The Creole general continued: "Accordingly, on the morning of the 17th ultimo [July], when the enemy appeared before that position, they were checked and held at bay with some confessed loss in a skirmish in advance of the works, in which Major Morgan and Captain Shelley, Fifth Regiment Alabama Volunteers, acted with intelligent gallantry, and the post was only abandoned under general, but specific, imperative orders, in conformity with a long-conceived plan of action and battle."[83]

General McDowell's Federals, meanwhile, reached Fairfax Court House around noon on the 17th. Daniel Tyler's division moved out to seize Centerville and carefully probe beyond. The main army, tired and hungry, reached the Centerville area late on the 18th after taking nearly three days to march twenty miles, a distance veterans later in the war would easily traverse in less than half the time. McDowell halted for two days to perfect his plans, which concurrently allowed his enemy to concentrate and prepare for him.[84]

When Ewell's brigade, about 2,500 strong, crossed to the south side of Bull Run on the morning of the 18th, Beauregard's entire army was behind the stream on a line stretching six miles long from Union Mills on the right to the Stone Bridge on the left. One mile to Ewell's left was Jones' brigade at

McLean's Ford. Beyond Jones was Longstreet's command at Blackburn's Ford. Bonham's regiments guarded Mitchell's Ford, while Cocke's brigade covered Island, Ball's and Lewis' fords. Beauregard's final two brigades included Shanks Evans' men defending the Stone Bridge and Jubal Early's command in reserve behind Ewell and Jones.

At Union Mills, Ewell held the Sixth Alabama in reserve. He put the Sixth Louisiana near the ford, above the Orange & Alexandria railroad bridge, and below the bridge he placed the Fifth Alabama. Rodes put part of the regiment in reserve and entrenched the rest along the water's edge, explaining to Company D that he wanted "to give the Greensboro boys a chance at the enemy the first opportunity." According to Campbell Brown, "Rodes was very strongly & skillfully posted. I remember Gen'l Ewell's praising his works for the engineering skill displayed."[85]

When McDowell sent Tyler on the 18th to probe from Centerville toward the stream, a hot skirmish broke out at Blackburn's Ford. Despite his proximity to the fight, Ewell obeyed orders to not get involved and stood firm. Accordingly, Rodes kept the Fifth Alabama under arms while desultory cannon and musket fire played on everyone's nerves until Longstreet finally threw back the enemy probe later in the day.[86]

In the Shenandoah Valley, meanwhile, events unfolded that would directly impact the developing battle on the plains of Manassas. A Federal diversionary force under Robert Patterson retreated to Harpers Ferry on the 17th, a move that freed General Joseph E. Johnston to transfer his Confederate army eastward to join Beauregard's command. A brigade under Thomas J. Jackson, the same man who eleven years earlier had received the VMI professorship so coveted by Rodes, arrived on the 19th, and Johnston himself reached the area the next day with two more brigades. Together with Beauregard, the two commanders developed a plan to strike McDowell's left flank.[87]

Beauregard expected the Federals to come straight down the Warrenton Turnpike and attack his left at Stone Bridge. His intent was to throw his right across Bull Run and hit McDowell's left and rear near Centerville. Ewell would open the attack, with support on his left from Jones, Longstreet, and Bonham, and with his rear covered by Theophilus Holmes' independent brigade just up from Fredericksburg. At 5:30 a.m. on Sunday, July 21, the Creole general sent Ewell instructions to be prepared with Jones to launch the strike toward Centerville "at a moment's notice."[88]

That morning McDowell struck first. However, he crossed Bull Run at Sudley Springs north of the Warrenton Pike and launched a powerful attack around Beauregard's left flank.

Soon after daylight, Rodes and Ewell heard the distant booming of cannon fire from that direction, but no orders arrived from Beauregard. Impatient to advance, Ewell sent a courier to McLean's Ford to get an update on the situation. Between 9:00 and 10:00 a.m., he received a copy of a dispatch Beauregard had sent Jones at 7:00 a.m., directing Jones to advance, with the assurance that Ewell had been ordered to do likewise. The news surprised Ewell, who had not received any such instruction. When he subsequently learned that Jones had indeed crossed the creek, Ewell prepared for immediate action. About 10:30 a.m. he notified Beauregard of his intention to advance on Centerville.[89]

Rodes' Alabama troops crossed first, followed by the Washington Artillery, the Sixth Alabama, and the Sixth Louisiana. After marching a short distance, Ewell received orders from Beauregard to turn around and recross the run and hold that position. Obedient to orders, Ewell about-faced his column and marched back to Union Mills.

Rodes and his men nervously marked time until about noon, listening all the while as the fight raged on the far left. Finally, Beauregard ordered Ewell, Jones, and Longstreet to cross their respective fords and demonstrate jointly against some troublesome Federal guns. Ewell's orders were to move across Bull Run for the third time that day, follow the creek north about one mile to McLean's Ford, and hit the Union battery in flank while Jones and Longstreet attacked it in front.

With the Fifth Alabama again in the lead, Ewell crossed the creek at 1:30 p.m. and advanced about one-half mile through some woods until he ran up against Federal pickets protecting the guns. He directed Rodes to deploy the Fifth and open fire. The Sixth Alabama was directed to rush up and form on Rodes' right, and the Sixth Louisiana on his left. Rodes was just beginning to spread out his men when Ewell received new orders from Beauregard to move back across Bull Run and report to General Johnston, who was directing reinforcements into position near the Lewis house on the left flank. Union pressure there was heavy and the situation was deteriorating.

Rodes pulled in his men as Ewell broke off from the Yankee pickets and reestablished his column by putting the Sixth Louisiana in the lead, the Fifth Alabama in the middle, and the Sixth Alabama in the rear. The brigade marched back across the creek about 3:00 p.m. and hurried westward on the

Manassas-Sudley Road toward New Market. When they stopped within one mile southeast of Henry House Hill at 4:00 p.m., the sounds of battle began dying away. "Just as we arrived at Lewis' the last cheer of victory greeted our ears," an officer recorded. Both Rodes and Ewell feared the cheers were from Yankee throats, and that the Confederates had been defeated. Was the brigade being thrown in to help stave off a complete disaster? Ewell passed the word for the column to make speed. The overeager Sixth Louisiana moved so fast that Ewell stopped it twice to allow the rest of the brigade to catch up. Two Union rifled guns fired at the brigade as it passed Mitchell's Ford, but the shots went long. Just beyond the Lewis house the brigade received startling news that the triumphant cheers ringing through the air were Southern voices of joy. The South had won a signal victory on the plains of Manassas.[90]

As is always the case on every battlefield, the joy and elation that spread through the ranks quickly tempered when the men saw the price paid for the victory. "I can give you no idea of the scene when we reached the battle ground about 5 o'clock in the evening as our column reached up the hill over looking the place of death below," Captain Webb of Rodes' staff wrote home. "I saw wounded men of our side every where it was terrible to be seen. I saw occasionally friends bearing off the body of a deceased comrade." Rodes had never beheld such a sight. He had not seen any casualties at Farr's Crossroads four days earlier (and certainly not up close). July 21 was different—a new form of baptism no combat soldier ever forgets. Before him lay acres of human carnage and suffering that left a deep and enduring impression.[91]

Instead of sending his unused brigades in pursuit of the beaten enemy, Johnston directed Ewell to return to Union Mills Ford. Rumors were circulating that the Federals were heading back in that direction. Ewell arrived there after dark, about 9:00 p.m., only to find a quiet sector. Rodes finally allowed his men to fall to the ground for a well-deserved rest. His Fifth Alabama had marched about twenty-two miles that day.[92]

The heavens opened that night with a heavy downpour that soaked man and beast to the bone. The Fifth Alabama spent July 22 bivouacked in the rain and mud, discussing the previous day's combat and stunning Confederate victory. The following day the men moved to a hill on the left of Union Mills station, where they remained in camp for several weeks.[93]

* * *

Not long after arriving in Virginia, probably sometime in early July, Rodes arranged for Hortense to live with his father and stepmother in Lynchburg. With her health improved somewhat, he wanted her closer to him should the opportunity for a visit arise. Another reason for the arrangement, however, may have been Rodes' concern for the care of his father, who some five years before had suffered a stroke that left him partially paralyzed. His condition had slowly worsened over the ensuing years, confining the elder Rodes to the house and making him increasingly dependent on others.[94]

In lieu of the opportunity to visit Hortense, Rodes paid a visit of a different kind. In mid-August, Ewell, Campbell Brown, and "Col Rodes of Alabama," Brown wrote home, "whom Genl Ewell thinks very highly of, as an able & efficient officer," rode to the Manassas battlefield for a tour of its already famous sites. Captain (later General) Samuel Wragg Ferguson of Beauregard's staff acted as their tour guide. Though the grounds had been cleaned up save for a number of horse carcasses still lying about, the trampled grasses had not yet fully recovered. The four officers could easily discern the battle's troop movements. A highlight of the tour included a visit to the spot, marked by a cedar post, where General Barnard Bee fell after delivering his famous cry, "There stands Jackson like a stone wall!"[95]

The tour served as a classroom in the course of combat instruction, one Rodes utilized in an attempt to understand and analyze the campaign as thoroughly as possible. It was a difficult, and even somewhat unpleasant course—not only because he had missed the great battle entirely, but because the heavy July 21 fighting reduced to insignificance his actions on the 17th at Farr's Crossroads. Frankly put, Rodes resented it. So strong was his resentment that it sometimes found expression in ways petty and even illogical. "Had anybody but Alabamians in the Regt. killed & wounded as many of the enemy as we did in the skirmish we had on the 17th," he complained in a letter written August 17 to his friend and attorney in Tuscaloosa, Philip Pitts, "the fight would have been set down as a fine glorious affair and the proper parties would have gotten the credit for it." Moreover, Rodes found it particularly galling that after leaving him in the lurch on the 17th, Bonham and his South Carolinians went on to play a significant part in the battle. "As it is," he continued in his letter to Pitts, "the S. Carolinians get the credit of it—and this too after leaving us fighting and utterly exposed to being cut off by a force so great that they thought 5000 strong retreated before us without firing a shot. We very narrowly escaped being cut off that day, our 600 men would have been awfully <u>handled</u> by a column of 20000 in rear and 5000 in front."

Though unable to avoid overestimations in his own accounts, Rodes quickly discovered similar miscalculations elsewhere. "Everything is exaggerated here except the merits of Genl Ewells Command," he told Pitts. "The great battle of the 21st is generaly [sic] exaggerated as to all its features except the hard fighting, especially as to the number engaged and those killed & wounded. My own opinion is that the killed of the enemy was no more than 800 and their wounded 2500. Ours 400 killed—1,200 wounded." Although his figures were also inaccurate, Rodes' take on the soldiery was solid. The men, he observed, "behaved very handsomely . . . except those who ran back (as some from every company did)." In his opinion one regiment stood out above all others. "The 4th Ala had covered Ala with glory," he told Pitts with obvious pride for his adopted state, "the other Ala Regiments look with envy at [the] fourths splendid reputation." The Fourth Alabama of Barnard Bee's brigade came in with Johnston from the Shenandoah and at a critical moment during the battle, with nearly all its officers down, stood firm until Beauregard and Johnston formed a new line that included the soon- to-be famous Stonewall Brigade. "No regiment," Rodes concluded "not even the S. Carolinian regiments which the S. Carolinians consider did all the fighting—did more service or fought better than the 4th."

Rodes also offered general praise to the leaders of the army. "Officers and all displayed great gallantry," he declared, though he quickly qualified that by adding, "Our Generals are gallant nay very splendid heroes in the field—but not yet are they Napoleons." He drew the general—and correct—conclusion that "on both sides the men could have been better handled."

As for the politicians now trumpeting the victory in an effort to claim some of its laurels, Rodes felt nothing but contempt. "War here is a mixture of broken down politicians," he scoffed, "struggling to be able to plead [that they] bled and died before the dear people."

In the end, Rodes believed he knew where to lay the credit for victory. "God saved us on the 21st," he declared. "He made the men fight like heroes whenever they could get a chance—And He taught them to run like the devil when they were 'surrounded' on 3 sides. Verily God is great," he concluded, "and so far we have been His people."[96]

The battle at Manassas had an obvious and profound effect on Robert Rodes. Though not a direct participant in the fighting, he had witnessed the horrible carnage left in its aftermath, its acres of dead and mangled men and horses. No sensitive, intelligent person could have been left unmoved by such a scene. It humbled and perhaps even frightened him. For the first time, his correspondence contained references to the Almighty and expressions of religious conviction that would continue to grow as the war progressed.

Moreover, Rodes was determined more than ever to preserve the lives of his own men. At the same time, he desperately yearned for the glory that had been denied him at Manassas. He knew of but one way to prepare for both: rely upon the two precious virtues that had sustained him throughout his adult life—discipline and drill. Only in this way would his men attain such "complete mastery of the subject" as to lessen their risks on the battlefield, while also enhancing his reputation as an efficient and capable commanding officer. Despite already being one of the severest taskmasters in the army, Rodes determined to push his men to their absolute limit. Three days after the battle, he put them on a new and intensified training program. Few in the regiment appreciated his good intentions.

"He seems to have 'turned over a new leaf,'" Private James Cowin observed in his diary in late July, "as he says he intends to deal more strictly than ever." Cowin woefully added, "Oh! who wouldn't be a soldier." The private continued: "This morning began our usual drills. Rodes I think had the drill-mania, for I think he had rather drill than eat a good dinner." Cowin, having also seen the aftermath of a battlefield, begrudgingly added, "I suppose however it is to our advantage." Not everyone in the regiment agreed with him. "The boys grumble considerably," he observed. "I suppose he [Rodes] intends us for regulars, and treats every one alike, and that is very cool." As Cowin observed, even officers grumbled. "I understand that two of the Captains have handed in their resignations," he reported. "They did not like such treatment as they get." Cowin speculated that more might have resigned, had they the nerve to do so. "Some of the captains would no more think of doing such a thing than attempt to fly. They are afraid of Rodes."[97]

The private went on to describe the manner of one of the drills the VMI graduate oversaw. "Col. Rodes had us trotting around on battalion drill, this evening. Our drill ground is very small and hilly, but it makes little difference with Col. Rodes for I think he can drill a regiment on a piece of ground that would puzzle many to drill a company."[98] Not surprisingly, men began finding ways to escape Rodes' increasingly harsh regimen. "A good many of the boys are on the sick list," observed Cowin on July 26, "though none of them seriously ill." Cowin, who had had some prewar medical training, succinctly explained the reason for the lengthy list—"drilling too hard."[99]

Rodes' reaction to the growing sick list is not difficult to imagine. In an attempt to give the men second thoughts about reporting themselves ill, he directed the orderly sergeants to report to him in person all the absentees from drill, beginning with the officers. "He seems to think that there are not so many sick as are absent," one private observed, adding, "Tighter and tighter on us every day."[100]

Rodes was going too far. On general inspection he checked each soldier individually, being "very particular about every thing, never passes over any thing and is always sure to reprimand a fellow, whenever there is any thing amiss." He risked severely damaging his soldiers' morale, which would cost him their indispensable support and confidence. On July 27, less than one week after the Manassas battle, he placed under arrest about forty men for being absent from duty. Some provided legitimate excuses and were released. Those who did not Rodes agreed to release if they promised not to plead ill again. Some accepted the easy bargain. Others, however, were so embittered toward Rodes that they preferred to "see him at the devil before they would promise him anything." Rodes kept these recalcitrants in the guardhouse, telling them that "they would tire of it before they got through"—a battle of wills Rodes eventually won.[101]

Unlike some officers, Rodes did not easily grant furloughs, however brief the time or good the reason. Captain Eugene Blackford of Company K complained bitterly when Rodes did not allow him time to slip over to Manassas to find out if his brothers Charles and William had survived the battle.[102]

Rodes was fully aware of the growing resentment against him. "Col. Rodes has discovered that he [is] in disfavor with the regiment, or at least a portion of it," Private Cowin confided to his diary on July 29. "He is under the impression that our company [D] is prejudiced against him."

As if to break the tension and relieve the growing stress against him, Rodes left on a seven-day leave to visit Hortense in Lynchburg. "Col Rodes has greatly over taxed himself," observed a sympathetic Captain Webb in a letter home. "[H]e is indefatigable in his efforts to drill & instruct his regiment [but] he shows the wear & tear that his labors has made on him."[103]

For five days during Rodes' absence, July 29 through August 2, Major Morgan drilled the regiment—much to the great relief and satisfaction of the men. "We are fortunate enough to have Major Morgan to drill us," a soldier gratefully observed in his diary. "He rests us oftener than Col. Rodes, and he drills very well. The men appear to try to do better for him, as he does not break us down. When a man gets tired he becomes careless."[104]

On Sunday, August 4, Rodes returned from his visit with Hortense. His reappearance caused quite a stir in camp, with much "running about" by the men. "They will go anywhere and at any time," observed a private, "just so they can get out of the sight of Col. Rodes." Then came the dreaded harbinger of things to come. "The first word he [Rodes] asked one of the boys whom he met, was if he had been drilling any since he left."[105]

Dissatisfied, perhaps even outraged, at Major Morgan's relatively easy treatment of the regiment, Rodes returned to drilling with a vengeance that could only have insulted the major and offended the men. Quite as if the last seven days had ruined all his previous hard work, Rodes treated the men as though they were new recruits, drilling them for hours every morning without guns and in small squads. He reserved the hot afternoon hours for company and battalion drill. "It is entirely too warm to drill at eleven o'clock," objected Private Cowin. "The officers now complain as much of Rodes as the privates. Do not know the object of so much drilling. In the battle [Manassas] the other day," he rationalized, "there was no necessity for the manual of arms nor any of the many movements we are put through. We all think Rodes is mad about something," he concluded, "and is giving vent to his spleen upon the men. If so he is a brave man."[106]

Predictably, the sick list swelled. Finally, on August 10, the regimental surgeons came to Rodes and complained "that the weather was too warm and that if he persisted in drilling so much he would kill all his men." This convincing protest, presented by educated men like himself, at last persuaded Rodes to back off from his near maniacal mission. To the great relief and satisfaction of the men, he limited drill to the morning hours. Afternoons were spent cleaning camp and resting, with formal parade done in the evening. This change of direction proved to be a major and even eye-opening turning point in Rodes' military career. He would always remain a strict taskmaster, but he never again imposed on his men such extreme measures.[107]

Along with the strain he had suffered in trying to set his men on the path of "striving for perfect mastery of the subject," Rodes endured significant stress from the home front. Though grateful that Hortense's health had improved, he continued to fret over the family's financial situation, which had yet to recover from his unexpected expenses in Pensacola. As chief engineer of the railroad, he had earned the respectable sum of $3,000 per year, or $250 a month. A colonel's pay was substantially less at $195 per month. Moreover, his civilian wages were paid on a consistent basis, but army paydays were irregular. He did not receive his first pay until July 13. The amount was $318.50, covering one month and nineteen days of service (May 13 to July 1). That money did not last long. On July 24, Hortense sat down in the house of her father-in- law in

Lynchburg and wrote a letter inquiring after the efforts of attorney Philip Pitts in Tuscaloosa to raise funds for the family. "War is very expensive," she emphatically reminded him, "and our money is going fast, and I wish very much to know if there is any prospect of my getting money from you." In particular, she wanted to know if Pitts had collected on any of the credit notes left in his hands by Robert. "This is a hard year," she explained, "and I am very sorry to be importunate, but my husband occupies a position that has to be supported, & money is all necessary & must be gotten in some way."

Then, as if to put the mundane problems of money in proper perspective, Hortense allowed herself to reflect on the recent, terrible battle at Manassas. Having already heard from Robert, she knew "that the 5th Ala. Regiment was safe & not a man hurt up to Monday Afternoon the 22nd." She also knew that other Alabama regiments had not been so fortunate. While her husband, with manly pride, had remarked in his letter to Pitts, "The 4th Ala has covered Ala with glory," she looked at the situation quite differently. "I am afraid to hear from the 4th Regiment, some say it is dreadfully cut up, & others that it was not. Accounts are so confused that we believe nothing, but this we know that as [President] Davis says— 'it is a dear bought victory.'"[108]

Hortense's letter to Pitts accomplished nothing. From Union Mills on August 17, Rodes followed up with one of his own, exhorting the attorney to secure the funds owed him. "I must have money sometime or other," he pleaded. He worried most about the near $1,400 due Mrs. Margaret Gooch next February, and his $480 share of the payment (in conjunction with Foster) on the property in Tuscaloosa. To help meet these obligations, Rodes tried to rent out his slave Hannah for $100 per year, but that fell through when the renter (a Mrs. Baird of the University of Alabama) failed to make any of the monthly payments. Rodes directed Pitts to reclaim Hannah and return her to Norton Whitfield, who Rodes in his will had appointed trustee with power to sell the slaves if need be to pay the debts. Rodes had stipulated that after his death, Hortense had the option of selling the slaves. He now believed the situation demanded immediate action. "Hannah and her children I wish to sell by next December at least," he declared. "I don't wish to die and leave my wife without money and in debt. . . . The Army [does not] pay [me] in money or glory either so far [so] I must if possible and as soon as possible sell the negroes." Rodes confessed that he and Hortense were very close to being destitute. "She and I have about $50 between us of which I have $17," he lamented. "We can get along perhaps until next winter 1st Dec. on my Army pay if I am not killed."[109]

While Rodes worried about providing for Hortense, she managed, in a sense, to provide for him. Captain Webb wrote home on August 15, "We had for breakfast this morning cantelope . . . tomatoe, eggs . . . hot rolls & good butter—the vegetables & such were sent to us by Mrs Rodes from Lynchburg—the first we have seen. We did not fail to make a display of our hospitality—we invited our Genl [Ewell] to breakfast with us." In another letter Webb mentioned the feast, adding, "We get no vegetables or fruit here."[110]

While matters of regimental and familial concern occupied Rodes, affairs on a grander scale concerned Richmond and army headquarters. The fighting had exposed deficiencies in command and control that prompted a reorganization of the army. Ewell's Second Brigade lost the Sixth Louisiana on July 25, but gained Lieutenant Colonel Theodore O'Hara's Twelfth Alabama and Colonel Richard Griffith's Twelfth Mississippi. Near the end of the month Ewell's reorganized command moved over from Union Mills to where the mouth of Pope's Head Run met the Occoquan River. There, it held the extreme right of Johnston's fifty-mile long defensive line that ended in the west at Leesburg.[111]

In mid-August, Johnston felt strong enough to move his main line forward to Fairfax Courthouse. Ewell's brigade moved up to Sangster's Crossroads, a mile-and-a-half south of Fairfax Station and seventeen miles west of Alexandria. On Friday, August 23, Rodes' Fifth Alabama occupied Camp Masked Battery (so named by Rodes) near Sangster's. "Thus we again take our stand in the advanced Corps of the 'Army of the Potomac,'" Captain Blackford proudly informed his mother. "We will now be within a mile or two of the Yankees, and will again have to exercise all that caution which distinguished our proceedings at Farr's X Roads, our former position."[112]

Having grown tired of their duty around Union Mills and Pope's Head Run, and eager to escape the clutches of typhoid and measles, Rodes' Alabamians gladly accepted the change. "Our men are as much delighted to get to a new place," Captain Webb wrote home, "put up tents & get everything fixed as little girls who have a new play house or a young married couple are when they set up for themselves & get to house keeping."[113]

Unlike his previous stay in this vicinity, Rodes found time for a special visit. "Day before yesterday [Aug.24]," wrote Captain Webb, "Col Rodes in company with Genl Ewell & five mounted men rode down to Pohick Church—the church in which Genl Washington was accustomed to worship. They were in sight of the broad Potomac—within four miles of Mt Vernon & within less than ten miles of Alexandria."[114]

Being so close to Alexandria, which was just across the Potomac from Washington, made many in the Fifth Alabama feel a bit edgy. On August 28, Eugene Blackford wrote home that "the men were anxious," and that there were "alarms every day."[115]

Shortly afterward, Rodes sent Blackford and his Company K on a scouting expedition toward the Potomac. "Our advance picket is not more than 400 yards from the Yankees," Blackford wrote his mother on September 5, "and both are churning up earth works, as hard as they can. Our men can see the Capitol at Washington plainly, the stripes in the flag can be distinguished, not being 4 miles off." Blackford and his men managed to capture three Yankees from the Fifth Maine. "I returned yesterday from my expedition toward Alexandria near Washington City and could hear the Yankees laughing and talking at night so near were their camps," he informed his father on the 10th.[116]

Four days earlier on September 6, the remainder of the regiment received a visit from Alabama Congressman J. L. M. Curry, who along with the regiment's Major Morgan, delivered a stirring speech to the men. "They made us feel as if we could whip all the Yankees that could be brought against us," Private Cowin exclaimed. He added, almost begrudgingly, "Col. Rodes also paid us a compliment."[117]

The reactions to the speeches were a reflection of how their morale had improved since Rodes eased up on drilling and the regiment had left its camps around Union Mills. "I wish you was hear this evening to see how the soldiers in Camp pass off the sabbath day," Private Jeremiah Tate wrote his cousin on September 8. "[Y]ou wood see them engaged in all kinds of amusements." Tate confessed that under Rodes' leadership, the Fifth Alabama had become a superb command. "I thought it hard," he reflected on his initial service with the regiment, "[but] since we have become acustom to it every man is prompt & performs his duty splendid. [W]e have the prase of being the best regiment in the state. [T]he old general says it is the best Drild that he has seen and it has got the name a broad of being the bravest of any. [E]ven the yankees tell us they speak often of the bluddy fifth, the desperados, the blood hounds. I guess we will make them think so if we ever git a chance at them." As for drilling, Tate was quite proud of the Fifth's efficiency. "I do wish you cood see us drill," he went on, "especially when we go on dress parade. [I]t wood be one of the most pleasing & effecting seens you ever witnessed to see one thousand men all in line & to hear the musicians perform on the brass instruments." Regarding this music, Tate favored one song in particular. "I want you to learn to sing the tune called Dixey," he told his cousin, "& think of me when you sing for it is a favorit tune amongst the soldiers."[118]

Despite all the scouting expeditions he sent out, Rodes remained desperate for accurate information. "We have had no end of alarms lately," Captain Blackford wrote his father on the 14th. "Yesterday the whole regiment had progressed a mile or more upon their journey to meet the enemy at Anandale when a countermarch was ordered and all hands returned to camp in high glee." About 10:00 a.m. the next morning, orders arrived from general headquarters to break camp and prepare to move out. After the men brought down the last tent, they received orders to cancel the movement.[119]

One false alarm hit Rodes hard and personally. Having gone back to Manassas to attend a court martial, he used the occasion to arrange for Hortense to come up from Lynchburg on September 13. The trip included sixty-three miles from Lynchburg to Charlottesville on the East Tennessee & Virginia Railroad, twenty miles over to Gordonsville on the Virginia Central, and sixty-five more miles up to Manassas on the Orange & Alexandria. Hortense was ill the entire trip. Barely an hour after the couple's first embrace at the depot, however, a courier with a telegram sent from Fairfax Station galloped into the junction looking for Rodes. According to the message, 5,000 Yankees were advancing and on the verge of cutting off the Fifth Alabama. Rodes tore himself from Hortense, leaped on his horse, and pounded up the road toward Sangster's Crossroads. Along the way he met Company D stationed out on the road "and was loudly cheered." After riding eleven miles at breakneck speed, he reached the camp of the Fifth Alabama, where he "found us all here as snug as you please," recalled Captain Webb.

The incident must have infuriated Rodes, who did not leave a record of his response. An investigation revealed that the alarm was raised by the panicked report of a cavalryman who had mistaken a friendly scouting party for the enemy. He then multiplied its numbers a hundred-fold. "True it is, that during the day we had received four orders to be ready to march in five minutes," Captain Webb wrote his wife of the incident, "so you see that here in sight of the enemy we can not hear the truth ten steps."[120]

Rodes brought Hortense into camp on the 14th. In eager anticipation of seeing her, he "had made great preparations by flooring his tent, and over hauling his premises generally," observed Captain Blackford in a letter to his father. Blackford added that "his tent is not more than twenty feet from me and I can now hear [them] laughing and talking at a great rate, you can't imagine how singular it sounds."[121]

On September 21, General Ewell dined with the couple. The occasion was apparently but one of many gatherings Rodes enjoyed with friends and fellow officers. As Private Cowin put it, "Rodes seems to be very popular as he has a great deal of company."[122]

Two days later, Hortense met with near disaster when her dress somehow caught fire. The flames spread quickly upward and might have engulfed her but for the fast action of a man named Simms (either a camp servant or a member of the regiment) who smothered the dress. The savior suffered a few burns in performing the heroic act. "She was very badly frightened," observed Cowin, "though was not at all hurt."[123]

By this time, Private Cowin had reached the conclusion that the cramped confines of camp life was an excellent teacher in the evaluation of character. He also had come to admire his regimental commander. "I find from observation that white men require watching as much so as negroes," he scribbled in his journal. "I think there are many who ought have masters over them at all times, and Col. Rodes is just the man to be over them, for if any could keep them straight he could."[124]

On October 2, an infuriated "Master" Rodes learned that men of his regiment had stolen and killed eleven hogs from nearby farms. He sent a squad to arrest them, but the offenders ran off, dropping the largest and heaviest of their booty. The would-be captors pounced on the hog and dragged it up to the guardhouse, where Rodes graciously allowed them to butcher and eat it. He was not so gracious with the commanding officers of the suspected thieves. Rodes placed three captains under arrest (Shelley, Dent, and Pegues), which in turn prompted a number of men into the wild talk of defying Rodes by refusing to drill the next morning. A good night of sleep, however, cooled their rebellious ardor. "Some trouble was anticipated in Camp this morning in regard to the arrest of the three Captains," a private wrote on October 3, "but all went off smoothly."[125]

Late in the month, Rodes took the Fifth Alabama north on another expedition toward the Potomac, this time to confiscate from the Yankees a large quantity of hay they had stored up for the winter. Things did not go as planned, which caused no little resentment among the men. "The whole regiment lay out of doors without fires even for 7 nights and days," Captain Blackford explained to his father. "The Yankees were near enough to be constantly firing at us with their long range guns and of course we could not expose our position with fires at night." As luck would have it, the week did not pass without a heavy cold rain. "I spent the night of the storm in the woods with my company," Blackford went on, "not more than 3 miles from Alexandria." The captain closed the letter on a lighter note, gratefully acknowledging the receipt from home of a cake, "which was much admired by us all, and by the Col. [Rodes] who partook."[126]

To his mother a few days later, Blackford resumed his complaints about the expedition:

> We suffered more hardships than we have ever done before, and that is saying a great deal I can assure you as we see more service than any other command in the service. We were exposed to a very cold rain for several days, doing guard duty constantly. Of course we could not sleep any to speak of as there was no shelter. . . . . What constitutes the particular hardship of such expeditions is the necessary absence of fire, which would draw the attention of the enemies [sic] scouts. The impression today is that a great battle will be fought tomorrow.

In neither letter did Blackford indicate whether the Fifth had succeeded in stealing the enemy hay.[127]

No battle occurred the next day, but the alarms continued. "The long rolls were beaten throughout the [Confederate] Army of the Potomac this morning at 3 o'clock and we were kept under arms until day," Blackford wrote his mother on October 7. "The cold was quite severe, and of course teeth chattered amazingly, there was quite a concert. You cannot imagine what a terrible sound the long roll is at night; it is the signal, you know, of danger, and the men are always kept under arms until the cause of the alarm is understood. I was laying awake when I heard one in camp some miles away from us, and I could hear them as they gradually came to the right, finally they commenced in our Brigade, and lastly in our regimental camp, thus in two minutes the whole Army was under arms."[128]

The next day, another wild rumor reared its head when the grumblings of a few soldiers for a transfer back to Fort Morgan turned into a report that Governor Moore had telegraphed President Davis to ask for the return of the Fifth regiment to Alabama. According to the rumor, the president had wired Rodes to see if he might be willing to go. Rodes and his staff quickly set the record straight, telling the officers and men who streamed into headquarters that the news was completely false.[129]

About the same time, unsettling (and true) news arrived. William Nelson, the husband of his beloved sister Sallie, had been arrested with a friend for using improper passes to go on leave from John Imboden's artillery company. Rodes rushed to his defense by writing a letter on October 10 vouching for the man's character. Private Nelson, he declared, was "a gentleman of high Character, accomplished education &c and I know would never violate knowingly any Army rule." As for Nelson's companion, Rodes argued that if he was his brother-in-law's friend, he must be a good man. The letter may have had the desired effect, for the men received only a mild punishment.[130]

Throughout these days in northern Virginia Rodes managed to keep the Fifth on a tight schedule of drilling, training, picketing, and other duty. In October, Captain Blackford wrote home that since moving up to Sangster's, the regiment had been "on the front line every day" picketing, foraging, opening and blocking roads, and building and burning bridges. The Fifth, he wrote, had torn up the railroad from Sangster's down to Union Mills. Rodes used his own specialized engineering skills to survey the surrounding area for the purpose of making reliable maps.[131]

Beginning at 6:00 a.m. on October 11, Rodes marched the regiment twelve miles to Pohick Church, where it acted as a guard for sixty wagons out on forage. Four days later, the Fifth's "front line" duty came to an end when the regiment moved back within two hundred yards of its old campsite at Union Mills. General Johnston had decided to withdraw the army to the vicinity of Centerville because he felt too weak to threaten the enemy's growing strength at Alexandria. The next day, the 16th, General Earl Van Dorn reviewed the Alabama regiment. Rodes prepared his men for the event by putting them through an arduous morning rehearsal.[132]

General Van Dorn's presence was no coincidence. A few weeks earlier, the War Department placed Ewell's brigade in Van Dorn's new division, one of four created to hold the thirteen brigades in Virginia. The other three divisions went to Longstreet, Gustavus W. Smith, and Thomas J. Jackson. In October, the four divisions were organized into two wings or corps, with the First Corps going to Beauregard and the Second Corps to Smith. Van Dorn's and Longstreet's divisions were in the former command, while Gustavus Smith's and Edmund K. Smith's (Jackson having been sent to the Shenandoah Valley) were dropped into the latter organization. With the elevation of four men to division command, the army needed as many new brigadiers. On October 22, Longstreet's brigade went to Ewell, who in turn relinquished command of his own brigade.[133]

To many observers, Rodes seemed the obvious choice to succeed "Old Baldy." The Alabama colonel had demonstrated solid command skills and a firm diligence in training, disciplining, and looking after his men. He also displayed a keen eye when selecting and fortifying a position. While not a West Pointer, Rodes was a graduate of the increasingly prestigious Virginia Military Institute. Though denied the opportunity of prominent combat on the field at Manassas, his delaying action on the morning of July 17 at Farr's Crossroads caught the attention and earned the respect of Ewell and Beauregard—both of whom now held a very high opinion of the colonel. Added to this were the invaluable assets of a distinct manner and attractive personal appearance. Rodes possessed what many at the time admiringly regarded as a natural martial bearing. Standing slightly more than six feet tall, the lithe and graceful officer with bright clear eyes, blond hair, and sweeping mustache cut an impressive figure. Many thought he was strikingly handsome. Simply put, he looked the part of a hero-soldier and exuded a contagious confidence.[134]

Rodes spoke very little about the possibility of promotion, and unlike many other officers in both armies, he refused to actively campaign to advance his own career. Though he must have coveted the position, he was uncomfortable with the idea of advertising himself for it. Along the way to adulthood Rodes had absorbed the virtue of humility (whether real or affected) from his father, who professed a strong disdain for ostentation. This seems especially true after having recently rediscovered the grace of God. Rodes quietly preferred to let promotion seek him rather than the other way around.

On Friday evening, October 25, Rodes received a letter from the War Department. The president had appointed him to the rank of brigadier general in the Provisional Army of the Confederate States, to date from October 21, 1861. Rodes drew his last pay as a colonel on October 29: $721.50 for three months and twenty-one days service stretching from July 1 to October 21. The months of hard work and dedication to duty were finally paying off.[135]

Robert Rodes' well deserved promotion to brigadier general in the Confederate army did not include an assignment. Adjutant General Samuel Cooper had yet to decide which of the then-available brigades should go to the newly-minted general. For a time, it appeared possible that Rodes might assume command of the Stonewall Brigade. Jackson himself had recommended the Alabamian (behind A. P. Hill) for the prestigious position. Whether Rodes knew this is unclear.[1]

If it were left to Rodes, he would have taken command of the brigade in which he had served the past four months—an assignment that would have kept him in direct contact with his beloved Fifth Alabama. Until officials in Richmond reached a decision, he remained in the familiar surroundings of his old regiment, nursing the effects of a severe cold.[2]

Rodes was sufficiently intelligent and sensitive to appreciate that his promotion had been the result of his close relationship with the Fifth Alabama. He had worked tirelessly to mold the Fifth into a well-drilled and disciplined outfit, and its men had done their part to make him look good as a commander. On the night of November 1, one week after receiving his letter from the War Department, Rodes felt well enough to stand before the entire regiment and express his gratitude. "He complimented us for our courtesy toward him," remembered one soldier, "also for bearing up under the many and toilsome and as he termed them 'famous' marches." Rodes went on to tell the men that he hoped to be their new brigadier, but if assigned elsewhere he "would never cease to feel a lively interest" in the old Fifth Alabama. "At the conclusion of his remarks," an impressed soldier acknowledged, "we cheered him lustily."[3]

Rodes quietly derived much satisfaction from the realization that his promotion had been based solely on performance, and not on any outside influence. It was a realization shared by many of his men. "This was a high but well deserved honor," Captain Webb wrote home in admiration of his commander. "[I]t was unsolicited—whilst others have been pressing their claims neither he or his friends have ever solicited promotion for him." Such respect on the part of Rodes' men proved to be deep and enduring. "Every contempt of counterfeit merit was his," artillerist Thomas Carter declared in a postwar speech in honor of Rodes, "every instinct of a true soldier was his! His laurels had to rest solely on the eternal foundations of truth! He refused to countenance any correspondence in his own behalf." Rodes seemed genuinely to despise "counterfeit merit." At every level of responsibility he insisted that his interests should be represented primarily by performance.[4]

Rodes' wish was about to come true. On Saturday, November 2, the day after he addressed the men of the Fifth, Rodes received official authorization to take command of Ewell's former brigade. The brigade was designated as the Third Brigade of Earl Van Dorn's First Division. To celebrate the event, and to express his great satisfaction at being able to remain close to his beloved Fifth Alabama, Rodes sent the regiment a barrel of whiskey. "We have just heard that Genl Rodes has been assigned to command this Brigade," Captain Webb happily wrote home the next day. "We are much pleased to have our late Col. to be continued with us."[5]

Webb expressed the sentiments of a great many soldiers in the Fifth who felt proud that their colonel had made brigadier. Some in the regiment, however, had reasons other than pride for deriving satisfaction from the promotion. Captain Webb's nephew, Private James E. Webb, was among those who welcomed the prospect of being taken out from under the direct eye of the strict disciplinarian. "You need not be regretting that Col. Rodes has been promoted," the younger Webb wrote his aunt in response to her concern that without Rodes the Fifth might suffer. "I was glad of it on our own account, for I like Col. Jones much better personally; and he has a big heart, while I think on the other hand Rodes has none at all, or if any a very small one." Then Webb drew this remarkable conclusion: "It is very true Gen'l Rodes is much the best military man, but that would make but little difference in the position of Col."[6]

Rodes agreed with Private Webb (though for different reasons) in his preference for who should command the Fifth Alabama. Consistent with his supreme virtue of discipline, Rodes believed that his former position should be filled by promoting the next senior officer. Despite his prior lack of confidence in him in the past, Rodes believed that the Fifth would best be served by promoting Lieutenant Colonel Jones.

Alabama law, however, stipulated that officer vacancies in volunteer regiments be filled by election. Rodes considered this policy acceptable for new unorganized regiments, but disastrous for veteran units. So strongly did he feel about this that when Governor Shorter insisted on adhering to the law, Rodes sent vehement protests to Montgomery and went outside state authority to appeal to the new national government. "Sometimes an election in an old regiment will put in good men," he conceded in a letter to Secretary of War Judah P. Benjamin, "[but] generally it will not. It will result in the discarding of strict officers in favor of a class of men utterly unfit for the position of commissioned officers." He offered this example: "In one case I have known an election to company officer to be used as a means of obtaining the discharge from the Army of a man who as a private applied in vain for discharge who had no good excuse for leaving. He was elected Lieut. upon the condition that he would resign at the end of two weeks."[7]

When Rodes learned that both Jones and Major Morgan planned to resign rather than submit to the "humiliation" of an election, his temper flared. Though convinced the two could easily win their respective contests for colonel and lieutenant colonel, he did not want to see them elevated by a process more appropriate for politicians than for soldiers. "That principle under the circumstances is monstrous," Rodes vented to Jones. "[It is] destructive to the army—it has seriously very seriously injured the efficiency of the regiments of this brigade and if persisted in will ruin them."[8]

Though the secretary of war declined to overrule Governor Shorter, Rodes refused to give up. Hoping to find a way around the technicalities of the law, he took the unusual step of "consulting prominent lawyers." Specifically, he sought legal support for his argument that the law applied only to units of the state militia, which the Fifth Alabama had ceased to be when it was sworn into Confederate service.[9]

When General Beauregard intervened to suspend all elections until the matter could be resolved, Rodes took the opportunity to send the Fifth's own lawyer, Major Morgan, to Montgomery for a final confrontation with the governor.

The men in the ranks followed these developments with great interest. "Many are of the opinion that vacancies should be filled by promotion and in regular succession," editorialized a Fifth Alabama private in the Montgomery *Daily Sun* in late November. "John T. Morgan . . . has gone to the proper authorities for the purpose of arguing the question in favor of promotion in succession by rank . . . he will not accept under an election, claiming the office by promotion."

The matter ended quickly. "John T. Morgan, of the 5th Alabama, has returned," declared the private's follow-up letter to the *Daily Sun*, "and brings the decision of Gov. Shorter, in relation to vacancies in Alabama Regiments. He decides that they are to be filled by election."[10]

Left without viable recourse, Jones and Morgan stood for election and won their respective "promotions." (Ironically, Jones would be defeated for reelection in the reorganization that would come the following spring). Though pleased at the outcome of the election, Rodes swallowed the bitter pill of having lost his battle against what he believed was an important principle.[11]

*   *   *

As Rodes quickly learned firsthand, the rank of brigadier general carried with it certain privileges, including better living quarters. He took down his tent and moved into a farmhouse near Union Mills Ford. "I am afraid of becoming spoilt if I stay here any longer," Captain Blackford wrote his mother about a visit to the new brigade headquarters. "[T]he style of living is very different from what I am accustomed to in my own quarters." However, Blackford observed that the "style" included some unpleasantness. "No one can tell the difference that there is between living in a house, and a tent at this season of the year," he continued. "There is no warmth in the sun even at midday so that when things become damp they are obliged to remain so until dried by a large fire, which we rarely have." Blackford offered his mother some idea of the close bond that had developed between himself and the new brigadier. "Gen. Rodes has been exceedingly kind to me since I have been an inmate of his house. [A]t some time before xmas I should like very much to have some nice things sent over for him, he is particularly fond of all kinds of cakes, sweetmeats & c, but I had better get oysters for him I suppose."[12]

In addition to the Fifth Alabama, Rodes' new command included Colonel John J. Seibel's Sixth Alabama, Colonel Robert T. Jones' Twelfth Alabama, and Colonel Robert Griffith's Twelfth Mississippi. (The Washington Artillery was no longer with the brigade, having been transferred to the Reserve Artillery in August.) Outside the Fifth Alabama, most soldiers in the brigade probably looked with indifference upon Rodes' promotion. Colonel Seibel, however, was one notable exception; he openly resented President Davis for not promoting him to command the organization. A few men formed an early and unfavorable opinion of their new brigadier when he continued the practice of dressing the headquarters guard in special uniforms, complete with red sashes and epaulettes. This may have been fine when drilling back home, some argued, but at the "front" it seemed gaudily inappropriate. "Mounting the guard so far from home is becoming quite unpopular in all the regiments," one soldier wrote his family, "and Gen. Rhodes [sic] more so. 'Tis true it makes a greater display but that is all."[13]

The headquarters guard, however, probably drew little of Rodes' attention at this time. In addition to the question of who should succeed him as colonel, he paid a great deal of attention to the formation of a new staff. In general, he sought to elevate his regimental assistants to brigade level. For the all-important position of assistant adjutant general, or chief of staff, Rodes secured his close friend Captain Henry Whiting, a twenty-nine-year-old VMI grad and former railroad engineering colleague. Except during periods of severe illness, Whiting would remain by Rodes' side for the rest of his life. Whiting was so devoted to the brigadier that he later would turn down a promotion to lieutenant colonel of the Forty- first Alabama Infantry to remain in his direct service. Commissary duties went to thirty-four-year-old Major Charles Force, a veteran of the Mexican War. Aides de camp who served as general assistants included Rodes' good friend from the NE & SW Alabama, Peyton Randolph, and twenty-nine-year-old Lieutenant John Mallett, a native of Ireland and erstwhile professor at the University of Alabama.

Rodes faced a challenge in convincing regimental quartermaster Captain John Webb to assume the added responsibility of looking after an entire brigade. Webb was reluctant to leave the Fifth Alabama. Rodes so valued Webb as an aide and quartermaster that he recently had intervened to keep him from accepting a line position as a company captain in the Fifth. "On the morning of the day of the election & before it was h[eld]," Webb explained to his wife, "Col Rodes heard that I would be elected & he came to me & urged on me not to permit it. . . . I told Mr Corwin not to permit the men to vote for me—he did so—that is the whole of it."[14]

The day after being notified of his promotion Rodes tried to convince Webb to join his brigade staff. "I have felt very much gratified to know that I have so large a share of the confidence of Col R," Webb wrote home. "[L]ast night he said to me that it would not only give him pleasure but that he would feel under obligation to accept any position on his staff that I would select. I thanked him kindly but declined to do so—he insisted that I should hold it under advisement. I consented to do so. My impression is that I cannot be induced to accept a place on his staff."[15]

Rodes refused to admit defeat and craftily placed the captain in a difficult situation: he directed Webb to become the brigade's temporary quartermaster. "I could not refuse to do so," Webb complained to his wife, "as he made an order that I should do so. This gives me a double duty not alone to act for my own Regiment but for three other Regiments. I have declined to accept the appointment tendered to me by him to go into his staff. I preferred to remain with my Regiment."[16]

For a time, neither man would yield. "Genl Rodes refuses to make the appointment of quarter master for his Brigade," Webb wrote six days later, "yet hoping to get me to consent to accept the appointment." Webb, however, finally gave in to the lures of a promotion to major, an increase in pay, a promise of release from service upon expiration of the one-year enlistment, an immediate furlough, and the expectation of good staff companionship. On November 16 he accepted Rodes' offer.

Not long afterward, however, Webb outmaneuvered Rodes at his own game when his friends Jones and Morgan were elected to colonel and lieutenant colonel, respectively. Their elevation allowed Webb to resign as brigade quartermaster and resume his position with the Fifth Alabama. Rodes "regretted it," Webb explained on November 30, "but yielded reluctantly to my wishes." As it turned out, Webb was not long for the service. Ill health forced his resignation on April 28, 1862. Rodes filled the position by turning to Captain Edwin Harris, a wealthy prewar cotton broker and four-term mayor of Montgomery.[17]

Through November of 1861, the brigade remained in camp around Union Mills Ford, where Rodes got acquainted with and drilled his new command. On the 24th he put his regiments on display for the first time in a grand review of the 10,000-man division. Beauregard, Van Dorn, and other notables observed the impressive martial display. "The scene was a very imposing one," Captain Blackford wrote his mother, "occurring as it did in a vast plain, the most level in the country—the most curious feature about it is the absence of the ladies, who are somehow intimately associated in every way with military displays."[18]

Eight days later on Monday, December 2, a larger military display took place when each regiment in Van Dorn's division received a new Confederate battle flag, replacing the national Stars and Bars that many believed might easily be confused on the battlefield with the federal banner. The presentation of these flags launched a grand review on the Yorkshire plantation along Bull Run southwest of McLean's Ford. With Bonham's South Carolina brigade on the right, Rodes in the center and Early on the left, the division that morning formed up into a single line extending nearly one-half mile. According to a Richmond reporter, at noon James Kemper's battalion of fifteen guns fired from a nearby hilltop to announce the arrival of Generals Johnston, Beauregard, and Van Dorn. While bands played spirited airs, the three officers and their staffs rode along the division line. When they were finished, Beauregard and Johnston trotted to a commanding hill and watched Van Dorn march by with the entire division, bayonets fixed and glimmering in the sunlight. The brigades formed a three-sided square around the generals. With every head uncovered and every voice silent, the Reverend E. Saunders, a Catholic chaplain of a Louisiana regiment, stepped up on a stand made from a caisson, blessed the new banners, and delivered a stirring address. When Saunders finished, Beauregard dismounted and walked to the center of the square. Each colonel solemnly approached and received from him the "Southern Cross," offering their patriotic pledges in return. The moving ceremony drew to a close when a band played an operatic air, followed by a relatively new song called "Maryland, My Maryland."[19]

About the same time, the government—as if to dash any lingering hopes for a short war—issued the men wool overcoats and other articles of winter clothing. This did not stifle rumors, many of which were generated within the upper command, of an impending clash with the enemy. "Our generals still persist in saying that there will be a great battle within a few days," Captain Blackford complained in a letter to his mother, "tho they have been persisting in the same story for more than four months, frequently even fixing the day on which all pickets are doubled, and every one kept on the alert. Of course the result had been that no one believes that the enemy intended to attack us this season, and were the longroll to beat tonight it would require the most strenuous exertions of the officers to get the men in line of battle." Instead of battle, most of Rodes' men at this time faced more pressing, and realistic, concerns. "The all prevailing topic of conversation in the Army now," continued Blackford in writing to his mother, "is when shall we go into winter-quarters, a question which no one can answer or even form a conjecture."[20]

The conjecture ended on Saturday, December 7, when Rodes marched the brigade to its newly assigned area for winter quarters at Davis Ford. The camp was near where the mouth of Bull Run opens into the Occoquan River about five miles east of Manassas Junction. There, his men built a number of wood or log shelters about fourteen feet square, with dirt floors. "There are now 150 or 200 little huts where but 10 days ago there was nothing but a dense pine thicket," one soldier wrote home on Christmas Eve. "The huts are covered with dirt or boards, according to the ability of the builder to obtain the latter."[21]

Winter quarters or not, rumors of battle persisted. "The most of our company is in & building houses for the winter," Private James Jones of the Twelfth Mississippi wrote home, "whitch [sic] we intend remaining in if old abe will let us but it is thought that he will give us a few shots in a short time as our pickets report the enemy advancing every day." Rodes, however, knew better. "On yesterday," Captain Webb wrote on December 9, "Genl Rodes called to see me for a few minutes & said if they [Yankees] did not advance to day he would give it up [the idea that the brigade would fight this winter]."[22]

Though its arrival may have ended the immediate prospect of battle, the winter would not be a season of idleness. With the occasional help of slave labor, the men worked on a variety of projects. As the supervisor of some of these projects, Rodes was quick to anger if he believed his men were shouldering an unfair amount of the burden. In a December 22 note to Van Dorn, for example, he complained that while his brigade held the responsibility of building the Davis Ford embankment and repairing the Manassas road, he also had to supply an entire regiment for picket duty. He wanted help from other brigades in the division—"Notwithstanding assurances that negroes shall finish the embankment at the [Davis ford] bridge—a heavy job."[23]

In addition to hard work, the men endured weather considered by many to be extremely harsh. In Virginia, most of the Mississippi and Alabama boys got their first real taste of a northern winter. Moreover, another epidemic of measles swept through the brigade, killing several men. None of this dissuaded Rodes from closing out the old year by holding a brigade review on Tuesday, December 31.[24]

*   *   *

The new year brought with it several changes to the army, to the division, and to Rodes' brigade. On January 30, 1862, President Davis reassigned Beauregard to Kentucky to give the Creole a command commensurate with his rank of full general (which dated from July 21, 1861). Thereafter the army abandoned the corps system and each division reported directly to Joe Johnston, who was also a full general. On January 10, Davis reassigned Van Dorn to the Western Theater, where the president hoped to put the

Gen. Joseph E. Johnston, commander of the Confederate army on the Peninsula.

National Archives

Mississippian's very substantial prestige to better use. Bonham commanded the division until early February, when he resigned to take his newly won seat in the Confederate Congress. General Jubal Early assumed temporary command of the division.

Meanwhile, the Third Brigade of that division acquired a new member and a new name. That January, Captain Thomas Carter's four-gun Virginia battery, the King William Artillery, joined what was now unofficially styled "Rodes' Brigade." From the "Lynchburg Beauregards" Rodes also acquired a new unpaid volunteer aide in the form of his nineteen-year-old cousin, Corporal Henry Yancey. At the same time, Rodes lost to illness his AAG Henry Whiting, whom he replaced temporarily with another old friend and railroad associate, Lieutenant Peyton Randolph.[25]

When the dust of all these changes finally settled, the high command began granting furloughs. So as not to dissipate the entire army, it allowed only one-fifth of the men in each veteran regiment to leave at any one time. Not surprisingly, every colonel and brigadier came under an immediate deluge of requests. "I am pressed to death," Rodes complained to Early on February 8, "with furloughs that came in last night & this morning."[26] So was Early, who refused the overwhelming majority of the requests and sent them back to Rodes, which made even more work for the brigadier. "Something is the matter, which seems to so vex Rodes," Captain Blackford observed in a letter written home, "as they are continually refusing every little paper sent up." Blackford added an interesting observation, one likely not shared by Rodes. "We have that wretch Early (Jubal) over us now as acting Division General," wrote the captain. "I won't serve long in his command, nor under that of any man whose private character is like that of Early."

Nor did Blackford wish to serve under an "inexperienced" colonel, which he expected to do when the one-year enlistment of the Fifth Alabama expired in the spring. When that transpired, his "in for the war" company would be placed in a new regiment. Rodes reluctantly agreed that many of the men of his beloved Fifth would go home rather than reenlist, and advised Blackford to apply for command of an artillery battery. "And by his advice also," Blackford wrote home, "I am to muster all the influence I can bring to bear in Richmond," a tactic Rodes ostensibly deplored, at least in so far as it pertained to himself.[27]

Shortly afterward Rodes took a furlough of his own, though he derived no pleasure from it. On Saturday, February 15, his father David Rodes died at his home in Lynchburg. Recent months had seen the rise of a new hope for recovery when the six-year-long advance of paralysis seemed to subside, but it cruelly resumed its progress to an inevitable end. Sustained by a strong religious conviction, the elder Rodes submitted to his fate "with the docility of a little child," and died quietly after uttering, "Jesus is with me, I know." He was laid to rest next to Robert's mother Martha in the Presbyterian Cemetery on the edge of town.[28]

The few extant letters exchanged over the years between father and son reveal a caring, mutually respectful relationship whose end could only have caused Robert a great deal of pain. Love cannot, in this case at least, be measured solely by money. From an estate valued at more than $31,000, the elder Rodes bequeathed to his three children by his first marriage—Virginius, Robert, and Sallie—$600 each from a note owed by former business partner Edward Burton. The rest of the estate, including six slaves and assorted real estate, went to David Rodes' second wife and their children.[29]

Soon after losing his father, Rodes faced the possibility of losing his brigade. On February 25, 1862, the Engineering Bureau's acting chief in Richmond, Major Alfred Rives, recommended his good friend and former VMI classmate as one of two candidates (General W. H. C. Whiting being the other) for the post of General Johnston's chief of engineers. "General Rodes is most admirably fitted for the position by talent, education, and experience," Rives wrote. "He is an engineer of great attainments, accustomed to organizing and directing engineering enterprises, and I feel perfectly certain, from personal knowledge, just such a man you need in this crisis." Johnston, however, did not want to put a line general in a staff position; neither Rodes nor Whiting got the job.[30]

The crisis referred to by Rives was the ominous buildup of federal strength in front of Washington and the consequent need for the Confederate army to evacuate its increasingly vulnerable position around Manassas. On February 25, the day Rives wrote to the commanding general about Rodes, Johnston began preparing to withdraw the army behind the Rappahannock River.[31]

The marching orders came at a bad time for Rodes' brigade. Despite the care he lavished upon his command, the winter had been hard on the men. "By March 1, 1862," remembered the Twelfth Alabama's James Howard, "we had lost quite a number of our company [E]. Some died from measles, some from pneumonia. Some of us had mumps and all had body-lice with 'IW' on their backs—that meant 'In for War.'"[32]

Moreover, the men and officers by this time had accumulated in camp a tremendous amount of personal baggage. They spent two or three laborious days packing and shipping this baggage to Manassas (where most of it would be burned when Johnston evacuated the place). In a similar vein, many officers, presumably including Rodes, scrambled to make arrangements to send home their wives. Rodes also lost the most important member of his staff, acting AAG Lieutenant Peyton Randolph, who transferred to the army's Engineer Department. The pair had been together nearly five years, first as railroad co-workers and then as army officers. After failing to persuade Randolph to remain on his staff, Rodes —who sincerely regretted losing the valuable services of his close friend—agreed to write him a letter of recommendation. "Mr. Randolph has been directly under my eye since the summer of 1857," he informed Secretary of War Benjamin, "and hence my opportunities of arriving at a fair estimate of his Character have been innumerable." Rodes went on to cite Randolph's many fine virtues and outstanding qualifications, including a "great natural quickness of apprehension," a specific type of intelligence particularly admired by Rodes. Until the return of Captain Whiting, Rodes employed Briscoe Baldwin, a VMI classmate and a distant relative of Jeb Stuart, as acting AAG. The brigadier affectionately referred to the thirty-four-year-old as "Buck." Rodes also lost to resignation his commissary officer, Charles Force, who was replaced by twenty-four-year-old Daniel Webster of the Fifth Alabama.[33]

On Saturday, March 8, Rodes took the brigade out of its camps along the Occoquan and led it for the first time on a long march. It had been some time since the the men had stretched their legs this aggressively, and many were loath to leave their comfortable winter cabins. The whole affair quickly turned into a trying ordeal. "We marched 10 miles by 3 in the morning, when we halted almost broken down under our heavy loads, and without fire or supper," wrote Captain Blackford, who left a detailed recollection of the excursion:

We were en route again at daybreak, no time being given to cook breakfast, because they said the enemys' cavalry was close behind, and away we went thro' a pouring rain & deep mud to a bivouac beyond Cedar run, where we had some fresh beef, but no bread or salt. This was a terrible day, I saw much suffering among the men from hunger & fatigue; many would lie down by the roadside to die as they affirmed, and really they looked like it. Of course we anticipated a rest until morning, but judge of our chagrin when the long rolls beat at 11 1/2 oclock and by midnight the whole division was en route. Owing to the darkness and an ignorance of the roads day found us not more than 3 miles from our Bivouac of the previous night. We having been all the time on our feet, stumbling over creeks & bushes. It was very cold but no fires could be made as we were not long enough in one place to kindle them. The column was not halted until 5 oclock in the evening, at which time the men, worn out with fatigue cold and hunger, could not be urged forward any further by their officers.

After covering twenty-five miles in two days, Rodes put his tired brigade into camp near Rappahannock Station, on the south bank of the Rappahannock River. Since they did not have any tents with them, the men were forced to sleep in a boulder-strewn meadow that quickly turned swampy under two days of heavy cold rain. "Of all the trials to which we are subject," concluded Captain Blackford, "being forced to lie out inactive in rainy weather is the greatest."

On March 17, Rodes began the twenty-mile leg of the journey to Orange Court House, where Johnston was concentrating the army. The brigade reached Brandy Station that evening. On Wednesday it trekked three miles to Culpeper, where it participated in an all-day, three-division grand display of marching through town with flags flying and bands playing. A thirteen-mile march on the 20th brought the brigade to the Rapidan, and the next day it moved into its camps near Orange Court House. "We have abandoned an immense portion of the State, and that one of the finest parts of the Confederacy," Captain Blackford lamented. "I shall never forget the sight I saw during our march. Hundreds of happy families abandoning their beautiful homes, and hastening to the rear."

Able at last to begin looking after the needs of his men, Rodes on the 24th dispatched a special four-day mission into Richmond. "Our party will consist of 3 captains and a Major," Blackford reported to a cousin, "and we are expected to buy all the shoes in the city, as our Brigade is barefooted."[34]

Maj. Gen. George B. McClellan, commander of the Army of the Potomac.

New Jersey Historical Society

* * *

Directing the massive federal buildup that triggered the Confederate retreat was the hero of Rich Mountain, Major General George B. McClellan. Summoned to Washington the day after Bull Run and given command of the Army of the Potomac, McClellan performed an invaluable service to his country by reorganizing the army and restoring its confidence and morale. Eventually, however, he frustrated the Lincoln administration with his apparent reluctance to use that army against the enemy. In early 1862, he developed a plan to advance on Richmond by moving the army down the Chesapeake to Urbana on the Rappahannock, and then overland to the rebel capital. He preferred this to the direct approach against Johnston, he explained, because he believed the Confederates at Centerville were too strong, both numerically and in position, and because the roads in northern Virginia were inadequate during the spring to sustain the movements of a large army. When Johnston's withdrawal behind the Rappahannock to the vicinity of Culpeper made the plan impractical, McClellan shifted his intended disembarkation farther south to Fort Monroe on the tip of a peninsula between the York and James rivers, about seventy-five miles southeast of Richmond. The Lincoln administration reluctantly agreed to the plan, with the proviso that McClellan leave behind enough troops to protect Washington. McClellan began putting his men into the Fort Monroe-bound boats on March 17.[35]

When the fear in Richmond finally turned into the conviction that McClellan intended to advance on the capital from the east, President Davis ordered Johnston to shift the army to the Peninsula. On Saturday, April 5, Jubal Early's division moved to Orange Court House and boarded trains for the sixty-five mile trip to Richmond. Rodes' brigade left first.[36]

With forty-five or so men crammed into each box car, tragedy struck unexpectedly when the train carrying the Sixth Alabama crashed head-on with an empty train heading north to get more troops. The collision completely destroyed both engines and killed or seriously injured many of the unlucky Alabamians.[37]

Notwithstanding this disaster, the rest of the brigade arrived without incident at the Broad Street Depot in Richmond about noon the following day. The capital welcomed the soldiers with open arms. We were "treated very hospitably by the Citizens," noted John Tucker of the Fifth, "who met us with Cakes, Bread, Meat & every thing good to eat." Rodes led the brigade through the city to the docks on the James, where about 3:00 p.m. they boarded steamers and set off down the river. After a twisting fifty- mile journey they landed about midnight on the southern side of the Peninsula just behind the Warwick River. Allowing no time for rest, Rodes set off on the thirteen-mile march across the Peninsula to the vicinity of Yorktown, where they arrived just after dawn. On the 8th, Rodes put them into camp, noted one soldier, "on the field that Cornwallis surrendered on and closed the first 'American Revolution.'"[38]

Rodes joined General John Magruder's 12,000 men on the defensive Warwick River Line, which stretched across the Peninsula from Yorktown to the James River. Magruder placed the brigade in support of Redoubt No. 4, which contained six heavy guns. The bastion was about 1,600 yards from the enemy line. Rodes quickly put his men to "work day and night to remedy the defects, strengthen the intrenchments and secure shelter."[39]

The Peninsula's harsh spring weather quickly attacked the new arrivals. "Rain, Rain, Rain," Private Richard Adams of the Fifth Alabama wrote in his diary. "Everybody wet and mad." Three days later he added, "Rain pouring down all the time. Every drop seemed to make our blankets 10 lbs heavier."[40]

On April 12, Jubal Early turned the division over to its new permanent commander, Major General Daniel Harvey Hill. A native South Carolinian, intellectual, and a devout Christian like his brother-in- law Stonewall Jackson , the forty-year-old Hill was an 1842 graduate of West Point. After being breveted major for bravery in the Mexican War, he resigned from the army to teach math at Washington College in Virginia and then at Davidson College in North Carolina. In 1859, Hill was made superintendent of the new North Carolina Military Institute. He entered Confederate service as a colonel from North Carolina and catapulted to national prominence with his skirmish "victory" at Big Bethel early in the war. Though resembling Rodes in the use of strict discipline, Hill differed vastly from him in temperament. He was much

Maj. Gen.
Daniel Harvey. Hill

National Archives

less gracious and more openly critical and sarcastic than Rodes. They eventually liked and admired each other, but their differences prevented the pair from ever becoming close friends. Hill arrived on the Peninsula not only to take over Van Dorn's former division, but to supervise the Yorktown fortifications, which would allow Magruder to concentrate on preparing and defending the remainder of the Warwick Line.[41]

Hill's division contained some 11,000 men—four brigades under Rodes, Early, Winfield Featherston, and Gabriel Rains. It held the left side of the Warwick Line, with Rodes' brigade standing between Redoubt Four and Redoubt Five, a section stretching from the defenses of Yorktown to the obstructions on the Warwick River. While a third of Rodes' men held the trenches at any one time, the others worked in the rear building traverses and epaulments. By mid-April, James Longstreet's division held the center of the line, with Magruder on the right and G. W. Smith's men in reserve.[42]

Against this still relatively meager force McClellan had at least 60,000 men, with more on the way. The federal commander was well aware he faced a Confederate enemy secure behind formidable works, and decided to use the federal navy to help him flank the position. When the navy refused to cooperate (as it had earlier agreed to do), and the weather turned the ribbons of dirt roads into steams of running mud, McClellan surrendered the initiative and called for his heavy guns.[43]

As the weeks passed, Rodes' men suffered terribly from the cold and rainy weather. Without tents or other substantial shelter, illness spread through the ranks. Limited rations, "consisting of the plainest and roughest food," compounded the problem. The soldiers survived without coffee, vegetables, or fresh meat, and there were no hospitals nearby to treat their illnesses. Like at Pensacola nearly a year before, Rodes could do no more than express his helplessness and frustration.[44]

Perhaps even more frustrating were the ever-present enemy sharp-shooters. At least something could be done about that menace. In the middle of April, Rodes sent a night expedition of two regiments to clear these annoying but deadly pests from a nearby orchard. In a few hours the men returned in triumph after cutting down the orchard and capturing a number of blankets, haversacks, and canteens. The next day, however, the sharpshooters returned with a vengeance, the fallen trees of the orchard providing them with better cover than before. The following night, Rodes sent a second expedition to burn the trees that proved more successful in providing some relief from enemy sharpshooters.

Nothing, however, could be done about the much more terrifying long-range enemy ordnance, which by some estimates sent a missile screaming overhead every two or three minutes. "The screaming of the shell sent from the heavy guns of the gunboats is awful," Captain Blackford informed his parents. "[W]e commence hearing it at the distance of a mile & a half, and by the time it reached us the noise is indescribable."[45]

The time spent waiting for McClellan to move against the works allowed the Confederate army some breathing space to reorganize itself. The government extended for the duration of the war all the one-year enlistments, which were about to expire. In exchange, the Davis administration granted the soldiers the right to choose their regimental and company officers. As he had six months before, Rodes strongly disapproved of "that system" of elections, particularly when it cast aside the Fifth Alabama's Colonel Jones in favor of Christopher C. Pegues.

General McClellan, meanwhile, with his big guns finally up in the front lines, prepared at the end of April to begin bombarding the rebel defenses. On May 1, however, Johnston, in consultation with his principle officers, wisely decided to abandon the Warwick Line before the enemy could act. Rodes' and Early's men unknowingly benefited the most from this decision, for McClellan's guns probably would have hit them the hardest.[46]

Johnston wanted Smith and Magruder to pull out first, followed by Longstreet, with D. H. Hill bringing up the rear. The heavy artillery Johnston left behind to open fire and cover the movement. Once their task was complete, the guns were to be spiked.

That night, D. H. Hill instructed his brigade commanders to prepare to move out after dark on the 3rd. Rodes gave the order for the men to cook three days' rations, and around noon the next day (May 2) the brigade wagons began rolling westward up the Peninsula. The following evening, Rodes marched his men through the night until they reached Williamsburg about daylight the next morning.[47]

By noon on May 4, the vast bulk of the Southern army had reached Williamsburg, twelve miles from Yorktown. After resting, it began pulling out with Magruder's men in the lead. Rodes put his men on the road about 2:00 a.m. on the 5th. While bringing up the rear, Longstreet came under increasing pressure from pursuing federals, who finally forced him to take up a position along a line of light field works previously built by Magruder two miles east of Williamsburg. Hill's division stopped to await the outcome of the developing rearguard engagement. "After standing under arms until 8 o'clock in a hard rain," Blackford wrote his mother, "we were ordered to stack and wait orders, so we stood until 2 p.m." About that time, McClellan threw Joseph Hooker's division against Longstreet, who called for Hill's assistance. Hill promptly led his division back through Williamsburg.[48]

Just before entering the town, Rodes ordered his to men drop their knapsacks and overcoats into a pile. In contrast to the sad faces seen on the townspeople during the retreat of the day before, Rodes and his soldiers saw "doors, windows, balconies and sidewalks crowded with beautiful women and children wild with excitement," noted Lieutenant Robert Park of the Twelfth Alabama, "waving handkerchiefs and flags and passing out sandwiches, water, etc. and giving us encouraging words. The men became enthusiastic, shouting and looking forward to the conflict."[49] "Who could not help fighting," declared an elated Richard Adams of the Fifth regiment, "when he had such ladies to cheer them on as we did and give such words of sympathy."[50]

Frequently urging his soldiers to double-quick, Rodes led his newly inspired men about two miles through fields sometimes shin-deep in mud. Around 5:00 p.m. he reached the front, where he received orders to form his brigade behind Early's regiments, which were deployed on Longstreet's left flank. Along with many of his men, Rodes believed that the moment of truth at last had arrived. "All were ready and thought the fate of war had gone in our favor," declared Adams. "We were to fight. What a glorious feeling."[51]

But that glorious feeling gradually sank into one of disappointment when the men slowly realized the brigade would have no greater share in the battle at Williamsburg than to stand in reserve and nervously endure the occasional shriek of a shell overhead or the sound of a stray bullet whizzing by. All the while they stood silently by as they witnessed "men in anguish going to the rear. We were in the midst of it," Blackford wrote his mother, "but as usual we fired not a gun, tho' many of the enemys' shot struck about us."

Longstreet eventually threw back the confused federal attack, and Early and Rains brought the fight to an inglorious end when they suffered a bloody repulse in an unwise attempt to seize an enemy battery located on the far side of a swampy wood. Rodes remained in line well past sundown. Because his men were not allowed fires, they suffered from the rapidly dropping night temperatures. "There we were forced to stand ankle deep in mud until 3 a.m. Tuesday morning," Blackford complained bitterly, "being unable to sit at all and exposed all the while to a cold wind rain." Rodes finally received orders from Johnston to pull back through Williamsburg and go into camp about one-half mile beyond the town. "Ah, too late, like at Manassas," Adams lamented that night in his diary.[52]

The retreat continued the following day. The men shuffled westward through a relentless cold rain that mercilessly tormented them the entire way. "Now was the time for one's patriotism to be tried," Private Adams confessed bluntly, adding, "I had rather be dead than alive cold and wet." With Hill bringing up the rear, the two divisions took all day to march about twelve difficult miles on muddy roads badly torn up by the shoes and wagons marching and rolling ahead of them. "The road could not have been known," observed Adams, "had we not known exactly where we were." Many men lost their shoes in the deep mud and went on barefoot. "The troops nearly all broken down from fatrigs [sic] hunger & want of sleep," Private John Tucker scribbled in his journal that night. "The road for 5 miles was strewn with Blankets, over coats, clothing, knapsacks, Cooking Utensils, Sick Men &c &c." And all through the day, Rodes and his men had nothing to eat.[53]

Beginning at 9:00 a.m. on Wednesday the 7th, Rodes marched the brigade six more miles to where Johnston was concentrating his command in the vicinity of Barhamsville. "We kept stamping our feet and crowding together to keep warm as we halted and moved on," remembered Lieutenant Park. For a second day they received no rations, being forced to subsist on parched corn, which further discomforted the men with unpleasant intestinal problems. Unable to withstand the march, many dropped out of the division column and took shelter in nearby barns, outhouses, and other buildings. Others, perhaps hundreds more, simply threw away their knapsacks and muskets and walked on alone. "Cold, tired, hungry, and jaded," General Hill observed, "many seemed indifferent alike to life or capture."[54]

At some point along the way Rodes met up with an old acquaintance, Captain J. W. Minnrich, who belonged to a heavy artillery battalion that for several months had been stationed in Yorktown. The two had met in the spring of 1861 while sharing the officers' car on the train up from Pensacola to Richmond, and had seen each other a few times at Yorktown. Minnrich and a comrade were hurrying by to catch up with their command. The night before they had made their way to a barn to get out of the rain, fallen asleep, and did not hear reveille the next morning. After a brief moment spent trying to decide whether to go after their battalion or join in the fight that could be heard to the rear, the two chose the better part of valor and headed west. Carrying eight-foot long pikes tipped with twelve-inch double-edged blades that had been issued to them the year before to "repel boarders," they came upon Rodes' brigade as it rested on the side of the road. Minnrich braced himself against the ribbing he expected the men to heap on him for being lost and for toting such a medieval weapon. To his great surprise, however, he escaped that fate, not only because the men were too cold, hungry, wet, and worn out to say much of anything, but because Rodes stood nearby "within earshot of them." Sixty years later, Minnrich fondly recalled the deep impression Rodes left on him at that moment. "Standing by the roadside with his arms folded under the cape of his great coat," he wrote, "he was listening to the sounds of battle in our rear. I never have forgotten the picture he made." When they recognized each other, the two saluted and exchanged pleasantries, wherein Minnrich "found him always the same genial and courtly gentleman." The captain ventured to ask if his artillery battalion had passed by. "A good while ago," Rodes answered. "They should be at least four miles ahead of you. But how did you happen to be so far behind your command?" The embarrassed captain explained the circumstances, including the moment given in consideration of joining a nearby fight. "At that," Minnrich wrote, Rodes "smiled his slow, genial smile," and jokingly asked, "And what did you expect to do with your pikes?" This brought a smile from Minnrich, who realized that he had not fully escaped the gauntlet of ribbing after all.[55]

On Thursday, May 8, improved weather allowed Rodes to pick up the pace. He marched his men until 3:00 a.m. the following morning. All were hungry, exhausted, and more than a bit irritable. When one of D. H. Hill's aides came along in the darkness to tell the men to close up, an incensed Captain Blackford, whom Rodes had put in charge of bringing up the rear, lashed out at him, threatening to "run him thro' if he interfered with my men." Fortunately, Rodes came along to diffuse the situation and send the aide on his way.

Returning to the road at 11:00 a.m., Rodes led his men to a point just east of Long Bridge on the Chickahominy River, a swampy wood-lined stream flowing southeast down the Peninsula. There, Johnston halted the army to set up a defensive line. Hill and Longstreet held the right near Long Bridge, and Huger and Smith deployed on the left near New Kent Court House. The men welcomed the stop. They received their first rations in three days, the army now supplied by the York River Railroad running out from Richmond. Many of the tired and filthy men used the Chickahominy for a quick bath. "Good gracious what a feeling," declared Private Adams. "So much like a white man after the best part of the soil of the Peninsula had been taken off my body." The men remained in bivouac a few days along the river, their spirits picking up despite Rodes occasionally putting them through drill or posting them out on picket duty.[56]

This welcome respite soon ended, however, when a Union gunboat flotilla tried to pass Drewry's Bluff on the James River, and the enemy attempted a landing at West Point on the York River. Though both attempts were failures, the efforts convinced Johnston of the prudence of continuing the retreat and pulling the army closer to Richmond. At 3:00 p.m. on May 15, Rodes complied with orders to cross the Chickahominy at Long Bridge on a pontoon his men had helped lay. Once across, he led his brigade four miles west on the Charles City Road. The following day he marched it from 2:00 p.m. until 10:00 p.m. that night, and on the 17th moved another five miles to the outskirts of Richmond. "We are now in sight of the 'seat of treason & rebellion,'" Private Adams joked in his diary, "where we expect to die in our tracks fighting for it."[57]

Though the Confederate retreat gave McClellan complete freedom of movement on the Peninsula, the cautious commander took fifteen days to reach the Chickahominy. Following in the wake of the retreating enemy was a laborious process, especially with poor maps. Despite outnumbering Johnston by roughly 100,000 to 60,000, he surrendered the initiative when he chose to approach the capital slowly in preparation to laying it under siege. By May 17, Johnston was ready for him, having set up a semi-circular line generally facing east, with Longstreet on the right five miles from Richmond, D. H. Hill on his left guarding the Charles City Road about three miles from the capital, G. W. Smith on the Williamsburg Road, and Magruder stretching from the Nine Mile Road to the Chickahominy.[58]

That same day, May 17, D. H. Hill put the Fourth Virginia Heavy Artillery Battalion and the Twenty-sixth Virginia Infantry under Rodes' command. Both outfits, together with the Forty-sixth Virginia, evacuated Gloucester Point during the retreat up the Peninsula and marched up the other side of the York River to join the rest of the army near King & Queen Courthouse. The Twenty-sixth remained under Rodes only a few days before reuniting with the Forty-sixth in Henry Wise's brigade. For the time being, Rodes kept the Fourth Battalion, which consisted of four independent artillery companies brought together at Gloucester Point to serve as infantry. They elected Captain C. C. Otey as their lieutenant colonel.[59]

The proximity to Richmond brought few benefits to Rodes and his men. "Altho we are so near the Capitol," Blackford wrote his parents, "our life is just the same as if we were at Yorktown, so far as camp discipline is concerned, the only difference being that no one man or officer is allowed to visit the city or even leave his camp. We have no tents." Blackford went on to express substantial bitterness at the top commanders, whose leadership during the retreat had allowed the men to suffer from hunger and from long hours of standing while the column barely moved. The poorly conducted retreat Blackford condemned as "shameful."[60]

As might be expected, Rodes used the waiting time in front of Richmond to resume drilling his men, much to their displeasure. On Tuesday the 20th, he went out to watch his former regiment perform "battalion drill." As colonel of the regiment the year before, he had brought the men to near "perfect mastery of the subject" when performing this exercise, and he eagerly looked forward to seeing them go smartly through their paces. What he witnessed greatly disappointed him. Having done relatively little drilling the past several weeks, and still recovering from their trying ordeal moving up the Peninsula, the regiment looked so sloppy that Rodes left in disgust. At least one soldier felt ashamed. "Our Regt made a complete failure out on Battalion drill," Private Adams lamented that evening. "The once proud & well drilled 5th Ala. with Rodes as Col had 'played out.' With Pegues as Col she has fallen, her proud mien is draging [sic] in the dust. Her officers & men can no longer speak of her with the same pride of former days. Her reputation & Songsters plus Rodes notoriety," continued the private, "left us with our much beloved Rodes. He came up with every confidence in his old Regt which he said made him what he is, to drill & show her off to the rest of the Brigade."[61]

The following day, a still irate Rodes demanded to see the entire brigade on drill. This time he witnessed a more satisfactory performance, particularly from the Fifth, which "Did very well on Brigade drill this evening," Adams proudly noted. The regiment "retriev[ed] its lost character somewhat." Two days later, Rodes called for another brigade drill, which this time came under the admiring eyes of many ladies out from Richmond. Again, the brigade did quite well, with Adams proudly characterizing the performance as "very tight."[62]

While Rodes watched the dismal performance of the Fifth Alabama on the 20th, McClellan's resolve stiffened with news from Washington that Irvin McDowell's powerful corps of some 35,000 men would soon march overland from the capital to join him. Little Mac edged his advance lines so close to Johnston's he set off near panic in Richmond. The move so unnerved President Davis that he considered contingency plans to move the government west into the mountains. Having decided that the best approach to the Confederate capital was a thrust below the Chickahominy River, McClellan sent Samuel Heintzelman's III Corps and Erasmus Keyes' IV Corps to seize bridgeheads on the southern shore. He kept the bulk of his army north of the river, however, in order to maintain communications with McDowell as well as to protect the army's supply lines along the Pamunkey River and the Richmond & York River Railroad, both of which ran east to his base at White House. In this vulnerable divided position he remained for several days, even after being informed on the 24th that McDowell's movement south had been cancelled.[63]

Fearing McDowell's arrival, Johnston began to shift his army northward on May 27 to strike above the river against McClellan's exposed right flank. Smith moved over to the river at Meadow Bridge. Rodes, who the day before had sent Captain Blackford and his company into Richmond to roust out the brigade's stragglers (he rounded up fifty-eight men), remained behind on the Charles City Road, while Hill took the remainder of the division to replace Smith on the Williamsburg Road. Longstreet swung around to the Nine Mile Road northeast of Richmond.

On the 28th, however, Johnston learned that McDowell's movement had been cancelled, and two days later received from Hill important information based on armed reconnaissances performed by Rodes and Garland on the Charles City and Williamsburg roads, respectively. Although Rodes' scouts had not spotted any Yankees, Garland reported the presence of what appeared to be an entire enemy corps strongly posted two miles west of Seven Pines and a mere five miles from Richmond. The recent heavy rains had swollen the swampy Chickahominy, which was now running out of its banks on a twenty-year flood tide. The newly widened river divided McClellan's army into two unbalanced wings, neither of which could now be readily reinforced. Having been pressed by President Davis for weeks to strike a blow against the approaching enemy, the defensive-minded Johnston finally saw an opportunity he liked. He changed his plans and resolved to strike at the exposed federal position dangling south of the river.[64]

*   *   *

Three miles below the Chickahominy, Darius Couch's 1st Division of Keyes' IV Corps held the Seven Pines area, so named for the seven loblolly pine trees that stood near the intersection of the Williamsburg and Nine Mile roads. The men were deployed behind a line of abatis, with pickets and flanking units posted on the Nine Mile Road to their right. Three-fourths of a mile in front of Couch, about five miles east of Richmond, was the 3rd Division under Silas Casey.

Fifty-five-year-old Casey was an 1826 graduate of West Point and a twice-breveted veteran of the Mexican War. He also was the author of *System of Infantry Tactics*, commonly called "Casey's Tactics," which the War Department adopted in 1862 as the training manual for volunteer soldiers. With three brigades totaling some 6,000 men, every one of them untried in battle, he held a strong defensive line stretching one mile from across the Williamsburg Road at Fair Oaks Station on the right to the edge of White Oak Swamp on the left. The entire position was lined with abatis, felled trees, entrenchments, and shallow rifle pits. Moreover, the center of Casey's position contained a small but strong pentangular redoubt holding nine guns. About half a mile in front of Casey's main line stood a formidable skirmish line complete with abatis. Behind Keyes's two divisions (Casey and Couch) stood Heintzelman's pair of divisions—one at Bottom's Bridge and the other farther back on the edge of White Oak Swamp.

Johnston planned to strike Casey's command along the three main roads that ran east out of Richmond and converged on Seven Pines. Longstreet, who was to lead the attack, would strike on the left down the Nine Mile Road. In the center, about two-and-a-quarter miles below Longstreet, Hill's division would assault along the Williamsburg Road. Two miles below Hill, Benjamin Huger's division of three brigades, just up from the now-untenable base at Norfolk, would advance on the right down the Charles City Road. W. H. C. Whiting, in command of G. W. Smith's division, would take a position at Old Tavern to watch for any Union advance from north of the river. Magruder would stand in reserve on the Nine Mile Road. Altogether, Johnston planned to hold six brigades along the river while committing his remaining twenty-two brigades to the offensive operation. This division of labor seemed more than sufficient to crush McClellan's left wing. Johnston set the attack for 6:00 a.m. on Saturday, May 31.[65]

Shortly after the sun set on the warm and sultry day of May 30, Rodes issued orders to ready rations for the next day. The men understood what this meant. Until very late in the evening they busied themselves with various preparations, but a violent, all-night thunderstorm robbed them of perhaps their greatest need—a decent rest. With nothing more to protect them than blankets stuck up on poles, the men by morning were tired, wet, cold, and miserable. Still, they realized that this was likely to be their day of inauguration into battle, and so they greeted the sunrise with special enthusiasm. "It was a lovely May morning," noted the Twelfth Alabama's James Howard, "and the sun rose bright and clear. Though they were wet and had enjoyed little rest, the men were full of life and courage, and the woods resounded with their cheerful voices and brisk movements." Some of the men of the Fifth took a more solemn approach to their day of reckoning. "Called from our wet & damp beds," Private Adams wrote in his diary. "[W]e buckled on our armor to advance against the enemy. Now the time had come. Everyone knew from the noiseless movements of the soldiers who spoke in subdued tones as they prepared their repast."[66]

D. H. Hill's division, fielding roughly 8,500 men, was tasked to deliver the main blow by driving straight up the Williamsburg Road and smashing into the center of the Union line. To better utilize the full weight of his command, Hill was ordered to delay the assault until Rodes' brigade joined him after an overland march from the Charles City Road. That movement, in turn, depended upon the arrival of Huger to relieve Rodes.

Johnston's complex plan relied upon a timetable of intricate marching, close cooperation, and skilled military judgment and command ability. As he was about to discover, the starkly different personalities leading his divisions had not yet developed the means to control large bodies of troops under combat conditions. For a largely green army, Johnston was asking too much of his men and their officers. An all-night rain muddied the roads and jeopardized the movement even before it began.[67]

And yet, somehow, it began well enough when Huger started his division before dawn south from its encampment at Oakwood Cemetery northeast of Richmond. When his men reached a makeshift wagon bridge over the normally fordable but now raging Gillies Creek near the Williamsburg Road, however, they spotted Longstreet's 14,000 men and their baggage wagons slowly crossing in single file. What was Longstreet doing here? As Huger understood the plan, Longstreet was supposed to be marching east on the Nine Mile Road so as to form the left punch of Hill's attack. He apparently misunderstood the verbal orders Johnston gave him the night before and was now marching south to get to the Williamsburg Road in order to come up behind Hill. Huger's men waited until 10:30 a.m. to begin crossing Gillies Creek. Because Johnston had not revealed to him the plan of battle, Huger assumed he was merely relieving a part of Hill's division. He thus lacked the sense of urgency required by the situation. Johnston's complex plan was unraveling.[68]

As the hours passed, Hill—already in a foul mood after having been up all night making preparations—grew increasingly impatient. He intended to launch the attack with Samuel Garland's brigade on the left of the Williamsburg Road (Garland had assumed command in Early's stead when that officer was wounded at Williamsburg) and Rodes' brigade on the right. The brigade under George Anderson (in place of the ill Featherston) would go in behind Garland, and Rains' men would do the same behind Rodes. To Hill's dismay, Rodes was nowhere to be seen.

Near 10:00 a.m., four hours after the attack was supposed to have begun, Hill sent an aide to inquire after the situation on the Charles City Road. Rodes, together with his aide Lieutenant Green Peyton, misunderstood the message to mean the brigade should move out, relieved or not, and that Rodes should ride personally to see Hill.[69]

After dutifully giving the order to begin marching, Rodes sped ahead through the difficult overland crossing along a narrow path to the Williamsburg Road and reported to Hill. The division commander was surprised to see him. Obviously there had been a misunderstanding. He had not given the order to march, Hill explained, but merely had inquired after the cause of his delay. Knowing Rodes, he probably offered his commander an explanation and an apology, and then directed Peyton to rush back to halt the brigade and return it to the Charles City Road. Rodes set off a short time later.[70]

About 11:00 a.m., elements of Lewis Armistead's brigade of Huger's division finally began arriving at Rodes' position. About the same time Rodes, his horse nearly worn out from the difficult ride to and from Hill's headquarters, received definite instructions from Hill to come up. Once more Rodes issued marching orders. Mindful, perhaps, of the recent misunderstanding with Hill, he gave specific instructions to each of his regimental commanders. Once again, the men rose to their feet. "With alacrity," Lieutenant Park of the Twelfth Alabama later jotted in his diary, "each man inspected his cartridges, and carefully loaded his musket. Pretty soon after, the command 'fall in' was given," and, in the cool, bracing air, Rodes led his men into the forest. "Thank God we open the battle," declared Private Adams.[71]

The feelings expressed by Adams were echoed in the Sixth Alabama, where one soldier remembered the seriousness of the moment. "At last we realized that we were to go into battle. Now all was still save the ringing of the steel ramrod as it clashed against the rifle barrel. No jesting now. Each man was busy with his own thoughts." All now agreed that it "begins to look like a fight! And then, again, the jest went round—for so often had Rodes' Brigade been marched out with the expectation of meeting the enemy and failed to get under fire, that the men had come to believe that it had been preordained that they should never share the dangers of the battle field." No one would be holding that view for long.[72]

The men faced a difficult three-and-one-half mile trek on a narrow path through woods, marshland, and the head of White Oak Swamp. The previous night's rain had made the soil soft and spongy, with standing water ranging from ankle to waist deep. To make matters worse, a washed-out bridge across the swamp forced the men to wade through murky water that in places rose up to their armpits. To save lives and ammunition, Rodes made sure the crossing went slowly and with great care. After the men were across, he double-quicked them to make up for lost time.[73]

Hill, meanwhile, continued to send messengers inquiring after Rodes' progress. Rodes answered each in turn the same way: he was coming on as fast as possible, though one reply carried the prediction that the brigade would be at least another thirty minutes late.[74]

Finally, about 12:30 p.m., ninety minutes after starting out, Rodes reached the Williamsburg Road at the head of his 2,200 tired and wet men, many of whom were black with mud up to their waists. He still needed time to get the brigade up and formed for battle, time that Hill might have saved by launching the attack with Rains' formed and waiting brigade taking the front position. Rodes' regiments could easily have gone in behind Rains in reserve. Hill, however, seems not to have considered this arrangement.[75]

Sitting in the saddle and surveying his command, Rodes steeled himself to lead his brigade into battle for the first time. He could not let this all-important moment pass without commemorating it in some fashion. He looked at the men of Colonel John B. Gordon's Sixth Alabama, the first of his column to reach the Williamsburg Road. "Gordon!" he cried out. "Halt your regiment a moment. I have a word to say to the men!" Rodes put the spurs to his sorrel nag

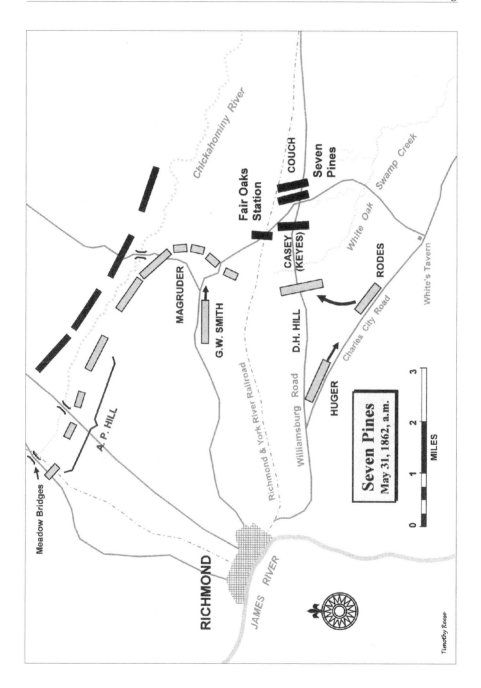

Seven Pines
May 31, 1862, a.m.

MILES

Timothy Reese

"Old Bob" and dashed to the front of the regiment. Every voice fell silent as the men turned a respectful gaze upon their general. "Sixth Alabama!" he called out, "you open the ball to day." Rodes paused for emphasis before adding, "Remember that you are Alabamians. You have bayonets, use them. If your brother falls, pass over him. If you see an enemy he is yours. Press on. Let no obstacle stand in your way!" With his short but inspiring speech finished, Rodes sent the Sixth Alabama forward to form a brigade-wide skirmish line about 150 yards in front of the main line.[76]

Next in line was Colonel William H. Taylor's Twelfth Mississippi. With no more time for speeches, Rodes simply ordered Taylor to line up the Twelfth with its left on the Williamsburg Road. The Mississippians had barely deployed when, about 1:00 p.m., word reached Rodes from Hill to launch the attack.[77]

Hill must have known that Rodes was not fully ready. The division commander had Rodes' note that he would need another half hour to get the brigade up on the line. With his division less than fully deployed, the impatient Hill took considerable risk ordering it forward. He evidently held great faith in Rodes' ability to improvise as best as possible.

Though only half his brigade was deployed, the situation left Rodes with no room for protest. To his left across the Williamsburg Road was Anderson's brigade, which already had stepped off toward the enemy. Rodes gave the order to do likewise. "Scarcely had the reverberation of the signal gun died away," remembered a soldier in the Sixth Alabama, "[when] the command: 'Skirmishers forward march' was given and we entered the dense swamps in our front."[78]

The formidable enemy abatis picket line lay distant about 1,000 yards. Between Rodes and the federals was a dense swampy pine forest choked with a thick undergrowth of tangled vines and luxuriant foliage. Not only was it difficult to keep order and move forward, but it was hard in many places to distinguish objects a mere ten paces in any direction. In anticipation of this problem, Hill earlier that morning had issued instructions requiring each man to wear on his cap an easily identifiable white strip of cloth.[79]

Rodes worked to get the other men up and into position as quickly as possible. Realizing the impossibility of establishing a straight line of battle, he prudently decided to deploy his remaining units en echelon as they arrived. He planned to advance in this manner until he seized the enemy picket line, when he intended to halt and reform the brigade into a straight line in preparation for the assault on the enemy's main position. This bold, complicated, and risky plan, would require the utmost skill and determination from both himself and his men.

As the Sixth Alabama and Twelfth Mississippi moved in line forward, the Heavy Artillery Battalion under Lieutenant Colonel Otey reached the front. Rodes dispatched it after the right-rear of the Twelfth Mississippi.

As Otey's men tramped ahead, loud explosions erupted to the left across the road in front of Anderson's men, who were now several hundred yards (or about fifteen minutes) in advance of Rodes' form-as- you-go battle line. Before long, artillery shells fell on the right side of the road, crashing their way through the trees. Rodes and his command were under direct enemy fire for the first time in the war.

As the Fifth Alabama arrived at the front, Rodes looked east toward his advancing lines, watching the Twelfth Mississippi pass into a storm of iron and falling tree limbs. Fearing the regiment might waver, he improvised his plan. Instead of sending the Fifth to form en echelon to the right of the Fourth Battalion, he personally led it up behind the Twelfth so to steady and reassure the Mississippians. To Colonel Robert Jones' Twelfth Alabama, the next regiment to arrive, he gave instructions to head to the right of the Fourth Battalion. The King William Artillery, the last unit of the brigade to come up, was ordered to advance directly on the Williamsburg Road.

All the men were now up. Rodes had coolly and efficiently deployed them in a prompt manner and sent them advancing toward the enemy. Using as guides the Williamsburg Road and the sound of the enemy's fire, he rode along directly behind his lines, calling out through the noise, the smoke, and the dense swampy forest to urge his men forward.[80] "Thick as hail fell the shot around us," recalled Private Adams of the Fifth, "more different tunes than were ever heard to them. Some burst as they struck, others a fluttering noise, & then the keen whistle of the minnie ball."[81]

Marshy ground appeared here and there, making it difficult to get a good foothold. Numerous trees lay about, deliberately felled by the enemy. In other places loomed hedges and briers, some so thick as to force the men to scramble around them and then quickly reform their line. "On we moved," remembered the Twelfth's Lieutenant Park, "over fences, through mud and water waist deep and almost impenetrable undergrowth, across fields and ditches and fallen trees, listening to the oft repeated command 'forward! close up! keep together!'"—commands that frequently came from the throat of Rodes.[82]

After what seemed an interminable time, the brigade emerged from the swampy woods and stepped out into the open on the Barker farm. Almost immediately, the men came under the direct musket fire of Casey's skirmish line. Men tumbled to the ground, among them Lieutenant Colonel Otey, who was killed on the spot. Many of his men, demoralized at the sight of their fallen commander, dropped out of line and sought cover. The trees and dense undergrowth had cut in two the Fifth Alabama, with five of its companies ending up to the right of the Twelfth Mississippi and five marching far behind it. With its organization jumbled and its men facing fire for the first time, Rodes' brigade faced a crucial test—would it fall into disorder and confusion or remain cohesive and follow orders?[83]

Rodes moved quickly to remedy the deteriorating situation. The five lagging companies of the Fifth were ordered to rush up and reunite with the rest of the regiment on the right of the Twelfth Mississippi. He found the Fourth Battalion's second in command, Major Bagby, and demanded to know why the battalion had stopped. Angrily rejecting Bagby's feeble explanation that they were acting under General Hill's instructions, Rodes directed the major to get his men up and move them forward, which was promptly done.

As he was riding about the field, a bit of good fortune smiled on Rodes. Carter's four guns came up and opened from the Williamsburg Road on the left, bringing a cheer from the men in the line. The brigade leader took advantage of the moment to renew his call for the entire brigade to move forward. The newly inspired men responded by lurching ahead. Within a few minutes Rodes' entire line caught up on the left flank of Anderson's brigade, which its commander had stopped to reorganize after it, too, became disordered while passing through the trees.[84]

With this seemingly irresistible two-brigade-wide line coming at him, Casey braced for the attack by pulling his skirmish line into the redoubt and rifle pits extending on either side of it. At the same time, he sent an urgent request for support from Keyes.[85]

Skirmishers from the Sixth Alabama were the first of Rodes' men to reach the enemy's abandoned line of abatis, followed quickly on the left by the Twelfth Mississippi and five companies of the Fifth Alabama. His attack having proceeded well thus far, Rodes called a halt to allow the rest of the brigade to catch up. According to Hill's earlier instructions, he was supposed to shift his entire brigade to the right to allow Rains to come up and take over this part of the line. Finding that Rains was behind and slightly to the right of his position, Rodes wisely decided to avoid Hill's complicated maneuver. After sending a request for Rains to move up on his right, Rodes set about readjusting his own line in preparation for rushing the next objective: the enemy's main position, which included a strong redoubt about one-third of a mile distant.[86]

To some observers, Rodes seemed to be everywhere. After issuing orders to establish his new line behind the protection of the captured abatis, Rodes made sure the Fourth Battalion took its place there. He then rode over to the right to bring back the Twelfth Alabama into line after it had gone about sixty yards too far in advance. He recalled the Sixth Alabama from the skirmish line and sent it to form up on the far right, then sped over to the left to bring back five companies of the Fifth Alabama which, like the Twelfth, had become over eager, stepped over the abatis, and gotten into a premature firefight with the enemy.

When all was ready to his satisfaction, Rodes cast his eyes across no-man's-land for one final study of the enemy position. To his satisfaction, he observed that the enemy line extended no farther than his own, which reduced his fear of being flanked on the right. He turned and gave the signal to advance, and then watched in admiration as his entire line pushed forward, a sight like nothing he had ever before witnessed.[87]

About the same time, Gabriel Rains' brigade, under orders from Hill, swept around to get behind the redoubt from the right, while from the left the Jeff Davis artillery (Bondurant's) and then the King William artillery (Carter's) opened fire from the Williamsburg Road. After driving off a column of federal reinforcements sent up the road by Couch, these guns turned their fire on the redoubt. The New Yorkers and Pennsylvanians of Palmer's brigade were doing their best to defend the position, but the converging artillery and infantry proved too much for them and they pulled out in a rush.[88]

Rodes' exuberant soldiers, whooping and screaming as they advanced, surged over the abandoned enemy breastworks. "Rodes," Hill later observed with well deserved admiration, "moved up his brigade in beautiful order and took possession of the redoubt and rifle-pits." Inside the redoubt were seven abandoned Napoleon field guns, several horses, and large amounts of equipment, supplies, and personal baggage.[89]

About the same time, around 3:00 p.m., Garland and Anderson broke through Casey's line on the left north of the Williamsburg Road. In two hours time, Hill's division had overrun the first enemy line and captured a total of eight guns, about 200 men, and tents and stores enough for a brigade of infantry.[90]

With several hours of daylight left, Hill asked Longstreet for support in assaulting the second federal line. The burly Georgian responded by starting

Robert H. Anderson's brigade down the Williamsburg Road. Longstreet, however, continued to make mistakes. On the extreme Confederate right, beyond Rains' position, Huger's three brigades removed themselves from the action when they marched down the Charles City Road to White Oak Swamp, where there were no federals, an error compounded by Longstreet when he dispatched three more brigades after him. This tactical error whittled away at Johnston's offensive punch, leaving only Robert H. Anderson's and James Kemper's brigades in reserve.[91]

Meanwhile, Casey's retreating Yankees quickly reached the abatis in front of their second line held by Darius Couch's 1st Division of Keyes' IV Corps. This division was deployed about 150 yards behind the captured redoubt. The federals gained their composure here and opened a deadly fire against Rodes' advancing line. Rodes watched as another column of enemy reinforcements pressed into the sector up the Williamsburg Road. As far as he could determine, Anderson had fallen behind on the left, and there was no sign of Rains' brigade on the right. Believing his flanks were in jeopardy, Rodes reluctantly decided to pull his regiments back. In so doing, he demonstrated for the first time his style of fighting while on the offensive, which emphasized a relentless hard-hitting thrust, often tempered with a concern—though sometimes excessive—for the integrity of his flanks.[92]

Unable to maintain the momentum of the assault, Rodes decided to wait for support and prepare for a possible counterattack. On the right behind a fence on the edge of a woods he put the Sixth Alabama. The Twelfth Alabama was placed in the enemy's abandoned abatis near the redoubt. Inside the redoubt he deployed the Fourth Battalion and the Fifth Alabama. In the rifle-pits to the left of the redoubt, stretching all the way to the Williamsburg Road, was the Twelfth Mississippi. He ordered the artillerymen of the Fourth Battalion to turn the captured guns in the redoubt on the Yankee column advancing up the road.[93]

Major Bagby barely managed to get two of the Napoleons into action before Carter's King William battery thundered into the redoubt. Unaware of the captain's useful action on the Williamsburg Road, Rodes chided his friend and former VMI classmate: "Carter, you are late. There's a battery at the edge of the woods that's been giving the Yankees hell." Carter laughed, bowed low, and replied, "Your right humble servant had the honor to command that battery!" Carter never forgot the look of surprise and pleasure those words brought to Rodes' face.[94]

Before long, General Hill reached the redoubt. After quickly surveying the situation, he ordered Carter to send one gun off to the right to enfilade the Williamsburg Road. When the piece unlimbered in its new position, however, an entire Union battery just 600 yards distant opened up a fire that "swept away nearly every man of the gun." The redoubt also came under tremendous fire. "The enemy were now bringing forward their reserves," recalled Thomas Coffey of the Twelfth Mississippi, "and as no reinforcements appeared to our rear, it seemed that, weary though all were, we should be compelled to 'stick it out.' [The] men were falling fast from fatigue and want of ammunition," he continued. "Although the enemy maintained a fierce triangular fire, he [Rodes] defied all efforts to dislodge him, and was lost in volumes of smoke."

The determined efforts of both Bagby and Carter finally took effect and the column of enemy reinforcements pulled back. "General Rodes," a corporal in Carter's battery proudly remembered, "sat on his horse behind a large pile of cord wood and directed matters. He was close enough to our position to observe how cool some of our fellows were." Those "fellows" also impressed Hill. "I would rather command that battery then be President of the Confederate States," he exclaimed.[95]

As Rodes' men battled to secure the area around the redoubt, Robert Anderson's brigade finally arrived from its reserve position. Hill placed it on the left of G. B. Anderson's command. After Rains came up on Rodes' right, Hill gave the order to attack the second enemy line which, in addition to some of Casey's rallied men, now consisted of a brigade from Couch's division and another from a division led by Philip Kearny.[96]

Rodes maneuvered his men into the open, carefully formed them for the advance, and rode along the line, bracing them for the attack. "Around his martial figure—six feet tall, clear-eyed, thin, with drooping mustache," wrote Lee biographer Douglas S. Freeman, "his men dressed their line for a second charge." When satisfied that all was ready, Rodes once again gave the signal to advance. "Every man rose to his feet and dashed forward," Lieutenant Colonel Gayle of the Twelfth Alabama proudly reported.[97]

The entire line immediately came under heavy fire. On the left, the Twelfth Mississippi and the Fifth Alabama advanced into another dense woods, while on the right the Twelfth and Sixth Alabama trudged through a swampy area with water several feet deep. Several of the wounded drowned when they slipped beneath its surface. The tragic scene caused many men to throw down their muskets in an effort to pick up their stricken comrades and carry them to dry land. Rains' men apparently failed to advance in unison to shield Rodes' right, and that portion of the line began to falter.[98]

Rodes dispatched a staff officer to urge Rains forward. When the attempt failed, Rodes turned his horse in a personal effort to locate Rains and demand that he bring up his lagging brigade and provide better cover on the right. Rains offered only excuses for his delay. His men were under too much pressure, he insisted. He would eventually have to contend with the rest of Kearny's division, which came up from Bottom's Bridge and formed on Casey's left. Hill was outraged by Rains' uninspired effort, and roundly condemned him in his after-action report. According to the division leader, Rains' dereliction cost Rodes an additional 500 casualties. Rodes agreed that support had been lacking. "I feel decidedly confident," he subsequently declared in his report, "that if we had been properly supported in the last charge the brigade would have marched on with uninterrupted progress." This "flank lesson" left a deep and lasting impression on him.[99]

Without support on his right flank, Rodes' right-most regiment, the Sixth Alabama, took a terrific beating. "Every moment now," remembered one veteran, "we could hear the soft thud that told too plainly that lead had encountered flesh." To avoid being turned, Colonel Gordon bent back Captain Thomas Bell's Company A at a near right- angle to the rest of the regiment. Heroic is an inadequate term to describe the stand made by this company. Of its fifty-five men, forty-four went down. Of those, twenty-one were killed, including Captain Bell, who fell but continued "to use his revolver with great effect upon the enemy" until he died. The eleven survivors of the company stood their ground and maintained their fire until orders came from Rodes to fall back to some cover at the edge of a nearby field. By then, the rest of the regiment had been shot up nearly as much as Company A: in three companies, every officer had been hit, and in four others all but one officer had gone down.[100]

Heroics were witnessed up and down the line. With the partial withdrawal of the Sixth, the Twelfth Alabama came under increasing fire. Colonel Robert T. Jones, considered by Rodes to be "the most accomplished officer in the brigade," fell dead leading his regiment. "But do they falter?" a proud Lieutenant Colonel Briston Gayle rhetorically asked in his report on the conduct of the men. "Not one!" was how he answered his own query. "They load, rise, take deliberate aim, and fire. 'I saw him fall,' they would exclaim and then repeat the same operation with equal coolness." Notwithstanding the "coolness" displayed by the men of the Twelfth, the regiment eventually did falter, gradually falling back to its original position in the abandoned entrenchments of the Union first line around the redoubt.[101]

On the left the situation looked equally bad. After losing six successive color bearers, a portion of the Twelfth Mississippi fell back to its original position in the rifle pits to the left of the redoubt. Moreover, most of the Fourth Battalion dropped back beyond the redoubt and took refuge in the ditches on the other side. When Rodes, riding back and forth along his line, discovered the retreat of the battalion, he became outraged. With much difficulty, he got them out of the ditches and up into the redoubt, marking the second time this day that unit had disappointed him. By 5:00 p.m. only the Fifth Alabama and portions of the Twelfth Mississippi and Fourth Battalion still held advanced positions, each taking heavy losses but "maintaining their posts without flinching," Rodes proudly reported. But a fragmented line made up of nothing more than clusters of fighting men standing in front of an enemy increasing in firepower would not carry the day, and Rodes knew it. The attack, which lasted barely an hour, had failed. Now Rodes faced the difficult problem of how to safely extract his men from their advanced position.

It was at this time that James Kemper rode up to make the surprising but very welcome announcement that his brigade had arrived as reinforcements. Rodes quickly decided to use the new men to replace his own so he could pull back and reorganize his command. He personally led Kemper forward to show where his regiments should go in.[102]

Rodes had been tempting fate all afternoon but somehow had escaped enemy lead. Aides had fallen all around him. Recently acquired ADC Lieutenant Philip Sutton received an ugly wound that would cost him an arm, and Major D. T. Webster and Captain H. A. Whiting both had horses killed under them. Now it was Rodes' turn. While riding forward with Kemper, a bullet ripped into his lower right arm, crippling the limb for several weeks.[103]

The impact of the slug staggered him. Private Thomas Coffey of the Twelfth Mississippi observed the immediate aftermath of the wound: "[I]t seemed a critical moment, he refused to leave the field, but still cheered on his men as if nothing had happened." This display of pride and bravery, however, carried Rodes only so far. When his sleeve filled with blood and he became faint, he dismounted. The situation might have turned critical but for the heroic action of a slave named Archie. The young man served as a cook with the Twelfth Mississippi and had refused to stay behind in camp. "Archie, a black boy," recalled Private Coffey, "volunteered to go for water and bandages, and, mounting a horse, plunged along across the line of fire, and soon returned. The general was much relieved, and remounted." However relieved and grateful he may have been, Rodes made no mention of "Archie" in his official report of the battle.

Rodes' refusal to leave the field at this time, preferring instead to control the situation by the use of a bandage and sheer willpower, deeply impressed those who witnessed it. "He has no fear," concluded the Fifth's Private Adams, who claimed to have seen Rodes get hit. Later in the battle, Adams took a bullet in the leg, a wound that forced him to leave the infantry. One year later he joined the cavalry and proudly named his new mount "Robert Rodes."[104]

Only after the fighting drew to an indecisive close ninety minutes later with the setting sun did Rodes, feeling faint and weak, consider leaving the field. He turned the brigade over to the Sixth Alabama's John Gordon, an officer he accurately judged to be the most capable colonel in the brigade.[105]

About the same time Rodes was wounded, General Joseph E. Johnston was felled by enemy fire. About 6:00 p.m., the general realized that his plan to crush one wing of McClellan's army was not going to be concluded before darkness put an end to the attempt. He decided to keep his men on the field and renew the contest the following morning. Too close to the front, a bullet thudded into his shoulder, followed by shrapnel from an exploding shell that tore into his chest and upper leg. Stretcher bearers carried the stricken commander from the field, and Gustavus Smith assumed command of the Confederate army.

By the following day, June 1, McClellan managed to shift enough troops south of the river to halt Smith's disjointed efforts to carry out Johnston's offensive. The battle sputtered to a close. Mercifully, Rodes' crippled brigade remained in reserve behind William Mahone's brigade of Benjamin Huger's division, and so missed the second day's action.

The first day at Seven Pines was a hideous introduction to war for Rodes and his large 2,200-man brigade. In five hours of fighting, almost exactly half of his men—1,049—became casualties. Most were struck down during the charge against the second federal line. Total Confederate losses for the battle were reported as 6,134, while the Federals lost 5,031 to all causes.

On the evening of June 1, the Twelfth Alabama's Lieutenant Park, who earlier had noted how eager for battle his comrades had been that beautiful morning, felt altogether differently. "The men were worn out, and were glad to stretch themselves upon the wet ground and slept soundly, though the air was filled with the agonizing cries and groans of the wounded and dying men and animals by whom they were surrounded." S. Q. Hale of the Sixth Alabama, recalling Rodes' speech to the men just prior to the battle, wrote after the war, "At last Rodes' men had been initiated into the misteries [sic] of the battle field. They had 'remembered that they were Alabamians,' and hundreds of the noblest sons of our mother state were resting in the bivouac of the dead."[106]

*   *   *

Before May 31, 1862, Robert Rodes held the well-deserved reputation for being an efficient and capable officer. Like so many other men in the army, however, he had never been tested in battle (the minor affair at Farr's Crossroads notwithstanding). Seven Pines forever changed that. The general had handled his brigade firmly and efficiently, guiding it with a steady hand while maintaining his composure in a situation that even veteran commanders would have found sorely trying. With an arm wound and hundreds of his men strewn about the bloody field, he now was a veteran in every sense of the word. He had been tested in the only classroom that mattered, and had passed the examination as well as anyone could have expected. The young general could rightfully lay claim to—and receive the honors of—being a courageous, inspiring, and hard-hitting combat leader. Nothing can prepare a man to pass such a sanguinary test; either he has the capability or he does not. Somewhere within the engineer-schoolteacher was a talent, unknown perhaps even to himself, for effective and even brilliant military command. By maintaining order and effectiveness as he led his brigade to the field of battle, formed it for attack, and advanced against an entrenched enemy, Rodes proved to men inside and outside his command the inherent value of his intense training and drill. His performance earned him the increased respect and confidence of his men. In the eyes of his fellow generals and superiors, he at last had proved worthy of the high rank he held. "I will mention Brigadier-General Rodes as distinguished for coolness, ability, and determination," General Longstreet wrote in his report. "He made one of the most important and decisive movements on the field and held his command some hours after receiving a severe wound." Division leader D. H. Hill agreed. In a letter to the secretary of war explaining the heavy losses in his command, Hill referred to Rodes as "a capital Brigadier." Coming from one of the most critical officers in the service, this was high praise indeed. [107]

In time, participants in the fight attached to Rodes and his command the loftiest praise for what they accomplished on the battlefield of May 31, 1862. "The charge of his brigade in single line," Captain Thomas Carter declared in a postwar speech in honor of Rodes, "unsupported on the right, at Seven Pines, through abatis, through water waist deep, over open fields, and the capture of rifle pits and redoubt fully armed with artillery and infantry, was next to Pickett's Division charge at Gettysburg, a feat of arms without a parallel in our army—an army as I believe without an equal in all the ages!"[108]

Shortly after the battle, an unknown scribe penned a long poem entitled "Rodes' Brigade at Seven Pines, May 31, 1862," which appeared in the July 4, 1862, issue of the Richmond *Daily Whig*. The last stanza of the poem read:

> Maidens of Southland! come bring ye bright flowers,
> Weave ye a chaplet for the brow of the brave,
> Bring ye the emblems of Freedom and Victory,
> Bring ye the emblems of Death and the Grave,
> Bring ye some motto befitting a Hero,
> Bring ye exotics that never will fade,
> Come to the deep crimsoned valley of Richmond
> And crown the young chieftain who led his brigade.[109]

Seven Pines provided Rodes with the glory he believed he had been unfairly deprived of at Manassas. Or so he thought. Praise from his superiors, Longstreet and Hill, was very gratifying, but in his opinion the newspapers fell far short of offering up the adulation Rodes believed he and his brigade rightfully deserved, the "crimson valley" ode notwithstanding. Hill agreed, complaining that his division had been characterized by some as skirmishers. Captain Blackford also protested, writing in a letter home, "Justice to Rodes' Brigade has not been done in the papers. Our Brig' alone made the first attack, and lost more men than any others." The perceived slight remained with Rodes for a long time. On his next battlefield just a few weeks later, he would inspire his men by telling them, at Seven Pines, "you did not get the credit you deserved."[110]

The wounded "young chieftain," meanwhile, remained in a Richmond hospital only long enough to have his arm properly cleaned and dressed. Luckily for him, the bullet had not broken any bones or damaged any nerves or arteries, which allowed him to avoid having to undergo the horrors and dangers of an amputation. Great danger, however, still lay ahead in the battle against infection. He transferred to General Hospital Number 1 in Lynchburg, but remained only long enough to get a basic examination. After demanding an immediate release, he finished recuperating at his father's house on Harrison

Street, where he came under the much more welcome care offered by his stepmother Fannie and his beloved Hortense.[111]

Though unable to write or get around very well, Rodes continued to work. His older brother Virginius came by to help by taking dictation and serving as a volunteer aide. Thirty-eight-year-old "Gin" had never married, "and it was known," recalled a friend, "he ever cared for but one fair lady. This was when he was young, before going to New Orleans." Having evidently failed after several years in the cotton compress business in New Orleans, Virginius became a planter on the Yazoo River in Carroll County, Mississippi. He had managed to stay out of the war up to this time, apparently because of poor health, but he jumped at the chance to help the younger brother he increasingly idolized. On Thursday, June 5, five days after being wounded, Rodes dictated a note to Secretary of War George W. Randolph asking for confirmation of the commissions for staff officers Philip Sutton and Henry Whiting. He praised both men for their conduct in the fight of the 31st. Twelve days later Rodes scratched out a note to Francis Smith of VMI. "My arm is nearly well," he declared, adding, "not entirely so, as you will see from this my first effort at writing since I was wounded." Rodes went on to explain why he must decline Smith's invitation to visit: "In a few days," he stated optimistically, "I shall be at my post again."[112]

Expecting another battle soon, many of Rodes' admiring men eagerly wanted him to resume his post. "We are all very impatient to have Gen. Rodes with us again," Major Blackford wrote his sister on June 12, adding, "there is a Col. Commanding the Brigade now, but may I be spared from fighting under him."[113]

Though his wound had not yet closed and still required bandaging, and infection-fighting fevers still tormented him, Rodes grew increasingly restive as the month of June slipped past. Convinced that a major campaign loomed on the horizon, he yearned to return to duty. Taking brother Virginius with him as a volunteer aide, Rodes went by train from Lynchburg to Richmond, and on Friday, June 20, one day short of three weeks after receiving his wound, he rode into the field and resumed command of his brigade.[114]

The brigade had undergone significant change during his twenty-day absence. In keeping with President Davis' wish to brigade regiments by state, the Twelfth Mississippi transferred to Featherston's Mississippi brigade in Longstreet's division. The Virginians of the Heavy Artillery Battalion relocated to Chaffin's Bluff on the James River, where they became a part of Henry Wise's brigade. In their stead, Rodes received Colonel Cullen Battle's Third

Alabama and Colonel Edward O'Neal's Twenty-sixth Alabama. The Third had spent twelve months at Norfolk before retreating up the Peninsula. As part of William Mahone's brigade, it suffered heavy losses at Seven Pines. The Twenty-sixth formed the previous December at Tuscumbia, Alabama. Brigaded with Rains' command, it also had been engaged at Seven Pines. Rodes was fortunate his replacements were two battle-tested regiments.[115]

"It was with no little pleasure that we took our place in a brigade composed entirely of Alabama regiments," the Third's Colonel Battle subsequently declared. Others in the regiment, however, strongly opposed the move. "This order was received with much disfavor by the regiment," asserted the Third's Major B. H. Powell. "The officers united in a protest and petitioned the Secretary of War to be allowed to remain with General Mahone." While many people back home in Alabama strongly supported the idea of an all-Alabama brigade, some did not think Rodes the appropriate commander to lead it. Congressmen William Yancey and Clement C. Clay took this opportunity to protest to President Davis. Rodes might be an excellent officer, they explained, but he was not an Alabamian but a Virginian merely "sojourning" in their state. They wanted the Alabama brigade to be commanded by a native Alabamian.[116]

Neither the petition nor the protest changed the situation, and Rodes apparently took little heed of either. Instead, he strove in his own inimitable fashion to get reacquainted with his new command. The manner in which he did this did not immediately win over Major Powell. "Our debut into Rodes' brigade and Hill's division," he wrote, "so far as we ever knew, was quietly made. There was no demonstration of welcome—no giving of the right hand of fellowship." Despite the unenthusiastic reception, Rodes quickly earned the respect of the men—including the initially displeased Powell. "This quiet was of short duration," continued Powell. "General Rodes, as we soon had occasion to know, was not at all inferior to General Mahone in energy and enterprise, and though, at this time, he was disabled by the wound he had received at Seven Pines, yet he was in camp and ever looking to the discipline and efficiency of his command." Rodes used "a large and roomy old field," remembered the major, "level, and without tree or stump, in which he could have his troops exercised."[117]

Along with the changes to Rodes' brigade came a restructuring of D. H. Hill's division. While gladly welcoming Rodes' return to duty, the division commander showed considerably less favor to his other brigadiers. His expressed dissatisfaction with fellow North Carolinian Gabriel Rains for not contributing more to the attack on the second enemy line at Seven Pines finally brought about Rains' reassignment on June 18 to river defenses. His brigade went to Alfred Colquitt, another North Carolinian. Hill had also had enough of Featherston, presumably because of that officer's frequent absences with illness. Featherston transferred (along with the Twelfth Mississippi) to Longstreet's division, with his old brigade going to George Anderson by way of promotion. Richmond's efforts to enlarge the Virginia army by bringing up troops from coastal states added a fifth brigade to Hill's division in early June when Roswell S. Ripley's command arrived.

Once the reorganization was complete, the First Brigade of Hill's division belonged to Rodes. The Second Brigade consisted of Anderson's four North Carolina regiments, while Garland's five North Carolina regiments composed the Third Brigade. Colquitt's one Alabama and four Georgia regiments made up Hill's Fourth Brigade, while Ripley's two North Carolina and two Georgia regiments formed the Fifth Brigade. Altogether, the division contained some 14,000 men, though probably no more than 8,000 would be available at any given time to take the field.

The army, too, had experienced important changes. President Davis' top military advisor, General Robert E. Lee, assumed command on June 1 after Johnston's wounding the evening before left a vacancy. (Gustavus Smith was a temporary solution as second in command, and quickly proved utterly unsuited for the difficult position.) Born in 1807, the son of Revolutionary War hero "Light Horse Harry," Lee graduated West Point in 1829. He served with distinction in the Mexican War and in a number of posts across the country prior to the outbreak of the Civil War. His service in the mountains of western Virginia was not one to inspire confidence in onlookers or subordinates, and his time spent along the South Atlantic coast seemed to reinforce such sentiment. President Davis, however, believed Lee to be one of the best officers in the Southern army, and in the spring of 1862 appointed Lee to the thankless job of his military advisor.

Lee had yet to create a favorable impression in the army by the time Rodes returned to duty. In reaction to McClellan's continued "shovel-and-spade" approach to Richmond, whereby the Federal commander slowly shifted his army south of the Chickahominy, Lee put his own men to work digging trenches and fortifying the defenses around the capital. This earned him the derisive nickname "King of Spades" from those who harbored doubts about a new commander who "made white men do Negroes' work." The skeptics included D. H. Hill, who told his wife he did not like to force this kind of work on "the brave fellows of my poor shattered and suffering Division." Preferring an immediate bold strike against the enemy, he lamented, "Gen Lee is so slow and cautious."[118]

Lee was about to prove that Hill and many others had greatly misjudged him. In a bold move that included bringing over Thomas J. "Stonewall" Jackson from the Shenandoah Valley, Lee planned to strike at McClellan's dangling right flank composed of Fitz Porter's V Corps, which was left north of the Chickahominy to protect the federal supply base at White House. After consulting with Davis and Longstreet, Lee decided to shift the bulk of his army, about 56,000 men including Jackson, above the river to fall upon Porter's 30,000, flank them if possible, and crush the enemy against the Chickahominy. The divisions of Huger and Magruder, totaling about 30,000 men, would hold the line of entrenchments south of the river against McClellan's remaining 75,000, maintaining a bold front to prevent a thrust against Richmond. The plan was a bold and even dangerous one, but with their backs to the capital, there was little else Lee could do but attempt to drive the enemy away. He sent for Jackson, who arrived at Ashland Station with his "foot cavalry" on June 23.

Unfortunately, Lee made the same mistake Johnston had made at Seven Pines. His plans were too complicated, the terrain too difficult, and the men and officers too inexperienced to pull it off. The series of maneuvers required the successful coordination of several columns on rather tight timetables. From Ashland, sixteen miles north of Richmond, Jackson would move southeast and swing beyond Porter's right flank to turn him out of his strong position. A. P. Hill's division, meanwhile, would cross north of the Chickahominy at Meadow Bridge and coordinate his moves with Jackson, striking Porter from the front. The divisions under Longstreet and D. H. Hill would both cross the river at Mechanicsville Bridge and support of efforts of A. P. Hill and Jackson to turn and destroy Porter. Lee optimistically set the morning of June 26 as the time for the attack.

In addition to the very real possibility that these marching timetables might easily go awry, Lee ran the risk that McClellan would realize that the bulk of the Confederates were north of the Chickahominy, conclude the defenders opposite his left were weak, and plunge straight ahead into Richmond. Although he eventually learned that Jackson had left the Shenandoah and correctly deduced the Confederates intended to attack his right wing, McClellan did not take the steps necessary to exploit this intelligence.[119]

In the meantime, skirmishing between the opposing lines became frequent and sometimes heavy. On Wednesday, June 25, the day before Lee intended to open his attack and five days after Rodes returned to duty, D. H. Hill's division marched out on the Williamsburg Road and took up a position in reserve behind the brigades of Ambrose Wright and Robert Ransom, which were skirmishing with the enemy near King's School House. Though Rodes did not get into the action, his men were somewhat unnerved when numerous shells flew over their position, a few landing among them.[120] That night, Hill issued orders for the division to make preparations to attack the following morning. "Brigade and Regimental Commanders," he decreed, "will institute a rigid inspection at once of the sick Camps and hospitals and drag out the drones and the Cowards."[121]

At 2:00 a.m. on June 26, Rodes' 1,460-man brigade left its position along the Williamsburg Road and began marching north for the Chickahominy. A small detachment remained behind to keep campfires lit to deceive the Yankees. By 8:00 a.m., the beginning of a clear day after two consecutive days of rain, Hill's and Longstreet's divisions were in position behind a crest of wooded hills just south of the river near Mechanicsville Bridge. Thick foliage protected them from the view of both the Union pickets across the river and the observation balloons farther away. With nothing left to do but wait for Jackson to turn Porter, the men remained in position—for much longer than they expected. Delayed by high water, muddy terrain, bad roads, his own fatigue, a lack of good maps, and General Lee's imprecise instructions that did not require him to be at a specific place at a specific time, Stonewall fell far behind schedule. The fiery energy displayed in the Shenandoah Valley a month earlier was conspicuously absent east of Richmond.

Hoping to ease the anxiety building in himself and others as the delay dragged on, Rodes decided to speak to the men. He drew up his regiments in close order. Riding before them, he explained, "General Lee is a little ahead of us watching for the dust of General Jackson's marching command, coming from the valley of Virginia, to turn McClellan's right flank by attacking its rear. We may soon receive orders to advance across the Chickahominy to attack in front." Recalling the scene many years later, a corporal in Carter's battery declared, "Rodes was a splendid looking officer, had a fine voice and I remember how he said 'Men you fought like hell at Seven Pines, but did not get the credit you deserved. I want you to do so again and I shall see that your gallantry is acknowledged."

The status quo north of the Chickahominy was broken not by Jackson, but by A. P. Hill. The high-strung and aggressive officer was worried that any further delay might jeopardize the whole operation. Unaware of Jackson's exact location or intent, Hill decided on his own hook to launch a frontal attack with his "Light Division" against Porter's strong position east of Mechanicsville at Beaver Dam Creek. The front was manned by George McCall's division of federal troops, and eventually supported by Brigadier General Charles Griffin's brigade and other troops.[122]

A. P. Hill's high-spirited but poorly coordinated attack across swampy terrain quickly reached the ears of Harvey Hill and James Longstreet. Likely thinking that Jackson was in position and turning Porter, the generals hurried their own men down to the river, only to discover that the Mechanicsville Bridge had been partially damaged by the enemy and could not be crossed without some repair. Jackson, meanwhile, finally showed up northeast of the headwaters of Beaver Dam Creek about 5:00 p.m., but the confused situation and his exhaustion convinced him to go into bivouac.

By the time D. H. Hill and Longstreet fixed the span, A. P. Hill was probably second guessing his decision to directly attack Porter, for his men were not making any headway but were falling by the hundreds. After making way for President Davis and staff to ride toward the battle, D. H. Hill rushed Ripley's brigade and five batteries to A.P. Hill's assistance. Hill threw Ripley's men into the offensive, but they did nothing more than add to the casualty rolls. When darkness put an end to the bloodshed, Porter ordered McCall to fall back several miles southeast to a strong prepared defensive position at Gaines' Mill behind Boatswain's Swamp. The movement was skillfully performed. Porter's losses were fewer than 400 from all causes out of some 15,600, while Hill lost approximately 1,400 men out of more than 16,000 engaged.

Having learned during the night of the 26th of Jackson's arrival beyond his right flank, McClellan convinced himself that he now faced an overwhelming Confederate force. He brushed aside suggestions to strike Magruder and Huger south of the Chickahominy the following morning and take Richmond. With his logistical lifeline at the White House on the Pamunkey River in jeopardy, Little Mac instead directed the entire army to fall back generally south by southeast toward the protection of the Union gunboats on the James River. All except Porter—whom he directed to protect the movement of the army by performing a delaying action.

With his enemy moving, General Lee developed a new plan to hit Porter the following day and crush him while he was still above the Chickahominy. With D. H. Hill in support, Jackson was ordered to attack Porter's right front while A. P. Hill and James Longstreet struck his left.[123]

After a fitful night's rest, Rodes got his men up well before dawn on Friday the 27th. The day promised no little agony, for the pain of his unhealed wound, coupled with a persistent nagging fever, drained Rodes of much-needed strength. Nevertheless, he stoically tried to shake off or ignore these problems in the hope of realizing the day's greater promise. In the pre-dawn darkness he put his brigade into column with the rest of the division and marched about four miles northeast on the Old Church Road to Bethesda Church, where Hill's men turned southeast and marched another four miles to a point in the road blocked by an entrenched enemy position defended by a few pieces of artillery. With the sun already above the horizon, Hill easily drove out the Federals by flanking them on the left with troops from Garland and Anderson's brigades. While waiting on the road, Rodes' men came under a brief fire that struck down one horse. With the Federals swept aside, Hill resumed the march and took his men to the edge of Powhite Swamp. Contrary to expectations, he saw no sign of Jackson's command.[124]

Once again, Stonewall was late. Because of poor maps and staff work, he took the wrong turn where two crossroads bore virtually the same name—marching toward New Cold Harbor, two miles west of his assigned destination of Old Cold Harbor. When he realized his mistake, Jackson doubled back, took the right road, and arrived behind D. H. Hill.

Jackson now possessed a powerful force of four divisions with which to pound and pursue Porter's command once A. P. Hill and Longstreet broke the left side of the enemy line. But as the sound of the fighting at Gaines' Mill soon revealed, Porter was holding his own just fine. When orders arrived from General Lee to assail Porter's right, Jackson quickly formed for the attack. On the extreme left he placed Hill's division at the edge of a woods, facing mostly south. Hill set up his brigades, from left to right as follows: Garland, Anderson, Rodes, Colquitt, and Ripley.[125]

About 3:00 p.m., an ill Rodes began organizing his regiments into line. He formed his regiments from left to right: Fifth, Twelfth, Twenty-sixth, Third, and Sixth. Under increasingly intense enemy shellfire, the men waited while the other divisions formed up. In this nerve-racking situation, Rodes and his colonels bravely held their men steady. Lieutenant Colonel Gayle of the Twelfth Alabama proudly reported after the fighting that only "two or three men" of his regiment ran away. Two others, in the Fifth, went down with severe wounds.[126]

Tension mounted as the minutes ticked past. Rodes put some of the time and tension to good use when he looked out over the field to get a measure of the task before him. It seemed daunting, even more so than at Seven Pines. Immediately to his front was swampy terrain, with a dense tangle of undergrowth choked with brushwood, felled timber, and enemy sharpshooters. Beyond that stretched an open field at least 400 yards wide, across which the men would have to rush in order to reach what appeared to be a strong enemy position. That formidable position was manned by native Southerner George Sykes, a roommate of D. H. Hill at West Point who now commanded a division of tough Regulars well- placed on elevated ground. His men and guns were deployed three tiers deep in several places.[127]

It was not until about 7:00 p.m. when Jackson finally gave the word to advance. Following instructions received through Ripley, Rodes called for the double-quick, believing this the best way to maintain order while passing through the swamp; it did little if any good. The tangled undergrowth, felled trees, and the heavy artillery fire threw the entire division into confusion. Only two regiments of Colquitt's brigade managed to get into action, but Ripley's entire brigade got lost and missed the fight altogether. Rodes emerged from the other side of the swamp with his three left regiments—the Fifth, Twelfth and Twenty- sixth—behind Anderson's left. The Third came out by itself behind Anderson's right, and the Sixth found itself ahead and to the right of Anderson's flank.[128]

From Rodes' vantage point, his two right regiments seemed to have "disappeared." Racing to find them, he quickly learned that the Sixth, under heavy fire along with Anderson's men, had been ordered by Colonel Gordon to lie down. Gordon then skillfully withdrew the regiment and realigned it with the Third Alabama. Though relieved to find both his regiments in good shape, Rodes noticed a huge gap opening to the right of Anderson. The Third and Sixth would not fill it. Behind him was most of Colquitt's brigade marking time at the lower end of the field. Rodes rode back and ordered these men to rush up and fill the gap, with his own Third and Sixth regiments moving with them.[129]

Once he was satisfied with the arrangement, Rodes sped back to check on the left side of his attenuated brigade line. Though his unhealed wound pained him greatly and he was feverish and weak, Rodes' spirits rose when he received news that his old regiment, the Fifth Alabama, had rushed forward with the support of the Twenty-sixth and seized an entire federal battery that had been hammering the whole line. It greatly distressed him, however, to learn at the same time that the Fifth's Colonel Christopher Pegue had been mortally wounded in the effort. Rodes later pridefully recalled Pegue's dying wish, expressed to Major Hobson, that the Fifth press on, allowing no other regiment to overtake it.[130]

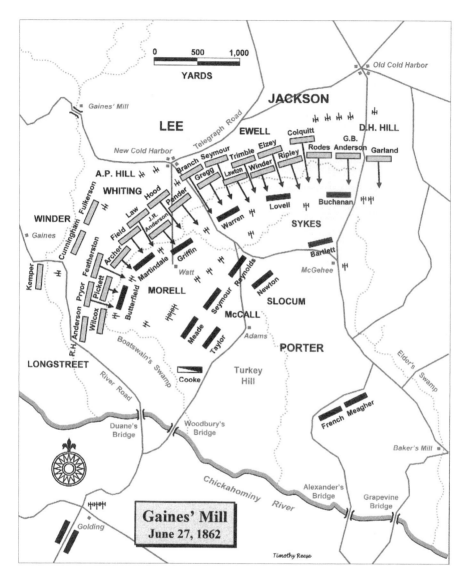

Gaines' Mill
June 27, 1862

Timothy Reese

Rodes' elation turned to concern a few minutes later when he witnessed droves of his own men streaming back from the enemy line, some running as hard as they could for the rear. He spurred his mount forward to rally them, but everything that could go wrong seem to do just that. His aide, Lieutenant Daniel Webster, took a bullet in the head and fell hard from his horse. As he was trying to rally his men, Rodes' arm wound ripped open and began bleeding. As he grew dizzy—either from the fever, loss of blood, or both—he lost strength and energy. He knew he could not remain mounted or in command. Trying to avoid slumping down in the saddle, he sent instructions for Colonel Gordon to take over the brigade. As he had at Seven Pines, Rodes refused to leave the field until darkness ended the fighting.[131]

The battle of Gaines' Mill ended at nightfall with a stunning Confederate victory. Under unrelenting pressure, Porter's line finally broke when W. H. C. Whiting's division followed natural folds in the land to cross the creek and pierce Porter's center. Artillery support and two brigades sent over from Bull Sumner's corps helped Porter withdraw most of his command. He crossed the Chickahominy about 4:00 a.m. on the 28th, burning the bridges behind him. Casualties on both sides were very heavy. Porter's command (about 34,000 engaged) suffered 6,837 killed, wounded, and missing, while Lee's divisions (about 57,000 engaged) lost 8,751 from all causes.[132]

After a short pursuit, D. H. Hill's division went into bivouac around 9:00 p.m. With their commander presumably still with them, Rodes' men bedded down for the night on the battlefield. They had again suffered heavily, losing thirty-one killed and 114 wounded. Hill offered praise to both the brigade and its commander, who "was on the field, and displayed his usual coolness and judgment, though very feeble from the unhealed wound received at Seven Pines."[133]

Finally, on the night of June 29, Rodes gave in and allowed himself to be carried by ambulance to a hospital in Richmond. His brigade remained in the charge of Colonel Gordon through the last few days of what became known as the Seven Days' Battles. In a series of confusing and bloody engagements, Lee pressed relentlessly forward in an attempt to catch and destroy the retreating Army of the Potomac before it reached the protection of federal gunboats on the James River.

As part of Jackson's pursuit, Hill's division with Rodes' brigade (under Gordon) remained out of the fighting until Malvern Hill on July 1. With its back to the James River, a portion of McClellan's infantry, together with heavy artillery support, beat back repeated uncoordinated attacks with heavy losses. Rodes' brigade was terribly shot up in the effort, losing 79 killed and 368 wounded. The brigade's total loss on the Peninsula from Seven Pines to Malvern Hill was nearly 1,650 men.[134]

Chapter 5

Maryland & Fredericksburg

Between the end of June and the end of August of 1862, it is difficult to determine the amount of time Rodes spent on duty and how much he spent convalescing. His wound continued to aggravate him, and its complications may have weakened his resistance to other illnesses that forced him occasionally to go on leave.

The written record shows that by July 15, eighteen days after he left the field at Gaines' Mill in an ambulance, Rodes was back at work in his brigade headquarters. On that Tuesday he wrote two letters, both replies to inquiries that had been in his hands for some time. To VMI superintendent Francis Smith, he explained that he would have answered the note sooner "but for the fact that from a few days after its receipt until now I have been knocking about in these interminable woods surrounded all the time with the discomforts and now the Conflicts of field life." Then he apologized for having no room on his staff for Smith's son Thurman. Rodes had more than enough volunteers, he explained, two of whom he took in when they failed to get reelected as officers in their own regiments and "who had no where else to go. One was my brother, another an old brother Engineer."[1]

The second letter went to General Robert E. Lee. The Virginian had taken command of the main Southern army in the Eastern Theater that spring and, through a series of large-scale combats, forged it into a weapon that mirrored his own aggressive battlefield prowess. Lee spent much of his time dealing with new enemy threats. On this day, however, he dropped his gaze to a query from one of his brigadiers about the fate of a horse loaned to a member of Rodes' staff, Lieutenant Eugene Webster—the "old brother Engineer" Rodes only recently took in as a voluntary aide. Before the war, Webster, now thirty-three years old, attended West Point and Yale and worked as a civil engineer in

General Robert E. Lee, commander of the Army of Northern Virginia.

National Archives

Maryland. Rodes informed Lee that at the beginning of the battle of Seven Pines on the morning of May 31, he had sent Webster with a dispatch to General Samuel Garland. To Rodes' surprise and dismay, Webster joined in a charge with Garland's brigade and was killed by a shell. The horse ran off, wrote Rodes, and no one had seen it since. "I would respectfully suggest," he continued, "that the surest plan to obtain the horse is to advertise [for] him. I shall cause a lookout to be kept up in the Div. for him." After devoting nearly a full page to the horse, Rodes remembered poor Webster. "I beg leave to bear testimony to Lieut. Webster's great gallantry and intelligence," he told Lee. "His service this day was to me and my command almost invaluable."[2]

Rodes' return to duty coincided with an increase in the intensity of training, despite the swarms of flies that tormented the men and made it difficult even to eat, sleep, or write a letter home. "Our camp duties are very onerous," a soldier complained in a letter home, "there being drill & parades from morning till night, tis all very necessary too, to a certain extent, but the thing is over done and the men are worried to death. Tis melancholy to look at the Regiments in our Brigade," he continued. "One year ago each would turn out some seven or eight hundred for drill merely, and once the 6th Ala. numbered 1300. The largest turnout now that any can bring is not more than 250."[3]

The previous April, the Confederate Congress passed the nation's first Conscription Act. With some exceptions, the legislation made liable for military service all men between the ages of eighteen and thirty-five. Seeing this as an opportunity to rebuild his shattered command, Rodes on July 29 sent a wire to Montgomery and asked Governor Shorter for some of Alabama's recently raised conscripts. The brigade commander obviously had failed to acquaint himself fully with the technicalities of the new law. That same day the governor's assistant inspector general, George Goldthwaite, wired back to set Rodes straight: the matter was out of the governor's hands. The War Department in Richmond, Goldthwaite explained, distributed the conscripts among depleted regiments as needed. With this explanation Goldthwaite thoughtfully included a copy of the regulations regarding the use of conscripts. He added, however, that if the War Department did choose to "discriminate," he hoped it would do so on the basis of officer merit. "Should this test be adopted," Goldthwaite assured Rodes, "you would have little to fear for your brigade."[4]

General McClellan, meanwhile, continued through the summer to maintain his Union army on the south side of the Peninsula at Harrison's Landing. From mid-July, Rodes' brigade and D. H. Hill's division remained in the area between Richmond and Hanover Junction, keeping a watchful eye on possible Union threats from either the Peninsula or Fredericksburg. On July 23, however, D. H. Hill went on detached duty as commander of the Department of the Southside, a sector extending from Drewry's Bluff to the South Carolina line. By order of General Lee, G. W. Smith took temporary command of the division on August 10. Hill's new responsibilities included harassing McClellan's supply line and encampment at Harrison's Landing. Hill was not enthusiastic about his new assignment, and after an unremarkable performance as department commander he was more than happy to return to his division in late August.[5]

On July 25, Rodes informed Hill by telegram that over the last three days, "An intelligent Marylander" had seen thousands of McClellan's troops disembarking at Aquia Creek. The man had witnessed the arrival of Fitz John Porter's V Corps, sent by McClellan from the Peninsula in response to General Lee's move northward with part of his Army of Northern Virginia. After sending Thomas Jackson in mid-July to secure the vital rail junction at Gordonsville against the growing threat of the newly created Army of Virginia under John Pope, Lee waited several weeks for an opportunity to strike a blow at one Federal army or the other. When McClellan began evacuating the Peninsula and sending his forces up the Potomac after Jackson's tactical victory at Cedar Mountain on August 9, Lee decided to concentrate his army for a move north and fall upon Pope as circumstances allowed.[6]

With Lafayette McLaws' division and the brigades of Rodes, G. B. Anderson, and Samuel Garland, D. H. Hill set out from Hanover Junction on August 26. Rodes, however, did not go with them. He had succumbed either to a further complication of his Seven Pines wound or to some other natural malady, quite possibly pneumonia. Only the severest circumstance could have removed from the opening of a major campaign the man who twice had refused to allow a wound to take him from the battlefield.

After picking up two brigades under Alfred Colquitt and Roswell Ripley at Orange Court House the following day (the 27th), Hill relentlessly pushed on in the hope of catching up with the rest of the army in time to participate in any upcoming battle. Despite reaching Chantilly on September 2 after a grueling sixty-mile march in three-and-one-half days, the North Carolinian missed Lee's magnificent victory over Pope at Second Manassas (August 29-30).[7]

With Pope's men retreating into the defenses surrounding Washington and McClellan's corps still largely in transit from the Peninsula to the capital, the rebel commander judged the time had come to take the war north of the Potomac and perhaps strike a fatal blow at Federal hopes of maintaining the Union by force. On Thursday, September 4, the Army of Northern Virginia began crossing the Potomac River into Maryland.

Men from D. H. Hill's division were the first of Lee's infantry to go over, crossing at White's Ford about thirty miles upriver from Washington. By all accounts, the men in the ranks fully appreciated the historic significance of the event, which they turned into a rather festive occasion, complete with joking, laughter, and rapid banter. In general, the men seemed confident and in high spirits. Some among them, and the numbers were not insignificant, disapproved of the operation on the principle that they enlisted to defend their homes, not invade the North. This feeling, together with the heavy recent fighting and poor food, contributed to the massive straggling problem that would plague Lee's army during its sojourn above the Potomac. Exactly how this sentiment affected either Hill's division in general, or Rodes' brigade in particular, is not known.[8]

That night the division, now part of Jackson's wing of the army, camped near Buckeytown alongside the Monocacy River and the B&O Railroad. On the 5th, the command moved within a few miles of Frederick, Maryland. The following day, a Saturday, Rodes arrived and resumed command of his brigade.[9]

*   *   *

Tormented by the prospect of missing a major and perhaps decisive campaign, Rodes endured his time convalescing as long as possible. Unable to remain behind, he stoically put aside his ailments and set out for Maryland, his most likely route straight up from Centerville through Leesburg. In this time of crisis, many throughout the brigade and the division gladly welcomed his return to duty. Lieutenant Park of the Twelfth Alabama probably expressed the feelings of many at this time when he observed, "General Rodes was a precise and somewhat stern military man, of resolute expression and soldierly bearing, and enjoyed the implicit confidence of his superior officers as well as his troops."[10]

Camped near Frederick, Rodes and his men enjoyed four days of relative inactivity, the rest and fair weather being generally agreeable to everyone. To keep Yankee cavalry videttes from getting too close to town, Rodes scattered patrols on all the nearby roads. Against his strong disapproval, however, some of these patrols turned into foraging expeditions. On one occasion two soldiers from the Sixth Alabama actually attempted to steal the lunches of thirty school children.[11]

After concentrating his entire army at Frederick, Lee intended to advance north on Hagerstown. When the sizeable Union garrison to his rear at Harpers Ferry failed to withdraw as expected, he crafted a plan to dispatch Jackson on September 10 with five divisions to seize the place. The following day Lee, James Longstreet, and the army's other four divisions marched through Turner's Gap to Boonsboro near the western base of South Mountain to await Jackson. Lee expected Stonewall to complete his mission in no more than two days. As events quickly would prove, that timetable was too optimistic.[12]

Soon after crossing South Mountain into Boonsboro, Lee received what would turn out to be a false report that Federals were moving on Hagerstown from Pennsylvania. To protect that vital point, he took Longstreet and three divisions thirteen miles north to Hagerstown, leaving behind at Boonsboro D. H. Hill's division, the army's supply train, and one battalion of the reserve artillery.

In addition to guarding the supply train, Hill's orders were to keep communications open between the two halves of the army, serve as Longstreet's rear guard, watch for Federals trying to escape on the roads coming north out of Harpers Ferry and, with Jeb Stuart's cavalry, guard the South Mountain passes against enemy attempts to push through them from the east. Convinced that the disaster of Second Manassas had thrown the Federals into such confusion that he could risk safely the separation of the army in enemy territory, Lee did not expect trouble to develop in Hill's area. The unexpected loss of Special Order 191, however, changed the dynamics of the campaign.

After two days of chaos and confusion in Washington, during which time Pope brazenly offered to take his army back out of the capital to fight Lee again, President Lincoln reluctantly turned once more to George McClellan. For a second time Little Mac performed a great service to his country by restoring order, discipline, and confidence in the demoralized Union soldiers. Despite his reputation for the "slows," he had that army in motion by September 6.

Cautiously moving northwest while believing he faced a superior enemy (which he estimated to be around 120,000 men), McClellan reached Frederick early on the 13th. There, he was handed a copy of Lee's Special Order 191, a document wrapped around three cigars found by a Federal soldier (probably in D. H. Hill's former camp). The order detailed the precise dispositions of the entire rebel army.

Despite this incredible piece of luck, McClellan waited most of a day before taking advantage of it. Late on the afternoon of September 13 he ordered Ambrose Burnside's "Right Wing," consisting of Joseph Hooker's I Corps and Jesse Reno's IX Corps, to march for Turner's Gap, while William Franklin's XII Corps made for Crampton's Gap. Both passes cut through the South Mountain range. McClellan had dispatched about 30,000 men to punch a hole in Lee's front by getting astride the twenty-five-mile line of march separating Longstreet from Jackson. Only D. H. Hill's division of 5,000 men and Stuart's cavalry stood in the way.

Lee learned of the intelligence leak around 10:00 a.m. the next morning, Sunday the 14th. He sent orders for Hill to hold the South Mountain passes while Longstreet and Lee started back toward Boonsboro.[13]

Hill already had been warned that the enemy was moving and had taken action to defend the passes. When informed by Stuart around noon on the 13th that two Federal brigades (of Alfred Pleasanton's cavalry) were pushing back the cavalry toward the eastern base of the mountain, Hill sent up to the 1,300-foot summit the brigades of Colquitt and Garland, along with two batteries (eight guns) under Bondurant and Lane. Hill held Rodes, Anderson, and Ripley at Boonsboro in reserve. Hill's action produced the desired effect. When the approaching enemy discovered Confederates in strength on the mountain, they backed off and went into camp for the night.

When Hill rode to Turner's Gap early the following morning, however, he decided the pass needed more protection—especially since Stuart had ridden farther south to cover Crampton's Gap. Anderson's brigade was called up and Hill shifted Garland about one-quarter mile to the right to guard the Sharpsburg Road snaking through Fox's Gap. After relieving Anderson about a half-mile west of Boonsboro, Rodes was ordered to remain behind with Ripley to guard the trains, maintain communications with Lee, and watch out for McClellan should he feint at Turner's Gap and pour through Crampton's.

Hill had done what he could, but he was enough of a soldier to know his command was woefully inadequate if the enemy intended to push through the South Mountain gaps. The North Carolinian climbed a lookout station near Mountain House Inn, a tollhouse at the apex of Turner's Gap, to scan the countryside. There, he discovered the astonishing sight of thousands of enemy troops coming up the mountain, many already in battle formation. Burnside had started Hooker's three divisions, about 13,000 men, up the Hagerstown Road for Turner's Gap; Reno's four divisions were moving up the Sharpsburg Road for Fox's Gap.

The battle commenced around 9:00 a.m. when Reno's command slammed into Garland's men. The fighting killed the promising brigadier and crippled his brigade. Hill responded by sending over Anderson and a battery of four guns, and the Yankees withdrew without comprehending the extent of their victory. Burnside, moreover, perhaps a bit unnerved by McClellan's warnings about large Confederate numbers, delayed pushing through Turner's Gap in order to allow his two infantry corps to concentrate.[14]

Hill, meanwhile, sent for Rodes and Ripley. "With characteristic promptness," remembered S. Q. Hale of the Sixth Alabama, "Gen Rhodes [sic] . . . ordered us into line, and had the brigade moving at double quick for the scene of action." So quick, in fact, that after the men dropped their knapsacks halfway up the mountain they easily caught up with and overtook, "almost contemptuously," Ripley's jaded troops, who were worn out after a night spent standing and sleeping in formation. Rodes' soldiers passed Garland's body as it was being transported down the mountain. Rodes himself arrived on the crest about 11:00 a.m.[15]

Hill sent Ripley to help Anderson on the right, and Rodes was directed to move to the left of Colquitt and take the high ground north of the Hagerstown pike, also called the National Road, the main thoroughfare through Turner's Gap. After quickly examining the ground with Hill, Rodes began placing his little brigade of some 1,200 men on a commanding ridge immediately left of the road. The Twelfth Alabama anchored the line, its right resting on the pike. To its left Rodes put the Twenty-sixth, beyond which he placed the Third, the Fifth, and, on the far left, the Sixth. For skirmishers he used the brigade sharpshooters, about two hundred men. Incredibly, he managed to do all this without interference from Burnside, who massed his forces without pressing the Confederates.[16]

Shortly after the Confederates went into position, Burnside unleashed a terrific artillery bombardment. The Alabamians hunkered down in the undulating ground, whose numerous dells, slopes, and gorges kept them fairly safe. About forty-five minutes into the cannonade, Rodes received from Hill instructions to seize a bare knoll about three-fourths of a mile north of the pike. During their initial examination of the ground, both Rodes and Hill somehow had missed the importance of this knoll. If the enemy grabbed it, Hill rightly believed, the position would jeopardize his entire line.[17]

Rodes gave the order and the men of the Sixth rose up amid the bursting shells and scrambled over to the unprotected knoll near the widow Main's farm. Rodes shifted the rest of his line until the Fifth held the hillside south of the Main farm, the Third spread itself out on the Haupt farm, the Twenty-sixth near the O'Neil farm, and the Twelfth placed its right in what the locals called the Frosttown Road gorge (which separated the two most prominent knolls north of the pike).[18]

Rodes' shift, however well executed, opened a huge gap between his right flank and Colquitt's left. This uncovered both the knoll closest to the pike as well as Captain John Lane's Georgia battery near it. Rodes seems not to have foreseen these problems before making the shift. When he learned of them and brought the matter to Hill's attention, the division leader ordered Rodes to correct the situation immediately. The Twelfth Alabama trotted back to the knoll closest to the pike.[19]

The Sixth Alabama now guarded the crest on the left, the Twelfth held the knoll on the right, the other regiments covered the two hillsides and the gorge in between. Lane provided artillery support with three guns near the pike and one firing from the gorge. Rodes' front was extremely wide—some 3,500 feet—and none of his regiments were in contact with any other. Moreover, the uneven ground and its many stone walls made it difficult for the regiments to maintain internal cohesion.[20]

Still, the position offered some advantages. The rough ground promised to make it very difficult for the Federals to maintain coordinated attack formations. At the same time, the rough terrain provided Rodes' men ample coverage among the numerous boulders, ledges, fences, and crests.

When the cannon fire slackened and the Yankee infantry started up the mountain, Rodes and his men beheld an incredible sight. The brigadier correctly accessed that the enemy marching in battle formation to sweep him

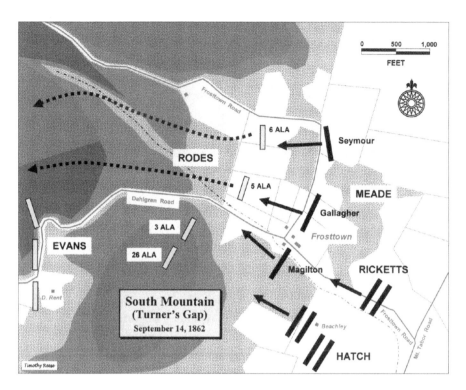

away comprised an entire Federal division. The Union attackers were led by forty-seven-year-old George Meade, a solid combat officer and West Point graduate of 1835. Rodes studied the approaching Yankee line as it came on in a strong three-brigade front. Meade's roughly 4,000 men included brigades under Truman Seymour, Albert Magilton, and Thomas Gallagher's Pennsylvania Reserves, nearly all veterans of Second Manassas. Off to the right, south of the pike, Rodes spotted yet another enemy division (this one under John P. Hatch) moving to meet Colquitt's brigade.

Concern for his own position elevated to some anxiety when the enemy advance gradually made it clear that their right flank overlapped his own left flank by several hundred yards. Rodes rode over to the point of danger, only to make the unsettling discovery of an unguarded pathway that led around and behind his position. In the evident conviction that envelopment is a greater danger than possible penetration, Rodes determined to keep the enemy off that lane by spreading his line even thinner. He quickly shifted the Sixth and part of the Fifth farther left to yet another knoll, and sent to Hill the first of three futile requests for reinforcements and artillery. About 3:00 p.m. the opposing skirmishers briefly peppered each other before falling back to their respective main lines.[21]

Earlier, Rodes issued his men instructions to let the Yankees come within 100 yards before opening fire. When they stepped within range, the Confederate line erupted with flames and smoke, dropping nearly two dozen enemy infantrymen holding the front of the Fifth and Sixth Pennsylvania regiments. Though stunned, the Yankees held on. The close action soon made it obvious that there were gaps in the Rebel line, and the Yankees surged forward. Disaster struck quickly when they rushed through the gorge in front of the Third Alabama and killed, wounded, captured, or drove away Captain E. S. Ready and his entire line of fifty defenders. "The gorge had become another 'Thermopylae,' and Ready was its Leonidas," the well-read Colonel Cullen Battle of the Third Alabama lamented after the war. The Yankees penetrated Rodes' thin line by sweeping past the left of the Third regiment and cutting off the right battalion of the Fifth regiment. Major Hobson managed to swing back the left battalion and unite it with the Sixth regiment, but disaster quickly struck on the right.[22]

Rodes was standing directly behind the Twelfth Alabama conversing with Colonel Briston Gayle and Lieutenant Colonel Sam Pickens. During the conversation, the regiment suddenly gave way and broke for the rear. There is no way of knowing how close Rodes was to Gayle when he was riddled with bullets and fell dead. Pickens, too, went down, shot through the lungs. Aides picked up the still-breathing lieutenant colonel and carried him to the rear while Rodes tried to rally the fleeing men.[23]

The crisis spread down the line when the Twenty-sixth Alabama "became completely demoralized," admitted Rodes. It, too, started to give way, its Colonel Edward O'Neal shot down with a severe wound. After penetrating the line beyond the Third Alabama, the Yankees began to swing around and head for the gorge near the pike, threatening to roll up the right side of Rodes' line. Only the Sixth Alabama under John Gordon on the far left, together with the left battalion of the Fifth Alabama, still held their positions.[24]

Together with the Third Alabama's Colonel Battle, Rodes—his thin figure seeming to appear everywhere—rode about calling for the fleeing men to halt. They used as inspiration the gallant stand of the Sixth Alabama, whose men were barely visible through the smoke on the left. Incredibly, clusters of men began gathering around the two officers, who quickly established an embryonic line that opened a ragged but effective flank fire against the Yankees fighting with Gordon's men. About this time, however, another Federal brigade under

Abram Duryea, part of James Rickett's division (which was held in reserve) surged up the hill. The fresh enemy troops decided the issue, and the men around Rodes and Battle gave up their position and resumed their flight. Rodes had no choice but to speed rearward and find good ground to set up a new defensive line for his men to rally upon. He needed help desperately.[25]

Help arrived on the mountain some time ago, but Rodes received none of it. About 3:30 p.m., shortly after the fight began on Rodes' front, two of Longstreet's brigades under Thomas Drayton and G. T. Anderson, John Hood's division, reached the mountain. Hill sent these men to shore up the line at Fox's Gap on the right. About 4:00 p.m., two more brigades arrived. Longstreet, who now took command of the field—much to the annoyance of Hill—used these men to fill the widening divide between Rodes and the fight at Fox's Gap.[26]

Rodes finally got some help about dusk when Longstreet sent Nathan Evans' South Carolina brigade (under the command of Peter Stevens). The South Carolinians filled in the gap on Colquitt's left. This did nothing, however, to relieve the pressure on Rodes' left, which he now began to pull back toward the pike. Moreover, Stevens' brigade was so small (perhaps 550 men in total), that when a portion of it arrived in time to get caught up in the retreat of the Twenty-sixth Alabama, Rodes assumed his men had become tangled up with "some South Carolina stragglers."

Meanwhile, Rodes skillfully marked out a new defensive line. The new position looked something akin to a rough L-shape, its left bent back facing north near Mountain House Inn about 200 yards from the pike and about one-half-mile behind his original position. With Stevens' small brigade serving as an anchor on the right, Rodes began to pull in his Alabamians and place them in the new line. Within moments, all of his regiments came in and formed up with the same alignment as before, save for the Third and Twelfth, which traded places in the line.[27]

This new line stood firm, the fight rippling up and down the entire front until darkness finally ended the battles for Turner's, Fox's, and Crampton's Gaps. Against overwhelming odds, the entire Confederate line had held. Though he captured the high ground, McClellan was unable to break through the Confederate lines on South Mountain. The Confederates remained in position for a brief time and when orders arrived, began pulling out shortly before midnight.

Once again Rodes' brigade suffered terribly. Sixty-one men were killed, 157 were wounded, and 204 were missing, a loss of 422. This number accounts for more than one-third of his brigade. Rodes' stout defenders had inflicted roughly equal damage against the enemy—Meade reported a total loss of 397—while holding off a full enemy division for several hours. "We did not drive the enemy back or whip him," Rodes confessed, "but with 1,200 men we held his whole division at bay for four hours and a half without assistance from anyone, losing in that time not more than half a mile of ground." It was a proud confession.[28]

His division leaders agreed. "Rodes handled his little brigade in a most admirable and gallant manner," D. H. Hill reported, "fighting, for hours, vastly superior odds, and maintaining the key points of the position until darkness rendered a further advance of the Yankees impossible." At South Mountain, continued Hill, Rodes' brigade had "immortalized itself." After the war, Hill expounded on his earlier observation: "It was pitiable to see the valiant but hopeless struggle of those Alabamians against such mighty odds."[29] After the war, James Longstreet used the pages of his autobiography to also heap praise upon Rodes: "In view of the great force approaching to attack him [Rodes], his fight seemed almost hopeless, but he handled his troops with skill and delayed the enemy, with the little help that finally came, till night, breaking from time to time as he was forced nearer our center at the turnpike."[30] Subsequent writers and historians agree with these assessments: at South Mountain, Rodes rendered to the Confederacy an invaluable service, and certainly his most important of the war to date.

Rodes, in turn, heaped praise on the Sixth's John Gordon, Edwin Hobson of the Fifth, and Cullen Battle of the Third, for "admirable conduct during the whole fight." Gordon, wrote Rodes, deserved special recognition. While his tired men rested within 100 yards of the Yankee line, Rodes, though also completely exhausted, refused to rest until he conversed with the commander of the Sixth Alabama. "Colonel Gordon," he called out, offering his hand for a firm grasp, "I congratulate you, and I do so heartily, upon your behavior and that of your regiment to-day. You have the staunchest regiment in my brigade." Rodes later wrote in his official report that the Sixth Alabama had been "handled in a manner I have never heard or seen equaled during this war."[31]

That night, General Lee authorized an immediate pullout after agreeing with Longstreet and Hill at a council of war in Boonsboro. Holding South Mountain for another day was out of the question. Although the Confederate defenders had fought well against heavy odds, South Mountain was a strategic defeat that dealt a critical blow to Southern plans. Simply put, it imperiled the still widely divided Army of Northern Virginia. With Jackson's men hovering around Harpers Ferry, McClellan's new advantage threatened to catch and destroy the Confederates in piecemeal fashion. About 10:00 p.m., Rodes roused his men from their desperately needed sleep and one hour later quietly led them to Fox's Gap and then down the Sharpsburg Road on the west face of the mountain. "Foot-sore and weary," remembered Colonel Battle, "hungry and almost naked, they had fought a great battle and added to their glory and fame."[32]

*   *   *

Forced to give up the South Mountain passes, and with Harpers Ferry still stubbornly holding out, General Lee reluctantly concluded he must withdraw the Army of Northern Virginia through Sharpsburg closer to Jackson, and probably concentrate on the south bank of the Potomac. Leaving the state without fighting a significant battle, however, was something Lee desperately wished to avoid. Part of his army was passing through Sharpsburg about noon on the 15th when word reached him that Harpers Ferry had fallen and Jackson was marching to rejoin him. Even though heavily outnumbered, Lee knew McClellan was not an overly aggressive general, and so he resolved to remain in Maryland. Lee halted the army's retreat and organized it in a defensive arrangement on the rolling hills behind Antietam Creek. It was a gambler's decision, for there was little left for Lee to gain in Maryland and much to lose— especially with a tired and understrength army deployed with its back to the Potomac River.

In the pre-dawn hours of Monday the 15th, Rodes led his tired men three miles to Keedystown, where they finally stopped for some much-needed rest. An hour later, however, he got them up again when new orders arrived to march with his own and Colquitt's brigade and drive off enemy cavalry reported to be four miles away in Sharpsburg. A short time later, however, Colonel R. H. Chilton of Lee's staff arrived with instructions for Rodes to send only part of his brigade for the task. The Virginian promptly stopped his men and dispatched the Fifth and Sixth Alabama. The situation changed again shortly thereafter when Longstreet directed Rodes to proceed with his entire brigade. Rodes dutifully complied. The result of this fitful stop and go was that none of the men got any rest after all.[33]

When he reached Sharpsburg from the northeast about daylight on the 15th, there was not a single mounted enemy cavalryman to be found. Rodes finally halted his men south of town "long enough to get a scanty meal and to gather stragglers," he reported, then moved back north of town to take up a position in the center of Lee's developing new line. That night he bivouacked the brigade in a field east of the Henry Piper house just behind a country lane known locally as the Sunken Road.[34]

With the main body of his army, McClellan arrived opposite Lee's position during the late afternoon of September 15. A determined effort the following day might have crushed the small Confederate force of fewer than 20,000 men, but McClellan wasted that day and all of the next skirmishing, planning his next move, and bringing up more troops. By the time the battle began on the morning of Wednesday, September 17, Confederate divisions marching from Harpers Ferry had nearly doubled Lee's strength. McClellan's nebulous battle plan called for attacking Lee's flanks in the hope of developing it into "something more." Even with all of his self-imposed delays, McClellan still held a two-to-one advantage over his opponent, which meant that "something more" could well be the destruction of the Army of Northern Virginia.

Stretching about four miles, Lee's line essentially paralleled the north-south course of the snake-like Antietam Creek. The position included numerous undulations and several large knots of timber, which promised to give most of his outnumbered men considerable shelter. But the position masked several weaknesses. It was too long for the number of men on the field, and the only avenue of retreat and reinforcement was across the deep and rocky Boteler's Ford one mile to the rear.[35]

D. H. Hill's division, about 3,000 strong and under Longstreet's tactical command, held the center of Lee's line about one-half mile northeast of Sharpsburg. Hill's front occupied flat ground in the angle of a V formed by two turnpikes—Hagerstown, running south into Sharpsburg, and Boonsboro, which slanted into town on a roughly northeast-southwest axis. Hill did not like the position and blamed Longstreet for placing his division "on the flats," with little or no natural cover.

Hill put Anderson's brigade astride the Boonsboro pike facing northeast. Rodes, whose five regiments totaled a scant 800 men—a number equal to what any of the regiments could have claimed to have in its ranks one year earlier—entered a sunken road on the left of Anderson. A slight gap separated the two brigades. Garland's brigade, under Duncan McRae, marched into the lane on Rodes' left. Colquitt and Ripley extended the line in that direction.[36]

After weathering a night of sleep-depriving rain, Rodes woke his men well before dawn on the 17th. They began a second day of subsisting on roasted corn, Rodes sharing his meager breakfast with Colonel Risden Bennett of the

Fourteenth North Carolina, George Anderson's brigade. The sun had not yet fully cleared the horizon when distant artillery and small arms fire erupted on the far left flank of the army. Unbeknownst to Rodes, McClellan had unleashed Joe Hooker's I Corps in a strong right hook that fell upon Jackson's men positioned farther north. The fighting escalated and continued, nearly without respite, for several hours as Rodes and his men listened to the battle and speculated on its progress. About mid-morning it became apparent the combat was not going well when Hill pulled Ripley, Colquitt, and McRae out of the Sunken Road position and marched them north into the smoking inferno. The move left a large gap in his line. To fill it, Hill sidled over his two remaining brigades, with Rodes taking up the position in the lane formerly held by McRae and generally facing north. About 9:00 a.m., Rodes' turn came when Hill told him to pull out his men and move into the fight.[37]

Rodes gave the word and his Alabamians rose to their feet. He quickly formed them in column and advanced generally north toward the raging combat. Within minutes, however, he came face to face with the disheartening sight of Colquitt's and McRae's men rushing headlong out of the smoke for the rear. Rodes halted his men and deployed in line to serve as a rallying point. Hill rode up and, although he approved of Rodes' decision to rally the men, he disagreed with his choice of position. Hill ordered the Alabamians to file back into the nearby zigzag sunken farm road they had just left.[38]

The narrow lane was about 600 yards south of a one-room white Dunker church. The sunken route broke off from the Hagerstown Road and extended 500 yards east, where it angled southeast another 500 yards to the crest of a ridge. From there, the lane continued in a series of turns to a crest at the Boonsboro pike, midway between Sharpsburg and Antietam Creek. Locals called the first 1,000 yards of the lane the Sunken Road, so named because generations of farmers had so worn down the surface by driving heavily laden wagons over it to a gristmill on the Antietam. Many points along the route were several feet below ground level—or deeper. The route now served as a good natural defensive position, protecting a standing man up to his knees in some places and up to his shoulders along much of the distance.[39]

Rodes hurriedly ran the Sixth Alabama up to the point where the lane turned southeast at a forty-five degree angle. To the left of the Sixth he placed the Fifth, then the Third, Twelfth and Twenty-sixth. Quickly and without instruction, the men set to work improving the position by piling up fence rails, dirt, and rocks to form a rough parapet facing the enemy. As the Alabamians labored, McRae's and Colquitt's shattered remnants streamed in on Rodes' left.

George B. Anderson's unbloodied brigade took up the line on Rodes' right (with the Second North Carolina to the right of the Sixth Alabama). Perhaps 2,500 men now were deployed in the lane.[40]

As the men worked, Lee, D. H. Hill, and Rodes rode along the front inspecting the position. Lee calmly reassured the men while stressing the importance of the line they held. A break here, he told them, might endanger the whole army. "These men are going to stay here," the Sixth's Colonel Gordon claimed he firmly assured the commanding general, "till the sun goes down or victory is ours." It was an audacious boast, especially since the line enjoyed no reserve or artillery support; both had been thrown into the grinding fight on the Confederate left.[41]

Soon after Lee and Hill departed, Rodes and his men heard the incongruous sound of music played by bands beyond the crest about 100 yards to their front. The mystery ended when enemy battle standards rose above the ridge, followed by a sea of Federal soldiers marching in perfect battle formation. William French's division of Edwin Sumner's II Corps, three brigades comprising about 5,700 Marylanders, Delawareans, New Yorkers, and Pennsylvanians, were aimed like a giant lance straight for the Sunken Road. A native of Maryland, forty-seven-year-old French was derisively called "Old Blinky" because of his annoying habit of blinking incessantly while talking. In Texas the previous year, French marched his 300-man garrison down the Rio Grande for embarkation to Federal-held territory. He now was in command of a division composed of ten well-trained and disciplined regiments, though only three had seen combat. They had begun the morning with orders to follow John Sedgwick's division in its attack into the West Woods. When the smoke and undulating ground swallowed up Sedgwick, French followed the natural lay of the land and angled his division southwest, marching through the orchards and pastures of William Roulette and across the fields owned by Samuel Mumma. When Rodes spotted the Union division, it was arrayed "in three beautiful lines" headed straight for the Sunken Road. With McClellan's right hook against the Confederate left spent, the fighting now shifted toward Lee's center. The battle about to engulf D. H. Hill's thinly held position was largely the result of an accident.[42]

As the blue host crested the ridge, officers halted the men to fix bayonets— an ominous indication of the expectation of closing with the Rebels before them. The men marched a little farther, halted again in perfect order about 80 yards off, raised their muskets, and fired a crashing volley into the Sunken Road position.[43] The small arms fire largely sailed over the heads of Rodes' and

Anderson's well-protected men, who unleashed a withering volley into the exposed Yankee line. The Confederates could hardly miss at that range, and large numbers of men fell, especially those in the First Delaware. After bravely withstanding the devastating fire for a full five minutes, the Federals fell back behind the crest, where they quickly rallied and, with the support of a fresh brigade, came on again.

Frantically loading and firing as fast as human muscle allowed, the Sunken Road defenders drove back French's men a second time, and then a third.

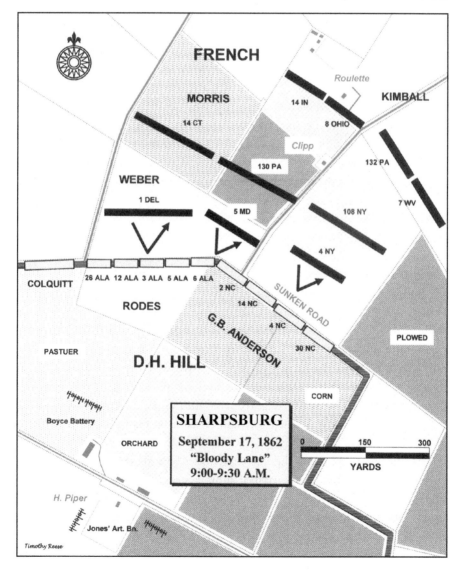

Duplicating his actions at Seven Pines, Gaines' Mill, and South Mountain, Rodes seemed to be everywhere. "Our gallant Brigadier Gen. Rodes by his own heroic example," remembered S. Q. Hale of the Sixth Alabama, "encouraged his men by moving up and down the line, while the brigade stood firm, repelling every onset of the enemy, breaking their lines and driving them back as a firm rock the waves of the sea." Despite heavy losses, the Yankees stubbornly refused to give up. They took cover behind the crest and engaged the defenders in a deadly small arms battle.[44]

General Longstreet watched the action from a position well behind the Sunken Road. He concluded the enemy had given up the offensive and it was time for a counterattack. Unaware that an entire Federal division under Israel Richardson had come up on French's left, Old Pete ordered Hill's men to leave their protected position and drive away the enemy.

Rodes duly ordered his men out of the lane. As his men were beginning to advance, he noticed that Colquitt's men on his left had "barely moved," and on the right, the Sixth Alabama had not moved at all. Racing over to the right, he discovered that in the din of battle the Sixth did not hear the order to charge. Before he could get the men moving, however, his other four regiments came tumbling back. Rodes spurred his mount toward the left and, after some effort, successfully prevented his men from fleeing beyond the Sunken Road. The fiasco embittered Rodes, who once more absorbed the bloody lesson that without support, particularly on the flanks, attacks held but little chance for success.[45]

Support finally arrived when Lee sent up Major General Richard H. Anderson's 4,000-man division, which had just arrived from Harpers Ferry. When Anderson fell almost immediately with a severe wound, command fell onto the shoulders of the senior brigadier, the inept Roger Pryor, who minimized the powerful impact the arrival of the division might have had on that sector by sending his troops into the fight piecemeal. The brigades of Carnot Posey and Ambrose Wright filtered into G. B. Anderson's portion of the line, while the brigades of Pryor and William Parham took up a position behind Rodes.[46]

Though gratified to see these troops, Rodes became visibly upset when he viewed one regiment and a portion of another stop in the safety of an orchard (Piper's) well to the rear. With his own men going through hell, how dare these troops take shelter in the shade where they could do no good at all? When the firing along his line slackened, Rodes seized the opportunity to ride back and flush out the pair of regiments. When low-ranking officers told him the troops belonged to Pryor's brigade, Rodes demanded to know why they had stopped in the orchard. Dissatisfied with the answer that "someone" had ordered them to do so, Rodes sought out Pryor, who promptly instructed the two regiments to move closer to the front.[47]

Satisfied, Rodes started back toward his own line. Along the way he met Lieutenant Colonel James Lightfoot, now in command of the Sixth Alabama after Gordon fell with five wounds (the last a bullet to the face that finally knocked him out of action). Lightfoot reported that the Yankees had penetrated a portion of Anderson's line and were pouring a deadly enfilade fire into the right flank of the Sixth Alabama. With less cover than Rodes' men, George Anderson's soldiers had suffered terribly. Federal numbers and constant pressure finally told, especially on his right flank, and his men began moving out of the line to the rear.

The Sixth Alabama held the far right of Rodes' brigade line, a shallow salient where the farm lane turned from its easterly course toward the southeast, rising to ground level as it did so. With Anderson's front collapsing and Federals on their right, the men of the Sixth—and Rodes' entire line—were now in mortal danger. Rodes instructed Lightfoot to "break back" the right of the Sixth by pulling its flank out of the road. Perhaps he misunderstood his orders. Perhaps the stress of the situation was simply too much for Lightfoot. Whatever the reason, when the officer returned to the Sunken Road, he stood behind the regiment and shouted, "Sixth Alabama, about face; forward march!" The entire regiment promptly evacuated the lane. Alarmed at the sudden gap opening on his right, Major Hobson of the Fifth Alabama dashed over to ask Lightfoot if that order applied to the entire brigade. Lightfoot, again for reasons unknown, answered in the affirmative.

Confusion and chaos coursed up and down the line. The Yankees poured into the road from which Anderson's and Rodes' men had fought and died for three hours in a defensive stand that would forevermore tag the position as the Bloody Lane. The triumphant Federals shot down scores of Alabamians, converting their withdrawal into a rout.[48]

Rodes might have prevented this tragedy by delivering the order himself, or by speeding after Lightfoot to ensure its proper execution. Unfortunately, just seconds after he sent Lightfoot back with instructions, a bullet whizzed by his head and struck his aide John Berney. The aide, "a handsome, pleasant fellow with a red head," as one observer described him, had joined Rodes' staff only five weeks earlier. Turning quickly in his saddle, Rodes watched as the lieutenant fell hard to the ground. Jumping from his own mount, Rodes ran to the fallen officer only to make the horrifying discovery that his aide had been shot in the face below the eye. The brigadier gently helped the semi-conscious lieutenant to his feet, carefully walked him over to the shelter of a nearby barn, and laid him down. Somehow, Berney would survive the wound and serve as a provost marshal in Alabama for the rest of the war.

While striding back to his mount, a razor-sharp fragment of shell struck Rodes in the thigh and knocked him down. The iron chunk opened a terrible gash in his leg, and no one was there to help him. The agonizing pain and profuse bleeding led Rodes to conclude the worst. He managed to fashion a bandage and apply it to his leg. When the bleeding slowed considerably, he discovered with great relief that the injury "was slight," no major artery had been severed, and no bones appeared to be broken. As he had done at Seven Pines and as he tried to do again at Gaines' Mills, Rodes refused to allow a wound to keep him from his duty. The general staggered to his feet, remounted his horse, and rode back toward his line.

Adding to the shock of his wound was the jolt that coursed through Rodes when he caught sight of his men fleeing in disorder for the rear, "without visible cause to me," he later reported. Quickly composing himself, he rode 150 yards west to the Hagerstown Road to head them off and attempt a rally. Only about forty men from the Third, Twelfth, and Twenty-sixth regiments, and a few under Major Hobson of the Fifth, heeded his call. The rest of the brigade, Rodes later confessed, "had completely disappeared from this portion of the field." The jubilant Yankees, pressing through R. H. Anderson's division, seemed on the verge of a complete breakthrough of Lee's center.

Gathering some Mississippians and North Carolinians about him, Rodes cobbled together a line of about 150 men. D. H. Hill continued to demonstrate his defensive skills when he brought up the Jeff Davis Artillery. Longstreet sent in another battery and held the reins of his staff officer's horses while they worked a field piece. Two of James Walker's regiments marched up from the left and delivered a devastating fire into the enemy's advancing right flank. Despite all odds, the tissue-thin Southern line held and the enemy attack ground to a halt. Rodes continued gathering stragglers and directing the fire of the artillery while Hill, with musket in hand, personally led some 200 men in a daring and successful countercharge. Hill was on foot because he had just lost his third mount of the day.[49]

Although McClellan had several fresh divisions available, he did not commit any of them to the action, where even one more might have smashed Lee's center and sent his army—or large portions of it—streaming for the single ford on the Potomac River. Instead, McClellan let the battle shift once again, this time to his far left, where fighting around the lower stone bridge across the Antietam finally opened the span to Ambrose Burnside's IX Corps, which streamed across and after some delay, made for Sharpsburg and Lee's thinly defended right. Late that afternoon, just as it looked as though Lee's right flank would be turned or crushed and the day lost, A. P. Hill's Light Division arrived from Harpers Ferry. Hill skillfully threw his men into the fight and brought the battle to a close.

In an act of pure defiance, Lee disregarded the sound advice of Longstreet and others to withdraw that night, and instead remained in position throughout the next day. The audacious commander even sought unsuccessfully to launch his own attack from his left. On the evening of September 18, Lee finally began withdrawing his army across Boteler's ford near Shepardstown. The following night the army camped within three to five miles of the Potomac, where D. H. Hill's division once again was placed under Jackson's command. After resting on the 21st on the Opequon below Martinsburg, Lee marched his army up the Valley unmolested to Berryville near Winchester.[50]

The fighting on September 17 remains the bloodiest day in American history. McClellan's army left more than 12,000 men on the field in killed, wounded, captured, and missing. Lee's army, which could ill afford such heavy losses, suffered about 13,500 from all causes. Rodes' brigade, like most brigades in the Southern army that day, lost heavily. He reported 50 killed, 132 wounded, and 21 missing, a total loss of 203, or roughly one-quarter of his command. Although his brigade eventually was driven from the Sunken Road, his stout defense, coupled with the brave stand of the mortally wounded George B. Anderson and his soldiers may well have saved Lee's army that day.[51]

*   *   *

For several weeks Lee remained in the Martinsburg-Bunker Hill-Winchester area of the Shenandoah Valley, feeding and resting his battered army. Stragglers filed in and replacements arrived, boosting his numbers. By November, the Army of Northern Virginia was nearly double the strength it carried into Maryland. On November 6, Lee's army was formally organized into two corps (which had not officially existed before this time). Officers leading them would do so with the rank of lieutenant general. Lee submitted the names of James Longstreet and Thomas Jackson (in that order) for promotion to lieutenant general to command the First and Second Corps, respectively. Old

Pete was given five infantry divisions; Jackson was allocated four divisions. D. H. Hill's division, its strength built up to some 7,000 men, was placed in Jackson's Second Corps. Rodes' brigade remained with Hill's division, resting and refitting first near Bunker Hill and then at Middletown. His thigh wound giving him but little trouble, the brigadier worked diligently drilling and rebuilding his command.[52]

Throughout these changes, D. H. Hill's close young friend and chief of staff, John W. Ratchford, somehow got it in his head that Hill meant to replace him with someone more experienced. He applied for a staff opening with Rodes, who lost to wounds at Sharpsburg not only Lieutenant Berney but Captain Whiting. The prospective move proved difficult for Ratchford, not only because it meant leaving his good friend Hill, but also because it meant entering the service of Rodes, whom he admired as a soldier while regretting that he was "anything but a Christian man." Ratchford's interesting observation reveals that, despite his "Verily God is great" epiphany following First Manassas, Rodes still impressed observers as a profane man.

"You are a fool to leave him," Rodes exclaimed "with an oath" when he learned of Ratchford's intentions. Despite claims of being "anything but a Christian man," the brigadier threaded God into his argument in an effort to persuade Ratchford to remain with Hill. "You would have been dead long ago had it not been for General Hill's prayers," he continued. "He exposes himself and staff so much that nothing but an overruling Providence has saved you. Go back to him and have a clear understanding with him and if things are as you think, come to me." Ratchford followed Rodes' advice and talked with Hill, who easily convinced the young officer to remain in his service.[53]

Major changes also were being implemented in the Federal army. After Antietam, and despite President Lincoln's suggestions to take the offensive, General McClellan and his army remained stationary for more than a month. McClellan finally put his army in motion on October 26, but consumed a full week to get it south of the Potomac River. Lee countered the move by sending Longstreet's First Corps to meet it, falling back slowly in the face of Little Mac's glacial advance. Until the intentions of the Federal commander became clear, Lee preferred to leave Jackson in the Valley between Winchester and the Shenandoah River. Stonewall, in turn, placed D. H. Hill's division near Berryville to keep an eye on the Federals gathered once again at Harpers Ferry.[54]

The quiescent situation gave Rodes the opportunity to settle a matter that had been troubling him for some time. With the passage last April of the country's first Conscription Act, all men in service over the age of thirty-five became eligible for immediate discharge. Rodes strongly disapproved of this part of the act because it deprived the army of thousands of invaluable combat veterans. While reluctantly endorsing the discharge of thirty-six-year-old Sergeant E. Kronberg of the Twelfth Alabama, he said as much, going so far as to make a few disparaging remarks about Secretary of War George Randolph. The comments eventually made their way to the secretary. Randolph shot off a letter to Rodes in which he made it clear he did not appreciate unkind words about him spoken behind his back. The missive infuriated Rodes, particularly the implication that he had done something dishonorable. He had tried twice unsuccessfully to arrange a meeting with Randolph, with the illness after Gaines' Mill and the Maryland Campaign intervening to make a meeting impossible. The matter remained unresolved when Randolph resigned because of ill health on November 15 and set sail for France. Instead of dropping the issue, Rodes persisted in trying to overturn this perceived slight. "I have had no fair opportunity until now," he wrote November 17 to the Adjutant General Samuel Cooper in Richmond, "to make a suitable reply to the remarks of the Secretary of War about my endorsement. A reply is necessary because the Secretary of War has, in his remarks, done me great injustice." Rodes also acknowledged that his own comments might have been discourteous. "I expressed myself broadly because of an honest, and at that time in the army, a common misconception of the Act," he continued. Particularly offensive to Rodes was Randolph's comment "that probably my endorsement 'was not intended to be seen by the Secretary and need not be noticed.'"[55]

There was nothing Cooper could do about the "injustice," and he likely gave it little or no attention. The matter is significant only in what it reveals about Rodes. As he was on the battlefield, in personal affairs he could be stubborn and determined to a fault. He easily took offense, particularly with regard to his honor even when, as appears in this case, he had been caught making intemperate remarks. It is more than probable that the disparaging remarks about Randolph, whatever they were, had not been intended for the secretary's eyes.

More important matters awaited everyone's attention. On November 5, Longstreet took up a position in front of the Federals at Culpeper. McClellan's refusal to decisively confront Lee's dispersed army led an exasperated President Lincoln to replace Little Mac two days later with Ambrose Burnside. The former IX Corps commander was a 1847 graduate of West Point, a veteran of the Mexican and Indian wars, and a genuinely likeable fellow. His independent operations earlier in the war along the North Carolina coast showed promise (and earned him promotions), but his less than inspiring leadership during the Maryland Campaign did not. Burnside had been offered the post of army command twice before, and had turned it down both times. He doubted himself capable of the responsible position and openly claimed exactly that. His fellow officers, however, urged him to accept the post, fearful that Joe Hooker would take the reins of command if he did not. Under tremendous pressure to act, Burnside reluctantly set aside his own doubts (at least temporarily) and accepted the command of the Army of the Potomac.

Instead of aggressively pursuing McClellan's viable operation, Burnside scrapped the plan and moved his army east with the intention of driving south from Fredericksburg. He reached the Rappahannock River opposite Fredericksburg on November 17, before Longstreet's First Corps reached the scene to oppose him, but the pontoons the Federals needed to span the river did not begin arriving from Washington until November 25.

The delay gave Lee more than enough time to decide upon his plan of action: he would contest the crossing of the river and meet Burnside at Fredericksburg. Jackson's Second Corps was called in from the Valley, while Longstreet's First Corps deployed on the strong defensive terrain above the city. Jackson directed D. H. Hill's division, which by now numbered some 9,000 men, to march independently of the corps and head south for New Market.

Though his men desperately needed shoes, Hill was determined, "by strict and sanguinary discipline," to prevent straggling. He directed that a provost guard follow behind each marching unit to pick up stragglers. He also ordered that a surgeon go along to examine those who claimed to be ill, and that ambulances be available for those too sick to march. Further, Hill threatened to arrest any company officer who allowed his men to fall out without cause.[56]

Hill, however, did not accompany his command when it began marching. Instead, he left to attend to another matter and placed the division in the hands of Rodes. This is the first documented occasion that Rodes assumed such a responsibility. Fully intending to enforce Hill's marching instructions, he "ordered the officers and non-commissioned officers to his Head Quarters," remembered a corporal in Carter's battery, "and gave us a talk, as to what we should do and not do." His list of do's and don'ts included the proper manner of referring to the men in the ranks. "I hear you calling your men 'boys,'" he protested to the assembled officers. "That will not do. They are not boys, they are men, and damned good men."[57]

Under Rodes' guidance, the division broke camp near Middletown on Friday, November 21, and marched south to the Shenandoah River. While sitting atop his horse on the riverbank, watching the men wade across the cold, waist-deep stream, he received a cordial greeting from the temporary commander of Stephen Ramseur's brigade, the Fourth North Carolina's Colonel Bryan Grimes. Unaware that Rodes was in temporary command of the division, Grimes began complaining, as one comrade to another might, about the harsh order that forbid the men to remove their shoes and pants before crossing. Instead of the expected sympathy and agreement, Grimes received a cold chastisement from the very man who had issued the order. In a sharp, authoritative tone Rodes replied that he was in command of the division, that he had issued the order, and that the commander of Ramseur's brigade had better see to it that the men obeyed. Taken aback by this stiff rebuke, Grimes sullenly rode down to the river to help supervise the crossing of his fully-clothed men.

For Grimes, unpleasant encounters with Rodes would not be limited to a single occurrence. When his brigade straggled badly during the crossing, Grimes ordered it to halt to allow the men to close up. While this was transpiring, Rodes rode onto the scene and angrily demanded to know why Grimes had disregarded Jackson's standing order to stack arms at all halts. Grimes duly gave the order. Rodes directed him to keep his brigade motionless until the artillery passed.

Hours passed with no sign of the artillery. As the high-strung Grimes marked time, a courier arrived from Rodes inquiring why his men were not on the move. Grimes sent the courier back to Rodes to explain that the artillery had not yet arrived. The courier returned with Rodes' order to bring up the brigade. When Grimes finally entered the small town of Paris, two miles from where he had stopped, he found Rodes standing on the porch of a hotel.

"What has kept you so long?" Rodes angrily called out.

"Obeying your order," replied an equally irritated Grimes.

"What was that order?" Rodes asked.

"To let the artillery pass me," Grimes stiffly reminded him.

"When you saw that no artillery came up, you should have come on, as the enemy are advancing," Rodes unfairly rationalized.

"You had just reproved me for not obeying [Jackson's] order," shot back Grimes, as if to remind Rodes of his previous inflexibility. He added somewhat testily, "[I]f you had not countermanded your order to await the arrival of the artillery, I should have remained there until General Hill resumed command."

Rodes tried to end the matter by ordering Grimes to "Halt your men here." When Grimes called out for his men to "Order arms" preparatory to stacking, Rodes interrupted with, "You need not stack arms."

"It is General Jackson's order," Grimes shot back, "and you have just reproved me for its violation, and I shall do it." By now, Rodes simply wanted Grimes and his men out of his sight. He ordered the brigade to move forward one mile beyond town, "to await the enemy." The incident demonstrated that Rodes could be both inflexible and unreasonable. The whole affair soured relations between the two men for nearly a year-and-a-half. It finally "ended," Grimes cryptically wrote his wife, "by a gentlemanly and chivalrous action on the part of General Rodes."[58]

This unfortunate episode with Grimes is illustrative of Rodes' continuing obsession with strictness and discipline. Indeed, his reputation as a harsh disciplinarian had become so well known by this time as to earn him a severe public rebuke in the Montgomery *Advertiser*. But while some despised Rodes for his methods, many others admired him. Using the pseudonym "Volunteer," an Alabama soldier (possibly a sympathetic staff officer) came to Rodes' defense by writing the Mobile *Evening News* on December 5:

> I have just been shown a very unjust and uncalled for letter in the Montgomery Advertiser, about our Brigadier General (Rodes). The epistle is filled with such sentences as the following: "Gen. Rodes is a strict follower and disciple of Gen. Hill (D. H.), punishing severely men for slight offenses. Gen. Rodes punishes without discretion or judgment, the innocent and guilty all suffering alike. No palliating or mitigating circumstances are listened to; his decision is law and his decree inexorable." The writer of the above knows little of what he says when he speaks of General Rodes as a "disciple of General Hill," for the nature and disposition of the two men are as diametrically opposed to each other as the opposite points of the needle. And he does him great injustice when he says Gen. Rodes punishes the guilty and innocent alike. While a strict and rigid disciplinarian, and a man who never disobeys an order himself, I have never met a more just, conscientious and impartial officer. Gen. Rodes, comparatively speaking, occupies a low position in the scale of rank, and receives his orders from three higher sources. Since our dearly bought experience in Maryland, necessity had forced strict discipline upon the army. Discipline, strict discipline was the only cure. Gen. Lee drew the

cure, and the consequence is the South to-day has one of the finest armies the world ever saw.

I have thought it due to Gen. Rodes to notice the statement of the Montgomery Advertiser's correspondent because I think few officers in the army have done as much as he has in promoting its efficiency. I mean as far as his brigade is concerned. A Division General with whom report says Gen. Rodes is no pet was forced to admit that he had one of the best regulated and disciplined brigades in this army. His, however, is one of the cases where merit has failed to meet its reward. Gen. Rodes deserves promotion, and it must be mortifying to his friends to see his juniors and inferiors made Major Generals when they know how well he has won his claim to advancement.[59]

Regardless of how deserving of promotion he may have been, Rodes remained in command of the division for only a short time. From Middletown on November 21, his brigade, with only about forty-five minutes rest the entire day, marched through Strasburg and Woodstock. "Nearly broke down &c sore stiff," the Fifth Alabama's Sam Pickens noted in his diary that night. The day marked the beginning of a terrible ordeal for many of Rodes' men. "On this march we suffered intensely," remembered a soldier in the Sixth Alabama, "the campaign in Maryland having worn out our shoes. The roads being stony and rough, blood from many feet marked our way. Many of us had to go to slaughter pens at night and get pieces of raw hide to sew around our feet, but it was miserable marching with these moccasins."

Beginning at sunrise on Saturday, November 22, Rodes moved the brigade through Edenburg and Mt. Jackson to New Market, where it left the Valley pike and headed east across Massanutten Mountain into the Luray Valley. The march that day consumed about twenty miles. After moving south up the Luray to Conrad's Store, then east through Brown's Gap, the men came out of the Blue Ridge on the 24th. The following day they passed through Madison Courthouse and camped within two or three miles of Gordonsville. After a welcome two-day rest, Rodes marched the brigade about eighteen miles on the 28th, passing through Orange Courthouse and onto the Plank Road. They covered about eighteen more miles on the 29th and fifteen the following day before reaching Guiney's Station near Fredericksburg. Their journey, however, was not over. The next day General Lee, who was very impressed with the condition of Hill's division upon its prompt arrival, started it for Port Royal, another twenty miles down the Rappahannock River. "We were disappointed in our expectations to stop," wrote the Fifth regiment's Sam Pickens, "and had to go on this morning again."[60]

Throughout the march General Burnside had not moved his Army of the Potomac in any substantial way. He had hoped to cross the Rappahannock on November 26, before Jackson could reinforce Lee, but his precious pontoons continued to arrive only in trickles.

With the Federals obviously intent on crossing somewhere, Lee spread out his forces to cover the potential sites. On Wednesday December 3, the date of the area's first deep snowfall, D. H. Hill's division reached Port Royal, the last potential crossing site to the east, beyond which the river was too wide and the banks too steep. To Hill's left was Richard Ewell's division under the temporary command of Jubal Early. The division covered a horseshoe bend in the river called Skinker's Neck about twelve miles downstream from where Longstreet's First Corps was arrayed in the high ground beyond Fredericksburg. A. P. Hill spread his "Light Division" around the Yerby farm, about two miles from Longstreet's right flank, and William Taliaferro's division held Guiney Station, roughly ten miles southeast of A. P. Hill.[61]

Unable to construct winter quarters because of the impending battle, the men camped out in the increasingly cold weather. Rations remained scarce. "Don't issue more than 2/3 our due & no salt," Sam Pickens complained to his diary on the night of December 3. He also noted that he had been part of a squad sent by Rodes to arrest men out foraging without permission. "We caught 25 or 30 & carried them up to Gen. Rodes Hd. qrs. sometime after darkening." What Rodes did with these men is unknown, but he likely meted out some form of strict punishment.[62]

At Port Royal on the night of December 4, D. H. Hill put his men to work building rifle pits above the town. Below the town he placed various artillery units, which twice the next day drove off Federal gunboats attempting to move upriver.[63]

Burnside, meanwhile, dropped whatever interest he had in these distant lower crossings and concentrated on laying his finally arrived pontoons at Fredericksburg. By December 10 he was ready to move, and during the next two days sent across the river roughly 100,000 men organized in what he grandiosely labeled "Grand Divisions."

Because of the imposing array of 150 Union guns on the commanding ridges of Stafford Heights across the river, Lee could not move up in strength to contest the crossing. William Barksdale's Mississippi brigade held the town, from which it harassed the pontoon construction crews before finally being driven out.

Convinced at last that Burnside's main assault would be directly in his front, with no serious effort downriver, Lee instructed Jackson to consolidate the Second Corps at Fredericksburg. Around sundown on the 12th, D. H. Hill received his summons to action. His division, spread out some eighteen to twenty-two miles from the town, struck out for Fredericksburg.[64]

After marching for hours through the bitterly cold night on difficult muddy roads, the division halted for a brief rest about three miles from Hamilton's Crossing around 3:00 a.m. Resuming the march at daylight, the men reached the vicinity of Fredericksburg a short time later. "The roads were terrible and we rested but twice in the whole march," wrote a member of the Sixth Alabama to the Montgomery *Advertiser* later that month. "If I were to live an hundred years I could not spend a more awful night." That morning Rodes, having had little or no sleep, set about putting his men into line.[65]

Lee held a formidable front about seven miles long. On the right were the 39,000 men of Jackson's Second Corps. Stonewall's men, however, covered only about two of those seven miles, a line so compact that Jackson stacked his divisions in three tiers. Three-quarters of that frontage was held by A. P. Hill's division, whose two lines of infantry ran on a line paralleling the Richmond & Fredericksburg Railroad. Behind him stood the divisions of Early and Taliaferro. D. H. Hill's men went in behind Early south of the Mine Road, acting as the corps' reserve.

Saturday, December 13, arrived as another foggy morning, the temperature eventually rising to a balmy thirty-four degrees. When the fog finally lifted around 10:00 a.m., Burnside launched his attack. The initial offensive fell against Jackson's front opposite Prospect Hill, who faced two corps from William Franklin's "Grand Division" spread one-and-a-half miles wide in three heavy lines. "From the hill on which we were posted," observed Major Blackford of Rodes' brigade, "the whole Yankee army could be seen in the plain below, drawn up in three lines of battle, their arms all glistening in the sun." From this bird's-eye view, Blackford watched the grand battle unfold beneath him. "I enjoyed the whole fight very much," he professed, despite the enemy shells that occasionally sailed overhead. Although he had some 55,000 men under his command, Franklin sent them forward in large dribbles instead of powerful hammer strokes. The attack was bloodily ineffective until George Meade's division discovered a gap that yawned wide in a stand of swampy woods in part of A. P. Hill's line.[66]

As the fighting tightened to close quarters, Jackson brought up Early's men to close the gap Meade had broken wide open. D. H. Hill's men were shifted to the right of Prospect Hill to watch for a possible flanking movement. "Gen. Rhodes [sic] was at the head of the Division," staff officer John Ratchford wrote D. H. Hill some twenty years after the war, "and you know he was always prompt." The flanking movement, however, never developed. Left isolated by Franklin's unwillingness or inability to exploit success, Meade had no choice but to fall back. Around 2:00 p.m. Burnside shifted the battle to Longstreet's First Corps along Marye's Heights opposite Fredericksburg. The fighting there, which would garner most of the headlines, consisted of a series of grand piecemeal wave assaults that broke apart in abject failure. When darkness brought a halt to the terrible ordeal, the sun set on another solid Confederate victory.[67]

When the fighting shifted to Longstreet's front, Jackson eagerly sought a way to hurl his four divisions forward to drive the Federals into the river. Apparently without securing Lee's approval, he moved up several batteries to prepare the way and called up D. H. Hill's division from reserve to spearhead the attack. Rodes, probably pleased to finally get a chance to enter the battle and deliver what promised to be a glorious and perhaps fatal blow to the enemy, led his brigade forward at the double-quick. When his men entered a thick woods, however, they became so scattered that he ordered a halt. "We started & soon got double quick & confused," Pickens of the Fifth noted in his diary that night, "& were about 8 or ten deep & comps. mixed & scatd." Rodes' decision to halt proved most fortunate, for Jackson's forward artillery brought down such a rain of shot and shell from the Union guns on Stafford Heights as to blanket the intended field of advance beyond the woods. Before Rodes could get his brigade reorganized, an order from Jackson came through D. H. Hill to suspend the attack. Rodes had but narrowly averted disaster.[68]

That night the men camped on the battlefield. "The cries of the wounded in the hedged old field in our front, where the enemy had charged," wrote Bryan Grimes, "was heart-rending and sickening— pleading prayers to the Almighty for mercy, and begging for water to quench their thirst, which was continued all night."[69]

The following day, December 14, Early and Taliaferro took over the front line while D. H. Hill moved up to the second line, and A. P. Hill fell back in reserve. The day was consumed with sharing stories of the battle and speculating on what the next hour might bring. About 5:00 a.m. on the 15th, D.

H. Hill took over the front line, where Rodes' brigade relieved Elisha Paxton's Stonewall Brigade.

The view from the new position left quite an impression on many of Rodes' soldiers. "On Monday morning before day we were moved up, and formed the front line of battle," a Sixth Alabama private wrote the Montgomery *Advertiser.* "We all expected the fight to commence at day-break, and it was a sublime sight to see the Yankee line as it then appeared only about four hundred yards distant." While regarding as "sublime" the sight of living Yankees in battle formation, the Alabamian held quite another opinion about their dead comrades. "I took positive pleasure in looking at them laid cold and ghastly in death," he declared. "This feeling is common in the army."[70]

About 10:00 a.m. that morning, the Yankees sent over a flag of truce. Rodes directed Major Blackford to go out and receive it. Ultimately, General Jackson refused the offer of a truce, claiming it was not done in proper form. At 3:00 p.m. the Yankees sent over another flag, this time "in grand style." Jackson accepted.[71]

Under the terms of the truce, Rodes' brigade received the grisly job of picking up the dead and wounded left lying between the lines. While the opposing pickets readily laid down their guns and met out in no-man's land, where they exchanged buttons, knives, pipes, salt, coffee, tobacco, and small talk, Rodes assembled a corps of litter-bearers. "Now, boys," he said before sending them out, "those Yankees are going to ask you questions, and you must not tell them anything. Be very careful about this."

"General," one of the men blurted out, "can't we tell them that we whipped them [day before] yesterday?"

"Yes, yes!" Rodes replied, laughing, "you can tell them that."

"General," asked another man, "can't we tell them that we can whip them tomorrow and the day after?"

Rodes laughed a second time and sent them out, saying, "Yes, yes! Go on, go on! Tell them what you please."[72]

With this friendly, if somewhat unusual, exchange, Rodes displayed a rare congenial sense of humor that transcended rank and social class. Moreover, by allowing the men to blurt out unsolicited informal comments, he revealed that occasionally he could see through the stiff martial trappings that surrounded his position.

"We carried all their wounded and a good many of their dead to them [Yankees at a halfway point between the lines]," declared one of Rodes' soldiers. "I got a good pair of boots from a dead Yankee for the trouble of pulling them off. . . . [O]ur boys and them mixed freely together exchanging tobacco for coffee and canteens."[73]

That night, Burnside withdrew his beaten army across the Rappahannock, bringing an end to his ill-conceived campaign. Though D. H. Hill's division was not directly engaged at Fredericksburg, it had suffered 173 casualties, mostly from long distance artillery rounds. Rodes lost two killed and fourteen wounded. The army's total losses were about 5,300 out of 72,500 engaged. Burnside's casualties were more than double that—12,700 killed, wounded, and captured out of 106,000. The figure reflects clearly the difference between fighting an offensive battle and standing on the defensive on good terrain to receive an attack.[74]

In the abandoned position in front of Rodes' brigade, the Yankees left behind a staggering amount of supplies and equipment. One member of the Fifth Alabama explained that he saw a field "full of boxes, tin plates, cups, pans & pieces [of] meat everywhere. guns cart. boxes knapsax, tents plenty. If [they] leave that much when [they] go off in order," he asked his diary rhetorically, "what must it be like when routed."[75]

The most precious items picked up were rifled muskets. Hill estimated the take at between 3,000 and 4,000, more than enough to allow Rodes to replace the smoothbores still carried by many in the Fifth Alabama. In keeping with his continued "lively interest" in his old regiment, he offered an oyster dinner to an entire company if any man in its ranks could use his new rifle to hit a block on top of a barrel at 100 yards. The regiment eagerly took up the challenge. Several men hit the barrel before a private in Company D finally hit the block and won the oysters for his comrades.[76]

At brigade headquarters on Thursday, December 25, the Fredericksburg slain less than ten days in their cold graves, Rodes held a Christmas party. It was attended by many officers in the division who enjoyed, among other treats, delicious eggnog provided in abundance by the host. As he had done twelve months earlier, Rodes closed out the year by holding a brigade review on December 31.[77]

W ith the Federals back across the Rappahannock, General Lee at last allowed his own army to build quarters for the war's second winter. D. H. Hill's division settled down in the vicinity of a small country house of worship called Grace Church on Bowling Green Road about five miles southeast of Fredericksburg.[1]

Once there, Rodes' men—or at least those from three of his regiments—thoughtfully took up a collection for the benefit of the people of war-torn Fredericksburg. In the second week of January, Rodes sent Major Eugene Blackford into town to present a grateful mayor with $1,950. More than $800 of that sum was contributed by Rodes' old command, the Fifth Alabama.[2]

When he returned to camp, Blackford was honored with a unique position of responsibility. Perhaps he considered doing so for some time, but now Rodes took advantage of the winter lull to create a special battalion of volunteer sharpshooters comprised of four of the best shots from each company in the brigade. On January 14, he gave command of this new unit to Blackford. "I esteemed it a great compliment from Gen. Rodes to have received the appointment," the major wrote his mother. Rodes intended to use the sharpshooters primarily in emergencies. On the march, for example, he wanted them to respond in an instant to a special bugle call developed by Blackford (and blown by Corporal Rail Grayson, who would always be at Blackford's side), leave their respective regiments, and dash "in front of the Brigade to protect them until the final advance of the enemy."[3]

Meanwhile, in the course of complying with General Lee's order to have a map created that detailed the location of each unit in the army, Jackson's excellent topographical engineer, Major Jedediah Hotchkiss, rode out on January 16 to D. H. Hill's headquarters at Grace Church. There, the mapmaker was surprised to learn that Hill had left just that morning to take up a new assignment in North Carolina. Robert Rodes now presided at division headquarters.[4]

Hill submitted his resignation after the first of the year. He had intended to do so for some time. Poor health—primarily a chronically aching back—was his official explanation. The general wanted to leave the service altogether, but General Lee and others persuaded him to take command of a department in North Carolina.[5]

Not everyone regretted his departure. Despite universal acclaim as an exceptionally brave and gallant commander, Hill possessed a brusque personality that strained relations with many fellow officers, including his immediate superior and brother-in-law, Stonewall Jackson. He had long been critical of others, including Lee, and his steady stream of negative comments had not endeared him to the army commander. Some of Hill's own men, many of whom derisively referred to him as "Old Rawhide," were not unhappy with the change. "Gen. D. H. Hill has been assigned to duty in N. Carolina," Major Blackford wrote his wife, "leaving his division behind much to our delight." In a letter written months later, a Third Alabama private reflected upon how glad he felt at the time to be out from under "that bundle of blundering prejudice and bad temper."[6]

In sharp contrast to Hill's cynicism, sarcasm, and "croaking" stood the affable, usually gracious, and reserved manner of Robert Rodes. "I like him so much," Captain James Power Smith of Jackson's staff wrote in a private letter. "He is very much admired by all and very popular."[7] However, a pleasant, charismatic manner and rank as senior brigadier in the division did not guarantee Rodes a promotion to major general to replace Hill. Other brigadiers in the army had to be considered. Private Thomas Coffey of the Third Alabama believed command of the division might fall upon Cadmus Wilcox. "I hope so," he wrote his wife regarding the rumor, "as he is considered one of the finest officers in Longstreet's Corps."[8]

Rodes, too, heard the gossip and the idea did not sit well with him. In a letter dated March 22 to the recuperating Richard Ewell (whose left leg had been amputated above the knee after a bullet shattered his kneecap at Groveton the previous August), Rodes wrote, "The latest information I have from Richmond as to my promotion shows that Wilcox and I are pitted against each other. As he is a West Point man he will beat me almost to a certainty."

Like Rodes, Wilcox began the war as a colonel of an infantry regiment, the Ninth Alabama. He received appointment as a brigadier the same day as Rodes, October 21, 1861, and he took command of an Alabama brigade that subsequently fought at Seven Pines. In the Seven Days Battles, Second Manassas, and Fredericksburg, Wilcox proved to be an efficient and capable— if not stellar—brigadier. For some unknown reason, however, Rodes detested the man. "I would prefer being beaten by a baboon," he bluntly informed Ewell, "but will submit to it quietly, unless they place him in command of the Div."

In lieu of getting the promotion for himself, Rodes hoped the division would go to Ewell, whom he grew to respect and admire while a colonel in his brigade. "To be frank with you," he penned in the same letter, "I consider my own chances to promotion and of assignment to the Command of this Div. so slight that I would hail with pleasure the announcement of your assignment here—The whole Division I doubt not would be delighted to have you as their Commander—Do not then hesitate to avail yourself of every means of procuring this result—and be assured that I will be personally gratified to be under your command again."

Despite words implying the contrary, Rodes not only wanted the promotion, but wanted it desperately. Lacking what he believed was the essential qualification of being "a West Point man," however, he did not allow his hopes to get too high. That and the still bitter memory of his humiliating rejection by the Louisiana Military Institute nearly four years before led him to profess that he still found it too distasteful to employ "every means" to secure advancement. "I cannot consent to obtain promotion by the steps resorted to by most men," he self-righteously told Ewell. Those steps typically included soliciting recommendations from influential politicians, colleagues, and friends.

Rodes possessed a sense of honor that required promotions be bestowed and not sought. He did not outwardly seek his brigadiership and he refused to do so now for a major generalcy. Still, the outcome was naturally of deep interest to him. He admitted to Ewell that he kept abreast of rumors "from Richmond as to my promotion." While refusing to seek out recommendations, he found it highly gratifying when they were offered unsolicited on his behalf. "Bye the bye," he told Ewell with pride, disguised as an afterthought, "My being unwilling to use Congressional and such influence at the War Office with the President has a single commentary, tho' one beyond my control, in the fact recently revealed to me since I wrote you in fact—that the Alabama delegation in Congress, the Governor of Ala. and the officers of my brigade have all I believe simultaneously expressed to the President a desire to have me promoted—I was surprised to hear it—really surprised."[9]

Surprised and undoubtedly very pleased. From the House of Representatives on February 13, the eight members of the Alabama congressional delegation sent to Secretary of War James A. Seddon a letter (composed by Representative Jabez L. M. Curry) asking for Rodes' promotion. "Gen R[odes] has been in service since the war commenced," it read, "and in camp or on the march and in battle he has distinguished himself by cool courage high soldierly qualities and rare skill and intelligence as an officer. Gen R. is an accomplished Engineer," Curry continued, "was educated at a military Institute and has too delicate a sense of honor to hound out recommendations from his superiors [and] he will not make a personal application or use the arts which so many officers use to get letters of recommendation from his superiors in command." Secretary Seddon politely promised to give Rodes "comparative consideration."[10]

That same day the delegation sent a similar letter to President Davis. "Gen. Rodes has so high a sense of honor, it is so repulsive to him [to seek recommendations]. . . . He is an accomplished Engineer—a fine scholar, well read in the profession of arms and has a brigade unsurpassed by any in Gen. Lee's army. In numerous battlefields his courage, coolness soldierly qualities and superior accomplishments have been tested. All his generals, ranking and commanding, speak well of him."[11]

Alabama's Governor John Shorter joined the movement when he sent a letter to the president on March 6. "The services and skills of this gallant officer," wrote the governor, "are not unknown to you or the Country. Virginia has been the field of his brilliant achievements. He is distinguished alike for his high administrative powers, and his cool judgment, daring bravery & military accomplishments. Alabama is proud of him, and the knowledge of his well earned promotion would give satisfaction to his people." President Davis politely vowed to "give it proper consideration in making future selections to fill vacancies."[12]

"We are all much interested in the appointment of our new Division General," Major Eugene Blackford wrote his father on March 8. "Yesterday this brigade sent up a petition signed by every officer in it asking that Rodes be made Maj. General, and assigned to this Command. I don't know whether it will do any good or not," Blackford concluded, "but it can't do any harm." Two days later Congressman Curry presented that petition to the president.[13]

Noticeably absent from the list of Rodes' supporters was Alabama Senator William Lowndes Yancey, who held such an extreme view on states' rights that he refused to support the advancement of anyone who was not a "pure" Alabamian. Yancey had opposed Rodes' promotion to brigadier, and he now spoke out against his elevation to major general. His action infuriated many in Rodes' brigade. "Yancey excited my indignation to the utmost by having said to the Alabama delegation that he was opposed to Rodes' promotion, that he was in the first place too severe a disciplinarian, and also a 'mere adventurer and not an Alabamian,'" Major Blackford wrote home in disgust. "[T]is very humiliating to a soldier that these vile politicians in Richmond should have to be consulted in regard to the appointment of a Maj General. Besides it is news home that being a Virginian is a reproach."

Like his brigade commander, Blackford believed that Rodes held the added "reproach" of not being a graduate of West Point. "They have missed it much in not making Rodes the Commander," he wrote his father, "but the prejudice in favor of West Pointers was too strong even for a man of his merit." Like many in the brigade, Blackford considered this a great injustice. "He has been in command of the Division for six weeks past," he explained, "and has shown even in these times of [relative] peace that he is the right man in the right place." Blackford sadly concluded, "It is thought that Gen Ed. Johnson will succeed to the command."[14]

Rodes, ever vigilant for developments on the subject, knew of the Johnson rumor. From North Carolina in mid-March, he received from his former commander, D. H. Hill, a request for someone to act as the department's chief of artillery. In a reply written March 22, Rodes discussed the possibility of sending either Thomas Carter (who refused) or John Bondurant (who was willing). "For some days after you began your advance on the enemy," Rodes wrote his former commander, "I expected to hear of a bloody assault upon Newbern by your troops. Glad you did not venture if what I hear of its defenses is correct." Inevitably, Rodes turned to the prospect, or lack thereof, of his own promotion. "Genl [Ed] Johnston [sic] has not reported for duty yet, and may not at all," he wrote with some satisfaction. In an undisguised attempt to discount his own chances, he added, "Wilcox and [William Dorsey] Pender are preeminent for your shoes now."[15]

In early April 1863, General Lee sent to Inspector General Samuel Cooper a request for two major generals, one to command D. H. Hill's division and the other to take over Isaac Trimble's. At that time, the Confederate service contained thirty-five divisions and thirty-five major generals, an even match.

Lee, however, was short two major generals because Edward Johnson had not yet recovered from an ankle wound received at McDowell the previous May, and Arnold Elzey was on detached duty as commander of the Richmond defenses. On April 6, Cooper sent Lee's request on to President Davis, adding that Johnson, "who is now walking with a cane," should be sent to Lee at once, but that in lieu of reassigning Elzey, who was too valuable in his present position, Rodes, "the senior brigadier of his division," should be promoted major general. Despite this impressive recommendation on Rodes' behalf, President Davis (and for that matter General Lee) did not yet have sufficient confidence in Rodes to act on Cooper's recommendation. They eventually gave command of D. H. Hill's division to Johnson, though Rodes would remain in charge until "Old Allegany" returned to duty.[16]

This temporary arrangement pleased Stonewall Jackson, who respected Rodes for his gallantry, hard-hitting tactics, and association with VMI. As for the men in the ranks, a letter sent by a soldier in the Sixth Alabama to a Montgomery newspaper in mid-April probably expressed the feelings of many. "If we could have John B. Gordon as our Brigadier General and R. E. Rodes Major General," the anonymous writer declared, "we would be as well satisfied as we could be with any arrangement, save an honorable peace."[17]

For the moment, however, none of these three wishes could be granted. An honorable peace seemed a long way off, Rodes remained a brigadier, and John B. Gordon was destined for command elsewhere. When he finally recovered that spring from the horrible wounds he received at Sharpsburg, Gordon advanced to brigade command. "D. H. Hill's Division," however, lost the services of that gallant and capable officer when he took charge of a Georgia brigade in a division led by Jubal Early. Rodes regretted the loss, even though he believed Gordon lacked an essential requirement for being a good general. "He is a magnificent officer in action," Rodes wrote Ewell, "but is a horrible disciplinarian I find."[18]

The uncertainty of the situation regarding Rodes' status troubled at least one man who had attached his star to him. "Although I have every reason to believe that Gen. Rodes feels kindly towards me and will do everything in his power to place me in a more pleasant position," declared a letter written home by George Rust, a non-commissioned officer with hopes of joining Rodes' staff, "it is impossible for him to do anything for me at this time as he is only commanding Division temporarily and he does not know what day some other person may be assigned to the command of this Division." Rust's grasp of the situation reveals a relationship based on great respect and admiration for Rodes.

"There is only the slightest possibility that he will be promoted to Maj. Gen., if he is he may make me one of his aids [sic] with the rank of Lieut," Rust continued. "Genl. Rodes is very cordial & treats me as a friend & his equal and makes it more pleasant than if I was serving in the same capacity under some other General who was a stranger to me. Genl. Rodes stands as high as any Brigadier Genl. in the service but there are Major Genl's without commands & one or two Brigs with older commissions and for these reasons he may not be promoted."[19]

Brigadier General Rodes had led five regiments, all from Alabama. Now temporarily in charge of a division, he commanded five brigades—twenty-two regiments and four batteries of artillery. Forty-four-year-old Colonel Edward O'Neal of the Twenty-sixth Alabama temporarily served as the head of "Rodes' Brigade." A lawyer before the war and a strong advocate of secession, O'Neal entered the service as a captain in the Ninth Alabama and rose to lieutenant colonel the following October. He was promoted to colonel of the Twenty-sixth on April 2, 1862, and was wounded at Seven Pines and again at South Mountain.[20]

Twenty-five-year-old Stephen Ramseur commanded one of the division's two North Carolina brigades. A member of the privileged slaveholding upper class, Ramseur before the war had been a firm supporter of slavery and Southern rights. After serving in the artillery through the first year of the conflict, he became colonel of the Forty-ninth North Carolina and was severely wounded in the right arm at Malvern Hill. Following a six-month period of recovery, he was promoted to brigadier general, and in January 1863 took command of George B. Anderson's brigade after that officer was mortally wounded at Sharpsburg.[21]

The division's third brigade was led by thirty-four-year-old Alfred Iverson. Like Ramseur's outfit, the all-North Carolina organization consisted of four regiments. A veteran of the Mexican War, "Bleeding Kansas," and the Mormon Expedition, Iverson at the start of the Civil War almost single-handedly raised the Twentieth North Carolina, for which he was made the regiment's colonel. Acknowledged as an excellent organizer and trainer, he led his regiment on the Peninsula and was wounded at Gaines' Mill. In November 1862, Iverson—who showed glimmers of promise—was elevated to brigadier general and succeeded the capable Samuel Garland, who was killed at South Mountain.[22]

Rodes' division also contained two Georgia brigades. Thirty-two-year-old George Doles led the smaller of the two. A Georgia bookkeeper and militia captain before the war, Doles was noted for his tall, erect military appearance that belied a quiet, gentle nature. He began the war as colonel of the Fourth Georgia, but did not see combat until the Seven Days' Battles, wherein he was wounded at Malvern Hill. After fighting at Second Manassas and Sharpsburg, Doles took over Roswell Ripley's brigade when that officer went down with a wound at Sharpsburg.[23]

The larger of the all-Georgia brigades was led by thirty-nine-year-old Princeton-educated Alfred Colquitt. Five regiments strong, the brigade was formerly led by Gabriel Rains, a brilliant scientist who proved incapable of field command. A militia captain and states' rights Democratic congressman before the war, Colquitt was noted for his sobriety and fervent piety. He began the war as colonel of the Sixth Georgia, with which he fought at Seven Pines and in the Seven Days' Battles. He became a brigadier on September 1, 1862, his command holding the far left of the Sunken Road at Sharpsburg. After the war Colquitt leveraged his piety to the rank of Methodist minister and governor of Georgia.[24]

Despite General Lee's defensive triumph at Fredericksburg, the men of "D. H. Hill's Division" did not look like a victorious army. Toiling in the cold without tents those first weeks of the new year, 1863, and ranging farther from Grace Church to find firewood, Rodes' ragged soldiers sported a haggard appearance. Constant hunger was a big part of their problem. "I am leaner than I have been in a long time," Thomas Coffey of the Third Alabama wrote his wife in mid-January, "and if you ever read Cervantes' description of Don Quixote, you have my photograph." A month later Coffey gave her an interesting picture of the sanitary conditions in camp. "A fellow sometimes don't get a chance to change his rags more than once per month," he declared, "and when such is the case the lice get so numerous that they tote a fellow clean away." The next day (Feb. 17) his message was even bleaker: "An intensely cold day. All suffered, as clothing is not heavy, and many have none or very poor shoes."[25]

Rodes, however, never let his men forget that they were soldiers. "We are drilling every day in Hardees Tactics," Sam Pickens of the Fifth Alabama told his diary on February 13. Written by William Hardee and published in 1855, the *Tactics* was an updated government subsidized version of the standard infantry manual. This newer version took into account the range and accuracy of the rifled musket when calling for increased speeds of march and deployment. Rodes remained diligent as ever in having his men practice these quick maneuvers. In addition to the Sabbath, however, he excused them from drilling on "wash day," which usually fell on a Saturday.[26]

Not everyone appreciated such diligence. After working ten days on his "crude but adequate hut," Private Coffey wrote his wife that he was glad for the break afforded by the recent five days of heavy rain, "as old Rodes would die if he could not have the men double-quicking five hours a day."[27]

The men inevitably found diversions from the miseries of camp and the monotony and strain of drill. Pickens scribbled in his diary that they occasionally played games, such as "cat," "Bull Pen," and "town-ball." With a foot of snow on the ground in early February, the brigades of O'Neal and Colquitt marched out from camp, formed up, and battled each other in a two-hour snowball fight. The most favored diversion, however, was leave time spent in Richmond. Lieutenant Park especially enjoyed attending the theatre there. He even had a favorite actor, a promising young and handsome man named J. Wilkes Booth.[28]

For Rodes, the best diversion was his beloved Hortense. With her health much improved, she joined him from Lynchburg in mid or late January. Rodes provided her with living quarters that proved comfortable enough to allow the two to at last conceive their first child, Robert Jr., who would be born the following September. Moreover, camp life seemed to agree with Hortense. She frequently enjoyed the company of other officer's wives, and that season she and Robert happily attended a number of social activities.[29]

Though probably irked at the temporary nature of the assignment, Rodes was pleased with the opportunity to handle an entire division. Coupled with that opportunity, however, was a certain degree of anxiety. General Burnside attempted to move upriver and flank the Confederate army, but the operation—derisively labeled the "Mud March"—came to an ignominious end on January 23. Although the fiasco would end Burnside's tenure as the commander of the Army of the Potomac, Rodes remained on edge for some time. "Gen Rodes thinks that a battle cannot be postponed longer than a day or two," Eugene Blackford wrote his mother on January 25. "He may have means of information of which we are not aware, but certainly there is nothing going on the opposite banks to justify any such opinion."

A native of Fredericksburg, Virginia, the twenty-two-year-old Blackford left school in Alabama in 1861 to join the Fifth Alabama, and subsequently rose to the rank of major in command of the brigade sharpshooters. In the course of nearly two years of service with Rodes, Blackford came to like and admire the brigadier—and perhaps even to understand him a little. "Gen R has always been remarkable for his extreme caution," continued Blackford's letter to his mother. "Most of us have set it down that now he is in command of a Division, his usual wariness has [increased]." Blackford knew Rodes better than most, but his description of the general is one most students would not associate with Rodes.[30]

Like D. H. Hill before him, Rodes made division headquarters in Grace Church. Also like his predecessor, he did not forget the sacred nature of the place. After attending Sunday services there on March 15, Sam Pickens proudly noted in his diary, "I shook hands with Genl Rodes who attended preaching." This brief entry reveals two interesting things about Rodes—the stern and officious general had no problem shaking hands with a private, and he was attending church services. Major Ratchford just the previous year had characterized Rodes "as anything but a Christian man." Whether his attendance was a one-off or something more lasting remained to be determined.[31]

Meanwhile, one of the many decisions required of Rodes as division commander included dealing with "labor" disputes. One in particular involved a talented black cook named Jim. Sometime in February, the Twelfth Alabama's Lieutenant Robert Park, acting regimental quartermaster, received an order to send his highly valued cook over to the brigade quartermaster for reassignment. Incensed at what he perceived was a covert attempt to steal the cook for personal use, Park jumped on his horse and rode straight to Rodes' headquarters at Grace Church.

Park so admired Rodes that in a diary entry commemorating the birthday of George Washington, he compared him favorably with the first president. "The great Virginian," Park wrote of Washington, "doubtless looks down approvingly upon the course of his successors, Lee, Jackson, A. P. Hill, Rodes and others."

When he learned that Rodes was holding a staff meeting at his headquarters in the church, Park entered the building, strode down the aisle to the altar, handed the order to Rodes, and firmly but politely asked for an explanation. Taking this abrupt intrusion in stride, Rodes read the note and told the incensed officer that he knew nothing about it. Instead of dismissing Park then and there, he put the matter to his staff. Major Whiting spoke up to say that he believed the order had been issued by the brigade quartermaster, Major James Bryan, who claimed the cook in question was to be used by him as a teamster. Park protested that the man was not a teamster, and that this was a blatant attempt by Bryan to steal his cook for his own use. Rodes, however, washed his hands of the whole affair. "The matter is between you and Major Bryan," he told Park. "I will have nothing to do with it." That satisfied Park, who took it to mean that Rodes would not interfere when he refused to obey this order. "I thanked him for his decision," Park explained in his diary, "and rode rapidly back to my tent, and told Jim to remain as cook, much to his delight."[32]

Rodes could be equally diplomatic when considering the feelings of his superiors. Later that spring he accepted an invitation to share a turkey dinner at Jackson's large tent headquarters at Moss Neck. Dinner guests included Jubal Early, Dr. Hunter McGuire, Lieutenant McHenry Howard, and others. When the abstemious Jackson excused himself and briefly stepped out of the tent to tend to some business, McGuire leapt to his feet. "Gentlemen," he cried, "wouldn't you like to have a drink before dinner?" Though the dumbfounded officers made no reply, their expressions told McGuire that they were up to the adventure. The doctor quickly pulled a canteen from under his cot. "Drink quick," he exclaimed, "the General will be back in a moment." Like schoolboys doing mischief, each guest hurriedly took a swig. McGuire shoved the canteen back under the cot and everyone straightened up in time for Jackson's reentry into the tent.[33]

Rodes, too, occasionally enjoyed serving drinks to guests, though in a manner not quite so harried as that of Dr. McGuire. During one evening that winter he and Hortense entertained General Early. They had both grown quite fond of him despite Hortense's initial dislike of the man (perhaps because of the bachelor's well-known disapproval of the practice of having wives in camp). "Mrs. Rodes desires to be remembered to you in the kindest terms," Rodes wrote Ewell on March 22. "She has forgiven old Jubal and has taken quite a fancy to the old bear. He actually dined with us one day—seduced by the promise of a good strong toddy."[34]

*   *   *

With the arrival of spring came ominous warnings of a renewed struggle with the enemy across the river. To meet that challenge, the army diligently prepared itself, both physically and spiritually. In accordance with President Davis's special proclamation, Stonewall Jackson on March 24 notified his commanders that three days hence, "all drills and Military Exercises will be suspended on that day in this Corps, and Chaplains will hold divine services in the Regiments." The following day, the 25th, Jackson issued General Order 22: "In addition to the careful study of tactics and the Army Regulations, required to enable officers to discharge properly the duties of their positions, it is hereby enjoined upon every officer of this Corps, to make himself, as far as practicable, thoroughly acquainted with the duties of the grade next above that which he occupies." In General Order 26, issued three weeks later on April 13, Jackson specified how he expected his command to perform on the march, specifications his famous "foot cavalry" generally adhered to in the Valley Campaign of the year before:

> Each Division will move precisely at the time indicated in the order of march, and if a Division or Brigade is not ready to move at that time, the next will proceed & take its place, even if a Division should be separated thereby. On the march, the troops are to have a rest of ten minutes. The rate of march is not to exceed one mile in twenty five minutes, unless otherwise specially ordered. The time of each Division commander will be taken from that of the Corps Commander. When the troops are halted for the purpose of resting, arms will be stacked and ranks broken and in no case during the march will the troops be allowed to break ranks without previously stacking arms. When any part of a Battery or train is disabled on a march, the officer in charge must have it removed immediately from the road, so that no part of the command be impeded in the march. Batteries or trains must not stop in the line of march to water. When any part of a battery or train from any cause, leaves its place in the column it must not pass any part of the column in regaining its place. Company Commanders will march at the rear of their respective companies. Officers must [be] habitually occupied in seeing that orders are strictly enforced; a days march should be with them a day of labor.[35]

On the other side of the Rappahannock River, the Army of the Potomac began to stir once more. After its sharp repulse at Fredericksburg and the embarrassing "Mud March," morale in the army sank to a new low. On January 25, President Lincoln replaced Burnside with Joseph Hooker who, like George McClellan after Bull Run in 1861, oversaw a remarkable transformation in the army's organization, fighting spirit, and logistical capabilities. By early spring, "Fighting Joe" commanded a well-trained, well-supplied, and well-disciplined army of some 134,000 men and 404 guns. As the end of April drew near and the northern Virginia roads began to dry, he devised an impressive plan to pin down Lee by pushing two corps across the river at Fredericksburg while stealing a march with the rest of the army upstream to turn Lee's left flank. Hooker's strategic envelopment was designed to pry Lee away from Fredericksburg and drive him back toward Richmond.

Major General Joseph Hooker,
commander of the
Army of the Potomac.

Generals in Blue

Hooker set the plan in motion on the morning of April 27. George Meade's V Corps, Oliver O. Howard's XI Corps, and Henry Slocum's XII Corps began the march for Kelly's Ford, twenty-seven miles upriver from Fredericksburg. The following day John Sedgwick moved his VI Corps and John Reynolds's I Corps, about 40,000 men, closer to the river and early the next morning the Federals crossed the Rappahannock at Fredericksburg. That same day, April 29, Darius Couch's II Corps started for United States Ford, followed on the 30th by Daniel Sickles's III Corps.[36]

The Confederate army numbered only about 62,000 men and 228 guns. Lee's ability to respond as aggressively as he might have liked was hampered by the absence of his senior corps commander, James Longstreet, and two of his First Corps divisions under George Pickett and John B. Hood. For several weeks, Old Pete and his veterans had been conducting widespread (and very successful) foraging operations south of the James River well below Richmond opposite Suffolk, Virginia. It was doubtful they would arrive in northern Virginia in time to join the army against Hooker. By the time Lee realized what Hooker was up to, the new enemy army commander had stolen a march and turned his flank. Devising a plan to confront and defeat an enemy more than twice his size—either wing of which presented a force larger or comparable to his own—was problematic. Most commanders in Lee's situation would have felt compelled to fall back. Lee, however, had other ideas.

Around 5:00 a.m. on the 29th, a courier galloped into the sleeping town of Fredericksburg, Paul Revere-style, shouting the stunning news that Yankees were crossing the Rappahannock. As planned, the Episcopal Church bell sounded the alarm and the townspeople sprang into action, preparing either to hide or evacuate.[37] Down Bowling Green Road, out near Grace Church, Rodes also received the news. In the predawn darkness, he sent out orders for the division to rouse itself and prepare to depart. Excitedly but professionally his men went about the business of packing equipment, loading wagons, cooking rations, dismantling tents, distributing ammunition, and inspecting weapons. Having sent back to Lynchburg by this time the three-months-pregnant Hortense, Rodes prepared for the journey that would lead him to the pinnacle of his military career.[38]

He began that momentous day well before dawn on April 29. "We had no idea where we were going," Captain William Calder of the Second North Carolina, Ramseur's brigade, later wrote. "A soldier never knows where he is going, nor what he is going to do, until the moment for action comes. They have only to trust in their commanders and blindly 'follow their leaders.'"[39]

Although Confederate commanders were still unsure what to make of the Federal movements, Lee ordered Stonewall Jackson to pull in his corps from around the Moss Neck area and concentrate it at Hamilton's Crossing, a depot on the Richmond & Fredericksburg Railroad three miles southeast of town. Jubal Early's division hit the road first, followed by Rodes and A. P. Hill. Isaac Trimble's division, commanded by Raleigh Colston, moved from Skinker's Neck.[40]

"On we went through mud and over stumps," remembered Calder of the march to Fredericksburg, "stumbling about in the dark, to the great danger of our heads and shins." One of the "casualties" of this march was the Third Alabama's Colonel Cullen Battle, who missed the coming battle because of injuries sustained in a fall from his horse. Along with having "no idea where we were going," Calder on this dark night (despite a bright moon two nights short of being full) had no idea of the extreme danger facing the depleted Army of Northern Virginia. He would have been more uncomfortable had he known how well the new Federal commander was executing his well-conceived plan.[41]

Aware that Hooker had sent a column upriver, Lee on the 29th pulled Richard Anderson's division back from United States Ford and sent it west a few miles along the south bank toward a minor crossroads known as Chancellorsville. Anderson would keep an eye on developments in that sector. The suspicion remained that Hooker's upstream march might be a feint designed to disguise his real intention of making a breakthrough at Fredericksburg. Jackson proposed an all-out attack against Sedgwick opposite the town. Lee seemed willing to consider the idea until both he and Jackson realized, as they had the previous December, that the commanding position of the Federal artillery across the Rappahannock on Stafford Heights rendered impractical any Confederate attack toward the river.[42]

Rodes, too, knew little about what was transpiring on the strategic level. He marched his division into Hamilton's around 10:00 a.m. on the 29th. Riding with him was his new aide-de-camp, the thirty-one-year-old Lieutenant James P. Arrington. A prewar merchant from Greene County, Alabama, Arrington was appointed just that day to replace Philip Sutton. Early the next morning, Jackson began placing his four divisions in a somewhat loose mile-long defensive line stretching from the left of Hamilton's Crossing to the right of Massaponax Creek. At 3:30 a.m. Rodes moved up to take the right flank, with Early on his left. With the assistance of Colonels Thompson Brown and artilleryman Tom Carter, Rodes laid out a good position for his men, who quickly fortified their line and settled down to wait for the Yankees to make the next move.[43]

Dawn of April 30 began cool and foggy, a touch of drizzle misting from the sky. Union guns on Stafford Heights opened fire. Rodes and his men watched the awesome display while Sedgwick's thousands continued crossing the Rappahannock. Rodes' division suffered its first casualties of the campaign when a number of shells struck Ramseur's position on the far right, where Rodes had posted it to guard a ford located where the Massaponax flows into the Rappahannock.[44]

When Lee learned around 10:00 a.m. that morning (April 30) that at least one Federal corps had crossed the Rappahannock well upstream at Kelly's Ford, he finally began to accept the possibility that Hooker's main effort might well come from that direction. The conclusion could not have been a welcome one. Lee sent Lafayette McLaws' three brigades to bolster Anderson's position around Chancellorsville.[45]

By 3:00 p.m. that afternoon, Hooker's brilliantly executed strategic envelopment seemed unstoppable. He had skillfully maneuvered two-thirds of his army into a position that promised to justify his boast, "May God have mercy on General Lee, for I will have none." Hooker, however, also had made two critical mistakes that soon would come back to haunt him. First, he had sent his powerful cavalry corps of 12,000 men on a distant ride to disrupt Lee's communications, leaving himself blind just at the time when he committed his second serious error. After crossing the Rappahannock River at Kelly's Ford on April 28-29 and moving southeast to a crossing of the Rapidan at Germanna and Ely's fords, Hooker headed for a concentration at an obscure crossroads in a heavily wooded region. He should have pressed on for a breakout into the open to bring to bear his overwhelming numbers to roll up Lee's left flank or crush whatever he faced when he emerged. Instead, for reasons unknown perhaps even to Joe Hooker, the Federal commander called a halt. Around Chancellorsville he set up a semi-circular line, with the XI Corps on the right, the XII Corps in the center, the V Corps on the left, and the II Corps in reserve, about 54,000 men altogether.

Hooker not only unilaterally cut the legs out from his own momentum, but he stopped his corps in the worst place possible—the middle of a seventy-square mile dense tangle of second-growth pine and oak. Laced with numerous small swampy streams cut by only a handful of roads and clearings, the "Wilderness" substantially negated his numerical superiority. In short, Hooker turned the initiative back to Lee, who gladly took it. Leaving Jubal Early's division and one brigade under William Barksdale (McLaws' division), perhaps 10,000 men all told, to confront Sedgwick at Fredericksburg, the Confederate commander made the daring decision to march the rest of Jackson's Second Corps west to join Anderson and McLaws and confront Hooker. Lee was breaking a cardinal rule of warfare by dividing his inferior numbers in the face of a larger enemy.[46]

On the eastern edge of the Wilderness, Anderson entrenched along a wooded ridge that extended from Tabernacle Church to Duerson's Mill. This excellent position commanded the two principal roads running through the Wilderness, the Orange Plank and the Old Turnpike, which came together at Chancellorsville before branching out again and reuniting midway to Fredericksburg. Anderson fought off a few cavalry probes by the time Jackson's corps set out to join him.[47]

In the midst of an all-night rain, Rodes got his brigades up around 2:00 a.m. on Friday morning, May 1. In compliance with orders, the men cooked two days' rations and put all excess baggage in the wagons for shipment to the rear. An hour later, an obligingly thick fog moved in to conceal Jackson's entire corps as it quietly pulled back from around Hamilton's Crossing and headed southwest on the Military Road. Rodes' division took the lead, his men in high spirits. Behind them trudged A. P. Hill, with Colston bringing up the rear.[48]

Ramseur's brigade marched at the head of the column, followed by Iverson, Doles, Colquitt, and O'Neal. Sensing an impending battle, the men maintained a brisk pace as they marched five-and-a-half miles before turning west onto the Orange Plank Road. Dawn was breaking as they filed into the road. A light breeze stirred, bringing with it the promise of a warm day and the

Lt. Gen. Thomas J.
"Stonewall" Jackson.

Generals in Gray

fresh scent of apple, peach, and cherry blossoms. After marching another two-and-a-half miles, the men heard gunfire erupt in the distance ahead to the right. The column halted and Rodes took the precaution of throwing out a line of skirmishers in the direction of the fire.[49]

Looking unusually resplendent this morning, having donned a new uniform recently given him by Jeb Stuart, Jackson rode ahead of the column and reached Anderson's position about 8:30 a.m. Taking advantage of the wide latitude granted him by Lee's instructions to "make arrangements to repulse the enemy," Stonewall ordered Anderson to stop entrenching and prepare to take the offensive. About 11:00 a.m. Anderson launched his advance down the Plank Road while McLaws set his division off down the Turnpike. Fifteen minutes later the two divisions smashed into a Federal line consisting of Slocum's corps and George Sykes' division of Meade's corps.[50]

The attack surprised the unsuspecting and overconfident Federals. Though stunned they did not break, and a bitter fight developed. The two sides fought a largely static affair for about three hours before Rodes received an order from Jackson to send up one brigade. Ramseur, being in the lead, stepped off about 2:30 p.m. Rodes' orders were to take the remainder of his division into the woods and deploy it in line of battle facing west between the two roads. New orders arrived thirty minutes later (roughly 3:00 p.m.) to move the division closer into a reserve position. Rodes carefully advanced his line a few hundred yards. Ramseur, meanwhile, went into the thick of it with Anderson and McLaws, and helped them drive back the Federals onto their main body. Around 6:30 p.m., however, the Southern attack petered out.[51]

Alhough the fighting was tactically indecisive that day, Jackson's steadfast confrontation shattered Hooker's vaunted confidence. Despite the arrival of the Federal III Corps, which increased Hooker's strength to roughly 73,000, "Fighting Joe" ordered his front withdrawn about two miles to the positions they had held the night before.[52]

Rodes kept his division in reserve until sunset, when he pulled it back onto the Plank Road and put it into bivouac in an opening on the John Alrich farm slightly more than one mile southeast of Chancellorsville. Ramseur's brigade remained on the front line through most of the night, where the men used for the first time the "sign" and "countersign" to identify each other—to the challenge "Liberty" came the response, "And Independence."[53]

"Remained all day in great expectancy from so-called 'Fighting Joe' Hooker, who succeeded Burnside," the Twelfth Alabama's Captain Park noted in his diary that night. Park and his comrades already had taken the measure of the Federal commander: "We feel he is no match for Rodes, Jackson, and Lee."[54]

*   *   *

Waking early, Rodes' first thoughts were of Hortense. "In the field, Early Saturday Morning, 2nd of May," was the headline of a quick note he penned to her. "My dearest wife. We had a little skirmishing yesterday in pressing the enemy back towards the Junction of the Rapidan & Rappahannock. We have the advantage so far and today we will whip them I believe if they fight us. We are very well," he concluded, "but hungry indeed, nothing to eat and all day ahead of us. Goodbye God bless you."[55]

Lee's daring decision to divide his army in the face of a superior foe had temporarily checked Hooker's flanking attempt. Still, he knew the enemy's overwhelming numbers could be brought to bear against his divided army. Somehow he had to maintain the initiative. But how? Hooker's left flank was snugly anchored on the Rappahannock River and his center strongly fortified. The status of his right flank, however, was unknown. As the night wore on, intelligence filtered into Lee's headquarters that, at first, must have seemed incredible. Had Hooker left himself vulnerable on that flank?

A reconnaissance conducted by Fitz Lee's cavalry revealed that the Federal right had not been bent back and secured against the Rappahannock, but was instead dangling somewhere in the angle formed by the Orange Plank Road and the Brock Road. Would it be possible to take advantage of this? The Reverend

Dr. B. T. Lacy, a chaplain in Jackson's Second Corps familiar with the country, together with local resident Charles Welford, assured Lee that troops could be conducted around Hooker's right via Wilderness Tavern. After a probe by Stuart confirmed this, Lee told cartographer Hotchkiss to mark out the route to the Orange Plank Road so the Southern infantry could strike the Federal flank.[56]

Jackson became so enthused with the idea that he proposed making the flank march with the entire Second Corps, leaving Lee with only about 14,000 men to face several times that many directly in his front. In practical effect, Lee once again would be splitting the Army of Northern Virginia in the face of the enemy, this time into three widely separated sections. The general approved the plan. He and Jackson had just conceived and agreed to implement one of the most daring plans of the war.

The specifics of the plan called for Rodes to take the head of the column, followed by Colston and A. P. Hill. This arrangement meant that Rodes, when the time came, would lead the attack. This honor derived at least in part from the tremendous confidence Jackson had in both Rodes and his men, but pure chance also played a major role; at the John Alrich farm, Rodes' division was the closest to the Furnace Road—the jump off point for the march.[57]

To prevent straggling during the march, Jackson directed that colonels with a guard of strong men with fixed bayonets bring up the rear of each regiment. He ordered that all baggage and commissary wagons remain behind. Because of the extremely narrow roads, he wanted the ammunition wagons, ambulances, and artillery to follow behind their respective divisions, which meant that Thomas Carter's artillery battalion of twenty guns would follow Rodes. Fitz Lee's cavalry, under Stuart, would screen the right flank of the march with the First and Fifth Virginia Cavalry and part of the Third Virginia Cavalry, and the head of the column with the Second Virginia Cavalry. In order to maintain secrecy, Jackson forbade advance scouting. If the Federals were other than where they were expected to be, the plan would be changed accordingly. Once formed, Jackson's column of 28,000 men (seventy regiments of infantry, four regiments of cavalry, and twenty-one batteries with eighty guns) stretched nearly ten miles. He faced a prodigious challenge in moving the whole roughly twelve miles along wilderness paths, deploying, and attacking—all before sundown and without alerting the enemy.[58]

After a cool damp night, Saturday dawn broke shortly after 5:00 a.m, by which time Rodes had his shivering men up trying to warm themselves with coffee. Because of the occasional shell thrown over by the Federals, few had enjoyed a good rest, particularly among Ramseur's brigade, which remained near the front line most of the night. Being seasoned veterans, the men realized something big was in the offing, especially when unusual orders came down from Jackson through Rodes. While on the march, they were instructed, they were to move briskly, carry only what was necessary, and make as little noise as possible.[59]

The Second Virginia Cavalry took the column's point, where it followed two guides: a renowned local hunter named Jack Hayden and local resident Charles Welford, the same man who had assured Lee of the feasibility of the whole undertaking. Behind them Rodes quickly and efficiently set up his portion of the column, putting Colquitt's Georgia brigade at the head, with the acclaimed division sharpshooters at the point, and Ramseur's tired men in the rear. Rodes' lean veterans stepped off in high spirits.[60]

Noted Chancellorsville historian John Bigelow asserted that Rodes began the march about 5:30 a.m. Rodes reported the time as "about 8 o'clock," which surely is in error. The column probably started moving around 6:30 a.m. Most sources agree that half an hour later, Rodes' men, after marching along the Plank Road for about one-half mile from the John Alrich farm, turned left and headed southwest on the Catherine Furnace (also known as Welford's) Road, at the intersection of which they saw Lee and Jackson conferring.[61]

It did not take long after that for Rodes to find trouble. A short march on the Furnace Road brought the head of his column at 8:00 a.m. to a clearing caused by Lewis' Creek (also called Scott's Run). The clearing was near Catherine Furnace, a former iron-smelting operation for the area's now played-out iron mines. Because the virgin timber had been used up many years ago to fire the furnaces, the area now was choked with a dense second growth that limited visibility in nearly every direction. According to Rodes, higher ground about one mile north of their position was visible from the clearing. As he subsequently learned, this piece of terrain was known as Hazel Grove and it was a perfect platform for artillery. Sure enough, not long after the column entered the clearing artillery shells from two guns unlimbered there began dropping close to the marching men. Rodes called for the double-quick. Jackson ordered him to post a regiment north of the clearing, and Rodes dispatched the Twenty-third Georgia of Colquitt's brigade.[62]

The artillery fire was significant because it meant the enemy had spotted Jackson's column. News of the movement slowly made its way up the chain of command to Hooker, but the southwest direction of the march led him to believe that the Confederates were executing a withdrawal. The Federal commander did, however, send a warning to O. O. Howard, whose XI Corps held the far right of the army, to be watchful for a possible flank march. He also authorized Slocum to advance a force from Hazel Grove into the Lewis Creek clearing. Howard turned two regiments and a pair of guns to the west. Beyond that, however, neither "Fighting Joe" nor Oliver Howard did anything substantial, despite other warnings that something was amiss, to impede or prepare for a Confederate flanking effort.

Later in the afternoon, David Birney's division of Slocum's XII Corps overran the Twenty-third Georgia, capturing some 300 men in the process. The regiment's colonel, Emory Best, escaped by running off with about forty others after the regiment retreated into a railroad cut. The dereliction would earn Best a court-martial and a one-way ticket out of the service. The colonel's poor judgment notwithstanding, the small tactical victory did not endanger the marching column. By the time the Georgians were scampering to safety, Lee was sending over from Anderson's division the brigades of Carnot Posey and Ambrose R. Wright, together with some artillery. The reinforcements not only saved the trains but prompted Slocum to call for help from Howard, who sent up the XI Corps reserve, a brigade under Francis Barlow. The decision, which seemed justified, further weakened Hooker's imperiled right flank.[63]

Rodes, meanwhile, continued the march unhindered. At noon he gave the men a twenty-minute rest, one of perhaps three such breaks authorized by Jackson, who did not want the troops worn out for the coming fight. A soldier in the Third Alabama who identified himself as "Willie" in a letter to a home newspaper, however, stated that he marched "from daylight Saturday until 2 1/2 oclock without a single halt for rest. Men fell by the roadside exhausted from hunger and fatigue." After another mile on the Furnace Road, the column turned left onto the Brock Road and marched about a third of a mile south around a small clearing. Rodes turned the head of the column again, this time west off the Brock Road onto a little-known dirt trail called the Brook Road.[64] Jackson still did not know the precise location of the enemy's right flank. He assumed it might be near the Carpenter farm, where Fitz Lee's cavalry skirmished with Federal infantry the day before. If so, the Brock Road heading north would bring the column within about 1,000 yards of the farm, too close to the enemy for comfort. To prevent that, Jackson authorized the detour, pointed out by the guide Charles Welford, which swung west of the Brock Road and then parallel to it heading north. After going beyond the Carpenter farm, the column swung back onto the Brock Road.[65]

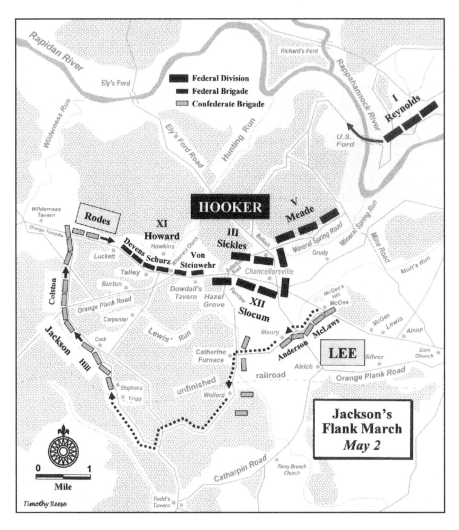

Jackson's Flank March May 2

Timothy Reese

"Road" seemed an inappropriate term for what was little more than a winding footpath barely wide enough in the dense spring undergrowth to accommodate a wagon. Some places became so tight that the men, marching only four abreast, found it difficult to shift a musket from one shoulder to another, and occasionally they fell out to remove stumps or clear brush.[66]

Hours passed as the men tramped on. Maintaining "route step" to save energy, the head of the column averaged about two-and-a-half miles per hour, while the rear managed about one-and-a-half miles per hour. "Strict silence was enforced, the men being allowed to speak only in whispers," remembered Captain V. E. Turner of the Twenty-third North Carolina, Iverson's brigade.

"Occasionally a courier would spur his tired horse past us as we twisted through the brush. For hours at a time we neither saw nor heard anything. Great was the curiosity to know where we were going and what 'Old Jack' was about."[67]

Eventually, heat, thirst, and exhaustion set in and struck down many. "I suffered exceedingly," remembered Captain William Calder of the Second North Carolina. "I was several times on the point of giving out, but persevered, and succeeded in keeping up."[68] Lieutenant William Reese of the Jeff Davis Artillery, which rolled behind Rodes' division, felt much the same way. "Never shall I forget that march," he declared. "The day was oppressively hot and many fell on the roadside from exhaustion. . . . [T]hey rushed forward throwing away blankets, knapsacks everything but their guns and ammunition. I blessed my stars that I had a horse to ride." Reese rode past "hundreds on the roadside perfectly unconscious and poured water on the faces of many who never knew where they received assistance. Many must have died from sun stroke."[69]

John McClendon of the Fourteenth North Carolina, part of Ramseur's brigade, recalled that when a comrade collapsed, his friends dragged him into the shade of some bushes, tried to cool him by removing his shirt, then moved on, "leaving him to die."[70] Many others confirmed McClendon's memory of the hardships endured along the flanking march. "Many fell out of ranks exhausted," reported Colonel Z. T. Zachary of the Twenty-seventh Georgia, Colquitt's brigade, "some fainting and having spasms; only a few had eaten anything since the morning before."[71] According to Captain F. M. Bonham of the Third Alabama, "many men fainted and fell by the roadside." After the war Bonham's comrade in the Third, Captain W. H. May, said what many others must have believed: "It was the most terrible march we made."[72]

In the heavy uniform of a brigadier general, Rodes became soaked with sweat and laden with fatigue. He registered no complaints, however, when about midway through that "terrible march" Jackson, Colston, and the Second Virginia Cavalry's Colonel Thomas Munford joined him at the head of the column. In the course of their ensuing discussion, someone remarked that all four men had been associated with VMI. This in turn led them to bring up the names of others in the column who also had been connected with the institute. They thought of Stapleton Crutchfield, the Second Corps' chief of artillery; Henry Whiting, Rodes' AAG and Munford's classmate; Brigadier General Jim Lane of the Class of 1854; Lindsay Walker, A. P. Hill's chief of artillery and an 1845 graduate. Perhaps a dozen other field officers also made the list. "The Institute will be heard from today," boasted Jackson. Munford saw this pleasant conversation as a reflection of the corps commander's general satisfaction with the progress of the march thus far.

Inevitably, Jackson returned the conversation to military matters. "I hear it is said," he remarked in his quiet voice, "that General Hooker had more men than he can handle. I should like to have half as many more as I have today, and I should hurl him in the river! The trouble with us had always been to have a reserve to throw in at the critical moment to reap the benefit of advantages gained. We have always had to put in all our troops," continued Stonewall, "and never had enough at the time most needed."[73]

About 2:00 p.m., the head of the column reached the Orange Plank Road. It was from that point Jackson intended to launch the attack against Hooker's exposed flank, reported to be about two miles to the east. Before Stonewall could deploy his men, however, Fitz Lee rode up with a critically important report: his reconnaissance revealed that an attack from that point would sweep across the enemy's front, not roll up his flank. Much greater advantage could be gained, explained Lee, by launching it from the Old Turnpike, another one-and-a-half miles farther north.

If Lee's report was accurate, an attack down the Orange Plank Road would prove disastrous. But to add another mile-and-a-half to the march also was risky. The rear of the column, which included the brigades of James Archer and Edward Thomas of Hill's division, was just clearing Catherine Furnace a full six miles back, and darkness was only about four hours away. Nevertheless, the column halted and Rodes waited while Jackson rode with Lee to the Old Turnpike. Gazing with binoculars at the relaxed and unsuspecting Federal soldiers in their camps two miles distant, Jackson concurred with Lee's assessment. After a short, silent prayer, he turned to a courier. "Tell General Rodes to move across the plank road and halt when he gets to the old turnpike," he ordered. "I will join him there."[74]

Upon receiving these instructions Rodes put the men in motion and pushed rapidly up the Brock Road to the pike. About 2:30 p.m. he met Jackson, who told him to move his division onto the pike and deploy it about one mile farther on. From the Brock Road, Rodes dutifully turned the column right at about a thirty-five degree angle and entered the turnpike just east of Wilderness Tavern. He led his men about a mile east to the vicinity of the John Luckett farm, about two-and-a-half miles west of Chancellorsville. For the men in his division, the eight-hour, twelve-mile march was finally over. They were now only about six direct miles from that morning's starting point.[75]

Not yet finished with taking risks, Jackson called for a division-wide front. He knew this would require precious time to establish, and during the attack it would be very difficult to control such a wide front in these tangled woods. But a wide line increased the chances of sweeping past Hooker's flank, and it reduced the possibility of being enveloped.

Rodes quickly brought up his brigades and quietly sent them north and south of the pike on the reverse slope of a long, low ridge that marked a watershed between the Rapidan-Rappahannock and the Mattapony-York rivers. Since the clearing around the Luckett farm was only about 400 yards wide, north to south, most of the deployment took place in thick forest.[76]

Under orders transmitted in low voice, the men silently took up their positions. No bugle sounded and no man cheered his general. To the immediate left of the road Rodes put O'Neal, beyond whom he sent Iverson, who detached the Twenty-third North Carolina to protect the left by marching in column. To the right of the road Rodes put the brigades of Doles and Colquitt. Instead of extending the line farther beyond Colquitt's right, Rodes placed Ramseur 200 yards behind him in order to avoid clashing with Frank Paxton's Stonewall Brigade, which had been sent by Jackson down the Orange Plank Road as protection for the right. For added security on that flank, Rodes extended Ramseur the length of one regiment beyond Colquitt's right. For a skirmish line, Rodes used his sharpshooters under Major Blackford, placing them 400 yards in front of the division, where they quietly laid down within sight of the enemy.

Rodes completed his deployment in about an hour, his line set around 4:00 p.m. With some 8,500 men in double rank (each regiment in two lines), his front extended one-and-a-half miles, three-fourths of a mile on either side of the pike. Jackson and Rodes had turned the dream of every military commander into reality: they had concentrated a large force on the flank of an unsuspecting enemy.[77]

While other troops arrived and deployed behind them, Rodes' men quietly bided their time. "Tired, breathless, but buoyant," wrote Captain V. E. Turner of the Twenty-third North Carolina, "we lay down in the woods near the unwary foe and waited till ordered to attack."[78] Captain W. H. May of the Third Alabama recalled the exhaustion most men felt when he stated simply, "In our wearied condition, most of us fell asleep in a few minutes." Over in the Fourth Georgia of Doles' brigade, Private Camp, "a good old man and Methodist preacher," led many men in quiet prayer.[79]

While Rodes arranged, Jackson oversaw, issuing his final instructions before the attack was to begin. About one mile to the east, the forest in front of Rodes gave way to a large clearing. On the western fringe of that clearing stood the Talley house, to the north lay the Hawkins farm, and on the eastern edge, in the triangle formed by the intersection of the Turnpike and the Plank Road, stood a place called Dowdall's Tavern. The latter place served as Howard's XI Corps headquarters. The advance toward this clearing would begin, decreed Jackson, with the sounding of a single bugle, whose call then would be picked up by others along the line. The whole line would push rapidly forward and "at all hazards" take the enemy's first position on the high ground at the Talley house, which commanded the second position about one-half mile beyond at Dowdall's Tavern. If Rodes encountered stiff resistance at the tavern, Jackson ordered, he was to seek shelter until the artillery came up to beat it down. Four sections of Stuart's horse artillery, lined up one behind the other on the pike, would advance with the division. Since the pike could accommodate only two cannons abreast, Carter's battalion of artillery parked in a clearing by the road, and would advance once the attack began. Under no circumstances was there to be any pause in the advance, insisted Jackson. If any of Rodes' brigades ran into trouble, they could send back for one of Colston's without going through the division commanders.[80]

After absorbing every word of Jackson's orders, and then studying the ground ahead, Rodes gave each of his brigade commanders "positive instructions, which were well understood." Doles' and O'Neal's brigades, aligned in the center, would anchor the front and spearhead the attack. Rodes depended on them to guide on the road in leading the way to the Yankee positions. "If any brigades can go there," he told Doles in a final vote of confidence, "yours and mine [O'Neal's] can." Rodes crossed to the left of the road. "He gave this his Brigade the post of honor," a private in the Third Alabama later proudly wrote to a home newspaper, "and made the Third Alabama the directing Regiment of the Division." When he rode upon Captain M. Ford Bonham, who was in temporary command of the Third Alabama (Cullen Battle having been injured near Fredericksburg when his horse fell on him), Rodes drew in his mount. "Captain Bonham," he said quietly, "one mile from this place, on a hill in a large field stands a white house; I want possession of it. I want my artillery planted on that hill. If you should meet any obstacle, sweep it before you."[81]

Around that white house stood Howard's XI Corps (minus Barlow's brigade sent earlier to aid Slocum) of about 11,500 men in twenty regiments of infantry and six batteries. Many of the men in these units were German-born immigrants. They served with John Fremont during Jackson's Valley Campaign, then fought in the disaster of Second Bull Run as part of the I Corps in John Pope's Army of Virginia. They held the defenses of Washington during the Antietam campaign, after which they became part of the XI Corps in the Army of the Potomac. Their lack of unqualified success thus far on the battlefield, coupled with their foreign birth, gave cause for much distrust among their fellow English-speaking soldiers. Thirty-three-year-old Oliver Otis Howard, who had lost his right arm at Seven Pines, had assumed command of the corps just one month earlier on April 2. Now, his men were lined up along the pike facing south, with Jackson's Second Corps forming on their right flank. Adolph von Steinwehr's division held the left near Howard's headquarters at Dowdall's, while Carl Schurz's division occupied the center of the line. Charles Deven's division was deployed to the right of Schurz. Per Howard's instructions, Deven had turned two regiments of Leopold Von Gilsa's brigade to face west—in the direction from which the storm was about to unfold.[82]

Around 5:00 p.m. Colston finished lining up his brigades to the left of Ramseur, about 200 yards behind Rodes' front line. A. P. Hill went to work spreading out his men behind Colston. The time to advance was close at hand. Tense and excited, Rodes, Blackford, and a bugler rode over to Jackson for his orders. They found him surrounded by a cluster of staff. All eyes now fixed upon the indomitable Stonewall. "I do not believe the most beautiful woman in the Confederacy could have diverted them from him," one of those officers later declared. Jackson's aide, Captain James Power Smith, left a vivid recollection of the momentous meeting: "Upon his stout-built, long-paced sorrel, Jackson sat, with visor low over his eyes, and lips compressed, and with his watch in his hand. Upon his right sat Robert E. Rodes, the very picture of a soldier, and every inch all that he appeared. Upon his right sat Major Blackford."

Jackson looked at his watch. It read 5:15 p.m., some one-and-a-half hours before the sun set at 6:48 p.m. "Are you ready, General Rodes?"

"Yes, sir."

Without changing his tone, Jackson gave the word, "You may go forward then." Rodes turned his penetrating blue eyes in Blackford's direction and nodded. Blackford relayed the signal to a bugler (possibly Rail Grayson of the Fifth Alabama), whose shrill tune then rang out, quickly followed by others up and down the line.[83] Thousands of men, their voices silent for so long, let out a tremendous shout and rushed forward. "We started as if by magic," wrote a soldier in the Third Alabama, "with yells like so many Indians."[84]

A problem arose almost immediately. Somehow, Blackford's skirmishers in front of O'Neal's brigade did not get the signal to advance, nor did they realize the attack was underway until the main line came slamming into their backs. Rodes spotted the confusion and sent up orders for the skirmishers to get going. The mess quickly sorted itself out and the advance went ahead in full force.[85]

To Rodes, it must have seemed like Seven Pines all over on a larger scale: his men were rushing headlong through dense growth, the thickets ripping and shredding their clothes, with the enemy in strength somewhere up ahead. Unlike Seven Pines, however, his men were moving against an exposed flank in massive force, and with the element of complete surprise on their side.

To the Yankees in their quiet camps, the first warning that something was badly awry arrived when wild animals began fleeing toward them in an effort to escape the thousands of rushing boots and shoes of Rodes' onrushing horde. "Like a cloud of dust driven before a coming shower," General Howard of the XI Corps later wrote, "the first lively effects of the steady Confederate advance appeared in the startled rabbits, squirrels, quail, and other game flying wildly hither and thither in evident terror, and escaping, where possible, into adjacent clearings."[86] Soon enough, Northern soldiers joined with the animals in the mad dash for safety. "The officers had hardly time to give a command," reported Carl Schurz, commander of the 3rd Division, "when almost the whole of General [Nathaniel C.] McLean's brigade, mixed up with a number of Colonel von Gilsa's men, came rushing down the road from General Deven's headquarters in wild confusion."[87]

"Charge, Alabamians, charge!" Rodes called out while riding directly behind the colors of the Third Alabama. The regiment quickly overran a six-pounder cannon before it could fire its deadly load of canister, with one of the Alabamians crushing the skull of an unfortunate gunner who remained too long at his post.[88]

On the left, Alfred Iverson's infantry halted to deliver a powerful volley that one private believed would "last them until peace is made." Another private of the Twentieth North Carolina characterized the ensuing chaos as "a running fight." From the woods "we emerged charging with a yell over their cooking detail routing their rear line which retreated with firing only a few shots at us, a great many of them not taking their guns which were stacked." One private in the Twenty-third North Carolina reached back and plucked a

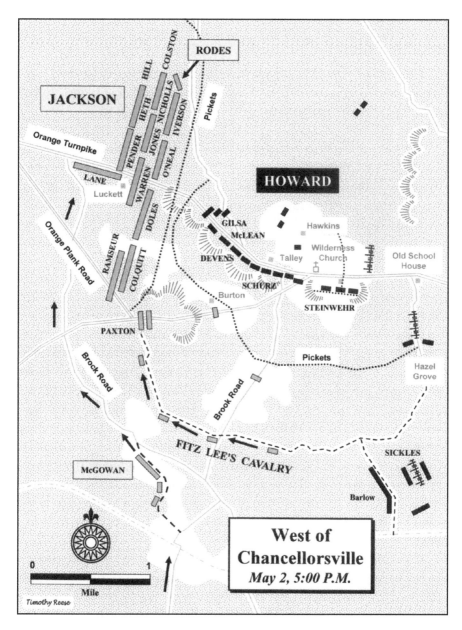

West of
Chancellorsville
May 2, 5:00 P.M.

memory for comparative purposes. The attack, he wrote, looked like "the second edition of the Bull Run races—I tell you we carried them two miles and a half at 2.40 speed, and would I believe have completely routed the whole army if we had made the attack three hours earlier." Presently, the Twenty-third came upon a cannon dangling in a tree, which apparently so objected to being run over that it snapped back, breaking the gun from its caisson and hanging it up in the branches.[89]

The air filled with noise and smoke as the Federal flight turned into a panic that became so severe one of Hooker's staff officers, Colonel Joseph Dickinson, allegedly implored Howard to fire on his own men to stop the stampede.[90]

The surprise was so overwhelming, and Rodes' pursuit so driven, that when two of his staff officers jumped down from their mounts to drink some abandoned Yankee coffee, they found the brew still too hot to handle. Other men, rushing through abandoned camps strewn with arms, accoutrements, clothing, caissons, and food, scooped up what "crackers" they could without breaking their momentum and pressed forward, eating, shouting, and firing at the same time.[91]

Iverson's brigade, together with Edward O'Neal's leftmost regiments, looped around succeeding Federal positions, enveloping them while Doles' Georgians hit them head-on. With the Fourth Georgia guiding on the pike and the Forty-fourth Georgia to its right, Doles smashed into two New York regiments, about 1,400 men of Von Gilsa's brigade, facing south. The unfortunate Germans had no time to respond; most simply ran away. Doles overran two guns after they had each fired but a single round down the road. North of the pike, the two Federal regiments Howard had turned to face west tried to put up a fight but broke when hit by O'Neal's right regiments and the Twenty-first Georgia, sent over by Doles to bolster that sector of the attack. With that regiment swinging left and the Twelfth Georgia going right, Doles enveloped one position after another. After sweeping up five more guns, the Georgians became the first of Rodes' men to break out into the open at the Talley house, easily securing Jackson's first objective in perhaps forty-five minutes.[92]

Rodes probably spent most of that time on or near the road, moving forward in the middle of the division, though there is some evidence he took the opportunity to range up and down the line to encourage his men. Now at the Talley house, he wasted no time. Without waiting for reports to come in, he took a risky ride up the pike to have a look at the second objective—Dowdall's Tavern, just one-half mile beyond. To his dismay, he saw through his binoculars an estimated 3,000–5,000 enemy soldiers. He did not know it at the time, but the force was a brigade from von Steinwehr's untouched division forming around the Hawkins farm. It was imperative that Rodes continue driving forward. Instead of wasting precious time trying to straighten his division, which was severely disrupted by the woods and pockets of enemy resistance, Rodes sent back to Colston for help (though Rodes made no mention of this appeal in his battle report). Within moments, Edward T. H. Warren's 2,125-man brigade (formerly Colston's, who was now leading a division) came up from behind Doles, John R. Jones's 1,800-man brigade moved up from behind O'Neal, and the rush continued toward Dowdall's. "Once more," Rodes proudly reported, "my gallant troops dashed at them with a wild shout, and, firing a hasty volley, they continued their headlong flight to Chancellorsville." About 6:30 p.m. Rodes' troops overran the second objective at Dowdall's Tavern.[93]

Because of a serious problem on the far right, however, not all of Rodes' regiments reached the tavern at this time. After advancing only a few hundred yards, Alfred Colquitt allowed a few Federal cavalry to spook him into thinking the enemy had swept around his flank. Despite knowing that Stuart or Paxton would have warned him if that were so, Colquitt defied orders from both Jackson and Rodes and committed a grave tactical error when he suspended the advance. The mistake compounded itself when Ramseur's brigade came up behind and partially intermixed with Colquitt's stationary lines, a situation that in turn prevented Frank Paxton's brigade (The Stonewall Brigade) from marching up the Orange Plank Road and cutting off the Federal escape route east of the Talley house. Colquitt's blunder removed more than 5,000 men out of the fight. These three brigades plus Archer's and Thomas' that lagged behind at the end of the column deprived Jackson of one-third of the fifteen brigades he set out with that morning. Moving over more open ground than the terrain confronting Rodes' other brigades, Colquitt probably could have cut off a large part of Daniel Sickles' force, in reserve behind Slocum. His position would have allowed him to rather effortlessly seize both Hazel Grove and Fairview, high ground that cost many lives to capture the following day. Indeed, the twenty-two Federal guns firing from Hazel Grove eventually stopped Doles' advance.[94]

Stephen Ramseur, who was even more aggressive than Rodes, was furious with the delay. When he found Colquitt, Ramseur forcefully pointed out that since the sound of heavy firing was coming from up ahead on the *left*, the advance must continue at once. Colquitt finally saw the light and the two brigades moved forward again, though they did not catch up to Rodes' line until the thickets were blanketed in darkness, around 7:15 p.m.[95]

By that time Rodes' other three brigades had lost nearly all cohesion, the thick woods and the varying levels of resistance having disrupted and broken up the line while gradually compressing it to the width of one-half mile. B. B. Carr of the Twentieth North Carolina, Iverson's brigade, described his segment as "a disorganized rabble, every one his own commander doing as pleased him but going forward all the time." Moreover, Colston's men had merged with Rodes', and the two division commands "mingled together in inextricable confusion." The men, increasingly beaten down with fatigue, found themselves bunched into clusters and knots, scattered here and there. According to Iverson, "no officer [was] able to tell what men he commanded." Private Sam Pickens clearly understood the situation. "Great pity theres so much confusion & men get scattered so badly," he lamented to his diary. "Several times men were stopped from firing into friends & I recollect joining in & screaming to them not to do it." Pickens added, "we went on till near dark when so exhausted we sat down in pines."[96]

Encouraged by the ease with which his men took the Yankee (Slocum's) log works at the tavern, Rodes tried desperately to maintain the momentum of the attack. The descending darkness, however, only added to the confusion. Word also arrived that ammunition was running low. (Doles later reported that his men at this time were "entirely out" of ammunition, and that it was "impossible to get ammunition to them.") Rodes realized the attack had spent itself. He sent a message to Jackson, asking for permission to pull back and reorganize while allowing A. P. Hill's division to come up and take over the front. Jackson reluctantly agreed, but with the added intention of having Hill continue the attack in the dark.[97]

At 7:15 p.m., roughly two hours after the attack began, Rodes sent out word for his men to halt. Stopping them was not that easy. When Colonel Samuel B. Pickens ordered his Twelfth Alabama to halt, only thirty men heeded his call; the rest were scattered in the darkness, many still moving forward. Pickens went after them and rounded up as many as he could, only to discover later that he had brought in men from several different regiments.[98] When a private in the Forty-fourth Georgia finally stopped, he recognized only one of the men around him. It took two hours to find his regiment. According to Sam Pickens of the Fifth Alabama (cousin to the colonel of the Twelfth Alabama) "Men from various regts. of different states were calling the name of [their] Regt. trying to get together. Never saw such confusion & scattering."[99]

Some writers have criticized Rodes for wanting to halt the attack, one declaring that "he was not gifted with the vision of his commander." The one critic who really mattered, to Rodes anyway, was his commander. Stonewall Jackson, one of the army's toughest taskmasters, offered nothing but the highest praise for the brigadier's conduct on this day.[100]

Having issued orders to halt, Rodes feared that the enemy might now try to take advantage of the lull and pull back. Riding out in the darkness about 8:00 p.m. on the same type of dangerous mission that would end so disastrously for Jackson a short time later, Rodes ventured down the Plank Road beyond his own lines in search of the enemy's position. After what must have been a harrowing experience, he returned to tell Jackson's artillery chief, Stapleton Crutchfield, that he could not find any evidence of an enemy line between his troops and the heights at Fairview, distant about 1,200 yards. Rodes missed the massive Federal buildup taking place just beyond the heights. Evidently to corroborate this claim, Crutchfield put three guns in the road and opened fire on the higher ground. The blasts brought in a devastating return fire that compelled James Lane to stop deploying his brigade, the first of A. P. Hill's division to come up. Hill angrily ordered Crutchfield to stop, and the Federals followed suit. About 8:45 p.m. Lane at last put out a line of skirmishers on either side of the Plank Road, and Rodes completed the withdrawal of his own men.[101]

Though the needless artillery duel delayed Hill's deployment, Jackson remained determined to resume the attack that night. He wanted his left flank to drive deep into Hooker's rear and his right flank to link up with Lee's body to the east. "Press them," he told A. P. Hill as he came up. "Cut them off from United States Ford. Press them!"[102]

Jackson intended Rodes and Colston, once they had reformed, to follow Hill in reserve. "Find Gen. Rodes," the corps commander instructed Captain J. G. Morrison, "and tell him to press forward, but to throw a line of skirmishers from his right perpendicularly to the rear and have them advance with the line and in sight of each other." Another version had Jackson instructing Major Norvell Cobb to "Find General Rodes and tell him to occupy the barricade at once!"[103] What was not in doubt was that Jackson expected aggressive action as soon as possible.

Rodes worked to bring in his men and put them to the right of the Stonewall Brigade, behind the abandoned Yankee barricades in the open ground around Dowdall's Tavern. Moving in the dark with the enemy so near, however, made the men so nervous and jittery that at one point many began firing wildly into the night. Moving down the line, Rodes offered a calming reassurance that quickly restored order. But when a few Federal guns boomed out, presumably from Fairview, it proved too much for some, who broke and ran back down the Plank Road into the darkness. Again Rodes acted swiftly, sending squads to block the road while he rode out once more to calm his jittery soldiers.[104]

As the seemingly tireless division commander went among his men time and again that night, he unknowingly created a deep and lasting impression on many who saw him. "General Rodes, though a martinet in discipline," the Fifty-third North Carolina's Sergeant Major Hampden Osborne recalled many years later,

> was always just and kind. We, his men, had absolute faith in him always. . . . None of those men can ever forget the confidence of victory Rodes would inspire when on many an anxious night, lying in line of battle, the men recognized their commander's presence by the faint but well-known sounds—the tinkling of Rodes' spurs—as with but a single orderly he rode along his entire front; for, like great Caesar in Gaul, every trench and every bastion received this faithful officer's personal inspection.[105]

Rodes' inspections were ever mindful of the incalculable value of morale. During his rides, the division leader made a point of offering his men encouragement and praise. "Rhodes [sic] complimented the Regt.," a soldier in the Third Alabama proudly remembered.[106]

Incredibly, others in the Third had not yet had enough fighting. Captain W. H. May came to Rodes with an astonishing plan to take fifty already secured volunteers out into the darkness with bowie knives to silently slit the throats of the Yankee pickets. Instead of humiliating May and his volunteers by flatly rejecting the outrageous plan, Rodes professed interest.

"Then what do you estimate their strength [of the Federals on picket in their immediate front]?" he asked the captain.

"A regiment," replied May.

Rodes moved in to let May off the hook. "Well, sir, you are greatly mistaken, they have a brigade."

Whether or not Rodes knew this was irrelevant, for it put an end to the wild scheme. May actually felt relieved. "A narrow escape, Tom!" he told his co-planner Captain Bilbro as the two walked back to camp.[107]

Meanwhile, Rodes realigned O'Neal's brigade, keeping its right on the road. He brought up Ramseur and squeezed him between O'Neal and Doles. Per orders, about 9:00 p.m. he sent Colquitt to guard a road coming in from the direction of Catherine Furnace to the south. The men of Iverson's brigade still were arriving.

Presently, along came Jackson. Rodes met him for the last time in front of an old school house near a trail that came in from Hazel Grove. "General Jackson," he called out impulsively, high levels of adrenaline obviously still coursing through his body. "My division behaved splendidly this evening and you must give them a big name in your report." The words likely pleased Old Jack. Though eager to continue the attack, he knew that it could not have gone this far without the aggressive determination of Rodes and his troops. "I shall take great pleasure in doing so," he replied, "and congratulate you and your command for it." The corps commander allegedly declared that he had never seen the enemy driven so far, so fast and in so short a time. Jackson and his staff left Rodes and rode east toward the front, disappearing in the darkness down the Plank Road.[108]

A short time later, Captain James Smith, a member of Jackson's staff who had remained behind as a liaison with the artillery and cavalry, came upon Rodes and asked him where the corps commander might be found. "General Jackson is just ahead on the road, Captain," said Rodes. "Tell him I will be here at this cabin [presumably the old school house] if I am wanted." The captain set off in search of his chief, but after going about 100 yards he drew rein at the startling sound of rifle fire just ahead.[109]

Colonel Bryan Grimes heard the fire, too, and ventured out beyond his line to learn its cause. Presently he came upon a group of men, including litter bearers carrying a wounded officer. They told Grimes that the injured man was a Lieutenant Sumter. The truth, however, reached Rodes sometime before 10:00 p.m.—it was General Jackson who lay critically injured on that litter, accidentally wounded about 9:30 p.m. by his own men. A.P. Hill, the corps senior division leader, would assume command. Rodes sent the stunning news on to his officers, adding that he "thought it advisable that it should be concealed from the troops, for fear of disheartening them, in view of the serious work ahead of us in the morning."[110]

Rodes' precautions, however, could not hold back the truth. "Attempts to keep the news from the men was unavailing," a Third Alabama private declared in a letter written after the battle. "[I]t soon spread like wildfire and cast a great gloom over the whole army. Strange to say, the effect was different from what was feared. With this great calamity staring them in the face, the idea of defeat in the end never once entered their heads, but seemed rather to inspire them with a determination to win the battle."[111]

*   *   *

Jackson's flank march and the attack led by Rodes was one of the most brilliantly conceived and executed in the annals of military history. It had not been, however, a complete success. The blow blew apart Howard's XI Corps and staggered Hooker, but the attack was not fatal to the Army of the Potomac's prospects by any means. The assault pushed back the XI Corps nearly two miles and peeled away roughly one-quarter of its strength, but the Federals managed to shoot down about 1,000 Confederates in the process, belying the notion that few Yankees made an effort to stand and fight back that day. When the attack drew to a disorganized halt, Jackson's Second Corps still was widely separated from General Lee. Given the long march and exceedingly difficult assignment, the Second Corps did all it could have on May 2. A number of factors—darkness, confusion and exhaustion among the men, the Federal artillery at Fairview and Hazel Grove, the presence of the unused V Corps and just-arrived I Corps—stood in the way of Jackson's plan for a successful night attack.[112]

Shortly after Jackson was carried away, another freakish occurrence compounded the disaster of Jackson's wounding: Federal shell fragments found their way into both lower legs of A. P. Hill. That left the Second Corps with neither a commander nor a major general. Because of its current detachment from the main (though smaller) body of the army operating under Lee, it could not readily be supplied with another high-ranking officer. This meant that, for the moment, command of the corps devolved upon its senior brigadier, Robert Rodes.

This sudden and certainly unexpected development stunned Rodes, yet he acted decisively. "Without loss of time," he subsequently reported, he turned his division over to Ramseur and established a makeshift corps headquarters. He also set up a meeting with Colston and Henry Heth, who now commanded Hill's division, to discuss the proper course of action. The triumvirate agreed to renew the attack in the morning at first light, "it being agreed that the troops were not in a condition to resume operations that night," explained Rodes. Moreover, despite lessons learned that day regarding the confusion that goes with attacking on a division-wide front through dense forest, Rodes wisely decided against shortening the line because he knew the arrangements would take most of the night and leave the men exhausted by morning.[113]

Rodes' tenure as commander of the Second Corps, however, was short lived. Barely two hours later, Jackson's chief of staff, Sandie Pendleton, and the wounded A. P. Hill evidently concluded that the responsibility was too great for a brigadier. They sent for cavalry leader Jeb Stuart, who was four to five miles away at Ely's Ford. Around midnight the cavalryman arrived at Rodes' field headquarters and assumed command of the Second Corps.

Though Stuart held the higher rank, army regulations made no provision for turning over an infantry corps to a cavalry officer. Without receiving official authorization for a transfer of command, Rodes technically did not have to step aside, but he did so without protest. To make sure he received proper credit for the nobility of the act, however, he included in his report a complete explanation:

> I deem it proper to state that I yielded the command to General Stuart not because I thought him entitled to it, belonging as he does to a different arm of the service, nor because I was unwilling to assume the responsibility of carrying on the attack, as I had already made the necessary arrangements, and they remained unchanged, but because, from the manner in which I had been informed that he had been sent for, I inferred that General Jackson or General Hill had instructed Major Pendleton to place him in command, and for the still stronger reason that I feared that the information that the command had devolved on me, unknown except to my own immediate troops, would, in their shaken condition, be likely to increase the demoralization of the corps. General Stuart's name was well and favorably known to the army, and would tend, I hoped, to reestablish confidence. I yielded because I was satisfied the good of the service demanded it.[114]

The statement produced the desired effect. "The history of war," wrote Major H. B. McClellan of Stuart's staff, who witnessed the transfer of command, "does not afford a more striking instance of magnanimous and patriotic self-sacrifice. . . . [Rodes] yielded the opportunity for personal distinction when he believed that the interests of his country so required . . . ."[115]

Others among the favorably impressed included Rodes' friend and staff officer, thirty-seven-year-old Captain Green Peyton, a pre-war engineer who had served with Rodes since before Seven Pines. "On this occasion," Peyton wrote after the war,

> Rodes exhibited conspicuously that noble spirit which ever actuated him during life. The 2d Corps had just gained a splendid victory, largely attributed to the good conduct of himself and his command. He was looking forward to a no less glorious morrow, when all the fruits of

success would be gathered, to be laid by him at the feet of General Lee, as some compensation for the irreparable loss he had sustained. The ambitions of this young general was sorely tempted. The command was his by military law, and he was conscious of the power to wield it loyally and well, but his love of country transcended his love of self, and he put the temptation aside.[116]

If Rodes felt indignant at the apparent lack of confidence shown him by Hill and Pendleton, he gave no outward indication of it. At least one of his colleagues, however, embraced that feeling for him. In memoirs written after the war, Thomas Munford loudly decried that at Chancellorsville, Stuart "was put over Rodes . . . which was a great piece of injustice!" Munford's remarks became one of many uttered by various commanders as they debated the somewhat controversial issue long after the war. Staff officer Henry Kyd Douglas, for example, concluded that Rodes made the right decision, being not yet "the man for the emergency." On the other hand, aide Randolph Barton believed that "Rodes distrusted his ability to take command," adding "I have always thought he threw away the opportunity of his life . . . modesty was a mistake in that crisis." Rodes' statement on the matter in his official report probably should be taken at face value. He believed "the good of the service demanded" the transfer to Stuart.[117]

Meanwhile, Second Corps signal officer Captain Richard E. Wilbourn carried to General Lee the sad news of Jackson's wounding. "Any victory is a dear one that deprives us of the services of Jackson, even for a short time," Lee lamented. After describing to the commanding general the incidents surrounding the tragic event, Wilbourn, who had been with Jackson when he fell, went on to report that A. P. Hill had taken Jackson's place, but that he, too, had been wounded. Rodes assumed command, continued Wilbourn, but Stuart had been summoned to take charge of the corps. "Rodes," remarked Lee, "is a gallant, courageous, and energetic officer." Despite these remarks, which might have made Rodes blush with embarrassment, Lee acquiesced in the wisdom of having sent for Stuart, and about 3:00 a.m. wrote an order conferring upon him command of the Second Corps.[118]

Shortly before Stuart arrived to take command, the Yankees made a somewhat feeble attempt to regain the rifle pits on the right of Lane's brigade. Though it came to nothing, the fight prompted Stuart to take the precaution of bending back the right of Heth's division. This episode, along with the continued confusion among the Confederate troops, some of whom still occasionally fired at each other in the dark, compelled Stuart to agree with Rodes' decision to delay the attack until morning.

Stuart also accepted Rodes' plan for the following day. "I had already made the necessary arrangements," Rodes reported, "and they remained unchanged." The plan called for the attack to resume in the morning with A. P. Hill's division, under Heth, in front about one mile west of Chancellorsville. Colston would follow Heth at a distance of 300 yards, with Rodes bringing up the third line, about 1,000 yards behind Colston. Straddling the Plank Road, the three divisions were ordered to drive east for Chancellorsville and the Federal lines. The arrival of the lagging brigades of Archer and Thomas brought Stuart's total strength to about 26,500 men. He set the attack to begin at 6:00 a.m.[119]

While heavy dew formed on the ground during the morning's pre-dawn hours, Rodes, who had had little if any sleep the past two nights, made preparations for the attack. Dowdall's Tavern served as the approximate center of his line. To the immediate left of the road he put O'Neal, with Iverson on his left. On the right of the road he placed Ramseur, Doles, and Colquitt, in that order. By 5:00 a.m. the division was ready.

One problem remained, and it was substantial: the men did not have any food. Some, including Rodes, ate nothing of substance the day before, while others had been fasting since before dropping their knapsacks to move up into the reserve line on May 1. Rodes took the matter to Stuart. "[A]s his men were entirely without food," Stuart later reported, "[Rodes] was extremely anxious to issue [rations]." Rodes evidently persuaded Stuart to delay the attack until after the men had been fed (something Jackson probably would not have agreed to do).

About 5:30 a.m., fighting erupted on the far right when Heth made contact with the enemy by bringing forward the regiments bent back the night before. This prompted Stuart to order the attack to begin immediately. Rodes and his men marched into battle on May 3 yet again with empty stomachs.[120]

The Federals waiting for the inevitable assault on May 3 were much better prepared than they had been the day before. They had spent the night profitably, using axe and spade to build two solid lines of defense that began at Hazel Grove southwest of Chancellorsville. The first line ran north across the Plank Road and stretched all the way to the Rappahannock River. The second line centered on Chancellorsville. Howard's battered XI Corps now held the Federal left, anchored tightly on a loop in the Rappahannock River facing southeast. Forming a tight perimeter around Chancellorsville on Howard's right flank was Darius Couch's II Corps, which faced east and southeast. Henry

Slocum's XII Corps continued the line facing mostly south and southwest, while Dan Sickles III Corps bent back again facing generally west and northwest. George Meade's V Corps and John Reynolds' I Corps extended the line northwest to the small creek called Hunting Run, where the line turned sharply northeast and ran the Federal right flank to the Rappahannock, where it was firmly anchored. While Lee's men attacked generally north against Slocum's front, Stuart's main attack drove due east against primarily Sickles' soldiers.[121]

At 5:30 a.m. Stuart's Confederate line surged forward. Heth and Colston achieved stunning initial success when they overran the first defensive line, including Hazel Grove, upon which Stuart promptly placed thirty guns. Federal resistance stiffened. With support from their superb artillery on the heights at Fairview behind Slocum's front, which stretched south of the road just west of Chancellorsville, counterattacks twice threw back the Confederates.[122]

Rodes stubbornly determined to keep his distance from Colston in order to avoid the messy entanglements of the day before. He slowly crept his division forward, using two hours to ease one-quarter mile beyond Dowdall's Tavern. An hour later, however, around 8:30 a.m., he came up on the backs of the intermingled commands of Colston and Heth, both stalled in the abandoned log works of the first Yankee line. Stuart ordered Rodes to add his weight to the stalled line and generate another general advance.[123]

Rodes, however, saw this as an opportunity to move up to the front and take over the attack. Roused by the prospect that his division might be able to complete the previous day's glorious work after all, he sent instructions for Colonel O'Neal on the left to meet him out on the road. Pointing in the direction of the Federal line, Rodes dramatically declared that upon the signal O'Neal was to pass through Colston's men and storm the enemy position straight ahead. To his other brigadiers Rodes sent a stirring appeal to prepare to attack the enemy. Careful later to include his orders in his official report of the battle, Rodes noted his directive was to "engage him vigorously, moving over friend and foe alike, if in the way." O'Neal, however, did not make the charge. While speeding back to the center of his brigade, he was struck by a shell fragment that knocked him down with a severe wound. Seventeen-year-old Edward O'Neal Jr., who had been serving as a volunteer aide on Rodes' staff for exactly one week, helped bear his stricken father from the field. When he heard the distressing news, Rodes sent a staff officer to confer command of the brigade upon the next senior colonel, Josephus Hall of the Fifth Alabama.[124]

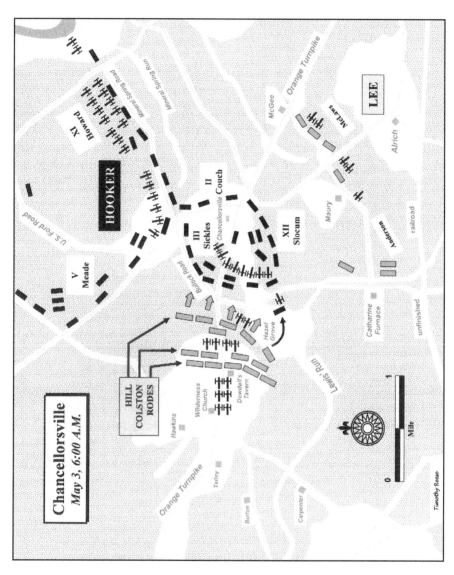

As he had the day before, Rodes positioned himself with the Third Alabama, whose right rested on the road. When at last all seemed ready, he gave the order to charge, and "His clarion voice," recalled a witness, rang out to "press on over friend and foe alike."[125] Colonel Cullen Battle recalled much the same thing. "Here Rodes, the ideal soldier of the South," wrote Battle, the future historian the Third Alabama, "leads the impetuous assault." Presently, they came upon their own comrades in the barricades directly ahead. In accordance with Rodes' orders, "We marched boldly over them," Captain Bonham of the Third bluntly stated.[126]

The bold march over their prone comrades, however, broke the cohesion of Rodes' mile-wide line, which became further disrupted by the thick forest. Within fifteen minutes after the charge began, none of his brigades remained in contact with any other in the division. Rodes resigned himself to the breakup. "On account of the dense forest, the undulating character of the ground, and the want of an adequate staff," he explained in his report, "it was not in my power, during the subsequent movements, to give a great deal of personal attention to the actions of any of my command, except Rodes' [O'Neal's] and Ramseur's brigades, which were next to the road, but my orders were faithfully executed by each brigade commander."[127]

Iverson separated from the far left, where he became involved in a hot fight that brought about the deaths of a pair of twins in the Twentieth North Carolina named Wilson, one brother falling across the body of the other. "Twins in birth, twins in death," the regiment's Colonel Thomas Toon sadly reported. On the far right, Colquitt's brigade drifted off until Stuart grabbed it and used it like a pendulum, swinging it from one flank to another as emergencies arose.[128]

Despite receiving Rodes' "personal attention," O'Neal's brigade came apart, the Fifth and Twenty-sixth Alabama regiments shifting leftward while the other regiments (Third, Sixth, and Twelfth) went ahead into the inferno raining down on them from the Union guns at Fairview. "The biggest tree offered no protection," recalled the Third Alabama's Private Nick Weeks. "One might as well have been in front as behind. Limbs and the tops were falling about us as if torn by a cyclone." The men hugged the ground, refusing or unable to leave. Weeks left a vivid account of his experiences that morning:

> We were enveloped, as it were, in dense fog, the flashing guns could be seen only a few feet away.... At every breath we were inhaling sulphurous vapor.... What a din. What a variety of hideous sounds. The ping of the minie ball, the splutter of canister, the whistling of grape, the 'where are you, where are you' of screaming shells.... [A]n arm and shoulder fly from the man just in front, exposing his throbbing heart. Another's foot flew up and kicked him in the face as a shell struck his leg. Another, disemboweled, crawled along on all fours, his entrails trailing behind, and still another held up his face with his hand, a piece of shell having carried away his lower jaw. I just about made up my mind that 'this is hell sure enough' when one, two, three and the fourth shell dropped almost in the

same spot as fast as I could count, exploding as they struck the ground—and all was dark around me. I should say blackness so black and thick I could feel it, and my feet seemed to rest on a sheet of flame.

When Weeks regained consciousness, he discovered lying around him fourteen dead and wounded comrades, some severely burned by brush fires that were quickly licking their way across the ground.[129]

Rodes did not go into this maelstrom with the Third Alabama. A report of the breakup on the left flank prompted him to speed off in that direction to reunite O'Neal's brigade for a concerted effort against the Yankee works. Colonel Hall had tried to bring back the leftward drifting Fifth and Twenty-sixth Alabama regiments by ordering them to advance by the right flank, but in so doing the two regiments came under a terrific enfilade fire. About this time, part of Iverson's brigade and a portion of Dorsey Pender's brigade of Heth's [Hill's] division arrived, scooped up the Fifth and Twenty-sixth, and successfully stormed the Federal barricade. The Twenty-sixth's Colonel John Gavin fell inside the works, together with scores of other soldiers. A counterattack, however, soon drove them out. Both regiments ended up losing about 100 men and their flags, though the Fifth's banner was not captured. Rather than have it seized, Color Bearer George Nuttling threw the banner into the woods.[130]

"At the barricades," reported Iverson after the battle, "I met General Rodes, and informed him that the enemy were threatening my flank." Rodes took charge. He skillfully set up a makeshift line that contained regiments from the brigades of O'Neal, Iverson, and Pender, and ordered the men forward. "My brigade pressed on," explained Iverson.

Having restored order on the left, Rodes gave supervision of that portion of the line to his AAG, Major Henry Whiting, and dashed back over to the beleaguered Third Alabama. He saw at once the necessity of getting the regiment out of its desperate situation. Refusing to pull it back, Rodes waded into the inferno, found its commander, Captain M. F. Bonham, and shouted for him to charge. "Forward, Third Alabama!" the captain cried out. "The order is forward! Follow me!" That was enough. The men sprang to their feet and rushed ahead.[131]

"The air seemed black with shot," remembered Private Weeks. A raging fire of dry leaves swept toward Weeks and his comrades. "Our line melted away, as if swallowed up by the earth," he wrote of the attempt by many to avoid the fire. Once the flames passed, the men reformed and vigorously resumed the charge. Many of the wounded, however, could not move to safety. "Their charred bodies dotted the ground," Weeks recalled in horror, "and we could see by the ashes where they had scratched the leaves away in a vain attempt to save themselves."[132]

Iverson's brigade and now all of O'Neal's as well pressed on until they struck the Yankee abatis, "which destroyed everything like order in our ranks," wrote Weeks, "and every man went on his own hook, crawling over and under the felled trees, not stopping to fire a shot till we struck the infantry and drove it back." Once again the Yankees rallied, counterattacked, and threw back the Confederates.[133] Rodes grabbed Colquitt's floating brigade from reserve and threw it in. That finally decided the matter. The Federals fled for good, leaving to Rodes their second line of defense north of the Plank Road.[134]

South of the road, meanwhile, Ramseur came up on the enemy's first line of abandoned works just after the Stonewall Brigade had been thrown back from an attack against the second line. He arrived in time to see a staff officer deliver Jeb Stuart's order for the men of John R. Jones' brigade to move out from behind the log works and make the next assault. But the leaderless brigade— Jones the night before went to the rear with an ulcerated leg (for which he would be dismissed from the service as a coward) and the next in command, Colonel R. T. Garnett, was dead—refused to move without orders from the division commander. Colston, however, was on the opposite flank. The next senior colonel was Alexander Vandeventer of the Fifty-first Virginia. Ramseur stepped forward to offer his brigade for the attack. The staff officer not only gladly accepted, but turned over to Ramseur the job of trying to get Jones' men (and apparently a smattering of the Stonewall Brigade, and perhaps others) to join in. When his efforts earned no more success than the staff officer's had, Ramseur obtained "cheerfully granted" permission from Stuart to pass through them and make the attack.[135]

After detaching the Thirtieth North Carolina to support the guns on Hazel Grove, Ramseur brought up his men. With open disgust they moved through Jones' prone brigade. "The brave, chivalric Virginians lay flat on the ground," the Second North Carolina's Captain William Calder later wrote in contempt, "and the tar-heels whom they so often ridicule walked over them to glory and to victory."[136]

"You may double-quick," a Virginian called out to the Fourth North Carolina's Colonel Bryan Grimes, "but you'll come back faster than you go!" Grimes, a man with a hearty temper and a combative soul, "put his foot on the back and head of an officer and ground his face in the earth."[137]

The North Carolinians burst out of the woods and stormed the Yankee line. The fight turned savage at close quarters and low ammunition forced Ramseur's men to scrounge cartridges from the dead. Twice Ramseur went back to Jones' brigade "and exhorted it (officers and men) to fill up the gap (some 500 or 600 yards) on my right, but all in vain." He somehow got a message through to the division commander. "I then reported to General Rodes," Ramseur later wrote, "that unless support was sent to drive the enemy from my right, I would have to fall back." Rodes hurried over and discovered, to his dismay, the Virginians crouching behind the works while others fought the battle to their front.[138]

Nearby at this time, an ambulance crew member poured water from a canteen onto the head and face of Colonel Bryan Grimes, the same officer who recently had ground into the soil the face of one of Jones' Virginians. Suffering from pain and deep exhaustion, Grimes lost consciousness after a shell fragment struck him in the leg. Carried to the rear, he revived in time to recognize the sound of Rodes' loud and angry voice. "What troops are these?!" Grimes heard him demand of a nearby Virginia officer, followed quickly by, "Why have you not joined in the charge?!" When Grimes heard the officer reply that they had no orders to advance Grimes became furious, roused himself, "and pronounced it a base lie." Grimes watched as Rodes pulled a pistol, put the muzzle to the Virginian's head, and, "with an epithet of odium," told him to order the men forward or he would blow out his brains. According to Grimes, the terrified officer jumped up and promptly led the men forward.

By that time, however, the Thirtieth North Carolina had stormed in from Hazel Grove on the right to tip the scales and force the enemy to leave the heights. Although Rodes stated in his report that the Stonewall Brigade also went in with the Thirtieth North Carolina, a letter written on May 29, 1891, by that regiment's Colonel Francis Parker refuted his claim. The Stonewall Brigade, declared Parker, "did not go on the field with us." Rodes made no mention of this dramatic episode in his report, other than to say that he tried unsuccessfully to get the men moving. Grimes, however, may be considered a reliable witness not inclined to exaggeration. That raises the interesting questions of whether Rodes really meant to "blow out" that officer's brains, and what judgment, if any, would have been passed on him had he done so.[139]

When Ramseur's men finally returned to their works after being relieved, Stuart ordered a cheer for the North Carolinians. Though gratified by this and the subsequent praise heaped on him by Rodes and others, Ramseur "wept like a child" when he later caught sight of the remnants of his shattered brigade.[140]

George Doles, meanwhile, after being deflected farther to the right by dense thickets, came up a ravine behind a graveyard on the Chancellor hill. He drove the enemy before him until he came out opposite the house almost in rear of the enemy position, where the Georgians fought hard until being forced back. General Lee, who had pushed forward with the force left to him until his left flank linked up with the advancing right flank of the Second Corps near Hazel Grove—one of the war's genuinely supreme moments—directed Doles and his men to fall back and take charge of the prisoners.[141]

By 9:30 a.m., about one hour after Rodes took over the attack, the divisions under Lee and Stuart formed one continuous line of battle. When Fairview and Chancellorsville fell to the Confederates thirty minutes later, Hooker rapidly pulled back northward toward the Rappahannock River and set up his corps in a tight defensive perimeter.

With the situation well in hand, Lee directed Stuart to contain this perimeter with his 25,000 men (against Hooker's roughly 75,000). A new threat, however, had developed that needed attention. John Sedgwick, whose Federal command was left opposite Fredericksburg to hold Lee in position, had successfully stormed Marye's Heights. With Jubal Early's defenders swept aside, Sedgwick could now advance in force against the Confederate rear. While Stuart was ordering Rodes to organize all the troops on Chancellor heights and prepare them for defensive operations, Lee scurried east and southeast with two divisions under McLaws and Anderson.

To confront Hooker's southward protruding perimeter, its flanks anchored on the Rappahannock, Rodes skillfully shifted the Confederate line to run parallel with the pike, facing north. On the far left he placed Doles' brigade, whose left linked up with Pender's brigade of Heth's division. Ramseur deployed his brigade to the right of Doles, followed by O'Neal's brigade under Colonel Hall. Rodes positioned Iverson's brigade on the right, between the Chancellor house and the Plank Road, with Colquitt's regiments 100 yards behind Iverson's right en echelon. Colston's division was stretched out to the right of Iverson. With bayonets, tin pans, and even fingers, the men went to work fortifying their lines.[142]

That night rations finally came in. For some men it was their first food in nearly three days. Though fed at last, many found it difficult to rest. "I could not sleep much that night," recalled the Second North Carolina's Lieutenant Norman, one of only two survivors in his company, "for the moment my eyes were closed I imagined I could see soldiers falling all around me, and their dying groans rang in my ears all the time."[143]

Others that night saw things even more horrible. "The burning of the deep, dry leaves had heated up the dead bodies and caused them to burn," remembered the Fourteenth North Carolina's John McClendon. "They were like lamps lighting up the woods."[144]

*   *   *

Rodes spent much of the night riding among his men, comforting and encouraging them. Nothing seemed too trivial to escape his attention. "Genl. Rodes says I must wear a light coloured hat," the Thirtieth North Carolina's Colonel Parker wrote his wife. "He thinks that a black hat will keep my head too warm." Parker added with obvious pride, "He says that he was very uneasy about me in this Sunday's fight. He seems to be much concerned about me." Such concern left a lasting impression on many of Rodes' soldiers. "Comrades," wrote the Forty-fourth Georgia's Major Key after the war, "you remember that in these battles [Chancellorsville] we belonged to D. H. Hill's division, but that that patriotic, heroic, unassuming, never tiring general, R. E. Rodes, commanded our division. Gen. Rodes was a grand character. In battle he would stand at the head of the command."[145]

Leaving Stuart thinly spread to face Hooker's six corps (Reynolds, Couch, Meade, Howard, Sickles and Slocum), Lee rushed McLaws and Anderson back to confront Sedgwick. In disjointed fighting along the Plank Road around Salem Church about four miles west of Fredericksburg on May 4, the Confederates boxed in a hesitant Sedgwick and stopped him cold. The Federal general re-crossed the Rappahannock that night.

The following morning, Rodes sent for Major Blackford. "After telling me of the splendid victory over Sedgwick," Blackford wrote his cousin, "he directed me to push forward my skirmishers to discover if the enemy were in force in our front." A deadly volley of grapeshot that struck down several of his men told Blackford all he needed to know.[146]

Having beaten back Sedgwick, Lee began concentrating his strength for a renewed attack against the well entrenched Hooker. Lee intended to deliver the fresh assault on the morning of May 6. Around 6:00 p.m. the night before, a rain began that filled the trenches with water. Still, Rodes' wet, sleep-deprived men cheered up when the outposts began reporting before dawn that the Yankee trenches were empty. Rodes cautiously sent forward another line of skirmishers, who quickly confirmed the report. Under cover of darkness and the blowing rain, Hooker had pulled back across the Rappahannock River, bringing the Chancellorsville fighting to an anti-climactic close.[147]

Around 2:30 p.m. that afternoon, Rodes' division left its muddy trenches, took up the march, and by 10:30 p.m. that evening most of the men arrived back in their old camps at Grace Church. For many, the march back through the driving rain was the most difficult part of the campaign. "Returning to this camp after the battle," wrote a soldier in the Third Alabama, "we had twenty-one miles to march, and the men were so completely broken down that they fell out all along the road." Some men took two days to find their way back to Grace Church. Rodes, however, managed to put an optimistic spin on this tragic epilogue. "It is worthy of remark," he added in his report, "that the enemy abandoned such a large number of knapsacks in retreating to his works that when this division began its homeward march in the rain it was thoroughly equipped with oil-cloths and shelter-tents of the best quality."[148]

Despite all the knapsacks, oil-cloths, and tents that came at the end of a great victory, many men returned to camp feeling anything but triumphant. "Everything and everybody seemed changed, sad and dejected," observed the Twelfth Alabama's Captain Park.[149]

The campaign had been a costly one for both combatants. Hooker lost slightly more than 17,000 men from all causes, abandoning a powerful entrenched position with tens of thousands of men who had not yet fired a shot. Lee's army suffered roughly 13,000 men lost from all causes. Rodes' division bore the brunt of much of the fighting. More than 8,500 men from his division had left their camps just eight days before. Only some 5,500 returned. Of the 3,000 men who did not march back to camp, 397 had been killed, 1,866 were listed as wounded, and 713 as missing, for a total of 2,976. Rodes believed enemy losses probably were not as high because of the advantage of entrenchments.

Although no one could have known it in the spring of 1863, Chancellorsville one day would be regarded by many veterans and civilians alike as General Lee's most magnificent field victory.[150]

Chapter 7

Across the Potomac, Again

The mortal wounding of Stonewall Jackson at Chancellorsville denied Robert Rodes the official praise he had so eagerly anticipated from his chief. "General Jackson," he impulsively expounded to the general on the night of May 2, "my division behaved splendidly this evening and you must give them a big name in your report." Jackson assured him, "I shall take great pleasure in doing so, and congratulate you and your command for it." But there would be no official praise from the pen of Thomas Jackson. Still, Rodes might have blushed with pride if he heard the remarks spoken by Jackson during the final days of his life.

After the amputation of his left arm, Jackson on May 3 endured a bumpy, agonizing ambulance ride to Guiney's Station. To help distract his patient from his suffering, Dr. Hunter McGuire engaged him in conversation. Inevitably, they discussed the recent battle and the role played in it by various officers of the Second Corps. Jackson reserved his highest praise for Rodes, "a soldier" who deserved promotion. On his deathbed a few days later, Jackson again spoke very highly of Rodes and of his wish to see him promoted as soon as possible.[1]

Rodes may have heard some of this praise from Jackson's own lips. A few days after his wounding, when it seemed Jackson was improving and might recover, Rodes visited his fallen chief. No reliable record of what the pair discussed exists, but it is more likely than not that before Rodes left the presence of his commander for the last time, he heard the words of praise that he would cherish for the remainder of his own life. Jackson lingered until May 10, when he expired.[2]

To please Jackson and reward his gallant brigadier, General Lee wrote President Davis on May 4 to request that Rodes immediately be made a major general in command of D. H. Hill's former division. Because such promotions required Senate confirmation, however, Davis was hesitant to act so swiftly. "There is difficulty in promoting Genl. Rodes owing to limitation of law," he wired Lee on May 6, "but if necessary, it must be done." Lee wired back the next day. "I desire Genl Rodes to command D. H. Hill's old Division," he reiterated. "He is a good soldier who behaved admirably in the last battles and deserves promotion." Davis relented. "Your recommendation of General Rodes is adopted," he wrote Lee the same day. "He is promoted accordingly."

The commission, however, bore the date of May 10. In an act of incredible nerve, Rodes refused it. He sent back the commission insisting that the promotion should bear the date on which his conduct had received special recognition from his corps commander. The forbearing Lee agreed, and the commission was confirmed by the Senate with the date of May 2—the day of Rodes' greatest triumph. The prompt appointment represented "the nearest approach the Army had known to promotion on the field for valor," observed Lee's biographer, Douglas S. Freeman.[3]

Well deserved accolades poured in. "While it is impossible to mention all who were conspicuous in the several engagements," Lee remarked at the end of his report on Chancellorsville, "it will not be considered an invidious distinction to say that General Jackson, after he was wounded, in expressing the satisfaction he derived from the conduct of his whole command, commended my particular attention to the services of Brigadier-General (now Major-General) Rodes and his gallant division."[4] A. P. Hill was likewise effusive: "Brigadier-General Rodes distinguished himself much," Hill noted in his report, "and won a proud name for himself and his division." The recuperating Richard Ewell, Rodes' former commander, wrote General P. G. T. Beauregard on May 8, "R. E. Rodes of Alabama, whose promotion to brigadier general was much owing to your efforts, had greatly distinguished himself and has been made major general, thus vindicating your recommendation. He seems after Jackson to be the hero of the fight."[6]

Though proud of their new major general, the first division commander in Lee's army who was not a graduate of West Point, many soldiers within its ranks held a somewhat different—and understandable—perspective on the reason behind Rodes' promotion. "Gen. Rodes was made a Major General on the field for gallantry, I suppose," wrote a soldier in the Third Alabama, identifying himself only as "Jimmie" to a local newspaper shortly after the battle, "but our brigade made him what he is, and he owes it all to us."[7]

"Justice," one of "Jimmie's" comrades in the Third Alabama, was even more caustic in his letter to the home newspaper.

> There is another point I wish to direct your attention to. The habit most of the press and public have of giving all the credit and gallantry to the Brigadier and Major Generals for victories which were won by the men. As in our case: The papers are teeming with all kinds of reports about the gallant and heroic conduct of Gen. Rodes. . . . It is true Gen. Rodes acted well, and did the post assigned to him, but his division was put in position by the lamented Jackson, and after the commands 'attention' and 'forward,' he became little more than a predator and his troops under him the eaters.
>
> I am particularly struck with this injustice by one instance alone, of Sgt. Hendrik Hardy, color bearer of the 3d Alabama. From the time the word forward was given, he dashed off in front of the regiment, waving his flag from right to left, and never faltered or hesitated until he had planted his standard upon a Federal battery. This was the emblem and spirit which led that body of men, and not the General. It is seldom that a General has to lead in this army. If he follows and keeps up with the impetuosity of the men, he does well. Give the Generals the credit due them, but do not let the deeds of the men go unwritten and unrecorded. They are the heroes of this war.[8]

Near the end of the war, a private in the Thirtieth North Carolina recorded in his diary that he admired Rodes as "Astute, capable, brave, conscientious—he made a fine commander, respected and honored, unselfish and devoted. . . . He was a fine officer, who had led us for years, had obtained our confidence, admiration and love." But that private did not forget to also note that Rodes was "whom we made a major-general on the field of Chancellorsville by the heroic conduct of our boys."[9]

Rodes held no delusions when it came to understanding the ingredients of battlefield success. He expressed his appreciation more than a year earlier to the Fifth Alabama for its role in helping him become a brigadier. Now, with his new promotion, he did not forget the men without whom he could not have been made a major general. We know he personally thanked the men of the Fourteenth North Carolina, for example, and almost certainly made similar gestures to other regiments in the division.[10]

Bursting with pride and gratitude, the major general on May 18 called for an inspection of his new command, now officially styled "Rodes' Division." It was by all accounts an impressive affair. "We have returned to camp from division review, which was the first time we have been reviewed by our new Gen. who now holds the position formally [sic] held by Gen. D. H. Hill our late commander," Captain William Haygood of the Forty-fourth Georgia's Company C wrote home that evening. "Gen Rodes was made Maj. Gen. on the late battel field [sic] in honor of his Gallant conduct on that memmorabel ocattion [sic]. We hope he will make a good and ifficient [sic] officer though we think he will be very strict with both men and officers which is all right in so large a crowd of men. We lost a great many men in the late battels though our Division is a very ifficient couple of men yet and can do good Service when we are called on."[11]

The division indeed looked very impressive, as did its commanding general. "Our new Major Gen. R.E. Rodes reviewed the division today," the Forty-fourth Georgia's Davis Tinsley wrote home. "He is a very young man— looks younger than I do, and is not more than 27 years old it is said. He is a fine officer."[12]

An observer of the review, the general's special guest, came away with an equally favorable opinion of the new division commander. As a standard bearer of Presbyterianism in Virginia, the renowned Reverend Dr. Moses Drury Hoge, pastor of Richmond's Second Presbyterian Church, had been a favorite of both Jackson and Ewell. Along with several matrons out from the capital, Hoge watched the review from a nearby hilltop. "The ladies and I occupied an eminence which commanded the whole field," Hoge wrote his wife from Rodes' headquarters on the 22nd. "The day was fine, the bands played well, and the young general [Rodes] acquitted himself very handsomely. The whole affair surpassed my expectations."

Also surpassing Hoge's expectations at this time was an extraordinary offer from the new division commander. "Did I tell you the General's admirable plan for my work?" he enthusiastically wrote his wife in the same letter. "I have heard of none like it in the army, and it seems to me all that any general could do, or any preacher could wish. A preaching camp is prepared by the pioneer corps in each brigade, and the whole brigade, officers and men, are marched to the place. This always secures me a good audience, and, as it takes the place of regular drill, is acceptable, I understand, to all concerned."[13]

The sermons, one for each brigade every five or six days, took place "in a beautiful amphitheater in the woods," shaded by magnificent hickory trees, the men lying in leaves around the speaker's stand, was how Major Blackford described it to his mother on May 26. "There is no time at which the minds of men are more impressible," Blackford observed, "than just after a fight, especially such an one as we have just gone through."

Not only Chancellorsville, but the horrors and harsh realities of the entire two years of war had softened many a heart and compelled men to seek comfort in the contemplation of a world of eternal peace. "I never saw so marked a change," Blackford told his mother, "as that which had come over the Division within the last six weeks." Though Blackford gave much of the credit for that change to Hoge, he apparently did not know that it was Rodes, the stern, seemingly cold, harsh disciplinarian, who had sought out the reverend and made these arrangements to provide for the spiritual comfort of the men. The move was a reflection of Rodes' own growing need, begun in earnest after First Manassas, for such comfort and reassurance.[14]

On Thursday, May 29, the division again went on review, this time in honor of Richard Ewell, the new commander of the Second Corps. As a partial means of improving the efficiency of the command structure while at the same time trying to compensate somewhat for the irreparable loss of Jackson, Lee divided the Army of Northern Virginia's infantry from two corps into three. Further juggling placed three divisions in each corps. James Longstreet, recently returned from his campaign in southeast Virginia, retained command of the First Corps. Ewell, despite Lee's concern that at times he might be indecisive and have unpredictable mood swings, succeeded Jackson as commander of the Second Corps. The newly created Third Corps went to A. P. Hill. Each corps received five battalions of artillery—one for each division, with two battalions in reserve. Thomas Carter's artillery was assigned to Rodes' division.

When he reported for duty on May 29, just three days after his marriage to the widow Lizinka Brown, Ewell literally stepped off the train and went straight to the review grounds. Nine months had passed since Old Baldy last commanded troops in the field. He had undergone a significant transformation during his absence. One leg had been amputated (a wooden prosthesis in its place), and he gained a wealthy wife whose strong influence so far had been successful in enabling him to take the difficult steps of accepting religion and giving up profanity. Ewell was eager to return to duty. With his own division in the hands of Jubal Early, he wrote Jackson back in April to express a desire to serve in some capacity in the Second Corps alluding, perhaps, to the command of D. H. Hill's division. Two months later he was tapped to command three divisions: Rodes, Early, and Edward Johnson, who had been given Isaac Trimble's former command.[15]

From its camps around Grace Church on the morning of May 29, Rodes' division marched three miles to the review grounds near the Rappahannock. Though Ramseur believed that, despite the tragic losses sustained at Chancellorsville, the troops made a "splendid appearance," some men resented having to stand several hours in the hot sun, waiting to get "properly aligned." In a private rehearsal, Rodes reviewed his own division with his new assistant adjutant inspector general, the Twelfth Georgia's Captain David Peden. Rodes rode down the line of each regiment, after which each brigade marched past him. After this rather laborious affair, the movements were repeated by the entire Second Corps, this time for the benefit of Generals Ewell, A. P. Hill, and the commanding general, Robert E. Lee, beside whom Rodes had the honor of sitting. The whole affair, from the beginning of the march at Grace Church to the end of the final corps review, took about seven hours (10:00 a.m. to 5:00 p.m.) "It was a most fatiguing day," Private Sam Pickens of the Fifth Alabama admitted to his diary, speaking no doubt for nearly everyone in the ranks that day.[16]

Rodes' division looked impressive, in part because new recruits already had made good most of the terrible losses sustained at Chancellorsville. There was another reason the division stood out: a large new brigade had been added to its

ranks. Dissatisfied with Alfred Colquitt's performance at Chancellorsville, Lee rid himself of the Georgian by taking advantage of a War Department proposal that allowed the exchange of depleted brigades in Virginia for full-sized brigades in North Carolina. In exchange for Colquitt and his entire brigade,

Brig. Gen. Junius Daniel,
one of Robert Rodes' finest
brigade commanders.

Library of Congress

the commanding general received from D. H. Hill the relatively inexperienced but large brigade of Brigadier General Junius Daniel, which arrived in Richmond on May 19. Ensuing events would prove that Lee and Rodes got the better end of the deal. (Hill wanted Stephen Ramseur's brigade, but Lee wisely refused.) Before the war, thirty-five- year-old Daniel, an 1851 graduate of West Point, served seven years on garrison duty in New Mexico, ran a Louisiana plantation for two years, and returned to his native state in time to get elected colonel of the Fourteenth North Carolina Infantry. After becoming a brigadier general the following winter, Daniel fought in the Seven Days' Battles and distinguished himself at Malvern Hill. Glory in Virginia that summer of the Confederate flood tide escaped Daniel, however, when his brigade was sent back to North Carolina to meet a threatened Federal invasion that failed to materialize. Rodes was fortunate to have this promising officer and his fine brigade join his division.[17]

*   *   *

Throughout the division and the army, belief in ultimate victory never seemed stronger then it did in the wake of Chancellorsville. But overconfidence can be a dangerous emotion, especially in the mind of the commanding general. Lee's string of successes against long odds, from The Seven Days' Battles near Richmond to the repulse of Joe Hooker at Chancellorsville, convinced him that the Army of Northern Virginia was virtually invincible if properly led. Although Jackson was dead, the new command structure and an influx of reinforcements infused him with a fresh confidence that the approaching summer months would likewise bring success—but how best to use the Virginia army?

With Vicksburg, Mississippi, threatened by U. S. Grant's invading army, many in the Davis administration clamored for Lee to detach troops to reinforce that theater. Lee, however, successfully argued to Davis that the decisive theater was in the East, where a decisive battlefield victory would compel Grant's withdrawal and perhaps convince foreign powers to recognize Southern independence. Besides, he argued, there was no guarantee troops from Virginia would arrive in Mississippi in time to help, or that the commanders there would employ them as effectively in Mississippi as Lee would use them in and around Virginia.

At a meeting June 1 with two of his three corps commanders (Hill was absent ill), Lee revealed his proposal to march the army down (north) the Shenandoah and Cumberland valleys and strike out into Pennsylvania. Ewell, having gained valuable experience in the Shenandoah during his service there with Jackson the year before, would lead the way with his Second Corps.

The following day Ewell met with his division commanders and, as if to honor the legacy of Jackson's secretive ways, instructed them to prepare for a march to Culpeper, and told them nothing more. To avoid being spotted by Federal observation balloons across the Rappahannock River, Rodes' men cooked three days' rations and broke camp in the darkness at Grace Church at 4:00 a.m. on June 4. Maintaining a practice begun by Jackson, Rodes gave the men a ten-minute rest every hour as they marched sixteen miles in a southwesterly direction to a bivouac two miles north of Spotsylvania Court House. "It was a warm day," the Fifth Alabama's Sam Pickens wrote in his diary that night, "and we were in a cloud of dust most of the time."[18]

The following day, June 5, Rodes turned the division right (north) at Verdiersville in order to head for a crossing of the Rapidan at either Raccoon or Somersville ford. By this time his men knew something big was in the offing. A number of them acted in such high spirits that they made at least one observer suspicious. "Gen Rodes Division had just passed," a member of Early's staff noted in his diary, "and some of his men having imbibed pretty freely from 'mountain dew' were in a happy state." A hot, dusty march of twenty-one miles brought these "happy" men to near Old Verdiersville. That same day, divisions under Early, Johnson, and George Pickett also began marching.[19]

After a march of only four miles on the 6th, Rodes received instructions to halt and await further orders. Lee learned the Federals were crossing the Rappahannock at Fredericksburg. Naturally, Rodes' men did not mind the stop, particularly after a hard rain blew in that afternoon. When he was satisfied the Federals were making nothing more than a probe around Fredericksburg, Lee ordered the march resumed the following day.

Before dawn on June 7, Rodes got the men up at 3:30 a.m. and put them on the road a little after 4:00 a.m. He took them across the Rapidan at knee-deep Somersville Ford northeast of Orange Court House and marched sixteen miles to a point on the Rixeyville Road, two miles north of Culpeper. Just before reaching camp, the men saw their corps commander ride by, waving his cap from inside a buggy. Ewell retreated inside the wheeled vehicle when the stump of his amputated leg began to cause troublesome discomfort. Despite the cheers of the men, Ewell felt embarrassed to be seen in such an unmilitary conveyance, and he sped on ahead of the column. Rodes allowed the men to rest all the next day while waiting for the corps to close up.[20]

Having executed the first leg of the march, Ewell allayed Rodes' suspicions by confirming that a major campaign indeed was underway. Accordingly, the division commander promptly ordered all excess baggage to the rear to make room in the brigade trains for three days' rations. He also wanted three days' worth of food put into the division's commissary train, and he ordered the men to stuff the same amount into their haversacks, for a total of nine days of rations.

The meaning of all this was not lost on the men of the division, who considered themselves "equal to any undertaking." Colonel Risden T. Bennett of the Fourteenth North Carolina, Ramseur's brigade, for example, judged the Army of Northern Virginia to be "as tough and efficient as any army of the same number ever marshaled on this planet."[21]

That very day, Tuesday, June 9, Rodes and his men heard the heavy sound of gunfire ahead to the northeast. Sensing that General Lee was up to something, General Hooker had sent out his cavalry on a reconnaissance-in-force that morning near Brandy Station, where his troopers ran into and surprised Jeb Stuart's mounted command. The clash produced the largest cavalry battle of the war.

In anticipation of orders not yet received, Rodes put his division on the road and marched toward the sound of the firing. Word arrived from Ewell to halt on the John Botts farm near the battlefield and await further orders. Stuart apparently was in some difficulty and needed help. About noon, orders came from Lee to prepare one brigade for battle. Rodes decided to test his newest brigadier, and issued orders for Junius Daniel to form up for the task.

Just then John Botts burst out the front door of his farm home, frantically waving his arms to angrily protest to Rodes that he was "a neutral, and I'll have no fighting around my house!" Rodes had little patience or sympathy for the man or his neutrality. "Make that damned fool go back and behave himself!" he shouted, whereupon a staff officer escorted Botts into his "neutral" farmhouse.[22]

Daniel's brigade moved out and took up a position behind Brandy Station, from which point it was to act as a potential rallying point for Stuart's beleaguered troopers. Presently, Ewell came up and bid Rodes go with him in search of Lee. They found the commanding general watching the battle from the porch of the Barbour House, an elegant mansion on top of a low ridge three-quarters of a mile north of Brandy Station. Moments after climbing the porch steps, however, the two officers saw an ominous line of Federal cavalry thundering straight for them. "Gather in the house," Ewell shouted, [we'll] defend it to the last!" Fortunately, a timely Confederate countercharge made it unnecessary for the generals to leave the porch. Not long afterward, the entire Federal force pulled back, making it unnecessary for Stuart, though roughly handled, to leave the battlefield. About 5:00 p.m. Rodes instructed Daniel to pull in his skirmishers and go into camp on the Botts' farm.[23]

Before dawn the following morning, Ewell met with his three division commanders—Rodes, Early, and Johnson—in order to lay out their paths to the Shenandoah Valley, Lee's preferred avenue of invasion. The corps commander told them that he intended to march toward the Valley in two columns. He gave Rodes the lead, instructing him to head north on the Old Richmond Road through Gourd Vine Church to Newby's Cross Roads, and then turn west and go on to Little Washington. There he was to hold until Early and Johnson, swinging up the turnpike through Sperryville, marched past on their way to Front Royal via Flint Hill and Chester Gap, when Rodes was to fall in behind them and bring up the rear.

With eager anticipation, Rodes sped back to his division, got his men up and by dawn had them ready to move. He did not, however, receive the order to march until mid-afternoon, when Lee finally determined the Union cavalry would not renew the fight with Stuart. The division managed only ten miles that day before going into camp on Hazel River near Gourd Vine Church. Early and Johnson, marching west of and parallel to Rodes, reached Woodville.

After an early start next morning, Thursday, June 11, Rodes marched up to Newby's on a washed-out, rutted road that exhausted his men. Because the road over to Washington appeared to be in the same horrible condition, Rodes decided to take the much easier Gaines Road north up to Flint Hill, where it met the Richmond Pike. There, per Ewell's orders, he halted to wait for Early's division to come up and pass through on the turnpike. An hour or so later, however, Ewell came along in his buggy and told Rodes that neither Early nor Johnson would be up, both having been delayed by bad roads. Rodes put the division into camp about one-and-a-half miles north of Flint Hill, his men having marched about fifteen miles that day.

That evening in camp, to the pleasant surprise of his division commanders, Ewell revealed his intention to attack Winchester in the Shenandoah Valley. He sold the idea two days before to a reluctant Lee, who preferred to have the Second Corps cross the Potomac as soon as possible in order to start gathering in much needed provisions. Lee remembered the near-disaster that nearly consumed his army after splitting it the previous fall to take Harpers Ferry during the raid into Maryland. He was not eager to assume that risk again. But

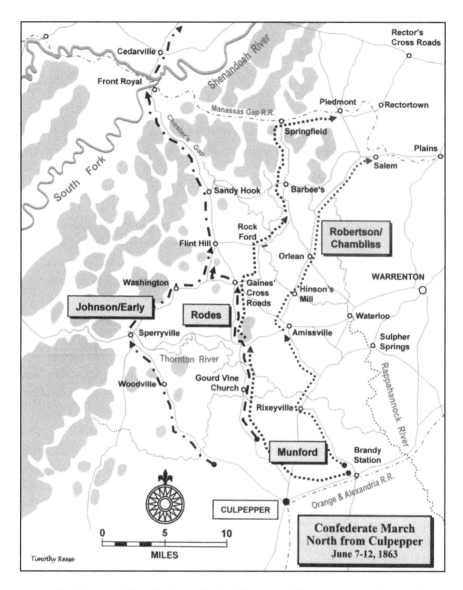

when Ewell argued that the large Federal force at Winchester—Robert Milroy's 2nd Division, VIII Corps—and the two smaller garrisons at Martinsburg and Berryville would pose a serious threat to Lee's rear, the commanding general relented on condition that the operation not delay the army's northward advance.

With Rodes' division still in the lead by virtue of the delays encountered the day before by Early and Johnson, the march for the Shenandoah Valley began at

4:00 a.m. on Friday, June 12. Later that morning near Sandy Hook, Ewell's buggy caught up with Rodes at the head of his division. Accompanying Ewell was the excellent map maker inherited from Jackson, Jedediah Hotchkiss, who presented Rodes with a just-finished map of the area he had been working on since 2:00 a.m. that morning. Rodes accepted Ewell's invitation to join him in the buggy, and together they rode north to Chester Gap, one of the eastern entrances into the Valley. The two officers obviously got along well and enjoyed each other's company.

Coming down into Front Royal about 11:00 a.m., the generals received from the townspeople the unpleasant surprise of an obviously planned and warm welcome. If the townspeople knew they were coming, so must Milroy, the Union commander at Winchester. When he learned that news of his appearance in Front Royal was revealed by the earlier arrival of the pontoons (sent by rail via Orange Court House to Culpeper) he intended to throw across the Shenandoah River, a frustrated Ewell changed plans and ordered Rodes to wade his men over immediately. Rodes pushed the division across both forks of the river and marched north about four miles to the little valley town of Cedarville. His men did not appreciate having to rush so quickly through the water. "The skin of feet is made tender & shrivels," the Fifth Alabama's Sam Pickens complained to his diary, "& then rubs off or blisters. It is bad policy to march troops thro water without giving them time to stop & take off shoes & socks."[24]

When Johnson's division arrived at Front Royal a short time later, Ewell crossed the river and went on to Cedarville, where he again met up with Rodes. In the course of a three-hour meeting, the corps commander went over the specifics of the plan for taking Winchester. While Johnson and Early moved directly against Milroy's large force of 7,000 men at Winchester, Rodes would fall upon the 1,800-man garrison at Berryville (comprised of a brigade from Milroy's division), immediately after which he was to seize the 1,300-man force at Martinsburg (one of six brigades from Benjamin Kelley's 1st Division, which was stationed about twenty miles northwest of Martinsburg at Harpers Ferry). Once that was done, Rodes would cross the Potomac River into Maryland and await further orders. For extra help, Ewell gave Rodes the 1,600 troopers of Albert Jenkins' cavalry brigade, just arrived in Cedarville from Middletown in the Valley.

Pleased with the relatively independent role given him, Rodes put his men on the road immediately after the meeting with Ewell. He wanted to get as close as possible to Berryville that night to shorten his thrust the next day. With

Daniel's brigade in the lead, the division left Cedarville and headed north in the direction of Millwood. John McCormack, "a most excellent guide and soldier," led the way over what was described as an "unfrequented road." To screen the movement, Rodes, in command of cavalry for the first time, sent Jenkins' troopers toward Millwood and Nineveh Church. After marching a total of seventeen miles that day, the division camped near Stone Bridge.[25]

*   *   *

Rodes set out for Millwood early the following morning. Not long afterward, Federal cavalry spotted the column. Though displeased with Jenkins for allowing the enemy to penetrate his screen, Rodes convinced himself that because the Federals (under Colonel A. T. McReynolds) had been at Berryville since March, they now were in a semi-permanent camp they could not easily or quickly move. Pushing the division with utmost speed through Millwood, he came up late that morning to Berryville, where he discovered that Jenkins, after driving the Federal cavalry into town, was being held off by the enemy's artillery.

Rodes quickly surveyed the situation and came up with a plan to surround the place and capture the entire Federal force. He directed Jenkins, followed closely by Daniel's brigade, to get behind the town and cut off the Federal retreat on the Winchester Road. With O'Neal holding in front, the other brigades would envelop the town on the right and left.

Just as these movements began, however, Rodes saw the Federal cavalry and artillery riding and rolling northward. Worse yet, he saw no sign of Federal infantry, making it now obvious that the cavalry and artillery had been waging a delaying action. It turned out that an hour before the Rebels appeared at Berryville, Colonel McReynolds had been warned, both by his cavalry patrol and two cannon shots fired from Winchester eleven miles to the west—which was Milroy's signal to evacuate. McReynolds accordingly started his train for Bunker Hill near Winchester, followed by the infantry. With his men exhausted after having marched about twenty miles that day, a disappointed Rodes decided against pursuit. He ordered O'Neal to move into and hold the town, and he put the remainder of the division into camp just beyond it near Summit Point.

Though "mortified" at the enemy's escape, Rodes found solace in the large amount of supplies and provisions left behind. He ordered a company of the Fifth Alabama to guard the captured stores, which included a number of items

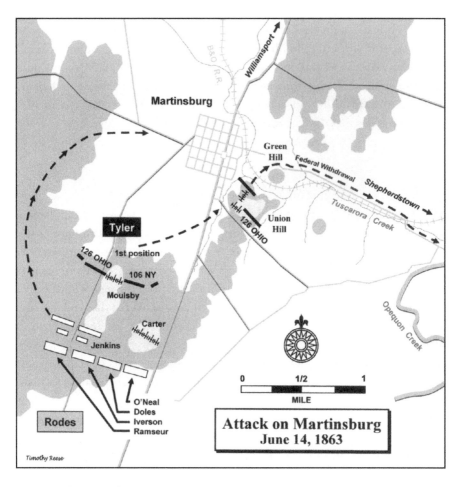

Attack on Martinsburg
June 14, 1863

set aside for the officer's mess. Sam Pickens, a member of the guard, told his diary that raiding comrades made the job very difficult, if not impossible: "We guarded several tents to the last for Gen. Rodes containing a great quantity sugar & coffee & barrels unopened."[26] The men took special pleasure in the confiscated food, especially the beans, which that night filled every pot. The boys in the Jeff Davis Artillery, however, made their beans hard and difficult to digest when they mistakenly added cold water to their pots after the hot water had evaporated. The gunners "paid for their temerity in the pains which followed."[27]

Ewell's orders specified that after Berryville, Rodes was to move immediately against Martinsburg. However, on the morning of Sunday the 14th, which dawned bright and clear after a drenching all-night rain, Rodes gave serious consideration to marching instead to Winchester. Despite sending several couriers to that place, he had heard nothing of Early's and Johnson's progress. Since the Federals at Berryville had fled in that direction, Rodes reasoned that Ewell might be in trouble. On the other hand, all could be well, in which case the division would have to countermarch toward Martinsburg. To avoid placing that strain on his men, Rodes decided to comply with his original orders. His men executed "a very fatiguing march of 19 miles" to Martinsburg.

Riding ahead of the column, Rodes and his staff reached the place that afternoon. He discovered that the Federal commander, Colonel B. F. Smith, had refused Jenkins' demand (delivered by Rodes' ordnance officer, Captain William Harris) to surrender and was drawn up for battle south of town. Delighted the Federals were not running away this time, Rodes determined to surround and bag the whole lot—provided his infantry came up in time. He sent Jenkins to swing around west of town to cut off any Federal attempt to retreat north toward the Potomac. Around 6:00 p.m. the infantry started coming in. Though quite fatigued, many having cut and bruised feet, the men promptly obeyed Rodes' orders to form a line of battle. "We had to march in quick time all day," a soldier in Daniel's brigade complained in his diary, "therefore we were not in the best of humor." With O'Neal's brigade in support, Carter's artillery came up and went into action against the troublesome Federal batteries. Ramseur arrived next. Rodes sent his brigade to the left of O'Neal. Iverson marched up, followed by Doles; Rodes sent them to the left of Ramseur. Daniel was the last to march up, around 9:00 p.m. The large brigade went into reserve.[28]

All this took far too much time. In an overcautious desire to use the entire division against a force less than half his size, Rodes consumed three precious hours. The Federals refused to oblige him and did not wait until his trap was ready to be snapped shut. Encouraged by the dramatic explosion of a limber struck by one of Carter's shells, they began a rapid pull-out before the Confederates finished deploying. Seeing another chance for glory slipping through his cautious fingers, Rodes in angry frustration called on Ramseur to double-quick through the town in pursuit. Despite their extreme fatigue, the North Carolinians rushed forward "with great enthusiasm," and kept up a running chase of two miles until the Federals split up—some heading east down the Shepardstown Road and others north for Williamsport. In a mostly fruitless pursuit to the Potomac River, Jenkins' troopers managed to intercept and capture only a few men and five artillery pieces.

With the enemy scattered and escaped, Rodes recalled Ramseur and moved the division into town just after dark. Although frustrated once again, he found large amounts of abandoned supplies, most of which the Federals might have carried off or destroyed had Rodes delayed the attack until morning. Among the treasures were 6,000 bushels of grain and 400 rounds of rifled artillery ammunition. When informed that a number of Federals had remained behind, hiding in town buildings, Rodes put Colonel Lightfoot's Sixth Alabama to work rooting them out.

The Virginian allowed his men to rest until 10:00 a.m. the following morning, June 15, when he finally received word of General Ewell's stunning success at Winchester. Old Baldy had executed a daring and decisive envelopment offensive that routed the Federals and captured about 3,000 men, twenty-three guns, and substantial supplies. General Milroy, however, escaped with most of his command to Harpers Ferry. Although Ewell had sent a message to Rodes for help in intercepting the fleeing Federals, the missive arrived too late to be acted upon.

In the eyes of many in the army, Ewell's impressive achievement was reminiscent of Stonewall Jackson. Perhaps Ewell would prove a worthy successor. That judgment was strengthened by the fervent nature of Ewell's General Order 44, in which he appealed to "the men & officers of the Corps to unite with him in returning thanks to our Heavenly Father for the signal success which has crowned the efforts of this command. In acknowledgment of Divine Favor, Chaplains will hold religious services in their respective regiments at such times as may be most convenient."

Unwilling to wait for that "convenient time," Rodes resumed his march to the Potomac. Leaving the Sixth Alabama under Colonel Lightfoot to protect the "pioneers" while they tore up the railroad around Martinsburg, he set out for Williamsport on the 10th. The difficult road and the intense heat made this, in Rodes' opinion, the most trying march yet on his increasingly ill-shod men. The tired command reached the town near sundown, about the same time Jenkins' brigade rode into Chambersburg, Pennsylvania.

Leaving O'Neal and Daniel on the south bank, Rodes used the pontoons that had pre-announced his arrival in Front Royal three days before to send across the Potomac three batteries and the brigades of Ramseur (the Fourteenth North Carolina having the honor of being the first to cross), Iverson, and Doles. The men set up camp in meadows along the north side of the river. Rodes' infantry were the first of the army's foot soldiers across the great river, the spearhead of General Lee's second raid into the North.[29]

* * *

"Being now within the limits of the enemy's territory," began Rodes' Special Order 85, issued on June 16, "punishments will hereafter be inflicted in a more summary manner than formerly. Instead of Courts Martial, Brigade Commanders will call together Military Commissions when necessary. All violence towards the persons or property of non-combatants is strictly forbidden & must be promptly punished. Property of any sort can only be taken under the authority of the heads of departments on the Division staff. This with other Gen. Orders issued since the march commenced & referring to the march, will be read at dress parade this afternoon."[30]

This marked the beginning of Rodes' efforts to ensure the proper behavior of his men while in "enemy territory." The military commission was a novel idea designed for the swift implementation of punishments. All of which, in eventual compliance with the orders of both Ewell and Lee, were intended to demonstrate clearly the superiority of Southern civilization over that of the despised Federal.

"I recon [sic] Genl Rhodes [sic] is waiting to know what to do &c," the Fifty-third North Carolina's James Green correctly surmised in his diary as the division settled down to a well deserved rest. While awaiting further orders and the arrival of the divisions of Early and Johnson, Rodes conscientiously tried to look after his men. He knew they had suffered greatly just getting to the Potomac. A ride through their camps on either side of the river raised both sympathy and admiration for them. "It was not until this day [June 15]," he subsequently reported, "that the troops began to exhibit unmistakable signs of exhaustion, and that stragglers could be found in the line of march, and even then none but absolutely worn-out men fell out of line." The rapid march from Culpeper to Williamsport, he continued, "was executed in a manner highly creditable to the officers and men of the division. A halt at Williamsport was absolutely necessary from the condition of the feet of the unshod men. Very many of these gallant fellows were still marching in ranks, with feet bruised, bleeding, and swollen, and withal so cheerfully as to entitle them to be called the heroes of the Pennsylvania campaign. None but the best soldiers," he concluded, "could have made such a march under such circumstances."[31]

Mercifully, these "best soldiers" now enjoyed a welcome three-day rest while waiting for Early and Johnson to come up. Relaxing, eating, washing in the river, they had little to do save for the division pioneers, who (under the supervision of Rodes' acting engineer officer, Captain Arthur Chichester) worked to destroy the nearby C & O Canal and the aqueduct over the

Conococheague River. On the 17th, Rodes ordered Daniel's brigade to the north side of the river.[32]

By that date a general feeling of refreshment and restoration prevailed throughout the division, with a corresponding effect upon its commander. "Gen. Rodes was in fine spirits," observed Jedediah Hotchkiss, who arrived in Williamsport to prepare detailed maps of Maryland and Pennsylvania for the division leader.[33]

When Hotchkiss and former Jackson staff officer Sandie Pendleton now serving under Ewell in a similar capacity, rode into Williamsport that June 17, Lee's army was strung out nearly 100 miles. Ewell's Second Corps held the lead, with Rodes out front at Williamsport, Johnson close behind, and Early at Bunker Hill near Shepardstown. Longstreet's First Corps held the middle of Lee's dispersed army, marching in the Shenandoah Valley between Ashby's Gap and Snicker's Gap. A. P. Hill's Third Corps brought up the rear. Hill had remained behind opposite Fredericksburg while the other two corps moved north. Once Hooker's rear guard pulled out of Falmouth, Hill began the journey north in the wake of his companion corps. By this date he was just entering the Valley at Chester Gap. Hooker, meanwhile, after being denied permission to ignore Lee's movement and head for Richmond, marched west toward the Bull Run Mountains, much of his army strung out along the Orange & Alexandria Railroad.

In addition to his effort to relieve Vicksburg by crossing the Potomac, Lee also wanted to take the conflict out of war-ravaged Virginia and into untouched regions of Pennsylvania, where he hoped to gather much-needed supplies for his army. In anticipation of the commanding general's orders that all appropriations be done "in a proper manner," Rodes at Williamsport began gathering supplies by securing the purchase of 5,000 pounds of leather— essential for shoes and shoe repair—and thirty-five kegs of gunpowder, all of which he sent to the "rear." Moreover, from the Chambersburg area, Jenkins sent in vast amounts of supplies until he became frightened by false reports of advancing enemy troops. Much to Rodes' displeasure, Jenkins returned to Williamsport.[34]

On June 18, Ewell and Major Moxley Sorrell of Longstreet's staff rode into Williamsport. Together with Rodes and Hotchkiss' new maps, they planned the route of advance into Pennsylvania. Rodes moved his division out the following morning, marching six miles up to Hagerstown, Maryland, where he received instructions from Ewell to continue toward Boonsboro in an effort to create a diversionary threat against Harpers Ferry. Continuing the practice of having each regiment followed by unarmed men with red badges in their hats—stretcher-bearers waiting to pick up soldiers who had collapsed from exhaustion—Rodes marched the division through town in column of companies. He stopped two miles out on the Hagerstown Road near Funkstown, where the men received another two-day rest, again for the purpose of waiting for Johnson and Early.[35]

The delay proved timely, for it rained hard on the 20th and 21st. On the latter day, a Sunday, Rodes allowed hundreds of his men to go into Hagerstown to attend church. Presbyterian services being either unavailable or unaccommodating, Rodes and Ewell rode in the corps commander's buggy to the Catholic church in town. Many from Company D of the Fifth Alabama attended as well. "Heard a very good sermon on the importance of prayer—St. Matt. 15th Chap. 21 to 29th verse," Sam Pickens told his diary. "After service a good many ladies & men went to the carriage & shook hands & conversed with the Gens. Most of the Catholics," he added, "are secessionists."[36]

Later that day Lee gave Ewell the final go-ahead to move in a general direction northeast toward the Susquehanna River. Ewell decided to advance his corps in three columns: (1) With Jenkins' cavalry in the lead, he wanted Rodes and Johnson to march north through the Cumberland Valley to Chambersburg, then head eastward; (2) One of Johnson's brigades under George H. "Maryland" Steuart would make for McConnellsburg to seize horses, cattle, etc.; (3) By order of Lee, Early was to quickly slip east of the mountains to prevent the Federals from cutting the lines of communication. Jeb Stuart's cavalry was expected to arrive and protect Ewell's flanks.[37]

On Monday morning, June 22, Rodes' division broke camp and resumed the march northward. At Middleburg, "Iverson's brigade was the first to touch Pennsylvania soil," Rodes later claimed with some pride. When the division caught up with Jenkins' brigade after a march of thirteen miles, Rodes went into camp at 12:30 p.m. around Greencastle, a quaint little town of about 2,000 people, most of whom "looked on us very grim," a North Carolina soldier recalled. "[T]hey had nothing to say to us only when we spoke to them."[38]

"Our advance has been wonderfully rapid and gloriously successful," Stephen Ramseur wrote from Greencastle to his fiancée. "Our troops are in the finest spirits and when we meet the enemy's horde we will give a good account of ourselves."[39] Others felt much the same. "I hail it as the proudest day of my life," Eugene Blackford wrote his father regarding the army's entry into Pennsylvania. "The secrecy with which our movements are conducted is wonderful. Gen. Rodes told me he did not know one evening which direction his march would turn the next day."[40]

After sending Jenkins back to Chambersburg, Rodes instructed Colonel Edward Willis of the Twelfth Georgia to act as provost marshal in charge of maintaining order in Greencastle. Rodes strictly forbade plundering. All "appropriations," he firmly stipulated, must be done "legally," by way of cash purchase or voucher.[41]

Many years later, Corporal J. S. Downs of the Forty-fifth North Carolina proudly recalled that while in Pennsylvania, the men "never broke ranks until a guard was placed at every house that could be seen from the camp." Rodes, he said, "allowed no pilfering, and no mistreatment of women and children," standards of action that helped explain why the general "was loved not only by his own men but by all who knew him."[42]

By most accounts, Rodes' men behaved very well during their visit to the Keystone State. "My best efforts were made to suppress all irregularities," Rodes stressed in his report,

> and, being very generally and cheerfully seconded by officers and men, they succeeded satisfactorily. Some few cases of fraud and (at Greencastle) some violence to property (the latter traceable to the cavalry) were heard of. A few instances of forced purchases were reported, but never established. I believe that one quartermaster seized such articles as velvet, & c, but could not find him out. In all cases of purchase that came before me, the parties were fully paid and satisfied.

Rodes went on to proclaim grandly that the conduct of his men "challenged the admiration of their commanding officers, while it astonished the people along the line of march. These latter very generally expected to be treated by us with the wanton cruelty generally exhibited by their troops when they are upon our soil."[43]

Ewell staffer Sandie Pendleton became one of those admiring officers after following directly behind Rodes' division for eighteen miles one day. He saw only one sign of devastation—a cherry tree with broken limbs. "This is literally true," he wrote in amazement to his wife on June 23, "and I am grateful for it."[44]

Though undoubtedly many more transgressions occurred than Rodes admitted in his report, most soldiers tolerated and abided by the restraints out of respect for Rodes and General Lee. They also followed the rules because, as

Captain Park noted with great satisfaction in his diary, "it is in accord with true civilization."[45]

However, Rodes was not against making heavy "legal appropriations." Among other essential items, he sent to the rear nearly 3,000 head of Pennsylvania cattle (much of it brought in by Jenkins). To the Greencastle town council Rodes' officers made hopelessly excessive demands for durable goods, including saddles, bridles, pistols, lead, and leather, not to mention perishables such as sauerkraut, which they believed the "Dutch" possessed in abundance, even during the summer months. When the council failed to fully comply, Rodes authorized a town-wide search that turned up little.[46]

On the evening of June 22, Rodes rode to Ewell's headquarters at Beaver Creek to attend a meeting of the division commanders. Early had reached Boonsboro and Johnson's men were not far from Greencastle. The meeting agenda probably included a review of each division's line of march, as well as General Lee's orders regarding troop conduct while in Pennsylvania, which Rodes ordered regimental officers to read to the men the next day in Greencastle.

With the First Battalion of Maryland Cavalry as an escort, Ewell the following morning accompanied Rodes back to Greencastle via Hagerstown. The corps commander decided to ride with Rodes' division until future events dictated otherwise.[47]

Colonel Cullen Battle of the Third Alabama reached the division about this time. Nearly two months earlier, Rodes had persuaded the capable officer to take a leave of absence in lieu of resigning. Battle had severely injured his back during a pair of falls from his horse during the Chancellorsville operations. With his division in good form, Rodes pulled it out of Greencastle at dawn on Wednesday, June 24. "The men, hardened into fine marchers, were in fine spirits," recalled Colonel Charles Blacknell of the Twenty-third North Carolina. "Despite the heat and dust and the rapid progress, not a straggler was to be seen."[48]

Sometime during the march, Rodes and Ewell, riding together at the head of the division, came upon an excited Bible-waving farmer standing by the road shouting at the Confederates. He opposed all war, he exclaimed, adding that his property should not be disturbed. "Though they cast glances at the talker as they passed," recalled a witness, Rodes and Ewell "made no halt or reply."[49]

Around 9:00 a.m. the two generals drew rein next to a Reformed Church standing on the brow of a hill affording a panoramic view of Chambersburg. Gazing down at this impressive Federal community of some 10,000 citizens, they readily agreed it deserved a proper display of Confederate strength, power, and discipline. Orders quickly rippled down the length of the column, calling for the men to go from route step to marching by brigades in column of fours, with arms at right shoulder shift. With regimental bands playing "Dixie" or "Bonnie Blue Flag," the men proudly strode over the hill and down onto Main Street. "Here's your played-out rebellion," jeered the Georgians of Doles' brigade to the gloomy-faced bystanders.[50]

The long column of infantry, artillery, wagons, ambulances, and droves of cattle took several hours to pass through town, after which Rodes put the division in camp on Shirk's Hill, two-and-a-half miles out on the Harrisburg Road near the Conococheague River. Rodes relieved Jenkins, who took his troopers eleven miles on to Shippensburg. "By the time we stacked arms," Sam Pickens told his diary, "the men went off by scores to the neighboring houses & brought back a great many hens, & milk, butter, &c. . . . The people gave everything to the soldiers as they said our money would do them no good." So much for Rodes' insistence on "legal appropriation."[51]

After establishing headquarters at the Franklin Hotel, Ewell assumed the role of an occupier "administering" the town. In Chambersburg's public school he set up a division hospital, its beds fashioned from mattresses provided by the hotels. Saloons were closed and the sale of alcohol prohibited. Ewell summoned the town leaders to the National Bank and presented them with a list of demands. Since most of the area's businessmen had fled with their property after Jenkins' first visit back on the 17th, Ewell's "requisitions" went largely unfilled. Unsatisfied, he authorized a search of the town. Confiscated foods and medicines went into a warehouse, but officers generously gave them back to the townspeople as needs arose. "Never were people more surprised than the citizens of Chambersburg when they found they were in the hands of gentlemen," Colonel Battle proudly declared in his report.[52]

Rodes' strict disciplinary precautions helped encourage that "gentlemanly" behavior. He assigned the Third Alabama as a guard "for the people, property, & c," an act that favorably impressed the townspeople. Particularly impressed was a grocer named Jacob Hoke, who professed astonishment at how quickly a Georgia officer received punishment for drunkenness. Hoke concluded that of all the Confederate troops that passed through Chambersburg, discipline seemed highest in the Second Corps.[53]

In its role as town guard, the Third Alabama took up quarters in a theatre decorated in honor of the "Heroes of Chancellorsville," the chandeliers displaying large letters that spelled "Hooker House." Naturally, this greatly amused the Alabamians, many of whom readily appreciated the irony of the situation. "The first inscription was appropriate," wrote the regiment's Lieutenant Colonel Charles Forsyth, "for it was fated that the real heroes—the Confederate troops—should be thrown into the very hall decorated for those who had been so severely defeated and punished by them at the Battle of Chancellorsville."[54]

When Jenkins sent a report (which ultimately proved unfounded) of approaching Federal cavalry, Rodes ordered Daniel to march his large brigade to Shippensburg. After starting just before midnight on the 24th, Daniel completed the eleven-mile trek around 5:00 a.m.[55]

With the arrival of Johnson's division in Chambersburg (minus Steuart's brigade, which was at McConnellsburg), and with Early at nearby Greenwood, Ewell on June 25 met with his division commanders at the Franklin Hotel. They discussed the exciting possibility of marching all the way to the Susquehanna and seizing Harrisburg. Despite the unexplained absence of Stuart's cavalry, the generals decided to first make for Carlisle, Rodes and Johnson to take the most direct route, Early to cross South Mountain and swing up through York in order to both protect the right flank and tear up the North Central Railroad. From Carlisle all three divisions would make the final, eighteen-mile lunge to the state capital. With the march set to resume the following morning, Major Hotchkiss went to work preparing the appropriate maps.[56]

The townspeople naturally felt greatly relieved to see their uninvited guests preparing to depart. Many realized the occupation might have been much worse. "When we were about to leave the town," reported the Third's Cullen Battle, "a number of citizens, headed by the Mayor, came and thanked the Commander and the regiment for the uniform courtesy and kindness shown the people."

Shortly after the march began, a gentle, steady rain swept in that quickly soaked the men. When they reached Shippensburg around 2:00 p.m., after a march of only eleven miles, Ewell allowed them to stop for the day and get out of the rain. Rodes, reuniting with Daniel (and Jenkins) put the division into camp at Dykerman's Spring about one-half mile south of town. He and Ewell authorized a search of the town's shops. As a soldier of Fifty-third North Carolina wrote, "The people of Shippensburg looked mad at us as usual in this Country."[57]

Lee's army was entirely across the Potomac, with Rodes and Johnson at Shippensburg, and Early at Mummasburg. Longstreet's First Corps divisions under Pickett and Hood were at Greencastle, with McLaws at Williamsport. A.

P. Hill's Third Corps was around Fayetteville, while Stuart's three cavalry brigades were operating near Wolf Run Shoals. Hooker, too, was north of the river; his army had begun crossing at Edward's Ferry two days before.

Starting at 6:00 a.m. on the rainy Saturday morning of June 27, Ewell set out for Carlisle. Johnson's division took the Baltimore Pike, while Rodes marched his men on Walnut Bottom Road. About 1:00 p.m. the town came into view. While Johnson's men went into camp on the McAllister place three miles west of town, Rodes prepared his own division for a grand entry into Carlisle, much as he had done three days earlier at Chambersburg. With bands playing and the men marching smartly, the column moved ahead. When it became clear the Walnut Bottom Road threatened to deflate the spectacle by running through the town's southern edge, Rodes turned the division left onto a side road and marched it up to Main Street (present day High Street), down which ran a railroad track. Here they turned right and, marching on either side of the track, moved directly through the center of town. Most citizens had taken refuge indoors with shutters closed and curtains drawn, some having fled in panic with their property. However, a few brave but gloomy Pennsylvanians stood on the streets—in marked contrast to the warm welcoming rays of the emerging sun.

To guard the town's western exit, Rodes put Doles' brigade onto the campus of Dickinson College. He placed O'Neal out on the Baltimore Pike, about two miles east of town. Daniel, Ramseur, and Iverson, meanwhile, turned north at the square in the center of town and took Hanover Street up to Carlisle Barracks, a Regular Army post built a century before as a frontier defense against Indians. It now was used primarily as a cavalry training school, its garrison of 268 men and six officers having evacuated the place two days before. Ewell and Rodes both set up headquarters in the officer's barracks, a large structure with wide verandas on each of two levels. Ironically, it was the same building "Old Baldy" Ewell had occupied many years before as a second lieutenant of dragoons.

After setting up camp in the barracks, in the public buildings, or out on the spacious lawns behind the officer's quarters, the men, mindful of their impressive marching accomplishments from Fredericksburg to Carlisle, and ever hungry for diversion, serenaded their generals with the bands of the Fourteenth and Twenty-third North Carolina. They called for Ewell to come out and give a speech, whereupon Old Baldy politely told the men his speaking days were over and excused himself. Undaunted, the men called for Rodes. Alluding to his chief's remark, Rodes proclaimed that his speaking days never had begun, "but if you'll whip the Federals," he promised, "when I get back to Old Virginia I will try to give you a speech."

Somewhat satisfied, the men dispersed. Many wandered to a nearby clear stream where they bathed for the first time since June 4, notwithstanding the wading of the Shenandoah and Potomac rivers. Spirits picked up even more when sacks of mail came in that day from Richmond.[58]

Years later, local boy James Sullivan recalled that Rodes' men appeared to be "a fit, well-fed, well-conditioned army," which implied that they benefited greatly from their trip up North, as indeed Lee intended they should. Sullivan also observed that the men generally wore new, albeit dusty, uniforms. "Knapsacks and the whole personal kit was in order," he recalled. "Arms were at every man's command. A significant touch to neatness was a toothbrush at hat band or buttonhole."

By order of Rodes, squads of these "fit, well-fed" men conducted a town-wide, house-to-house search for concealed weapons, food, shoes, and cooking utensils. This led to the somewhat surprising discovery that many townspeople had fled. "So hurried was the flight of the Yanks," concluded Ramseur in a letter to his fiancée, "that many household ornaments & luxuries were left behind. This morning," he added by way of emphasis, "I breakfasted on salmon left in ice."

Citizens who remained in their homes generally received polite treatment. "When the two young officers assigned to search the houses in our block for arms and provisions came to our home," recalled James Sullivan, "they spoke to my mother with grave politeness. . . . They took nothing from us. Mother wept as she told them of her son killed in battle and hoped they would get back to their mothers safely. They were thoughtfully silent."[59]

Among other things, the search parties gathered large amounts of cattle, horses, flour, grain from the barracks stables, and an estimated $50,000 worth of medicines. And though the men stripped the town's stores and tore up the track, bridge, and 600-foot trestle of the Cumberland Valley Railroad, they damaged little else. The soldiers took good care of Dickinson College, many proudly professing that they or their fathers were alumni. Moreover, though Carlisle Barracks was an enemy military installation, Ewell refused to burn it. He even went so far as to stop unscrupulous local civilians from looting the abandoned public buildings. And, of course, Rodes strictly forbade looting. When four of his men were caught in the act, they were tied together and marched through the streets wearing signs on their backs that read: "These men have disgraced themselves by pillaging women's gardens." A band preceding them was supposed to play "The Rogues March," but when the civilian spectators seemed to enjoy this a little too much the band switched to "Yankee Doodle," and the crowd dispersed.[60]

In general, the visiting Southerners treated the civilians, especially the women, with great courtesy, though the reverse was not always the case. Captain Park of the Twelfth Alabama, for example, noted in his diary that when he ventured alone into the National Hotel, he found himself "in the midst of an unfriendly and rough looking crowd," adding, "Had a poor dinner rather ungraciously served by a Dutchy looking young waitress." Park's opinion on the appearance of the local ladies was by no means the harshest offered. A soldier of Twenty-first Georgia wrote home that "there are some of the ugliest women here I ever saw."[61]

Ewell set aside the following day, June 28, for rest and observance of the Sabbath. He directed the clergy in town to hold services as usual, promising at the same time that no one would disturb them. Confederates attending these services noted that "the preachers, though nervous, prayed for their country in peril and their friends in danger; they also prayed for the strangers that were among them; some of them prayed for peace."[62]

Most of Rodes' men, however, attended one of two services held at the barracks. The first, conducted by the Reverend B. Tucker Lacy, the Second Corps' unofficial chaplain (so appointed by Jackson), took place at 11:00 a.m. The Reverend A. D. Betts led the afternoon service. With most of his staff (including John Cabell Early, the fifteen-year-old nephew of Jubal), Ewell attended the first session, as did Rodes and his brigade and regimental commanders. Afterward Rodes hosted in the barracks a bountiful dinner using the linen and tableware of the departed Federal commander, Captain Hastings. The guests included the recently arrived Major General Isaac Trimble, who reached the army without a command. Slated to take back the division now led by Edward Johnson, the sixty-one-year-old Trimble had been forced aside by the lengthy recovery from a wound he took at Groveton the previous August. Not wanting to lose his valuable services, however, Lee sent the aged officer on to Ewell as a voluntary aide.[63]

The solemn religious services, the fine dinner, and the rousing band renditions of Dixie and Bonnie Blue Flag served as a prelude to a grand, elaborate ceremony that most in the division acknowledged as a monumental historic occasion. Before the invasion of Pennsylvania, patriotic ladies of Richmond sent President Davis their hand-sewn version of the new national flag, recently approved for adoption by the Confederate Congress. The banner consisted of an all-white field containing in the upper left corner the battle flag stars-and-bars. In compliance with the ladies' wish that it be presented to the regiment deemed most worthy, the president gave the flag to General Lee who, in honor of the fallen Jackson, sent it on to Ewell. The Second Corps chief passed the flag on to "his favorite division commander"—Robert Rodes. Apparently to avoid offending his other brigadiers, Rodes gave the banner to his most senior in rank, Junius Daniel, who finally bestowed it upon the Thirty-second North Carolina. Someone determined that the new flag deserved to be honored at some special, appropriate time, preferably in a flag-raising ceremony deep in enemy territory. All agreed that special time had arrived.

Ewell, however, thought the flag too small for such a big occasion. To avoid offending the Thirty-second North Carolina, he thoughtfully directed that a new ceremonial national banner be improvised using the regiment's full battle flag. While waiting for "two or three tailors" from the ranks to do their work, the officers scheduled to make speeches passed the time tapping a huge keg of recently discovered lager beer. Rodes and his aide Green Peyton agreed that the brew was good, though a bit strong—they did not realize that the local "Dutch" added whiskey to their lager, with the inevitable inebriating results. Rodes liked a drink now and then, but the renowned disciplinarian never let it get the best of him—until now. "I never saw Rodes intoxicated before or since," Ewell's staff officer Campbell Brown declared seven years later.[64]

Finally, about 4:00 p.m., the improvised grand banner went up the flagpole. "And thus it was," the Thirty-second regiment's historian proudly wrote, "that North Carolinians can boast that it was the flag of one of their regiments that defiantly waved on the enemy's soil at a point farther north than any other Confederate flag during the whole war."[65]

"Oh! it was a grand occasion," recalled Private Henry A. Loudon of the Thirty-second's Company I, ruefully adding, "in striking contrast with the sad scenes witnessed by the same soldiers, two days thereafter, on the blood-stained heights at Gettysburg."[66] A soldier in the Forty-third North Carolina agreed: "Food, drink, music, oratory, this was almost like the war young men had expected in 1861."[67]

Despite having just one day earlier proclaimed that his speaking days were over, Ewell delivered a brief oration in front of about 8,000 men, before promptly retiring to seek relief from a severe headache. Reverend Lacy followed Ewell, offering a moving speech about the late Stonewall Jackson. "The magnificent blond Rodes spoke in his turn," recalled a soldier in the Forty-third North Carolina. Daniel was next, with a few patriotic remarks of his own. "Everything the generals said," remembered a North Carolinian, "was greeted by storms of applause from the listening troops, and certain Carlisle townsfolk clapped hands as well." So far none of the speakers gave any indication they had tasted the "Dutch brew," and up to this point the troops considered the affair to be rather inspiring. A member of the Forty-third North Carolina wrote, "I felt like going on to New York on the occasion." But then up to the platform stepped Isaac Trimble, who appeared in the words of one observer "quite jolly." Trimble delivered an oration that was "not too neat." Though the audience got a kick out of Old Isaac, they loved it when Major Ben Greene of Georgia stepped up and seized the podium. Grinning and waving out to the men, Greene, who in addition to the beer had imbibed a shot of strong brandy, began speaking in an "utterly incoherent" manner. The troops jeered when someone grabbed Greene by the coattail and pulled him back, but a cheer broke out when the major escaped and returned to the podium to continue his rambling. The affair came to an unceremonious end when a storm broke out and aides at last were able to lead Greene away to bed.[68]

Inevitably, intoxication found its way into the ranks. In addition to lager beer, a fair amount of Federal whiskey was hidden in and about town. While out foraging, a North Carolina private discovered a full barrel hidden in a haystack, a happy discovery he did not hesitate to share, with "mint juleps in tin cans [becoming] plentiful." Captain Vines Turner of the Twenty-third North Carolina sadly confessed, "Here many of our jaded, weary boys drank too much United States Government whiskey and a battle with a Georgia regiment, for the time likewise drowning their weariness, was narrowly averted." The alcohol consumption led a comrade in Ramseur's brigade later to angrily speculate that the loss at Gettysburg may have been due in part to the alcohol found in Carlisle. Brigadier General Alfred Iverson, he declared, was the principal abuser.[69]

Meanwhile, the end of the month required a head count that constituted the June return of Rodes' division. The tally showed that Ramseur's brigade was the smallest, with but 1,130 men. Iverson's brigade was next with 1,356, Doles' had a few more at 1,373, and O'Neal's substantially more with 1,791. With 2,304 men, Junius Daniel commanded the largest brigade. Including fourteen staff members, Rodes' division fielded 8,125 men, making it not only the largest division in Lee's army, but nearly as large as the entire Union I Corps under John Reynolds. In terms of both size and quality—nearly all of the officers and men were proven combat veterans—the division was one of the best under Lee's command.[70]

* * *

Alcohol and revelry notwithstanding that day of June 28, the strategic pieces of the campaign were beginning to unfold rapidly. Ewell's Second Corps was the farthest north, with the divisions of Rodes and Johnson at Carlisle and Early's men holding York. Jenkins' troopers were reconnoitering toward Harrisburg. A. P. Hill's Third Corps was near Fayetteville, while James Longstreet's First Corps was in the vicinity of Chambersburg. Jeb Stuart's missing cavalry, however, was still trying to get around the moving Army of the Potomac and was operating near Rockville, Maryland. "Are you surprised to find that we are so far advanced into the Enemy's territory?" Ramseur wrote from Carlisle to his fiancée. "We are; or rather we are surprised that we have met with feeble resistance so far." As for Lee's plans, "Let this suffice," Ramseur discreetly assured her, "they are bold and well conceived."[71]

The Army of the Potomac was generally strung out between Frederick and South Mountain (which meant that it was also between Jeb Stuart and Lee's army). "Fighting Joe" Hooker, however, no longer was in command. A dispute with the administration regarding his authority over the garrison at Harpers Ferry led to his resignation, which was promptly accepted by Abraham Lincoln. Equally prompt was the selection of his replacement. Pennsylvanian George Gordon Meade, the commander of the Federal V Corps and the same officer who had thrown his division against Rodes on South Mountain, was tapped to lead the Army of the Potomac in the middle of a complex and fluid campaign.

Unaware of any of this, Ewell on the morning of June 29 received from Jenkins the exciting news that only a few militia defended Harrisburg. The Second Corps commander promptly ordered Rodes and Johnson to prepare for a march on the Pennsylvania capital, distant a mere eighteen miles, "a step," Rodes asserted, "which every man in the division contemplated with eagerness." Before the operation could get underway, however, stunning orders came in from General Lee—the army was to concentrate at Chambersburg.[72]

While at Chambersburg with Longstreet's corps, Lee learned from a "scout" named Harrison that the Federal army had crossed the Potomac and was centered around Frederick, Maryland. This placed his own army, strung out some fifty miles from Chambersburg to Harrisburg, in a very dangerous position. Lee sent out orders for all three of his corps to concentrate near Chambersburg.

In a cold rain, Johnson's division, along with the Second Corps train (fourteen miles long) and two battalions of artillery, marched west out of

Carlisle at 1:00 p.m. Rodes' men had not yet taken a step when new orders came in for Ewell. Lee had had second thoughts about giving up so much and concentrating the entire army at Chambersburg. Instead, he would keep the Second Corps operating east of South Mountain to provide greater flexibility in dealing with a Federal march north from Maryland. He instructed Ewell to march down to Heidlersburg, where he would have the discretion, as circumstances might require, to move southwest to Cashtown or nine miles south to Gettysburg.

Too late to recall Johnson, whose division went on to spend the night at Shippensburg, Ewell decided to move out with Rodes for Heidlersburg the following morning, June 30. He would rendezvous there with Early, whom he ordered to come in the same day from York and the outskirts of Harrisburg. Deeply disappointed with this turn of events, Rodes decided to make his last night in Carlisle a memorable one. At his barracks headquarters he spread out another lavish dinner, this time for the officers of his division.[73]

The pullout began shortly after 7:00 a.m. the following morning. Maintaining a lively pace, the men marched south into a gap in the Cumberland Valley, crossed Yellow Breaches Creek, then went two miles on to Papertown (now part of Mt. Holly Springs), "where many of our men obtained a supply of writing paper" from the town's prosperous little paper mill, Captain Park noted in his diary. Like many roads they traveled upon in Pennsylvania, this one possessed a temptation irresistible even to Ewell. "Cherries were ripe along the rock-walled lanes," recalled a captain in the Twenty-third North Carolina. "Bringing camp hatchets out, fruit ladened limbs were severed and we regaled ourselves as we swung onward."[74]

Other acts were not so easily tolerated. Along the road to Papertown, a few of Rodes' more enterprising men managed to secure a handout at the farm home of a Mrs. John S. Motts, who served them large slices of bread right out of the oven. When the men used up all her butter, she gave them molasses. One of her children, Sarah, recalled many years later that eventually "the commanding general [Rodes] came along, and he, seeing what was happening, told his men to desist; it was not a stern, harsh command, but was given in soft, quiet tones, and we saw a soldiers' instant obedience in action; in the presence of the men the general said, 'MY men must not annoy you.' It was not 'My MEN,' but 'MY men.' And the men passed on the road."[75]

From Papertown, Rodes' division marched into a gap between Mt. Holly on the right and Piney Mountain on the left, where ran a tributary of Yellow Breach called Mountain Run. Here Rodes allowed the men to rest, fill their canteens, and wash their feet. Taking the Baltimore- Harrisburg Pike, he led them into Petersburg just before noon, about which time they ran into a battalion of young school cadets. In a fair exchange for their shoes and socks, · the boys received from Rodes' men a good scolding for being out on the road and not at their studies.[76]

Refreshed, Rodes put the division on the Frederick City Road and headed for Heidlersburg. The day was humid and the men became increasingly weary. Ewell rode to the head of Doles' brigade and ordered the band of the Fourth Georgia—reputed to be one of the best in the division—to stop and play for the men as they marched by. It seemed to have a good effect. The music, particularly the tune "Tom, March On," noticeably lifted the spirits of many passing marchers.[77]

After a fatiguing trek of nearly fourteen hours and twenty-two miles, some of it through rain and mud—under better conditions Rodes' veterans could have covered this distance in about ten hours—the division entered Heidlersburg just before dark. The same evening, June 30, Early's brigades arrived from the east, the division going into camp three miles outside Heidlersburg.

Ewell called several of his generals to a meeting. To Trimble, Rodes, and Early (Johnson was absent), the Second Corps commander expressed consternation at Lee's discretionary orders to "march to Cashtown or Gettysburg as circumstances may dictate." Extreme fatigue underscored that consternation. As if to compensate for the loss of his leg, Ewell had driven himself to the point of exhaustion, a situation made worse near Winchester by a hard fall from his horse. Moreover, having served under the exacting Jackson, Ewell was not accustomed to working with discretionary orders. Again and again he read Lee's order, as if it might somehow explain itself. He asked, perhaps with a dollop of sarcasm, if anyone knew where they should go. Trimble suggested Gettysburg, since reports indicated that elements of the Union XI Corps were near there. Rodes and Early, however, preferred Cashtown, since that would bring them closer to Lee and the other two corps. Ewell finally resolved on a compromise: they would march for Middletown (an appropriate name for Ewell's compromise), midway between Cashtown and Gettysburg, and march from there "as circumstances might dictate."

By that evening, the divisions of Dorsey Pender and Harry Heth of A. P. Hill's Third Corps were already at Cashtown, eight miles west of Gettysburg. Hill's third division under Richard Anderson, together with First Corps divisions led by John Hood and Lafayette McLaws, were near Fayetteville, between Cashtown and Chambersburg. Longstreet's other division under George Pickett was at Chambersburg. Ewell's remaining division under Edward Johnson was not far from Heidlersburg at Scotland on the foot of the west slope of South Mountain. Jeb Stuart's troopers were near Jefferson.[78]

What was missing from the equation was the exact location of the Army of the Potomac. Though rumors abounded, the disposition of the enemy was unclear. What time would prove certain, however, is that no one in the Army of Northern Virginia expected that one of the most important battles of the war would begin on the morrow.

Chapter 8

Gettysburg

Wednesday, July 1, dawned with a drizzling mist, but as the morning progressed the weather cleared, the sun came out, and the heat and humidity became intense. With Ewell accompanying the division, Rodes moved out of Heidlersburg at 7:00 a.m. and headed southwest for Middletown (present day Biglerville). To avoid congestion on the roads, Early headed south on the Harrisburg Pike. When he reached Hunterstown, about four miles north of Gettysburg, he would turn west and head toward Mummasburg and Cashtown.[1]

The van of Rodes' column reached Middletown about 8:00 a.m., though with the stage of time-keeping in the 1860s, some sources claim it was 9:00 a.m. or even as late as 10:00 a.m. Fifteen minutes later, Ewell received word that A. P. Hill was marching his corps from Cashtown to Gettysburg. That finally decided the matter for Old Baldy, who ordered Rodes to take the Middletown Road south to Gettysburg. Ewell sent instructions for Early to continue south on the pike for the same place. Ewell informed Lee of these moves.[2]

In a reconnaissance-in-force approved by A. P. Hill, Heth's division had set out from Cashtown about 5:00 a.m. that morning, followed later by a division under Dorsey Pender. Heth's destination was Gettysburg, the seat of Adams County with a population about 2,400. Though it had much to recommend it, including a fine college and some industry, its importance was not what was in the town, but what led into and out of it. Gettysburg was a major road hub, with ten different avenues of approach converging on it from every direction of the compass. Why Hill allowed Heth to push ahead with so many men is unclear, for the larger the force under one's command, the higher the odds of triggering a serious engagement. About 8:00 a.m., Heth ran into John Buford's division of Federal cavalry, 2,700 carbine-wielding men posted west of Gettysburg. Instead of identifying his enemy and withdrawing, or holding his position and sending back a detailed report, Heth deployed his brigades and drove forward. The advance triggered a meeting engagement that intensified when John Reynolds's I Corps arrived after a forced march, just in time to support Buford's gallant holding action.[3]

Rodes was riding at the head of his division as it marched south from Middletown. The faint sound of distant gunfire to the southwest filled the air. He looked at his watch. It was about noon, and he figured he was about four miles north of Gettysburg. Rodes hurried the column along, but at some point he must have ridden ahead with his staff as the sound of battle grew louder with every step of his horse down the Middletown Road. He finally pulled up on some high ground about one-half mile north of town. From there, he could see the relative positions of the combatants west of town, though at this point the morning fight had ended and only the artillery was engaged. Rodes quickly realized an opportunity lay before him, the likes of which few military commanders ever see.

Rodes' division was arriving on the right flank and rear of the enemy engaged with Hill's Third Corps troops. The Union line ran generally north to south, while Rodes' would run, when deployed, east to west— perpendicular to the defending enemy front. If he quickly brought down his division from the north, he could smash the enemy flank and drive deeply into his rear. Given the lay of the terrain and road network, he also realized he would have to shift his arriving division west to a wooded hill, across the wide base of which the Mummasburg Road ran in a northwest- southeast direction. North of the road, a rising hill crowned with trees (Oak Hill) offered not only concealment for his movement and deployment but the advantage of high ground from which he could take the enemy directly in flank. No doubt thrilled by the prospect of pulling off a flank attack greater even than the one he had so brilliantly spearheaded just one month before in the woods west of Chancellorsville, Rodes sped north to fetch his division. At the same time he sent a courier to find Early and hurry him along.[4]

The shift to the high ground would not be easy. After Iverson's skirmishers flushed out a light screen of Union cavalry, Rodes began the movement about two miles north of town. "On the run," the men sped through the woods, crossed wheat fields, darted through orchards and leapt over stone fences to the reverse slope of Oak Hill. Like he had at Chancellorsville two months before, Rodes pushed and urged his men forward into position, the strain of which caused "many of them to faint from exhaustion." Iverson's brigade led the column. It deployed in the Forney Woods south of Mummasburg Road, as the rest of the division arrived behind it. Rodes' front was a mere 800 yards away from the combatants. "The whole portion of the force opposing General Hill could be seen," he later wrote in his after-action report. A soldier in the Sixth Alabama later recalled plainly seeing Hill's troops "away to our right across broad fields of ripe wheat . . . moving slowly but steadily on the long blue lines. It was the only time during the war that we were in position to get such a view of contending forces." On this commanding knob, with all of its thrilling potential for a great victory, Rodes planted his division flag, a blue banner diagonally crossed with white stars, and set up his field headquarters.[5]

His arrival on Oak Hill was even more important than he might have realized. In taking the high ground, Rodes preempted any men from O. O. Howard's XI Corps from seizing it. Howard's men were moving north as fast as possible, passing through town to protect Reynold's exposed right flank from exactly the threat Ewell's arrival posed to the developing Federal position. Rodes' division not only threatened the Union I Corps (which now was under Abner Doubleday after Reynolds fell early in the action), but compromised Howard's left flank in the undulating and generally open ground north of town.

As the rest of his division arrived, Rodes about 1:00 p.m. called for Carter's battalion of sixteen guns to set up on Oak Hill and open on enemy infantry deployed north of the Chambersburg Pike facing west toward Hill's Third Corps. The Union infantry comprised the battered remains of Brigadier General Lysander Cutler's brigade, part of James Wadsworth's division, Reynolds' I Corps. After being hit hard earlier in the fields a few hundred yards to the west, they had fallen back to take up a position on Oak Ridge. Rodes' call for Carter to open fire was unwise: it accomplished nothing, but alerted the enemy to his presence and allowed them time to redeploy to meet him.

O'Neal's brigade formed on partially open ground to the left and slightly in advance of Iverson. Worried about his left flank, Rodes sent George Doles' Georgians east toward Carlisle Road to keep an eye on the arriving Federal XI Corps. Daniel's large brigade arrived next and formed 200 yards behind Iverson. Ramseur's brigade was still moving into position behind Oak Hill.[6]

As his men deployed, Rodes spotted additional Federal troops arriving on Oak Ridge on Cutler's previously exposed right flank. As he soon would learn, the Union infantry was John C. Robinson's division, part of Reynold's I Corps. The fresh division included two brigades under Henry Baxter and Gabriel Paul. They had been sent by Abner Doubleday to extend the Federal position and prevent an enemy turning movement. Baxter arrived first and formed his men into a wide arrowhead pointing generally north, one side of the tip facing northwest and the other northeast. Rodes and his men had never faced any soldier from the I Corps, whose total strength on July 1 was roughly equal to his own division. The corps, however, possessed relatively little combat experience, but Reynolds' rigorous training and inspired leadership had molded it into a confident and efficient fighting machine. Two of its divisions were putting up a stubborn and skillful fight west of Gettysburg, where they had chewed up Heth's division and stymied every effort to thrust them aside. John Robinson's 2,500 men were preparing a similar hard lesson for Rodes.

Even though he had three fully deployed brigades ready to advance (plus Doles some distance to the east), Rodes hesitated. Robinson's men were still arriving and the available Confederates substantially outnumbered him, but caution whispered in Rodes' ear. What was the strength of the enemy behind the wooded ridge to his front? He did not know. Rodes had learned bitter lessons at Seven Pines, Gaines' Mill, and Sharpsburg about attacking the enemy without full support. He wanted everything in order, everyone to understand his orders, and his entire division up, if possible, before moving forward.

As Ramseur's men threaded their way onto Oak Hill (they had been back with the wagons) and Baxter deployed his Federal brigade on the ridge to the south, Confederate aides escorted into Rodes' presence a few soldiers the enemy had captured earlier that morning in the fighting west of town. Somehow they had escaped and made their way to Oak Hill. Rodes knew A. P. Hill's Third Corps had arrived from the west but he did not know which of Hill's units were in the fight. "Who is in front of the enemy on my right?" he asked the escaped soldiers. When they told him the Southern brigades were from the divisions of Heth and Pender, Rodes, thinking aloud to himself, said, "All right, I'll send word to Heth [that I am going to attack]." Wanting to also keep his fellow Second Corps division commander apprised of the developing situation, Rodes turned to two of Jubal Early's recently arrived staff officers. "I have a message for Early," he said. Taking out a pencil and small piece of paper, he wrote: "Heth and Pender are in Reynold's front. I can burst through the enemy in an hour." (When he read this a short time later, Early endorsed it on the back, and then wrote on the front: "All right, burst through," and sent it back to Rodes.)[7]

While waiting in line, some of Rodes' men took a severe pounding from Federal artillery. Having relatively little cover, O'Neal's brigade was the hardest hit. Captain Park of the Twelfth Alabama saw a cannon ball ricochet off the ground and hit Captain James Davis in the head, "and his brains splattered upon me." Over in Daniel's brigade on Rodes' right, Lieutenant Colonel Wharton of the Second North Carolina Battalion watched as a shell flew in and took down nine men at once. Lieutenant Wharton Green, a member of Daniel's staff, suffered a shrapnel wound in his head. "I ordered the Alabama brigade [O'Neal] from the line it had occupied to fall back abreast with Iverson," wrote Rodes, "so as to obtain some little shelter for the troops." Rodes ordered O'Neal's right-most regiment, Cullen Battle's Third Alabama, to take up a position "on a line with Daniel's brigade." Rodes ordered O'Neal "to form the balance of the brigade upon it." O'Neal's left-most regiment, the Fifth Alabama, was held back "under my own immediate command," Rodes later explained, as a mobile reserve to fill, if necessary, the wide gap between O'Neal and Doles. These actions either confused or angered O'Neal, as events would soon make clear. Regardless, the suddenly complicated arrangement courted trouble—especially since it involved Rodes' least experienced brigade commander. And trouble was not long in coming.[8]

The still-outnumbered Federals in front of him had taken up a strong if exposed position on the Forney farm property. A surprised Rodes believed the enemy was "rash enough" to come out of the woods and attack his position. Indeed, some Federal infantry was advancing toward the gap between O'Neal's left and Doles' right. Rodes determined to break up the assault with a preemptive strike. "Boys," he called out to the Twelfth North Carolina of Iverson's brigade, "the enemy are advancing upon us, [we are going to] go ahead and meet them."[9]

It was about 2:00 p.m. or slightly later, and Rodes' division now occupied a front about one mile wide. Doles held the far left facing generally southeast in an open plain between the Middletown Road and the foot of Oak Ridge. On his right was Blackford's sharpshooter battalion, spread thin to cover the several hundred yards separating Doles' right from O'Neal's left. O'Neal extended Rodes' front westward up the slope of the hill. Iverson held the right front of Rodes' line, deployed south of Mummasburg Road. Daniel was in the second line 200 yards behind and shifted some distance to the right of Iverson. Ramseur's men were standing in reserve.

Rodes' plan of attack was relatively straightforward. While Doles held on the left to await Early's arrival, O'Neal would advance south with four of his five regiments (the Fifth Alabama being held in reserve on his left) down the steep slope of the hill. Iverson, meanwhile, would move south and southeast toward the ridge held by the newly arrived enemy. Daniel would advance en echelon behind Iverson's right, protecting the division's right flank, while

Ramseur moved up in close reserve. There is some confusion whether Rodes expected Cullen Battle's Third Alabama to advance with Daniel or under O'Neal's command. Rodes instructed Colonel Battle to "keep well up on Daniel's left." In his report, he noted (apparently in some surprise) that O'Neal had not moved out with the regiment, "the Third having been permitted by Colonel O'Neal to move with Daniel's brigade." Still, if all went according to plan, the attack would put Robinson's Federals in a vice, O'Neal squeezing their flank from the north, and Iverson and Daniel with heavy numbers thrusting from the northwest and west.

But almost nothing would go according to plan. When the attack order arrived, O'Neal was at Rodes' headquarters. The colonel informed the general that neither he nor his staff officers had horses. Without them, communication with his regiments and the brigades on his flanks would be nearly impossible. How a brigade commander could be in such straits on the eve of an attack has never been satisfactorily explained. O'Neal also demanded the return of the Third Alabama to his line. Undoubtedly surprised and perhaps a bit irritated to see O'Neal only moments before the attack was to begin, and without horses no less, Rodes brusquely told him to attend to the attack. Relenting slightly, Rodes told him that with the colonel's "permission," he would send a staff officer, Lieutenant James P. Arrington, to make sure the Third advanced with Daniel. This failed to satisfy O'Neal, which may explain why he made what can only be described as the drastic decision to dissociate himself from the attack. Without telling Rodes, he stalked off—not to prepare his three (or four) regiments to go into the fight, but to the Fifth Alabama on the far left, which Rodes was holding in reserve. There was no reason for the colonel to attach himself to that regiment. "Why my brigade was thus deprived of two regiments, I have never been informed," O'Neal disingenuously, and with obvious bitterness, wrote in his after-action report.

The attack began about 2:30 p.m. Nothing went right. O'Neal's three leaderless regiments (aligned left to right as follows: Sixth Alabama, Twenty-sixth Alabama, Twelfth Alabama), jumped off by themselves. Iverson somehow missed the signal to advance altogether. In his official report, the North Carolinian claimed that when he received orders to advance, he sent a staff officer to watch for O'Neal's movement so as to conform to it. Almost immediately, however, the officer returned with the startling news that O'Neal had already gone forward. By the time Iverson's 1,450-man brigade set off, O'Neal's regiments were hopelessly jumbled, confused, and taking enemy fire. Moreover, despite Rodes' instructions to O'Neal to advance toward a specific

Brig. Gen. Alfred Iverson, in a postwar image. His performance on July 1, 1863, can only be labeled as disastrous.

Generals in Gray

point—probably the left side of Baxter's line, so as to converge there with Iverson's left flank— the leaderless Alabamians veered to the east, leaving Iverson's men isolated in their attack. "It was soon apparent," Rodes reported, "that we were making no impression upon the enemy."

O'Neal's fitful attack fell against the right wing of Baxter's Federal arrowhead. These four regiments deployed with the 12th Massachusetts holding the left, followed by the 90th Pennsylvania, 83rd New York, and the 88th Pennsylvania on the right. The 12th Alabama's Col. Samuel Pickens recalled that they "attacked them [Baxter's men] in a strong position. After a desperate fight of about fifteen minutes, we were compelled to fall back, as the regiments on our left gave way, being flanked by a large force." Because O'Neal did not advance far, if at all, with his three regiments, no one seems to have identified the 45th New York deployed on the Hagy farm on Baxter's right flank. The New Yorkers were part of Col. George von Amsberg's brigade, Carl Schurtz's division, Howard's XI Corps. Von Amsberg's regiments were spread thinly across a wide front, with the 45th New York battling Blackford's sharpshooters. As they were doing so, the XI Corps was pouring through the town to take up a position north of it. Supporting the 45th New York was Dilger's battery. The New Yorkers and artillery opened an enfilade fire into the Sixth Alabama's left flank. Baxter's regiments fired from the front. Rodes ordered the Fifth Alabama under Colonel Josephus Hall out of reserve to the Sixth Alabama's assistance. There he made the startling discovery that O'Neal was with the regiment and not up front leading the attack. With no time to berate the sulking colonel, he sent him forward with the Fifth, only to see the old regiment quickly get caught up in the general repulse. "My command was under a front and enfilading fire, with no support, and suffering a very severe loss," Hall later reported. Rodes rode out to help O'Neal rally the brigade and steady its line as it fell back. "The whole brigade . . . was repulsed quickly, and with loss," Rodes tersely stated.[10]

Iverson's attack on the right of Rodes' line looked much better than O'Neal's hapless effort, but it would suffer a far worse fate that history would never forget. Iverson's North Carolina brigade advanced in parade-like formation, its regiments aligned from left to right as follows: Fifth, Twentieth, Twenty-third, and Twelfth. The brigade attacked on an oblique, veering in a southeast direction. The advance leaned its left side regiments into a Federal line strengthened by two regiments, the Ninetieth Pennsylvania and Twelfth Massachusetts. Both Federals units had recently moved into position after their fight against O'Neal. Iverson, however, made a crucial mistake that would cost the lives of hundreds of good men: he failed to make sure that skirmishers advanced ahead of his battle line. None of the North Carolinians knew that many hundreds of Federals were crouched in the edge of the woods behind a stone wall, waiting for them to step into point blank killing range.

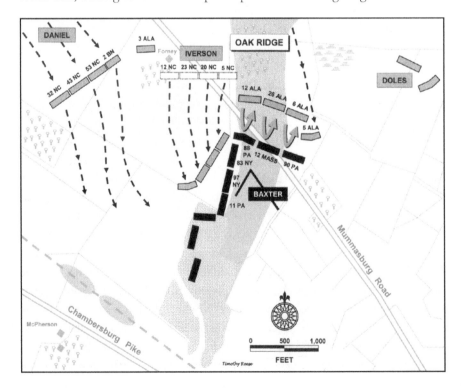

Blissfully unaware of their pending fate, the North Carolinians came on "as evenly as if on parade" through an open field of timothy, with the Forney buildings between their left and O'Neal's right. "There was not a bush nor a tree between the place where Iverson formed and the Federal line, a distance of nearly half a mile," observed Lieutenant Walter Montgomery of the Twelfth North Carolina. "Iverson's men," observed one of Baxter's Pennsylvanians, "with arms at a right shoulder, came on in splendid array, keeping step with an almost perfect line . . . as orderly as if on brigade drill, while behind the stone wall the Union soldiers, with rifles cocked and fingers on the triggers, waited and bided their time, feeling confident." That time arrived when the North Carolinians came within 100 yards of the wall. Baxter's men rose as one and unleashed one of the most devastating fires in the entire war. Scores of North Carolinians went down together, with one private in the Twenty-third taking five bullets in the head. "I believe every man who stood up was either killed or wounded," declared Lieutenant Oliver Williams of the Twentieth North Carolina.[11] "Iverson's line," a Union soldier wrote after the battle, "was indicated by the ghastly row of dead and wounded men, whose blood detailed the course of their line with a crimson stain clearly discernable for several days after the battle, until the rain washed the gory record away."[12] A Virginia artillerist later counted that, "within a few feet . . . seventy nine North Carolinians laying dead in a straight line [that] was perfectly dressed. Three had fallen to the front, the rest had fallen backward; yet the feet of all these dead men were in a perfectly straight line."[13]

Lying among the near-perfect rows of their fallen comrades were the living, some of whom opted out of this hopeless situation by raising bits of cloth in surrender. News of this tragic development reached Rodes by way of a message from Iverson. After ordering his men forward with a "Give them hell!" cheer, he chose to remain behind and watch the battle from the rear. Perhaps the painful groin wound suffered at Chancellorsville changed the officer who once offered some promise. Whatever the reason, Iverson was not on hand to correct his brigade's faulty alignment or see that it did not stumble into a trap. "Unarmed, unled as a brigade," lamented Captain Vines Turner of the Twenty-third North Carolina, "we went to our doom. Deep and long must the desolate homes and orphan children of North Carolina rue the rashness of that hour." From his position far to the rear, Iverson was unable to distinguish that the long line of men laying on the ground was not there by choice. When he discovered that some of the men were trying to surrender, Iverson rashly assumed they were displaying cowardice on the field in the face of the enemy.

Closer examination, however, revealed that those men lying in neat rows on the battlefield had not disgraced their brigade commander after all; they were dead.[14]

"When I saw white handkerchiefs raised," Iverson later reported, "and my line of battle still lying down in position, I characterized the surrender as disgraceful; but when I found afterward that 500 of my men were left lying dead and wounded on a line as straight as a dress parade, I exonerated, with one or two disgraceful exceptions, the survivors, and claim for the brigade that they nobly fought and died without a man running to the rear. No greater gallantry and heroism," he concluded, "has been displayed during the war." Rodes agreed the men fought well, even if he believed their commander had not. "Iverson's brigade attacked handsomely," he wrote in his report, the men "fought and died like heroes. His dead lay in a distinctly marked line of battle." Meanwhile, the shattered remnants of the brigade sought the relative safety of a shallow gully, where it suffered further humiliation when the Federals stormed the position and captured about 400 men, plus the flag of the Twenty-third North Carolina, before being driven off.[15]

While Iverson's brigade was marching to its slaughter, Junius Daniel was advancing his brigade behind it en echelon. He did so without O'Neal's Third Alabama, fearing the extra regiment might come up against Iverson's men on his left. (Colonel Battle later offered his regiment to Stephen Ramseur, who gladly accepted it.) As Iverson moved southeast, Daniel's brigade continued due south, widening the distance between it and Iverson's left flank. Within a few minutes, Daniel's men were completely in the open and unsupported on either flank. Daniel divided his command into two wings, with one heading east southeast toward Cutler's men in Shead's Woods, and the other south against Colonel Roy Stone's brigade aligned near the Chambersburg Pike. After his right wing hit Stone's Federals in a railroad cut and was thrown back, the resourceful Daniel adjusted his line and swung around two companies to enfilade the cut. A long and bitter fight followed as Daniel sought to fulfil his orders to retain the integrity of the right side of Rodes' division and drive away the enemy.[16]

Rodes' attack began with substantial promise but had thus far failed miserably. Not only did he fail to get off in time to flank the exposed Federal right facing Hill's Third Corps, but his piecemeal frontal assault against a much weaker opponent had been bloodily (and rather easily) repulsed. Although two of his brigadiers amply demonstrated their inept leadership abilities, much of the blame for not conducting a thorough reconnaissance and for not properly coordinating the general advance rested on Rodes' shoulders.

Douglas Southall Freeman, the Army of Northern Virginia's biographer, criticized the alignment of Rodes' division that afternoon. "Within the time available," wrote Freeman, "this deployment probably was unavoidable, but it was far from ideal. It left the well-tested Brigadiers, Ramseur and Doles, out of the first attack and put the direction of the assault on O'Neal and Iverson, who had not distinguished themselves in the battles of May." Freeman was right to consider the deployment unavoidable. It had been Iverson's turn that morning, without the expectation of combat, to lead the march, and for Ramseur to bring up the rear. Freeman also is right in proclaiming Ramseur and Doles "well-tested," but so were Iverson and O'Neal, both of whom, despite Freeman's contrary inference, fought well at Chancellorsville. Their brigades led the attack of May 2, and eventually went into the thick of it the next day, both men falling with wounds. Only in retrospect can the judgment be made that Rodes' deployment on July 1 "was far from ideal." No one on the scene would have thought that was the case at 2:00 p.m. on July 1, 1863.[17]

General Lee, meanwhile, had arrived on A. P. Hill's Third Corps front. He seemed willing to let Rodes' attack carry its own water. "Rodes is heavily engaged," the repulsed Heth pleaded with him. "Had I not better attack?" Lee answered in the negative. "I am not prepared to bring on a general engagement today—Longstreet is not up." For the moment, Rodes would have to sink or swim on his own, though it should have seemed obvious that with Ewell's men striking from the north, and Heth's division already chewed up, a general engagement was well underway whether Lee liked it or not.[18]

Although his attack had not gone off as he had hoped, Rodes refused to give up. It now was Ramseur's turn. As the survivors from Iverson's, O'Neal's, and Daniel's brigades pulled back to reorder themselves, Ramseur's roughly 1,000 men prepared to attack "just where he [the enemy] had repulsed O'Neal and checked Iverson's advance." Baxter's exhausted Federals had moved south a bit to make room for Gabriel Paul's newly arrived 1,500-man brigade, which formed a U-shaped line along the Mummasburg Road. Whether Ramseur would have any more luck than the others remained to be seen. Paul's arrival certainly was not welcome news, and neither was Howard's presence. The vanguard of his XI Corps, which Rodes' division had handled so roughly at Chancellorsville, was quickly deploying on the right of the I Corps beyond Rodes' left. The XI Corps threatened to turn and crush Doles' Georgians and perhaps Rodes' entire position.

The situation from Oak Hill through Rodes' binoculars before Ramseur's brigade stepped off to the assault must have looked much more desperate than it does today. In the mid-afternoon of July 1, 1863, Rodes, whose heroic acclaim earned at Chancellorsville was second only to that of the semi-deified Jackson, stood face-to-face with humiliation and disaster.

And then the situation changed. Around 3:00 p.m., Ramseur ordered his men forward. His situation, too, was initially confused because his brigade was divided. On Rodes' earlier orders, the Second and Fourth North Carolina regiments tramped east to support O'Neal's failed effort, leaving Ramseur with the Fourteenth and Thirtieth regiments. These he guided south and east in conjunction with Daniel and bits of Iverson's command. On the way, Ramseur encountered Colonel Battle's orphaned Third Alabama (O'Neal's Brigade). When he inquired whether Battle would join him (or when Battle asked for permission to do so), the combative officer agreed and the trio of regiments formed a line of battle. Before Ramseur advanced across the same terrain where Iverson's men had come to grief, he shifted his line to his left (northeast) so his assault would fall upon the apex or point of Paul's newly-formed defensive line. Ramseur's missing two regiments (the Second and Fourth), meanwhile, were recalled by Rodes to watch the division's exposed left flank. Orders quickly arrived for the North Carolinians to ready themselves for the attack.

Rodes watched with satisfaction as large numbers of Confederate soldiers on his left surged south and began forming into lines of battle beyond Doles' exposed flank. These were John Gordon's men, the advance of Early's division. Disconsolate spirits, including Rodes' own, soared. This time another golden opportunity would not be squandered waiting for an entire division (this time Early's), to come up. Rodes ordered his brigades to advance.

And so Ramseur's right wing (the Third Alabama on the right, Thirtieth North Carolina in the center, and Fourteenth North Carolina on the left) stepped off against Paul. On Ramseur's left, remnants from O'Neal's brigade moved up (perhaps without orders), with Ramseur's Second and Fourth regiments advancing on O'Neal's left, attacking nearly due south. To the right of Cullen Battle's Third Alabama were the remains of Iverson's outfit (including the relatively fresh Twelfth North Carolina, which had escaped most of the carnage of the earlier surprise ambush) and Daniel's reorganized brigade. On the left, Doles plunged ahead with Gordon. In the center, Ramseur, apparently with Iverson's and O'Neal's remnants under his command, shoved forward. Daniel on the far right was also moving again, this time southeast into the woods north of the railroad bed. Rodes' division was moving in concert, the coordinated attack he had been so desperately seeking finally at hand.

If Rodes was confident of success, so was General Lee. A short time earlier he had come to realize the potential of what was unfolding before him and authorized Hill to resume his attack. The Third Corps troops launched a bloody series of assaults that cracked open the Federal line holding Seminary Ridge. The coordinated Southern assaults from the west, northwest, and north were too much for the Federal defenders, who began making for the rear individually, followed by small groups, and finally en masse. North of town, Early's division, with substantial assistance from Doles' Georgians, crushed elements of the XI Corps. By 4:00 p.m. the headlong flight to and through Gettysburg was well underway, the Federals running for the safety of the high ground just south and southeast of town. Oliver Howard had had the foresight to place one of Steinwehr's brigades there as a possible rallying point, and that decision may well have saved Cemetery Hill for the Army of the Potomac.

Though many Confederate units claimed to be the first to enter Gettysburg, it is difficult to determine which holds that honor, particularly since the pursuers became nearly as disorganized and confused as the pursued. Doles' men raced through the center of town while Ramseur's and a few of O'Neal's men came in through the west side, sweeping up hundreds of prisoners. Both Rodes and Early would later boast that their men together collected some 5,000 Federals, but the best estimates place the figure at 3,665.

As his men swept forward in obvious victory, Rodes, forever abhorrent of confusion and disorder, sent orders for his brigades to stop at the southern edge of town. "The troops being greatly exhausted by their march and somewhat disorganized by the hot engagement and rapid pursuit," he explained in his report, "were halted and prepared for further action." He went to work restoring order by setting up a line extending from the streets in the center of town to the countryside west of it. To get into that line, however, many of his tired men had to struggle through hordes of Federal prisoners, "so many," explained Rodes, "as to embarrass its [the division] movements."

While Rodes reorganized his division, he watched as hundreds of Federals fled up and over the slope of Cemetery Hill. Enemy defenses on the high ground were growing in strength, and artillery pieces rolled into line. "By the time my line was in a condition to renew the attack," Rodes continued, "he [the enemy] displayed quite a formidable line of infantry and artillery immediately in my front, extending smartly to my right, and as far as I could see to my left, in front of Early." Hill's troops had not yet come up on his right, and Early's brigades were not in line on his left. Rodes believed he faced the reinforced heights alone. "[T]o have attacked this line with my division alone would have been absurd," he concluded. Without orders from either Ewell or Lee to attack, Rodes drew the remarkable conclusion that he must abide by the commanding general's earlier wish (communicated through Ewell during the attack off Oak Hill) to avoid a general engagement—as if such a thing had not already transpired. "I concluded that the order not to bring on a general engagement was still in force, and hence placed my lines and skirmishers in a defensive attitude," he reported, "and determined to await orders or further movements either on the part of Early or of the troops on my right."

It is difficult to determine how such an aggressive commander schooled at the elbow of Stonewall Jackson could draw such a conclusion once his division reached the southern outskirts of Gettysburg. The reasons listed in his report were offered after the battle was lost, of course, so perhaps post-battle guilt in not having pressed the attack played a part in his explanation. With plenty of daylight left, and with a beaten enemy still within reach, would a determined effort by even part of his division have driven away the Federals tasked with the defense of the high ground? We shall never know, but if such an attack had failed, the overall situation would not have been altered. Rodes simply could not find the wherewithal to press the attack.[19]

Although a detailed discussion of whether Cemetery Hill was susceptible to attack is beyond the purpose of this study, a general overview of how the participants acted as the sun began moving toward the western horizon that day is appropriate.

Jubal Early followed his own men into town and rode in search of Rodes, Ewell, or Hill. According to Early, his purpose was to work with them in organizing an attack before sunset. About thirty minutes after the Federal collapse, he met Rodes in the town square. The two readily agreed the Federal line south of town looked strong. "The enemy had fallen back to a commanding position known as Cemetery Hill," Old Jube later reported, "and quickly showed a formidable front there. . . . I could not bring artillery to bear on it." Still, Early and Rodes agreed they could take Cemetery Hill provided their divisions were supported on the right by A. P. Hill's Third Corps. When the generals found Ewell under a shade tree in the town square, they urged him to present their case to General Lee, for the Second Corps commander did not have any authority over Hill's troops.[20]

On the march from Carlisle to Heidlersburg, Ewell remained in his buggy at the rear of Rodes' column. From Heidlersburg to Oak Hill north of

Gettysburg, he rode his horse at the van of the division. After approving Rodes' battle plan, he allowed him to implement it without interference. That was Ewell's style of command. "You are the operator now," he had told Ed Johnson at Winchester, "I am only a looker on." Having acquired a new mount after a cannon ball smashed the head of the horse he had been riding near Oak Hill, Ewell entered Gettysburg amid the surging tide comprised of the intermingled divisions of Rodes and Early. Sometime before 5:00 p.m., Colonel Walter Taylor, one of Lee's staff officers, arrived to express General Lee's opinion that "it is only necessary to press those people in order to secure the heights beyond the town." Lee wished Ewell to do so "if practicable." Ewell gave a nod, which Taylor interpreted as a willingness to comply, though the corps commander evidently meant it as an expression of understanding and nothing more. He wanted to consult with Early and Rodes regarding the feasibility of attacking Cemetery Hill before deciding upon a course of action.[21]

When he met the two division commanders in the town square, Ewell listened to each express the view that the heights could be taken, provided they got support on the right from A. P. Hill. Rodes explained that his division was too exhausted and bloodied to go in without that support, and that only three of his brigades (Doles, Ramseur, and Daniel) could handle the assault even with Hill's cooperation. Early professed to be in a similar situation. He claimed to have only two combat-worthy brigades under Harry Hays and Robert Hoke (led by Colonel Isaac Avery) at hand.

Ewell turned to Lieutenant James Power Smith, a staff officer who left Lee in a field about three miles west of Seminary Ridge around 3:00 p.m. "You have seen General Lee a little while ago," said Ewell. "Will you be kind enough to find him and tell him what these gentlemen say?" To be absolutely certain of their position, Smith moved closer to Early and Rodes and asked them to repeat their views. When he was sure he understood, Smith rode off to find the commanding general.[22]

With their respective staffs, Ewell, Early, and Rodes rode south on Baltimore Street to get a closer look at the Federal position on Cemetery Hill. After crossing High Street and passing over a crest just south of the alley beyond, they abruptly drew rein when a fusillade of bullets whizzed by, fired by Federal sharpshooters from Steinwehr's division hiding about 500 yards distant in the buildings at the foot of the hill. One bullet hit the stirrup of Major John Daniel of Ewell's staff. The close call prompted the officers to wheel left and ride behind the cover of buildings along the alley. At the risk of drawing more fire, however, they occasionally ventured out into yards on High Street, where excellent views of Cemetery Hill and Culp's Hill were available. To their dismay, they saw at least one enemy brigade holding a very secure position behind a stone wall, supported by about forty guns. The enemy was too high for Confederate guns to reach.[23]

Lieutenant Smith, meanwhile, found General Lee with Longstreet on the Cashtown Road and informed them of his meeting with Ewell, Rodes, and Early. Despite the proximity of Richard Anderson's unused division, Lee concluded that Hill's men were too "exhausted by some six hours of hard fighting." Longstreet also begged off on the grounds that his lead division under Lafayette McLaws still was six miles away. Although there was still plenty of daylight left, Lee did not order Longstreet or Hill to mount an assault. His knowledge of what had transpired on Ewell's front, and what exactly he was facing there now, was sketchy at best. Lee sent Smith back to give Ewell "discretion whether to advance alone or not."[24]

The delay in attacking once the division was formed generated strong reactions within Rodes' ranks. The always-combative Ramseur wanted to keep going. John Stikeleather of the Fourth North Carolina, part of Ramseur's brigade, concluded that prompt action by only 500 men could have taken Cemetery Hill. "The simplest soldier in the ranks felt it," he angrily wrote his mother after the battle. "But, timidity in the commander that stepped into the shoes of the fearless Jackson, prompted delay, (and all night long the busy axes from tens of thousands of busy hands on that crest, rang out clearly on the night air, and bespoke the preparations the enemy was making for the morrow)." William Calder, an officer with the Second North Carolina, felt the same way. He wrote his mother on July 8 that the delay was a tragic error. "It was here that the great mistake was made which lost us all the advantage we had gained and caused the subsequent death of so many gallant men," he explained. "Our generals should have advanced immediately on that hill. It would have been taken then with comparatively little loss and would have deprived the enemy of that immense advantage of position which was afterward the cause of all his success." Corporal B. B. Ross, one of Stikeleather's comrades in the Fourth North Carolina, agreed. "Had Stonewall Jackson been in command of the 2nd corps on the 1st of July," he grumbled, "we would have taken these heights, and Gettysburg would have been a Confederate victory instead of a drawn battle." Captain W. H. May of the Third Alabama felt the same way. "If Stonewall had been alive," he wrote after the war, "we never would have spent a minute in that manner." Of course, each of these conclusions were put into tangible form after the fact.[25]

Colonel O'Neal reported that he ordered up artillery and prepared with Doles to charge Cemetery Hill, when Rodes' orders stopped him. This is the same report, however, that expressed strong bitterness at Rodes for depriving O'Neal of two regiments prior to that afternoon's attack. An unconfirmed story in *Confederate Veteran Magazine* carried that bitterness further by claiming that O'Neal pleaded with Doles to ignore Rodes' orders and charge anyway, and that Doles refused.[26]

Not everyone agreed a successful attack upon Cemetery Hill was possible. Junius Daniel reported that when ordered to halt he did so "agreeably." Colonel Bennett of the Fourteenth North Carolina, part of Daniel's brigade, was more emphatic. "It was a hot day," he reported, "and our men were much distressed by the heat and work. We straggled into town and then formed as quick as possible. Many of our command were overcome by the heat, and I go upon record now and here as saying that immediate and effective pursuit of the enemy was out of our power."[27]

Ewell, exhausted after having passed nearly forty hours without sleep, drew the same basic conclusion as Colonel Bennett. By now the Federal position on the heights appeared quite strong, making it a very dangerous prospect to bring the troops through town and form them up in full view of the enemy guns, which held an advantage in elevation over his own. The strength of the position and the lack of support from Hill convinced Ewell the proper course was to flank the enemy position by taking nearby Culp's Hill with Ed Johnson's fresh division, which he erroneously expected to arrive momentarily.[28] "It was, as I have always understood," wrote Campbell Brown after the war, "with the express concurrence of both Rodes and Early, and largely in consequence of the inactivity of the troops under Gen'l Lee's own eye . . . that Gen'l Ewell finally decided to make no direct attack, but to wait for Johnson's coming up and with his fresh troops seize and hold the high peak. . . ."[29]

Another matter also gave Ewell pause. Federal troops were rumored to be moving beyond his far left on the York Road. If that was true, the enemy in strength could get into his rear and turn his entire corps. Though Early doubted the report, he went with Ewell and Rodes to check out the situation on that flank. With their staffs in tow, the three generals rode about 5:30 p.m. to the high ground east of Gettysburg overlooking Rock Creek. From that vantage point they gained a long view of the York Road. Though admitting that distance made it impossible to distinguish uniform color, Rodes concluded that the troops appearing in his field glasses indeed were Federals. Early didn't believe it. If they were Federals, he vehemently protested, there would have been firing in that direction from Gordon's brigade. Rodes persisted. "There they come now!" he suddenly cried out. Using "somewhat emphatic language," Early strongly disagreed. Ewell intervened to send one of his staffers, Lieutenant Thomas T. Turner, and one of Early's, Lieutenant Robert D. Early, to investigate. The two lieutenants quickly returned to vindicate Early. The men on the road were Confederates, they said, troops from William "Extra Billy" Smith's brigade (Early's division), whom Gordon was repositioning.

Ewell allowed no time for gloating or recrimination. After promptly sending the two staff officers to determine if the enemy occupied Culp's Hill, he went to await a meeting with General Lee. Early started back to his own division, while Rodes rode to finish overseeing the formation of his men. The separation of these high ranking Second Corps officers ended the possibility of an attack against Cemetery Hill that day. It also triggered the decades-long debate over whether a major blunder had been committed by not attacking that afternoon or evening. The situation is open to endless analysis, and there is no meaningful way to conclude satisfactorily when, or even whether, such an attack would have been successful.[30]

Rodes, meanwhile, finished deploying his division. "My skirmishers were promptly thrown out so as to cover more than half the town and the front of the division," he wrote. The brigades of Doles, Iverson, and Ramseur were ordered to hold a line that began at the center of town and extended west of it along the Cashtown or Fairfield Road. Daniel and O'Neal aligned their brigades about 200 yards behind them, this second line running along the railroad to a point considerably beyond the right of the first line. "In this position we remained quietly, but with considerable annoyance from the enemy's sharpshooters and artillery, until the morning of the next day," was how Rodes quietly concluded the report of the momentous first day at Gettysburg. With that, Rodes rode to Ewell's designated meeting place with General Lee just north of town at the stone house of a Mrs. Blocher, about 100 yards beyond where the Carlisle Road split into two forks.[31]

According to one eyewitness, Rodes looked noticeably ill and was flushed with fever. He must have been ailing for some time, perhaps with an intestinal problem. Ewell suggested he lie down in the house. Rodes declined; the rooms were full of wounded soldiers who needed the space more than he did. General Lee arrived shortly thereafter and the discussion quickly turned to matters of strategy.[32]

Given Lee's battlefield comportment, he probably was disappointed that Ewell did not press that afternoon's attack. Having already uttered the

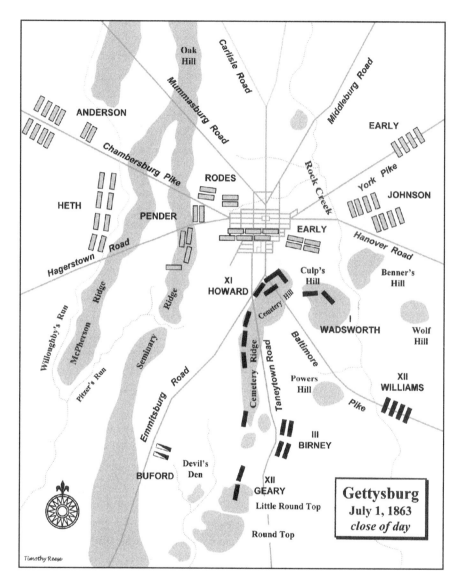

combative rebuttal, "If the enemy is there tomorrow, we must attack him," to reject Longstreet's proposal to pull the army back and maneuver around the right, the commanding general tried to put Ewell to work. Sitting out on the back porch of the house, using the shade from a a grape arbor for relief from the heat, Lee asked about the condition of the troops. Rodes replied that his division had been badly mauled, losing perhaps 2,500 men.

Lee turned to Ewell. "Can't you, with your Corps, attack on this flank at daylight tomorrow?" Having gone nearly two days without sleep, Ewell seemed nearly unable to speak. Rodes was feverish and languid. That left the just-arrived Early (at least according to his own often suspect account) as the de facto spokesman for the Second Corps. As Early puts it, he explained that by morning the Federal position would be far too strong to attack. Ewell and Rodes, noted Early, nodded in agreement. Early went on to say that there might better prospects for success on the Confederate right, with an attack to secure the two round tops. "Then perhaps I had better draw you around towards my right," Lee countered, "as the line will be very long and thin if you remain here, and the enemy may come down and break through it?"

Again Ewell and Rodes maintained a supportive silence while Early protested that a move around to the right might demoralize the men while also leaving thousands of wounded in the hands of the enemy. The present position, Early declared, was strong enough to stop any enemy attempt to break through.

Unable to persuade his generals that something noteworthy could be accomplished on the Confederate left, Lee ended the frustrating meeting and left the Second Corps in its present position. That decision meant that his army occupied a dangerously long concave exterior line wrapped around a more compact Federal defensive front with the advantage of interior lines of reinforcement. The strategic situation was less than ideal.[33]

After Lee left the Blocher house, the three tired generals tarried a bit in the warm evening air. While sitting in a fence corner of the yard, they received lieutenants Turner and Early, the two staff officers sent to examine Culp's Hill. They reported that the wooded heights remained unoccupied. (Somehow their mounted reconnaissance—which itself has generated much debate—missed the Iron Brigade.) Ewell supposedly sought Rodes' opinion on whether Ed Johnson's division, which had arrived about dusk after a grueling twenty-five mile march from near Greenwood, should be sent to immediately occupy the hill. If we are to believe Early, Rodes gave a reply that was completely out of character. According to Early, Rodes stressed that Johnson's men had to be utterly exhausted, and that the occupation of the wooded high ground could wait until morning. Perhaps it was the illness speaking, or perhaps Early was mistaken. Or, perhaps the general used Rodes after the war in his account to set himself up as the only one favoring what hindsight demonstrates was the better course. "If you do not go up there tonight," Early jumped up in protest, "it will cost you 10,000 lives to get up there tomorrow." Ewell agreed and authorized the move. According to this version of events, twice in one evening "the Old Bear" (as Rodes playfully referred to Early in a private letter) had vehemently contradicted his fellow division leader. Rodes did not leave an account of the meeting, and not a word of this exchange appears in his official report.[34]

With that, the three generals parted, Early heading back to his division and Ewell leaving with Rodes. Colonel Charles Marshall of Lee's staff found the latter two exhausted generals resting by a roadside. Marshall offered the rather startling news that Lee had changed his mind about moving the Second Corps around to the right. Ewell discussed the order with Rodes and sent for Early. Both officers (according to Early's version of events) strongly advocated remaining in their present position. Ed Johnson was not consulted because that officer had no familiarity with the ground or the situation. Suddenly finding his voice, Ewell rode to Lee to protest the order. He argued that with Johnson's division now in hand, he could take Culp's Hill and flank the Federal position on Cemetery Hill. Ewell, of course, knew much more about the possibilities on that flank than did the commanding general. Lee relented a second time.[35]

When Ewell arrived back at his own headquarters just after midnight, however, fresh reconnaissance reports and a captured dispatch indicated that the enemy was in force on Culp's Hill—and two divisions were within close supporting distance. This left the corps commander no choice but to cancel Johnson's orders to occupy the high ground. Lee was duly notified. With this disappointing news, Lee later changed his plans again. After deciding to send Longstreet's First Corps against the Federal left the next day, he instructed Ewell to "make a simultaneous demonstration upon the enemy's right, to be converted into a real attack should opportunity offer."[36]

* * *

The line in town held by George Doles' brigade ran along Middle Street, from Stratton Street in the east to the Seminary Building in the west. But that evening the men did not confine themselves to this narrow passageway. Many went out to explore the town. According to one witness, they "were seen to be running all over the place, mingling with the citizens. At every corner, and dotted all along the streets, could be seen little groups of 'Johnnies' freely conversing and disputing with the citizens, male and female, on the merits of their respective armies, and especially of their officers." Professor Jacobs, who taught at the local college, was told that the Confederates would win a great victory the next day. The Southern soldiers found the place to their liking. "The town afforded us any quantity of butter and preserves of all kinds, on which we supped most sumptuously," William Calder later wrote his mother. When it was time to end the sightseeing and scrounging, the men bedded down for the night. One soldier of the Fifty-third North Carolina noted in his diary that the men, though without blankets, slept soundly that night, for they were "much fatigued."[37]

Along with Early, Rodes evidently spent the night at Ewell's headquarters inside a barn standing at the junction of the Carlisle and Middletown roads. His fever persisted, and may have worsened. Whenever possible, noted one eyewitness, he would spend the following day riding or resting in an ambulance, a drastic step for the man who had twice refused to allow a wound to remove him from the battlefield. Rodes' illness not only reduced his energy level, but may well have had an adverse affect on his judgment. Events of the morrow would seem to confirm that.[38]

Before dawn Ewell invited the ailing Rodes to go with him and Early to beg a breakfast from Mrs. Blocher, who had been so gracious and hospitable the day before. Rodes gathered his strength and joined the expedition, which turned out well when Mrs. Blocher set out hot coffee and biscuits. At daylight Rodes returned to his men.[39]

His division was not well positioned to allow Ewell to use the men "should opportunity offer." One reason Rodes deployed his brigades far from the front was to keep them beyond the range of the Federal guns on Cemetery Hill. Facing south, Doles remained in line on the streets in town. Iverson was on his right just outside town, with Ramseur on the right of Iverson. O'Neal's brigade was back behind the railroad cut facing southwest. Daniel's men had the most trying experience that day. "The rest of the men generally were only disturbed by the occasional skirmishing and desultory firing of the opposing sharpshooters," explained Rodes, "but Daniel's brigade, which had been early in the morning moved by my order so as to connect with Pender's division, on the crest of the ridge before spoken of, was subjected to a galling artillery fire, especially in the afternoon." Facing almost due east, Daniel was behind Seminary Ridge, his right abutting Pender's left. The entire day of July 2 passed without Ewell or Rodes noticing that the division was so poorly aligned it could not accomplish much of anything—especially an attack against the enemy. The men could not be needlessly exposed to sharpshooters and artillery fire, but their deep placement made effective use of the division nearly impossible. In many respects the division fell prey to happenstance, which dropped it into a nearly untenable location.[40]

In what would prove to be Rodes' only substantive contribution that day, he ordered Major Eugene Blackford's battalion of sharpshooters to move into the two- and three-story brick row houses lining the southern edge of town. The men knocked out the room partitions and the walls between the houses in order to make one continuous block-long corridor. For extra protection they overturned beds and mattresses, and cut holes in the wall facing the enemy for additional firing space. Stripped to the waist and blackened with powder, Blackford's men kept up an incessant fire on the Federals atop Cemetery Hill. When Captain William Blackford of Stuart's staff visited later that day, he found his brother Eugene "in a room in the middle of the block, lolling with some of his officers on sofas in a handsome parlor. On the marble table were all sorts of delicacies taken from a sideboard in the dining room—including decanters of wine."[41]

"Nothing of importance transpired in my front," was how Rodes described the day's events in his after-action report. The statement was true enough if measured against the intensity of the fighting elsewhere later that afternoon and evening. Unfortunately for the Confederates, there was much of importance that *should* have transpired on his front.[42]

While Rodes marked time in the outskirts of town, Lee's plan of attack eventually called for Longstreet to conduct a march around the army's right and attack George Meade's ill-defined left flank. With most of his army on the field by the morning of July 2, Meade ordered Dan Sickles' III Corps to shift to the left and extend his line south, anchoring it on the high rocky hill known today as Little Round Top. To his right was Winfield Hancock's II Corps, running up Cemetery Ridge. Sickles, however, disliked his line and, in an effort that has been debated from that day to this one,

Maj. Gen. George G. Meade, commander of the Army of the Potomac.

National Archives

advanced about 1,200 yards to what he believed was more defensible ground along the Emmitsburg Road and the Sherfy Peach Orchard. The left wing of his line bent back at a wide angle, but was too short to cover the Round Tops. Sickles had unwittingly created a large salient in Meade's otherwise strong front, with the high ground in his left-rear undefended. When Longstreet discovered the new tactical arrangement later that day, he believed Sickles' deployment offered an opportunity to be exploited, and set about to do just that.

Although there is some debate on this point, the evidence strongly suggests the Confederate attack was designed to unfold *en echelon*, from right to left. The grand rolling series of well-timed punches was crafted to hit hard and either break through or wear down the Federals at the point of impact and suck reinforcements from distant (temporarily quiet) sections of the Federal line that would be hit with heavy attacks as the hours wore on. If all went well, somewhere the Confederates would achieve penetration, triggering an opportunity that could be exploited for decisive gain. Ewell was ordered to cooperate with the effort by launching his own forceful demonstration on the far left against Culp's Hill, to be turned into something more as opportunity allowed.

It took Longstreet most of the day to get his two large divisions into position. The long delay led many to believe there would be no action of significance on July 2. "[A] band in Rodes' division, from a ravine on the left, began to play lively polkas and waltzes," remembered one witness. About 4:00 p.m., however, Longstreet launched his attack, opening the effort with John Hood's division, which swept forward toward the Round Tops. Although Little Round Top remained in enemy hands, the Peach Orchard, Devil's Den, Wheatfield, and the Emmitsburg Road were overrun after some of the heaviest fighting of the war. Ewell emboldened himself to convert his demonstration into a full-scale attack. He directed Johnson to move his division ahead and carry Culp's Hill. Jubal Early was directed to join in from the center of Ewell's line and strike East Cemetery Hill, with Rodes striking heavily from the northwest, coming in on Early's right flank.[43]

It is clear that Rodes was unsure about his exact orders, believing them to be somewhat nebulous and open to interpretation. His situation demonstrates well just how little even high-ranking officers knew or understood about what was transpiring around them. "Late in the afternoon . . . an attack was made upon the enemy's position by some troops of the right wing of the army [Longstreet's First Corps], which produced some stir among the enemy in my immediate front, and seemed to cause there a diminution of both artillery and infantry," observed Rodes. "Orders given during the afternoon," he continued, "and after the engagement had opened on the right [Longstreet's attack], required me to co-operate with the attacking force as soon as any opportunity of doing so with good effect was offered." When the afternoon expired and early evening arrived, Rodes believed "that opportunity had come, and [I] immediately sought out General Early, with a view of making an attack in concert with him."[44]

After giving assurances to Early, Rodes, as he had the day before, sought support on his right for the offensive. By this time the rolling Confederate attack had moved north from Longstreet's sector and now was firmly embedded on Hill's Third Corps front. Unfortunately, Hill was conspicuously inactive (and perhaps himself quite ill), and the attack was breaking down, his men attacking piecemeal against Cemetery Ridge—or not attacking at all. Holding Hill's left flank was Dorsey Pender's division. Unfortunately for Southern arms, about this time Pender fell with a mortal shrapnel wound to his leg, and his senior brigadier, James Lane, assumed command. Instead of attacking, the division remained stationary: Lane had no idea what to do. When Major Whiting from Rodes' staff arrived with a plea from Rodes for support, Lane equivocated. "I did not give him a definite answer then," he reported truthfully. Lane already had sent a staff officer to notify Hill of Pender's wound and was awaiting instructions. Neither Rodes nor Ewell seem to have communicated directly with A. P. Hill on the matter.[45]

With Johnson's division trying to scale the smoky wooded heights of Culp's Hill in the face of determined opposition, and Early poised to strike at East Cemetery Hill, Rodes at last began moving his own men into position. Doles believed the move did not begin until "about 8 p.m.," while Ramseur simply noted it was "at dark." Only now did Rodes discover how hard his task would be. In order to clear the town, whose streets still were congested with ambulances and wounded soldiers, he had to march the men west in a column of fours. Once beyond the town limits, his division formed for battle, with Doles, Iverson, and Ramseur in front from left to right, with Daniel behind Ramseur and O'Neal behind Iverson. Somehow or another, orders did not reach every brigadier. "I had received no instructions," Iverson claimed in his report, "and perceiving that General Ramseur [from whom Iverson learned of the pending attack] was acquainted with the intentions of the major-general commanding the division, I raised no question of rank, but conformed the movements of my brigade to that of Brigadier-General Ramseur."[46]

Once in position, the division wheeled about forty-five degrees to the left and, aligned generally southeast, advanced on its long fitful march toward

Cemetery Hill. These complicated maneuvers, though skillfully executed, took a great deal of time. And time was not something the Confederates had to spare. It now was nearly dark. Early's division had less than half the distance to traverse, with no complicated movements to perform beforehand. The result was that while Rodes was moving into position, Early was attacking. Two of his brigades (under Harry Hays and Isaac Avery) spectacularly knocked the defenders off the top of East Cemetery Hill. While the Federals were funneling reinforcements toward this dangerous breach in their line, Early's men were looking anxiously for support that would never arrive. Rodes' division moved toward the high ground in the rapidly fading light as the fighting on the far left seemed to be dying out. Hill's men on the right were nowhere to be seen.[47]

Rodes designated Ramseur's command, which held the right front of the advancing division, as the brigade upon which the advance would be directed. "Boys," Ramseur told his men before they moved out, "I want you to take off your canteens and haversacks and leave them in a pile right here. We've got to take those breast-works up yonder, and we don't want any noise. Take nothing but your cartridge boxes and guns. The Federals have got a strong picket-line out and if they shoot don't return the fire, but keep advancing until you've driven them back into the works. North Carolina to the rescue! will be the watch-word." Spirits were high. Our "great hearts thump and beat within our bosoms as if they would leap out," wrote one soldier.[48]

The southeastwardly advance carried the front of the division within a couple hundred yards of the base of the hill. Word came down the line for the men to halt and lie down. The skirmishers were drawing a terrific fire. Ramseur wanted a closer look at what his men were marching into. "For ten minutes," remembered a North Carolinian, "we lay in dire suspense" while Ramseur and others studied the enemy position. In the bright glow of the moon the general spotted several batteries waiting to pour "direct, cross, and enfilade fires" on his men. "Two lines of infantry behind stone walls and breastworks were supporting these batteries," continued Ramseur. Other than fitful small arms fire on the far left, the entire battlefield was largely silent. That was enough for Ramseur. "The strength and position of the enemy's batteries and their supports induced me to halt and confer with General Doles, and, with him, to make representation of the character of the enemy's position, and ask further instructions." Ramseur, Doles, and Iverson discussed the situation and agreed the attack would be exceedingly dangerous. With their men still lying in the fields, the three brigadiers sent their assessment to Rodes.[49]

Exactly where the messenger found Rodes is open to some question. Did he advance with his men that evening? The evidence is unclear on the point. The movement (and apparently authority) of the division had been placed in the hands of a brigadier (Ramseur). Rodes was almost certainly still ill that evening, which might explain the unusual delegation of authority.

Although the sequence of events that followed is murky at best, definitive word from James Lane reached Rodes about this time: expect no support on the right. Given Rodes' combative character, he must have experienced a deep sense of frustration, perhaps even humiliation. His division alone had not fulfilled its part in Ewell's offensive. Would his participation have made a difference? This may have been why Rodes told Early, who rode earlier to find out what was going on, that he still would advance if Early "thought it proper." When Early received word that his own brigades had been repulsed, Rodes concluded that "it would be a useless sacrifice of life to go on" and called off the attack. Down the line ran the order to "Fall back without noise." The entire affair had been a fiasco from beginning to end.

Many men were pleased the attack fizzled. "[P]erceiving, as I believe every one did, that we were advancing to certain destruction," reported Iverson, "when other parts of the line fell back, I also gave the order to retreat." A soldier in the Thirtieth North Carolina agreed. "The idea of charging strong fortifications in the night time was an awful thing," he wrote, "but everyone was willing to follow our brigadier-general [Ramseur] wherever he would lead us."

Rodes pulled back about 300 yards to a little-used and but recently discovered sunken road known as Long Lane, located in a swale 600 yards west of and parallel to the northeast-southwest running Emmitsburg Road. Iverson, Ramseur, and Doles deployed there, while O'Neal and Daniel returned to the positions they had held before the attack. With its excellent cover, the lane offered a good position from which to launch the just-aborted attack, but for some reason no one knew of its existence until it was too late to use it. "This position was nearer the enemy, was clear of the town, and one from which I could readily attack without confusion," Rodes reported, as if to say that despite his failures that day, he had achieved something positive. "Everything was gotten ready to attack at daylight."[50]

Daylight offered a clear view of the strong enemy position and a corresponding relief over the cancellation of last night's attack. "Our general [Rodes] saw the foolhardiness and madness of the attempt," was how one officer characterized it. "For that act there are many Carolina mothers, wives, sisters and children who should pray blessings on his head."[51] William Calder agreed. "It was well for us that we did [not attack]," wrote the North Carolina captain to his mother, "for in the confusion of the darkness we would have lost nearly every man and gained nothing whatever."[52] Long after the war, North Carolinian Fred Phillips recalled, "[T]he only thing to be done, and which was done with amazing rapidity, was for the men to bury themselves in the farm road, using as implements of excavation, pocket knives, bayonets, swords, tin cups and everything else at command."[53]

Though Carolina mothers may have gratefully brought down "blessings on his head," others in the army were not as kind when it came to Rodes' role in the failed attack, Jubal Early among them. Rodes fretted about support on his right, this time perhaps excessively, implied Early. "He was new in his position of division commander at Gettysburg," Old Jube condescendingly and erroneously wrote after the war, "but [by the time he had been] killed at Winchester . . . he had learned to be less sensitive about his flanks." Though protesting that he did not wish to impugn Rodes, "for whom I had a very high appreciation as a man and a soldier, and to whose skill, gallantry and efficiency I have borne the fullest testimony," Early went on to make the fantastic postwar assertion that Rodes' failure on July 2 "was the solitary instance of remissness on the part of any portion of the corps in the battle." With that single statement, Early exempted himself from any personal blame for the failures that day. Rodes had not performed well, but the record is clear that Early's own actions on several occasions were suspect.[54]

A question few ask concerns Rodes' poor use of intelligence on July 2. Why did Ramseur have to stop the advance and personally examine the ground? Rodes' skirmishers had spent the entire day in front of Cemetery Hill, so he must have been intimately familiar with the terrain and the nature of the Federal defenses he was tasked to assault. Evidently, Rodes did not use that information or communicate what he knew to his brigadiers.

After-action reports penned by other generals damned Rodes with faint praise or by implication. "No attack was made on the immediate right, *as was expected* [emphasis added]," Early wrote with barely concealed disappointment, "and not meeting with support from that quarter, these brigades [Hays and Avery] could not hold the position they had attained."[55] Ewell was a bit kinder in his report, writing, "Major-General Rodes did not advance, for reasons given in his report." Campbell Brown of Ewell's staff was more forthright. Privately, maintained Brown, Ewell "always thought Rodes fairly censurable. . . . Ewell and Early both thought Rodes had been too slow."[56] The usually forbearing Lee included an undisguised and, for Lee, strong censure in his report. "When the time to attack arrived," he wrote, "General Rodes, not having his troops in position, was unprepared to co-operate with General Early, and before he could get in readiness the latter had been obliged to retire for want of the expected support on his right."[57]

Rodes' harshest critic was Colonel Charles Marshall of Lee's staff. "If General Rodes had prepared his troops to advance on the right of General Early," he bitterly charged after the war, "the latter would not have been compelled to withdraw from a successful attack, and the position on Cemetery Hill would have been held. The capture of that hill would have enabled General Early to have enfiladed the Federal troops opposed to those of General Longstreet, and the effect of such fire at that time might have changed the result of the day. At one time on July 2nd," continued Marshall, "victory was within our certain reach. It was lost by delay and by the failure of co-operation on the part of the troops."[58]

"The whole of the three days' battle," declared Douglas Southall Freeman in his biography of Lee, "produced no more tragic might-have- beens than this twilight engagement on the Confederate left. For Early's right regiment had been within 400 feet of the flank of the Federal batteries commanding the approaches to the hill from Rodes' front. Had Rodes' 5,000 men been at hand to support Early for even an hour," Freeman concluded, not unreasonably, "the Federal guns could have been captured and turned on the enemy." In *Lee's Lieutenants* Freeman concluded simply, "Rodes' 2nd of July was in disappointing contrast to his 2nd of May. Dash was lacking."[59]

It wasn't simply dash that was absent, but thoroughness and judgment as well, important traits Rodes failed to utilize on both July 1 and July 2. If eyewitness accounts are accurate, Rodes was quite ill by the evening of July 1, and this remains the most viable reason for his uncharacteristic battlefield lapses. To his credit, Rodes did not use this as an excuse, but Confederate success that day may have been sacrificed to his stubborn pride, which prevented him from relinquishing command to someone better able to make the exertions required by the situation.

*   *   *

Shortly after establishing a new line on the night of July 2, Rodes received orders from Lee to immediately reinforce Johnson on the far left with as many troops as possible, though without jeopardizing his own position. Because of their relative proximity to Johnson, Rodes dispatched his second line, Daniel

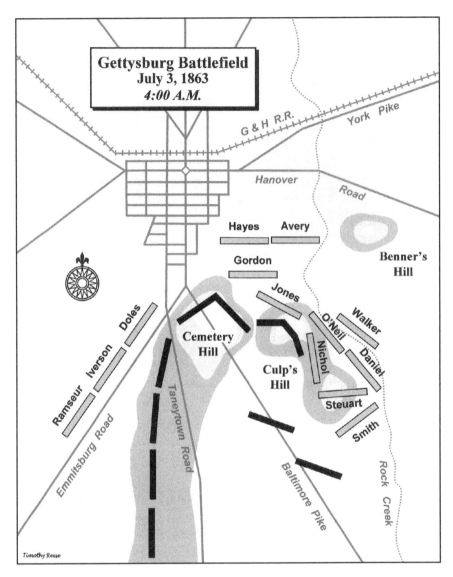

Gettysburg Battlefield
July 3, 1863
4:00 A.M.

Timothy Reese

and O'Neal (minus the Fifth Alabama, which Rodes always preferred to keep under his own eye, this time to guard the streets of Gettysburg). Leaving around midnight, the two brigades reached Johnson about two hours later after a march of four miles. Lee wanted Johnson's reinforced division to renew the fight for Culp's Hill by attacking at dawn from the breastworks captured on the hill's south shoulder the previous evening. The Federals, however, preempted that plan by launching their own attack against Johnson in the predawn darkness. For the next six hours the battle raged on with varying intensity, with both

Daniel and O'Neal hotly engaged. By 11:00 a.m., Johnson's effort was repulsed decisively for the last time.[60]

Having set up his line the night before with the hope of attacking Cemetery Hill on the morning of July 3, a disheartened Rodes felt "powerless to do more than hold my position." He estimated that without Daniel and O'Neal, his thin line contained no more than 1,800 men, though he faced "the most impregnable portion of the enemy's line of intrenchments." Several times that morning the enemy pushed forward and then withdrew a line of skirmishers, each line of which Rodes believed equaled or exceeded his entire strength.

After failing to break apart the Army of the Potomac by attacking its flanks, General Lee decided to use George Pickett's recently arrived fresh division (part of Longstreet's First Corps), together with troops from Hill's Third Corps, in a grand assault on July 3 against the right-center of Meade's line on Cemetery Ridge. About 1:00 p.m. that afternoon, the massive artillery bombardment intended to knock apart the Federal defenses at the point of the attack erupted with what Rodes called "the fiercest and grandest cannonade I have ever witnessed." The effort marked the prelude to what became popularly known as Pickett's Charge. One battalion of Second Corps batteries contributed to the bombardment by firing over the heads of Rodes' men, a nerve-racking experience made even more terrifying by the thunderous reply of the Federal guns, some of whose shells fell among the troops. The Southern army's artillery chief, William Nelson Pendleton, squandered an excellent opportunity to enfilade the Union line by not using more of the Second Corps artillery; four additional battalions of guns did not fire a shot during the cannonade.

Federal sharpshooters peppered Rodes' line with an irksome and occasionally deadly fire. The men "underwent this terrible trial not only without murmuring or faltering," Rodes proudly reported, "but with great cheerfulness and with the utmost coolness." When the artillery bombardment ended (estimates of its length vary widely, but it was probably about one hour in duration), three divisions of Southern infantry (plus two additional brigades from another division that would also advance later) stepped forward in a grand attack against Cemetery Ridge.

For Rodes, confusion and uncertainty ruled the third day at Gettysburg, just as they had on the first two days. His orders that day, he recalled, "were general, and the same as those of the day before, and accordingly, when the heavy cannonade indicated that another attack was made from the right wing of our army, we were on the lookout for another favorable opportunity to co-operate." Rodes' report is clear: he was not briefed on the specifics of the attack against the Federal center, and was unsure whether he was to directly cooperate, and if so, when such cooperation was expected. "When the sound of musketry was heard, it became apparent that the enemy in our front was much excited," he observed. "The favorable opportunity seemed to me close at hand."

Rodes reached the rather remarkable conclusion that the time had arrived to launch his own attack. "I sent word to Lieutenant-General Ewell by Major [H. A.] Whiting, of my staff, that in a few moments I should attack, and immediately had my handful of men, under Doles, Iverson, and Ramseur, prepared for the onset," he wrote in his report, "but in less than five minutes after Major Whiting's departure, before the troops on my immediate right had made any advance or showed any preparation therefor, and just as the order forward was about to be given to my line, it was announced, and was apparent to me, that the attack had already failed." Rodes looked on the shocking spectacle of Confederate infantry tumbling backward in confusion as the grand attack collapsed. In "a silence that was almost stunning," remembered one of his soldiers, Rodes held his position for the rest of the day.[61]

*   *   *

Lee knew the opportunity to crush his opponent and win a decisive victory north of the Potomac River had failed. It was time to withdraw from the field, a difficult proposition in the face of a victorious enemy. To shorten, straighten, and strengthen his line in anticipation of a counterattack by Meade, Lee instructed Ewell to take up a position along Oak and Seminary ridges. Around 3:00 a.m. on Saturday morning, July 4, Rodes pulled his division back north of town near Oak Ridge, where three days earlier it had stepped off with such high hopes. Just before dawn the division welcomed back the battered brigades of O'Neal and Daniel after their disappointing experience under Johnson's command on Culp's Hill, where many of their comrades still lay. Rodes spread out his five brigades along the railroad cut, where they dug in and built up a long line of breastworks and rifle pits. When dawn arrived he expected a fourth day of battle, but as the hours quietly passed he began to suspect otherwise.

He put the time to good use by moving to the rear both the walking wounded and those able to ride in an ambulance. Hundreds of his men, however—760 by Rodes' estimate—could not be moved, their injuries too severe. Most of these unfortunates were left in fields, surrounded by a sea of dead men and horses, to await stretcher bearers and transport to a makeshift hospital. The decision anguished Rodes, who wrote about leaving their fate "in the hands of the enemy." To help care for them he left behind four surgeons, six assistant surgeons, three hospital stewards, ninety-four attendants, plus ten days' supply of food and medicine. "This painful result was, of course, unavoidable," he wrote. "This was all we could do for them."[62]

When it became clear that Meade would not commit the folly of Pickett's Charge in reverse, Lee prepared to withdraw. The wagons left first. In a driving rain, ambulances and supply vehicles that eventually formed a line seventeen miles long, rumbled off that afternoon toward Cashtown. John Imboden's 2,100 cavalrymen escorted the train. After passing through Greencastle during the night, the train took the road to Williamsport. For added protection, and almost as an afterthought, Iverson's brigade was pulled out of the line late that afternoon and sent after the wagons. Though the brigade marched quickly, it arrived too late to save the train from Judson Kilpatrick's cavalry, which fell upon it about 3:00 a.m. on July 5. Before being driven off, the Federal raiders inflicted severe damage and captured many prisoners, stealing, among other things, a money chest carrying the precise amount of $11,235 intended as pay for O'Neal's men. Iverson was too late to prevent the attack, but he managed around dawn to help break up another raiding party near Hagerstown. "By forced march, [Iverson] arrived at Hagerstown soon after the passage of the train, and found a heavy force of the enemy's cavalry driving back our cavalry through the streets. Making a hasty but skillful disposition of his troops, he soon routed them, capturing a considerable number," Rodes noted in his report. "Great credit is due Brigadier-General Iverson for the handsome and prompt manner in which this affair was managed." Coming as it did on the heels of Iverson's disastrous showing in the fields below Oak Hill, Rodes' praise deserves special notice. Curiously, Iverson did not even mention the affair in his report. Given his lamentable performance at Gettysburg, one might have expected him to use the opportunity to mitigate his less-than-stellar July 1 showing.[63] Lee, meanwhile, began pulling his infantry out after dark on July 4. Hill went first, marching west on the Fairfield Road followed by Longstreet, with Ewell bringing up the rear about midnight. Jeb Stuart's two brigades of cavalry screened the left flank while Fitz Lee's men covered the right.

Despite the disastrous results of the Gettysburg battle, few in the Army of Northern Virginia willingly labeled it an outright defeat. Mapmaker Jedediah Hotchkiss wrote in his diary on July 3, "There was a general feeling of despondency in the army at our great losses, though the battle is regarded as a drawn one." A North Carolinian felt the same way. "The battle is over," wrote a Tar Heel of Daniel's brigade on July 4, "and although we did not succeed in pushing the enemy out of their strong position, I am sure they have not anything to boast about." Ramseur, however, confessed in a letter to his fiancée that his optimism had been severely shaken. "Our great campaign, admirably planned & more admirably executed up to the fatal days at Gettysburg, has failed. Which I was not prepared to anticipate." The surgeon of the Fourth North Carolina of Ramseur's brigade, John Shaffner, felt much the same way. He wrote home on July 17, "Our men are somewhat disheartened at the result of the campaign, having heretofore been accustomed to nothing but success."

Many of the men marched out of Pennsylvania with much more respect for their enemy than they had when they marched in. "I think they fight harder in their own country than they do in Virginia," a soldier in the Twenty-first Georgia concluded in a letter home dated July 8. "I would rather fight them in Virginia." Some, and perhaps all, of these sentiments ran through Rodes' mind as the army painfully wound its way back toward Virginia.[64]

With Daniel in the lead, the division marched through the night and much of the day of July 5. "After a most wearisome march in mud and rain," the division went into camp around 4:00 p.m. on a hill two miles west of Fairfield. The next day, Rodes took his turn bringing up the army's rear, relieving Early of that thankless job. The duty proved hazardous, with Federals constantly nipping at their heels. Daniel, marching at the end of the column, lost during the day two killed, two wounded, and five missing. At one point near the Emmitsburg Road an exasperated Rodes stopped the division and formed Daniel and Doles in line of battle. When the enemy withdrew in the face of this show of force, Rodes pulled in his men and resumed the march around 3:30 p.m. After crossing a mountain near Monterey Springs, he stopped for the night at Waynesboro, Pennsylvania. About noon the following day, July 7, the division tramped into Hagerstown, where the men received the disheartening news that Vicksburg, Mississippi, had fallen to the enemy. Thankfully, the news was followed by a very welcome four days of relative quiet.[65]

Unfortunately for the beleaguered Army of Northern Virginia, the Potomac River was swollen by recent rains and too high to safely cross. Lee was trapped north of the river with Meade's army moving against him. Rodes marched southwest through Hagerstown and took up a position about one-and-a-quarter miles out on the National Road, where he formed the extreme left end of Lee's line. Hotchkiss noted in his diary, "[R]ode over a line selected by the Engineers and the Generals, in the morning, with Generals Ewell, Rodes, Early and Johnson and the positions for the troops were chosen and they were assigned to their places and put in position and commenced fortifying."[66]

Lee's position stretched for about eight miles. It was good ground, well chosen and powerful. On his right was Longstreet's First Corps, whose right rested on the Potomac below Falling Waters near Downesville. A. P. Hill's Third Corps held the center, his line extending to the Funkstown Road. Ewell's Second Corps stretched from that point across the National Road just west of Hagerstown. For two days Lee waited for the river to fall and the Federals to attack him. "They have but little courage," he finally concluded, and with the Potomac having fallen to an acceptable level, he began pulling the army back across the river early on July 14.[67]

"On the memorable night of July 14," Rodes noted in his report, the Second Corps fell back to Williamsport. Beginning at midnight, Rodes' men waded across the river on a sandbar located above the aqueduct that ran over the mouth of the Conococheague River. Carter and the artillery crossed on a pontoon at Falling Waters, four miles below Williamsport. "The operation was a perilous one," Rodes recorded:

> It was very dark, raining, and excessively muddy. The men had to wade through the aqueduct, down the steep bank of soft and slippery mud, in which numbers lost their shoes and down which many fell. The water was cold, deep, and rising; the lights on either side of the river were dim, just affording enough light to mark the places of entrance and exit; the cartridge-boxes of the men had to be placed around their necks; some small men had to be carried over by their comrades; the water was up to the armpits of a full-sized man.

Rodes maintained, however, that his men endured all this "with cheers and laughter." Though no one suffered serious injury, the division did lose about 30,000 rounds of ammunition, ruined by the water. "We waded two & two side by side," Sam Pickens wrote in his diary, "holding on to each other in order to resist the current better & be more steady. There were orders for the men to hang their cartridge boxes around their necks, but a great many failed to do it & there was a considerable amount of ammunition damaged & destroyed by getting wet."[68]

Once across, the men marched about one hour before being allowed to collapse into bivouac. "And there," Rodes concluded, "ended the Pennsylvania campaign, so far as this division was concerned."[69]

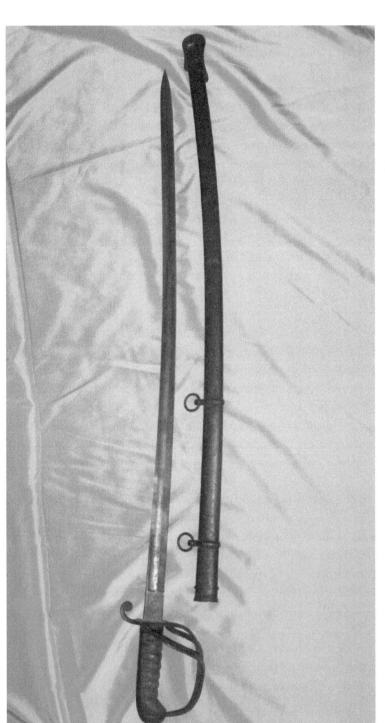

Maj. Gen. Robert E. Rodes' sword, in what is believed to be the first published photograph of the weapon.

Mary Rodes Dell, and the Rodes Family

Chapter 9

Bristoe, Kelly's Ford, and Mine Run

Though the Pennsylvania campaign was effectively over, it carried enough momentum to compel both sides to remain in motion for some time. On Wednesday, July 15, Rodes' command, marching between Johnson's and Early's divisions, reached Big Spring three miles from Martinsburg. The following day eight more miles brought it to Darkesville about noon. Ewell's Second Corps then marched back to the outskirts of Martinsburg in a futile attempt to bag about 6,000 Federals reported to be hovering around the B&O Railroad. This wild goose chase left the Second Corps dangerously far behind the rest of the Army of Northern Virginia at a time when Meade was swiftly marching down the east side of the Blue Ridge in an effort to block General Lee's exits from the Shenandoah Valley. Though A. P. Hill and James Longstreet managed to slip their corps through Chester Gap and go on to Culpeper on July 24, Ewell faced the prospect of being cut off by the Union III Corps at Manassas Gap, which was held only by Ambrose Wright's brigade of Richard Anderson's Third Corps division.

With Rodes in the lead, Ewell on July 22 began a dramatic race for the gap. Rodes reached Abraham's Creek near Winchester, and in terrific heat the following day his men executed an incredible twenty-three-mile march to arrive at the gap about 4:00 p.m. Rodes, who had ridden part of the way with Ewell in his buggy, quickly deployed about 300 yards behind Wright, who maintained a tenuous hold on the gap against large enemy numbers. "These dispositions," Ewell reported, "were made by General Rodes with his usual promptness, skill, and judgment."

Almost immediately after sending up Eugene Blackford with about 250 of the division sharpshooters, Rodes saw Wright's men come tumbling out of the gap with the Federals close behind. When the Confederates rallied at the base of the gap, Rodes put Carter's artillery on the pursuing Federals, who "fled in a most cowardly manner." Despite having an entire corps, new III Corps commander William French (the same officer who had attacked Rodes and the Sunken Road at Sharpsburg) gave in to caution and did not press the issue. His tentative performance allowed Wright and Rodes to withdraw safely. Though Rodes' main line was not engaged, his sharpshooters lost fifteen men killed, wounded, or missing.[1]

That night Rodes marched his exhausted men another four or five miles south on the Luray Road to a bivouac two miles from Front Royal, where they received a welcome three-day rest. On the 27th the division took its turn bringing up the rear of the corps as it moved east through Thornton's Gap to near Sperryville. Two days later Rodes brought his men to the west bank of Robertson River, a tributary of the Rapidan near Madison Court House. Here, at last, the last gasp of momentum in the Gettysburg campaign came to an end.[2]

Losses in the campaign were heavy for both sides. For the Federals, who had some 88,000 men engaged, casualties totaled 3,155 killed, 14,329 wounded, and 5,365 missing or captured, a total of 23,049. Confederate losses were heavier. General Lee's army numbered about 75,000 men, of whom 3,900 were killed, 18,735 were wounded, and 5,425 were missing or captured, a total of 28,063.

Rodes' division entered the fighting on July 1 seventeen men shy of 8,000 effectives. The battle peeled away nearly thirty-nine percent of them, or 3,116. The campaign ripped apart Rodes' magnificent division. Broken down, the numbers looked like this: 602 killed, 1,684 wounded, and 830 missing or captured. Brigade losses varied considerably. Iverson's brigade took 1,384 men into the fighting and lost 903 of them (182 killed, 399 wounded, and 322 missing), or nearly sixty-six percent of its effective strength. Daniel marched 2,162 men off Oak Hill and lost 950 (231 killed, 583 wounded, and 136 missing), or forty-four percent. O'Neal's losses were similarly heavy. His brigade began with 1,688 effectives and lost 696 of them (90 killed, 422 wounded, and 184 missing), for a percentage loss just north of forty-one. Ramseur's small command began with 1,027 men and left 275 in Pennsylvania (39 killed, 149 wounded, and 87 missing), or just under twenty-seven percent. Doles' Georgians escaped with the lowest number of casualties. Doles led 1,323 men south toward Gettysburg off Oak Hill and lost 219 of them (46 killed, 106 wounded, and 67 missing), or sixteen and one-half percent. By way of comparison, Ed Johnson's division numbered 6,433 men and lost 1,936 (thirty-percent), while Jubal Early's smallish division of 5,460 lost 1,476 (twenty-seven percent).

The eight-week campaign taught Rodes another important lesson about the remarkable capabilities of his men, whom he now held in even greater awe, respect, and gratitude. "In concluding what I have to say about this campaign," he added at the end of his report, "I beg leave to call attention to the heroes of it; the men who day by day sacrificed self on the altar of freedom; those barefooted North Carolinians, Georgians, and Alabamians who, with bloody and swollen feet, kept to their ranks day after day for weeks. When the division reached Darkesville, nearly one-half of the men and many officers were barefooted, and fully one-fourth had been so since we crossed the Blue Ridge."[3]

*   *   *

After moving down through Warrenton, Meade began arriving at the north bank of the Rappahannock on July 26. Lee responded by putting his own army into defensive positions south of the river in the area around Culpeper. On Saturday, August 1, Rodes brought up his division and placed it in the line.[4]

After an inspection with Ewell on August 3 confirmed the security of his position, Rodes obtained permission for a short leave. From Orange Court House the following day he took the Orange & Alexandria train twenty-five miles down to Charlottesville for a quick check on Hortense, who expected to deliver the couple's first child in less than two months. The couple had not been together for months, probably since before Chancellorsville. They had decided that, in order to be closer to each other at this critical time, Hortense should spend her confinement with friends in Charlottesville. All must have been well, for Rodes did not tarry long there, spending less than two days with his beloved wife before returning to camp on the 6th. On the train ride back from Charlottesville he kept company and shared a "snack" with Major Hotchkiss, who was returning from a visit to Staunton.[5]

Rodes returned to a division whose men had had time in their quiet camps around Orange Court House not only to receive the kind and generous hospitality of the community, but also to reflect on how things stood in the late summer of 1863. "Our troops are very much disheartened since the downfall of Vicksburg and our Retreat from Pennsylvania," the Twenty-sixth Alabama's W. H. Terrill wrote home on August 15. "[T]here is a great many deserting from all portions of the army. Last winter spirits were higher. Lots of men in the regiment are talking about the futility of going on and will go home when their time expires." Despite a unanimous vote of condemnation in Ramseur's brigade, the peace movement in North Carolina, led by the Raleigh *Standard's* William Holden, remained fairly strong there. The movement had an adverse affect upon some Carolina soldiers at the front. In some parts of the army, morale seemed dangerously low.[6]

Rodes acknowledged the morale problem, but not the cause, attributing most of it to President Davis' recent proclamation of amnesty for deserters. The general expressed as much in a letter written to the father of his friend and subordinate, Major Eugene Blackford, the commander of the division sharpshooters. The letter was in response to an inquiry the elder Blackford had made of Rodes regarding the condition of Eugene's ulcerated leg. After having Dr. William Mitchell, the division surgeon, examine the major, Rodes—much to the embarrassment of Eugene—reported the results to the father. It was a friendly letter, indicating that the two previously had corresponded. "Nothing of interest transpiring here," Rodes added in the same August 13 letter. "I know nothing at least. As for the next grand battle I think we will force it on and hence that it will be fought on the other side of the Rappahannock—Who knows? There is no indication of the intention to attack on the part of either army so far as I know." Rodes then touched upon the problem of morale.

> The stories you hear about desertions are exaggerated I imagine. The North Carolinians are deserting and so are the Virginians but neither to a greater extent than they did last Spring whilst we were at Fredericksburg—excepting our Div wherein it seems the President's proclamation caused some 100 or more men to leave. The evil is not going on to an alarming extent I think—Nor to an extent which is not perfectly natural under the system adopted by our Pres. of pardoning all men who are condemned to be shot and finally releasing all deserters unconditionally. We are all in hopes that this last proclamation [will be replaced by] the rule with the strong hand.[7]

Rodes, however, fervently wished to be rid of at least two men in camp: Brigadier General Alfred Iverson, whose men now openly refused to serve under him, and Colonel Edward O'Neal who, in Rodes' opinion, also had done poorly at Gettysburg. General Lee agreed the men were not suited to lead brigades in his army. He conveniently removed Iverson by making him provost marshal. Though pleased with this arrangement, Rodes strongly objected to the commanding general's intention to consolidate Iverson's brigade (which now

Col. Edward A. O'Neal in a postwar image. His poor display at Gettysburg resulted in his acrimonious transfer out of Rodes' division and the Army of Northern Virginia.

Generals in Gray

had 1,855 men present for duty) with Ramseur's. "This brigade has fought well generally and fought with distinguished gallantry at Chancellorsville & Gettysburg," Rodes pleaded with Lee on August 19. "[I]ts espirit de corps is such as to make the loss of its individuality a matter of great mortification to its men and officers—to consolidate it with another brigade will tend to demoralize it—such a step just at this moment when desertions are so common will be particularly dangerous. In truth," Rodes concluded, "in my opinion it is necessary just now to encourage it by all legitimate means." Lee gave in to the wishes of his young major general and agreed to leave the brigade intact.[8]

Iverson, however, still needed a replacement. Rodes recommended twenty-six-year-old Colonel Robert D. Johnston of the Twenty-third North Carolina. An attorney before the war, Johnston served a year as a company captain before being elected colonel of the Twenty-third at its reorganization. At Seven Pines he gallantly led the regiment to within fifty feet of the Union line before falling with three wounds. Johnston recovered in time to stand among his men in the Bloody Lane at Sharpsburg. He fought well again at Chancellorsville and received a severe wound at Gettysburg on July 1. The colonel had just returned to duty when Rodes nominated him for promotion. "[T]he good of the service demands that he shall be placed in command of the Brigade in preference to all others," explained Rodes. After both Ewell and Lee endorsed Rodes' recommendation and President Davis approved it, Johnston received the appointment on September 8.[9]

The situation with Colonel O'Neal would not be settled quite so easily. Rodes saw to that. His controversial involvement more than a year earlier with the question of who should succeed him as commander of the Fifth Alabama replayed itself, though with much greater drama and complexity, regarding who should be made the permanent commander of his brigade.

Soon after O'Neal took temporary command of Rodes' brigade at the beginning of the year, Alabama politicians began a relentless campaign with Richmond to get him promoted to brigadier general. When Rodes became a major general in May, those same politicians and many officers and men in and out of the brigade assumed O'Neal finally would get a wreath around his colonel's stars. As a matter of course, however, Lee and A. P. Hill, the acting commander of the Second Corps at that time, sought out Rodes' opinion on who should take over his old brigade. Rodes' answer surprised both officers.

"After mature reflection," Rodes wrote the commanding general on May 13, "I have come to the conclusion that General John B. Gordon . . .

> is the best man the service considered, and for the good of the brigade to succeed me. I have the honor therefore to solicit most earnestly his immediate return to the brigade (he has been in it always and commands its confidence fully) as its commander. I am of course conscious that the brigade or Div. which the General serves in now will be loth [sic] to give him up, and that it will be difficult to supply his place there, but the service and this Army will be equally well served by his taking the position I ask for him. He himself prefers to command my brigade to any other—has identified himself thoroughly with it—a portion of it has fought him up to his position & I as his brigade commander knowing his merit have taken great interest in improving and helping him to his present position. And under the circumstances I respectfully submit that we have the best right to his services.[10]

Rodes' preference for the capable and courageous Gordon, the former commander of the gallant Sixth Alabama, is understandable. But the wisdom of it was highly questionable since it carried the risk of controversy and damage to morale in Gordon's current command. In response to this rather surprising request, Lee took the equally surprising step, apparently to please Rodes, of promptly writing the president to secure Gordon's transfer from temporary command of Alexander Lawton's Georgia brigade. When Gordon's Georgians found out about the proposed transfer, they drew up a petition, signed by every officer in the brigade, to retain him as their commander. To avoid damaging the morale of an entire brigade, Lee gave in to the petitioners. Gordon would have to stay put.[11]

Rodes expected something like this might happen, but he remained determined to stir up controversy by reaching outside the brigade to find his permanent replacement. "Failing [to get] Gordon," he told Hill on May 13, "my choice is confined to Col. O'Neal now commanding the brigade, Col. Battle [whom Rodes a few months before had dissuaded from resigning in favor of a medical leave of absence] Comd 3rd Ala. and Col. John T. Morgan now on Conscript duty in Ala. but Comdg a Cavalry (Ala.) regiment in the Tennessee Army. I would prefer Morgan who is an able officer and one well known to the brigade if he can be had promptly. Between the other two gentlemen who are both good men, but who are not in my opinion equal to Morgan as brigade Comdr generally and as a disciplinarian."[12]

General Lee replied by inquiring about the capabilities of Colonel Samuel Pickens of the Twelfth Alabama. "In all the positions he has filled," Rodes replied carefully on May 30, "he has proved himself a first rate disciplinarian and manager of men." But Rodes had real reservations about Pickens, who was "not a man of high order of talent." Still, Rodes averred unpersuasively that if the native South Carolinian and graduate of the Citadel in Charleston had "been from Alabama or ever lived in it at all, I should have recommended him then as the next best man to Morgan."[13]

Though he had been willing to accommodate Rodes' somewhat controversial desire for Gordon, Lee drew the line with Morgan, whom he did not know at all. On May 26, the commanding general brushed aside Rodes' request for that officer and took the most logical next step by writing the president that he now preferred "O'Neal as perhaps the most fit—as he has been identified with his regiment and the brigade by long service as Lieut. Col. and Col." Davis approved O'Neal's promotion to brigadier general, to date from June 6.[14]

Before Lee could present the commission to O'Neal, however, Rodes made a dramatic last minute protest. "The more I see of Col. O'Neal's conduct in the office and especially in the field," he wrote Lee on June 10, "the more I am satisfied that he ought to be confined to his regiment. He has not self reliance enough, nor is [he] quick enough of apprehension to manage any but a small command. He will not do as well as I thought he would."[15]

Lee could not ignore such a candid assessment. Promptly, if somewhat hastily, he looked into the matter personally, going so far as to interview

O'Neal. "Since my first letter to his Excellency the President," he wrote Secretary of War Seddon on June 11, the day after receiving Rodes' letter, "I have seen Col. O'Neal and I made some particular inquiries into his capacities to command the brigade and I cannot recommend him to the command." Based largely on Rodes' protests, Lee took the unusual step of returning O'Neal's commission to the War Department. Not unexpectedly, this move unleashed a firestorm of protest.[16]

Though his performance at Gettysburg seemed to vindicate Rodes' suspicions about O'Neal's unfitness for brigade command, severe personal disagreements between the two men may have led Rodes to be less than objective when assessing the colonel's capabilities. Evidence of this is found inside a stinging letter President Davis received from Mississippi Senator James Phelan, a former Alabamian who now took up the cause of defending O'Neal. "I have been informed that your refusal to appoint him," Phelan wrote the president on August 23, "was probably thro' the opposing influence of Genl Rhodes [sic]. Genl R. is the enemy of Col O'Neal I am assured, because Col O'Neal has criticized his failures & drunken debaucheries. The person who thus writes me will not shirk the contention, in my opinion and Genl R. may have to guard his own honor upon confirmation of his new honors."[17]

These astonishing assertions indicate that an intolerable tension had strained beyond repair the relationship between Rodes and O'Neal. Rodes was known as a man who rarely turned down a drink, but he was not known—save for the inadvertent incident at Carlisle the previous June, of which Ewell's staff officer Campbell Brown remarked after the war that he had never seen Rodes intoxicated before or since—as a man who indulged in excessive drinking, let alone "drunken debaucheries." As for "criticizing his failures," this probably refers to an issue Rodes stressed with many of his officers—discipline. Rodes looked after his old brigade, and he no doubt pridefully believed that it had been in its best condition when under his direct and firm control. Such an attitude understandably would have aroused O'Neal's strong resentment, and set the two men on the path of irreconciliation.

Next in line of brigade seniority after O'Neal stood Cullen Battle of the Third Alabama. "Col. Battle has ability," continued Rodes in his June 10 letter to Lee, "but is not a number one disciplinarian . . . and his health are the only objections to him that I have noticed." Despite these objections, Rodes preferred Battle to the alternative. "He will do now I think better than Col. O'Neal."[18] After this less than ringing endorsement of Battle, Rodes relentlessly returned once again to what he really wanted. "But I find it my duty to insist as far as I may with propriety," his letter went on to Lee, "upon Jno. T. Morgan's appointment in preference to either of those two gentlemen and to any other officer whatever."[19]

This was the same Morgan who served with Rodes two years before in the Fifth Alabama. As colonel of the Fifth, Rodes had relied heavily on Major Morgan to help run the regiment, often preferring his advice and guidance to that of Lieutenant Colonel Jones. With Rodes' elevation to brigade command, Morgan had been elected lieutenant colonel, though rather than endure the indignity of another election, he resigned upon the regiment's reorganization the following April. Morgan returned to Alabama to recruit a new regiment, which became the Fifty-first Alabama Partisan Rangers. While serving in varying capacities with the cavalry of Joseph Wheeler and Bedford Forrest, Morgan's Fifty-first saw relatively little action through the remainder of 1862 and early 1863. It is thus somewhat surprising that Rodes preferred him, particularly after having officially commended O'Neal for his conduct at Chancellorsville (though before witnessing his poor performance at Gettysburg).[20]

To further justify his controversial preference, Rodes made the somewhat dubious claim, "The whole Brigade knows Morgan and would like very much to have him command it." Though he had seen Morgan in very light combat only once, more than two years before in the skirmish at Sangster's Crossroads, Rodes declared, "I know [him] thoroughly [as] an able man—cool and reliable in action, stern and just in his judgments and actions and is altogether the best man that can be gotten for the place. It will not do," Rodes concluded with a dramatic flourish, "for this good brigade to be paralyzed by an incompetent Comdr."[21]

In an evident desire to satisfy his persistent new division commander, the tactful and forbearing Lee finally gave in to Rodes. On June 11, he recommended Morgan's appointment as "the best which can be made." Davis and the War Department complied and promoted Morgan to brigadier general, his commission to date from June 6, 1863—the date O'Neal's commission was to have taken effect.[22]

Rodes finally got what he wanted—at least until an unusual circumstance intervened to undermine his efforts. When he reached Richmond en route to take up his new command, Morgan learned that his beloved Fifty-first Alabama had become leaderless after losing its lieutenant colonel in a tough fight at Elk River Ford. On July 14, he wrote the War Department that he wished to decline the promotion to brigadier and return to his old regiment. At least that was Morgan's official excuse.[23]

Almost immediately, other more sinister rumors took hold among those who found it difficult to understand why anyone would turn down the opportunity to become a general. Sides were drawn in the growing bitter controversy, with Alabamians, including Governor John Shorter, increasingly lining up against Rodes and for O'Neal. "Alabama is proud of him," the governor had declared of Rodes back on March 6 to President Davis. On July 28, the governor came out solidly behind O'Neal in a letter written to him. "I have heard that Col. Morgan, recognizing the injustice to your command, has declined to accept the appointment tendered to him." In his August 23 letter to President Davis, Senator Phelan related another rumor with a similar theme. "It is also asserted," he wrote, "that the unwillingness of the Brigade to be commanded by any other officer [than O'Neal] was the cause of Morgan's refusal to accept." Led by Representative Thomas Foster of O'Neal's congressional district, Alabama politicians used these rumors in a relentless campaign on behalf of the colonel that vexed Lee, Davis, and the administration right up to the last days of the Confederacy. "It is feared," Foster wrote the president on September 8, 1863, "that Genl Rhodes [sic] failed to do justice to a meritorious officer from motives of unkindness." Colonel Morgan turned down the promotion, declared Foster, "because on his arrival in Richmond [he] learned that all the Officers had handed Genl Rhodes [sic] a written protest against his [Rodes'] conduct."[24]

If the brigade's officers had presented Rodes with a "written protest," there is no evidence of it today. We do know that when they learned O'Neal had demanded a transfer, a handful of his subordinate officers on July 24 signed a sort of "to whom it may concern" petition, wherein they expressed their admiration for the colonel, making no overt criticism of Rodes. It also is known that Rodes did not stand in the way of that demand.[25]

Rodes wrote to Secretary of War Seddon on August 1 in an obvious attempt to facilitate O'Neal's transfer. ""I have the honor to call your attention respectfully to the desire of Col. Ed. A. O'Neal to be promoted to the Command of some Alabama brigade in the Western Army," explained Rodes, "and I beg to say in the Colonel's behalf that he has served with me thro the various Campaigns of the Army of Northern Virginia with great credit to himself and to his state." Subtly but obviously, he praised O'Neal's qualifications, but only at the regimental level. "As a regimental commander in action he has acquired and deservedly a reputation of which any soldier might be proud." After a few more obligatory platitudes Rodes concluded, "I have not recommended the Col. to promotion and assignment to my old brigade because I consider the officers whom I have recommended for this position as better suited for it than the Col."[26]

More than five months later on January 21, 1864, Rodes again wrote the secretary regarding O'Neal, who was still with the army in Virginia. This time Rodes discussed an old obsession—discipline. "I hope I may with propriety state that whilst I opposed the promotion of himself and Genl. Battle (both on same grounds bye the bye) and would under the same circumstances do so again," he continued, "justice to them and truth, required me to say that my requirements as to the qualifications of my brigade commanders, and especially of those of the commander of my old brigade, were much severer, and in accordance with a much higher standard than is usual in our armies."[27]

In February 1864, Edward O'Neal's transfer finally was authorized, though it did not include a brigadier's commission. Disgusted by what he believed was a grave injustice, the colonel apparently submitted his resignation. He would have had the commission, he bitterly complained to Secretary of War Seddon on May 29, 1864, except that Rodes had intervened to get Morgan, "who after he reached Richmond declined the honor because of the injustice to me. Genl Rodes confessed that the charge I made with the Brigade at Chancellorsville—when it broke & routed the 11th Army Corps of the enemy—won for him his spurs as Maj. Genl. and Col. now Genl. Battle told him on the field that the same order announcing his promotion should have announced mine." Rather than resign, however, O'Neal ended up recruiting men in Alabama before handling a regiment in James Cantey's brigade during the Atlanta campaign. When Cantey assumed division command, O'Neal received command of the brigade and led it in heavy fighting before being relieved for reasons that remain unclear. His three wounds may have had something to do with it, but more likely it was an unsatisfactory field performance. He finished the war chasing deserters in his home state. One historian put O'Neal's curious officer rank purgatory thusly: "His commission as a brigadier was never confirmed by the Senate, nor was the document itself ever given to him, making him, in a way, a general who never was."[28]

Rodes, meanwhile, still needed a brigadier confirmed. Gordon was always a longshot, and Morgan failed to work out as expected. In mid-August, Rodes traveled to Richmond to argue for his next choice. "Colonel Battle's appointment," he declared, "[must] be made promptly, because until the Brigade has a permanent commander, and [in another dig at O'Neal] a better one in a disciplinary character than it has had lately it is likely to continue in a condition that is not at all satisfactory to any one concerned." This time there was no drama or controversy. On August 25 the appointment went to thirty-four-year-old Cullen Battle, a battle-tested veteran who gladly accepted, regardless of the feelings he may have held about the "injustice" done to O'Neal.[29]

During his return from Richmond, Rodes ran into Captain Robert Park of the Twelfth Alabama, the same officer who back in February had successfully protested to the acting division commander the transfer of Jim, the black cook. "I can never forget a brief conversation with General Rodes while at the depot at Orange C. H. on his return from a visit to Richmond," Park fondly recalled years later. "He told me of the appointment of General Battle to the command of the brigade, and stated that Colonel O'Neal of the Twenty-sixth Alabama, had asked for a transfer to the Western Army." Rodes' next remarks, however, made the occasion especially memorable. "During the conversation," Park continued, "General Rodes spoke most affectionately of my former captain, R. H. Keeling [killed at Seven Pines], saying that he knew him at the Virginia Military Institute, and that he should have entered the army as a brigadier general instead of a first lieutenant."[30]

Meanwhile, the fight to restore the army's damaged morale was well underway. Knowing his men were emotionally and physically exhausted, Lee authorized a system of furloughs in mid-August that allowed two men in every 100 to take a month-long leave. About the same time, President Davis proclaimed Friday, August 21, as a day of fasting, prayers, and offerings of thanks. At Ewell's headquarters, Reverend Lacy delivered a moving sermon to a large audience that included Lee, Ewell, Rodes, Johnson, Ramseur, Robert Hoke, and others. According to mapmaker Jedediah Hotchkiss, Lacy confirmed to his approximately 1,500 listeners that "God must be on our side because we are in the right as proven by our deeds, and our enemies had shown themselves cruel and blood-thirsty. Our army had not been defeated [at Gettysburg]," the reverend added reassuringly, "but had been asked to do an impossible thing and had not done it." One cannot help but wonder what General Lee thought upon hearing those words.[31]

Having prayed, given thanks, and fasted, the army turned to reviews as the next step in rebuilding its morale. On the afternoon of the 26th, Rodes brought out the brigades of Battle, Ramseur, and Daniel. "About three o'clock we were drawn up in line with some stakes placed to mark our place of alignment, the 5th Ala occupying the right, the 3rd Ala the next on the left, the 6th next & the

12th & 20th [26th] combined on the left," explained an Alabama soldier in a letter home. He left a long a detailed description of the review that is worth reproducing:

> After being framed in our proper position we attached arms & rested that is lay around loose each one sitting, lying, standing, going after water or anything else he wished until . . . Gen. Ewell appeared at his position at the blue white star cross flag, which was planted about a hundred paces in front of the center of the brigade. The flag was blue. The cross on it was composed of white stars & extended from corner to corner. It was the flag that usually marks Gen. Rodes headquarters. Gen. Ewell accompanied by Gen. Rodes having taken their position we were called to attention & prepared for review.
>
> Having formed in open order the Gen. accompanied by Gen. Rodes commenced [with] the 5th Ala., [riding] along in front of the brigade talking to the commanders of each regt. And for the sake of having something to say asked each some little pleasing or agreeable question, that keen teaching eye examining all the guns & accoutrements, clothing, and appearance of the privates who looked at him as he passed with that criticizing gaze that is common with most persons when they are deeply interested in the person looked at. They looked at him as if they respected him, but not as if looking at a managerie [sic] nor from mere vulgar curiosity.[32]

"The soldiers presented a very fine appearance," thought Hotchkiss, who watched the proceedings along with Ewell and the rest of the Second Corps staff. The generals apparently looked very fine as well, especially Ewell. "He was dressed up much better than I ever saw him before," wrote Private Sam Pickens. "A Splendid sword & yellow sash & fancy saddle & bridle set him off to advantage. He is a good rider although he has a wooden leg. Gen. Rodes is a fine rider, too, & looked well on his splendid black—Maryland—horse." The following day Doles' and Johnston's brigades went on review with the rest of the corps.[33]

Though others thought Rodes "looked well" on review, he was unhappy with the state of his own and his staff's apparel. On August 30, he sent his aide, Lieutenant James Hutchinson, a pre-war lawyer who had been with him since the first of the year, to Richmond to get new uniforms, eight or nine altogether, for the division commander and his staff. Hutchinson went to Philip Sutton, the same who had lost an arm at Seven Pines and who now was engaged in private business in the capital. "Please assist him all in your power," Rodes instructed his friend and former staff member, "and furnish him with money enough to pay for all the cloth and hold me responsible for the money which shall be refunded to you as soon as I can ascertain the amount."[34]

Sometime in early September, Rodes finished his report on the Gettysburg campaign. Working on it reminded him again of the incredible suffering his men had endured and the remarkable bravery they had displayed. On the 5th, he issued a division-wide circular praising the men who served under his command:

> History has seldom recorded an instance in which soldiers of any nation or in any cause had evinced so many of the highest qualifications of men, patriots & soldiers as were shown in the conduct of the Confederate troops in the Pennsylvania Campaign. To those who, with ragged clothes and feet bare, bleeding & swollen, cheerfully kept their place in the ranks during marches remarkable for their length, rapidity & fatigues & then fought resolutely an enemy superior in numbers, position, and all the advantages of war, the impartial observer must award the credit of being heroes, the true heroes of this bloody war. As no scheme for conferring honorable badges of merit has yet been put into operation, it is ordered that each company commander shall cause to be entered upon the rolls whether or not each individual man, officer, non commissioned officer or private was present in his place in the contest of each day at Gettysburg and that such entries are to be made upon the rolls of the regiment.

> Hereafter in every case of an engagement with the enemy, it is ordered that a similar registry of present & absent shall be made upon the Company and Regimental rolls of each regiment in this Division.

> It is always a matter of congratulations to win the approval of our lawful superior, & it is announced with pride to a Division which received the highest praise from the late lamented Gen. Jackson for their achievements at Chancellorsville, but on the field of Gettysburg the illustrious soldier Commanding the Army of Northern Virginia sent, through a staff officer, to the Commander of this division, the message "I am proud of your Division."

Rodes so cherished Lee's remark that he included it not only in the circular but also in his official report of the campaign. Five days later, Rodes ordered that "Gettysburg" be inscribed upon every regimental flag in the division.[35]

On September 8, Rodes issued another division-wide circular directing that select infantrymen should be trained as artillerists. He ordered that a battery of four guns be made available to each brigade for one day, with one company from each regiment selected for training on the pieces. This innovative and unique order was Rodes' way to make it possible in the heat of battle to keep guns operating even after their crews had been killed or wounded.[36]

The next day, the army began shedding thousands of men for service in the Western Theater. With the strategic situation stable on the Virginia front, the commanding general reluctantly agreed to the temporary transfer of two of Longstreet's divisions (John Hood's and Lafayette McLaws') west to Braxton Bragg's Army of Tennessee. A large Federal force under William S. Rosecrans was moving against Bragg in North Georgia. President Davis hoped to use the advantage of interior lines of communication to reinforce Bragg in time to defeat Rosecrans, and return the troops to Virginia as circumstances warranted.

That same day Lee, as if to reassure himself of his remaining strength, called for another grand review. In perfect late summer weather, Ewell's three divisions lined up behind each other on a large piece of open undulating land just east of Orange Court House. Early's division stood in front. After marching three miles from camp, Rodes' division, the corps' largest, formed up two hundred yards behind Early. Johnson's men held the rear. "I witnessed, on Wednesday evening, the grandest military display that I have ever before seen," reported a correspondent of the Petersburg *Express*. He continued:

In a large and beautiful field just east of the court house, General Ewell's entire corps, consisting of three divisions, commanded respectively by Major-Generals Early, Rhodes [sic] and Johnson, was reviewed by General Lee in person. About noon, large bodies of troops could be seen wending their way across the field to the place designated for them, and wishing to be in at the commencement of the show, I immediately repaired thither, and wishing to hear what was going on, as well as to see, I took my stand by the large flag, designating the general's stand point. By this time three lines of troops, each some mile and a half in length, and one behind the other, was stretching out to the right and left, and now they are halted, arms stacked, and the men are lying down awaiting the movements of the generals. The crowd around my stand point was now augmenting rapidly, and on looking around I beheld a large body of ladies on horseback, and in carriages and buggies, who had been drawn thither to witness the scene. Just then a number of officers came dashing up, who proved to be Generals Ewell, Early and Rhodes [sic], and a number of their respective staffs. Never having seen General Ewell before, my eyes were riveted upon him. He is a tall, slim individual, with extremely sharp features, and his Frenchified moustache and whiskers, make him look the warrior that he is; but the most remarkable feature about him is his restless eyes, which were constantly wandering over the field, and ever and anon some courier would be hastily despatched [sic] to some point to order some movement or other. General Early is a most husky looking person, and seemed as one who would not be brooked in any thing he wished, while General Rhodes [sic] is one of the most pleasant looking men that I have seen for many a day.

The bugle soon announced all in readiness, and General Lee was despatched [sic] for, who soon came riding up, and now the cavalcade, composed of General Lee and staff, General Ewell and staff, and the division commanders, started off at a swift gallop to the right of the first division, and soon they are seen coming down the front of the line, each brigade coming to a present as the cavalcade passed, and as they swept by us the strains of music were swelling up all along the line. They passed round the left of the line, dashed back to the right of the second division, and reviewed the second and third divisions in the same manner as the first, and once more came back to the original starting point, the riders and horses both looking much jaded, the distance they had gone so swiftly over being fully nine miles.

General Lee immediately dismounted and came to his carriage, which was only a few steps distant, and in which were two of his daughters, and in a few minutes he called to his side many of his generals, among them Generals Ewell, Longstreet, Hill, Stuart, Wilcox and others, and gave his daughters an introduction to them. His daughters, though not over handsome, have exceedingly pleasant and intelligent countenances, both having dark and piercing eyes, and both bearing some resemblance to their father.

The generals now took a stand just by the flag, and the troops commenced passing in review before General Lee, and as each flag in passing would be lowered as a salute, the general in response would take his hat off. And now I got a close view of the men composing this gallant corps. Here passed those men who had so often followed General Jackson in his numerous battles, and who had won for him that renown which will live through ages to come; and now passes Jackson's old division, at present commanded by the gallant General Johnston [sic], and here comes the "Stonewall Brigade," which was composed of veteran looking soldiers. Many of the banners of the corps bore evidence of having been often borne to the breeze amid the whistling of bullets, and all of them contained some dozen or fifteen names to mark the different battles the respective regiments had distinguished themselves in.

The review being now over, the crowd of spectators dispersed, and the troops, with three hearty cheers for General Lee, commenced wending their way back to their camps. . . .

It is surprising to see how eager the men of this army are always to get a good view of General Lee, for though a person may have seen him a hundred times, yet he never tires looking at him, and this was noticeable as the many thousands passed by, to see how eagerly they would peer to the right to get a glance at him.[37]

*   *   *

With two divisions of Longstreet's First Corps detached on operations in the Western Theater, Lee decided to withdraw to a stronger position. At 7:00 a.m. on September 14, Rodes led his division on "a hurried march" of twelve miles to a crossing on the Rapidan River at Racoon Ford. After getting his men safely over, he saw the enemy in some strength approaching the river's far side. He called up his artillery and after a three-hour duel the enemy batteries retired. Rodes put his division in a woods in rear of the ford and guarded against a thrust across the river.[38]

In somber contrast to the grand review held a few days earlier, Rodes assembled his division on September 15 to view the execution of a deserter from the Second North Carolina of Ramseur's brigade. "A Chaplain prayed with him & then he was blindfolded," Sam Pickens wrote of the condemned man, "his hands tied behind his back, & kneeling was fastened to a stake. In a few moments more the command 'fire' was given & 1/2 dozen or more musket balls passed thro' his breast—killing him instantly."[39]

"It was a sad sight," concluded Captain Park of the Twelfth Alabama, "but his death was necessary as a warning and lesson to his comrades. Each regiment was marched in front of the dead body, and his breast was pierced by several balls."[40]

On Friday the 18th, Rodes received orders to proceed down to Morton's Ford on the same river. "When we came down it was raining hard and very dark & muddy so that it was impossible to get a place to lie down, or even make a fire," Major Blackford wrote home. The strength of the Federals gathered on the far side of the Rapidan genuinely concerned the division commander. "Gen. Rodes was positive that the enemy would attempt to cross before day," Blackford went on in is letter home, "but I could not agree with him from the signs visible on the opposite banks, however the same watch & ward had to be kept up." Blackford's conclusion was the correct one. Though within easy range of each other, the enemy did not try to cross, nor did they wish to exchange fire, preferring instead to exchange newspapers and coffee until Rodes put a stop to the fraternization.

The "enemy" that occupied everyone's interest—for the time being, at least—was Mother Nature. "The storm continued for several days," lamented Blackford when writing about a particularly heavy downpour, "causing us to spend a miserable time having no shelter at all." As if out of pity for their tent-less adversaries, the well-sheltered Yankees often sent over consoling music. "To our special benefit, I suppose," observed Blackford, "we are regaled by their national airs, and to crown all, they struck up Yankee Doodle yesterday evening."[41]

While marking time below the Rapidan preparing for an enemy movement and trying to stay dry, glorious news arrived for Rodes. At Charlottesville on Wednesday, September 30, Hortense delivered a healthy baby boy. After six years of marriage, during much of which Hortense had been severely ill, the Rodes' at last became a family. The young boy was named Robert Jr.[42]

With the opposing lines relatively stabile, the excited new father easily obtained leave to make a quick dash to Charlottesville to see Hortense and the baby. After a brief and pleasant visit, he returned on the Orange & Alexandria railroad. Mapmaker Jedediah Hotchkiss met Rodes on the train on October 7. "Gen. Rodes got on the cars at Charlottesville," he wrote his own wife. "He said he had just got a fine boy! & his wife was doing well. Aint he a lucky man?"[43]

Hundreds of miles to the west, meanwhile, Longstreet and his men helped Braxton Bragg's Army of Tennessee in North Georgia secure a stunning victory at Chickamauga. The Confederates pursued the defeated Federals north to Chattanooga, Tennessee. The stunning defeat—it was the Army of the Tennessee's only clear-cut, large-scale battlefield victory of the war—created deep concern in Washington, D.C. In response to the disaster, General Meade was ordered to dispatch to Tennessee two corps (XI and XII). Their removal from the ranks of the Army of the Potomac reduced Meade's effective fighting force to about 77,000 men. Although he could field only some 47,000 of his own combat soldiers, Lee interpreted the reduction as an opportunity to go over to the offensive. After sifting through a wide variety of intelligence reports, Lee resolved to swing his army west around Cedar Mountain and in doing so turn Meade's right flank. If all went well, Lee hoped to position his army between Meade and Washington, which might provoke the Federal commander into doing something hasty and foolhardy. With Jeb Stuart and Fitz Lee shielding the front, Lee's army prepared to move in a wide arc around the mountain, with Ewell's men marching on an inner line and A. P. Hill's divisions assuming a wider trek.

Rodes put his division in motion at 4:00 a.m. on Friday, October 9. After crossing the Rapidan at Barnett's Ford, he marched within three miles of Madison Court House. The following day he led the division down byroads, across old fields, and on new roads cut by pioneers, to reach the Sperryville Pike eleven miles northwest of Culpeper. "Rodes displayed untiring energy and sagacity in dodging about the hollows and never following the main road, in order to avoid the Yankee signal operators at Thoroughfare Gap," Major Blackford admiringly wrote home. "Thus we moved on for a day or two," he added in a separate letter, "working around our unsuspecting enemy, in true 'Stonewall' style."[44]

On the 11th, Rodes took the division across the Robinson River to the abandoned camps of the Union VI Corps. That morning, Meade initiated a three-day retreat that would take him all the way back to Centerville. Getting the men up at 2:00 a.m. the following morning, Rodes started the division for the Rappahannock at Jeffersonton, where about noon he ran into a strong contingent of Federal cavalry. Rather than challenge them with a potentially costly infantry attack, he brought up the artillery. "I was then in Gen. Rodes' company," wrote one of his officers, "& at once remarked that I would 'amuse' them [the enemy] for him, at the same time making a signal for my corps to come up at the 'double-quick.'" Rodes agreed to send Major Blackford and his sharpshooters on a six-mile flank march around Jeffersonton in order to cut off the Yankee retreat. After waiting the appropriate length of time, Rodes opened with an artillery barrage. Twenty minutes later the enemy broke and ran, heading straight for Blackford's flanking force. They "came tearing through the woods towards the river," wrote the major, "where we easily bagged them, killing & wounding a good many, besides taking about 100 prisoners." The tactic worked well. At little cost to himself, Rodes took Jeffersonton and went on to Warrenton the next day.

"Gen. R was much pleased and spoke of us in high terms," Blackford proudly wrote his cousin. The major's gratification with the praise offered by Rodes, however, was somewhat offset by his perceived lack of recognition from the Richmond papers. "One piece in the Sentinel of yesterday was decidedly rich," he complained bitterly in the same letter to his loved ones. From Rodes, however, Blackford gratefully received the consolation that all would be made right in the end. "Gen. R says that justice will be done some day," explained the major.[45]

A. P. Hill, meanwhile, after moving on the outer arc around Cedar Mountain, caught up with Meade's rear at Bristoe Station on October 14. Hill believed the troops he faced comprised only the Federal III Corps. Divided by Broad Run, Hill saw an opportunity to attack the corps vigorously and defeat it. Unfortunately for the Confederates, the Union II Corps (temporarily under General John Caldwell) was deployed behind a railroad embankment. Hill quickly ordered Harry Heth's division to attack. As his three brigades (two in front, one following behind) struck out east, much of the Union II Corps opened fire on them from the south. Heth's men turned in an effort to confront the fire, but were decimated in their attempt to do so. By the time Heth pulled his brigades back, nearly 1,400 men (hundreds of whom were captured), were no longer on the Confederate muster rolls. Later that day, when Hill was guiding General Lee across the field in an effort to explain how he had essentially repeated his mistake west of Gettysburg on July 1, Lee uttered his famous rebuke: "Well, well, general, bury these poor men and let us say no more about it."[46]

Early on the morning of October 14, Ewell's Second Corps set out from Warrenton Springs on the road to Auburn. The enemy was soon discovered to be in a good position on a ridge covering the road passing through Auburn. To break through, Ewell brought up Ed Johnson's division to deploy in his center straddling the road, while Rodes moved his division to the right, and Jubal Early marched around the left to gain the enemy's rear. Before these troops could get

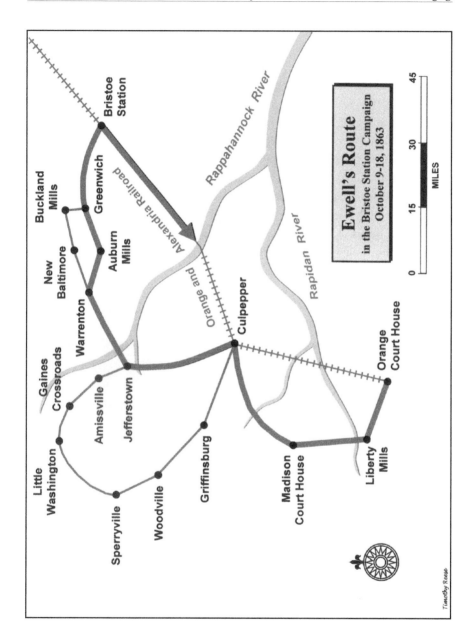

into position, however, the enemy infantry and cavalry pulled out, leaving some batteries behind to cover the retreat. Johnson's artillery (Anderson's battalion) opened with long range guns and a brisk duel ensued lasting several minutes until the Federal guns withdrew.[47]

By the following morning Meade had established a strong defensive line along Bull Run. Intensive probes throughout that drizzly day convinced Stuart that the Yankee position contained no exploitable weaknesses. With no real chance to hurt the enemy with a dramatic Third Manassas, and having outrun his supplies, Lee reluctantly decided to withdraw, his effort to flank Meade and trigger a favorable battle stymied. On October 16, Ewell started his men south. Some spent hours working in the rain tearing up the tracks of the Orange & Alexandria line along the way. With Hill's corps close behind, Rodes camped that night two-and-a-half miles from Catlett's Station.

After destroying more track on the 17th, Rodes' men resumed their march at 4:00 a.m. the following day. Up at 3:00 a.m. on the 19th, the division was on the road thirty minutes later, marching through driving rain and sleet to cross the Rappahannock on pontoons that afternoon. On the 20th, Rodes' men marched downstream to Kelly's Ford, where they prepared to go into winter quarters. The inglorious and inconclusive Bristoe Campaign had cost Rodes nineteen men killed and seventy-one wounded.[48]

*   *   *

The anti-administration Charleston *Mercury* saw the Bristoe Campaign as a failure of leadership. It was not as critical of the much-revered General Lee, but of his two corps commanders, Richard Ewell and A. P. Hill. The newspaper cried out for their replacement. "His [Lee's] plans are admirably conceived, that which ended with the ugly affair at Bristoe, was all that could be desired," the paper editorialized on November 21, "but he is compelled to entrust the execution of them to his Lieutenants, and we have no Jackson now. The truth is," the writer cleverly continued, "we want a new cut, shuffle and deal in Lieutenant Generals. Ewell's great physical sufferings have impaired his efficiency; he seems to lack decision; but he had Early and Rhodes [sic], men of excellent judgment. A. P. Hill has not risen to the requirements of a corps commander." The editorial was extraordinarily prescient, if ultimately ineffective.[49]

In lieu of a "new cut, shuffle and deal" that might reward him with a lieutenant generalcy, Rodes received a special gift of a different sort. Although his popularity in Alabama suffered as a result of the Edward O'Neal affair, in Virginia—particularly in his hometown of Lynchburg—his reputation soared. "We have been deputed by a portion of your friends in this city in their behalf," declared an official letter dated October 30 that accompanied the gift (the letter was later published in the Lynchburg *Virginian* on November 24),

> to present you a handsome bay Gelding; young, strong, active and very suitable, we hope, for service under the saddle. In their name, we now perform this agreeable task, and, request that the compliment be accepted as an earnest of their high estimate of your devoted and arduous service in the army of the Confederacy. From the commencement of the atrocious war, your friends have marked and admired the steady steps you have taken in the line of duty, in every way favorable to yourself and gratifying to them. Whether leading regiment, brigade or division, you have shown ability and fidelity equal to all the emergencies encountered; and, your gallant course thus far, whether on the march or in the field, has been onward and upward, continually reflecting credit on your name, conferring obligation on your country and cheering all your friends, at this your early home, with the cheering assurance that their high confidence in your character and conduct had been worthily bestowed.

To his proud fellow citizens of Lynchburg, Rodes' accomplishments must have seemed prodigious. In two-and-a-half-years, the vicissitudes of war had transformed him from an obscure and frustrated railroad engineer hoping to be a teacher, to national renown as a major general in command of a division in the Confederacy's most prominent and successful army. Rodes was an efficient killer of the enemy, a virile virtue his fellow citizens so admired that they hoped to share in it by lavishing praise upon him as one of their own.

From near Morton's Ford on the Rappahannock, Rodes sent his thanks on November 14. "Gentlemen," began his reply,

> The pressure of other duties has prevented me from sooner acknowledging the receipt of your beautiful and well chosen present, the most suitable a soldier could receive, and from expressing as well the gratitude I feel to its donors as the pleasure I take in its acceptance. A peculiar value attaching to the gift, coming as it does from citizens of the town of my nativity and youth, and from those who are associated with my early recollections. It assures me that my name is not forgotten there,

and that my efforts to serve my country, poor as they may be, have found recognition among the scenes of my early years, an assurance dear to the heart of every man, and especially so to me, a son of this noble old Commonwealth, whose lot has been cast at a distance from her borders.

Accept, gentlemen, for yourselves and those you represent, my kindest regards, and well wishes, and believe me to be,

Your friend and ob't serv't,

R.E. Rodes.[50]

During the final days of October, meanwhile, General Lee finished reestablishing his line along the Rappahannock. The position contained one major weakness: possession of the high ground north of the river at Kelly's Ford enabled the enemy to command the crossing. To deal with that problem, Lee established a bridgehead upstream where the Orange & Alexandria crossed the river at Rappahannock Bridge. From there, he could strike at the flank of any Union attempt to move up and cross at Kelly's.

The bridgehead marked the approximate center of Lee's line, with Hill spread out to the west of it and Ewell to the east. Longstreet's men were still on detached service in the Western Theater. To Rodes went the job of holding the critical point at Kelly's Ford, as well as nearby Wheatley's, Norman's and Steven's fords. He encamped his division between the Rappahannock River and Mountain Run, about one-and-a-half miles behind Kelly's Ford.[51]

Always vigilant against shirking, and wishing to strengthen the division as possible combat approached, Rodes on November 5 ordered all men on detached service to report to his headquarters at once. If they could not walk to the nearest train station, he decreed, transportation would be provided. During the ensuing days, scores of men reported for duty.[52]

Meanwhile, about noon on November 7, Rodes received an ominous report from the Second North Carolina's Colonel William R. Cox. The colonel was temporarily in command of Ramseur's brigade, who was home on leave to get married. After several days of picketing, warned Cox, the Federal cavalry had disappeared and been replaced by infantry. Rodes hurried to the ford to see for himself. Cox was right, he concluded; the enemy intended to force a crossing. He ordered his brigades, many of whose men were then trying on their just-issued winter clothing, to move up and assume pre-assigned positions at the edge of a woods south of the ford on a line that ran from the river to Stevensburg Road. He notified Lee, who in turn instructed the division commander not to attack until the Federals had crossed the river and given up the advantage of the high ground on the far side.[53]

Along the river, meanwhile, the Second North Carolina's 322 men held Rodes' picket line. Some of the men were deployed three-quarters of a mile upriver at Wheatley's, with others slightly more than one mile downstream watching Steven's. Most, however, were in rifle pits at Kelly's Ford. At the edge of a woods about three-quarters of a mile behind the Second, Rodes placed the Fluvanna artillery under Captain John Massie, supported by 500 men of the Thirtieth North Carolina.

As expected, Federal artillery that afternoon opened fire from the high ground across the river. The intense bombardment drove off all but three or four companies of the Second North Carolina. Rodes reacted to the bombardment hastily. Instead of withdrawing the rest of the Second to save the men while complying with Lee's order not to contest the enemy crossing, he ordered the Thirtieth to move up to the ford, to no good purpose. When they came under the intense fire of the Federal guns, the North Carolinians predictably scattered and ran for the shelter of the buildings and houses near the ford—behavior Rodes unfairly condemned as "disgraceful." The situation worsened when Federals belonging to William H. French's III Corps, under the protection of their artillery, laid a pontoon and crossed over the river, scooping up some 300 prisoners of the Second and Thirtieth regiments, most of whom had been hiding in nearby buildings.

As the shells were raining down, Rodes was busy putting into line the rest of his division, with his left anchored on the river near Wheatley's and his right, held by Junius Daniel's brigade, extending beyond the Stevensburg Road. When the Federals appeared to be massing for an attack against his left, however, he shifted Daniel to that flank, with the added intention of launching his own attack from that point. When the enemy quickly built their strength beyond his own, however, Rodes decided not to attack until Ed Johnson's division arrived. Neither side moved, each staring down the other through the remaining hours of daylight. Johnson finally arrived after dark and formed on Rodes' right, extending the line to Mountain Run.

Sometime during the night, Rodes received the somewhat surprising order to fall back on the Stevensburg Road to Pony Mountain. Setting out in the dark, he marched the division by the right flank across Mountain Run at Stone Mills, leading it through Stevensburg. About daybreak, the division halted on Pony Mountain, two miles from Culpeper Court House. With Early on his left, Rodes put the division into line of battle, his exhausted men feverishly working with bayonets and tin cups to throw up breastworks and trenches.

The retreat was triggered by the shocking loss of Lee's bridgehead at Rappahannock Station. In a brilliant *coup de main*, troops from John Sedgwick's VI Corps used speed and surprise to collapse the ill-conceived position. The Confederates there, two brigades under Harry Hays and Robert Hoke (led by Colonel Godwin) from Jubal Early's division were nearly eliminated from the army's muster rolls. Hays' brigade lost 702 of its 900 men (684 of whom were captured). Godwin's command suffered even more so, losing about 900 captured. When Rodes' losses of five killed, forty-five wounded, and 309 missing, are added to the Second Corps casualties, the inconclusive fighting shaved about 2,000 men from the Army of Northern Virginia to no purpose whatsoever. Federals losses, by comparison, numbered only forty-two.

Forced to abandon the Rappahannock line, Lee moved back to his old position behind the Rapidan River. Around 9:00 p.m. on the night of November 8, Rodes' men waded through the cold water at Racoon Ford. Ninety minutes later they stumbled into their old camps around Morton's Ford, where they promptly went to work building huts for winter quarters.

The fighting did not showcase Early or Rodes at their best. For the disaster at Kelly's Ford, Rodes unfairly tried to shift blame to the Thirtieth North Carolina. Though he graciously reported that the mortally wounded Lieutenant Colonel William Sillers (who died November 9) had "acted gallantly," he went on to write that the regiment as a whole "did not sustain its reputation." In his own report, however, Lee distributed the blame more judiciously. "It was not intended to attack the enemy," he wrote, "until he should have advanced from the river."[54]

* * *

By the second week of November, it appeared as though both sides were more than ready for winter quarters. President Davis paid a morale-boosting visit to the army that was supposed to culminate in a glorious grand review in his honor on the 24th. When a cold drenching rain intervened to cancel the review, the president retreated to Richmond.[55]

At his austere headquarters near Morton's Ford the following evening, Rodes sat down to write Reverend Moses Hoge, whose sermons many of Rodes' men attended following the battle of Chancellorsville. Although regular attendance was disrupted by the Pennsylvania campaign and subsequent movements to the Rapidan, Rodes and Hoge remained in touch during those months. Their letter-writing relationship likely included a fair amount of religious counseling from the man who enjoyed a strong spiritual influence on both Stonewall Jackson and Richard Ewell. With the army settling down for the winter behind the Rapidan, Hoge took the opportunity to extend that influence by sending Rodes a gift. On a recent trip to England, the Reverend had obtained several beautifully crafted Bibles, which he now took great pleasure in presenting one each to Lee, Ewell, and Rodes.

"My Dear Sir," Rodes wrote in acknowledgment of the gift. "Captain Smith delivered to me a few days ago the tasteful and valuable present you did me the honor to make me. I assure you that such a gift at your hands gives me great pleasure. I will prize it highly, and read it, I hope, with profit to my soul. I feel sure that in my promising you this I appreciate your kindness," he continued, "and that I am sincerely obliged to you for the interest you have taken in my welfare."

Twelve years later, Rodes' staff officer and close friend, Captain Green Peyton, explained how as the war progressed, Rodes became increasingly interested in spiritual matters and the salvation of his soul. The horrors of the battlefield, coupled with the wonderment at the birth of his son, deeply intensified his concern with the question of life's true meaning. Perhaps Reverend Hoge had been the final catalyst that set Rodes on the path of spiritual awakening.[56]

As Rodes knew full well, the war and all its evils were far from over. Instead of wintering, the enemy appeared to be preparing to take the offensive. "We are all on the lookout today for a fight," he penned on November 25 to his friend and former railroad colleague George Robertson, "as it is reported that Meade is advancing. So far I have seen nothing of him."[57]

Rodes did not have long to wait. The following day, November 26, Meade began crossing the Rapidan along the river's lower fords in an effort to turn Lee's right flank. Meade's intent was to turn and defeat Ewell before A. P. Hill's Third Corps reached the scene. The Confederate commander hastened to respond, shifting his army to the right to intercept the advancing enemy. Ewell was ordered to pull back his division from the river while Hill was directed to come up from around Orange Court House. Lee favored holding a strong entrenched position along the west bank of Mine Run creek.

Around midnight on the 26th, Rodes received orders from acting corps commander Early (Ewell having gone to Charlottesville to receive treatment for his ailing and painful stump) to move the 7,100-man division from its

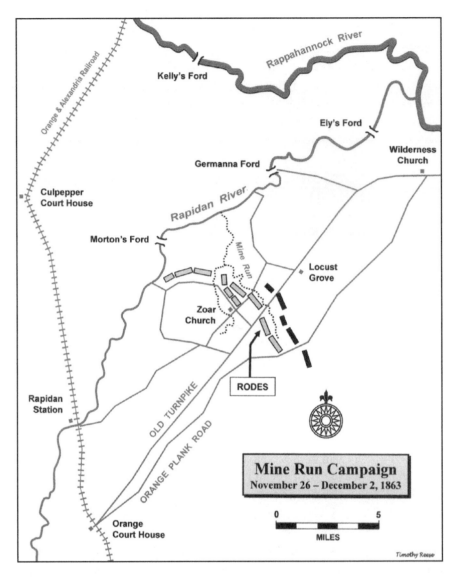

Mine Run Campaign
November 26 – December 2, 1863

breastworks at Morton's Ford to a ridge between Mine Run and Walnut Branch, and there to take up a line extending from the branch to Zoar Church. In frigid temperatures under a lunar halo, Rodes moved out an hour later. With his men still fortifying their new line, he received from Early about 8:30 a.m. instructions to move up to a concentration of the corps at Locust Grove.

With Daniel in the lead, Rodes began the march around 9:00 a.m. An hour later Locust Grove came into view about one mile ahead. To Rodes' surprise, the enemy was already their in force. With the center of his line across

Germanna Road, Rodes quickly posted his brigades in line of battle facing northeast. From left to right he placed Johnston, Daniel, Battle, and Ramseur, with Doles' Georgians in reserve. With Early at Lee's headquarters in Verdiersville, Rodes was the senior commander on the field. He expected to launch an attack once Harry Hays (temporarily in command of Early's division) finished deploying on his right. When Hays reported that the Federals in his front were strongly posted in a line that extended beyond his right, Rodes decided to await the arrival of Johnson's division.

Rodes used the time to strengthen his line and study the ground. To his dismay, word arrived that Johnson had been delayed when his men stumbled into the Federal III Corps under William French in their march along Racoon Ford Road. The aggressive-minded Johnson turned his four brigades from column into line and launched an attack. Although ill-conceived and hastily mounted, the assault blunted French's timid advance (as well as Sedgwick's VI Corps, which clogged the roads behind French). Usually wrongly portrayed as nothing but a skirmish, the bitter fighting that erupted late that afternoon at Payne's Farm was a very sharp meeting engagement that threw Meade's critical timetable completely off schedule. While the fighting raged, explained Rodes, "I sent General Doles' brigade, which had been placed so as to cover, as far as possible, the interval between Johnson's division and mine, to General Johnson's assistance." By the time the sun set a few hours later, Johnson was still firmly in position along Racoon Ford Road, and the opportunity French may have had to pry him loose and open an avenue deep into the Confederate left-rear had passed. Johnson's division lost about 550 in two solid hours of fighting, while French's corps lost nearly double that number. Payne's Farm was no mere skirmish, but a battle. Once darkness set in, Johnson moved up on Rodes' left. Doles did not return to Rodes until 1:00 a.m. the next morning.[58]

While Johnson was battling French, Rodes faced his own problems around Locust Grove. Enemy sharpshooters took up a position on a nearby ridge and opened a hot fire on Daniel's skirmishers. Rodes ordered the brigadier to clear the high ground. Daniel moved forward in strength and the Federals pulled back. Another brigadier, Bradley Johnston, sent Rodes word the enemy was deploying beyond Rodes' left. Rodes sped Ramseur's brigade to the threatened point from the right, and he set up Carter's artillery to return the fire coming down on Hays' line.

Shortly after Johnson's division came up around noon on November 28, Jubal Early reached the field and resumed command of the corps. Rodes had done an admirable job in his absence, marching his men well and securing the corps line promptly and efficiently. Old Jube promptly met with his division commanders to discuss the feasibility of attacking the enemy. Everyone agreed that the strong enemy position on high ground at the far side of a dense forest could only be carried by a very costly attack. Unwilling to make that sacrifice, Early held his line as night fell. All told, Rodes' division sustained about twenty casualties that day, mostly from artillery fire.

After midnight, orders came in from Lee for the corps to fall back to a stronger position behind Mine Run. Following behind Johnson, Rodes began to pull out about 2:00 a.m. Marching by the right flank, Cullen Battle took the lead, with Ramseur in the rear. After crossing Hays' former position, the men moved onto the old turnpike, where they turned and re-crossed Mine Run at Rowe's Mill. After a few hours' rest, Rodes deployed on the right side of Johnson and the left of Hays. His line stretched along the west bank of the stream overlooking the valley of Mine Run, with his right resting on the old turnpike and the left on the country road on which he had advanced the day before from Zoar Church.

The position, however, had a serious flaw. "The whole position was so much exposed to the enemy's artillery," explained Rodes, "that the troops were ordered to intrench. This they did with great energy and success, though the enemy was in sight on the opposite side of the run before a shovelful of earth was thrown." While the enemy continued to deploy, Rodes' men labored. In a driving rain, the veterans quickly threw up a formidable line made of logs and earth. Within hours, Rodes later boasted, "the intrenchments . . . were generally artillery proof, and on that day they were repeatedly tested by the enemy's artillery." Rodes unlimbered his artillery along the line, "and when permitted to fire," he reported, "did good work."

For four agonizing days they held this position, during which time the rain stopped, the temperature dropped, and the enemy continually tested them with artillery and skirmish fire. Though the fierce cold winds "made sleep light and uncomfortable," Rodes kept the men at work improving their line, until by the 29th he considered it "generally artillery proof." Waiting for an attack, however, was a nerve-racking ordeal. One of Ramseur's men complained of having to "keep all our things on all the time and one-half of the men are up all night in case of an attack."[59]

Meade was in favor of launching an attack, and orders to that end were issued, but at the last minute the assault was called off because of the strength of Lee's position. Lee, however, contemplated delivering an attack of his own. He shifted Early's [Ewell's] corps to the right to enable two of A. P. Hill's divisions to attack Meade's left flank. About 3:00 a.m. on December 2, Rodes sidled over until his left moved into the line formerly held by the center, and the rest of the division moved into the position vacated on the right by Richard Anderson's division. When daylight arrived, Meade was gone.

As part of Lee's organized pursuit, Rodes concentrated his division, crossed Mine Run and marched down the Germanna Road toward Spottswoods. Moving quickly, the division scooped up about two hundred Yankee prisoners, including 137 captured by only nineteen of Doles's sharpshooters after a brief skirmish. Soon it became apparent, however, that Meade's army had escaped across the Rapidan. What would become known as the Mine Run campaign was over.

After camping that night about one mile from Locust Grove, Rodes the following day returned the division to Morton's Ford. The fitful fighting cost the division eight killed, twenty-five wounded, and twelve missing, a total of forty-five men. Although the campaign was not a particularly bloody one, it was an exhausting exercise for both sides. In the end, all the marching, sleepless freezing nights, and hardships bore no fruit whatsoever for either side.

On December 4, Ewell resumed command of the Second Corps. For more than two weeks quiet prevailed at Morton's Ford. Rodes used the time to write Secretary of War Seddon to recommend VMI alumnus Matthew Cullen, "an employee of the War Department," for appointment as the military judge of the Second Corps. He characterized Cullen as "just, firm, and merciful." Rodes, ever loyal to deserving fellow alumni, declared to the secretary, "You will do us this Corps a great favor by sending him here as Judge." Cullen did not get the appointment.[60]

At 11:00 a.m. on December 20, Rodes broke camp and marched his men within six miles of Orange Court House, where they at last went into winter quarters along the Plank Road. That same day back in Tuscaloosa, Alabama, agents closed the deal that, for $1,700, made Rodes the new owner in town of two half-acre lots and a three-and-a-quarter acre lot. Like his father before him, the major general considered real estate a wise investment, especially now as a hedge against rising inflation and a corresponding depreciation of Confederate currency. In sharp contrast to his financial situation two years before, Rodes was doing quite well on the $328 a month pay of a major general.[61]

Once the Army of Northern Virginia settled into winter quarters, Major Eugene Blackford decided, against the advice of Division Chief Surgeon Mitchell, to have surgery on the ulcerated leg that had been causing him such severe pain for so long. Blackford chose to recover at the home of his parents in Lynchburg. To help pass the time, he took up a rather unusual hobby. "I have made two large Confederate flags with white fields," he wrote his cousin Mary, "to drape on each side of Gen. Rodes' picture." When he felt stronger later in the spring, Blackford had his own photograph taken, which he framed and placed on the wall of the family library, "vis-a-vis to Gen. Rodes."[1]

The flag-adorned photograph Blackford so honored was a copy of one of only three known wartime images taken of Rodes. It is possible that all three were taken during the same session. Because they each show Rodes wearing the tunic of a brigadier general, they probably were taken during the late fall of 1861 or early winter of 1862. In the first, and perhaps best known image, Rodes is intently gazing slightly off to the side, hands resting in his lap, mouth firmly set beneath a tawny, drooping moustache, with a strong dimpled chin and square jaw. His light-colored hair curls up above the ears and, even though the photo is black and white, reveals unmistakably blue eyes. In the second image, he is looking directly into the camera, the intensity of his gaze giving way to a more relaxed and even friendly expression, complete with a hint of that "slow, genial smile" for which he was so well known. For the third shot, the camera was pulled back to show Rodes sitting bolt upright with legs crossed, one arm resting on a side table and the other hand firmly planted on the hip—a military bearing somewhat offset by his understanding and even sympathetic gaze. All three portraits present a striking image of Rodes as the mid-nineteenth century personification of a military hero. The photos also dutifully reflect his temperament, which contemporaries labeled as "firmness tempered by kindness." His bearing won for Rodes tremendous loyalty, devotion and respect at all rank levels.[2]

Among the most devoted of his fans was Major Blackford, who sent Rodes a note to inform him of the success of the leg operation. Mindful of the major general's fondness for sweets, Blackford thoughtfully included a cake, which Rodes promised to share with Hortense, who recently had arrived at his headquarters on the Plank Road near Orange Courthouse. It troubled Blackford's conscience to enjoy the comforts of home in Lynchburg while his comrades continued to suffer at the front. "A letter from the Surgeon says that the officers have drawn nothing but flour since the 29th ultimo," he wrote his cousin on January 14, "[and] that a very little coffee & sugar was issued to the enlisted men in lieu of meat."[3]

During the winter of 1863-1864, food indeed was in short supply. From December through most of January, daily rations consisted of but two to four ounces of bacon or salt pork and eighteen ounces of flour. At the end of January the ration increased to between four and eight ounces of meat with a pint of cornmeal, still barely enough to keep a man alive. "We eat everything they give us and feel hungry all the time," complained a private in Ramseur's brigade. And what they ate wasn't always of the highest quality. After vomiting up his sour rations, a soldier in the Fourth Georgia wrote home that the bacon smelled so bad, "The boys say it outranks General Lee."[4]

Other afflictions included the weather and the lack of basic supplies. "It is extremely cold, below zero," Captain Park noted in his diary on January 1. "Major Whiting, Division Inspector, examined the arms and clothing of the men, and found them sadly in need of shoes, many of them barefooted, and the others having no soles to their shoes, the uppers only remaining." Six days later Park wrote that because of the lack of shoes, most men had to remain in camp when the brigade took its turn doing picket duty on the Rapidan.[5] On January 15, Thomas Coffey of the Third Alabama wrote home that when his shredded shoes finally broke apart he would have to, "like hundreds of others in this brigade—go barefooted." To spare their raggedly dressed men from the cold, officers often suspended drill.[6] Desertions rose, as did the punishments carried out to stop them. On January 8 Rodes again drew up the entire division to witness an execution, this time of men from Daniel's brigade.[7]

One case in particular hit Rodes personally when his ordnance officer, twenty-two-year-old Captain William A. Harris, a VMI graduate who had been with the division for some time, deserted to the enemy. "It was a great shock," Major Blackford wrote of the feeling at division headquarters, "as he was an elegant young fellow—very handsome, and a favorite with all." Blackford believed Harris did it because, "He was married last August, and had been completely demoralized ever since—worthless as a soldier, but I could not conceive that it would extend so far." Moreover, Harris, though Virginia born, had been "corrupted by many years residence in Missouri."[8]

The horrid conditions suffered by Rodes' men made it easier for many to listen to the rising tide of anti-war propaganda, particularly that spewed out by William W. Holden, editor of the Raleigh *Standard*. Increasingly, men no longer scoffed when Holden argued that sacrifices on the battlefield were in vain, not only because the Confederacy had little chance to succeed, but because the "despotism" of the Richmond government made life worse in the South than it had been before secession. Holden even went so far as to demand that North Carolina enter separate peace negotiations with Washington. Ominously, such demoralizing sentiments were beginning to take hold among Rodes' men. At least one soldier, the Fourth North Carolina's Private James King, allegedly confessed just before being executed in early February that Holden's writings had inspired him to desert.[9]

If a man did not feel inclined to take the drastic step of desertion, he still might find other ways to avoid harsh service. On February 15, General Lee informed Secretary of War Seddon that the Second Corps rolls contained no fewer than 11,610 absentees, including 4,102 from Rodes' division. Though acknowledging the legitimacy of most excuses, the commanding general believed that many men were lingering in hospitals as patients or workers.[10]

Building on the revivals that took place in the army during the past two years, religion became ever more important as a salve to ease the suffering. In Ramseur's brigade, men of the Fourteenth North Carolina put together a makeshift shack to serve as a chapel, where a chaplain presided over nightly prayer meetings that eventually included men from many different regiments. Beginning in the Twelfth Alabama, the men of Battle's brigade formed a "Christian Association," whose members took the drastic step of pledging not to use profanity or intoxicating liquor.[11]

In taking note of his men's deepening interest in religion, Battle was particularly impressed by the effects of a sermon delivered to them by the Reverend Hoge, the same man with whom Rodes had made arrangements to preach to the division after Chancellorsville. "Lift up your heads, O, ye gates, and be ye lifted up, ye everlasting doors, and the King of glory shall come in,"

Battle quoted Hoge. "Who is the King of glory? The Lord of Hosts, Mighty in battle, He is the King of glory." Battle was completely taken by the message. "The sermon was powerful," he confessed, "and the effect was wonderful. Many, perhaps hundreds, came out on the Lord's side that day."[12] The question remained, however, whether the men would come out on the side of the Confederacy. With thousands of three-year enlistments about to expire, "even the heart of Lee," observed Battle, "was convulsed with apprehension."

Rodes' heart, too, trembled at the thought of losing so many of his battle-hardened veterans. To head off that disastrous possibility, he went on campaign, tirelessly speaking with several captains, appealing to them to encourage their men to reenlist. Moreover, he put out a circular, "which appealed in eloquent terms to the patriotism of his command." On January 26, Battle read it to each of his regiments in turn, after which he delivered his own stirring plea. He invited all those willing to reenlist to take two steps forward. Each of the regiments did so as an entire unit. (In such an open circumstance, who would have dared do otherwise?). "This is an act," observed Captain Park, "of which we may well be proud to our dying day."[13]

No one was prouder of the brigade, and especially of the Fifth Alabama, than its former commander. "I was extremely gratified," Rodes wrote the convalescing Major Blackford, "at the prompt manner it [the Fifth Alabama] and the whole brigade acted upon my appeal." On the 26th, Rodes sent a stirring letter of congratulation to General Battle, who proudly read it aloud to each regiment in turn:

> Headquarters Rodes' Division, January 26, 1864.
> Brigadier-General Battle, Commanding Battle's Brigade:
>
> General, I have just received your message by Captain J.P. Smith, informing me of the glorious conduct of my old brigade in re-enlisting for the war without conditions. Conduct like this, in the midst of the hardships we are enduring, and on the part of men who have fought so many bloody battles, is in the highest degree creditable to the men and officers of your command. I always was proud, and now still more so, that I once belonged to your brigade. As their division commander, and as a citizen of Alabama, I wish to express my joy and pride, and as a citizen of the Confederacy, my gratitude at their conduct. The significance of this grand movement, when considered in connection with the circumstances accompanying it, will not be underrated, either by the enemy or our own

people. They will, as I do, see in this the beginning of the end, the first dawn of peace and independence, because they will see that these men are unconquerable. To have been the leaders of this movement in this glorious army throws a halo of glory around your brigade which time will not dim. Convey this evidence, feebly at best, but doubly so in comparison with what I would express of my appreciation of the course you and your men have pursued in this matter, and see now, having written 'Excelsior' in the records of your camp history, that your fighting record shall hereafter show you, not only to have been among the brave, but the bravest of the brave.

And now, dear sir, let me congratulate you upon being the commander of so noble a body of gallant and patriotic men!

R. E. Rodes, Major-General[14]

With Rodes' circular serving as the incubator and Battle's brigade as the host, the contagion of patriotism rapidly spread. The following day the men of Ramseur's brigade unanimously passed a "resolution" proclaiming that they were "in for the war without condition." Then, save for about one hundred recalcitrant men in Johnston's brigade, Rodes' other brigades quickly followed suit. "Our glorious Division," a proud Ramseur wrote a friend, "has shown the world that we intend to fight the thing out—that we won't be whipped as long as anybody is left to fight."[15]

The example drew much praise from not only a grateful commanding general but also from the local newspapers. "Gen. Rodes has commanded his division with success and ability," the February 15 issue of the Richmond *Daily Whig* quoted General Lee, "and I am gratified to state this division re-enlisted for the war, Battle's brigade of Alabamians having set the example. Instead of raising new brigades, I think it would be far better to recruit to the fullest numbers those veteran brigades, whose whole conduct is worthy of the admiration of their countrymen." Lee reminded readers that "Gen. Rodes' whole division acted at Chancellorsville with distinguished gallantry, and that officer owes his promotion to Gen. Jackson's observation of his skill and conduct. You will see in my report of that battle that one of his dying messages to me was to the effect that Gen. Rodes should be promoted Major General."[16]

Using Rodes' division as an example, Lee on February 3 called on other units in the army to reenlist. Three days later the Confederate Congress passed a joint resolution of thanks for Rodes' division. As a final reward for their loyalty, the men over the next nine months would march more than 2,000 miles, fight in some three dozen skirmishes and battles, and lose thousands in killed, wounded, missing, and to disease.[17]

*   *   *

Rodes, however, would not have shared those 'rewards' had the division lost the commander who had been so inspirational in saving it for future agonies. Though he probably did not know it, Rodes' name appeared on a list of candidates to replace the head of the Department of Southwest Virginia, Sam Jones. President Davis had had enough of the man after William Averell's successful December raid on the vital Virginia & Tennessee Railroad at Salem. Lee, of course, did not want to give up any of his veteran officers. "But so important do I consider the maintenance of western Virginia to the successful conduct of the war," he wrote the president on January 27, "that I will relinquish any of them you may select for its command, though I do not know where to replace them." Ewell might be a good choice, thought Lee, but for his health. "I have also great confidence in the ability of Genls. Early, Rodes, Edward Johnson, & Wilcox. Of the brigadiers, I think Genl. Gordon of Alabama one of the best." Rodes undoubtedly would have been very reluctant to leave his division and take the post. In the end, Davis decided not to deprive Lee of so valuable a combat leader, and the position went to John Echols, one of Jones' subordinates.[18]

Unaware that he was up for consideration for the Southwest Virginia post, Rodes sent for Hortense. She arrived from Lynchburg in late December or early January with their three-month-old son, Robert Jr. Rodes originally planned for her to share a house with the newlywed Ramseurs in Charlottesville, only some forty miles south of Orange Courthouse, but for some reason the arrangements did not work out. Mrs. Rodes stayed with her husband at his headquarters on the Plank Road near Orange.[19]

This was not the only arrangement that fell through for Rodes that winter. Apparently because of Hortense's delicate health, he purchased a cow to provide milk for the baby. In doing so, however, he tempted fate far beyond what he had risked thus far on the battlefield. "Some of the boys a few nights ago wanted fresh meat," the Third Alabama's Thomas Coffey wrote home on January 15, "and after prowling around a good while they made a raid on the cowpen of General Rodes and killed the milk cow of the Mrs General. This little act of larceny has raised the indignation of the General and his spouse up to fever heat, and they both swear vengeance on the luckless thieves if they can only find out who they are."[20]

More ignominious losses followed. After somehow managing to procure a twenty-five-pound turkey, Rodes offered to share it with some of his fellow officers, who readily gathered at his headquarters tent in eager anticipation of the rare, sumptuous meal. When the cook at last announced that the steaming hot bird was ready, "done to a crisp" and complete with dressing and gravy, Rodes and his guests walked to the feast tent only to make the disheartening discovery that the bird had disappeared. Rodes was outraged. Though unable to prove it, he suspected the blame for the pilfered bird rested with the headquarters guard, which that day consisted of the Twelfth Alabama's Corporal Henry Fowler and two privates. To those three the general "expressed himself in very positive language," blasting them for belonging to "the damned thieving Twelfth Alabama," a title the regiment adopted and proudly held onto until the end of the war.[21]

Judging by the observation of others, as expressed in their diaries, letters and memoirs, Rodes rarely lost complete control his temper. Equally rare were were the moments when he displayed an appreciation for the humorous or ironic side of life. One of those moments occured when Rodes was out inspecting pickets one morning and came upon a young country boy who was relaxing on the ground with his musket leaning against a tree instead of standing at his post. Witnesses waited for the stern, officious general to severely reprimand the boy and draw him up for punishment.

"Did you know," Rodes began sternly, "you could be court-martialed for lying about while on picket"?

"No, I did not," the boy innocently replied, without getting up.

"When did you enlist?" Rodes asked, suspicious that the boy was too green to comprehend the severity of the situation.

"Last week," came the confirming answer.

"When were you assigned on picket duty?" continued Rodes.

"This morning," replied the new recruit.

"Do you know who I am?" Rodes asked.

"No, sir."

"I am General Rodes."

With that, the boy jumped up, walked over to Rodes, stuck out his hand and answered, "Glad to know you, General Rodes; I'm Dick Maness. How's your folks?" Even Rodes could not help but find this amusing.[22]

An unpleasant situation for Rodes finally came to an end on February 13. On that day, Colonel Edward A. O'Neal left the Army of Northern Virginia when the Alabama legislature successfully petitioned to have the Twenty-sixth Infantry return home to recruit its thinned ranks. The regiment and its colonel would never rejoin the Virginia army. As part of James Cantey's brigade, they would serve during the Atlanta campaign and beyond, up to and including the surrender at Greensboro, North Carolina. In exchange for the departing Twenty-sixth, Battle's brigade received the Sixty-first Alabama, a new regiment organized at Pollard the previous September.[23]

The Sixty-first joined a brigade that in early February suffered the misfortune of being pulled away from its winter quarters to bolster the defenses of Richmond against an anticipated Union raiding strike. Moreover, orders required Rodes for the same reason to take two other brigades up to Hanover Junction, where he assumed command over all Confederate troops in the area. He made no secret of his displeasure with these arrangements. "Battle's men will suffer terribly in this weather," he wired on February 15 to Arnold Elzey, commander of the Richmond department. "[I]f possible please send them up to their cabins here." The protests may have paid off somewhat when later that month two of Rodes' three brigades (Johnston's being left at Hanover by order of President Davis) were returned.[24]

During a visit to Richmond to check on Battle's brigade—and possibly as well to see his friend and former staff member, the one-armed Philip Sutton— Rodes received a special honor. "On motion of Mr. [William R.] Smith, of Alabama," read the Congressional minutes for February 11, "an invitation was extended to Major-General Rodes to a seat on the floor during his stay in this city."[25] Rodes also used the visit to submit a personal order to the quartermaster of the War Department. Considering the inflation then rampant in the Confederacy, he paid astonishingly low prices for some new clothing: ten dollars for a pair of shoes, fourteen dollars for a jacket, and twelve dollars for a pair of pants.[26]

Meanwhile, just as Rodes' men were finally settled into their relatively comfortable winter quarters, he pulled them out on the last day of the month and marched the division through a blinding snowstorm to Madison Courthouse to meet an alleged enemy movement toward Charlottesville. Two days later he pushed the division down the Plank Road in the vain hope of intercepting Judson Kilpatrick's cavalry as it returned from its celebrated raid toward Richmond.[27]

At the end of all this marching Rodes became involved in another unpleasant situation with Bryan Grimes, with whom he had had an angry exchange nearly two years before at the crossing of the Shenandoah while in temporary command of D. H. Hill's division. This time Rodes went so far as to put Grimes under arrest. The official document read:

Charges & Specifications vs Col. Bryan Grimes 7 Mar 1864

Charge—Conduct prejudicial to good order and military discipline.

Specification—In this that the said Bryan Grimes Colonel Commanding the Fourth North Carolina Regiment having been left with his Regiment by order of Maj Genl Rodes to protect the bridge over the Rapidan river at Liberty Mills did permit men of his command to build fires on the floor of the said bridge, exposing it to the danger of destruction by fire, and actually burning the floor of said bridge in several places. All this at Liberty Mills Orange County, Virginia, on or about the night of March first, in the year of our Lord, eighteen hundred and Sixty four.

Regardless of how far Rodes meant to carry this, General Lee intervened to bring the matter to a swift conclusion. "While the zeal of Col. Grimes in behalf of his men is duly appreciated as commendable," Lee wrote on the back of the above charges, "still his own statements show that sufficient precautions were not taken to prevent injury to the bridge which might have resulted in serious advantage to the enemy. Nevertheless in view of his explanation, his high character as an officer [illegible] of his Comdg officers," Lee continued, "the charges are withdrawn & Col Grimes will retain his Comd."[28]

Once his temper cooled, Rodes seems to have put the matter behind him. Moreover, he did not, perhaps as he had with O'Neal, allow such differences to cloud his judgment regarding the capabilities of the North Carolinian. On April 27, for example, Rodes recommended him for promotion. Grimes, he wrote, "has shown himself, under all circumstances, to be a good and reliable officer. He is a thorough gentleman, brave to a fault, invaluable in an action, and his habits are worthy of imitation."

Grimes so appreciated the flattering remarks he promptly included them, word for word, in a letter to his wife. Rodes' strong recommendation may have been the "gentlemanly gesture" that Grimes told her had smoothed over the differences between the two men.[29]

Back on March 23, meanwhile, the dreariness of camp life lifted temporarily when two of Ed Johnson's brigades (the Stonewall Brigade and Stafford's Louisiana outfit) went up against two of Rodes' brigades (those of Doles and Ramseur) in a two-hour snowball fight, complete with battle lines, officers' shouted commands, and flank marches.

Three days later the men drew more entertainment from a visit by Governor Zebulon Vance, who came "hoping to rekindle the fires of patriotism in the hearts of North Carolina troops." That afternoon he gave a two-hour speech to a large audience that included Lee, Rodes, A. P. Hill, Stuart, Ewell, Wilcox, and perhaps a dozen other generals. Two days later the governor dined with the Fourteenth North Carolina, after which he delivered a four-hour speech to the Tarheels of the Second and Third Corps. At least one listener, however, was not impressed. "Vance made a tolerably good speech," the Forty-eighth North Carolina's Colonel Samuel Walkup wrote home, "but had too little seriousness and too much buffoonery in it for a Governor on so solemn an occasion."[30]

Wanting more, the diversion-starved troops "lustily" called out for General Lee, who "simply blushed," recalled a witness, "and retired from the scene." More calls went out for other generals "who seemed special favorites with the army." Irascible General Early stepped forward, and "being a lawyer by profession spoke with force and fluency, paying many handsome compliments to the soldiers, and especially lauding the heroism of those from North Carolina. He was warmly received and enthusiastically cheered throughout."

Next came the flamboyant General Stuart, "with all that ease and grace for which he was so remarkable, and, lifting his long-feathered hat, bowed, and bowed again in return for the loud shouts which greeted him. 'Fellow-soldiers,' he said, 'I am a cavalryman, and, consequently, not an orator, but I should be untrue to myself if I failed to command words enough to thank you for your kind reception, and to say that I have commanded many soldiers, but never braver and more trusty than those who hailed from the Old North State. God bless her!'"

After the cheering finally died down, Rodes "arose in a very modest and hesitating way," recalled an observer of the occasion. "I never attempted but one speech before this in my life," the general began, "and that was at Carlisle when we raised a Confederate flag over its arsenal last year." Rodes added this puzzling remark: "I did not finish that speech," he declared, "because an attack was made upon us while I was in the midst of it, but with God's help I intend to finish my speech at Carlisle."

Though Rodes' comment regarding his unfinished Carlisle speech was not entirely accurate, it did have the desired dramatic effect. "This reference to a possible forward movement was received with the greatest manifestations of delight," a soldier later wrote. "At Carlisle! At Carlisle!" the men shouted, "and the army seemed ready to begin its march northward at once and with as much pleasure as if some great feast had been prepared for it over the border."[31]

Quieter but no less important diversions occurred every Sunday, when dozens of officers, including Rodes, attended church in Orange Court House. In addition to the religious services, these occasions provided a day of affable relaxation. "It is curious and very interesting to look around that church on Sunday morning," observed Major Blackford. "Long before the appointed hour the seats are crowded. There are a few residents of the village . . . the rest of the seats, and the aisles being filed [sic] up with soldiers, and officers of every grade, from the Commdg General down. At any time you can count two Lt. Generals (Gen. Lee is always there) five or six Maj. Generals, & a host of Brigadiers—while the number of field officers and staff captains is innumerable."[32]

April 1864 brought the promise of fine weather, the ominous signs of a new campaign, and for Rodes, a pair of unpleasantries. On the 15th he received a telegram from Major Blackford's mother asking Rodes to perform the sad task of telling her son Eugene that his father had died the night before. The death hurt Rodes, too, for through their correspondence the past few months the two men had become friends. "Dear Blackford," Rodes wrote on the back of the telegram, "I am sorry to be compelled to send you this dispatch. I can only offer sympathy for you in your grief. Yours very sincerely, R. E. Rodes."[33]

The second unpleasantry came from complying with Lee's order for all wives to leave camp. That month, Rodes and his wife had conceived their second child. With what could only have been a heavy heart, the general placed Hortense and six-and-a-half-month-old Bobby on a train bound for Lynchburg. Like many Second Corps officers, however, he probably welcomed the departure of one wife. Lizinka Ewell, who in camp had so dominated her compliant husband that Rodes on one occasion inquired sarcastically of Reverend Lacy "who commanded the Second Corps, whether Mrs. Ewell, General Ewell, or Sandy Pendleton, hoping it was the last."[34]

*   *   *

On April 25, one of Rodes' soldiers took pen in hand to inform the folks at home about the status of the war. "Soon yea very Soon we Shall have to meet

Maj. Gen. Ulysses S. Grant, the new general-in-chief of the Union armies.

Library of Congress

the Great Army of the Potomac," he wrote, "and God may See fit to turn the tide of Favor against us."[35]

Unable to take the war into enemy territory, General Lee waited for the Federals to make the next move. The Confederates now faced yet another enemy commander in Ulysses S. Grant. The architect of a number of victorious campaign battles in the Western theater, Grant headed east as general-in-chief of the Union armies (some 500,000 men spread across the country), a position bestowed on him by President Lincoln that March. Grant decided to make his headquarters with the Army of the Potomac, but leave George Meade in command. Grant intended to issue broad strategic objectives, leaving Meade responsible for tactical decisions. The army was reorganized into three corps for the coming campaign: the depleted I and III Corps absorbed into the II Corps, the V Corps, and VI Corps. The IX Corps under former Army of the Potomac commander Ambrose Burnside arrived from Kentucky, giving Grant and Meade a total of about 118,000 men and 316 guns.

Grant planned to use his sizable advantage in manpower to pressure Confederate forces simultaneously on multiple fronts to make it difficult or impossible for the Southerners to use interior lines to reinforce various sectors. While Meade went after Lee in Virginia, Grant wanted William T. Sherman to take on Joseph E. Johnston's Army of Tennessee in Tennessee and Georgia, Franz Sigel to pressure the Rebels in the Shenandoah Valley, Ben Butler to come up the James River toward the Confederate capital, and Nathaniel Banks to advance deep in Louisiana up the Red River and capture Shreveport.

Although the Army of Northern Virginia contained only about 65,000 men (including James Longstreet's First Corps, which returned from Georgia in mid-April) and 227 guns, Grant knew Lee's position behind the Rapidan River was too strong to assault frontally. He also ruled out a westward move around Lee's left flank because it risked exposing his communications with Washington. Grant therefore determined to move around Lee's right. This plan would preserve his line of communications and also shift his army closer to Butler's army as it advanced up the James River.

Grant's decision required that the Army of the Potomac pass through the same heavily wooded terrain known as the Wilderness, ten miles west of Fredericksburg, that had been the ruin of Joe Hooker one year before. The idea was to get the army through the area as quickly as possible before Lee could concentrate and offer resistance.

On May 2, Rodes attended a meeting of Lee's corps and division commanders at a signal station on Clark's Mountain. The station, located south of the Rapidan, afforded the Confederates a clear view of the thousands of white tents in the distant Yankee camps. Demonstrating keen strategic insight gleaned from a variety of sources and years of experience, Lee told the generals that he expected the Federals to cross the river, probably at Germanna or Ely's Ford, and try to turn his right.[36]

And that was exactly what happened. Near midnight on Tuesday, May 3, Gouverneur Warren's V Corps started for Germanna Ford and Winfield Hancock's II Corps set out for Ely's Ford. Though the crossings occurred without incident, the supply trains lagged far behind. Grant ordered a halt to allow his forces to close up. Warren's corps stopped at Wilderness Tavern while Hancock's men paused at Chancellorsville. The opportunity for Lee to offer battle in the Wilderness was at hand.[37]

Mindful to resolve personal matters on the eve of battle, Rodes arranged to settle a $185 debt he owed to his friend and staff member, Major Green Peyton. Rodes instructed his former staff member Phillip Sutton, with whom Rodes maintained an account with which to purchase various items in Richmond, to pay Peyton. "Should you not have done so before the big battle we are expecting comes off," instructed Rodes, "and should anything happen to me please see that Peyton gets it in my name at once through Mrs. Rodes."[38]

Two days later, Lee began shifting the Army of Northern Virginia east to meet the Union army. Speed was essential. If Lee hoped to use the tangled Wilderness as he had the previous spring to negate much of the Federals' superiority in artillery and manpower, he had to get there before Grant.

While Stephen Ramseur's brigade remained to picket the river from Rapidan Station to Mitchell's Ford, Rodes' division of fewer than 4,000 men (not including Robert D. Johnston's brigade at Hanover Junction) broke camp on the cool foggy Wednesday morning of May 4 to fall in between Jubal Early's and Edward Johnson's soldiers on the march south for the Orange Turnpike. "The troops were never in better spirits," recalled the Fifth Alabama's Captain J. W. Williams after the war, "but [they] did not present a very martial or soldierly appearance, as no two were dressed alike, haversacks empty, but with bright and well kept guns to do the deadly work before them." Its ranks full with well-dressed and untried men, the new and large Sixty-first Alabama stood out in sharp contrast to Rodes' lean, veteran units.[39]

About noon, Richard Ewell's Second Corps, comprised of no more than 13,500 men, turned east on the Orange Turnpike at Verdiersville. Ewell's men headed for Locust Grove, an old stage stand marked by a little branch called Wilderness Run about two-and-a-half miles west of the Wilderness and five-and-a-half miles from Wilderness Tavern. Locust Grove was also the location of Warren's V Corps. About five miles to the south, A. P. Hill's Third Corps followed the Orange Plank Road on a roughly parallel course to Ewell's march. At 4:00 p.m., 42 miles to the southwest, Longstreet's First Corps commenced its march up from Gordonsville via the Catharpin Road.

Jubal Early's division and the corps artillery reached Locust Grove around sunset. Rodes and Johnson camped for the night about two miles behind Early, while A. P. Hill stopped on the Plank Road five miles to the south. Longstreet halted his men far to the south on the Old Stone Road.[40]

The men of the Second Corps, stretched out in a column three miles long, resumed their eastward march on the Orange Pike at 5:00 a.m. through wispy clouds of morning fog. Johnson's men led the way, followed by Rodes and Early. Lee directed Ewell to keep pace with A. P. Hill, whose men remained five miles to the south on the Plank Road, and to avoid a general fight until Longstreet's corps came up. Chance intervened, as it did so often, when two opposing lines of march intersected.

Just before 11:00 a.m., the lead elements of Johnson's division ran into Charles Griffin's V Corps division marching south on the Germanna Plank Road. Because the thick and tangled area prevented thorough screening and reconnaissance, the encounter surprised both sides. The Confederates and Federals scrambled to deploy for battle.

Johnson formed his division with the lead brigade under John M. Jones on his right, straddling the pike and facing east. In compliance with Ewell's order, Rodes brought up Cullen Battle's brigade and positioned it about 100 yards

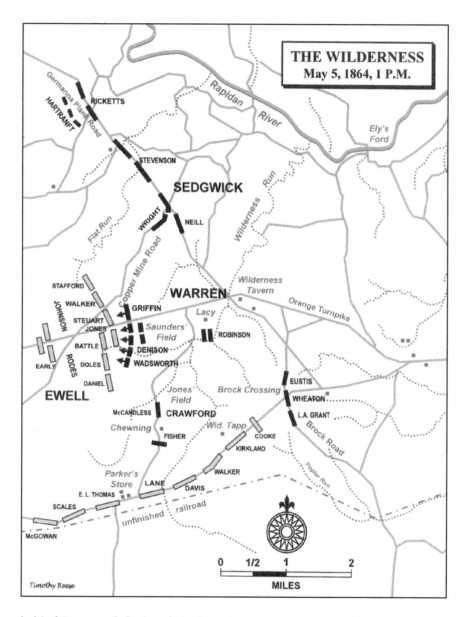

THE WILDERNESS
May 5, 1864, 1 P.M.

behind Jones and deployed the brigades of Doles and Daniel to the right of
Battle. Ewell placed Early's division in reserve.

While his men hacked away at vines and saplings in a desperate attempt to
align themselves, Rodes headed out on the pike to confer with Ewell, Early, and
Jones. About 1:15 p.m. "a heavy skirmish fire opened on the front," recalled
Early's aide, Major John Daniel, "swiftly followed by volleys along the line."

Suddenly, from across both sides of the pike appeared Griffin's 6,000 veterans, charging through the brushy woods.[41]

Jones' men quickly gave way despite the valiant efforts of their brigadier, who fell dead trying to rally them. They poured back into Battle's line, causing confusion and scattering many of the Alabamians. Only with some difficulty did Rodes and Battle manage to reestablish order, positioning the men near the edge of an 800-by 400-yard clearing known locally as Saunders' Field. "Those of us who remained," remembered Sergeant J. B. Stamp of the Third Alabama, "were deployed at intervals of fifteen or twenty feet, and the first intimation I had of the proximity of the enemy, I was covered by the gun of a soldier, who, under concealment of the chaparral, had approached to within ten feet of me."[42]

As the potential disaster was unfolding along Ewell's front, Rodes coolly indulged in a brief moment of levity. "General Battle," he called out, "where is the Third Alabama?" as if to insult the brigadier by implying that his former command had deserted him. "Retired with the 5th, General Rodes!" Battle shot back with equal effect. "You see," Battle explained in a post-war memoir, "Rodes had been Colonel of the 5th, and I of the Third, and we frequently exchanged compliments."[43]

The battle quickly expanded with increasing ferocity. Warren positioned James Wadsworth's division on Griffin's left and Horatio Wright's recently

arrived VI Corps division on his right. Ewell countered by deploying Gordon's brigade on Daniel's right and the rest of Early's division on Johnson's left, leaving only Jones' shattered brigade as a reserve behind a line that now extended some 2,700 yards.[44]

Brig. Gen. Cullen Battle. The hard-hitting native of Alabama fit comfortably into Rodes' division at the head of a brigade.

Library of Congress

On horseback when possible and on foot when necessary, Rodes ceaselessly moved up and down his line, encouraging the men to hold steady. Some soldiers in the Fifth Alabama discovered in the tangled underbrush a Federal with an abdominal would so painful that he begged the Rebels to kill him. When they refused, he allegedly slit his own throat with a file. "I have heard," recalled Captain J.W. Williams of Company D, "that Gen. Rodes had him buried, and pine straw strewd over the grave for fear the enemy might recover the body and think that our soldiers had killed him."[45]

About 4:00 p.m. Hancock's II Corps came up on Warren's left and assaulted A. P. Hill's just-formed position astride the Plank Road, located about one mile from Ewell's right. About 7:30 p.m., Grant threw John Sedgwick's VI Corps at Johnson and Early, and again sent Hancock against A. P. Hill. Warren was held back, sparing Rodes' portion of the front. In desperate fighting, the Confederates held all along the line until the battle finally petered out around 9:00 p.m. Fires ignited in the leaves and dry grass in Saunders' Field, compounding the horrors of the day when the flames engulfed many wounded, filling the air with the stench of burning flesh and the screams of the terrified injured.[46]

Spared from attack for several hours, Rodes used the time to dig in. By 10:00 p.m. his hungry men—they had not eaten all day—had established a formidable line that arched around the Hagerson farm south of the pike facing Griffin's division and that of their old Gettysburg foe, John Robinson. North of the pike stood Johnson, with Early's brigades on his left.[47]

Rodes' remaining two brigades arrived during the night. The general sent Johnston's men, on the heels of their grueling 22-mile march from Hanover Junction, to the left of Ewell's line. Ramseur's men, who appeared about 3:00 a.m. from their picket post on the Rapidan, were held in reserve, a decision the feisty North Carolinian protested. As if to say that there would be plenty of fighting for everyone soon enough, Rodes pointed out a strong enemy position and jokingly informed Ramseur that if he "would move those Yankees away from there, he would place his brigade in line."[48]

Much like he had the previous spring, the outnumbered General Lee successfully tied up the Army of the Potomac in the Wilderness. Still, Lee knew he was heavily outnumbered and so must maintain the initiative and find a way to quickly defeat the enemy. Longstreet's corps was due to arrive at any time, and when it did Lee intended to attack the Federal left and roll it up northward toward the Rapidan. As the Confederates soon would discover, Ulysses Grant was no Joe Hooker. This time, Grant struck first.

The Federal line extended from Sedgwick's VI Corps on the right to Hancock's II Corps on the left. Warren's V Corps occupied the right-center, with a space for Burnside's IX Corps between it and Hancock. Burnside, however, got bogged down and failed to arrive in time, leaving his spot in the line unoccupied. Even so, about 5:00 a.m. Grant launched an all-out attack.

Ewell's men stubbornly held their ground against heavy assaults by Sedgwick and Warren, with Rodes' men suffering heavy losses in the close-action fighting. While Ewell's line held, however, A. P. Hill's did not. Chaos best described Hill's front the night before, but the corps leader refused the entreaties of subordinates to wake the men and rectify it. When Hancock's heavy attack struck, Hill's front crumbled like dust before a stout wind. Lee's entire right flank was collapsing. Only the arrival of Longstreet's men about 6:30 a.m. stabilized the critical situation. Fighting raged on the Confederate right, the attacks surging back and forth without visible advantage until 11:00 a.m. About 2:00 p.m., Burnside finally came up and shoved his 2nd and 3rd divisions under Robert Potter and Orlando Willcox, respectively, into the mile-wide gap yawning between Junius Daniel's right and A. P. Hill's left. Another crisis was at hand. Rodes countered the move by bringing up Ramseur from reserve and sending him to extend Daniel's right southward. Finally getting his wish to be on the firing line, Ramseur arrived just in time to plug the gap and stop the enemy onslaught.

Having fought the enemy to a standstill, Lee boldly went on the offensive, sending Longstreet's corps against Hancock's exposed left flank about 4:00 p.m. The attack rolled up the flank and promised significant success reminiscent of Jackson's victory a year earlier. Unfortunately for the Southern cause, the advancing Confederates ran into strong Federal works, and Longstreet, while on a reconnaissance, was critically wounded when his own men unloaded their rifles in his direction.

Another Confederate opportunity of a more localized potential was lost when Ewell refused to sanction John Gordon's request to attack the Federal right. Gordon was convinced the enemy flank was "dangling," much like Hooker's had near the same ground at Chancellorsville the year before. After several hours of delay, Lee intervened around 5:00 p.m. and authorized Gordon, with Johnston in support, to make the attack. The Georgian swept up about 600 prisoners before darkness and enemy reinforcements brought the daring movement to an end.

Throughout the following day, Saturday, May 7, each side held its well-entrenched ground and waited for the other side to attack. The only action on

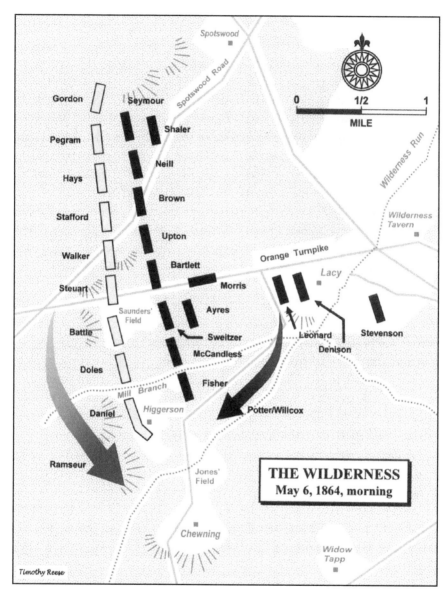

THE WILDERNESS
May 6, 1864, morning

Timothy Reese

Rodes' front occurred when Ramseur's skirmishers drove off their counterparts from Burnside's command and captured a number of tents and knapsacks. That night, Lee ordered Ewell to extend his right flank, informing the general that if in the morning he saw no enemy to his front he was to follow the First Corps (now under Richard Anderson after Longstreet's wounding) to Spotsylvania Court House.[49]

* * *

When Joseph Hooker met strong resistance in this same Wilderness the year before, he pulled his army back across the Rapidan. Ulysses Grant had no intention of repeating the maneuver. Forced to concede that he could not penetrate Lee's strong position with a frontal assault—and that Lee also was a commander unlike any other he had faced in the Western Theater—Grant issued orders on the evening of May 7 for his army to move around the enemy right. At 8:30 p.m. Warren and Sedgwick pulled out of their lines and took up the march, heading southeast on the Brock Road toward Spotsylvania Court House. Many of Grant's men, fearing another retreat and a consequent endless extension of the war, cheered when the Army of the Potomac's vast marching columns turned south. Ironically, Lee's men, who also expected the Yankees to pull back, gave out a cheer of their own when false word of an enemy retreat swept along the line.[50]

When he learned that evening that the Federals had severed their supply line at Germanna Ford, Lee concluded correctly that Grant intended to move east or southeast. There would be no enemy retreat this time around. At 7:00 p.m. the Army of Northern Virginia commander directed Richard Anderson to pull back his men from its position on the right after dark, assemble them for a rest in some quiet area in the rear, and then start sometime before 3:00 a.m. for Spotsylvania. A. P. Hill's corps spread out to cover Anderson's vacated spot in the line, and Ewell moved Rodes' division to fill the space left by Hill.

Anderson began his movement at 11:00 p.m. Thick undergrowth, choking smoke from smoldering fires, and the stench of dead bodies made it impossible to find a suitable area to rest his men. The South Carolinian made the fortuitous decision to keep marching for Spotsylvania. The decision put the head of his column at Laurel Hill five hours ahead of schedule—and just in time to meet the van of Grant's approaching column and prevent it from turning Lee's flank.[51]

Rodes began his own pullout at 8:00 a.m. the following morning, in compliance with Lee's order for Ewell to slip his corps behind Hill's and march to join Anderson. Johnson pulled his division out at 9:00 a.m. Early followed at 10:00 a.m., and A. P. Hill's Third Corps waited until 3:00 p.m. "The cries of the wounded day and night were awful," the Fifth Alabama's Captain Williams wrote after the war, "and we were happy when orders came on the morning of the 8th for us to leave for Spotsylvania Court House."[52]

Rodes placed Ramseur in the lead, followed by Daniel, Doles, and Battle (Johnston's brigade remained with Early's division). He proceeded along the path hacked out by Anderson's pioneers to the Catharpin Road near White Hall, then angled left toward Shady Grove Church. Frequently calling for the double-quick, Rodes brought his men to the church between noon and 1:00 p.m., just in time to disturb Sabbath services. He led the column southeast on Shady Grove Church Road. Though finally clear of the stench of the recent battlefield, Rodes' men suffered from the day's intense heat and the thick dust kicked up by their advance. Within a couple of hours, soldiers began to succumb to exhaustion.[53]

Along the march, Rodes received word that his division had been reduced in size by one brigade. The loss was the end result of a chain reaction that began the day before when A. P. Hill fell sick. Lee elevated Jubal Early to assume temporary command of Hill's Third Corps, and John Gordon, who in the Wilderness again displayed remarkable courage and leadership, to lead Early's division. However, Harry T. Hays, the senior brigadier in Early's division, outranked Gordon. To get around this technicality, Lee put Hays in command of a consolidated brigade consisting of his own Louisiana regiments and those of Leroy Stafford, who was mortally wounded in the Wilderness, and shifted it to Johnson's division. This left Johnson with four brigades, Gordon with three, and Rodes with five. Lee evened things out by transferring Robert Johnston's brigade to Gordon's new command.[54]

Not everyone was happy with the move. "It was while on the march to Spotsylvania that Johnston's brigade was, much to their regret, transferred from Rodes' division to Early's," wrote a captain in the Twenty-third North Carolina. "The men were much troubled over losing their identity with Rodes' Division," declared Lieutenant Walter Montgomery of the Twelfth North Carolina.[55]

As he neared the Block House Bridge around 6:00 p.m., Rodes heard firing in the distance. Anderson was under tremendous pressure from the enemy and desperately needed help. Ewell directed Rodes to head north on the Old Court House Road for about one mile and come in on Anderson's right.

With time of the essence, Rodes pushed his dead-tired men ever harder. As they neared the battlefield Rodes halted the division and sent word for each regiment to close up and dress on center. Astride his magnificent black stallion, he rode along the line shouting words of encouragement to his men, who lustily cheered as he passed. Rodes stopped in front of Company D of his old regiment, the Fifth Alabama. "Boys!" he called out, "you played hell the other evening; now, when the order is given I want you to run over those Yankees in front!" Many members of the Fifth proudly took this as special recognition from Rodes. "Our colonel (Hall)," wrote Company D's Captain Williams after the war, "always said that Co D were Rodes' pets; that he never wanted a man for a responsible place that he didn't call on Williams for one of the company."[56]

With his men regrouped and ready, Rodes guided the division into position. Anderson's men formed to the left of Rodes' line, while Dole's secured the right. The brigades of Ramseur and Daniel (left to right) constituted the center, with Battle's men in reserve.

As he had against Burnside two days before, Ramseur arrived in position without a moment to spare, this time to stop the Yankees from turning and crushing Anderson's right flank. An energized Rodes seized the initiative, calling up Battle's men from reserve and sending them charging forward with Ramseur's brigade toward enemy lines.

Battle's eager Alabamians took the lead in a 600-yard push against the Pennsylvanians of Samuel Crawford's 3rd Division of the V Corps, a charge one of Battle's soldiers later wrote "made the saucy Yankees 'about face' and hunt a more comfortable position a short distance further back." Though the retreating Federals found protection behind some recently constructed earthworks, the Alabamians did not stop their advance. With bayonets fixed and shouts of "Forward!" filling the air, Battle and men from the Sixth and Sixty-first Alabama slammed into the enemy trench line. Though the Confederates fought hard, some of it hand-to-hand, they were too few. The Alabamians of the Sixth fell back without their flag.

Despite the fact he had been shot in the foot, Battle called for another charge, grabbing the banner of the Third Alabama and imploring the men to follow him. He received virtually no response. Ramseur arrived and added his own pleas, again to no effect. The Alabamians were too exhausted and battle-weary to engage the enemy again. Although Battle felt humiliated by what he viewed as a failure, he and his men had helped save the Confederate right flank from a serious setback.[57]

When he learned of Battle's wound, Rodes sent a staff officer to inquire of his brigadier's condition. Battle and his men had performed "highly creditable and arduous services . . . for twelve consecutive hours," prompting Rodes to offer to relieve the brigade if Battle so desired. He refused.[58]

Farther to the right, meanwhile, Doles' and Daniel's brigades, along with Johnson's division, stubbornly held against fierce enemy attacks until darkness finally intervened. Rodes' rapid march and decisive deployment, combined with the determination and bravery of his men, had helped save the day.

Rodes and his division received little or no rest the night of May 8-9. Seeking to improve his army's overall position, Lee directed Ewell to move the Second Corps slightly forward to a low ridge and dig in, a difficult and dangerous task given the darkness and proximity of the enemy. Rodes sent Ramseur up to the newly designated line, where the left of his brigade was to connect with Joseph Kershaw's division of Anderson's [Longstreet's] corps. Daniel was ordered to take up a position on Ramseur's right. Daniel summoned one sergeant from each of his regiments to brigade headquarters and directed them to follow staff officers to their new positions. Once there, the sergeants were to stand and guide their respective regiments forward by calling out in a low voice. Sergeant Cyrus Watson of the Forty-fifth North Carolina remembered how he was advised not to sit down for fear of falling asleep. For one hour Watson stood nervously and alone in the dark woods, surrounded only by the groans and wails of the wounded, including one delirious man who barked out like a dog.[59]

Rodes deployed Doles' brigade on Daniel's right and held Battle's battered regiments in reserve. Edward Johnson's division formed into line on Doles' right, while Ewell designated Gordon's division as the corps' reserve. On Johnson's right, Early led A. P. Hill's Third Corps in an extension of the Confederate line. With a renewal of hostilities expected in the morning, the men worked through the night, using bayonets, tin cups, or whatever else proved useful to dig trenches and traverses, construct log works, and build abatis.

Dawn on May 9 revealed that Ewell's portion of the line included a half-mile-wide salient. Though a potential weak point, this area included some high ground that Lee wanted kept out of enemy hands. Rodes held the western face of the salient, called the "Mule Shoe," his line extending through the woods about one-half mile north by northeast. Doles' brigade occupied the apex of the "shoe." On his and Daniel's front was an open field 200 yards wide. Johnson's division held the eastern face, a one-half mile stretch of trench front, with James Walker's Stonewall Brigade connecting with Doles' right. Gordon's division held the base of the salient. About 250 yards behind the apex of the salient stood the Harrison house, where Ewell established his headquarters.[60]

That afternoon, Ewell's gunners and those of the VI Corps commenced an artillery duel that picked up again the following morning and lasted into the early afternoon. Though stressful, the enemy barrage inflicted little damage. Of more concern were Yankee sharpshooters, one of whom killed Rodes' aide, Lieutenant James Hutchinson, with a bullet through the head.[61]

As the opposing armies solidified their new positions and traded fire, Captain Ronald MacKenzie of the U.S. Corps of Engineers determined that the weakest point in the Confederate salient was a narrow protuberance in its northwest face. Concentrate a strong force against that point, he advised, and a breakthrough would inevitably result.[62]

Such an operation seemed especially suited to the talents of 24-year-old Colonel Emory Upton, commander of the 2nd Brigade, Horatio Wright's 1st Division, VI Corps. The previous November, Upton had employed a concentrated force to successfully storm Lee's bridgehead at Rappahannock Station in a daring assault at dusk. Thrilled with the opportunity to win a brigadier's star, Upton assembled a special strike force of twelve picked regiments, about 5,000 men who in Upton's estimation comprised the cream of the VI Corps. Concealed in a thick belt of timber 200 yards across an open field from the point of attack, Upton organized his men into a dense column of four lines. Each line contained three regiments separated by only ten feet.

Upton instructed the men in the first line to load and cap their muskets, and for the men in the remaining three to load only. He took each regimental officer forward to the edge of the woods and showed them the ground over which they would charge. He informed them that three VI Corps batteries would pound the Confederate defenses for ten minutes. When the guns fell silent, they would attack, rushing ahead without stopping to fire. Upton directed the officers to repeat the command "Forward!" until they hit the enemy positions. When the first line reached the Confederate works, it was to split to the right and left so as to widen the penetration and allow the second line to push through and seize the second Confederate line. Upton's third and fourth lines were to hold near the breastworks and be prepared to exploit any advantages. Gershom Mott's division of the II Corps was to come up on Upton's left and act as a general reserve. "I will carry these works," the young colonel boasted to Wright's chief of staff. "If I don't, I will not come back."[63]

Upton's designated point of attack aimed straight at the portion of Rodes' line held by George Doles' brigade, which broke camp six days before with 1,567 men. After May 10, the "protuberance" in the Confederate line forever would be known as "Doles' Salient."[64]

When the Yankee bombardment opened at 6:00 p.m., Rodes alerted his commanders to brace for an attack. Doles, in turn, ordered his men to load

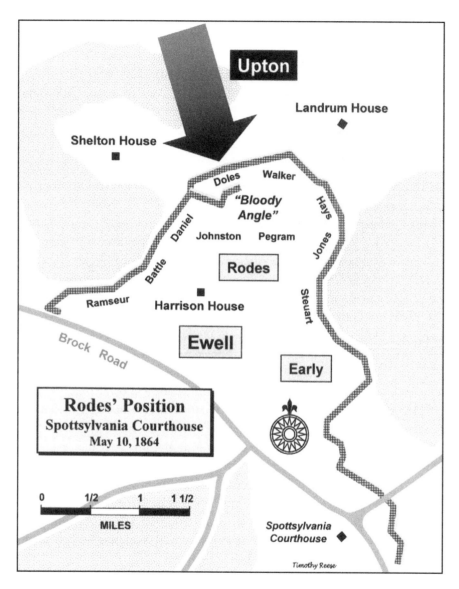

Upton

Landrum House

Shelton House

Doles   Walker

"Bloody
Angle"

Hays

Daniel

Johnston   Pegram

Jones

Rodes

Battle

Ramseur   Harrison House

Steuart

Brock Road

Ewell

Early

Rodes' Position
Spottsylvania Courthouse
May 10, 1864

0   1/2   1   1 1/2

MILES

Spottsylvania
Courthouse

Timothy Reese

rifles and fix bayonets. Ten minutes later, when the firing abruptly stopped, both generals concluded that there would be no more fighting that day.[65]

Suddenly, thousands of shouting Yankees burst from the woods 200 yards distant. In no more than 90 seconds, they reached Rodes' line. Hundreds of Federals poured over the parapet and began a vicious fight with Doles' stunned Georgians. While defiantly waving his regiment's flag, 21-year-old Thomas Dingler of the Forty-fourth Georgia received fourteen bayonet wounds before he went down. Another Georgian took a bayonet through the eyes, and still another had his head split open by an enemy sabre.[66]

The shear weight of the Federal numbers proved too much for Doles' men, who broke and ran for the second line. The pursing Yankees scooped up about 300 prisoners, including Doles himself. At one point so many gray-clad captives were being led back to Union lines that gunners in the Richmond Howitzers gave a cheer at what they believed was a Confederate countercharge.[67]

The collapse of Doles' brigade exposed the right of Junius Daniel's line. The Second North Carolina Battalion, "my little mob," as Daniel affectionately called it, took the brunt of the expanding Yankee attack. The North Carolinians "fought almost hand-to-hand with the enemy until nearly annihilated," remembered one soldier. The firing became so intense that "the immense volumes of smoke which rose from the musketry so darkened [the sun's] rays as to give the appearance of a bright moon-shining night." Now many of Daniel's men broke and ran for the second line.[68]

With his line cracking, Rodes rode "up as close as he could get," remembered the Fifth Alabama's Captain Williams, to assess the situation and help realign and steady Daniel's men. Then he made a daring decision. Quickly and accurately comprehending the narrow, punch-like nature of the enemy attack, Rodes ordered Ramseur to pull out of the line and come over from the left. He sped back to get Battle's brigade from reserve, telling it "to move forward quick!" Comprehending the urgency of the situation, the Alabamians went ahead on the run, wasting no time to form up. Presently they came out into an open field. "Which way, general?" someone called out to Rodes. "Into the pine thicket and retake those works!" he shouted back. "Soon began the bravest fighting I ever saw," noted Captain Williams. "Not a Yankee bent his body that I could see, and I know our men stood perfectly erect, loaded and fired. . . . We returned shot for shot, yell for yell. . . . A humming bird could not have lived at the edge of that little field in their rear."[69]

Ewell, meanwhile, brought up Johnston from reserve and Walker from the right, while Lee threw in the brigades of George Steuart and Clement Evans (successor to Gordon). Under the weight of these reinforcements the tide of battle quickly turned. Upton's Yankees fell back to the parapets (freeing Doles from his captors), where the young colonel found himself isolated and surrounded on three sides (Mott's reserve division had been driven off by Confederate artillery). Taking terrible losses while fighting his way out of a closing trap, Upton barely managed to get his command back across the field and into their own lines. By 7:30 p.m. the fight was over. It cost Upton about

1,000 men. Ewell lost about 1,500, including 600 from Doles' brigade and 400 from Daniel's.[70]

Lee was not pleased. "General," he asked of Rodes during a meeting that evening at the McCool house, which stood within the salient's perimeter, "what shall we do with General Doles for allowing those people to break over his lines?" By inference, Lee may also have been saying to Rodes "what shall I do with you?" as a means of expressing displeasure with him for not being better prepared. Lee apparently did not yet comprehend that Rodes' line had sustained a very powerful and potent attack. "We shall have to let Doles [me] off this time," Rodes responded, "as he has suffered quite severely for it already." Lee, however, showed his displeasure again that evening when at 8:15 p.m. he instructed Ewell to re-establish his whole position. "I wish General Rodes to rectify his line and improve its defenses," the commanding general stressed, "especially that part which seemed so easily overcome this afternoon."[71]

Though Lee seemed somewhat disappointed in Rodes, others in the division, particularly those who saw him in action that day, were not. "Gen. Rodes displayed great skill and courage in this fight," the Sixth Alabama's James Roberts scribbled in his diary that night, "and proved himself worthy of the praise he has received from so many sources. He remained in the thickest of the fight, cheering the men to deeds of valor." Moreover, Rodes' daring redeployment of Ramseur's brigade at a critical time had helped save the day.[72]

That night, a Confederate band gathered in the salient and played "Nearer My God to Thee." Across the way a Yankee band responded with "Dead March." The Confederates came back with "The Bonnie Blue Flag," and a few hearty rebel yells. The Yanks took their turn with "The Star Spangled Banner" and some huzzahs of their own. The rebels brought the program to a close with "Home Sweet Home." Both sides cheered, as if to say goodnight.[73]

*   *   *

Rodes "rectified" his line during the night by having his men dig a ditch outside the works and add a barricade of felled trees. He pulled back into reserve Doles' three shattered regiments (the Fourth, Twelfth, and Forty-fourth Georgia), which now totaled no more than 550 men. He put Battle's brigade on the left of the division line, Ramseur's in the center, and Daniel's on the right. Daniel's men connected with the left of Harry Hays' brigade (commanded by William Monaghan, who succeeded the wounded Hays), which at 10:00 a.m. moved to the left of Henry H. Walker.[74]

The only fighting of note that broke out on dreary, rainy May 11 was a clash of cavalry at Yellow Tavern, where Phil Sheridan gave Jeb Stuart's horsemen a drubbing and mortally wounded Stuart himself. Both sides used the lull to improve their lines and take stock of their situation. Hundreds of dead and wounded Federals lay about on the ground in front of Doles' Salient, a ghastly scene made worse by sharpshooters, who thwarted efforts to succor the wounded. The result, explained one witness, was that "the poor fellows were left to die in agony."[75]

Rodes spent the day looking after his men. When he saw Battle still suffering from the wound he had received on the 8th, Rodes urged, but did not order, the brigadier to go at once to the hospital. The tough fighter refused. "I told him I could not leave the front for such a wound, while better men were dying on the field," recalled Battle.[76]

A light rain persisted during the night of May 11. Inside the Mule Shoe, Sergeant Cyrus Watson of the Forty-fifth North Carolina of Daniel's Brigade sat on picket with the rest of his comrades, gun in hand, listening attentively to the nearby Yankees chatter and open cracker boxes. All along the lines, one man in each company held the job of keeping the others awake so that they would not be surprised by the Yanks during the night. Little could any of them know the terrible storm that awaited them in the morning.[77]

Though it had not succeeded, Upton's attack had so impressed Grant that he wanted to try it again—but on a much larger scale. He determined to bring Hancock's entire II Corps around from its position on the right under cover of darkness and throw it against the apex of the Mule Shoe at 4:00 a.m. on the 12th.[78]

The Union commander could not have chosen a better time to strike. At the Harrison house on the evening of the 11th, Lee met with Ewell, Rodes, and the Second Corps artillery chief Armistead Long. Mistakenly thinking that Grant's wagons sent to the rear to remove Federal wounded and bring up supplies signaled an enemy retreat toward Fredericksburg, Lee set about organizing a pursuit. He instructed Long to have the guns ready to roll early the following morning. Long in turn decided to pull back 22 pieces (the battalions of Richard Page and William Nelson, which had supported Johnson's division) from the toe of the salient that night, leaving only eight guns (from the battalions of Wilfred Cutshaw and Robert Hardaway) in support of Rodes' position. A fierce storm blew in with the darkness, overruling Lee's wish to have the Second Corps pull back that night to the village of Spotsylvania.[79]

Throughout the chilly final minutes of May 11 and first few hours of May 12, Rodes' and Johnson's men clearly could hear the Yankees moving about in the woods from which Upton had so aggressively leapt just two days before. Correctly interpreting the meaning of the sounds, Johnson around midnight sent a frantic call through Ewell to bring back the guns. In part because the couriers got lost in a heavy fog, three-and-a-half hours passed before the gunners received the order to head back for the salient.[80]

That same fog also compelled Hancock to delay his attack for thirty minutes. At 4:35 a.m. a dense column of about 20,000 Federals consisting of John Gibbon's 2nd Division, David Birney's 3rd Division, and Gershom Mott's 4th Division—four times the number of men used by Upton—burst from the trees and rushed headlong for Johnson's left front. Before more than a few shouts and shots could be fired, the Yankees poured over the works and broke through what only seconds before had appeared to be an impregnable front. The Federals quickly captured about 2,000 of Johnson's men, including Johnson himself, seizing also 20 of the just-returning pieces of artillery (12 of Page's guns and eight of Cutshaw's). Though Ewell threw Evans' brigade from Gordon's division into the fight, the Yankees seemed unstoppable. The screaming infantry rolled down the line, barreling over the Stonewall Brigade and heading for the exposed right flank of Daniel's brigade.[81]

Daniel ordered his rightmost regiment, the Forty-fifth North Carolina, to right wheel, align itself astride the works and face the oncoming onslaught. "We dropped upon our knees and opened fire upon the enemy," remembered Sergeant Cyrus Watson, "every man loading and firing as rapidly as possible." Two of Hardaway's batteries opened fire with canister. The Yankees, "in unbroken lines reaching back as far as we could see[,] came sweeping on in our front, but this combined fire of infantry and artillery was more than human flesh could stand and it was impossible for them to reach our lines."[82]

As he had on so many other battlefields, Rodes "seemed to be everywhere." He sped up to the point of attack and ordered Daniel, only moments away from receiving a mortal abdominal wound, to swing around his other regiments, while Major Whiting instructed Battle to charge toward the works. Once again, Rodes pulled Ramseur out of the line, telling him to "Check the enemy's advance and drive him back." Without any additional reserves to plug the line, Kershaw's division extended itself to fill the vacancy left in the works by Ramseur's departure.[83]

Ramseur led his men east into the clearing at the McCool house and realigned them facing north toward the enemy. "We were out in the open field with no breastworks in front, save those held by the Federals. Thro [sic] the lifting fog the stars and stripes were seen waving over the captured works," recalled one of Ramseur's soldiers. Looking like "an angel of war" as he rode along the line, Ramseur told his men to advance without firing. When he gave the signal, they were to charge while screaming at the top of their lungs.

Ramseur's line moved forward, slowly at first. The captured works ahead appeared to contain "a living mass of Yankees," making the prospect of success "a gloomy one for the boys in gray." At the signal, the North Carolinians rushed forward with a shout. "For a moment," recalled a private in Daniel's brigade, "it seemed to me our brigade ceased firing and held its breath as those men [Ramseur's] went forward, apparently into the very jaws of death." With equal intensity and admiration, Rodes and Ewell "breathlessly" watched the gallant charge.

As his men swept forward, Ramseur took a bullet in the right arm below the elbow. He remained with his men until pain and bleeding forced him to turn the brigade over to Bryan Grimes. The Confederate counterattack overran the first line of works. The men pulled bodies from the pits. Rainwater "red with human gore" awaited them in the breastworks, along with a ghastly scene of scattered fugitives, mingled shouts, cries of agony, and endless fusillades of musketry.[84]

Battle's brigade soon joined the charge, forming, in Battle's words, "a solid wedge driven into the very heart of the enemy." Still, Battle's and Ramseur's

men faced tremendous pressure from enemy soldiers shooting over the outer edge of the works and from nearby trenches. Cyrus Watson sympathized with the five captured Federals he was instructed to send to the rear. As the firing intensified, Watson's

Brig. Gen. Stephen D. Ramseur, perhaps the best brigade commander in Rodes' division, would outlive his superior by only a single month.

Library of Congress

captives vehemently protested that such a move was suicidal and that he may as well shoot them now. Orders were orders, however, and Watson forced them to go. Sure enough, all five were shot down. "Such was war," he lamented. "I never regretted any incident of the war more than this one."[85]

About 6:00 a.m., Grant threw in a second wave comprised of Thomas Neill's 2nd Division of the VI Corps. The insertion of a fresh division was like pouring fuel on steady fire, and the battle quickly flared up with renewed intensity. "It was here for the first time," wrote Bryan Grimes of the Fourth North Carolina, "I ever knew the enemy to run upon our bayonets, but they came down with such fury that we pitched many of them with the bayonet right over into the ditch." The brigades of Ramseur, Battle, and Daniel suffered punishment that pushed them near the breaking point and from which they would barely recover.[86]

While Grimes' men were skewering enemy soldiers on cold steel and tossing them "right over into the ditch," Abner Perrin's Alabama brigade (William Mahone's—formerly Anderson's—division, Hill's Third Corps) arrived from the far left, where it had been guarding the Block House Bridge over the Po River until Lee ordered it into the salient. Perrin arrived on the field to find Rodes, Gordon, and Ewell "engaged in an earnest and animated discussion" at the McCool house. "Things looked desperate," recalled one of Perrin's soldiers, "and there was a considerable show of excitement. Perrin was looking from one to the other as if at a loss for his orders. Gordon was talking rapidly and literally foaming at the mouth." When the generals finally reached a consensus, they directed Perrin to fall in behind Doles. Perrin was killed shortly thereafter.[87]

The massive enemy surprise assault showed few if any signs of faltering. There was no way around it: Rodes needed more men. Knowing that Ewell was out of reserves, he sent directly to Lee for help. The commanding general responded by ordering his chief of staff, Colonel Charles S. Venable, to pull reinforcements from the Shady Grove area four miles away on the Confederate right. Venable reached Rodes' position about 8:00 a.m. with Nat Harris' Mississippi brigade (Mahone's division, Third Corps) in tow. As Rodes sat waiting for the Mississippians by a spring in the woods, he received word from Ramseur that his men were falling so fast that the end of his ability to maintain the line was approaching rapidly. That morning, for example, the Fifth North Carolina had 450 men in its ranks; that evening only forty-two would answer the roll. As quickly as he could, Rodes sent Harris' men forward toward Ramseur's right. The Mississippians, however, went in too far left and partly overlapped

Ramseur's position. After sliding his men to the right, Harris managed to regain part of the works, though at a loss of about one-third of his brigade.[88]

About 10:00 a.m. Rodes spotted additional reinforcements coming in from the right flank. He rode up to the column and called out for the name of the command. "McGowan's South Carolina Brigade!" replied the men. Rodes turned to a staff officer, and with calculated effect loudly proclaimed, "There are no better soldiers in the world than these!" "We hurried forward," a South Carolinian later declared, "thinking more of him and ourselves than ever before."[89]

Somehow, against odds that seemed steeply aligned against them, Lee's men regained the initiative and the tide of battle shifted slowly in their favor. Around 10:30 a.m., Rodes and Gordon sutured closed the initial one-half mile tear in the Confederate line to no more than a few hundred yards. Grant, however, refused to quit. About 3:00 p.m. he fed two more divisions from the V Corps into the seething mass of men jammed into the trenches, but they had little effect as their was no good way to manage the stacked up commands. At 5:10 p.m., more than twelve-and-a-half hours after the fighting began, Wright called off the attack. Although reliable records do not exist, the Federals lost about 9,000 men in the effort to punch through Lee's lines; Confederate losses approached that count.[90]

"The restoration of the battle line on the 12th was a wonderful feat of arms in which all troops engaged deserve the greatest credit for endurance, constancy and unflinching courage," Colonel Venable later wrote, "but without unjust discrimination, we may say that Gordon, Rodes and Ramseur were the heroes of this bloody day." With regard to Rodes in particular, Venable declared, "at the beginning of the campaign [Rodes' division contained] about six thousand five hundred muskets, and it had already done some heavy fighting in the Wilderness and on the Spotsylvania lines. The brigades sent to his assistance did not number twenty-five hundred men. So that Rodes, with less than ten thousand men, kept back for eighteen hours more than one half of General Grant's infantry, supported by a heavy fire of Federal artillery."[91]

Lee's biographer, Douglas Freeman, added to Venable's statement. "That can scarcely be disputed," wrote Freeman. "Rodes' conduct, like his military bearing, was flawless. In the crisis, which allowed no time for deliberate reflection, he displayed the soundest economy of force. His tactics were those of protecting his flank by drawing a line perpendicular to the west front of the salient, while the greater part of his Division fought its way up the earthworks.

The achievement was reassuring proof that Rodes had learned much since Gettysburg in the handling of a Division."[92]

Indeed, Rodes had maneuvered his brigades masterfully—shifting Ramseur, for example, like a knight on a chessboard: one space over and two spaces up—all the while keeping a close handle on the larger situation while repeatedly exposing himself to danger. One soldier declared that he witnessed Rodes riding up and down the line "within rods of the firing." Declared artillerist Colonel E. P. Alexander, "There were never anywhere two better fighters than Rodes and Ramseur or two more attractive men."[93]

The most interesting observation of Rodes during the battle comes from artillerist Robert Stiles. "We saw nothing of the major-general of our division," wrote the captain regarding the action on the morning of May 12. "General Rodes, of Ewell's corps, was the only major-general we saw. He was a man of very striking appearance, of erect, fine figure and martial bearing. He constantly passed and repassed in rear of our guns, riding a black horse that champed his bit and tossed his head proudly, until his neck and shoulders were flecked with white froth, seeming to be conscious that he carried Caesar. Rodes' eyes," continued Stiles, "were everywhere, and every now and then he would stop to attend to some detail of the arrangement of his line or his troops, and then ride on again, humming to himself and catching the ends of his long, tawny mustache between his lips."[94]

After nearly 14 hours of savage fighting, the survivors of Rodes' division were exhausted beyond any previous combat experience. Finding some level of comfort proved nearly impossible. Dead men from both sides littered the ground and bloody water filled the trenches. From all around rose the pitiful groans of the wounded and dying. Throughout the night deadly stray bullets whizzed about as the enemy clung to the outer edge of the Mule Shoe only a scant few yards distant. "There is not a man in this brigade [Ramseur's]," Walter Montgomery of the Fourth North Carolina wrote home, "who will ever forget the sad requiem, which those minie balls sung over the dead and dying for twenty-two long hours." Rodes singled out the men of Ramseur's brigade for praise, telling them they had saved the Second Corps and deserved the thanks of the entire nation.[95]

*   *   *

While the fight was still raging late that afternoon, Lee wisely decided to give up the untenable Mule Shoe and shorten his line. Under Gordon's supervision, the remnants of Johnson's division put in hours of backbreaking labor building a line of trenches across the base of the salient behind the Harrison house. About 3:00 a.m. on the 13th Johnson's men began pulling back into the new trenches 1,320 yards from the salient's apex. An hour later, Rodes ordered his men to do the same. In total darkness they quietly set out in twos and threes, groping their way rearward across ground covered with trenches, shell holes, and dead bodies. Getting little or no sleep that night, Rodes kept busy making sure everyone reached the rear safely.[96]

A drizzly rain moved in and persisted throughout the 13th. Though the fighting had stopped, the dying had not. Among the mortally wounded who perished that day was Junius Daniel. Rodes turned over the dead man's brigade to Bryan Grimes of the Fourth North Carolina.[97]

With clear weather came a new effort from the seemingly indefatigable Grant, who instructed Warren to swing round behind the army, form up across the Fredericksburg Road, and attack Lee's right at 4:00 a.m. on the 14th. Grant ordered Wright to move out after Warren and form on his left. For a variety of reasons, including exhaustion of their own, Warren and Wright did not get into position until the evening of the 14th. By that time Lee was ready for them. The Confederate commander sent Charles Field's division of the First Corps from its position on the left to the right, extending the army's entrenchments two miles south of Spotsylvania. During the night the remainder of Anderson's First Corps joined Fields, and the following day (the 16th) Lee extended Anderson's right to the Po River. This arrangement left Ewell's corps holding the army's left flank and Early (Hill's) holding the center.[98]

All the while, skirmishing, sharpshooting, and artillery duels added to the casualty figures on both sides. Through it all Rodes strove to maintain a vigilant front under difficult conditions. "The ghastly and upturned faces of the numerous dead stared grimly at us between our lines, the bountiful fruit of the harvest of death, and until the 17th, their decomposed and worm eaten bodies lay uncovered, filled with worms and polluting the atmosphere with their foul stench," recalled T. M. Gorman of the Second North Carolina of Ramseur's Brigade.[99]

The ghastly field exploded the following morning, Wednesday the 18th, when the Federals opened a massive artillery barrage at 4:00 a.m. Grant directed Hancock and Wright to deliver a crushing blow on what he believed was Lee's weakened left flank. After a fierce hour-and-a-half artillery duel, three divisions under Francis Barlow and John Gibbon of the II Corps, and Thomas Neill of the VI Corps, advanced at 5:30 a.m.

Rodes held the extreme left of the Confederate line, with Gordon on his right. From the Old Court House Road on the left, their line ran along a rise on the southern base of the former salient about three-quarters of a mile behind the McCool house. From left to right, Rodes placed the brigades of Ramseur, Battle, Grimes, and Doles. The men were well protected, having dug traverses every 10 to 15 feet and more across the rear. Abatis guarded their front out to a distance of 100 yards. Twenty-nine guns supported the line. Rodes and Gordon maintained a formidable position.

When the advancing Federals tried to thread themselves through the thick abatis, the Confederate guns opened on them with canister, mowing down hundreds. Rodes' and Gordon's men did little more than watch as the enemy infantry approached, leaving the deadly work to their field pieces. By 9:00 a.m., the attack was over. Rodes' men crowded around the artillerists to shake their hands and affectionately pat the smoking gun tubes.[100]

Undeterred, Grant resumed his efforts to slip around Lee's right flank. On the 19th he sent Hancock on a rapid march south along the line of the Fredericksburg & Potomac Railroad. That same day, Lee ordered Ewell to demonstrate in his front to determine if the enemy had abandoned their line. Ewell protested that since the Second Corps now contained fewer than 6,000 effectives, a demonstration in force might prove disastrous. (Ewell did not know that Hancock had been gone for more than 12 hours.) He secured Lee's permission instead to sweep west around the enemy's flank and proceed northeast for a glimpse across the Ny River.

The Second Corps set out at 2:00 p.m. Rodes' division led the way, with Ramseur's brigade out front, followed by Battle, Grimes, and Doles. Gordon's division followed. The corps proceeded northwest along the Brock Road to the Gordon Road, which turned northeast past the Couse farm. Since recent downpours had turned the roads into quagmires, only six guns accompanied the column; even these turned back after slogging through two or three miles of sticky Virginia mud. Just beyond the western face of the salient, at the clearing on the Spindle farm, the pace picked up considerably as the men hurried to escape the stench of decomposing bodies unearthed by recent rains. At the Armstrong farm the column turned southeast onto a narrow path. About 3:00 p.m. the men crossed the Ny and marched about one mile to the Harris farm. And there, finally, the enemy came into view.

Ewell's reconnaissance had stumbled upon some rearguard Federal artillery units (the First Massachusetts Heavy Artillery Regiment, Maine Heavy Artillery, and New York Heavy Artillery) consisting mostly of raw recruits recently transferred from Washington D.C., where they had manned heavy guns in the city's defensive perimeter. Both sides rushed to deploy for what promised to be an uneven contest.

First on the field about 4:30 p.m., Stephen Ramseur secured permission— either from Ewell or Rodes, the record is unclear—to attack the Federals immediately. After initial success against the green troops of the First Massachusetts, pressure on Ramseur's flanks forced him to pull back 200 yards and settle into line between Grimes on his left and Battle on his right.

The thrust had not gone as Ramseur intended. To the surprise of many, these Yankees proved to be tough, capable fighters. When they flanked Gordon and forced him to fall back, the withdrawal exposed Grimes' brigade on Rodes' left. Grimes averted disaster by maneuvering and fighting skillfully until Rodes ordered him to fall back. When Hancock and Warren sent in reinforcements, Ewell's situation turned critical. Rodes and Gordon quickly put their men to work building a defensive line that discouraged the enemy from making further attacks. The lull allowed Ewell to slip away in the darkness. About 10:00 p.m. the Confederates quietly began pulling back. After reassembling in the rear, they marched south for their old lines.[101]

Though this Harris farm fiasco cost the Second Corps some 900 men (the Federals lost approximately 1,500), Ewell unknowingly had disrupted Grant's plan by compelling him to delay Hancock's southward march by one day. Rodes, however, strongly disapproved of the way Ewell had handled the situation. He blamed his commander for not maintaining a firmer control of the developing crisis. Though he did not air his concerns publicly, his observations that day may have raised serious doubts in Rodes' mind about Ewell's ability to continue in command of a corps. On the other hand, Rodes heaped unqualified praise upon Bryan Grimes. "You have saved Ewell's Corps," he said while shaking the colonel's hand, "and shall be promoted, and your commission shall bear date from this day." Two weeks later, Grimes received a well deserved brigadier's commission. It was dated May 19.[102]

*   *   *

"This is the fifteenth day since we have met them," newly minted Brigadier General Bryan Grimes wrote his wife on the 19th. "Have been fighting more or less every day," the North Carolinian wearily continued. "If they would retire beyond the river and give us a breathing spell, it would be decidedly advantageous. Nearly all fagged out and need rest."[103]

The enemy, or more specifically the imperturbable Grant, had no intention of re-crossing the river. On the night of May 20 Hancock started marching southeast for Guiney's Station, whence he could turn directly south and make for Richmond. By noon of the following day Hancock's lead division reached Milford and crossed to the west side of the Matapony River. Warren, Burnside, and Wright followed.

At daylight on the 21st, Lee ordered Ewell to move down the Telegraph Road and into a line to the right of Charles Field's division near Hanover Junction. Ewell's new position was on the south bank of the Po, between Snell's Bridge and Stanard's Mill. The commanding general intended to take up a solid defensive position two miles behind the North Anna River at Hanover Junction. The opposing armies were now just 22 miles north of Richmond.

Ewell did not begin his move until about noon. The men of the Second Corps marched steadily for 11 hours throughout the pleasantly cool afternoon and evening. After an early start the following day on May 22, the men proceeded through Mud Tavern to Hanover Junction, where Ewell set up a line on Doswell's farm. Ewell's men spent the night in tents for the first time since breaking camp on May 4.[104]

Also on the 22nd, Lee took in substantial reinforcements for the first time since the start of the campaign. From P. G. T. Beauregard's command at Bermuda Hundred—where Benjamin Butler had been "bottled up" after frittering away several opportunities to move aggressively against either Petersburg or Richmond itself—Lee received George Pickett's division and, from the Shenandoah, where Franz Sigel had been defeated at New Market, arrived John C. Breckinridge's command. Together, these outfits added nearly 9,000 additional men to the depleted ranks of the Army of Northern Virginia.

Behind the North Anna Lee set up a smartly designed inverted V-shaped defensive line that permitted the rapid shift of troops from one flank to reinforce the other. The Third Corps, again under the command of the still quite ill A. P. Hill, held the Confederate left up to Little River. Anderson held the center, his line running southeast along the North Anna. Ewell held the right, with Rodes on the extreme end at Hanover Junction.

Lee's position forced Grant to take up a line that straddled the North Anna. Any Federal flank reinforcements would be required to cross the river twice. After several days of fruitless skirmishing and maneuvering in this undesirable manner, the Union commander finally realized that Lee's line was unassailable. After sunset on May 26 he withdrew and moved southeast toward Cold Harbor.

Once again, Lee moved quickly to counter Grant. By the 28th he had taken up another strong position, this time behind Totopotomoy Creek five miles northwest of Cold Harbor. From that point he was able to block all direct approaches to Richmond from the Pamunkey River crossings.[105]

That same day a significant change occurred in the Second Corps. Richard Ewell was an ill man. Weak from diarrhea and scurvy, exhausted by the physical exertions required from a general in his position, the once vigorous subordinate of Stonewall Jackson left on what he assumed was temporary sick leave. Lee, however, seized the opportunity to remove Ewell permanently from command. It was readily apparent to Lee, Rodes, and probably many others as well, that Ewell no longer possessed the energy and state of mind required of a corps commander. Lee also was displeased with Ewell's recent field performances. According to the army's chief of ordnance, Colonel William Allan, Lee explained in a postwar conversation that on May 12, he had "found Ewell perfectly prostrated by the misfortune of the morning, and too much overwhelmed to be effective." Lee purportedly told Allan that he observed Ewell cursing his fleeing men and swinging his sword at them. "How can you expect to control these men," Lee scolded, "when you have lost control of yourself? If you cannot repress your excitement, you had better retire!" Allan related that at the Harris farm on May 19, Ewell "lost all presence of mind, and Lee found him prostrate on the ground, and declaring he could not get Rodes' division out (Rodes being heavily engaged with the enemy)." Lee angrily informed Ewell that if he "could not get him out he (Lee) would."[106]

Lee, of course, was nowhere near the Harris farm on May 19, but there may be an element of truth in Allan's story. Evidence of this is Lee's remarkable statement to Allan concerning Rodes' strong objection to the prospect of Ewell returning to duty from sick leave, which in turn influenced the commanding general to remove Ewell from command. Before making the decision, however, Lee undoubtedly would have required Rodes to provide reasons for his objection, which may have included the account of Ewell losing "all presence of mind" at the Harris farm. If so, it meant Rodes may have taken the drastic step of turning against the man he had so admired as a brigade commander and whom he at one time had hoped would take over D. H. Hill's division. Rodes would never have taken such a step without deep and careful consideration. His sarcastic remark made months before about Lizinka Ewell commanding the corps indicates that he may have been harboring doubts about the capacity of his superior for some time.[107]

Ewell, meanwhile, remained in command limbo. After only two days on leave he applied to return to duty. Lee tactfully advised him to take more time to recover. When Ewell produced a medical certificate stating that his health was fine, Lee countered by arguing that he did not wish to change commanders while the troops were in line of battle. The message the army commander was sending was loud and clear, if not directly spoken: Ewell would not be invited back with the Army of Northern Virginia. The one-legged hero of Second Winchester spent the remainder of the war commanding the Richmond defenses.[108]

Jubal Early's experience as temporary commander of both the Second and Third Corps made him the obvious successor to Ewell. Rodes apparently never entered the equation. His experience in corps command totaled no more than a few hours on the night of May 2 more than one year before, and another few hours at Locust Grove the previous November. Moreover, despite Rodes' steady performance as a division commander at Chancellorsville and Spotsylvania, Lee probably remembered his poor showing on the second day at Gettysburg, his disregard of orders that resulted in serious losses at Kelly's Ford, and his "lack of preparedness" that allowed Doles' brigade to be "so easily overrun" at the Mule Shoe. Rodes not only failed to receive the position of corps commander, but he also lost his best brigadier when Lee put Ramseur in command of Early's old division. William R. Cox assumed command of Ramseur's brigade.[109]

As Lee was dealing with Ewell, two Union corps crossed to the south side of the Totopotomoy. To prevent the Federals from extending their left to the Chickahominy, Lee on May 29 directed Early to turn the flank of the V Corps at Bethesda Church. Early selected Rodes to spearhead the attack east down Old Church Road. Upon reaching Bethesda Church, Rodes was to turn north and sweep in behind the V Corps. Ramseur would follow in support.

Just before noon, Rodes started down the Old Church Road with Doles' brigade leading the column. When he spotted Federal skirmishers about one-half mile from Bethesda, Rodes ordered the division to deploy. As always, he took great care with his preparations. Like he had done at Seven Pines and again at Chancellorsville, Rodes stipulated that the attack should be guided on the road. At 2:00 p.m. he sent the men forward.

Advancing quickly and with spirit, Rodes' division slammed into Martin Hardin's Pennsylvania brigade of Samuel Crawford's 3rd Division. "The volley or two delivered by our feeble force," reported Colonel Hardin, "made no impression on the enemy; he ran over and around . . . [us], and his division headquarters arrived amidst the headquarters of the First Brigade before the latter could extricate itself. The enemy was so confident of its ultimate success, he did not stop to secure the First Brigade prisoners, but continued on his charge down the pike."[110]

After sweeping aside Hardin's brigade, Rodes' Confederates smashed into two others near the church. If these broke, Rodes could turn north and sweep the field. But the Yankees, stiffened by reinforcements, held firm and the fighting bogged down into a stalled small arms fight. Under increasing pressure, Rodes pulled back slightly in an effort to consolidate his line until Ramseur arrived. Hours passed, however, before Early finally got the North Carolinian into the fight. By then it was too late. About 6:00 p.m. the Federals delivered a relentless counterattack that drove Early's entire line backward. The Second Corps was not at its best at Bethesda Church. Reliable records tabulating the losses from this engagement are not available, but Rodes' division suffered heavily.[111]

In his continuing quest to break down Lee's army, Grant set his sights on Cold Harbor to the southeast. Drawing reinforcements from their respective forces around Bermuda Hundred, both sides began gathering there on the 30th. By June 2, Lee's line ran from Totopotomoy Creek on the left to the Chickahominy on the right, a nearly impossible position to flank.

Although his army had been seriously weakened and its command structure decimated, Lee remained vigilant for opportunities to disrupt Grant's movements. To that end, he once again ordered Early to execute a preemptive strike, this time by attacking Burnside's corps on Grant's right.

After arriving from Hundley's Corner on the Shady Grove Road, Rodes filed in between Harry Heth's First Corps division on his left and Gordon's on his right. Ramseur lined up to Gordon's right. The line advanced at 2:00 p.m., a fierce thunderstorm gathering in the skies above them.

Spearheading the assault, Rodes plunged his men into a gap between the IX and V corps. From his own IX Corps, Burnside sent Thomas Crittenden's 1st Division to meet the threat. Rodes pushed on, flanking two brigades (Sudbury's and James Ledlie's of Crittenden's division) before the Federals finally stiffened. The tide gradually turned. Rodes, outnumbered and without any reserves to call upon, ordered his brigades to fall back. Before they did, a Federal sharpshooter's bullet struck and killed George Doles as that officer was inspecting his lines.[112]

At 4:30 a.m. on Thursday, June 3, Grant sent three Union corps, the II, VI, and XVII, altogether some 40,000 men, across no-man's land in a grand attempt to smash Lee's center and throw his army into the Chickahominy. Lee's men required little more than half an hour to shoot down 7,000 of those Federals. At the same time, Rodes and Early easily turned aside Burnside's feeble attempts to swing out and hit Lee's left flank north of the Old Church Road.[113]

Once again, Lee successfully parried Grant's thrust. And once again, he called upon Early to execute a disruptive strike. On June 7 Lee sent the Second Corps on a turning movement near Metadequin Creek. At 8:00 a.m., "Rodes' division packed up their baggage," Captain Park noted in his diary, "and marched down the breastworks near Richmond, and turning to the left at the same point as we did on 30 May, and continuing nearly a mile under a hot, broiling sun, when we came up with the divisions of Ramseur and Gordon. We halted a few hours; skirmishing, shelling, we expected a fight but there was none." With Grant evidently having pulled out of this part of the line and moved farther south, Rodes' division went into camp along the Mechanicsville Pike.

Unbeknownst to Rodes, a surprising and new duty beckoned. On June 12, Lee ordered Early to prepare his Second Corps for a special assignment in the Shenandoah Valley.[114]

An undated image of Robert Rodes as a brigadier general.

| Into the Valley

O n Wednesday, June 8, 1864, in new trenches about one half-mile behind the front line, Rodes' men savored their first day of rest in the last thirty-five. "Many reading their Bibles," observed Major Blackford, "some singing hymns, some sleeping, some cooking, and all as jolly and confident of ultimate victory as possible."

Blackford took the opportunity to pay a friendly visit to division headquarters, where he and Rodes "enjoyed a dish of onions and vinegar." The two men relaxed and indulged in pleasant conversation, Rodes displaying his cordial off-duty manner that had won him numerous friends and admirers. The two friends inevitably talked about a subject dear to Rodes' heart: the Fifth Alabama, his original wartime command. "Gen. Rodes spoke of my Regiment in the highest terms," Blackford proudly informed his sister, "and evinced great interest in all that appertained to it." Then he added, "It is really extraordinary to notice how accurately he remembers every thing about every man that belonged to it when it was under his command. This frequently annoys the men very much, when they attempt in any way to practice deception upon him. He recollects distinctly that A used to shirk duty in 61, and that B did not go into the battle of Manassas &c, & much to the disgust of these men an unfavorable endorsement is placed upon their applications."[1]

Along with his beloved Fifth Alabama, Rodes in three full years of service in the army of the Confederate States had participated in nine campaigns embracing some twenty battles, actions, and skirmishes. During that time the twice-wounded officer had proven himself a brave, intelligent, and capable leader. His dramatic rise from captain to major general had been equaled by a rise in esteem among not only his superiors and fellow commanders, but also among those whom he commanded. In the cool pre-dawn hours of June 13, Rodes set out on his tenth campaign.

This latest turn in his destiny was determined by General Lee's decision to send the Second Corps to save the Shenandoah Valley from yet another Federal invasion. After the defeat of Franz Sigel at New Market on May 15 and the subsequent transfer of John C. Breckinridge's command from the Valley to Lee's army, the Federals regrouped for another effort. In late May, 8,000 Union soldiers under a new commander, David Hunter, began marching up the Valley Pike. At Piedmont on June 5, Hunter defeated Grumble Jones's small force of 4,000 men. Six days later, Hunter entered Lexington and burned Rodes' beloved Virginia Military Institute. Reinforced to 18,000 men, Hunter drove for the great prize of Lynchburg, where three vital railroad supply lines intersected (Orange & Alexandria, Virginia & Tennessee, and the Southside). It also was the home of Rodes' two-months pregnant wife Hortense, his infant son Bobby, stepmother Fannie, and half-sister Lucy.[2]

Added to the outrage at what had been done to his alma mater, Rodes now carried the anxiety of what might happen to his family. Revenge and worry weighed heavily upon his mind as he led his men from their camps near the old battlefield of Gaines' Mill at 3:00 a.m. on the morning of June 13.

Scarcely two months before, his magnificent division numbered 7,100 men. Now it contained barely 3,000. Moreover, Rodes no longer enjoyed the services of four officers who had been among the army's ablest brigade commanders: Robert Johnston and his brigade had been transferred, Stephen Ramseur had been promoted, and George Doles and Junius Daniel had been killed. Rodes was fortunate, however, to receive capable replacements. Bryan Grimes assumed command of the fallen Daniel's brigade. Ramseur's brigade went to thirty-two-year-old William R. Cox, a lawyer who had served with distinction as major and colonel of the Second North Carolina. The leadership of Doles's Georgia brigade passed to forty-six-year-old Philip Cook, also a lawyer, who had enlisted as a private in the Fourth Georgia and risen through the ranks.[3]

As much could be said of the Second Corps. In April it boasted a strength of about 17,000 men. Now it contained less than half that number—fewer men than marched in Rodes' division during the Gettysburg campaign. With the exception of the now senior division commander Rodes, the corps' high command presented a completely different look. Jubal Early had succeeded Richard Ewell, Ramseur had taken over Early's division, and John Gordon had assumed command of what was left of Ed Johnson's old division.

Lt. Gen. Jubal Early assumed command of Ewell's Second Corps in May 1864, and led it, with reinforcements, into the Shenandoah—and beyond.

Library of Congress

After weeks of nearly relentless attacks by the Army of the Potomac General Lee assumed a bold gamble in sending away the Second Corps. His hope was that Early not only would stop Hunter, but also draw off some of General Ulysses S. Grant's strength. Perhaps Early's presence in the Valley would equal what Thomas Jackson had accomplished there two years before. Old Jube, however, had very little with which to accomplish those great tasks. In addition to his own 8,000 men, only John C. Breckinridge's small command of 2,000 and some 4,000 cavalry already in the Valley (the brigades of John Imboden, William L. Jackson, John McCausland, John Vaughn, and Bradley Johnson leading Grumble Jones's old command) and forty guns (nine batteries in two battalions under Lieutenant Colonels Carter Braxton and William Nelson, all under the command of Armistead Long), were available to augment it.[4]

Inspired by the invigorating cool pre-dawn air and the anticipation of delivering some great blow upon the enemy, Rodes' men maintained a brisk, jaunty pace as they set out for the Valley. Speculation ran along the column as to where the division was headed. "Some said to assume its position on the right of the army," Captain Park recorded in his diary, "and others to the south side of the James; still others thought it was a grand flank movement, in which Grant was to be outgeneraled as McClellan was, and Lee, as usual, grandly triumphant."[5]

With Rodes' division in front of the corps, Battle's brigade in the lead and the Twelfth Alabama at the point, the column marched west through Mechanicsville, crossed the Chickahominy River at Meadow Bridge, and picked up the Brook Pike five miles north of Richmond. Settling into route step, the men marched north to the Plank Road, then northwest to the Old Mountain Road where, sweltering from the heat and choking on the dust, they began to wonder when they would stop. After twenty-five miles, the column finally jostled to a halt at Auburn Mills, twenty miles from Richmond.[6]

The following day brought another hot, dusty march of twenty-two miles. On the 15th the men covered only seven miles, stopping near Trevillian's Depot seven miles from Gordonsville, but on the 16th they stepped off another twenty-fives miles to Shadwell Station on the Virginia Central Railroad, six miles from Charlottesville.[7]

In four days the division covered an incredible eighty miles. Along the way, everyone came to realize they were going to the Shenandoah to face Hunter. As usual, the men eagerly and optimistically looked forward to this next challenge. "If he doesn't mind," Cary Whitaker of the Forty-third North Carolina recorded in his diary regarding Hunter's chances, "he may find himself about wound up before he thinks of it."[8]

From Shadwell Station, Early intended to transport the corps sixty miles down to Lynchburg via the Orange & Alexandria Railroad. He became infuriated, however, upon discovering there were only enough "cars" to send little more than one division. He selected Ramseur's and one brigade of Gordon's, instructing Rodes to march down the line with his own division and the rest of Gordon's and catch the train on its return from Lynchburg.[9]

This arrangement did not suit Rodes, and he let Early know it. Fretting over the safety of his family, Rodes demanded that his division be allowed to go first on the train. Early's refusal to revise his orders provoked an exchange of "hot words" between the two men. It is the only known recorded instance of Rodes openly displaying anger toward a superior officer. After the train pulled out, the still-upset division commander pushed his men (many of whom had just received from the good citizens of Charlottesville a bountiful treat of cherries and cream) rapidly down the roadbed. That night he stopped near North Garden to await the train's expected arrival the following morning.[10]

During the initial trip down to Lynchburg, meanwhile, the train's dilapidated rolling stock triggered a derailment that killed two men. A journey that normally took three hours stretched into five. Ramseur and Gordon did not reach Lynchburg until 1:00 p.m., whereupon they quickly marched three miles out on the Salem Road to join Breckinridge in a defensive line facing

Hunter. Although the Federal commander still had an excellent chance to overwhelm the weaker Confederates, Hunter remained stationary.[11]

He still was waiting when Rodes finally arrived around 4:00 p.m. the following afternoon. After riding several uncomfortable hours out in the open on flatcars, where the passengers battled hot cinders that stuck in their hair and beards, Rodes' men quickly detrained and moved briskly through the hilly streets and out onto the Forest Road to reinforce the right side of Early's line. Rodes, however, clearly indicating his true priorities at this time, initially did not go with his men. Leaving the division in the hands of Bryan Grimes, he broke off from the column for a quick dash up to Harrison Street to make a reassuring check on his family.[12]

With the command united, Rodes, Gordon, Ramseur, and Breckinridge hoped and expected to launch an attack against the lethargic Hunter. Early, however, prudently decided to wait until the artillery came up the following morning.[13]

That night the generals gratefully enjoyed a few baskets of "good edibles" provided by the patriotic ladies of Lynchburg. Contributors to this bounty quite probably included Hortense and Lucy Rodes. The thoughtful gesture certainly would have been in character for Rodes' half sister. While a student at the Lynchburg Female Seminary two years before, fifteen-year-old Lucy had proven both her patriotism and her compassion when she helped organize a concert that raised $125 for the benefit of wounded and sick soldiers convalescing in Lynchburg.[14]

With the dawn came the startling discovery that Hunter had fled. After correctly interpreting the meaning of the cheering announcing Rodes' arrival the day before, the Federal commander pulled out during the night and retreated west along the Salem Road.

With Ramseur in front, the Army of the Valley, as Early now styled his command, moved out the morning of the 19th on the Salem Road and took up the pursuit. Despite encountering burned bridges along the way, Ramseur managed a respectable twenty-five miles to overcome Hunter's rear guard at Liberty, though nothing more than a brief skirmish ensued. Rodes and the others came up that night and the army camped near the town.[15]

Gordon's turn to lead the column came on the 20th. The pursuit continued just east of Salem at Buford's Gap, where Hunter stopped and made a show of resistance. Early deployed with Gordon on the left and Rodes on the right, but darkness fell before anything happened. The small army camped in the gap.[16]

With Rodes scheduled to take the van the following day, Early sent a courier that evening to instruct him to pull in his skirmishers and be prepared to move out at daybreak. For some reason, however, the courier told Rodes to advance his skirmishers at daybreak. Instead of getting back to Early to verify this strange order, Rodes sent an inquiry over to Ramseur, who replied that he, too, had been ordered to advance his skirmishers. Satisfied the order was correct, Rodes did not have his men ready to march at the appointed hour. Sometime after daybreak, Early sent an aide to inquire after the delay, only to see Rodes shortly afterward arrive at headquarters to receive his orders for the day. The misunderstanding was sorted out (in an undoubtedly strained atmosphere) and Rodes hurried his men into march formation. To head off the Federals, he left the main road at Big Lick and raced for Mason's Gap, only to discover that Hunter already had passed through. By the following morning (22nd), it became evident that the Federal commander had left the Valley altogether and was heading west. Unbeknownst to the Confederates, Hunter had begun an exhausting, precipitate ten-day trek that would take him through Lewisburg and all the way to Charleston in the Kanawha Valley. "The night after Rodes' Invincibles got there," the Fourth North Carolina's John Anglin proudly wrote home, "he [Hunter] took the back track & farely flew."[17]

To Rodes' great relief, Lynchburg had been saved.

*   *   *

Hunter's flight offered the aggressive Lee an opportunity to seize the initiative in the Valley. He gave Early the option to either return to the Army of Northern Virginia or build upon his success by moving farther north down the Valley. Not surprisingly, Old Jube set his sights on the Potomac River.[18]

That day, June 22, the army camped at Botetourt Springs, where Early granted a day of rest to allow for the supply wagons to come up. Except for some scant bacon found in Liberty, his men had not eaten for quite some time. "Rodes had now been nearly 3 days without rations," Early's aide, Captain William Old, recorded in his diary. "Troops very tired & fagged." Not knowing when those supply wagons might arrive (they came in that evening), those tired, fagged, famished soldiers throughout the day agonizingly cried out for "bread, bread, bread!" whenever they caught a glimpse of Rodes or Early.[19]

The next day, the army marched north to Buchanon. Beginning at 3:00 a.m. the following morning, Rodes led the way up to Buffalo Creek, near Lexington. On June 25 the Confederates entered the town.

The blackened ruins of Governor Letcher's house, the charred remains of his beloved VMI, and the final resting place of his revered former commander certainly had an emotional impact upon Rodes. He led his division off the main street and through the gate of a small cemetery. Just inside stood a mound of dirt adorned by numerous flowers and a tiny Confederate flag. The wooden headboard that once stood over Thomas Jackson's grave had long ago been chipped away for souvenirs. Rodes directed the band of the column's lead regiment, the Fourth North Carolina, to stop at the site and play a dirge while the rest of the men passed by. Officers dismounted and each man uncovered his head, reversed his rifle, and walked by in a silence described by one impressed soldier as "a hush as deep as midnight."[20]

After camping that night eight miles north of Lexington, the army, with many men now barefoot, reached Staunton on the 26th. Early used the following day to give them a much-needed rest and await the arrival of shoes by rail from Richmond and for other supplies to arrive from Waynesboro. He also used the time to reorganize his little command to make it look more like an army. With the divisions of Gordon and Breckinridge he fashioned a "corps" and assigned it to the former vice president in order to give him a command commensurate with his rank. Breckinridge's division passed into the hands of Gabriel Wharton. Early's reorganization extended to his cavalry. The horse brigades were pulled together into a single division under Robert Ransom. Early also issued orders that restricted the army's baggage. He limited the train to one wagon carrying cooking utensils for every five hundred men, and one four-horse wagon for every brigade or division commander. Regimental and company officers were ordered to carry only such underclothing as needed for the expedition. Though generally unpopular with the men, these orders clearly expressed Early's firm determination to maintain the utmost speed and efficiency during the army's march to the Potomac.[21]

Though the shoes did not arrive by the following morning as expected, Early was unwilling to delay the expedition any longer. Thoughtfully leaving behind several wagons to bring up the desperately needed footwear when it came in, he resumed the march north on the 28th. With five days' rations in their wagons and two in their haversacks, the unevenly shod soldiers tramped on, reaching the vicinity of North River that evening. The following day they made Sparta, and on the 30th they covered eighteen miles to reach New Market. Twenty-two more miles on July 1 brought them to Fisher's Hill. The following day the army liberated Winchester, whose 5,800-man garrison under Robert

Milroy had fled to Harpers Ferry. "The good people [of Winchester]," Captain Park noted in his diary, "received us very kindly and enthusiastically."[22]

With Winchester once again under the Southern banner, Early set his sights on Franz Sigel's Federals at Martinsburg. On July 3, Early dispatched Breckinridge directly against the place while Rodes and Ramseur swung to the east in an effort to cut off Sigel's escape route to Harpers Ferry and force him north into the waiting arms of the cavalry. Although a clever plan, Early was simply asking too much of his men. The twenty-four-mile march so exhausted Rodes' and Ramseur's foot soldiers that they did not arrive until after dark, by which time Sigel had slipped across the Potomac at Shepardstown.[23]

That left Harpers Ferry as the last remaining Federal outpost in the Shenandoah. On July 4, Early sent Ramseur through Flowing Springs to Halltown, where he met up with Rodes coming in from Charlestown. Together, they marched up to Bolivar Heights overlooking Harpers Ferry. From the town and nearby Maryland Heights, the Federals tried to shell the newly-arrived Southerners with 100-pound Parrotts, though with little effect. After sunset the Federals quickly but quietly evacuated their position and Rodes moved in.[24]

Moving in the dark into an area that might yet contain enemy sharpshooters and even a sizeable enemy force required strong nerves. Rodes knew exactly who to rely upon—his favorite Alabama brigade. "Where is Colonel Sands?" he called out to the thirty-eight-year-old commander of the Third Alabama, which was positioned to lead the advance into town. "Here I am!" Sands replied.

Rodes twice before had removed the intrepid Robert Sands from the field. The first episode came about during the retreat from Gettysburg when he ordered the lieutenant colonel, ailing from a knee wound, into an ambulance after finding him riding at the head of the regiment. The second occurrence took place later in the year when Rodes discovered that Sands was suffering so severely from an attack of bronchitis that he could not speak and needed an interpreter to express his orders. Against the subordinate's protests, Rodes ordered him examined by a medical board and sent home to recover. Both displays of concern left Sands favorably impressed with his major general. Despite mildly protesting that the Third might be too "cut up" to deal with any firm resistance in the town, Sands obeyed Rodes' orders and took in the men.[25]

The heavy atmosphere quickly took a festive turn when the Alabamians discovered that the Yankees had abandoned not only the town but numerous Fourth of July dinners. And there was more. "After dark," Captain Park told his diary, "General Rodes took his old Alabama brigade (now under Cullen Battle) into the town, where a universal pillaging of United States Government property, especially commissary stores, was carried on all night." Rodes put his other brigades in nearby Charlestown, where local secessionists happily regaled the men until they became "half demoralized" by all the food and drink lavished on them. Drunkenness became such a problem that Rodes established a guard from the Forty-third North Carolina to prevent "rioting and pillaging."[26]

* * *

Like the sorely-missed Stonewall Jackson and his "Foot Cavalry" two years before, Early's little army had achieved significant results by clearing the enemy from the Shenandoah Valley. Circumstances in 1862, however, had confined Jackson's operations south of the Potomac River. Early faced no such restrictions. On July 5 he sent Breckinridge across the Potomac at Boteler's Ford near Shepardstown.[27]

After waiting an extra day in Harpers Ferry for the arrival from Staunton of the hoped-for shoes (which failed to arrive), Rodes and Ramseur crossed the river on Wednesday the 6th. For the third time in the war the Second Corps entered Maryland. Unlike the previous two occasions, this crossing was not witnessed by large crowds or accompanied by glamour or fanfare. The tone of the war had changed too much for that. That night Rodes camped his men on the banks of Antietam Creek not far from the "Bloody Lane" where so many Confederates had fought and died nearly two years before. "Memories of scores of army comrades and childhood's friends slain on the banks of this stream, came before my mind, and kept away sleep for a long while," Captain Park sadly noted in his diary, [28]

On July 7, Rodes marched to the Rohrersville area three miles from Crampton's Gap, where that night the army's long-awaited shoes finally arrived from Richmond. The following day he crossed over the old battlefields of South Mountain and pitched camp near Jefferson. Less than forty miles to the east was the enemy capital, and Old Jube was determined to at least have a closer look.[29]

On July 9, Early's command came up against Lew Wallace's small force of 5,800 Federals positioned in a defensive line along the Monocacy River. A tributary of the Potomac east of Frederick, the Monocacy was a mere thirty-five miles from Washington. Determined to force a crossing, Early sent Ramseur straight ahead on the Washington City Road while Rodes moved to the left to act as a diversion along the Baltimore Pike.

Against Ramseur, Wallace put up a stubborn resistance until Gordon and McCausland arrived from downstream on the Federal left. After his stiff and even gallant display, Wallace wisely retreated north along the river to the Baltimore Pike and then east across Stone Bridge (also called Jug Bridge). Rodes caught up with Wallace after marching southeast through Frederick. In order to take the bridge, Rodes deployed Cox's brigade on the left of the pike and Cook's on the right, while Grimes and Battle kept their brigades in column behind. Once the skirmishers battled their way across, the two lead brigades poured over and scooped up about two hundred Federal prisoners before the remainder of Wallace's force escaped. That night Rodes bivouacked his division along the pike east of the bridge.[30]

Although Early emerged as the clear tactical winner of the brisk Monocacy fight, the engagement delayed by one crucial day his advance on Washington. That delay, however, did not dissuade him from entertaining the breathtaking possibility of seizing the Federal capital. With Gordon in the lead, followed by Rodes and Ramseur, Early set out at sunrise on Sunday, July 10. A grueling twenty-mile march along the Georgetown Pike via Urbana and Gaithersburg carried the Southerners to the outskirts of Rockville. Sustained by a drought that stretched back to June 3, the heat became so oppressive that several men, including many Union prisoners, fell out from heat prostration. The hot and humid night brought little relief.[31]

With Rodes in the lead, followed by Ramseur and Gordon, the final drive for Washington began at 3:30 a.m. on July 11. Early called for a quick pace, hoping this with the early start might beat not only the heat but also the reinforcements he expected would soon file into the capital's defenses. As the morning wore on, however, and the temperature rose to ninety-four degrees, Early reluctantly granted requests to slacken the pace. The column approached Washington from the northwest on the Georgetown Road (now Wisconsin Avenue). Three forts guarded this route near Tannallytown, however, forcing Early to shift east to an easier approach from the north that boasted only one fort.[32]

After turning east at Rockville and crossing upper Rock Creek, Rodes turned his division south onto the Washington and Brookville Turnpike, known in Maryland as Union Road and in the District of Columbia as the Seventh Street Road (now Georgia Avenue). On both sides of the road stood tall, lush fields of ripening corn. About 1:00 p.m. Rodes, riding at the head of his division, reached Sligo Post Office (now Silver Springs) "on the borders of the District of Columbia."[33]

As if to absorb the significance of having arrived on the outskirts of the enemy's capital, Rodes called a halt. Up the road he could see Fort Stevens, and beyond that, the Soldiers' Home. Presently, Early rode up and ordered his division leader to deploy and take the works directly ahead. While Rodes went to work bringing up his brigades, Early sped down the column to inspire the men with the exciting—if nearly impossible—prospect of capturing Abe Lincoln in the White House.

Rodes, however, quickly discovered what Early had yet to realize: the unbearable heat and grueling pace of marching had caused severe straggling, and Rodes' command was hopelessly strung out for miles. Although his skirmish line was but barely formed, the impatient Early ordered Rodes to probe Fort Stevens' defenses.

Gamely, Rodes' tired, sweat-drenched men advanced and drove back the Federal skirmishers that had marched out to meet them. The gray line slowly but steadily moved forward until about 1:30 p.m., when surprising orders arrived from Rodes to break off the advance and pull back. Thick clouds of dust rising to the east of the capital indicated the imminent arrival of massive Federal reinforcements. Risking a battle now, with his divisions strung out across the countryside, was to invite disaster. The consequences of the long day of delay along the Monocacy were now painfully obvious.[34]

Two miles behind Rodes' skirmish line Early established army headquarters at a place called "Silver Spring," the fine estate of Francis Blair (the father of Lincoln's postmaster general Montgomery Blair), who conveniently was away on a fishing trip in Pennsylvania. There, as if to seek reassurance about his decision to call off the attack, Early took the unusual step of convening a council of war. Meeting at the Blair house just after dark, the generals readily agreed that since Rodes probably could have committed no more than 3,000 men by late afternoon, the army commander had made the right choice. The generals also agreed that they needed time to study the city's obviously formidable defenses, which included 643 guns and forty-three mortars in sixty forts spaced 1,000 yards apart across a thirty-seven mile perimeter connected by earthworks. At the hour of Early's approach some 10,000 men manned those defenses, though substantial reinforcements in the form of two divisions from the VI Corps also had arrived. More were on the way. The XIX Corps, called up to Virginia from Louisiana, was diverted by Grant to the Northern capital. Early also knew from newspaper reports that Hunter had returned to the lower Shenandoah after being recalled from Charleston by a worried Lincoln, and now posed a threat to the rear of the

Southern Valley Army. Despite these formidable odds, the Confederate generals meeting in the Blair house agreed that they had come too far, with too much at stake to give up now.

Having resolved in their minds an issue that they believed had placed them on the eve of a momentous date in history, the men relaxed, conversation lightened, and the evening took on the air of a festive occasion. With wine pilfered from the Blair cellar, the officers toasted each other on the pending capture of Washington, former Vice President Breckinridge taking special ribbing over the prospect of returning to his presiding seat at the Senate. Satisfied with the night's proceedings, the generals left their empty bottles and dirty dishes on the dinning room table and retired for the night.[35]

"The men are full of surmises as to our next course of action," Captain Park penned in his diary that night, "and all are eager to enter the city. We can plainly see the dome of the Capitol and other prominent buildings." While lounging about the Blair estate picking blackberries and bathing in Cool Springs, Park and his comrades speculated on how much money they might liberate from the U.S. Treasury.[36]

At dawn on July 12, Rodes and Gordon deployed their men on a two-mile-wide front and sent forward their skirmishers. They waited and waited, but the order to attack never arrived.

Sometime during the night Early received a dispatch from Bradley Johnson, whom Early had sent on a daring but futile attempt to free Confederate prisoners at Point Lookout near Baltimore. From Northern newspapers Johnson learned of the arrival in Washington of two corps (VI and XIX) sent by Grant. Since the Federal ramparts did indeed seem to be packed with enemy soldiers, Early feared that Johnson's report must be true. With his own strength estimated at only 12,570 men (Rodes 3,013, Ramseur 1,909, Gordon 2,544, Breckinridge 2,104, cavalry 3,000), Early wisely concluded that an attack would be very costly. Even if he got into the city, he reasoned, it might be at the expense of his entire army. When presented with these cold facts, Rodes' eager expectations quickly dissolved. "General Rodes," aide Green Peyton later confirmed, "was decidedly of the opinion that it [Washington] could not [be taken]." Early decided to hold his position until evening and then withdraw under cover of darkness.[37]

All through that hot day Rodes and his men watched those ramparts, which continued to fill with Federal soldiers, and even a few civilian observers. "Some of the enemy, seen behind their breastworks," Park remarked in his diary, "were dressed in citizens' clothes, and a few had on linen coats." Though the

Confederates did not know it, for a time those well-dressed citizens observing them included President Lincoln.[38]

As if to break the day-long tension, Daniel Bidwell's 3rd Brigade, 2nd Division, VI Corps, about 1,000 men, sortied out of the fort at 6:00 p.m. and advanced up the Seventh Street Road. When Bidwell's regiments pushed back Rodes' skirmish line, composed of the Thirty-second North Carolina, Rodes threw forward the Forty-third and Forty-fifth North Carolina regiments. After an intense but brief fight in the vicinity of what is now Walter Reed Army Medical Center, the Federals retreated into Fort Stevens with a loss of some 250 men.[39]

With the darkness came preparations to withdraw. Among Rodes' many concerns was the preservation of a Christian code of honor that forbade the breaking of any but one of the Ten Commandments. Forever at war against the evil of plundering, he now made the remarkable gesture of placing in the hands of neighbors for safekeeping several articles of silver and other valuables that "stragglers" had taken from the Blair house and other nearby homes. He became especially upset when he later learned that "Falkland," the Montgomery Blair home, had burned down. Given his long resume of strictness regarding the protection of private property, he refused to believe his men had had anything to do with the destruction of the house. He may have been right. Lieutenant Joshua Lee of the Fifty-third North Carolina later claimed that three times that day he and his men put out fires started in the house by enemy shells. There was more than enough on Rodes' plate that day, however, and investigating the matter was not one of them.[40]

Around midnight, Early began to pull back from the outskirts of Washington. His army had come closer than any other Southern command to the Federal capital. Although he did not secure the great prize, he could take consolation from the fact that he forced Grant to divert large numbers of troops from in front of General Lee's besieged army hugging the trenches in Richmond and Petersburg.

Moving back onto the Georgetown Road, Breckinridge's corps (the divisions of Wharton and Gordon) took the lead in heading northwest toward Rockville, followed by the divisions under Rodes and Ramseur. With much regret, Rodes left behind a field hospital filled with fifty-eight of his wounded and seven sick. Added to his column, however, were hundreds of prisoners and captured cattle, encumbrances that considerably slowed the pace of the division as it marched through the night to reach Rockville about dawn of July 13. Fortunately, the Federals pursued so cautiously that nothing more than a brief

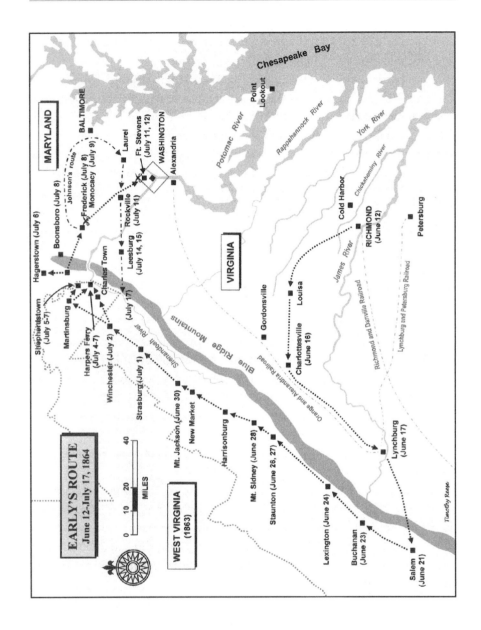

skirmish at Rockville with William Jackson's rearguard brigade of cavalry broke out.[41]

Pushing westward, the tired command reached Seneca about noon, where Early finally allowed the men to rest until dark. Rodes put his division into camp around Darnestown. After sunset the army pushed on through Poolesville to arrive about midnight at White's Ford near Leesburg, where Early halted for the night. At dawn on the 14th, the army waded across the Potomac and camped between it and Leesburg. For the third time in two years Rodes re-crossed the river. And on all three occasions, he did so with a heavy heart after failed expeditions.[42]

*   *   *

Once south of the Potomac River, Early fully expected to return to the Army of Northern Virginia. General Lee, however, decided to keep him in the Shenandoah in an effort to draw off more troops from Grant. His presence also would protect the Valley's precious wheat crop, thought to be the largest in years. To accomplish all this without getting caught by the enemy, Early readily understood that he must keep his little army on the move.[43]

Though the Federals occasionally disturbed the peaceful day by lobbing shells across the river, Early prepared his men for their coming exertions by allowing them to rest in camp through the 15th. The following day, the small army pushed westward through Leesburg and Purcellville to Snicker's Gap. On the 17th it reached the Shenandoah River, where Rodes' division waded across at waist-deep Rock's Ford before marching on westward to within five miles of Berryville.[44]

On that same day, Grant recalled to the Petersburg front the VI and XIX Corps, one day after they had crossed the Potomac at White's Ford. But with Hunter's division, Sigel's division, and William Averell's cavalry, the Union commander forged a new VIII Corps under George Crook. Grant had a special task in mind for Crook and his roughly 9,500 men: track down and defeat the troublesome Early. With unusual vigor for a Federal commander in the Shenandoah, Crook drove ahead in close pursuit. At 3:00 p.m. on the 18th he crossed Snicker's Gap and sent Joseph Thoburn with three brigades to establish a bridgehead across the Shenandoah River at Cool Spring farm.[45]

Early watched the gathering Federal host with deep interest. Thoburn had to be punished and thrown back. Gordon and Wharton set out from Berryville, and Rodes marched from Gaylord. Arriving first on the field, Rodes discovered that Thoburn—a physician before the war described by an admirer as a "rock" on the battlefield—held a good position made up of two lines. The first stretched across the Westwood farm behind a bluff seventy-five yards from the river. The second ran behind a low fence that followed a road on the riverbank. Despite the obvious positional and numerical strength of his enemy, Rodes did something astonishingly out of character. In contrast to past tendencies, he decided not to wait for additional Southern troops to arrive and protect his flanks. Convinced he could crush the enemy before help could arrive, Rodes formed his men on a low ridge. His front was aligned, from right to left as follows: Cox, Grimes (under Colonel William Owens), Cook (under Colonel Philip Pickens), and Battle (under Cook). At 4:00 p.m., Rodes threw his entire division against Thoburn's right.

Thoburn's men, mostly West Virginia veterans, denied Rodes. For two hours they held off the Virginian's repeated attacks. Finally, around 6:00 p.m., Wharton came up on the right and together with Rodes stormed Thoburn's position one final time. The concerted effort broke the stubborn Federal defensive position. The enemy ran for the river, where several drowned in a frantic, confused crossing. Rodes moved up to finish the job, but Federal artillery on the opposite shore forced him to pull back to the cover of the nearby heights. The bold attack cost both sides about four hundred men, but the Southern attack stung the head of the rapid Federal advance. From now on, Crook would keep a more respectful distance from the Valley Army.

After resting undisturbed near Cool Spring through most of the 19th, Rodes pulled out after moon rise in compliance with Early's order for the army to concentrate at Strasburg. After passing through Berryville, Rodes halted to allow his men to cook rations and rest from 2:00 a.m. until dawn.[46]

Near Winchester on July 20, meanwhile, Averell's Federal cavalry got the jump on Ramseur's division, flanked its left, and caused a panic that netted the Federals four guns and 267 men. The loss devastated Ramseur, who until now had known only success and nearly universal acclaim. "I am greatly mortified at the result," he sadly confessed in a letter to his wife, adding ruefully, "My men behaved shamefully." He took great comfort, however, in the prompt and unqualified emotional support given him by Rodes and others. "I have great satisfaction in telling you that none of my superiors blame me," he wrote his wife nearly a month later, the memory of the affair still obviously with him. "I have had the kindest expressions of sympathy & confidence from Genls Early, Rodes, & Gordon!"

Upset at what he perceived was a great injustice to the man he had breathlessly watch lead the gallant charge that helped save the day at the Mule Shoe during the fighting at Spotsylvania in May, a man he had come to know and greatly admire, Rodes took special efforts to defend Ramseur. Rodes wrote Ewell on September 12, for example, to profess his conviction that the disaster was not the fault of Ramseur, but of his panicky troops. "Now sir, this result would not occur one time in a hundred with these same troops under the same circumstances," Rodes averred, "and ought never to have occurred with old troops at all. Ramseur acted most heroically, as usual exposed himself recklessly, but could do nothing with the men; they were under the influence of panic. I do not hesitate to record my belief," added the division leader, "that the cause of the disaster was the conduct of the men." Rodes also told Ewell why Ramseur was still being shamefully tormented in public:

> With their superior opportunities and urged by a natural desire to shirk the responsibility for the disaster, and the less laudable one inspired by their dislike of Ramseur, to throw the blame upon Ramseur, the men and main officers concerned have succeeded in winning public opinion to their side, and have very nearly ruined Ramseur. He of course is perfectly powerless. He degrades himself to a newspaper controversy, or is driven to ask when a suitable time comes, a court of inquiry may be called. In the mean time his reputation is ruined, and he is deprived of his permanent promotion. My statements are, I am aware, in conflict with the popular and general version of the occurrences of that day; but they embody the substance the main facts of the case. I feel it is due Ramseur as my friend, and as an admirable officer that I should make some effort to relieve him at once of the embarrassing situation he finds himself in at Richmond.

Though it is impossible to measure the effect of Rodes' loyal defense, the controversy eventually died down and Ramseur's reputation survived intact.[47]

At dawn on July 20, the same day Averell's troopers struck Ramseur's infantry near Winchester, Rodes put his own foot soldiers back on the road south of Berryville and marched all day to reach Newtown. Beginning at daylight the following morning, his division led the army south to Cedar Creek, and on the 21st reached Fisher's Mill northwest of Strasburg.[48]

Once he learned Grant had recalled the VI and XIX Corps, Early daringly reversed course and set out north on July 24 to attack Crook at Winchester. The Federal commander obligingly came out to meet him on the old Kernstown battlefield. Holding Rodes in reserve, Early sent Gordon in a direct attack along the pike while Wharton moved around to strike Crook's left and Ramseur swept around his right. When the Federals broke and fled in confusion, Early sent Rodes to cut them off at Mrs. Hamilton's farm. Most of the enemy, however, escaped the trap. "It seems impossible to catch a running Yankee," Captain Park scoffed in his diary. "They are as fleet almost as race-horses." The Federals tried several times to rally and make a stand, but Rodes and Gordon kept up the pressure until nightfall. After a heavy morning rain, Early resumed the pursuit at 3:00 p.m. on the 25th by pushing Rodes up to Bunker Hill and the cavalry on to Martinsburg. Crook, however, escaped across the Potomac after suffering losses of about 1,200 men from all causes.[49]

"We drove the Yankees from Kernstown, 4 miles south of Winchester, to a point 5 miles beyond—9 miles in all," Major Blackford proudly wrote his mother. "We only stopped then because human muscle could do no more. We had marched 27 miles—the latter 10 miles almost at a run." Blackford continued, describing the division's march up from reserve to the Hamilton farm and what he witnessed that day:

> To show you the impetuosity of Rodes, tho' he started in rear, having that position in the column that day, he soon joined the front and when the pursuit ended was 3 miles in advance of any other Division. The Yankees forsook all organization, the whole country was one mass of horse foot and artillery. The infantry threw away their arms by thousands. The wagoners cut the teams from their wagons & made off." Then in a letter to his cousin, Blackford added, "It was scarcely safe to pass near the road for many of these wagons were of their Ordnance Train, and contained shell, which were bursting at intervals all night long. We bivouacked within a few hundred yards of one of these, which kept up an incessant fire all night, one fragment striking very near my horse, much to my disgust.[50]

*   *   *

Once again, Early had achieved remarkable results. His energetic handling of his Valley command cleared the enemy from the Shenandoah. Feeling justifiably triumphant, Old Jube concentrated his divisions at Martinsburg on July 26, and for the next two days put the men to work tearing up the tracks of the B&O, "much to the disgust of the good Union people of the town, who showed their feelings by hearty curses upon the heads of our men," gloated Major Blackford. Early also dispatched McCausland's cavalry across the Pennsylvania line to burn Chambersburg, a vengeful act launched in retaliation for David Hunter's depredations in the Valley. To protect McCausland's rear, Early sent Rodes and Ramseur to the Potomac, where on the 29th they threw skirmishers across the river at Williamsport.[51]

While waiting for McCausland to complete his controversial mission, Rodes found time to invite a number of officers to share the bounty of a table a slave servant had set up under the shade of a large oak. This was another of those instances when the general displayed a charming affability that included a willingness to indulge, even during the afternoon, in a bit of social drinking. Apparently little had changed in that regard since serving friends champagne in his tent one hot afternoon near Pensacola more than three years earlier. As far as is known, however, only one officer, Colonel Edward O'Neal of the Twenty-sixth Alabama, believed Rodes imbibed to excess—and he went so far as to accuse Rodes of "drunken debaucheries." O'Neal harbored serious grievances against Rodes for blocking his promotion to brigadier general. Since the colonel apparently is alone in making such accusations, it is fair to assume that he exaggerated the severity of Rodes' indulgences in, and preference for, adult libations.

On the pleasant Saturday afternoon of July 30, Rodes was about to begin serving his grateful guests when up rode the temporary commander of the Forty-third North Carolina, Captain Cary Whitaker. Without dismounting, Whitaker asked Rodes for permission to ride into Winchester and visit a mortally wounded cousin. Rodes denied the captain's request. With the enemy so near, he explained, the regiment might require its commander at a moment's notice. The denial stunned and angered Whitaker. "Gen R was just in the act of mixing and taking a drink no doubt made of the best liquor while the balance of us, that is we poor subordinates and soldiers, can hardly ever see a drop of mean whiskey, even when wounds and sickness require such stimulants," Whitaker resentfully noted in his diary that night. "I sat on my horse at a respectful distance and wished I had a good drink too, but the General didn't think proper to ask me to indulge so I had to forego the pleasure." Despite the refusal and the snub, Whitaker tempered his harsh remarks and hurt feelings by telling his diary that he still considered Rodes an "ideal of a commander." Such was the remarkable effect Rodes had on many of his men.[52]

On July 31, McCausland crossed below the Potomac, his historic mission against Chambersburg a great incendiary success. Early pulled back Rodes and

Ramseur to Winchester. Through the following week, Old Jube freely moved about the lower valley with impunity. On August 4, he dispatched Rodes and Ramseur back up to Williamsport. "[I am] now about to start on my fourth trip across the Potomac," Rodes' ordnance officer, Captain James Garnett, noted in his diary. "Hope 'Old Jubal' knows what he is about." While the cavalry rode yet again to Sharpsburg the following day, Rodes and Ramseur led their men across the Potomac and camped at Claggett's Mill near St. James College, five miles from Funkstown.[53]

General Grant, meanwhile, suffering a difficult summer outside Petersburg and Richmond, decided he had had enough of Early and the 1862 gambit being replayed in the Valley. The Union commander started the VI and XIX Corps back to the Shenandoah. On August 5, Grant combined the Shenandoah's four overlapping jurisdictions into one called the Middle Military Division, and put the entire area into the hands of one of his favorite rising stars: Phillip Sheridan. The blustery cavalry commander of the Army of the Potomac set out with specific instructions to catch and destroy Jubal Early. Eager to accomplish his objective, "Little Phil" arrived in the Valley on August 7. As Early and the Confederates soon would discover, Sheridan bore little resemblance to George Crook.

At his new headquarters at Halltown, four miles southwest of Harpers Ferry, Sheridan assumed command of a motley gathering called the Army of the Shenandoah. His new army eventually swelled to some 35,000 infantry, 8,000 cavalry, and sixty-two guns. Notwithstanding faulty intelligence that put Early's strength at 30,000 men, and Grant's dire warnings about the disastrous political consequences of a serious reverse in the Valley, Sheridan launched his campaign against Early on August 10. At 5:00 p.m. that afternoon, his army arrived at Berryville, ten miles east of Winchester.[54]

Early had in the ranks but 9,000 men to confront these overwhelming odds. His strategy, as related in his memoir, "was to use my forces so as to display them at different points with great rapidity, and thereby keep up the impression that they were much larger than they really were." With the Army of the Shenandoah threatening his rear by concentrating at Halltown, Early pulled Rodes, Ramseur, and Breckinridge back across the Potomac on August 6. When Sheridan advanced to Berryville on the 10th, Early concentrated at Winchester in order to keep the north-south running Opequon River as a barrier between himself and the Federals.[55]

The next day, August 11, Sheridan moved aggressively for the Opequon fords in an effort to cut off Early and block his retreat up the Valley. Early slipped past the move and pulled back to Newtown. With Sheridan in close pursuit, the following day Early marched his men through Strasburg and took up a strong position on Fisher's Hill, a steep bluff overlooking the town. He remained in this position until the 16th, when he received welcome reinforcements sent from Richmond by General Lee ten days before. The infusion of infantry, cavalry, and artillery was comprised of Joseph Kershaw's infantry division, Fitz Lee's cavalry division, and Wilfred Cutshaw's artillery battery, in all about 6,000 men under the overall command of Richard Anderson.[56]

Sheridan completely misinterpreted the situation. Convinced Early had just been reinforced with numbers that swelled his army to 40,000 men, the Union leader began on the 17th to pull back for Halltown, burning barns, hay, and grain as he withdrew.[57] Proving that miscalculations are common in war, Early quickly returned the favor. Judging that Sheridan "possessed an excessive caution which amounted to timidity," Old Jube set out vigorously after the Federal commander. With each of his divisions marching on a different road, Early approached Kernstown that evening.[58]

"My good mother says Rodes' division is in every battle her papers mention," Captain Park told his diary that rainy night, "and that such expressions as 'Rodes bore the brunt of the battle,' 'Rodes began the action,' 'Rodes' command suffered severely in killed and wounded,' 'Rodes' division led the advance,' or 'Rodes conducted the retreat, serving as rear guard,' are constantly in the telegraphic column, and to be found in 'Letters from War Correspondents.'" Obviously proud of what the papers had been saying, whether accurately or not, Park concluded, "It is true that our gallant and beloved Major-General is usually foremost at the post of honor and danger."[59]

While Captain Park was scribbling in his diary, Major Blackford was writing a letter home to his sister. The seemingly incessant marching and countermarching in unbearable heat, he explained, was driving his ragged, unshaven men to exhaustion. "It will be better when the weather becomes cooler," he reassured her, "but the intense heat of the sun, aided by the reflection from the white limestone of which the pikes are made, renders marching almost intolerable." Blackford begged his sister to send newspapers. Without them, he lamented, he and his uninformed men were subject to the wildest rumors about the war in general and their own situation in particular.[60]

On Thursday the 18th, Rodes marched through Winchester, whose citizens, for one final time, offered a warm welcome to the liberating Confederates. He stopped his men a mile or so east of town on the Berryville

Road. Early brought up and concentrated his army around Winchester, and attacked Sheridan three days later on August 21.[61]

Rodes' division led the assault. About 9:00 a.m. that morning, he caught up with Sheridan's rearguard two miles from Charlestown. After losing about 250 men in a tough fight, Sheridan pulled back. The sharp attack cost Rodes about 160 killed and wounded. The action was waged with such intensity that Rodes' ordnance officer, Captain Garnett, estimated that the division "expended about 60,000 rounds of ammunition." The expenditure, he adding disapprovingly, was "very extravagant."[62]

A chastised Sheridan reached his old camps at Halltown on the 22nd and dug in. Early wisely chose not to attack him there, opting instead for yet another crossing of the Potomac. Leaving Anderson to hold the works at Charlestown, Jubal marched up to Shepardstown on the 25th. In a minor skirmish at Leesburg that day, Rodes' friend and aide, Lieutenant James P. Arrington, took a bullet that broke the kneecap and thighbone, a painfully agonizing wound that eventually would kill him.[63]

With most members of his staff Rodes enjoyed a relationship of mutual trust and admiration, even fondness. Whenever one of them fell on the field, he took it hard. Many had fallen during more than three years of war. Philip Sutton left an arm at Seven Pines, where a shell killed Eugene Webster. At Gaines Mill, Daniel Webster fell with a shot in the head. John Berney was shot in the face at Sharpsburg. Spotsylvania took its toll when an enemy bullet struck James Hutchinson in the head and killed him. And now Arrington.

As these personal losses mounted, Rodes became increasingly concerned about one aide in particular: his brother Virginius. Because of delicate health, Virginius had stayed out of the army, serving only intermittently on his brother's staff the past two years as an unpaid voluntary aide, a clerk, and a courier. Hoping to dissuade him from doing even that, Rodes all the while had resisted Virginius's unrelenting pressure to secure for him an officer's commission. For some, probably compassionate, reason Rodes finally gave in. On June 7, 1864, he wrote the War Department and one month later Virginius became a first lieutenant and an official aide-de-camp on his brother's staff. In a letter written nearly forty years after the war, Hortense Rodes remembered to a friend how her husband fretted over his brother and how he tried to keep him out of harm's way. "General Rodes, without telling him why," she explained, "when he knew that a battle was coming on, would use some pretext for sending him to some town—this I've never told & tell you only to explain why I cannot say something about his fighting. Virginius ought not to have been in the army, he was <u>very</u> <u>delicate</u>, but <u>would</u> follow his idol Gen. Rodes."[64]

Whatever personal losses or anxieties Rodes may have suffered during the war, he always remained optimistic, at least outwardly. With Grant and Sherman stymied before their respective objectives of Richmond-Petersburg and Atlanta, Rodes believed an honorable peace was a real possibility. During this latest march to the Potomac, he flatly predicted to Ramseur that an armistice would be signed by the end of the year. To another officer he made the rather surprising confession that his days with Early in the Shenandoah had been the proudest of his military career, and the campaign there "the grandest of the war" considering the lopsided nature of the forces engaged. It was an odd remark. He ranked a campaign still underway above his gallant charge at Seven Pines, his stubborn fight on South Mountain, and his staunch defense of Bloody Lane at Sharpsburg. The Valley marches and fights, he claimed, were more important to him than the great flanking march conducted under the watchful eye of Stonewall Jackson on May 2, 1863—the date Rodes insisted be placed on his major general's commission—the crushing (if disjointed) blows he delivered on the first day at Gettysburg, and his heroic counterattacks at the Mule Shoe at Spotsylvania. Those other bloody campaigns had not brought about peace. Perhaps he measured the significance of Early's Valley operations not only in terms of the forces engaged, but also in the hope that they might, finally, be the last of the war.[65]

On August 26, Early put an end to his Maryland ruse by recalling his extended forces and concentrating them the following day in their old camps around Winchester and Bunker Hill. "Hitherto it has been the regular programme for us to camp at Bunker Hill after the 'taking' of Winchester," Major Blackford wrote his cousin. "This time however we had every prospect of avoiding that hated camp, by our taking the Berryville pike—on which we camped that night. However," he continued, "next morning we came back to the old Valley road & moved on to Bunker Hill & camped in the same old field, in which we have bivouacked 5 times this summer."

In "that hated camp" all remained relatively quiet until the last day of the month, when Early sent Rodes eleven miles up to Martinsburg to chase away William Averell's horsemen. When he arrived, Rodes again called on his favorite command to do the job. "General Rodes," Captain Park told his diary that night, "seems to think his old brigade of Alabamians entitled to the post of honor, and usually sends them to the front in times of danger." Fortunately, Averell's cavalry put spur to horse flesh before any real danger developed.[66]

One of those who made the march to Martinsburg included Sergeant Henry Donnelson of the Third Alabama. Donnelson owned what had become the unofficial regimental mascot, a dog named Colline. The dog went everywhere with the men, even into battle, where incredulous observers often saw her "snap furiously at the bullets as they whizzed by."

"She was brave," Cullen Battle fondly recalled, "never skulked, and always obeyed orders." Having such admirable virtues, the dog attracted many admirers, including Rodes. "Donnelson," he asked of the dog's owner one evening in camp, "where is Colline?" Though Donnelson replied that he did not know, he did not intend to let this opportunity slip away. "General Rodes," he quickly added, "do you know the boys say you and Colline are just alike?"

"No," answered Rodes.

"Well, they do," Donnelson continued. "Every morning Custer, or some other Yankee comes galloping down the road with his cavalry, and you go after them as hard as you can split, and you ain't cotched a single cavalryman yet, and Colline, a dratted fool, every time a train passes shoots out after it, and she ain't cotched narry train yet. You and Colline are just alike."

According to Battle, "Rodes took the jest in the spirit of the occasion and laughed with the rest of us." In a postwar memoir, Battle fondly remembered this incident for the way it revealed an endearing aspect of Rodes' personality. "The General," he explained, "although a strict disciplinarian, was, when off duty, one of the most genial of men."[67]

Sheridan, meanwhile, finally decided on September 1 to begin a cautious advance along the Opequon. By the 3rd he had built an eight- mile line of field works in front of Berryville. The following day Early approached to have a look. After probes by skirmishers determined that the line was too strong to assail, he pulled back on the 5th.[68]

Rainstorms came in on the 6th to drench Rodes' tentless men, a miserable experience made worse the following day by news of the fall of Atlanta, one of the two lynchpins upon which Rodes had attached his hopes for peace. Spirits rose somewhat on the 9th, however, when cash boxes arrived from Richmond carrying several months' pay for the men.[69]

But more than money, the men needed food and clothing. "Our entire army is getting its supplies of bread by cutting and threshing the wheat in the fields," Captain Park told his diary on the 9th, "and then having it ground at the few mills the enemy have not yet destroyed. . . . It shows to what straits we have been reduced. Still the men remain cheerful and hopeful." Two days later Park added, "Nearly all of my company are barefooted, and most of them are almost destitute of pants. Such constant marching on rough, rocky roads, and sleeping on the bare ground, will naturally wear out the best of shoes and the thickest of pants."[70]

On September 10, Rodes again set out to chase away enemy cavalry, this time two miles north at Darkesville. After the enemy fled across the Opequon, Rodes, who still "ain't cotched a single cavalryman yet," returned to Bunker Hill that evening and pitched his tent on the same spot for the ninth time since mid-July.[71]

The next day, however, Early again uprooted him and posted his division at nearby Stephenson's Depot. A vicious rain twenty-four hours later gave Rodes the opportunity finally to respond to Ewell's request for reports on the Wilderness and Spotsylvania battles. "I have not had the time and the courage at the same moment to undertake it," he explained to his former commander, "and in truth our life here is one of such constant motion, and constant separation from baggage, as to make it, together with the constant expectancy of a cavalry fight, which belongs to this division now, even when in camp, that I am unable to concentrate my thoughts upon anything except my immediate military duty. . . . I hope soon, however, to send you the whole budget [all the reports]." Perhaps keeping in mind that Ewell resented not being in command "of such constant motion," Rodes did not elaborate on the current campaign. Instead, from the man he had helped remove from that command, Rodes sought recognition universally craved by members of his species in general and military leaders in particular. "I hope you will not send in yours till mine is before you," he went on, "for I depend upon you alone to get my share of the glory of the actions of the Wilderness, and 12th of May, which have so far reflected glory on all concerned on our side except me. I claim to have been your right-bower on the 12th May, and feel that I did my duty that day fully." Unfortunately for history, Rodes would never write those reports.[72]

Wednesday, September 14, the two-year anniversary of Rodes' stubborn fight on the slope of South Mountain, marked a turning point in Early's Valley Campaign that eventually would lead to disaster for the army in general and for Rodes in particular. On that day the reinforcements sent to Early the month before began the return trip to Lee's lines at Petersburg. Their transfer reduced the Valley Army's strength to a mere 12,500. Early compounded this misfortune by dividing his small command, shifting part of it more than twenty miles up to Martinsburg for the relatively unimportant task of burning a bridge over Back Creek and chasing off repair crews mending the B&O line. Until now

Early had conducted his campaign with consummate skill. Contempt for his enemy and overconfidence in himself finally got the better of him.

Leaving Ramseur on the Berryville Pike two miles east of Winchester, and Breckinridge with Wharton at Stephenson's six miles north of town, Early set out on September 17th with the divisions of Rodes, Gordon, together with William Jackson's brigade of cavalry. The following morning he left Rodes at Bunker Hill and moved on to Martinsburg. After burning the Back Creek bridge but finding no sign of repair crews, Early marched back to Bunker Hill the same day. Leaving Gordon there, he went on with Rodes' division that evening to Stephenson's.[73]

*   *   *

As Early later explained it, throughout the Valley Campaign, "[I tried] to use my forces so as to display them at different points with great rapidity," a remarkably successful strategy thus far. "General Early outgenerals all of us," General Bryan Grimes wrote home in admiration on August 12. "No one can guess when he is going to move, or where he will next bring up. The Yankees begin to think him ubiquitous." Others, however, worried that Early might someday take one chance too many. One of Rodes' brigadiers, William Cox, flatly predicted as much. The next time Early took the risk of separating the

army, Cox explained, Sheridan would attack and crush him in detail. Rodes thought so as well. "I know it," a visibly irritated Rodes responded to Cox. "I have told Early as much. I can't get him to believe it." Now, in the

Brig. Gen. Bryan Grimes. Although Rodes and Grimes had moments of personal turmoil, the pair put their differences behind them before Rodes fell at Winchester.

Generals in Gray

presence of a numerically superior enemy, "General Early had us scattered from Dan to Bersheba," the Third Alabama's Captain W. H. May declared.[74]

Sheridan became aware of his tantalizing opportunity to do just that around midday of the 18th. Just two days before, General Grant directed Sheridan "to move out and whip Early." The chance to do so arrived sooner than Little Phil likely expected. He quickly formulated a plan to strike west from Berryville, drive through Ramseur's position, and cut off Early by getting across his communications with the upper valley.

Sheridan's cavalry, a division under James H. Wilson, started out at 2:00 a.m. on September 19. Wilson had orders to cross the Opequon, pass through two-mile-long Berryville Canyon, sweep aside Ramseur's pickets, and hold a line about two miles west of the Opequon until the arrival of 20,000 infantry from the VI and XIX Corps. The VIII Corps' 8,000 men would remain in reserve east of the river waiting to march southwest and cut off Ramseur's escape. Averell's and Wesley Merritt's cavalry would have the same job to the northwest.[75]

Ramseur had but 2,000 men to confront Sheridan's overwhelming force. His line faced east, straddling the Berryville Pike about two miles east of Winchester. His left was anchored on Red Bud Run and his right on Abraham's Creek, both tributaries of the Opequon.[76]

About 4:30 a.m., Wilson's cavalry reached the Opequon at Spout Spring near the entrance to Berryville Canyon. For some reason, Ramseur made Wilson's job easier by not picketing Spout Spring or barricading the narrow passageway. Wilson rode quickly out of the canyon around 6:00 a.m. and easily pushed aside Jackson's much weaker skirmish line.

After struggling several hours to pass through the canyon, the VI Corps deployed on a wide plateau and attacked the Confederate position. The heavy attack cracked Ramseur's thin line. Faced with another humiliation like at Stephenson's Depot two months before, the North Carolinian bravely rallied his men and withdrew a few hundred yards west to more favorable ground, where Southern resistance stiffened.[77]

While encamped at Stephenson's, his tent pitched in Rodes' bivouac, Early got word about daybreak of the disaster unfolding east of Winchester. He immediately instructed his widely separated army to coalesce. Early ordered Rodes to march as fast as possible to Ramseur's assistance, about six miles distant. To Gordon and Breckinridge word was sent to hurry down fourteen miles from Bunker Hill. With his orders issued, Early rode to join Ramseur, who by now was putting up a stubborn fight.[78]

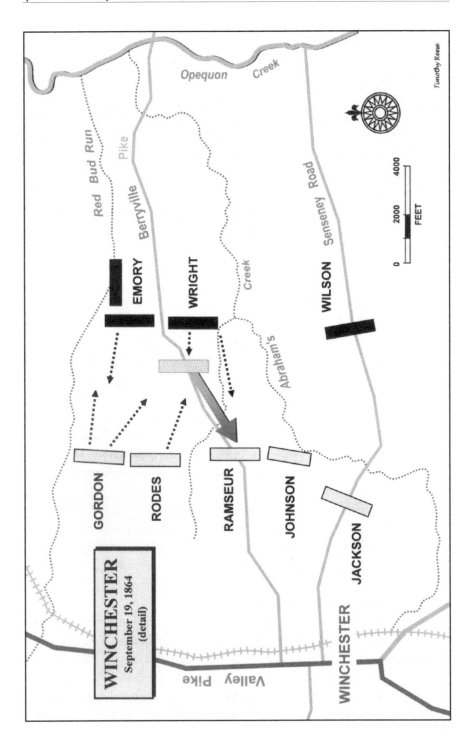

WINCHESTER
September 19, 1864
(detail)

With his usual efficiency, Rodes quickly got his division going. "The health and spirits of the men were good," a North Carolina soldier remembered of the march that Monday morning, "and they were always pleased to be in motion." Allowing nothing to disrupt their momentum, not even the carriage of Gordon's wife thundering by them toward the rear, Rodes brought the men to the field sometime between 9:00 a.m. and 10:00 a.m.[79]

The situation seemed quite clear. Across the field Rodes saw the enemy rapidly deploying for another attack. Through a patch of woods and an open field, he quickly set up his line three to four hundred yards north and west of Ramseur's left flank. Rodes put Grimes on his right, Cox in the center behind a stone wall, Cook on the left, and Battle in reserve behind and beyond Cook's left. After placing a battery on each end of the division line, Rodes sent the division's sharpshooters forward as skirmishers.[80]

Around 10:00 a.m. Gordon arrived and began deploying his men on Rodes' left. Breckinridge, however, did not. Early had diverted the former vice president and his men to deal with Federal cavalry trying to cross the Opequon farther north. An hour later, Early's line ran from Ramseur on the right (straddling the Berryville Pike around the Dinkle farm), through Rodes in the center (slightly behind and to the left of Ramseur), to Gordon on the left extending to Red Bud Run. Cavalry guarded both flanks, with Johnson and Jackson covering the right south of Abraham's Creek and Fitz Lee and one battery on the left north of Red Bud Run.[81]

Though considerably slowed by the bottleneck formed in Berryville Canyon, Sheridan eventually managed to put on the field fourteen brigades in five divisions. They formed into a line that ran from the XIX Corps anchored on Red Bud Run on the right through the VI Corps extending to Abraham's Creek on the left. When satisfied that all was ready, Sheridan set 11:40 a.m. as the time for the attack to begin.[82]

Federal artillery fire blanketed the ground as the infantry moved out under the cover of the barrage. The heaviest blow fell against Gordon, whose men fought desperately and threw back an attack that was joined by Cuvier Grover's Second Division, XIX Corps.

As the enemy recoiled and opened a four-hundred-yard-wide gap in their line, the naturally aggressive Gordon spotted a window of opportunity that offered some hope of success against heavy odds. He was veteran enough to know that if he did not act quickly, his chance would forever pass by. "In the absence of specific orders from the commander-in-chief," he related in his memoirs, "I rode up to Rodes for a hasty conference. A moment's interchange of views brought both of us to the conclusion that the only chance to save our commands was to make an impetuous and simultaneous charge with both divisions, in the hope of creating confusion in Sheridan's line, so that we might withdraw in good order."[83]

It now was about 12:30 p.m. Rodes, sitting astride the magnificent black stallion that had become an inspiring symbol of his leadership, sent his ordnance officer, Captain Garnett, riding to bring up Battle's brigade. "Charge them, boys! Charge them!" Rodes cried out when he saw the Alabamians approach.[84]

With great satisfaction and expectation, the two generals watched as the men set off toward the enemy. Rodes, however, became momentarily distracted from the grand spectacle when the crashing, whizzing sounds of battle triggered an unusual skittishness in his horse.

As he was trying to control his mount, Rodes' head snapped violently forward. A bullet or shell fragment (the record is unclear) had struck him in his skull behind the ear. The general hesitated for a brief moment, then tumbled hard to the ground.[85]

*   *   *

"There are times in battle—and they come often," General Gordon recalled after the war, "when the strain and the quick shifting of events compel the commander to stifle sensibilities and silence the natural promptings of his heart as cherished friends fall all around him. This was one of those occasions. General Rodes was not only a comrade whom I greatly admired, but a friend whom I loved. To ride away without even expressing to him my deep grief was sorely trying to my feelings; but I had to go."[86]

Rodes made not a sound as he lay on the ground, blood oozing from the back of his head. If he was still alive, he probably lived no more than a few minutes as his heartbeat became feeble and his life ebbed away. Sometime around 1:00 p.m. on Monday, September 19, 1864, Robert Emmett Rodes died. He was thirty-five years old.[87]

Stretcher bearers arrived and gently lifted Rodes' corpse onto a stretcher, which they carried to an ambulance waiting on the Martinsburg Pike. Under the command of Rodes' signal officer, Captain Lewis Randolph, the wagon turned and made its way two miles back to Winchester. Randolph oversaw the transfer of the general's body to a private home. News of his arrival spread quickly through town, and soon "A great many ladies were around his body with tears in their eyes," recalled an observer.[88]

"For some months previous to his death," Rodes' friend and aide, Major Green Peyton, wrote after the war, "he wrote much and earnestly to his wife of his soul's salvation, and said that he had a faint hope that God had forgiven him. Amid the package of papers and maps found on his person, were two earnest prayers printed on cards." It seemed appropriate now that a chaplain, Alexander Betts of the Thirtieth North Carolina, should be among the first to visit Rodes in Winchester, where he prayed for his salvation. "It was my fortune to have had the most intimate and confidential relations with him during the greater part of the war," Peyton added. "I shared his blanket and, I believe, his heart. Upright, truthful, just, stern in the discharge of duty and in expecting it of others, but soft and genial in his hours of ease and relaxation, he was universally beloved."[89]

Word of the general's death was suppressed, as far as such a thing was possible, for fear of its disheartening effect. The attack went forward in good order, explained Major Osborne, because the men "did not observe [Rodes' mortal wounding] at that time." The sight of Rodes' black stallion bolting riderless across the field might have alerted some to the tragedy, but the Thirtieth North Carolina's Marcus Herring quickly removed the animal and took it to the rear. Another clue of what had transpired, however, could not be hidden. After driving back the enemy, the men looked in vain for their general to ride among them as he usually did. Nor did they hear his voice encouraging them as they rallied at the edge of a nearby woods to finish the job. The expression on the face of one of Rodes' closest aides revealed to one soldier, at least, the reason for the unusual absence. "Major Peyton, A.A.G. to General Rodes, rode up," Captain Park recalled after the war, "and an indescribable, unexplained something, I know not what, carried to his side as he sat upon his horse. I had heard nothing, not even a rumor nor whispered suggestion, yet something impelled me to ask, in a low tone, 'Major, had General Rodes been killed?' In an equally low, subdued tone, that gallant officer answered, 'Yes, but keep it to yourself; do not let your men know it.' The news distressed and grieved me beyond expression. There was no better officer in the entire army than he. . . . His men regarded him as second only to General Lee, excelled by none other."[90]

Most of Park's comrades did not learn the truth until after they had been defeated and driven from the field by Sheridan's Federals. Despite this disaster and the wound it had inflicted on him, Park, while lying in a Winchester street waiting to be treated, could not help but think of Rodes. He inquired of a helpful lady as to what had become of him. She replied that his body had been sent on to Lynchburg. "Many of my wounded comrades wept loud and bitterly on learning for the first time the fate of their brave and beloved commander," Park remembered. "All seemed overcome with real, unaffected grief."[91]

"When General Ramseur alluded to General Rodes, in speaking to Battle's brigade," Captain Garnett penned in his diary a few days later, "I could not refrain from tears, and there were many other wet eyes."[92]

Though Rodes could not have changed the outcome of the battle of Third Winchester (where his division lost eighty-nine men killed and 597 wounded), many of his soldiers were convinced that his untimely demise led to the disaster. "But for his death," artilleryman Thomas Carter declared thirty years later, "I shall forever believe Sheridan would have been defeated that day." North Carolinian Thomas J. Watkins wrote on the very day of the battle that "it would seem that the death of Genl Rhodes [sic] was a calamity never repaired on this field, [we] felt the great loss sustained to day, by Early's forces not having his wisdom to guide them. Such is war."[93]

When staff officers that afternoon finally secured a coffin for their slain commander, they removed his body from the house in Winchester and placed it in an ambulance for the first leg of the journey to Lynchburg. Getting out of Winchester, however, proved difficult. "I found everything coming through town in the greatest confusion," recalled Captain Garnett. "Market street was filled with medical and ordnance wagons and ambulances three deep. I met the ambulance with General Rodes' body." After struggling through these crowded streets, the ambulance set off on the road south.[94]

The following day at Rude's Hill near New Market, the wagon crossed paths with Major Hotchkiss, who was on his way to rejoin the army after having been home in Staunton since the 13th. Having just learned of Rodes' death, the mapmaker stopped to pay his respects. "A severe loss," he recorded in his diary, "his men along the road lamenting it deeply." In a letter to his wife, Hotchkiss added, "We have never suffered a greater loss save in the Great Jackson. Rodes was the best Division Commander in the Army of N. Va. & was worthy of & capable for any position in it." Presumably Hotchkiss considered Rodes qualified not only for corps command, but also command of the entire army, a rather remarkable statement.[95]

Cullen Battle echoed Hotchkiss' sentiments when he wrote in his memoir that Rodes' death "shook the whole corps," and that "the whole army mourned his death. No single death—save that of Jackson, caused such deep regret and bitter sorrow."[96]

On the evening of Tuesday the 20th, the wagon bearing Rodes' body rumbled into Staunton. Early the following day mourners put his remains on the Virginia Central for the thirty-five-mile ride to Charlottesville. Hortense, five months pregnant with Belle, and seventeen-year-old Lucy Rodes stood on the platform as the train pulled into the depot. They accompanied the coffin to a hotel in the center of town, where it remained on display from 10:00 a.m. until 3:00 p.m. A family friend, Mrs. Kate McKinnie, placed on it a beautiful wreath made of evergreen branches, white roses, and rose buds. Because the newspapers mistakenly reported that the body would not arrive until the following day, few people attended the ceremony.

"I know how to feel for his poor widow," wrote another family friend in Charlottesville, Mrs. Francis Pollard. "She has been so kind & feeling to me and mine, that I can't help from feeling more than ordinary interest in her. She expects in the course of a few weeks to return to her parents in Tuscaloosa. I've seldom seen a more attractive woman & [I] liked him particularly."[97]

After the sparsely attended viewing, staff officers, accompanied by Hortense and Lucy took the coffin to the depot of the Orange & Alexandria and put it on a train for the final, sixty-mile leg to Lynchburg. Upon pulling into town that evening, they were met at the depot by "the Ambulance Corps and a number of personal friends." The coffin was placed in an ambulance and taken up to Rodes' boyhood home on Harrison Street, where it remained through the following day while scores of visitors came by to pay their respects. The funeral was set for Friday the 23rd.[98]

"To the Citizens of Lynchburg," proclaimed the Lynchburg *Virginian* that morning. "Our city has lost one of its noblest and patriotic sons, Major Gen'l Robert E. Rodes, whom we all honored and respected whilst living. He is now dead; let us show the respect which is due to his memory by the suspension of all business during his funeral obsequies."[99]

Down on Main Street near the river, the huge funeral procession formed up early that morning. "Never was there a larger turnout or a more impressive demonstration," declared the *Virginian*. Chief marshals and staff led, followed by a military escort, Masonic members and then the hearse with pall bearers. Following the horse-drawn hearse came Hortense and a number of other family members, then the clergy and officers of the navy and marine corps. Next in line were a number of Confederate officers, cadets, and soldiers, followed by the ambulance corps, judges of the Court of Appeals and circuit courts, then the mayor, aldermen, and other city officials and the city council. Officers and employees of the Northeast and Southwest Alabama Railroad were next in line, with hundreds of citizens on foot, in carriages, and on horseback, bringing up the rear. From Main the long procession made the difficult, steep climb up Federal Hill to the Rodes house on Harrison Street. "Here the body of the lamented hero was taken in charge," reported the *Virginian*. Then the multitude made the long trek back down the hill to the Presbyterian Cemetery on the edge of town. At the grave site, located in front of the resting sites of Rodes' parents and grandparents just beyond the cemetery gate, Reverend James Ramsey presided over a very moving and solemn service. A Masonic ceremony followed, after which the body was lowered into the ground.[100]

"He has gone down to the grave," declared the *Virginian*, "but his memory and service will not be forgotten by a grateful country."[101]

T he circumstances of Rodes' death immediately gave rise to an enduring controversy. Many of his soldiers firmly maintained a lifelong conviction that the untimely loss of their division commander deprived them of victory at Third Winchester. Other, more rational observes, usually officers of higher rank, knew better. Despite the tremendous value Rodes provided on virtually every battlefield he stepped foot on, his presence could not have held back Phil Sheridan's overwhelming numbers on September 19, 1864. Everyone agreed, however, that the Virginian's death was a tragic loss for the army and for the Confederacy. Many, including civilians, believed the blow to the South was second only to the loss of the "Great Jackson."[1]

Later that same afternoon after Rodes fell, Sheridan advanced George Crook's III Corps, which moved beyond Early's exposed left flank. About 3:00 p.m., Crook's men, supported by a pair of Union cavalry divisions, fell upon the vulnerable Southern line. Early's men tried to defend their positions, but were outnumbered and outgunned and unable to stand. The legendary Second Corps was, for the first time, driven from a battlefield in full flight. After the disastrous defeat at Third Winchester, the command of Rodes' division went to his staunch friend and capable commander, Stephen Ramseur. Within one month Ramseur would be killed at Cedar Creek.

A few days later, a committee of officers led by the new division commander, Phillip Cook, drew up a "Tribute to the Memory of Maj.- Generals Rodes and Ramseur." It contained five "Resolutions" attesting to the great sorrow of the men and officers of the division at the tragic double loss of their "beloved," "brave," and "gallant" commanders. The committee sought permission from General Early for the division to set aside Tuesday, November

1, as a day of observance, complete with religious services and the suspension of military duties. Early readily agreed and endorsed the "Tribute" with lavish praise for the two fallen generals.[2]

Though the general's men grieved at his loss, no one suffered more than Hortense Rodes. A widow at thirty-one, with a one-year-old boy and another child due in a few months, she now faced the terrifying prospect of what to do with her life. She lost no time in reaching a decision. Before her husband's body arrived in Charlottesville, Virginia, on its journey to Lynchburg, she decided to return home to Tuscaloosa.[3] There, on January 11, 1865, she gave birth to Belle Yancey Rodes. Hortense quietly lived out her life in Alabama, where she raised her two children. She never remarried and rarely received public attention. In 1866, she signed a petition to have President Johnson release ex-Confederate President Davis from prison.[4]

Hortense's father died in 1876, and her mother eight years later. By that time, 1884, twenty-one-year-old Robert Jr. was able to support her. Nineteen-year-old Belle married that year and moved to Savannah, Georgia, where she would give birth to five children.[5]

Like the father of whom he had no memory, Robert Jr. became an engineer, working mostly for the city of Tuscaloosa. He also served for a time as city alderman. He finally married in 1896, a union that produced eight children. The family lived with Hortense in the Woodruff house, valued at $1,000 in the Tuscaloosa County tax assessment of 1894.[6]

When the Alabama Division of the United Daughters of the Confederacy formed the Robert Rodes Chapter in Tuscaloosa, it seemed only fitting that Hortense should be its first president. She served from May to November 1896, and ten years later she became an Honorary Lifetime President.[7]

Hortense Rodes died in Tuscaloosa in 1907 at the age of seventy- four. She is buried near her parents in Greenwood Cemetery on the edge of town.[8] She was not laid to rest next to her husband in Lynchburg, Virginia, because Robert's brother had taken that spot many years before. After the war, Virginius returned to his farm in LeFlore County, Mississippi, where he died, alone in 1879 at only fifty-five years old. Apparently, at his own request, he was brought to Lynchburg and buried in the Presbyterian Cemetery next to the younger brother he had so idolized in life.[9]

That same year, the home in which the two boys had grown up on Harrison Street atop Federal Hill in Lynchburg was sold after being in the Rodes family since 1833. A cousin, David Rodes (the son of uncle Robert) sold it for $2,900 to a family that kept it well into the 1940s. The ensuing decades, however, have not been kind to the once-magnificent structure. Though still privately owned, it is unoccupied because of its decrepit condition.[10]

According to the Greek storyteller Herodotus, when Xerxes, the mighty King of Persia, stood atop a hill to view the magnificent million-man host he had assembled for the conquest of Greece, he was moved to tears by the thought that one hundred years hence all those men would be dead and forgotten. And so it is with all of us. But whereas we inevitably must die, a few, a very select few, make such an impact upon their times that the memory of them continues to reverberate through the years, the centuries, and even the millennia.

Like the home he had known as a boy, the memory of Robert Rodes passes from generation to generation, always changing along the way. Hopefully, long after the old family house has fallen into dust, the reverberations of Rodes' impact will remain as strong as ever.

Robert Emmett Rodes IV, the general's great grandson,
proudly holds his ancestor's sword.

Mary Rodes Dell, and the Rodes Family

Introduction

1. Willis Brewer, *Alabama, Her History, Resources, War Record, and Public Men* (Montgomery, AL.: Barrett & Brown, Steam Printers and Book Binders, 1872), 568; Jedediah Hotchkiss to wife, September 20, 1864, Jedediah Hotchkiss Papers, Library of Congress, Washington, D.C.

2. Thomas M. Owen, ed., *Report of the Alabama History Commission to the Governor* (Montgomery: Brown, 1901), 184.

3. Brewer, *Alabama*, 458; Charles D. Walker, *Memorial, Virginia Military Institute* (Philadelphia: J.B. Lippincott, 1875), 457; Preston L. Ledford, *Reminiscences of the Civil War, 1861-1865* (Thomasville, N.C.: News Printing House, 1909), 79.

Chapter One

1. Howard J. Rhodes, comp., *The Rhodes Family in America* (New York: Greenwich Book Publishers, 1959), 18-19, 393; Joseph Hunter, comp., "The Rodes Family," *The Virginia Magazine of History and Biography*, vol. vii (June 1900): 188-191; W. Paul Treanor, great-grandson of Robert Rodes, papers regarding Rodes genealogy, Robert Rodes file, Archives of the Virginia Military Institute, Lexington, Va. (all references to these archives hereafter cited as VMI Archives); unp. letter of Jennie H. Fletcher, Blackwell-Rodes file, Manuscript Dept., Alderman Library, University of Virginia, Charlottesville, Va.

2. The other cooler head being John Coles. Edgar Woods, *History of Albemarle* (Charlottesville: Michie Co. Printers, 1900), 306; W. Paul Treanor unp. papers regarding Rodes genealogy, Robert Rodes file, VMI Archives; "A List of Taxable Articles Taken by Magistrates appointed April 10th 1782, Together with the Amount of Tax Thereon," *Magazine of Albemarle County History*, vol. 5 (1944-45): 61.

3. Hunter, "The Rodes Family," 203-204; Woods, *History of Albemarle*, 306; W. Paul Treanor unp. papers, Robert Rodes file, VMI Archives.

4. *Ibid.*

5. V. W. Southall, sheriff, to David Rodes, May 2, 1822, Matthew Rodes will, Sept. 30, 1833, both from David Rodes Collection, Handley Regional Library, Winchester-Frederick County Historical Society, Winchester, Va. (all references to this source hereafter cited as David Rodes Coll.).

6. Various letters exchanged over a number of years between David and his brother Robert Rodes, David Rodes Coll.

7. W. Paul Treanor unp. papers, Robert Rodes file, VMI Archives.

8. While building up and running his own plantation, Joel Yancey also served as the chief overseer of Jefferson's nearby second home, "Poplar Forest" (1815 to 1821). Rosa Faulkner Yancey, *Lynchburg and Its Neighbors* (Richmond, Va.: J.W. Ferguson, 1935), 29, 99, 269, 440-442; Lynchburg *Virginian*, Nov. 29, 1822; Rothsay destroyed by fire in 1912—W. Paul Treanor unp. paper in Robert Rodes file, VMI Archives.

9. Rhodes, *Rhodes Family*, 393; Deed Book P and will of David Rodes, Lynchburg Circuit Courthouse, Lynchburg, Va.; Edward Burton to David Rodes, March 3, 1838 (describes trip to Richmond, Phila., & N.Y), Burton to Rodes, March 11, 1839 ("how are improvements in our store going, will they be completed by the time new goods arrive?"), Anthony M. Duprey to David Rodes, Feb. 12, 1839 (regarding store competition in Martinsburg), all from David Rodes Coll.; W. Paul Treanor unp. papers, Robert Rodes file, VMI Archives.

10. On March 8, 1825, Capt. David Rodes of 2nd Bn., 53 Va. Reg., issued battalion orders for muster and drill later that month, and later that year he issued regimental orders. David Rodes Coll.; Yancey, *Lynchburg and Its Neighbors*, 402; Christian W. Asbury, *Lynchburg and Its People* (Lynchburg, Va.: J.P. Bell Company, 1900), 84-86. The three other men appointed with David Rodes to assess Jefferson's estate were Archibald Robinson, William Gough and Henry Langhorne. R.H. Early, *Campbell Chronicles and Family Sketches* (Lynchburg, Va.: J.P. Bell, 1927), 276.

11. Asbury, *Lynchburg and Its People*, 92-96.

12. Thomas M. Owen, *History of Alabama*, 4 vols. (Chicago: S.J. Clark Pub. Co., 1921), vol. 4, 1456; Presbyterian Cemetery, Lynchburg, Va.; Yancey, *Lynchburg and Its Neighbors*, 99.

13. Allen S. Chambers, *Lynchburg: An Architectural History* (Charlottesville, Va.: University of Virginia Press, 1981), 54; James K. Swisher, *Warrior In Gray: General Robert E. Rodes of Lee's Army* (Shippensburg, Pa.: White Mane, 2000), 3; Frances Robertson unp. paper, "The Rodes Family," Jones Memorial Library, Lynchburg, Va. According to Robertson, in 1879 David Rodes (son of Lafayette) sold the house for $2,900 to Mr. & Mrs. Fernando C. Wood, who owned it until 1941.

14. Swisher, *Warrior in Gray*, 4.

15. *Ibid.*, p. 108; opera invitation in David Rodes Coll.

16. Yancey, *Lynchburg and Its Neighbors*, 61; Dorothy T. Potter and Clifton W. Potter, *Lynchburg: The Most Interesting Spot* (Lynchburg, Va.: Progress Printing Corp., 1976), 51; Phillip L. Scruggs, *The History of Lynchburg, Virginia, 1786-1946* (Lynchburg, Va.: J.P. Bell, 1972), 81.

17. David Rodes to Martha Rodes, May 4, 1833, David Rodes Coll.

18. Joel Yancey to Martha Rodes, April 2, 1837, David Rodes Coll.

19. Membership notice in David Rodes Coll.; Christian, *Lynchburg and Its People*, 123, 167; David Rodes to Francis Smith, May 23, 1848, VMI Archives.

20. Deed Books, Lynchburg Circuit Courthouse, Lynchburg, Va.; 1860 Federal Census of Campbell Co., Slave Schedule, lists David as the owner of two males, ages 55 and 5, four females, ages 70, 50, 45, and 15, and one mulatto female, age 10.

21. Virginius Rodes to David Rodes, Aug. 14, 1841, David Rodes Coll.; Chambers, *Lynchburg*, 54-55.

22. Unable to handle the rigors of the institution, young Burton dropped out of the academy in 1828. The first person the humiliated youth wrote to for comfort was not his father, but David Rodes, to whom he touchingly apologized. Robert Burton to David Rodes, no day or month, 1828, David Rodes Coll. Burton wrote, "You took an active part in procuring my appointment," and, "You got me my appointment."

23. Virginius Rodes file, VMI Archives; Virginius Rodes to David Rodes, Jan. 25, 1842, David Rodes Coll.

24. Jennings C. Wise, *The Military History of the Virginia Military Institute from 1839-1865* (Lynchburg, Va.: J.P. Bell Company, 1915), 24, 30, 32-34; Thomas M. Boyd in *Southern Bivouac*, 2 (1885-1886): 212-214; William Couper, *One Hundred Years at VMI* (Richmond: Garrett and Massie, 1939), vol. 1, 5.

25. Couper, *One Hundred Years*, vol. 1, 8, 169; Swisher, *Warrior in Gray*, 6.

26. Couper, *One Hundred Years*, vol. 1, 60-62.

27. VMI Curriculum Guide, 1848, VMI Archives; James I. Robertson Jr., *Stonewall Jackson: The Man, the Soldier, the Legend* (New York: Macmillan Library Reference, 1997), 111-114; Couper, *One Hundred Years*, vol. 1, 62.

28. Virginius Rodes to David Rodes, May 8, 1841, David Rodes Coll.

29. Joel Yancey to Martha Rodes, Oct. 1837, and Cousin Mary to Martha Rodes, July 31, 1841, David Rodes Coll.

30. Virginius Rodes to David Rodes, Aug. 14, 1841, David Rodes Coll.

31. Virginius Rodes to David Rodes, Jan. 20, 1842, David Rodes Coll.

32. Walter Coles to David Rodes, Feb. 5, 1842, David Rodes Coll.

33. Virginius Rodes file, VMI Archives; Presbyterian Cemetery, Lynchburg, Va.

34. Virginius Rodes file, VMI Archives; Virginius Rodes to David Rodes, Aug. 1847, David Rodes Coll.

35. Couper, *One Hundred Years*, vol. 1, 31, 68, 167, 188, 232.

36. VMI Class Standings, 1846, VMI Archives; Thomas H. Carter, "Remarks on the Presentation of a Portrait of Gen. Robert Rodes to Lee Camp, Sons of Confederate Veterans," VMI Archives; Swisher, *Warrior in Gray*, 8.

37. VMI Class Standings, 1846; Robert Rodes file, Francis Smith to David Rodes, Feb. 11, 1847, both from VMI Archives; Couper, *One Hundred Years*, vol. 1, 35.

38. John S. Wise, *The End of an Era* (Boston: Houghton, Mifflin and Company, 1899), 245-246; Edwin L. Dooley Jr., "Gilt Buttons and the Collegiate Way: Francis H. Smith as Antebellum Schoolmaster." *Virginia Cavalcade,* 36 (1986): 30-39.

39. VMI Class Standings, 1847, VMI Archives; Couper, *One Hundred Years*, vol. 1, 167.

40. Couper, *One Hundred Years*, vol. 1, 168-168, 233.

41. *Ibid.*, 167-169.

42. VMI Class Standings, 1848, VMI Archives.

43. *The Virginia Magazine of History and Biography,* "The Rodes Family," vol. vii, 82-87, 203-205; Swisher, *Warrior in Gray*, 5; Presbyterian Cemetery, Lynchburg, Va.; W. Paul Treanor unp. papers, Robert Rodes file, VMI Archives.

44. Robert Rodes file, David Rodes to Francis Smith, May 23, 1848, VMI Archives.

45. Francis Smith to David Rodes, Feb. 22, 1848, VMI Archives.

46. Francis Smith to Thomas S. Bocock, Feb. 22, 1848, David Rodes Coll.

47. Robert Yancey to Thomas Bocock, Feb. 28, 1848, David Rodes Coll.

48. Unsigned letter from Richmond, Va., to David Rodes, March 20, 1848; Robert Yancey to David Rodes, May 28, 1848; five years later Yancey had a slight change of heart about Robert's chances for survival in Missouri. On April 27, 1853, he wrote David, "If Robert should be out of employment, both Engineers and Surveyors are in demand here, and as are teachers, preachers, doctors and blacksmiths, in short it is hard saying what is not wanted here, but long practice has enabled us to [survive] upon what you Virginians would perrish on." All of the above from the David Rodes Coll.

49. Robert Rodes file, David Rodes to Francis Smith, May 28, 1848, VMI Archives.

50. Francis Smith Order #42 and Order #43, VMI Archives.

51. Couper, *One Hundred Years*, vol. 1, 232.

52. *Ibid.*, vol. 1, 182-187.

53. *Ibid.*, 189.

54. Richmond *Whig and Public Advertiser*, Dec. 19, 1848, the notice read: "MARRIED. At Lexington, Va. on the 12th inst. by the Rev'd R. Nelson Lieut. R.E. Rodes of Lynchburg to Miss Mary Jones of Lexington"; Richmond *Examiner,* Dec. 22, 1848; The Rockingham *Register*, p. 2, col. 5, Oct. 13, 1849.

55. Couper, *One Hundred Years*, vol. 1, 223.

56. Francis Smith to Robert Rodes, Sept. 24, 1850, VMI Archives; Swisher, *Warrior in Gray*, 9.

57. Couper, *One Hundred Years*, vol. 1, 214.

58. *Ibid.*, vol. 1, 215-221.

59. *Ibid.*, vol. 1, 229; Wise, *Military History*, 63.

60. Couper, *One Hundred Years*, vol. 1, 230.

61. Robert Rodes to David Rodes, May 21, 1850, David Rodes Coll.

62. *Ibid.*

63. *Ibid.*

64. 1850 Federal Census, Campbell Co., VA.

65. Wise, *Military History*, 63-64; Couper, *One Hundred Years*, vol. 1, 247-248.

66. Couper, *One Hundred Years*, vol. 1, 248.

67. Robert Rodes to Francis Smith, Sept. 23, 1850, VMI Archives.

68. Francis Smith to Robert Rodes, Sept. 24, 1850, VMI Archives.

69. Couper, *One Hundred Years*, vol. 1, 248-249.

70. Wise, *Military History*, 68-69; Couper, *One Hundred Years*, vol. 1, 249-251.

Chapter Two

1. Elizabeth Dabney Coleman and W. Edwin Hemphill, "Boats Beyond the Blue Ridge," *Virginia Cavalcade*, vol. iii, no. 4 (Spring 1954): 8-9.

2. *Ibid.*; Swisher, *Warrior in Gray*, 10-11.

3. Swisher, *Warrior in Gray*, 12; Coleman, "Boats Beyond the Blue Ridge," 10. By 1857, only eight miles of the canal had been completed. It ceased operating in 1881, having never done well financially.

4. Robert Rodes to David Rodes, Jan. 3, 1851, David Rodes Coll.

5. *Ibid.*

6. *Ibid.*

7. *Ibid.*; Southside Railroad Company Record Book 64.1, University Libraries-Special Collections Department, Virginia Tech, Blacksburg, Va. (this source hereafter cited as SSRR Co. Records).

8. SSRR Co. Records.

9. *Ibid.*

10. *Ibid.*; Robert Rodes to David Rodes, Jan. 3 and Dec. 7, 1851, David Rodes Coll.

11. Robert Rodes to David Rodes, Jan. 3, 1851, David Rodes Coll.

12. Peyton Randolph to his sister, May 25 and July 31, 1860, John T. Harris Papers, SC #2025, Special Collections, Carrier Library, James Madison University, Harrisonburg, Va. (this source hereafter cited as Harris Papers).

13. Robert Rodes to David Rodes, Nov. 17, 1851, David Rodes Coll.

14. Robert Rodes to David Rodes, Nov. 17 and Dec. 7, 1851, David Rodes Coll.

15. Robert Rodes to David Rodes, Dec. 7, 1851, David Rodes Coll.; William Foster to Robert Rodes, May 6, 1858, Records of the Northeast & Southwest Alabama Railroad Co., Robert Jemison Papers, W. Stanley Hoole Special Collections Library, University of Alabama, Tuscaloosa, Alabama (this source hereafter cited as Jemison Papers).

16. Report of Chief Engineer Charles O. Sanford, Nov. 12, 1851, SSRR Co. Records.

17. *Ibid.*; Report of Chief Engineer Charles O. Sanford, Oct. 18, 1852, SSRR Co. Records.

18. Robert Rodes to David Rodes, June 15, 1852, and C. P. McKinnie to David Rodes, June 25, 1852, David Rodes Coll.

19. C. P. McKinnie to David Rodes, June 25, 1852, David Rodes Coll.

20. Robert Rodes to David Rodes, June 5, 1852, David Rodes Coll.

21. *Ibid.*; "The Rodes Family," *The Virginia Magazine of History and Biography,* vol. vii, 205.

22. C. P. McKinnie to David Rodes, June 25, 1852, David Rodes Coll.; "The Rodes Family," *The Virginia Magazine of History and Biography,* vol. vii, 205. In November 1856, Sally married William James Nelson, for whom she bore twelve children.

23. David Rodes will, on file at the District Courthouse, Lynchburg, Va.; Robert Rodes to brother David Rodes, March 7, 1849, April 4, 1850, among others, David Rodes Coll.; 1860 Federal Census, Campbell Co., Va.

24. Report of Chief Engineer Charles O. Sanford, Oct. 18, 1852, and Report of President Pannill, Oct. 20, 1852, SSRR Co. Records.

25. *Ibid.*; Report of Chief Engineer Charles O. Sanford, Oct. 18, 1853, Report of President Pannill, Oct. 19, 1853, and Committee Report, Oct. 1853, SSRR Co. Records.

26. Robert Rodes to Alfred Rives, Sept. 24, 1854, Rives Family Papers, Virginia Historical Society, Richmond, Va. (this source hereafter cited as Rives Family Papers).

27. *Ibid.*; Stewart Sifakis, *Who Was Who in the Civil War* (New York: Facts on File Publications, 1988), 546.

28. *Who Was Who,* 546.

29. Charles D. Walker, *Memorial, Virginia Military Institute* (Philadelphia, J.B. Lippincott, 1875), 440-441. If the company had been as successful as he had hoped and expected, it is conceivable that Rodes might have entered the coming war as a member of a Texas regiment.

30. Swisher, *Warrior in Gray,* 13

31. Wayne Cline, *Alabama Railroads* (Tuscaloosa, Al.: The University of Alabama Press, 1997), 38-39; James Harold Carter, *History of the North East and South West Alabama Railroad to 1872,* Master's Thesis, University of Alabama, 1949, 8-10.

32. Report of Chief Engineer Edward D. Sanford, July 5, 1855, Jemison Papers.

33. Carter, *History of the North East and South West Alabama Railroad*, 10; Matthew William Clinton, *Tuscaloosa, Alabama: Its Early Days, 1816-1865* (Tuscaloosa: The Zonta club, 1958), 1-10; G. Ward Hubbs, *Tuscaloosa: Portrait of an Alabama County* (Northridge, CA.: Windsor Publications, 1987), 11-12, 21; Marilyn D. Barefiled, comp., *Old Tuscaloosa Land Office and Military Records, 1821-1855* (Easley, S.C.: Southern Historical Press, 1984), xvi.

34. Pauline Jones Gandrud, comp., *Marriage, Death and Legal Notices From Early Alabama Newspapers, 1819-1893* (Easley, S.C.: Southern Historical Press, 1981), 200; DAR application of Louise Rodes Schoch, Rodes file, VMI Archives; Clinton, *Tuscaloosa*, 95; Owen E. Adams, *Confederate Major General Robert E. Rodes: A Civil War Biography*, Master's Thesis (The University of Southern Mississippi, 1995), 20-25 (cited hereafter as Adams thesis). The 1640 Woodruff homestead remained a prominent landmark in the community for many years until it was destroyed by fire.

35. Robert Rodes to Francis Smith, Aug. 28, 1857, VMI Archives; Adams thesis, 20-25.

36. Report of Chief Engineer Edward D. Sanford, Jan. 15, 1857, Jemison Papers.

37. *Second Annual Report of the President and Directors to the Stockholders of the Western North Carolina Rail Road Company* (Salisbury, N.C., 1856), 2-24.

38. *Ibid.*

39. Robert Rodes to Francis Smith, Oct. 18, 1856, VMI Archives.

40. Cline, 39; Carter, *History of the North East and South West Alabama Railroad*, 13.

41. Robert Rodes to Francis Smith, Oct. 8, 1856, VMI Archives.

42. Robert Rodes to Francis Smith, Nov. 27, 1856, VMI Archives.

43. Francis Smith to Robert Rodes, Dec. 6, 1856, VMI Archives.

44. Francis Smith to Robert Rodes, Oct. 17, 1856, and Robert Rodes to Francis Smith, Nov. 27, 1856, VMI Archives.

45. Robert Rodes to Francis Smith, Nov. 27, 1856, VMI Archives.

46. Adams thesis, 20-25.

47. Francis Smith to Robert Rodes, Nov. 3, Dec. 6, Dec. 9, 1856, and Robert Rodes to Francis Smith, Aug. 28, 1857, VMI Archives.

48. Robert Rodes to Francis Smith, Aug. 28, 1857, VMI Archives.

49. *Ibid.*

50. *Ibid.*

51. *Ibid.*

52. *Ibid.*

53. *Ibid.*; Marriage Warrant on file at Tuscaloosa Co. Courthouse, Tuscaloosa, Al.

54. Peyton Randolph to Robert Rodes, Sept. 6, 1857, Jemison Papers.

55. Peyton Randolph to Mother, June 7, 1857, Harris Papers.

56. Peyton Randolph to Robert Rodes, Dec. 12, Dec. 22, 1857, Jemison Papers.

57. Charles Derby to Mary [Stancell], Jan. 20, 1858, Charles Derby file, VMI Archives.

58. Robert Rodes to Francis Smith, Aug. 28, 1857, VMI Archives.

59. Tuscaloosa *Independent Monitor,* Jan. 28, 1858, ADAH.

60. Letterbook 1857-60, Executive Committee Meeting Resolutions, NE & SW RR, Box 3570, Jemison Papers; Robert Rodes to Francis Smith, Jan. 2, 1859, VMI Archives.

61. James Corry to Robert Rodes, May 25, June 19, Dec. 6, 1858, Jemison Papers.

62. The trip to New York is alluded to in Rodes' annual report, delivered on October 11, 1858, to the NE & SW Alabama Board of Directors, Jemison Papers. It also is referred to in Peyton Randolph's August 7, 1858, letter to his sister "Nannie," wherein he complains that, "I am constantly interrupted by the Contractors coming in and as the Chief Engineer [Rodes] has gone on a trip to the North I have to attend to his Correspondence and do the talking with the folks that come in." Harris Papers.

63. James Corry to Robert Rodes, July 24, Sept. 21, 1858, Jemison Papers.

64. James Corry to Robert Rodes, Oct. 11, 1858, and William Foster to Robert Rodes, Oct. 15, 1858, Jemison Papers.

65. James Corry to Robert Rodes, Dec. 6, Dec. 20, 1859, Jan. 23, 1860, Peyton Randolph to Robert Rodes, Dec. 8, 1859, George W. Robertson to Robert Rodes, Aug. 3, 1859, Jemison Papers.

66. Francis Smith to Robert Rodes, Sept. 30, 1859, and Robert Rodes to Francis Smith, Oct. 8, 1859, VMI Archives.

67. *Ibid.*

68. Report of Chief Engineer Robert Rodes, Oct. 11, 1858, Jemison Papers.

69. Robert Rodes to Francis Smith, Jan. 2, 1859, VMI Archives.

70. Peyton Randolph to "Dear Nannie," August 7, 1858, Harris papers.

71. Peyton Randolph to friend, Jan. 9, Feb. 8, 1859, Jemison Papers.

72. Records of NE & SW RR Co., and Robert Rodes to George W. Robertson, Aug. 3, 1859, Jemison Papers.

73. Records of NE & SW RR Co., Jemsion Papers.

74. Peyton Randolph to Robert Rodes, Feb. 7, 1859, Jemison Papers.

75. Carter, *History of the North East and South West Alabama Railroad,* 22.

76. Deed Book 5, p. 343, Deed Book 4, p. 235, Tuscaloosa County Courthouse, Tuscaloosa, Al.

77. Peyton Randolph to Robert Rodes, June 6, Sept. 6, 1857, Jemison Papers. Three months later on September 6, 1857, Randolph complained about Gene being unbearable to work with. "I have come to the same conclusion with you that his Conceit together with his being so abominably needlesome have caused me not to be very anxious to keep him."

78. James Corry to Robert Rodes, Nov. 30, 1857, May 31, 1858, Jemison Papers.

79. Peyton Randolph to Robert Rodes, Jan. 27, 1859, Oct. 11, 1860, Jemison Papers.

80. Peyton Randolph to George W. Robertson, Jan. 9, Feb. 8, 1859, Jemison Papers.

81. George W. Ross to Robert Rodes, April 4, May 5, June 17, 1858, Jemison Papers; Robert Rodes to Francis Smith, Nov. 27, 1856, VMI Archives.

82. James Corry to Robert Rodes, June 21, 1859, Jemison Papers.

83. Robert Rodes to Francis Smith, Jan. 2, 1859, VMI Archives.

84. Robert Rodes to Francis Smith, May 4, 1859, VMI Archives.

85. *Ibid.*

86. *Ibid.*

87. Robert Rodes to Francis Smith, July 4, July 16, 1859, VMI Archives.

88. Francis Smith to the Louisiana State Seminary Board of Directors, June 12, 1859, VMI Archives.

89. Francis Smith to Robert Rodes, June 20, 1859, VMI Archives.

90. Robert Rodes to Francis Smith, July 4, 1859, VMI Archives.

91. *Ibid.*

92. Robert Rodes to Francis Smith, Aug. 17, 1859, VMI Archives.

93. *Ibid.*

94. Robert Rodes to Francis Smith, Aug. 17, Sept. 23, 1859, VMI Archives; Asbury, *Lynchburg and Its People*, 229-230.

95. Francis Smith tribute to Rodes, Richmond *Enquirer*, October 4, 1864.

96. Swisher, *Warrior in Gray*, 15; Couper, *One Hundred Years,* vol. 1, 351.

Chapter Three

1. Tuscaloosa *Independent Monitor*, November 19, 1861.

2. Report of Historical Committee to the United Confederate Veterans, Camp Rodes, No. 262, April 27, 1896 (hereafter cited as Report of Historical Committee).

3. James Corry to Rodes, October 25, 1859, Peyton Randolph to Rodes, February 5, 1860, all from Jemison Papers.

4. Francis Smith to Rodes, September 9, 1860, VMI Archives.

5. RR Records, Jemison Papers.

6. Rodes' Report, October 1860, Jemison Papers.

7. Tuscaloosa *Observer*, November 21, 1861; Rodes to Francis Smith, January 13, 1861, and Hortense Rodes to Mrs. Anderson, September 19, 1904, VMI Archives.

8. Report of Historical Committee.

9. Peyton Randolph to Rodes, December 20, 1860, Jemison Papers.

10. Rodes to the Trustees of the Lounsboro Male Academy on behalf of William G. Williamson, December 25, 1860, Compiled Service Record of William G. Williamson, National Archives.

11. Clinton, *Tuscaloosa*, 133-135.

12. Rodes to Francis Smith, January 13, 1861, VMI Archives.

13. Rodes to Francis Smith, August 17, 1859, January 13, 1861, VMI Archives.

14. Clinton, *Tuscaloosa*, 135; Rodes to Francis Smith, January 15, 1861, VMI Archives.

15. Report of Historical Committee.

16. Patricia Faust, ed., *Historical Times Illustrated Encyclopedia of the Civil War* (New York: Harper & Row, 1987), 276.

17. Peyton Randolph to "Dear [sister] Nan," March 24, 1861, Harris Papers.

18. Tuscaloosa *Independent Monitor*, February 1, 1861.

19. Report of Historical Committee.

20. Peyton Randolph to Rodes, January 19, 1861, Jemison Papers.

21. Rodes to Peyton Randolph, March 19, 1861, Harris Papers.

22. Rodes to Peyton Randolph, March 29, 1861, Harris Papers.

23. Report of Historical Committee.

24. Tuscaloosa *Independent Monitor*, March 29, 1861.

25. Report of Historical Committee.

26. Peyton Randolph to Rodes, April 17, 1861, Jemison Papers.

27. Rodes to Peyton Randolph, April 18, 1861, Harris Papers.

28. Cline, *Alabama Railroads*, 38-39; Rodes to Peyton Randolph, April 29, 1861, Harris Papers.

29. Rodes to Peyton Randolph, April 29, 1861, Harris Papers.

30. Robert Rodes' will, Will Book 3, Tuscaloosa County Courthouse; Jemison Papers, box 2819; Tuscaloosa County Deed Book 4, p. 235 and Deed Book 5, p. 343.

31. Eugene D. Genovese, *A Consuming Fire: The Fall of the Confederacy in the Mind of the White Christian South* (Athens, Ga.: University of Georgia Press, 1998), 18-22.

32. Tuscaloosa *Independent Monitor*, May 10, 1861.

33. *Ibid*; William E. Tarrant, unp. memoir, n.d., Nan Neblett Maxwell Coll., Gorgas Library, University of Alabama, Tuscaloosa (hereafter cited as Tarrant memoir).

34. Tarrant memoir; G. Ward Hubbs, ed., *Voices from Company D: Diaries by the Greensboro Guards, Fifth Alabama Infantry Regiment, Army of Northern Virginia* (Athens, Ga.: University of Georgia Press, 2003), 4.

35. Willis Brewer, *Brief Historical Sketches of Military Organizations Raised in Alabama During the Civil War* (Montgomery, AL.: Alabama Civil War Centennial Commission, 1962), 596-597; Hubbs, *Voices from Company D*, 5.

36. *Ibid.*

37. *Ibid*; Captain James D. Webb to his wife, May 12, 1861, Walton Papers, Southern Historical Collection, University of North Carolina, Chapel Hill (this source hereafter cited as Walton Papers); Grady McWhiney, *Braxton Bragg and Confederate Defeat*, 2 vols. (New York: Columbia University Press, 1962), vol. 1, 155-175.

38. Webb to wife, May 13 and May 14, 1861, Walton Papers; Hubbs, *Voices from Company D*, 5.

39. Webb to wife May 14, 1861, Walton Papers.

40. Willis Brewer, *Alabama-Her History, Resources, War Record and Public Men*, 458.

41. Charles D. Walker, *Memorial, Virginia Military Institute* (Philadelphia: J.B. Lippincott, 1875), 457, 475.

42. Webb to wife, May 19, 1861, Walton Papers; Hubbs, *Voices from Company D*, 5.

43. Webb to wife, May 19 and May 21, 1861, Walton Papers.

44. Hubbs, *Voices from Company D*, 5-6.

45. Webb to a friend, May 16, 1861, Walton Papers.

46. Webb to wife, May 23, 1861, Walton Papers.

47. Rodes to Secretary of War Leroy P. Walker, Microfilm Group M437-Letters Received by the Confederate Secretary of War, 1861-1865, National Archives, Washington, D.C.

48. Webb to wife, May 23, 1861, Walton Papers; Rodes to Secretary of War Walker, May 2, 1861, National Archives.

49. Rodes to Secretary of War Walker, May 2, 1861, National Archives.

50. Webb to wife June 3, 1861, Walton Papers; Fifth Alabama Infantry Record of Events, Microfilm Group M861, National Archives, Washington, D.C. (hereafter cited as Fifth Alabama Record of Events, NA).

51. McWhiney, *Braxton Bragg*, 177.

52. Webb to wife June 3, 1861, Walton Papers.

53. *Ibid*; Robert E.L. Krick, *Staff Officers in Gray: A Biographical Register of the Staff Officers in the Army of Northern Virginia* (Chapel Hill, N.C.: The University of North Carolina Press, 2003), 298.

54. Fifth Alabama Record of Events, NA; Tarrant memoir; Hubbs, *Voices from Company D*, 6, 9.

55. Fifth Alabama Record of Events, NA; Tarrant memoir; Hubbs, *Voices from Company D*, 6-7.

56. Captain Eugene Blackford to The Greensboro *Beacon*, June 18, 1861, Fifth Alabama history file, Alabama Department of History, Montgomery; Hubbs, *Voices from Company D*, 7.

57. Fifth Alabama Record of Events, National Archives; Donald Pfanz, *Richard S. Ewell: A Soldier's Life* (Chapel Hill, N.C.: University of North Carolina Press, 1998), 129;

Samuel J. Martin, *The Road to Glory: Confederate General Richard S. Ewell* (Indianapolis: Guild Press of Indiana, 1991), 18-19; Hubbs, *Voices from Company D*, 7.

58. Vincent J. Esposito, ed., *The West Point Atlas of American Wars*, 2 vols. (New York: Praeger Publishers, 1959), vol. 1, maps 19-20 (hereafter cited as Esposito, *West Point Atlas*, all references are to vol. 1).

59. *Ibid*; Fifth Alabama Record of Events, National Archives; Pfanz, *Richard S. Ewell*, 130.

60. Fifth Alabama Record of Events, National Archives; Hubbs, *Voices from Company D*, 7.

61. Fifth Alabama Record of Events, National Archives; Hubbs, *Voices from Company D*, 7, 12.

62. Webb to wife July 16, 1861, Walton Papers.

63. Hubbs, *Voices from Company D*, 8, 10.

64. *Ibid.*, 10-11.

65. Blackford to "My dear Uncle," July 12, 1861, Gordon-Blackford Papers, Maryland Historical Society, Baltimore (this source hereafter cited as Gordon-Blackford Papers).

66. Blackford to "My dear Mary," July 15, 1861, Gordon-Blackford Papers.

67. Hubbs, *Voices from Company D*, 12, 15.

68. Blackford to "My dear Uncle," July 12, 1861, Gordon-Blackford Papers.

69. Fifth Alabama Record of Events, National Archives; United States War Department, *War of the Rebellion, A Compilation of the Official Records of the Union and Confederate Armies*, 128 vols. (Washington: U.S. Government Printing Office, 1880-1901), Series I, vol. 2, 459-460 (hereafter cited as *OR*; all references are from Series I); Hubbs, *Voices from Company D*, 15.

70. Hubbs, *Voices from Company D*, 18.

71. *OR* 2, 460; Fifth Alabama Record of Events, National Archives; Hubbs, *Voices from Company D*, 18-19.

72. *OR* 2, 460.

73. Esposito, *West Point Atlas*, maps 19-20.

74. *OR* 2, 460; Fifth Alabama Record of Events, National Archives.

75. *Ibid.*

76. *Ibid.*

77. *Ibid.*

78. *Ibid.*

79. *OR* 2, 447, 460; Fifth Alabama Record of Events, National Archives; Blackford to "My dear Mother," July 20, 1861, Gordon-Blackford Papers; Hubbs, *Voices from Company D*, 19.

80. *OR* 2, 447, 460; Fifth Alabama Record of Events, National Archives; Blackford to "My dear Mother," July 20, 1861, Gordon-Blackford Papers.

81. *OR* 2, 460; Ewell to Lizinka Brown, July 31, 1861, Richard S. Ewell Papers, Library of Congress, Washington, D.C.

82. Ewell-Stewart-Brown Papers, box 2, folder 4, Tennessee State Library, Nashville (hereafter cited as Ewell-Stewart-Brown Papers).

83. *OR* 2, 446.

84. Esposito, *West Point Atlas*, maps 19-21.

85. Esposito, *West Point Atlas*, maps 20-21; Pfanz, *Richard S. Ewell*, 130; Ewell-Stewart-Brown Papers; Hubbs, *Voices from Company D*, 21.

86. Esposito, *West Point Atlas*, maps 20-21; Fifth Alabama Record of Events, National Archives.

87. Esposito, *West Point Atlas*, maps 20-21.

88. Pfanz, *Richard S. Ewell*, 135.

89. *Ibid.*

90. Martin, *Road to Glory*, 24-25; Pfanz, *Richard S. Ewell*, 137-138; Fifth Alabama Record of Events, National Archives.

91. Webb to wife July 1861, Walton Papers.

92. Pfanz, *Richard S. Ewell*, 138.

93. Fifth Alabama Record of Events, National Archives.

94. Based on evidence found in Hortense Rodes' letter to P.A. Pitts, July 24, 1861, A. Cole Hargrove Papers, William Stanley Hoole Special Collection Library, University of Alabama, Tuscaloosa (this source hereafter cited as Hargrove Papers); and in Webb letters; David Rodes obituary, Lynchburg *Virginian*, March 27, 1862.

95. Polk-Brown-Ewell Papers, Southern Historical Collection, University of North Carolina, Chapel Hill; Pfanz, *Richard S. Ewell*, 143.

96. Robert Rodes to P.A. Pitts, August 17, 1861, Hargrove Papers.

97. Hubbs, *Voices from Company D*, 25.

98. *Ibid.*

99. *Ibid.*, 26.

100. *Ibid.*

101. *Ibid.*, 26-27.

102. Blackford letter July 24, 1861, Lewis Leigh Collection, United States Army Military History Institute, Carlisle, Pa. (this source hereafter cited as Leigh Coll., USAMHI); Charles Minor Blackford, ed., *Letters From Lee's Army* (New York: Charles Scribner's Sons, 1947), 46-47. Blackford's brothers survived, and a mutual respect eventually developed between Blackford and Rodes. After a visit with Eugene on October 9, William, a member of Jeb Stuart's staff, wrote home that his brother and

Rodes "seemed to be on the very best terms, from which I inferred Eugene had his confidence."

103. Hubbs, *Voices from Company D*, 28; Webb to wife, August 1, 1861, Walton Papers.

104. Hubbs, *Voices from Company D*, 28-29.

105. *Ibid.*, 32.

106. *Ibid.*, 32-33.

107. *Ibid.*, 34.

108. Jemison Papers; Rodes' Compiled Service Record, National Archives; Hortense Rodes to P.A. Pitts, July 24, 1861, Hargrove Papers.

109. Robert Rodes to P.A. Pitts, August 17, 1861, Hargrove Papers. Though no record has been found for the sale, Rodes evidently did sell the slaves, for he paid his debt to Mrs. Gooch by December 1862.

110. Webb letters of August 1861, Walton Papers.

111. OR 2, 999-1000; Pfanz, *Richard S. Ewell*, 142.

112. Pfanz, *Richard S. Ewell*, 142-143; Fifth Alabama Record of Events, National Archives; Blackford to "My dear Mother," August 21, 1861, Gordon-Blackford Papers; Hubbs, *Voices from Company D*, 40.

113. Webb to wife, August 26, 1861, Walton Papers.

114. *Ibid.*

115. Blackford letter, August 28, 1861, Leigh Coll., USAMHI.

116. Blackford to "My dear Mother," September 5, 1861, and to "My dear Father," September 10, 1861, Gordon-Blackford Papers.

117. Hubbs, *Voices from Company D*, 44.

118. Jeremiah Tate to "Dear Cousin Marcus," September 8, 1861, Gilder Lehrman Collection, GLC 2082.08, New York, NY.

119. Blackford to "My dear Father," September 14, 1861, Gordon-Blackford Papers.

120. Webb to wife, September 14, 1861, Walton Papers; Hubbs, *Voices from Company D*, 47.

121. Blackford to "My dear Father," September 14, 1861, Gordon-Blackford Papers; Webb to wife, October 10, 1861, Walton Papers.

122. Hubbs, *Voices from Company D*, 50.

123. *Ibid.*, 51.

124. *Ibid.*, 52.

125. *Ibid.*, 55-56.

126. Blackford to "My dear Father," October 1, 1861, Gordon-Blackford Papers.

127. Blackford to "My dear Mother," October 7, 1861, Gordon-Blackford Papers.

128. *Ibid.*

129. Fifth Alabama Record of Events, National Archives.

130. Rodes letter October 10, 1861, B.T. Johnson Collection, Duke University.

131. Blackford letter, Leigh Coll., USAMHI; Rodes to Beauregard, October 5, 1861, Rodes' Compiled Service Record, National Archives.

132. Fifth Alabama Record of Events, National Archives; Webb to wife, October 27, 1861, Walton Papers; David Rodes obituary, Lynchburg *Virginian*, March 27, 1862; Hubbs, *Voices from Company D*, 60, 62.

133. Pfanz, *Richard S. Ewell*, 144.

134. Jeffrey D. Wert, "Robert E. Rodes," *Civil War Times Illustrated* (December 1977): 8.

135. Webb to wife, October 27, 1861, Walton Papers; Rodes' Compiled Service Record, National Archives.

Chapter Four

1. Faust, *Historical Times*, 640; Webb letters to wife, October 27, October 30, 1861, Walton Papers; OR 5, 914; Robert K. Krick, *The Smoothbore Volley That Doomed The Confederacy* (Baton Rouge, La.: Louisiana State University Press, 2002), 125-126.

2. Webb letter to wife, October 30, 1861, Walton Papers.

3. Webb letter to wife, November 3, 1861, Walton Papers; Richard Adams diary, Ms 940013, Special Collections Library, Virginia Polytechnical and State University, Blacksburg, Va. (hereafter cited as Adams diary); Hubbs, *Voices from Company D*, 69.

4. Webb letter to wife, October 27, 1861, Walton Papers; Carter speech in Rodes' file, VMI Archives.

5. OR 5, 935-936; Webb letter to wife, November 3, 1861, Walton Papers; Hubbs, *Voices from Company D*, 72.

6. Pvt. James E. Webb to mother, November 24, 1861, Walton Papers, Southern Historical Collection, University of North Carolina.

7. Rodes to Secretary of War J. P. Benjamin, October 29, 1861, Record Group 109, M437, National Archives.

8. Rodes to Jones, November 15, 1861, Record Group 109, M437, National Archives; Alabama AAG George Goldthwaite to Rodes, November 6, 1861, Record Group 109, M437, National Archives.

9. Rodes to Jones, November 15, 1861, National Archives; Rodes to Shorter, November 1861, National Archives.

10. *The Daily Sun* (Montgomery), December 10, December 13, December 25, 1861, Alabama Department of Archives and History (ADAH).

11. Robert K. Krick, *Lee's Colonels* (Dayton, Ohio: Morningside, 1992), 213; Faust, *Historical Times*, 510-511.

12. Blackford to "My dear Mother," November 25, 1861, Gordon-Blackford Papers.

13. *OR* 5, 1029; John J. Thompson letter, January 28, 1904, 6th Alabama History File, ADAH; Thomas R. Lightfoot letter, November 15, 1861, 5th Alabama History File, ADAH.

14. Joseph J. Crute Jr., *Confederate Staff Officers* (Powhatan, Va.: Derwent Books, 1982), 167-168; Krick, *Staff Officers in Gray*, 131, 212, 249, 301; Webb to wife, October 25, 1861, Walton Papers.

15. Webb to wife, October 27, 1861, Walton Papers.

16. Webb to wife, November 8, 1861, Walton Papers.

17. Webb to wife, November 14, November 16, November 30, 1861, Walton Papers; Webb Compiled Service Record, National Archives; Krick, *Staff Officers in Gray*, 150.

18. S.Q. Hale letters to Macon Co. *Democrat*, July 15, August 12, 1892, 6th Alabama History File, ADAH; Blackford to "My dear Mother," November 25, 1861, Gordon-Blackford Papers.

19. Joseph Mills Hanson, *Bull Run Remembers* (Manassas, Va.: National Capitol Publishers, Inc., 1953), 99-100. The Richmond reporter signed his article "Kiawah."

20. S.Q. Hale letters to Macon Co. *Democrat*, July 15, August 12, 1892, 6th Alabama History File, ADAH; Blackford to "My dear Mother," December 4, 1861, Gordon-Blackford Papers.

21. Fifth Alabama Record of Events, National Archives; 5th Alabama History File, ADAH; *Daily Sun* December 20, 1861; 6th Alabama History File, ADAH; James Madison Howard, *A Short Sketch of My Life* (Alberville, AL.: 1917), 30; Blackford to "My dear Mother," December 24, 1861, Gordon-Blackford Papers.

22. James T. Jones Collection, John Davis Williams Library, University of Mississippi, Oxford; Webb to wife, December 19, 1861, Walton Papers.

23. Rodes to Early, December 22, 1861, Jubal Anderson Early Papers, Virginia Historical Society, Richmond (hereafter cited as Early Papers).

24. "Private" to *Daily Sun*, January 8, 1862.

25. *OR* 5, 1029; Greensboro *Beacon* July 19, 1903; Fifth Alabama History File, ADAH; Jubal A. Early, *Autobiographical Sketch and Narrative of the War Between the States* (Philadelphia: J.B. Lippincott, 1912), 52; Lynchburg *Virginian*, January 25, 1862; Randolph Compiled Service Record, National Archives.

26. Rodes to Early, February 8, 1862, Early Papers.

27. Blackford to "My dear Father," February 9, 1862, Gordon-Blackford Papers.

28. David Rodes' obituary, Lynchburg *Virginian*, March 27, 1862; Rodes' furlough is confirmed by Blackford to "My dear Father," February 28, 1862, Gordon-Blackford Papers.

29. David Rodes Coll.; David Rodes' will, Will Book E, Tuscaloosa Co. Courthouse.

30. *OR* 5, 1081-1082.

31. Esposito, *West Point Atlas*, map 39; OR 5, 1080-1083.

32. Howard, *A Short Sketch*, 32.

33. Early, *Autobiographical Sketch*, 53-54; Peyton Randolph Compiled Service Record, National Archives; Krick, *Staff Officers in Gray*, 66, 298.

34. Early, *Autobiographical Sketch*, 54-56; Blackford to "My dear Mary," March 23, 1862, Gordon-Blackford Papers.

35. Esposito, *West Point Atlas*, map 39.

36. Robert Johnson and Clarence C. Buell, eds., *Battles and Leaders of the Civil War*, 4 vols. (New York: Century Co., 1887-1888), vol. 2, 203; Early, *Autobiographical Sketch*, 57; Stephen W. Newton, *The Battle of Seven Pines, May 31-June 1, 1862* (Lynchburg, Va.: H.E. Howard, 1993), 157-159.

37. John B. Gordon, *Reminiscences of the Civil War* (New York: Charles Scribners Sons, 1903), 52-53; Blackford to "My dear Mary," April 26, 1862, Gordon-Blackford Papers.

38. Diary of John Tucker, *The Alabama Historical Quarterly* (Spring 1981): 7-8 (hereafter cited as Tucker diary); OR 11, pt. 3, 426; Blackford to "My dear Mary," April 26, 1862, Gordon-Blackford Papers.

39. Esposito, *West Point Atlas*, map 39; OR 11, pt. 1, 601; Newton, *The Battle of Seven Pines*, 159; Blackford to "My dear Mary," April 26, 1862, Gordon-Blackford Papers.

40. Adams diary.

41. Hal Bridges, *Lee's Maverick General* (Lincoln, Neb.: University of Nebraska Press, 1961), 5-36, 151-152.

42. Early, *Autobiographical Sketch*, 59-60; OR 11, pt. 1, 601-602.

43. Esposito, *West Point Atlas*, map 40. Deep and thorough new research on McClellan's campaign on the Virginia peninsula can be found in Russel H. Beatie, *The Army of the Potomac: McClellan's First Campaign, March – May, 1862*, vol. 3 (Savas Beatie, 2007). According to Beatie's research, the role of the federal navy was more perfidious than previously believed.

44. Early, *Autobiographical Sketch*, 62-65; Esposito, *West Point Atlas*, map 41.

45. Blackford to "My dear Father and Mother," April 22, 1862, Gordon-Blackford Papers.

46. Early, *Autobiographical Sketch*, 62-65; Esposito, *West Point Atlas*, map 41.

47. Early, *Autobiographical Sketch*, 65; Adams diary; OR 11, pt. 1, 602.

48. Bridges, *Lee's Maverick General*, 10; Blackford to "My dear Mother," May 11, 1862, Gordon-Blackford Papers.

49. Blackford to "My dear Mother," May 11, 1862, Gordon-Blackford Papers; Park, *Southern Historical Society Papers*, vol. 33, 217 (hereafter cited as Park, *SHSP*); Tucker diary, 10.

50. Adams diary.

51. *Ibid;* Letter of Private Green Polkiss, 12 AL., May 12, 1862, Confederate Miscellany, Virginia State Library, Richmond (hereafter cited as Polkiss letter).

52. OR 11, pt. 1, 603-604; Newton, 161; Adams diary; Park, *SHSP*, vol. 33, 217; Polkiss letter; Blackford to "My dear Mother, May 11, 1862, Gordon-Blackford Papers.

53. Adams diary; Tucker diary, 11; Park, *SHSP,* vol. 33, 218; Blackford to "My dear Mother," May 11, 1862, Gordon-Blackford Papers.

54. Adams diary; *Battles & Leaders*, vol. 2, 221; Park, *SHSP*, vol. 33, 217-218.

55. *Confederate Veteran Magazine*, vol. 30, 55.

56. Blackford to "My dear Father and Mother," May 20, 1862, Gordon-Blackford Papers; Tucker diary, 11; Adams diary; *Battles & Leaders*, vol. 2, 220.

57. *Battles & Leaders*, vol. 2, 222-223; Tucker diary, 11; Adams diary.

58. *Battles & Leaders*, vol. 2, 223; David G. Martin, *The Peninsula Campaign, March-July, 1862* (Conshohocken, Pa.: Combined Books, 1992), 102.

59. Stewart Sifakis, *Compendium of the Confederate Armies,* 10 vols. (New York: Facts on File, 1992-1995), vol. 4, 154-156; Alex L. Wiatt, *26th Virginia Infantry* (Lynchburg, Va.: H.E. Howard, 1984), 4-5; Darrell L. Collins, *46th Virginia Infantry* (Lynchburg, Va.: H.E. Howard, 1992), 34-35; OR 11, pt. 3, 525, vol. 11, pt. 1, 968.

60. Blackford to "My dear Father and Mother," May 20, 1862, Gordon-Blackford Papers.

61. Adams diary.

62. *Ibid.*

63. Esposito, *West Point Atlas*, maps 43-44; Martin, *The Peninsula Campaign*, 101.

64. *Battles & Leaders*, vol. 2, 224; Martin, *The Peninsula Campaign*, 104-105; Blackford to "My dear Mother," May 26, 1862, Gordon-Blackford Papers. Blackford wrote, "Of course the delinquent can see us at any distance, and would scatter where our men could not find them." In addition to his own company, Blackford took into Richmond a non-commissioned officer from each company of the brigade.

65. Craig L. Symonds, *Joseph E. Johnston: A Civil War Biography* (New York: W.W. Norton and Co., 1992), 160; Martin, *The Peninsula Campaign*, 109; *Battles & Leaders*, vol. 2, 211, 226.

66. S.Q. Hale to Macon Co. *Democrat*, May 21, 1892; Howard, *A Short Sketch*, 33; Park, *SHSP*, vol. 33, 218-219; Adams diary.

67. OR 11, pt. 1, 943-944; Bridges, *Lee's Maverick General*, 38-39.

68. Symonds, *Joseph E. Johnston*, 163-164; Martin, *The Peninsula Campaign*, 108.

69. Bridges, *Lee's Maverick General*, 40; *OR* 11, pt. 1, 943, 971.

70. *OR* 11, pt. 1, 971.

71. *Ibid.*; vol. 11, pt. 3, 563; Park, *SHSP*, vol. 33, 219; Adams diary.

72. S.Q. Hale to Macon Co. *Democrat*, May 21, 1892; 6th Alabama History File, ADAH.

73. *OR* 11, pt. 1, 971; *Battles & Leaders*, vol. 2, 229.

74. *OR* 11, pt. 1, 971.

75. *Ibid.*; Christian G. Samito, "Warrior In Gray," *America's Civil War* (Jan. 1995): 49; 6th Alabama History File, ADAH.

76. S.Q. Hale to Macon Co. *Democrat*, May 21, 1892.

77. *OR* 11, pt. 1, 943, 971.

78. *OR* 11, pt. 1, 971; *Battles & Leaders*, vol. 2, 230; S.Q. Hale to Macon Co. *Democrat* May 21, 1892; Newton, *The Battle of Seven Pines*, 191.

79. *Battles & Leaders*, vol. 2, 229; *OR* 11, pt. 3, 564.

80. *OR* 11, pt. 1, 971-972; Newton, *The Battle of Seven Pines*, 191-192.

81. Adams diary.

82. *OR* 11, pt. 1, 979; Park, *SHSP*, vol. 33, 224.

83. *OR* 11, pt. 1, 968; Newton, *The Battle of Seven Pines*, 192.

84. *OR* 11, pt. 1, 972; Thomas Carter to Richard L. Maury, May 29, 1891, Maury Letters, Duke University.

85. *Battles & Leaders*, vol. 2, 230-233.

86. *OR* 11, pt. 1, 972; Newton, *The Battle of Seven Pines*, 192-193.

87. *OR* 11, pt. 1, 972.

88. *OR* 11, pt. 1, 978.

89. *OR* 11, pt. 1, 943, 973.

90. Bridges, *Lee's Maverick General*, 44.

91. *OR* 11, pt. 1, 944; Martin, *The Peninsula Campaign*, 108-109.

92. *OR* 11, pt. 1, 973.

93. *Ibid.*

94. *Ibid.*; Bridges, *Lee's Maverick General*, 44.

95. *OR* 11, pt, 1, 973, 976; Bridges, *Lee's Maverick General*, 44; [Thomas E. Coffey] *Battle-Fields of the South* (New York: John Bradburn, 1864), 252; War Reminiscences of Corporal Thomas Catesby Jones, Parry Family Papers, United States Army Military History Institute, Carlisle, Pa. (cited hereafter as Jones Reminiscences, USAMHI). Rodes later gave too much credit to Carter for driving the Yankees out of the redoubt, and he criticized Hill for not acknowledging Carter's effort in that regard. Carter's greatest contribution, however, was in twice driving off federal reinforcements coming up the Williamsburg Road.

96. *OR* 11, pt. 1, 944; Stephen W. Sears, *To the Gates of Richmond: The Peninsula Campaign* (New York: Ticknor and Fields, 1992), 131.

97. Douglas S. Freeman, *Lee's Lieutenants*, 3 vols. (New York: Charles Scribner's Sons, 1942), vol. 1, 240; *OR* 11, pt. 1, 977-981.

98. *OR* 11, pt. 1, 943, 973, 980; Jeffry Wert, "Robert E. Rodes," *Civil War Times Illustrated* (Dec. 1977): 6.

99. *OR* 11, pt. 1, 974, 976; *Battles & Leaders*, vol. 2, 234-236.

100. S.Q. Hale to Macon Co. *Democrat*, May 28, 1892; *OR* 11, pt. 1, 980.

101. *OR* 11, pt. 1, 973, 981.

102. *Ibid.*, 974.

103. *Ibid.*, 974-975. Although it is unclear which limb suffered the wound, the general was unable to write for several weeks. If Rodes was right handed (that, too, is not known with certainty, though probable), the injury would have been to his right arm.

104. *Ibid.*; Coffey, *Battle-Fields*, 252; Adams diary.

105. *OR* 11, pt. 1, 974, 977; Gordon, *Reminiscences*, 58-59.

106. *OR* 11, pt. 1, 976; Park, *SHSP*, vol. 33, 219-221; S.Q. Hale to Macon Co. *Democrat*, August 5, 1892.

107. *OR* 11, pt. 1, 940-941; Wert, "Robert E. Rodes," 8; D.H. Hill to Secretary of War George W. Randolph, June 6, 1862, in Compiled Service Record of George B. Anderson, National Archives.

108. Rodes' file, VMI Archives.

109. Richmond *Whig*, July 4, 1862.

110. Blackford to "My dear Father," June 6, 1862, Gordon-Blackford Papers; Hill to George W. Randolph, June 6, 1862, in Compiled Service Record of George B. Anderson, National Archives; Jones Reminiscence, Parry Family Papers, USAMHI (hereafter cited as Jones Reminiscence).

111. Robert Rodes' Compiled Service Record, National Archives.

112. Virginius Rodes file, VMI Archives; Rodes to Randolph, June 5, 1862, Record Group 109, M474, National Archives; Rodes to Smith, VMI Correspondence.

113. Blackford to "My dear Mary," June 12, 1862, Gordon-Blackford Papers.

114. Robert Rodes' Compiled Service Record, National Archives; Walker, *Memorial*, 443.

115. Bridges, *Lee's Maverick General*, 59-60; 3rd Alabama History File, ADAH; 26th Alabama History File, ADAH. In 1864, the battalion became the Thirty-fourth Virginia Infantry.

116. Cullen Andrew Battle, "The Third Alabama Regiment," unpublished manuscript, 3rd Alabama History File, ADAH (hereafter cited as Battle, "The Third Alabama Regiment"); Samito, "Warrior In Gray," 48-49; B.H. Powell, "Reminiscences

of Army Life, Camp Scenes and Personal Sketches," series of articles written in 1866 for the *Union Spring Times*, 3rd Alabama History File, ADAH (hereafter cited as Powell, "Reminiscences").

117. Powell, "Reminiscences," 3rd Alabama History File, ADAH.

118. Bridges, *Lee's Maverick General*, 59-61.

119. *Battles & Leaders*, vol. 2, 352; Bridges, *Lee's Maverick General*, 62-63.

120. *OR* 11, pt. 2, 623.

121. Bridges, *Lee's Maverick General*, 65.

122. *OR* 11, pt. 2, 623-624, 630-631, 638-639; *Battles & Leaders*, vol. 2, 351; Jones Reminiscence.

123. *OR* 11, pt. 2, 622, 674; *Battles & Leaders*, vol. 2, 352; Bridges, *Lee's Maverick General*, 68; Walker, *Memorial*, 443.

124. Walker, *Memorial*, 443; *OR* 11, pt. 2, 624, 631; Bridges, *Lee's Maverick General*, 68-71.

125. *OR* 11, pt. 2, 624.

126. *Ibid.*, 631, 638.

127. *Ibid.*, 625; *Battles & Leaders*, vol. 2, 355.

128. *OR* 11, pt. 2, 624-625; Faust, *Historical Times*, 295.

129. *OR* 11, pt. 2, 631-632; Walker, *Memorial*, 443.

130. *Ibid.*

131. *OR* 11, pt. 2, 632; Yancey, *Lynchburg and Its Neighbors*, 100; Walker, *Memorial*, 442-443.

132. Esposito, *West Point Atlas*, map 45.

133. *OR* 11, pt. 2, 626, 632.

134. *Ibid.*, 632-633, 976; Yancey, *Lynchburg and Its Neighbors*, 100-101; Walker, *Memorial*, 443.

Chapter Five

1. Rodes to Francis Smith, July 15, 1862, VMI Archives.

2. Lee Family Papers, Virginia Historical Society; Krick, *Staff Officers in Gray*, 298.

3. Blackford to "My dear Mother," July 18, 1862, Gordon-Blackford Papers.

4. *OR*, Series 4, vol. 2, 20-21.

5. Walker, *Memorial*, 443; *OR* 19, pt. 1, 1029, vol. 11, pt. 3, 671, vol. 51, pt. 2, 611; Bridges, *Lee's Maverick General*, 89.

6. Esposito, *West Point Atlas*, map 57; *OR* 19, pt. 1, 144.

7. *OR* 19, pt. 1, 145, 1019; Bridges, *Lee's Maverick General*, 89-90.

8. *OR* 19, pt. 1, 144-145; Freeman, *Lee's Lieutenants*, vol. 2, 146-153.

9. *OR* 19, pt. 1, 1019; Walker, *Memorial*, 443.

10. Park, *SHSP*, vol. 33, 282.

11. John M. Priest, *Before Antietam: The Battle for South Mountain* (N.Y.: Oxford University Press, 1996), 21.

12. *OR* 19, pt. 1, 145.

13. *Ibid.*, 145-147, 1019, 1022; *Battles & Leaders*, vol. 2, 570; Edward Stackpole, *From Cedar Mountain to Antietam: August-September, 1862* (Harrisburg, Pa.: The Stackpole Co., 1959), 363; Esposito, *West point Atlas*, map 65.

14. *OR* 19, pt. 1, 146, 1019-1020, 1033-1034; *Battles & Leaders*, vol. 2, 560-564.

15. *Battles & Leaders*, vol. 2, 572; S.Q. Hale, 6th Alabama History File, ADAH; *OR* 19, pt. 1, 1034; Freeman, *Lee's Lieutenants*, vol. 2, 180; Priest, *Before Antietam*, 174-175.

16. *OR* 19, pt. 1, 1020, 1034.

17. *Ibid.*

18. *Ibid*; Priest, *Before Antietam*, 227, 236.

19. *OR* 19, pt. 1, 1034.

20. Priest, *Before Antietam*, 227, 234.

21. *OR* 19, pt. 1, 1034; *Battles & Leaders*, vol. 2, 574.

22. *OR* 19, pt. 1, 1034; Battle, "The Third Alabama Regiment," 3rd Alabama History File, ADAH.

23. *OR* 19, pt. 1, 1034-1035; Priest, *Before Antietam*, 244. Captain Park of the Twelfth describes Gayle's death thus: in the fading light Rodes, Gayle and Pickens stood in front of the Twelfth peering between the rocks in an effort to determine enemy movements. Seeing a smattering of troops approaching, Rodes said, "What troops are those?" Gayle replied, "I don't know, sir, I'll see." He stepped forward over some rocks, when he realized they were Yankees. They demanded his surrender, but he pulled his pistol and began firing. But by the time this would have happened, Park was a captive, having been taken while a skirmisher as the battle opened.

24. *OR* 19, pt. 1, 1034-1035.

25. *Ibid.*, 1036; *Battles & Leaders*, vol. 2, 574.

26. *OR* 19, pt. 1, 1020-1021.

27. Priest, *Before Antietam*, 240, 263; *OR* 19, pt. 1, 941, 947.

28. *OR* 19, pt. 1, 1036; *Battles & Leaders*, vol. 2, 574.

29. *OR* 19, pt. 1, 1021; *Battles & Leaders*, vol. 2, 574.

30. James Longstreet, *From Manassas to Appomattox: Memoirs of the Civil War in America* (Philadelphia: J.B. Lippincott, 1896), 224.

31. *OR* 19, pt. 1, 1036; S.Q. Hale, 6th Alabama History File, ADAH.

32. Bridges, *Lee's Maverick General*, 113; Battle, "The Third Alabama Regiment," 3rd Alabama History File, ADAH.

33. *OR* 19, pt. 1, 1036.

34. *Ibid.*

35. Esposito, *West Point Atlas*, map 67; Bridges, *Lee's Maverick General*, 115.

36. *OR* 19, pt. 1, 1022-1023; Bridges, *Lee's Maverick General*, 116.

37. Ralph Lowell Eckert, *John Brown Gordon: Soldier, Southerner, American* (Baton Rouge: Louisiana State University Press, 1989), 33; *OR* 19, pt. 1, 1036; Robert Krick, "It Appeared as Though Mutual Extermination Would Put a Stop to the Awful Carnage: Confederates in Sharpsburg's Bloody Lane," in Gary W. Gallagher, ed., *The Antietam Campaign* (Chapel Hill, N.C.: University of North Carolina Press, 1999), 224.

38. *OR* 19, pt. 1, 1036-1037.

39. Stephen W. Sears, *Landscape Turned Red: The Battle of Antietam* (New Haven, CT.: Ticknor and Fields, 1983), 236; John M. Priest, *Antietam: The Soldiers' Battle* (N.Y.: Oxford University Press, 1994), 142-143.

40. *OR* 19, pt. 1, 1037; Sears, *Landscape Turned Red*, 238; James Murfin, *The Gleam of Bayonets: The Battle of Antietam and Robert E. Lee's Maryland, September 1862* (N.Y.: Thomas Yoseloff, 1965), 246; Priest, *Antietam*, 136, 142; Krick, *Confederates in Sharpsburg's Bloody Lane*, 229-230.

41. Gordon, *Reminiscences*, 84.

42. Murfin, *The Gleam of Bayonets*, 246; Sears, *Landscape Turned Red*, 236-237; Priest, *Antietam*, 139, 142; Sifakis, *Who Was Who*, 229-230.

43. *OR* 19, pt. 1, 1023, 1037; Sears, *Landscape Turned Red*, 237; Priest, *Antietam*, 142-143.

44. *OR* 19, pt. 1, 1037; Sears, *Landscape Turned Red*, 238; Priest, *Antietam*, 142, 145; S.Q. Hale, 6th Alabama History File, ADAH.

45. *OR* 19, pt. 1, 1037.

46. *OR* 19, pt. 1, 1023; Priest, *Antietam*, 158; Krick, "Confederates in Sharpsburg's Bloody Lane," 239-240.

47. *OR* 19, pt. 1, 1037.

48. *OR* 19, pt. 1, 1037-1039; Sears, *Landscape Turned Red*, 242; Gordon, *Reminiscences*, 89-90; Krick, "Confederates in Sharpsburg's Bloody Lane," 232, 245.

49. *OR* 19, pt. 1, 1037-1039; Sears, *Landscape Turned Red*, 248; Bridges, *Lee's Maverick General*, 122; Krick, "Confederates in Sharpsburg's Bloody Lane," 226; Krick, *Staff Officers in Gray*, 73.

50. Esposito, *West Point Atlas*, map 69.

51. *OR* 19, pt. 1, 1038; Krick, "Confederates in Sharpsburg's Bloody Lane," 247. George Anderson was wounded in the ankle joint by a musket ball while defending the Sunken Lane position. Infection set in, the limb was amputated, and Anderson died on October 16, 1862. Robert K. Krick, "George Burgwyn Anderson," in William C. Davis, *The Confederate General* , 6 vols. (National Historical Society, 1991), vol. 1, 19.

52. *OR* 19, pt. 1, 152; Walker, *Memorial*, 444; Esposito, *West Point Atlas*, map 70.

53. Bridges, *Lee's Maverick General*, 152.

54. Esposito, *West Point Atlas*, map 70.

55. Letters to the Confederate Inspector General, M474, National Archives.

56. Bridges, *Lee's Maverick General*, 154.

57. Jones Reminiscence.

58. The "gentlemanly and chivalrous action" mentioned by Grimes may have been Rodes' strong endorsement of Grimes for promotion to brigadier general. Pulaski Cowper, ed., *Extracts of Letters of Major Gen'l Bryan Grimes to His Wife, Written While in Active Service in the Army of Northern Virginia: together with some personal Recollections of the War, Written by Him after Its Close, etc.* (Raleigh, N.C.: Edwards, Broughton and Co., 1883), 22-24 (hereafter cited as Cowper, *Grimes Letters*).

59. Mobile *Evening News*, December 14, 1862.

60. Samuel Pickens diary, William S. Hoole Special Collections Library, University of Alabama (hereafter cited as Pickens diary); Cowper, *Grimes Letters*, 25; James Monroe Thompson and William S. Hoole, eds, *Reminiscences of the Autauga Rifles (Co. G) Sixth Alabama Volunteer Regiment, C.S.A.* (Pratville, Al.: 1879), 5.

61. OR 21, 642; Stackpole, *From Cedar Mountain to Antietam*, 110-114; Pickens diary.

62. Pickens diary.

63. OR 21, 642.

64. *Ibid.*, 643; Bridges, *Lee's Maverick General*, 158; Esposito, *West Point Atlas*, maps 71-72.

65. Annette Tapert, ed., *The Brother's War: Civil War Letters To Their Loved Ones From The Blue and Gray* (N.Y.: Times Books, 1988), 119; Montgomery *Weekly Advertiser*, December 31, 1862.

66. Stackpole, *From Cedar Mountain to Antietam*, 149-153; Esposito, *West Point Atlas*, map 72; Blackford to "My dear Mary," December 19, 1862, Gordon-Blackford Papers.

67. Stackpole, *From Cedar Mountain to Antietam*, 149-153; Rathcford to D.H. Hill, July 2, 1886, Bound Volume 56, Fredericksburg & Spottsylvania National Military Park; Esposito, *West Point Atlas*, map 72.

68. Bridges, *Lee's Maverick General*, 159-160; OR 21, 643; Pickens diary; Tapert, *The Brother's War*, 121.

69. Cowper, *Grimes Letters*, 25.

70. OR 21, 681, 684; Montgomery *Weekly Advertiser*, December 31, 1862.

71. Blackford to "My dear Mary," December 19, 1862, Gordon-Blackford Papers.

72. G.W. Wright letter, December 17, 1862, Ralph Brown Draughon Library, Auburn University.

73. James Watt letter, December 21, 1862, J.H. Scruggs Collection, Birmingham Public Library, Birmingham, AL.

74. OR 21, 560, 644.

75. Pickens diary.

76. *OR* 21, 644; Pickens diary.

77. Pickens diary; Blackford to "My dear Mary," January 19, 1863, Gordon-Blackford Papers.

Chapter Six

1. Henry W. Thomas, *The History of the Doles-Cook Brigade, Army of Northern Virginia, C.S.A.* (Atlanta: The Franklin Printing & Pub. Co., 1907), 171.

2. Blackford to "My dear Mother," January 15, 1863, Blackford to "My dear Mary," January 19, 1863, Gordon-Blackford Papers.

3. *Ibid.*; Fifth Alabama History File, ADAH; Greensboro *Beacon*, July 19, 1903.

4. Archie McDonald, ed., *Make Me a Map of the Valley: The Civil War Journal of Stonewall Jackson's Cartographer, Jedediah Hotchkiss* (Dallas: Southern Methodist University Press, 1973), 109; Walker, *Memorial*, 445.

5. Bridges, *Lee's Maverick General*, 146-147, 162-163.

6. Blackford letters, Brake Collection, United States Army Military History Institute (this source hereafter cited as Brake Coll.); Mobile *Advertiser & Register*, May 24, 1863.

7. William C. Davis, ed., *The Confederate General*, 6 vols. (The National Historical Society, 1991), vol. v, 108; James P. Smith to "My Dearest Sister," January 21, 1863, as quoted in Krick, "The Smoothbore Volley."

8. Thomas Coffey to wife, February 16, 1863, *Confederate Veteran Magazine*, vol. 26, 198.

9. Rodes to Ewell, March 22, 1863, Polk-Brown-Ewell Papers, Southern Historical Collection, University of North Carolina (this source hereafter cited as Polk-Brown-Ewell Papers); Sifakis, *Who Was Who*, 712-713.

10. Robert Rodes' Compiled Service Record, National Archives. Representatives signing the letter included E.S. Dargan, William P. Chilton, James L. Pugh, John P. Ralls, David Clopton, Francis S. Lyon, Thomas J. Foster, and William R. Smith.

11. *Ibid.*

12. *Ibid.*; Haskell M. Monroe, James T. McIntosh, Lynda Lawell Crist, Mary Seaton Dix, and Kenneth H. Williams, eds., *Jefferson Davis, Constitutionalist: Letters, Papers and Speeches,* 9 vols. (Baton Rouge: Louisiana State University Press, 1973), vol. 5, 447 (hereafter cited as *Jefferson Davis*).

13. Blackford to father, March 8, 1863, Brake Coll.; Robert Rodes' Compiled Service Record, National Archives.

14. Blackford to father, March 8, 1863, Brake Coll.

15. Rodes to D.H. Hill, March 22, 1863, D.H. Hill Papers, North Carolina State Archives; Montgomery *Weekly Mail,* April 15, 1863.

16. Cooper to Davis, April 6, 1863, Davis Papers, RG109, National Archives; Douglas S. Freeman, ed., *Lee's Dispatches* (N.Y.: Putnam's Sons, 1915), 92; Stephen W. Sears, *Chancellorsville* (Boston: Houghton and Miflin, 1996), 50; Sifakis, *Who Was Who,* 343.

17. James I. Robertson, *Stonewall Jackson: The Man, The Soldier, The Legend* (N.Y.: Simon & Shuster Macmillan, 1997), 698; 6th Alabama History File, ADAH.

18. Sifakis, *Who Was Who,* 255; Rodes to Ewell, March 22, 1863, Polk-Brown-Ewell Papers.

19. George Rust to "Dear Beckie," May 1, 1863, Rust Papers, Virginia Historical Society, Richmond.

20. Sifakis, *Who Was Who,* 447; Davis, *Confederate General,* vol. IV, 204-205.

21. Sifakis, *Who Was Who,* 529; Davis, *Confederate General,* vol. V, pp. 74-75.

22. Sifakis, *Who Was Who,* 332; Davis, *Confederate General,* vol. III, 142-143.

23. Sifakis, *Who Was Who,* 186; Davis, *Confederate General,* vol. II, 72-73.

24. Sifakis, *Who Was Who,* 134; Davis, *Confederate General,* vol. II, 9-10.

25. *Confederate Veteran Magazine,* vol. 26, 198-199.

26. Pickens diary, 46.

27. *Confederate Veteran Magazine,* vol. 26, 157.

28. *Ibid.*; Pickens diary, 46; *SHSP,* vol. 26, 3.

29. Frank E. Vandiver, *Mighty Stonewall* (N.Y.: McGraw-Hill, 1957), 450; Walker, *Memorial,* 445.

30. Blackford letter, Jan. 25, 1863, Brake Coll.

31. Pickens diary, 53.

32. *SHSP,* vol. 26, 4, and vol. 33, 232.

33. McHenry Howard, *Recollections of a Maryland Confederate Soldier and Staff Officer under Johnston, Jackson, and Lee* (Dayton, Ohio: Morningside Bookshop, 1973), 191.

34. Rodes to Ewell, March 22, 1863, Polk-Brown-Ewell Papers; T. Harrell Allen, *Lee's Last Major General: Bryan Grimes of North Carolina* (Mason City, Iowa: Savas Publishing, 1999), 220.

35. Henry A. Whiting Papers, Chicago Historical Society; Junius Daniel Brigade Order Book, Wilson Library, University of North Carolina, Chapel Hill, NC.

36. Esposito, *West Point Atlas,* map 84; *SHSP,* vol. 7, 553-554; Robertson, *Stonewall Jackson,* 698.

37. John Bigelow, Jr., *The Campaign of Chancellorsville: A Strategic and Tactical Study* (New Haven, CT.: Yale University Press, 1910), 207.

38. Earnest B. Furguson, *Chancellorsville, 1863: The Souls of the Brave* (N.Y.: Alfred A. Knopf, 1992), 120.

39. *Ibid.*; *OR* 25, pt. 1, 939.

40. Furguson, *Chancellorsville*, 120; Bigelow, *The Campaign of Chancellorsville*, 207-208.

41. Captain William Calder letters, SHC, UNC (hereafter cited as Calder letter); Robertson, *Stonewall Jackson*, 699.

42. *SHSP*, vol. 7, 562; Bigelow, *The Campaign of Chancellorsville*, 208-209.

43. *OR* 25, pt. 1, 939, 950; James P. Arrington Compiled Service Record, National Archives; Mobile *Advertiser & Register*, May 19, 1863; Krick, *Staff Officers in Gray*, 63.

44. *OR* 25, pt. 1, 939; Gary W. Gallagher, *Stephen Dodson Ramseur: Lee's Gallant General* (Chapel Hill, N.C.: University of North Carolina Press, 1985), 53.

45. Bigelow, *The Campaign of Chancellorsville*, 207, 232.

46. Esposito, *West Point Atlas*, maps 84-85; Vandiver, *Mighty Stonewall*, 459; Robertson, *Stonewall Jackson*, 701.

47. Esposito, *West Point Atlas*, map 85.

48. *OR* 25, pt. 1, 939, 950, 983, 995; Bigelow, *The Campaign of Chancellorsville*, 232; William M. Norman, *A Portion of My Life* (Winston-Salem, N.C.: John F. Blair, 1959), 169.

49. *OR* 25, pt. 1, 939-940; Gallagher, *Stephen Dodson Ramseur*, 53.

50. *OR* 25, pt. 1, 939-940; *SHSP*, vol. 7, 564.

51. *OR* 25, pt. 1, 940, 950, 995; Bigelow, *The Chancellorsville Campaign*, 249-250; Gallagher, *Stephen Dodson Ramseur*, 57.

52. Esposito, *West Point Atlas*, map 85.

53. *OR* 25, pt. 1, 940; Walter Clark, ed., *Histories of the Several Regiments and Battalions from North Carolina in the Great War, 1861-1865*, 6 vols. (Wendell, N.C.: Broadfoot, 1982), vol. 2, 169.

54. *SHSP*, vol. 26, 7.

55. Rodes to "My dearest Wife," May 2, 1863, Simon Gratz Collection, Historical Society of Pennsylvania, Philadelphia.

56. Edward Stackpole, *Chancellorsville: Lee's Greatest Battle* (Harrisburg, Pa.: The Stackpole Co., 1958), 232; *SHSP*, vol. 7, 567; Bigelow, *The Chancellorsville Campaign*, 264; McDonald, *Make Me a Map*, 137

57. Robertson, *Stonewall Jackson*, 714.

58. Furguson, *Chancellorsville*, 241; Bigelow, *The Chancellorsville Campaign*, 274-275; Robertson, *Stonewall Jackson*, 714.

59. Clark, *Histories,* vol. 2, 228.

60. Robertson, *Stonewall Jackson*, 715; *Confederate Veteran Magazine*, vol. 28, 450; Davis, *Confederate General*, vol. V, 107.

61. *OR* 25, pt. 1, 940; Furguson, *Chancellorsville*, 240.

62. *OR* 25, pt. 1, 940; *SHSP*, vol. 7, 571; Bigelow, *The Chancellorsville Campaign*, 274-275.

63. OR 25, pt. 1, 981-982; Furguson, *Chancellorsville*, 267; Bigelow, *The Chancellorsville Campaign*, 281; Krick, *Staff Officers in Gray*, 74.

64. OR 25, pt. 1, 940; Montgomery *Weekly Advertiser*, June 3, 1863.

65. Furguson, *Chancellorsville*, 241.

66. Robertson, *Stonewall Jackson*, 717.

67. *Ibid.*; Clark, *Histories*, vol. 3, 228.

68. Calder letter.

69. Lawrence R. Laboda, *From Selma to Appomattox: The History of the Jeff Davis Artillery* (Shippensburg, Pa.: White Mane, 1994), 108-109.

70. Reminiscences of John J. McClendon, William Alexander Smith Papers, SHC, University of North Carolina (hereafter cited as McClendon Reminiscences).

71. OR 25, pt. 1, 981.

72. *Ibid.*, 956; Reminiscences of W.H. May, 3rd Alabama History File, ADAH (hereafter cited as May Reminiscences).

73. "Jackson's Last Battle," *Confederate Veteran,* vol. 28, 94; Robertson, *Stonewall Jackson*, 718.

74. *SHSP*, vol. 7, 572-573.

75. Furguson, *Chancellorsville*, 234, 258; Bigelow, *The Chancellorsville Campaign*, 289.

76. Furguson, *Chancellorsville*, 260; Freeman, *Lee's Lieutenants*, vol. 2, 555.

77. OR 25, pt. 1, 940-941, 995, 1004; Furguson, *Chancellorsville*, 260-261; Bigelow, *The Chancellorsville Campaign*, 292; Lenoir Chambers, *Stonewall Jackson*, 2 vols. (N.Y.: William Morrow, 1959), vol. 2, 397.

78. Clark, *Histories*, vol. 3, 229.

79. May Reminiscences; *Confederate Veteran Magazine*, vol. 8, 408.

80. OR 25, pt. 1, 940-941, 999, 1004; Furguson, *Chancellorsville*, 235, 261; Bigelow, *The Chancellorsville Campaign*, 293.

81. OR 25, pt. 1, 940; 3rd Alabama History File, ADAH; Montgomery *Weekly Advertiser*, June 3, 1863; Thomas, *Doles-Cook Brigade*, 72.

82. Esposito, *West Point Atlas*, map 87.

83. OR 25, pt. 1, 940-941, 1004; *Battles & Leaders*, vol. 3, 208; *SHSP*, vol. 43, 48-49; Freeman, *Lee's Lieutenants*, vol. 2, 557; Robertson, *Stonewall Jackson*, 721.

84. Montgomery *Weekly Advertiser*, June 3, 1863.

85. OR 25, pt. 1, 941.

86. Furguson, *Chancellorsville*, 238.

87. G.F.R. Henderson, *Stonewall Jackson and the American Civil War,* 2 vols. (London: Longmans, Green and Co., 1898), vol. 2, 503-504.

88. Montgomery *Weekly Advertiser*, June 3, 1863; James Tate, "A Historical Record of the Tuskagee Light Infantry, Co. G 3rd Regt. AL.," 3rd Alabama History File, ADAH.

89. Furguson, *Chancellorsville*, 278; Clark, *Histories*, vol. 3, 229; Pickens diary, 65.

90. Bigelow, *The Chancellorsville Campaign*, 297.

91. *OR* 25, pt. 1, 985; Walker, *Memorial*, 446.

92. *OR* 25, pt. 1, 941, 967; Jasper Co. *News*, Dec. 8, 1893.

93. *OR* 25, pt. 1, 941, 1004, 1009, 1031; Bigelow, *The Chancellorsville Campaign*, 301; 6th Alabama History File, ADAH.

94. *OR* 25, pt. 1, 942; Bigelow, *The Chancellorsville Campaign*, 298.

95. *OR* 25, pt. 1, 995.

96. *Ibid*, 941, 985; Furguson, *Chancellorsville*, 278, 287; Pickens diary, 67.

97. *OR* 25, pt. 1, 941, 967.

98. Bigelow, *The Chancellorsville Campaign*, 308; Chambers, *Stonewall Jackson*, vol. 2, 406.

99. W.B. Hagood letter, May 13, 1863, Harden Collection, Duke University (hereafter cited as Hagood letters); Pickens diary, 68.

100. *OR* 25, pt. 1, 946; Bevin Alexander, *Lost Victories:: The Military Genius of Stonewall Jackson* (N.Y.: Henry Holt and Co., 1992), 313.

101. *OR* 25, pt. 1, 941-942, 999; Bigelow, *The Chancellorsville Campaign*, 312-314.

102. Furguson, *Chancellorsville*, 256-257.

103. *Confederate Veteran Magazine*, vol. 13, 231; Bigelow, *The Chancellorsville Campaign*, 323.

104. *OR* 25, pt. 1, 942.

105. *Confederate Veteran Magazine*, vol. 25, 227.

106. Letter of May 8, 1863, Bound Volume 241, Fredericksburg & Spottsylvania National Military Park; Mobile *Advertiser & Register*, May 24, 1863.

107. May Reminiscences.

108. *OR* 25, pt. 1, 995; Robertson, *Stonewall Jackson*, 724; Thomas, *Doles-Cook Brigade*, 72; Mobile *Advertiser & Register*, May 24, 1863.

109. *Battles & Leaders*, vol. 3, 209.

110. Cowper, *Grimes Letters*, 30; Robertson, *Stonewall Jackson*, 727-728.

111. Mobile *Advertiser & Register*, May 24, 1863.

112. Bigelow, *The Chancellorsville Campaign*, 337; Robertson, *Stonewall Jackson*, 724.

113. *OR* 25, pt. 1, 942; Furguson, Chancellorsville, 266-267.

114. *OR* 25, pt. 1, 942-943; Bigelow, *The Chancellorsville Campaign*, 339; Chambers, *Stonewall Jackson*, vol. 2, 424.

115. *SHSP*, vol. 8, 444-445; *Confederate Veteran*, vol. 16, 269-270. This is in sharp contrast to a dubious story found in *Confederate Veteran*, which claimed that at the beginning of the Chancellorsville campaign Rodes refused to turn over the division to Edward Johnson upon that officer's return to duty. "General Rodes," claimed an

alleged witness, "coolly told him that, as he had started in the fight, he would not be relieved until it was over unless he was put under arrest."

116. Walker, *Memorial*, 446-447; Krick, *Staff Officers in Gray*, 242.

117. Munford to J.W. Daniel, March 22, 1907, J.W. Daniel Papers, Duke University; Krick, *The Smoothbore, Volley* 128.

118. *Battles & Leaders*, vol. 3, 211; Bigelow, *The Chancellorsville Campaign*, 341.

119. OR 25, pt. 1, 885, 887, 942; Bigelow, *The Chancellorsville Campaign*, 339.

120. OR 25, pt. 1, 887, 943, 946; Bigelow, *The Chancellorsville Campaign*, 346; Montgomery *Weekly Advertiser*, June 6, 1863; Gallagher, *Stephen Dodson Ramseur*, 60.

121. Gallagher, *Stephen Dodson Ramseur*, 59; Esposito, *West Point Atlas*, map 87.

122. OR 25, pt. 1, 887.

123. OR 25, pt. 1, 896, 943, 996; Bigelow, *The Chancellorsville Campaign*, map 26.

124. OR 25, pt. 1, 943, 952; Notebook of Edward O'Neal, John Coffee & Family Papers, Library of Congress.

125. 3rd Alabama History File, folder 7, ADAH.

126. *Ibid*; Mobile *Advertiser & Register*, May 19, 1863.

127. OR 25, pt. 1, 943, 946.

128. Clark, *Histories*, vol. 3, 118.

129. OR 25, pt. 1, 943; 3rd Alabama History File, folder 7, ADAH.

130. OR 25, pt. 1, 943; Montgomery *Weekly Advertiser*, April 11, 1905.

131. OR 25, pt. 1, 986; 3rd Alabama History File, folder 7, ADAH.

132. 3rd Alabama History File, folder 7, ADAH.

133. *Ibid*.

134. OR 25, pt. 1, 944.

135. Gallagher, *Stephen Dodson Ramseur*, 60-62; Allen, *Lee's Last Major General*, 96-99.

136. Calder letters.

137. Cowper, *Grimes Letters*, 33.

138. OR 25, pt. 1, 996.

139. *Ibid.*, 944, 996; Francis M. Parker letter, May 29, 1891, Stephen Ramseur Papers, SHC, UNC; Grimes, 34.

140. Norman, *A Portion of My Life*, 174.

141. OR 25, pt. 1, 944.

142. *Ibid.*, 886, 945, 987; Bigelow, *The Chancellorsville Campaign*, maps 31 & 33; *SHSP*, vol. 40, 89.

143. OR 25, pt. 1, 974; Montgomery *Weekly Advertiser*, June 5, 1863; Norman, *A Portion of My Life*, 176.

144. William Alexander Smith Papers, SHC, UNC.

145. Parker letter, May 9, 1863, Parker Papers, North Carolina Department of Archives and History; Jasper Co. *News*, Dec. 8, 1898.

146. Blackford to "My dear Mary," May 21, 1863, Gordon-Blackford Papers.

147. *OR* 25, pt. 1, 945, 989; Furguson, *Chancellorsville*, 403.

148. *OR* 25, pt. 1, 945; Montgomery *Weekly Advertiser*, May 21, 1863; Mobile *Advertiser & Register*, May 19, 23, 1863.

149. *SHSP*, vol. 26, 8.

150. *OR* 25, pt. 1, 946-947.

Chapter Seven

1. Robertson, *Stonewall Jackson*, 742; Burke Davis, *They Called Him Stonewall* (N.Y.: Wings Books, 1988), 439-440; Walker, *Memorial*, 447.

2. Jones Reminiscence. In this postwar reminiscence, Thomas Jones, a member of Carter's battery, wrote, "Major Whiting, who was Gen. Rodes's A.A.G., told me after the war, that Rodes called to see Gen. Jackson several days after he was wounded, when it was thought he would get well. . . ."

3. *OR* 25, pt. 2, 774, vol. 51, pt. 2, 703; *Jefferson Davis*, vol. 6, 48; Freeman, *Lee's Lieutenants*, vol. 2, 640; Memoirs of Clement D. Fishburne, 81, Alderman Library, University of Virginia, Charlottesville. Fishburne wrote:

> I heard this and the report that Gen. Rodes returned the commission & declined it with the statement that if he earned promotion and was entitled to it for gallant services, they were rendered on the 3rd of May and he would not have the commission without some recognition of that fact. Afterwards I saw Rodes & asked him about it and he confirmed the report I had heard & said that he declined the commission, stating briefly the reasons of what I had heard as his reasons for so doing. The Commission was returned through the usual regular channels & of course passed through the office of Gen. Lee, who is said to have approved Rodes' course and to have made such an endorsement that very soon the department at Richmond sent back a Commission dated 3 May giving some recognition to him for gallant services.

Major Blackford was among those who believed that Rodes won his promotion based upon his actions of May 3, wherein he had advanced "over friend and foe alike"—Blackford to My dear Mary, May 21, 1863, Gordon-Blackford Papers.

4. *OR* 25, pt. 2, 803.

5. *Ibid.*, 886.

6. Percy Gatling Hamlin, *"Old Bald Head" (General R.S. Ewell): The Portrait of a Soldier* (Strasburg, Va.: Shenandoah Publishing House, 1940), 134.

7. Montgomery *Weekly Advertiser*, May 21, 1863.

8. Mobile *Advertiser & Register*, May 26, 1863.

9. William A. Smith, *The Anson Guards, Company D, Fourteenth Regiment North Carolina Volunteers* (Wendell, N.C.: Broadfoot, 1978), 181, 279.

10. Clark, *Histories*, vol. 1, 716.

11. Haygood letter, Harden Collection, Duke University.

12. Davis Tinsley letters, Georgia Dept. of Archives & History, Atlanta.

13. Hoge letters, Brake Collection, USAMHI.

14. Blackford letters, USAMHI.

15. *OR* 25, pt. 2, 810, 840; Pfanz, *Richard S. Ewell*, 271-276.

16. Park, *SHSP*, vol. 26, 10; Pickens diary, 80; Gallagher, *Stephen Dodson Ramseur*, 67; *Confederate Veteran Magazine*, vol. 16, 269-270; Manly Wellman, *Rebel Boast: First at Bethel—Last at Appomattox* (N.Y.: Henry Holt, 1956), 109.

17. *OR* 25, pt. 2, 798, 851; Gallagher, *Stephen Dodson Ramseur*, 67; Davis, *Confederate General*, vol. 2, 46-47.

18. Pfanz, *Richard S. Ewell*, 280; *OR* 27, pt. 2, 545, 592; Pickens diary, 82.

19. *OR* 27, pt. 2, 546; George Greer diary, CWTI Collection, USAMHI.

20. *OR* 27, pt. 2, 293, 546; Samuel J. Martin, *The Road to Glory: Confederate General Richard S. Ewell* (Indianapolis: Guild Press of Indiana, 1991), 178.

21. *OR* 27, pt. 2, 546; Clark, *Histories*, vol. 1, 717.

22. *OR* 27, pt. 2, 546, 564; Martin, *The Road to Glory*, 179.

23. *OR* 27, pt. 2, 564, 592; Martin, *The Road to Glory*, 179-180.

24. *OR* 27, pt. 2, 546; McDonald, *Make Me a Map*, 150-151; Pickens diary, 84; Martin, *The Road to Glory*, 180-182.

25. *OR* 27, pt. 2, 546; Martin, *The Road to Glory*, 182-183.

26. *OR* 27, pt. 2, 546-548, 565; Pickens diary, 86-87; William Sturtevant Nye, *Here Come the Rebels!* (Baton Rouge: Louisiana State University Press, 1965), 86-87.

27. *Confederate Veteran*, vol. 30, 384.

28. *OR* 27, pt. 2, 548-549, 594; Louis Leon, *Diary of a Tar Heel Confederate Soldier* (Charlotte, N.N.: Stackpole, 1971), 31; Krick, *Staff Officers in Gray*, 150.

29. *OR* 27, pt. 2, 442, 548-550, 594; Nye, *Here Come the Rebels*, 134; Junius Daniel Brigade Order Book, Wilson Library, University of North Carolina, Chapel Hill, NC.

30. Junius Daniel Brigade Order Book, Wilson Library, University of North Carolina, Chapel Hill, NC.

31. James E. Green diary, Wilson Library, UNC (hereafter cited as Green diary); *OR* 27, pt. 2, 550.

32. OR 27, pt. 2, 550; Chichester Compiled Service Record, National Archives; Krick, *Staff Officers in Gray*, 95.

33. McDonald, *Make Me a Map*, 153.

34. Esposito, *West Point Atlas*, map 93; OR 27, pt. 2, 305, 550.

35. OR 27, pt. 2, 307, 550-551; McDonald, *Make Me a Map*, 153.

36. Pickens diary, 90-91.

37. OR 27, pt. 2, 297, 443.

38. *Ibid.*, 551; Green diary, UNC.

39. Ramseur letters, UNC.

40. Blackford letters, USAMHI.

41. OR 27, pt. 2, 551.

42. *Confederate Veteran*, vol. 35, 318.

43. OR 27, pt. 2, 551.

44. William B. Bean, *Stonewall's Man: Sandie Pendleton* (Chapel Hill, N.C.: University of North Carolina Press, 1959), 135.

45. Park, *SHSP*, vol. 33, 242.

46. OR 27, pt. 2, 550.

47. *Ibid.*, 551; *Confederate Veteran*, vol. 30, 384.

48. OR 27, pt. 2, 594; Battle, "The Third Alabama Regiment," ADAH.

49. *Confederate Veteran*, vol. 30, 384.

50. Hamlin, "*Old Bald Head*," 141; Thomas, *Doles-Cook Brigade*, 7.

51. Hamlin, "*Old Bald Head*," 141; Pickens diary, 91-92.

52. Battle, "The Third Alabama Regiment," ADAH; Pfanz, *Richard S. Ewell*, 297-298.

53. OR 27, pt. 2, 551; Hamlin, "*Old Bald Head*," 141.

54. William Stanley Hoole, *History of the Third Alabama Regiment, C.S.A.* (Montgomery, Al.: Confederate Publishing Co., 1982), 41.

55. OR 27, pt. 2, 566.

56. Pfanz, *Richard S. Ewell*, 298; McDonald, *Make Me a Map*, 154.

57. Battle, "The Third Alabama Regiment," ADAH; Green diary, UNC; Martin, *The Road to Glory*, 194; Nye, *Here Come the Rebels*, 301.

58. OR 27, pt. 2, 551; Reminiscences of John J. McClendon, William Alexander Smith papers, SHC, UNC; *Confederate Veteran*, vol. 30, 384; Smith, *The Anson Guards*, 201.

59. Nye, *Here Come the Rebels*, 304-307; Glenn Tucker, *High Tide at Gettysburg* (N.Y.: The Bobbs-Merrill Co., 1958), 62.

60. OR 27, pt. 2, 443; Hamlin, "*Old Bald Head*," 143; Pfanz, *Richard S. Ewell*, 299-300.

61. Park, *SHSP*, vol. 26, 12; Thomas Hightower letters, Ga. Dept. of Archives & History, Atlanta.

62. Pfanz, *Richard S. Ewell*, 299.

63. *Ibid.*, 300; Davis, *Confederate General*, vol. 6, 60-61.

64. Campbell Brown diary, Tennessee Historical Commission Collection, USAMHI; McDonald, *Make Me a Map*, 155; Martin, The *Road to Glory*, 195-196; Tucker, *High Tide*, 63.

65. Tucker, *High Tide*, 64; Clark, *Histories*, vol. 2, 526.

66. Tucker, *High Tide*, 63-64.

67. Wellman, *Rebel Boast*, 119.

68. Campbell Brown diary, Tennessee Historical Commission Collection, USAMHI; Wellman, *Rebel Boast*, 119; George Whitaker Wills papers, UNC.

69. Wake Forest student newspaper, April 1897, Brake Collection, USAMHI (hereafter cited as Wake Forest paper).

70. OR 27, pt. 2, 562.

71. Esposito, *West Point Atlas*, map 94; Ramseur letters, UNC; Tucker, *High Tide*, 62-63.

72. OR 27, pt. 2, 443, 552; Martin, *The Road to Glory*, 197.

73. OR 27, pt. 2, 301, 444; *Confederate Veteran*, vol. 8, 25.

74. Park, *SHSP*, vol. 33, 244; Clark, *Histories*, vol. 2, 234.

75. Nye, *Here Come the Rebels*, 358.

76. *Ibid.*, 358-359; Hamlin, *"Old Bald Head,"* 144.

77. *Confederate Veteran*, vol. 5, 614-615.

78. Trimble in *SHSP*, vol. 26, 121-122; Martin, *The Road to Glory*, 184, 203-204; Harry W. Pfanz, *Gettysburg: Culp's Hill and Cemetery Hill* (Chapel Hill: University of North Carolina Press, 1993), 32-33; Nye, *Here Come the Rebels*, 359.

Chapter Eight

1. OR 27, pt. 2, 444.

2. *Ibid.*, 444, 468; Pfanz, *Gettysburg*, 33.

3. Edwin B. Coddington, *The Gettysburg Campaign: A Study in Command* (N.Y.: Charles Scribner's Sons, 1968), 29-30.

4. OR 27, pt. 2, 552; *Southern Bivouac*, 6 vols. (Wilmington, N.C.: Broadfoot Pub. Co., 1992-93), vol. 4, 439 (hereafter cited as *Southern Bivouac*).

5. OR 27, pt. 2, 552, 596; Thompson, *Autauga Rifles*, 7; Massy Griffin, "Rodes On Oak Hill: A Study of Rodes' Division on the First Day of Gettysburg. *Gettysburg Magazine*, no. 4 (Jan. 1991), 34-36 (hereafter cited as Griffin, "Rodes On Oak Hill"). Rodes' division flag is described in Newton Davis to sister, August 28, 1863, ADAH.

6. OR 27, pt. 2, 552; Pickens diary, 94; Coddington, *The Gettysburg Campaign*, 63, 87.

7. *Southern Bivouac*, vol. 4, 440.

8. Park, *SHSP*, vol. 26, 12-13; Clark, *Histories*, vol. 4, 255; *Confederate Veteran*, vol. 16, 269-270; Krick, *Staff Officers in Gray*, 142.

9. OR 27, pt. 2, 552; Clark, *Histories*, vol. 1, 634.

10. OR 27, pt. 2, 552-553, 579, 592, 595-596; Griffin, "Rodes On Oak Hill," 36; Pickens diary, 95; Hoole, *History of the Third Alabama*, 41, 70; Clark, *Histories*, vol. 2, 119, 635.

11. Warren Hassler, *Crisis at the Crossroads: The First Day at Gettysburg* (University, Al.: University of Alabama Press, 1970), 272.

12. Gary W. Gallagher, ed., *The First Day at Gettysburg: Essays on Union and Confederate Leadership* (Kent, Ohio: Kent State University Press, 1992), 134.

13. Clark, *Histories*, vol. 2, 235.

14. OR 27, pt. 2, 553-554, 579-580; Clark, *Histories*, vol. 2, 637. These dead their comrades buried that night in four shallow depressions directly behind their line of battle, a location known for decades as the "Iverson Pits."

15. OR 27, pt. 2, 554, 566-567.

16. Freeman, *Lee Lieutenants*, vol. 3, 83.

17. *Ibid*, 86.

18. OR 27, pt. 2, 307, 492, 554-555, 587, 595; Coddington, *The Gettysburg Campaign*, 309.

19. *Ibid.*, 469, 555.

20. *Ibid.*, 318, 445; McDonald, *Make Me a Map*, 156; Martin, *The Road to Glory*, 184, 205.

21. Pfanz, *Gettysburg*, 73.

22. *Ibid.*

23. *Ibid.*, 76; Smith in *SHSP*, vol. 33, 144-145.

24. John A. Stikeleather, Reminiscences, NCDAH (hereafter cited as Stikeleather); B.B. Ross letters, Brake Collection, USAMHI; Calder letters, Brake Coll.; W.H. May memoir, Georgia Dept. of Archives & History, Atlanta.

25. *Confederate Veteran*, vol. 5, 614-615.

26. OR 27, pt. 2, 567; Clark, *Histories*, vol. 1, 719.

27. OR 27, pt. 2, 445.

28. Ewell-Stewart-Brown Papers, Tenn. State Library.

29. OR 27, pt. 2, 445, 469.

30. *Ibid.*, 555; Martin, *The Road to Glory*, 215.

31. Martin, *The Road to Glory*, 219.

32. *Ibid.*, 220; Charles C. Osborne, *Jubal: The Life and Times of General Jubal A. Early, C.S.A.* (Chapel Hill, NC.: Algonquin Books, 1992), 195-196; Pfanz, *Gettysburg*, 83;

Clifford Dowdy, *Death of a Nation: The Story of Lee and His Men at Gettysburg* (N.Y.: Alfred A. Knopf, 1958), 155.

33. *OR* 27, pt. 2, 503-504; Osborne *Jubal*, 197.

34. *OR* 27, pt. 2, 446; Pfanz, *Gettysburg*, 84-85.

35. *Ibid.*, 85.

36. Hamlin, *"Old Bald Head,"* 150; Green diary, UNC; *Southern Bivouac*, 443; Calder letters, Brake Coll., USAMHI.

37. Hamlin, *"Old Bald Head,"* 150; Pfanz, *Gettysburg*, 282; John C. Early, "A Southern Boy's Experience at Gettysburg." *Journal of the Military Service Institution of the United States*, 43 (Jan.-Feb. 1911): 422.

38. Martin, *The Road to Glory*, 229.

39. *OR* 27, pt. 2, 555.

40. Charles Minor Blackford, ed., *Letters From Lee's Army* (N.Y.: Charles Scribner's Sons, 1947), 231-232.

41. *OR* 27, pt. 2, 555.

42. *Ibid.*, 318-319, 446-447; Douglas S. Freeman, *R.E. Lee: A Biography,* 3 vols. (N.Y.: Charles Scribner's Sons, 1943-35), vol. 3, 96.

43. *OR* 27, pt. 2, 556.

44. *Ibid.*, 556, 666.

45. *Ibid.*, 580.

46. *Ibid.*, p. 556; *Southern Bivouac*, vol. 4, 497.

47. *OR* 27, pt. 2, 588; Stikeleather; Wake Forest student paper.

48. *OR* 27, pt. 2, 568, 588; Stikeleather; Freeman, *Lee's Lieutenants*, vol. 3, 171.

49. *OR* 27, pt. 2, 556, 666; Stikeleather; Early, *Autobiographical Sketch*, 274.

50. Stikeleather.

51. Calder letters, Brake Coll., USAMHI.

52. Ramseur papers, UNC.

53. *OR* 27, pt. 2, 659, 666; Pfanz, *Richard S. Ewell*, 280-282; Dowdy, *Death of a Nation*, 233; *SHSP*, vol. 4, 279.

54. *OR* 27, pt. 2, 470; Pfanz, *Richard S. Ewell*, 281.

55. *OR* 27, pt. 2, 447; Ewell-Stewart-Brown Papers, Tenn. State Library.

56. *OR* 27, pt. 2, 319.

57. Frederick Maurice, ed., *Charles Marshall, An Aide-de-Camp of Lee* (Boston: Little, Brown, 1927), 237.

58. Freeman, *R.E. Lee*, vol. 3, 102; Freeman, *Lee's Lieutenants*, vol. 3, 178.

59. *OR* 27, pt. 2, 556, 594, 596.

60. *Ibid.*, 556-557; Pickens diary, 97.

61. *Ibid.*

62. *OR* 27, pt. 2, 558.

63. *Ibid.*, 557-558, 593, 703.

64. Diary of a Tar Heel, 37-38; McDonald, *Make Me a Map*, 158; Ramseur papers, UNC; Sidney Richardson diary, Ga. Dept. of Archives & History, Atlanta; Shaffner letter, Brake Coll. USAMHI.

65. OR 27, pt. 2, 558, 570; Battle, "The Third Alabama Regiment," ADAH.

66. McDonald, *Make Me a Map*, 160.

67. Freeman, *R.E. Lee*, vol. 3, 140-141.

68. OR 27, pt. 2, 558-559; Pickens diary, 99-100.

69. OR 27, pt. 2, 559.

Chapter Nine

1. OR 27, pt. 2, 324, 448-449, 560-561.

2. *Ibid.*, 448-450, 560-561.

3. John W. Busey and David G. Martin, *Regimental Strengths and Losses at Gettysburg* (Longstreet House, 1986), 288-289; OR 27, pt. 2, 561.

4. Esposito, *West Point Atlas*, map 117; Pickens diary, 107; Norman, *A Portion of My Life*, 192.

5. McDonald, *Make Me a Map*, 164-165.

6. Terrill letters in 26th Alabama history file, ADAH; Gallagher, *Stephen Dodson Ramseur*, 76-78.

7. Blackford to "My dear Mother," August 12, 1863, Gordon-Blackford Papers; Rodes to William Blackford, August 13, 1863, Lewis Leigh Coll., USAMHI. Dr. Mitchell advised against surgery to remove a vein from Blackford's leg, but Blackford went ahead with it the following winter.

8. Davis, *Confederate General*, vol. III, 143, 198-199; OR 29, pt. 2, 706; Rodes to Major Walter H. Taylor, August 19, 1863, Wade Hampton Compiled Service Record, National Archives.

9. Davis, *Confederate General*, vol. III, 143, 198-199; OR 29, pt. 2, 706. Though not without protest from Governor Vance, who accused Davis of overlooking native North Carolinian Colonel Thomas Garrett because of that officer's pre-war anti-secessionist sentiments. To this Davis indignantly replied on March 31, 1864, "I must beg that a correspondence so unprofitable in its character, and which was not initiated by me, may here end, and that your future communications be restricted to such matters as may require official action." See *Jefferson Davis*, vol. 6, 216.

10. Compiled Service Record of Edward A. O'Neal, Sr., National Archives (hereafter cited as O'Neal CSR, NA).

11. *Ibid.*

12. O'Neal CSR, NA; 3rd Alabama History File, ADAH.

13. Compiled Service Record of Samuel Pickens, NA.

14. *Ibid.*

15. Compiled Service Record of John T. Morgan, NA (hereafter cited as Morgan CSR, NA).

16. Morgan CSR, NA.

17. Jefferson Davis Papers, Duke University.

18. Morgan CSR, NA

19. *Ibid.*

20. Davis, *Confederate General*, vol. IV, 190-191, 205.

21. Morgan CSR, NA.

22. *Ibid.*

23. *Ibid.*

24. O'Neal CSR, NA; Phelan letter, Jefferson Davis Papers, Duke University.

25. *Ibid.*

26. *Ibid.*

27. Rodes to J.A. Seddon, January 21, 1864, Houghton Library, Harvard University, Cambridge, Mass.

28. O'Neal CSR, NA; Phelan letter, Jefferson Davis Papers, Duke University; William C. Davis, "Edward Asbury O'Neal," in William C. Davis, *The Confederate General*, 6 vols. (National Historical Society, 1991), vol. 4, 204-205. O'Neal enjoyed a successful legal and political career after the end of the war. He held various state offices including two terms as governor. He died in 1890.

29. Davis, *Confederate General*, vol. I, 75; Park, *SHSP*, vol. 33, 247.

30. Park, *SHSP*, vol. 33, 247.

31. McDonald, *Make Me a Map*, 168-169.

32. Newton Davis to sister, August 28, 1863, ADAH.

33. *Ibid.*, 171; Pickens diary, 112.

34. Rodes to P.T. Sutton, August 30, 1864, Jubal A. Early Papers, VHS; Krick, *Staff Officers in Gray*, 168.

35. Junius Daniel Brigade Order Book, Wilson Library, University of North Carolina, Chapel Hill, NC.

36. *Ibid.* The circular read: "A Battery of four (4) guns and artillery officers are now stationed near these Hd Qrs for the purpose of instructing of each Infantry Command in the Manual of the Piece. Each Brigade Commander will in turn have the use of these guns for a day—Daniel Sept. 10—Doles Sept. 11—Ramseur Sept. 12 and 14th &c. The guns can be used each day as long as the officers are able to give instructions; it is recommended that at least one company for each Regiment be drilled during the intervals the men can be sent from time to time under officers to the Camp of Maj. McIntosh Comdg Arty."

37. Pickens diary, 115; Park, *SHSP*, vol. 26, 17; [James D. McCabe], *The Grayjackets: And How They Lived, Fought and Died* (Richmond: Jones Brothers, 1867), 229-230.

38. Blackford to "My dear Mary," September 27, 1863, Gordon-Blackford Papers.

39. Pickens diary, 116. The man executed was Private James Foulkes, Co. E, 2nd North Carolina Infantry.

40. Park, *SHSP*, vol. 33, 248.

41. Blackford to "My dear Mary," September 27, 1863, Gordon-Blackford Papers.

42. *Dictionary of Alabama Biography*, 1456; Louise Rodes Schoch application for membership in the DAR, Rodes' file, VMI Archives.

43. Hotchkiss to wife, October 7, 1863, Hotchkiss Papers, LC.

44. Blackford to "My dear Father," October 20, 1863, Blackford to "My dear Mary," October 28, 1863, Gordon-Blackford Papers.

45. Blackford to "My dear Mary," October 28, 1863, Gordon-Blackford Papers.

46. A. L. Long and Marcus J. Wright, *Memoirs of Robert E. Lee* (N.Y.: J. M. Stoddart and Co., 1886), 311.

47. OR, 29, 417-418, 423.

48. Esposito, *West Point Atlas*, map 118; OR 29, pt. 1, 412, 416.

49. Charleston *Mercury*, November 21, 1863.

50. Christian, *Lynchburg and Its People*, 213; Lynchburg *Virginian*, Nov. 24, 1863.

51. OR 29, pt. 1, 611, 631.

52. Junius Daniel Brigade Order Book, Wilson Library, University of North Carolina, Chapel Hill, NC.

53. OR 29, pt. 1, 631; Gallagher, *Stephen Dodson Ramseur*, 86; Martin F. Graham and George F. Skoch, *Mine Run: A Campaign of Lost Opportunities, Oct. 21, 1863-May 1, 1864* (Lynchburg, Va.: H.E. Howard, Inc., 1987), 1-50.

54. OR 29, pt. 1, 611-613, 616, 631-633.

55. *Ibid.*, 823; Park, *SHSP*, vol. 33, 254.

56. Rodes to Hoge, November 25, 1863, MC-3 Series, Museum of the Confederacy, Richmond.

57. Rodes to Robertson, November 25, 1863, Talcott Family Papers, VHS.

58. OR 21, 1, 877.

59. OR 29, pt. 1, 827-836, 846-847, 876-887; Laura Elizabeth Lee, *Forget-Me-Nots of the Civil War: A Romance Containing Reminiscences and Original Letters of Two Confederate Soldiers* (St. Louis, 1909), 101.

60. Rodes to J.A. Seddon, December 13, 1863, Matthew Cullen CSR, NA.

61. OR 29, pt. 1, 829, 838, 886; Deed Book 8, 352, Tuscaloosa County Court House.

Chapter Ten

1. Blackford to "My dear Mother," August 12, 1863, Blackford to "My dear Mary," December 20, 1863, Blackford to "My dear Mary," March 25, 1864, Gordon-Blackford Papers.

2. Walker, *Memorial*, 457.

3. Blackford to "My dear Mary," January 14, 1864, Gordon-Blackford Papers; Robert Rodes to "Dear Major," February 9, 1864, Gilder-Lehrman Coll., GLC 2615, New York, NY.

4. Gallagher, *Stephen Dodson Ramseur*, 90; Laura Elizabeth *Lee, Forget-Me-Nots of the Civil War: A Romance Containing Reminiscences and Original Letters of Two Confederate* Soldiers (St. Louis, 1909), 103; Eli Glover letter, April 17, 1864, Georgia Dept. of Archives & History, Atlanta.

5. Park, *SHSP*, vol. 33, 257.

6. *Confederate Veteran*, vol. 26, 353.

7. Pickens diary, 128.

8. Blackford to "My dear Mary," January 14, 1864, Gordon-Blackford Papers; Krick, *Staff Officers in Gray*, 150.

9. *North Carolina Civil War Documentary*, 99, 290-305.

10. *OR* 33, 1173.

11. Gallagher, *Stephen Dodson Ramseur*, 94; Park, *SHSP*, vol. 33, 289-290.

12. Battle, "The Third Alabama Regiment."

13. *Ibid.*; "Spectator" to Montgomery *Daily Post*, February 7, 1864, 6th AL. History File, ADAH; Park, *SHSP*, vol. 33, 258; Robert Rodes to "Dear Major," February, 9, 1864, Gilder-Lehrman Coll., New York, NY. Rodes tells Blackford that regarding reenlistments he talked to various captains.

14. *SHSP*, vol. 26, 30-31; Robert Rodes to "Dear Major," February 9, 1864, Gilder-Lehrman Coll., New York, NY.

15. Rodes to R.H. Chilton, January 26, 1864, Lee Family Papers, VHS; Gallagher, *Stephen Dodson Ramseur*, 92-93.

16. Richmond *Daily Whig*, February 15, 1864.

17. *OR* 33, 1150.

18. *Ibid.*, 1124.

19. Gallagher, *Stephen Dodson Ramseur*, 94-95; Robert Rodes to "Dear Major," February 9, 1864, Gilder-Lehrman Coll., New York, NY.

20. *Confederate Veteran*, vol. 26, 353.

21. Park, *SHSP*, vol. 33, 206.

22. Smith, *The Anson Guards*, 223.

23. Davis, *Confederate General*, vol. IV, 204-205; Sifakis, *Compendium*, vol. 1, 94, 128.

24. *OR* 33, 1175, 1176, 1181; Robert Rodes to "Dear Major," February 9, 1864, Gilder-Lehrman Coll., New York, NY, in which Rodes tells Blackford that "Getting here [Hanover Junction] I was put in command of all the troops. . . ."

25. *SHSP*, vol. 50, 410.

26. Rodes payment statement, February 24, 1864, Record Group 109, Confederate Unfiled Papers, National Archives.

27. Walker, *Memorial*, 450.

28. Grimes Papers, SHC, UNC, Chapel Hill.

29. Cowper, *Grimes Letters*, 49.

30. Samuel Walkup diary, FSNMP; Lee, *Forget-Me-Nots*, 110; Pickens diary, 148; Joseph T. Durkin, ed., *Confederate Chaplain: A War Journal of Rev. James B. Sheehan, 14th Louisiana, C.S.A.* (Milwaukee, The Bruce Co., 1960), 78; Gallagher, *Stephen Dodson Ramseur*, 91-94.

31. Edward Warren, *A Doctor's Experiences in Three Continents* (Baltimore: Cushings & Barley, 1885), 316-320.

32. Blackford to "My dear Mary," April 25, 1864, Brake Coll.

33. Blackford letters, Brake Coll., USAMHI.

34. Davis, *Confederate General*, vol. V, 108.

35. George Rooker letter, April 25, 1864, Jesse F. Newsome Papers, Duke University.

36. Esposito, *West Point Atlas*, map 123; Osborne, *Jubal*, 230-231.

37. *OR* 36, pt. 1, 1070; Gordon C. Rhea, *The Battle of the Wilderness, May 5-6, 1864* (Baton Rouge: Louisiana State University Press, 1994), 25.

38. Rodes to "Dear Sutton," May 2, 1864, BR Box 287, Huntington Library, San Marino, CA.

39. *OR* 36, pt. 1, 1081; Capt. Williams to The Greensboro *Beacon*, June 29, 1903, in 5th AL. History File, ADAH (hereafter cited as Williams to The *Beacon*); Early, *Autobiographical Sketch*, 345.

40. *OR* 36, pt. 1, 1070; Rhea, *The Battle of the Wilderness*, 85-86.

41. *OR* 36, pt. 1, 1070; Rhea, *The Battle of the Wilderness*, 123, 153.

42. J.B. Stamp Reminiscences, in 3rd AL. History File, ADAH.

43. Battle, "The Third Alabama Regiment."

44. Edward Steere, *The Wilderness Campaign: The Meeting of Grant and Lee* (Harrisburg, Pa.: The Stackpole Co., 1960), 178-179.

45. Williams to The *Beacon*, July 2, 1903.

46. John M. Priest, *Nowhere to Run: The Wilderness, May 4th & 5th, 1864* (Shippensburg, Pa.: White Mane, 1995), 104-130; Martin, *The Road to Glory*, 286.

47. Steere, *The Wilderness Campaign*, 238-241.

48. *OR* 36, pt. 1, 1081; Clark, *Histories*, vol. 1, 278.

49. OR 36, pt. 1, 1071, 1081; Esposito, *West Point Atlas*, maps 123-124.

50. Gallagher, *Stephen Dodson Ramseur*, 103-104.

51. Freeman, *Lee's Lieutenants*, vol. 3, 375-385.

52. Williams to The *Beacon*, July 2, 1903.

53. Gallagher, *Stephen Dodson Ramseur*, 104; Gordon C. Rhea, *The Battles for Spottsylvania Court House and the Road to Yellow Tavern* (Baton Rouge: Louisiana State University Press, 1996), 77-78; Lee, *Forget-Me-Nots*, 114.

54. OR 36, pt. 2, 974, vol. 51, pt. 2, 902-903.

55. Clark, *Histories*, vol. 2, 241, vol. 1, 641.

56. Williams to The *Beacon*, July 19, 1903.

57. OR 36, pt. 1, 1071, 1081, 1083-1084; James W. Roberts diary in *The Florida Historical Quarterly* (Oct. 1932), 66 (hereafter cited as Roberts diary).

58. Battle, "The Third Alabama Regiment."

59. OR 36, pt. 1, 1081; Clark, *Histories*, vol. 2, 46.

60. Rhea, *The Battles for Spottsylvania*, 89-90; Freeman *Lee's Lieutenants*, vol. 3, 394-395.

61. Hamlin, *"Old Bald Head,"* 176-177.

62. Rhea, *The Battles for Spottsylvania*, 164.

63. Esposito, *West Point Atlas*, map 129; Rhea, *The Battles for Spottsylvania*, 161-165.

64. Jackson letter, May 11, 1864, Duke University.

65. Esposito, *West Point Atlas*, map 129; Freeman, *Lee's Lieutenants*, vol. 3, 394-395.

66. Rhea, *The Battles for Spottsylvania*, 170

67. OR 36, pt. 1, 1072; Rhea, *The Battles for Spottsylvania*, 170.

68. Clark, *Histories*, vol. 4, 259; Roberts diary.

69. Williams to The *Beacon*, July 19, 1903.

70. Esposito, *West Point Atlas*, map 129; Rhea, *The Battles for Spottsylvania*, 173-176.

71. Rhea, *The Battles for Spottsylvania*, 187; OR 36, pt. 2, 983.

72. Roberts diary.

73. Martin, *The Road to Glory*, 302-303.

74. Jackson letter, May 11, 1864, Duke University; Rhea, *The Battles for Spottsylvania*, 219-220.

75. OR 36, pt. 1, 1073; Rhea, *The Battles for Spottsylvania*, 219.

76. Battle, "The Third Alabama Regiment."

77. Clark, *Histories*, vol. 2, 50.

78. Esposito, *West Point Atlas*, map 130; Rhea, *The Battles for Spottsylvania*, 215.

79. OR 36, pt. 1, 1086-1087; Hamlin, *"Old Bald Head,"* 178; Rhea, *The Battles for Spottsylvania*, 220-221.

80. Rhea, *The Battles for Spottsylvania*, 226-227.

81. OR 36, pt. 1, 1073; Esposito, *West Point Atlas*, map 130.

82. Clark, *Histories*, vol. 2, 51.

83. *OR* 36, pt. 1, 1082; Clark, *Histories*, vol. 1, 257; Battle, "The Third Alabama Regiment."

84. *OR* 36, pt. 1, 1082; Clark, *Histories*, vol. 2, 51.

85. Battle, "The Third Alabama Regiment"; Clark, *Histories*, vol. 2, 51-52.

86. Allen, *Lee's Last Major General*, 157-158.

87. Alfred Lewis Scott memoir, VHS.

88. *OR* 36, pt. 1, 1091-1092; Venable in *SHSP*, vol. 14, 531; Clark, *Histories*, vol. 1, 289.

89. *OR* 36, vol. 1, 1073, 1093-1094; Clifford Dowdy, *Lee* (Boston: Little, Brown and Co., 1965), 212.

90. Rhea, *The Battles for Spottsylvania*, 304-312.

91. Venable in *SHSP*, vol. 14, 531-533.

92. Freeman, *Lee's Lieutenants*, vol. 3, 448.

93. Williams to The *Beacon*, July 19, 1903; Gary W. Gallagher, ed., *Fighting for the Confederacy: The Personal Recollections of General Edward Porter Alexander* (Chapel Hill, N.C.: University of North Carolina Press, 1989), 373.

94. Robert Stiles, *Four Years Under Marse Robert* (N.Y.: Neale Pub. Co., 1903), 261.

95. Lee, *Forget-Me-Nots*, 116; Gallagher, *Stephen Dodson Ramseur*, 111-112.

96. Rhea, *The Battles for Spottsylvania*, 304-312; Martin, *The Road to Glory*, 309.

97. Davis, *Confederate General*, vol. II, 47.

98. Esposito, *West Point Atlas*, maps, 131-132.

99. T.M. Gorman memoir, NCDAH, Raleigh.

100. *OR* 36, pt. 1, 1073; Esposito, *West Point Atlas*, map 132.

101. *OR* 36, pt. 1, 1073, 1082-1083; Esposito, *West Point Atlas*, map 133; Gallagher, *Stephen Dodson Ramseur*, 113-114.

102. *OR* 36, pt. 1, 1073; Cowper, *Grimes Letters*, 55.

103. Cowper, *Grimes Letters*, 53.

104. Esposito, *West Point Atlas*, map 134; D. Pfanz, *Richard S. Ewell*, 395.

105. Esposito, *West Point Atlas*, map 134; Allen, *Lee's Last Major General*, 163.

106. *OR* 36, pt. 1, 1074, 1076; Gary W. Gallagher, *Lee the Soldier*, excerpts and review of book, in *Civil War History*, vol. 36 (Sept. 1997).

107. Pfanz, *Richard S. Ewell*, 402.

108. *CW History*, 114-115; Pfanz, *Richard S. Ewell*, 402-403.

109. *OR* 36, pt. 1, 1083.

110. *OR* 36, pt. 3, 854; Noah Andre Trudeau, *Bloody Roads South: The Wilderness to Cold Harbor, May -June, 1864* (Boston: Little, Brown & Co., 1989), 252-255.

111. R. Wayne Maney, *Marching to Cold Harbor: Victory and Failure, 1864* (Shippensburg, Pa.: White Mane, 1995), 80-81.

112. Louis J. Baltz III, *The Battle of Cold Harbor, May 27-June 13, 1864* (Lynchburg, Va.: H.E. Howard, 1990), 125-127.

113. *Ibid.*, 161-173.

114. Park, *SHSP*, vol. 33, 259.

Chapter Eleven

1. Blackford to "My dear Mary," June 5, 1864, June 8, 1864, Gordon-Blackford Papers.

2. Osborne, *Jubal*, 246-252.

3. *OR* 43, pt. 1, 1018; Davis, *Confederate General*, vol. II, 21-22, 39-40.

4. *SHSP*, vol. 3, 112; Osborne, *Jubal*, 263-265; Millard K. Bushong, *Old Jube: A Biography of General Jubal A. Early* (Shippensburg, Pa.: Beidal, 1985), 193.

5. Benjamin F. Cooling, *Jubal Early's Raid on Washington, 1864* (Baltimore: Nautical and Aviation Pub. Co., 1989), 26; Park, *SHSP*, vol. 1, 373.

6. Colling, *Jubal Early's Raid*, 27; Park, *SHSP*, vol. 1, 373.

7. *OR* 43, pt. 1, 1018; Wellman, *Rebel Boast*, 160.

8. Early, *Autobiographical Sketch*, 373; Wellman, *Rebel Boast*, 161.

9. *OR* 43, pt. 1, 1018; Colling, *Jubal Early's Raid*, 36; Early, *Autobiographical Sketch*, 373.

10. Colling, *Jubal Early's Raid*, 36; Wellman, *Rebel Boast*, 161; Yancey, *Lynchburg and Its Neighbors*, 81-82.

11. *OR* 43, pt. 1, 1018; Colling, *Jubal Early's Raid*, 36; Osborne, *Jubal*, 255.

12. Colling *Jubal Early's Raid*, 50-51; Cowper, *Grimes Letters*, 56.

13. Colling *Jubal Early's Raid*, 50-51.

14. Cowper, *Grimes Letters*, 57; Lucy Rodes to Alexander Brown, May 6, 1862, Alexander Brown Papers, Duke University.

15. *OR* 43, pt. 1, 1019; Early, *Autobiographical* Sketch, 376; Osborne, *Jubal*, 261.

16. *OR* 43, pt. 1, 1019; Colling, *Jubal Early's Raid*, 56.

17. *OR* 43, pt. 1, 1019; Colling, *Jubal Early's Raid*, 56-57; Brown Reminiscences, Ewell-Stewart-Brown Papers, Tennessee State Library, Nashville; John S. Anglin letters, Library of Congress.

18. Early, *Autobiographical Sketch*, 382.

19. *OR* 43, pt. 1, 1019; Cowper, *Grimes Letters*, 56.

20. *OR* 43, pt. 1, 1019; Colling, *Jubal Early's Raid*, 63; Osborne, *Jubal*, 261; Clark, *Histories*, vol. 2, 275.

21. *OR* 43, pt. 1, 1019; Don Lowry, *Fate of the Country: the Civil War from June to September 1864* (N.Y.: Hippocrene Press, 1992), 102; Early, *Autobiographical Sketch*, 382; Osborne, *Jubal*, 265.

22. *OR* 43, pt. 1, 1019; Park, *SHSP*, vol. 1, 377; Osborne, *Jubal*, 263.

23. *OR* 43, pt. 1, 1019-1020; Colling, *Jubal Early's Raid*, 27.

24. *OR* 43, pt. 1, 1020; Lowry, *Fate of the Country*, 124-125.

25. Letters of Lt. Col. Sands to New Orleans *Daily Picayune* March 15, 1903, in 3rd AL. History File, ADAH.

26. Park, *SHSP*, vol. 1, 377; Colling, *Jubal Early's Raid*, 27-28.

27. *OR* 43, pt. 1, 1020.

28. *Ibid*; Park, *SHSP*, vol. 1, 378.

29. *OR* 43, pt. 1, 1020; Early, *Autobiographical Sketch*, 385.

30. *OR* 43, pt. 1, 1020-1021, vol. 37, pt. 1, 348-349; Osborne, *Jubal*, 271-275.

31. *OR* 43, pt. 1, 1021; Peter J. Meaney, *The Civil War Engagement at Cool Spring July 18, 1864* (Berryville, Va.: Clark County Historical Association, 1980), 5.

32. *OR* 43, pt. 1, 1021, vol. 37, pt. 1, 348; Colling, *Jubal Early's Raid*, 149; Early, *Autobiographical Sketch*, 389; Osborne, *Jubal*, 282.

33. *OR* 43, pt. 1, 1021, vol. 37, pt. 1, 348.

34. *OR* 37, pt. 1, 348; Colling, *Jubal Early's Raid*, 153-155.

35. *OR* 43, pt. 1, 1021, vol. 37, pt. 1, 348; Colling, *Jubal Early's Raid*, 116-117, 155; Early Reminiscences, 392; Osborne, *Jubal*, 278-279.

36. Park, *SHSP*, vol. 1, 379.

37. Early, *Autobiographical Sketch*, 392-394; Walker, *Memorial*, 454; Colling, *Jubal Early's Raid*, 232.

38. Park, *SHSP*, vol. 1, 380.

39. *OR* 43, pt. 1, 1021; *Colling, Jubal Early's Raid*, 148-149, 170.

40. Bushong, *Old Jube*, 210; Walker, *Memorial*, 455.

41. *OR* 43, pt. 1, 1021, vol. 37, pt. 1, 349; Colling, *Jubal Early's Raid*, 182-183; Park in *SHSP*, vol. 1, 380-381.

42. *OR* 43, pt. 1, 1021-1022.

43. Osborne, *Jubal*, 298.

44. *OR* 43, pt. 1, 1022; Park, *SHSP*, vol. 1, 381.

45. *OR* 43, pt. 1, 1022; Meaney, *Cool Spring*, 10-20; Lowry, *Fate of the Country*, 198-199.

46. *OR* 37, pt. 1, 291; Colling, *Jubal Early's Raid*, 200-201; Meaney, *Cool Spring*, 22-26; Park, *SHSP*, vol. 1, 384.

47. *OR* 43, pt. 1, 1022; vol. 37, pt. 1, 353-354; Ramseur papers, UNC.

48. *OR* 43, 1022; Park, *SHSP*, vol. 1, 384.

49. *OR* 43, 1022-1023; Park, *SHSP*, vol. 1, 384; Early, *Autobiographical Sketch*, 385.

50. Blackford to "My dear Mother," August 3, 1864, Blackford to "My dear Mary," August 14, 1864, Gordon-Blackford Papers.

51. *OR* 43, pt. 1, 1023; Blackford to "My dear Mother," August 3, 1864, Gordon-Blackford Papers.

52. Wellman, *Rebel Boast*, 187.

53. *OR* 43, 1023; Garnett, *SHSP*, vol. 27, 1; Early, *Autobiographical Sketch*, 402.

54. *OR* 37, pt. 1, 233; Osborne, *Jubal*, 312-319.

55. *OR* 43, pt. 1, 1023; *Battles & Leaders*, vol. 3, 522.

56. *OR* 43, pt. 1, 1023-1024; Early, *Autobiographical Sketch*, 403-407.

57. *OR* 43, pt. 1, 1024; Osborne, *Jubal*, 325-326.

58. *OR* 43, pt. 1, 569, 1024; Early, *Autobiographical Sketch*, 404-407; Osborne, *Jubal*, 325-326.

59. Park, *SHSP*, vol. 1, 386.

60. Blackford to "My dear Mary," August 14, 1864, Gordon-Blackford Papers.

61. *OR* 43, pt. 1, 569-570, 1024.

62. *OR* 43, pt. 1, 1024-1025; Garnett, *SHSP*, vol. 27, 2.

63. *OR* 43, pt. 1, 570, 1025; Walker, *Memorial*, 456.

64. Virginius Rodes Compiled Service Record, National Archives; VMI Correspondence, Hortense Rodes to Mrs. Anderson, Sept. 19, 1904.

65. Gallagher, *Stephen Dodson Ramseur*, 136; [Alexander M. Garber], *A Sketch of the Life and Services of Maj. John A. Harmon* (Staunton, Va.: "Spectator" Job Print, 1876), 32, as cited in Krick, *The Smoothbore Volley*, 139.

66. *OR* 43, pt. 1, 571, 1025-1026; Park, *SHSP*, vol. 1, 432; Blackford to "My dear Mary," August 28, 1864, Gordon-Blackford Papers.

67. Battle, "The Third Alabama Regiment," 3rd AL. History File, ADAH.

68. *OR* 43, pt. 1, 572, 1026; Early, *Autobiographical Sketch*, 412.

69. *OR* 43, pt. 1, 572, 1026; Wellman, *Rebel Boast*, 206.

70. Park, *SHSP*, vol. 1, 434-435.

71. *OR* 43, pt. 1, 573, 1026; Walker, *Memorial*, 455.

72. *OR* 43, pt. 1, 573, 1026, vol. 37, pt. 1, 354.

73. *OR* 43, pt. 1, 554-555, 1027.

74. Cowper, *Grimes Letters*, 8; May Reminiscences, Georgia Dept. of Archives & History; George F. Pond, *The Shenandoah Valley in 1864* (N.Y.: Scribner's and Sons, 1883), 154.

75. *OR* 43, pt. 1, 1027; Roger U. Delauter and Brandon H. Beck, *The Third Battle of Winchester* (Lynchburg, Va.: H.E. Howard, Inc., 1997), 23; Osborne, *Jubal*, 333-335.

76. Osborne, *Jubal*, 333.

77. Delauter, *The Third Battle of Winchester*, 25-33; Don Lowry, *Dark and Cruel War: The Decisive Months of the Civil War, September-December 1864* (N.Y.: Hippocrene Press, 1993), 74.

78. *OR* 43, pt. 1, 554.

79. *OR* 43, pt. 1, 1027; Gordon, *Reminiscences*, 320; Clark, *Histories*, vol. 2, 261; various sources contend with each other as to who arrived first on the battlefield, Rodes or Gordon. Though Early reported that it was the latter, it seems more reasonable to trust the account of Gordon, who stated that he arrived on the field after Rodes.

80. Lowry, *Dark and Cruel War*, 76.

81. Delauter, *The Third Battle of Winchester*, 32-35.

82. *Ibid.*, 35-38.

83. Gordon, *Reminiscences*, 321; Delauter, *The Third Battle of Winchester*, 38-43.

84. *Confederate Veteran*, vol. 28, 184; Garnett, *SHSP*, vol. 27, 5.

85. Wert, "Robert E. Rodes," 45; Samito, "Warrior in Gray," 90; *Confederate Veteran*, vol. 16, 269-270.

86. Gordon, *Reminiscences*, 321-322. There exist several known accounts of Rodes' last moments, the most reliable of which probably is that of Gordon. Ramseur, however, stated in his official report that "Rodes was shot in the head by a ball, and caught by [my aide] Lieutenant [J.S.] Battle as he fell from his horse. The fall of Rodes was not observed by the troops, who pushed on. . . ." Yet another source claims that "General Rodes was bending from his saddle and giving instructions to Colonel Thurston [3 NC] when the fatal bullet pierced his brain. He fell, without a groan, in the arms of the colonel, saturating him with the warm life current." Terry L. Jones, ed., *The Civil War Memoirs of Captain William J. Seymour: Reminiscences of a Louisiana Tiger* (Baton Rouge, La.: State University Press, 1991), 141—"While this movement was in progress, a bullet pierced the brain of the gallant Gen. Rodes & he fell from his horse about ten paces from where I was standing. Thus died one of the best Division Commanders in the Army of Northern Virginia—an intrepid & accomplished soldier, and a gentleman of many noble qualities & of unaffected & attractive manners." Col H.A. Brown to "My Dear Mother," Sept. 30, 1864, James B. Gordon Papers, NCDAH—"Gen. Rodes was killed at Winchester in the early part of the engagement. The ball passed through his head he never spoke but died without a struggle."

87. *OR* 43, pt. 1, 574; McDonald, *Make Me a Map*, 229.

88. Garnett, *SHSP*, vol. 27, 6; Samito, "Warrior in Gray," 52; Hubbs, *Voices from Company D*, 313.

89. Walker, *Memorial*, 457; Alexander Betts, *Experiences of a Confederate Chaplain* (Ann Arbor, Mi.: University Microfilms, 1973), 65.

90. *Confederate Veteran*, vol. 28, 185; Park, *SHSP*, vol. 2, 26.

91. Park, *SHSP*, vol. 2, 29; Garnett, *SHSP*, vol. 27, 5.

92. Garnett, *SHSP*, vol. 27, 10.

93. *OR* 43, pt. 1, 557; Thomas Carter to John W. Daniel, Nov. 28, 1894, Daniel Papers, Duke University; Thomas J. Watkins memoir, NCDAH.

94. Garnett, *SHSP*, vol. 27, 6.

95. *OR* 43, pt. 1, 573-574; Jedediah Hotchkiss to wife, Sept. 20, 1864, Jedediah Hotchkiss Papers, LC.

96. Battle, "The Third Alabama Regiment," ADAH.

97. Mrs. F.C. Pollard to "My Dear Warner," Sept. 23, 1864, Baylor Family Papers, VHS.

98. Lynchburg *Virginian*, Sept. 22, 1864.

99. Lynchburg *Virginian*, Sept. 23, 1864.

100. Lynchburg *Virginian*, Sept. 24, 1864; Asbury, *Lynchburg and Its People*, 228-229.

101. Lynchburg *Virginian*, Sept. 24, 1864.

Epilogue

1. For example, see: Jedediah Hotchkiss to "My Dear Sara," Sept. 21, 1864, Hotchkiss Papers, LC. Hotchkiss wrote, "We have never suffered a greater loss save in the Great Jackson"; *SHSP*, vol. 37, 233; various items in history files of the 3 AL., 5 AL., and 6 AL., ADAH; *Richmond Daily Whig*, October 4, 1864: "There is no officer since the great and lamented Jackson fell a sacrifice to this country whose death is so deeply felt as General Rodes. As a tactician, strategist, and disciplinarian, he had no superior and but one or two equals in the whole Confederate army. He never exposed his troops needlessly and never struck a blow that was not effective. Bold and daring as a Lion when occasion required it—he was noted for his caution and prudence, in reconnoitering in person the ground his Division had to fight over. No one under him had the least fear of surprise. It was these qualities that made him so successful, and earned for him a reputation that will make one of the brightest pages in the history of the war."

2. Richmond *Daily Whig*, November 8, 1864; John T. Gay [44 Ga.] to "My Dear Wife," November 1, 1864, Mary Barnard Nix Collection, Ms 20, Hargrett Library, University of Georgia, Athens.

3. Mrs. F.C. Pollard to "My Dear Warner," September 23, 1864, Baylor Family Papers, Virginia Historical Society, Richmond.

4. Genealogical data found in Rodes' file, VMI Archives; Yancey, *Lynchburg and Its Neighbors*, 246.

5. Genealogical data found in Rodes' file, VMI Archives; Owens, vol. iv, 1456; according to the Tuscaloosa *Gazette* of February 17, 1876, David Woodruff died of "consumption."

6. Genealogical data found in Rodes' file, VMI Archives; The Tuscaloosa Genealogical Society, *Abstract of Tax Assessment For Collector—Tuscaloosa County, Alabama, 1894* (Tuscaloosa: The Tuscaloosa Genealogical Society, 1989).

7. United Daughters of the Confederacy 50th Anniversary
Scrapbook, 1896-1946, Box 2554, Hoole Collection, Hoole Library, University of Alabama, Tuscaloosa.
8. Genealogical data found in Rodes' file, VMI Archives; Owens, vol. iv, 1456.
9. Virginius Rodes file, VMI Archives; genealogical data found in Robert Rodes' file, VMI Archives; Presbyterian Cemetery, Lynchburg.
10. The house sold on October 15, 1879, to Mr. & Mrs. Fernando C. Ford.

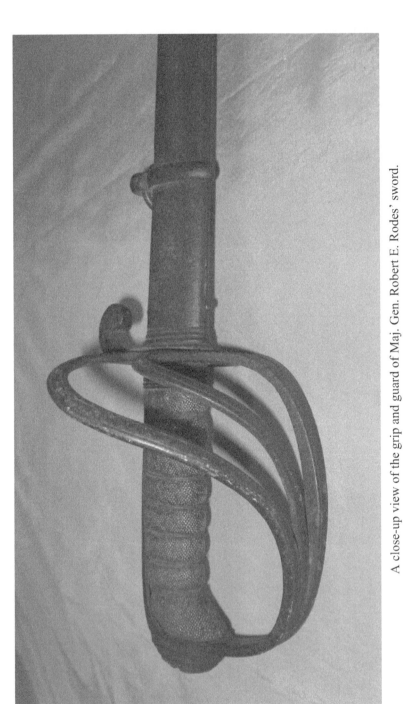

A close-up view of the grip and guard of Maj. Gen. Robert E. Rodes' sword.

Mary Rodes Dell, and the Rodes Family

Bibliography

NEWSPAPERS

The Daily Sun (Montgomery, Alabama)
Greensboro (Alabama) *Beacon*
The Independent Monitor (Tuscaloosa, Alabama)
Jasper County (Missouri) *News*
Lynchburg *Virginian*
Macon County (Georgia) *Democrat*
Mobile *Advertiser and Register*
Mobile *Evening News*
Montgomery *Daily Post*
Montgomery *Weekly Advertiser*
New Orleans *Daily Picayune*
Petersburg *Express*
Raleigh *Register*
Raleigh *Standard*
The Rockingham (Virginia) *Register and Village Advertiser*
Richmond *Examiner*
Richmond *Whig and Public Advertiser*
Staunton *Vindicator*
Tuscaloosa *Observer*

OFFICIAL PUBLICATIONS

United States War Department. *The War of the Rebellion: A Compilation of the Official Records of the Union and Confederate Armies,* 128 vols. Washington, D.C.: U.S. Government Printing Office, 1880-1901.

MANUSCRIPT COLLECTIONS

Alabama
Alabama Department of Archives and History, Montgomery
    Cullen Andrew Battle Papers
    Newton Y. Davis Letters
    Rev J.H.B. Hall Papers
    3rd Alabama Infantry Regiment history file
    5th Alabama Infantry Regiment history file
    6th Alabama Infantry Regiment history file
    12th Alabama Infantry Regiment history file

26th Alabama Infantry Regiment history file
62nd Alabama Infantry Regiment history file
Samuel Pickens diary

Birmingham Public Library, Birmingham
    J.H. Scruggs Collection
Ralph Brown Draughon Library, Auburn University, Auburn
    G.W. Wright letter
Gorgas Library, University of Alabama, Tuscaloosa
    Nan Neblett Maxwell Collection
William Stanley Hoole Special Collections Library, University of Alabama,
Tuscaloosa
    A. Cole Hargrove Papers
    Robert Jemison Papers
Tuscaloosa County Courthouse, Tuscaloosa
    Deed Books 5, 7, 8
    Robert Rodes will
    Rodes Marriage Bond

California
The Huntington Library, San Marino
    BR Box 287

Georgia
Georgia Department of Archives and History, Atlanta
    Eli Grover letter
    Thomas Hightower Letters
    W.H. May Memoir
    Sidney Richardson Diary
    Davis Tinsley Letters
University of Georgia, Athens
    Mary Barnard Nix Collection

Illinois
Chicago Historical Society, Chicago
    Henry Whiting Collection

Maryland
Maryland Historical Society, Baltimore
    Gordon-Blackford Papers

Massachusetts
Houghton Library, Harvard University, Cambridge
    Frederick Dearborn Collection

Mississippi
John Davis Williams Library, University of Mississippi, Oxford
    James T. Jones Collection

New York
Gilder-Lehrman Collection, New York Historical Society, New York
    Jeremiah Tate letter
    Robert Rodes Letters

North Carolina
William L. Perkins Special Collections Library, Duke University, Durham
    Alexander Brown Papers
    I.H. Carrington Papers
    John W. Daniel Papers
    Jefferson Davis Papers
    Jubal Early Papers
    Edward Hardin Papers
    D.H. Hill Papers
    Bradley T. Johnson Collection
    Richard L. Maury Papers
    Jesse F. Newsome Papers
North Carolina Department of Archives & History, Raleigh
    Thomas Pollock Devereux Letter Book, 1863-1865
    James B. Gordon Papers
    T.M. Gorman Memoir
    D.H. Hill Papers
    Francis Parker Letters
    Stephen Ramseur Papers
    John A. Stikeleather Reminiscences
    Thomas J. Watkins Memoir
Southern Historical Collection, Wilson Library, University of North Carolina, Chapel Hill
    William Calder Letters
    James E. Green Diary
    Bryan Grimes Papers
    Polk, Brown, Ewell Family Papers
    Stephen Ramseur Papers
    William Alexander Smith Papers

Walton Papers
George Whitaker Wills Papers

Pennsylvania
Historical Society of Pennsylvania, Philadelphia
    Simon Gratz Collection
The United States Army Heritage and Education Center, Carlisle
    Robert L. Brake Collection
    Civil War Times Illustrated Collection
    Lewis Leigh Collection
    Parry Family Papers
    Tennessee Historical Commission Collection

Tennessee
Tennesse State Library and Archives, Nashville
    Ewell-Stewart-Brown Papers

Virginia
Special Collections Department, Alderman Library, University of Virginia, Charlottesville
    Blackwell Family Papers
    John W. Daniel Papers
    Jubal A. Early Papers
    Clement D. Fishburne Memoir
Eleanor S. Brockenbrough Library, Museum of the Confederacy, Richmond
    James P. Smith Letters
    MC-3 Series
Special Collections Department, Carrier Library, James Madison University, Harrisonburg
    John T. Harris Papers
Fredericksburg and Spottsylvania National Military Park, Fredericksburg
    Bound Volumes
    Samuel Walkup diary
The Handley Regional Library, Winchester-Frederick County Historical Society, Winchester
    David Rodes Collection
Jones Memorial Library, Lynchburg
    "The Rodes Family," unp. paper by Frances Robertson
Lynchburg Circuit Courthouse, Lynchburg
    Deed Books
    Will Book E, David Rodes will

Library of Virginia and Virginia State Archives, Richmond
    Confederate Miscellany
Virginia Historical Society, Richmond
    Baylor Family Papers
    Jubal A. Early Papers
    Hobson Family Papers
    Lee Family Papers
    Rives Family Papers
    Rust Papers
    Alfred Lewis Scott Memoir
    Talcott Family Papers
Archives, Preston Library, Virginia Military Institute, Lexington
    Class Standings
    Correspondence of the Superintendant
    Charles Derby File
    Robert Rodes File
    Virginius Rodes File
Special Collections Department, University Libraries, Virginia Polytechnic and State University, Blacksburg
    Richard H. Adams diary
    Records of the Southside Railroad Company

Washington, D.C.,
Library of Congress, Manuscripts Division
    John S. Anglin Letters
    John Coffee & Family Papers
    Richard S. Ewell Papers
    Jedediah Hotchkiss Papers
    William Old diary
National Archives
    1850 Federal Census, Campbell Co., Va.
    1860 Federal Census, Campbell Co., Va.
    1860 Federal Census, Tuscaloosa Co., Al.
    Record of Events, 5th Alabama Infantry Regiment
    Record Group 109
    Compiled Service Records of Confederate Generals & Staff
        Officers, & Non-regimental Enlisted Men
    Confederate Records, Correspondence of the Adjutant General
    Letters Received by the Confederate Secretary of War, 1861-1865
    Letters and Telegrams Sent by the Confederate Adjutant and Inspector
        General, 1861-1865

PUBLISHED PRIMARY SOURCES

Articles

Cunningham, Sumner Archibald, and Edith D. Pope, eds. *Confederate Veteran Magazine,* 40 vols. Nashville: S.A. Cunningham, 1893-1932.

Early, John Cabell. "A Southern Boy's Experience at Gettysburg." *Journal of the Military Service Institution of the United States,* 43 (Jan.-Feb. 1911), pp. 415-423.

Garnett, Capt. James M. "Diary." *The Southern Historical Society Papers,* vol. xvii, pp. 1-16; vol. xviii, pp. 66-71.

Park, Robert E. "Diary." *Southern Historical Society Papers,* vol. 1: pp. 370-386, 430-437; vol. 2: pp. 25-31, 78-85, 173-180, 232-239,306-315; vol. 3: pp. 43-46, 55-61, 123-127,183-189, 244-254; vol. 26: pp. 1-31.

Roberts, James W. "Diary." *The Florida Historical Society Quarterly,* vol. xi, no. 2 (Oct. 1932), pp. 58-73.

Tucker, John S. *"Diary."* The Alabama Historical Quarterly. vol. xliii, Spring 1981; pub. by Alabama Dept. of Archives & History.

Books

Beck, Brandon H., ed. *Third Alabama! The Civil War Memoir of Brigadier General Andrew Cullen Battle, CSA.* Tuscaloosa, Al.: The University of Alabama Press, 2000.

Betts, Alexander. *Experiences of a Confederate Chaplain.* Ann Arbor, Mich.: University Microfilms, 1973.

Blackford, Charles Minor, ed. *Letters From Lee's Army.* N.Y.: Charles Scribner's Sons, 1947.

Blackford, William W. *War Years With Jeb Stuart.* N.Y.: Charles Scribner's Sons, 1945.

Cowper, Pulaski, ed. *Extracts of Letters of Major-Gen'l Bryan Grimes to His Wife, Written While in Active Service in the Army of Northern Virginia: together with Some personal Recollections of the War, Written by Him after Its Close, etc.* Raleigh, N.C.: Edwards, Broughton and Co., 1883.

Dowdy, Clifford, and Louis H. Manarin, eds. *The Wartime Papers of R.E. Lee.* Boston: Little, Brown and Co., 1961.

Durkin, Joseph T., ed. *Confederate Chaplain: A War Journal of Rev. James B. Sheenan, 14th Louisiana, C.S.A.* Milwaukee: The Bruce Co., 1960.

Early, Jubal A. *A Memoir of the Last Year of the War for Independence, in the Confederate States of America, Containing an Account of the Operations of his Commands in the Years 1864 and 1865.* Lynchburg, Va.: Bulton, 1867.

———. *Lieutenant General Jubal Anderson Early, C.S.A: Autobiographical Sketch and Narrative of the War Between the States.* Philadelphia: J.B. Lippincott, 1912.

Freeman, Douglas S., ed. *Lee's Dispatches.* N.Y.: G.P. Putnam's Sons, 1915.

Gandrud, Pauline Jones, comp. *Marriage, Death and Legal Notices From Early Alabama Newspapers, 1819-1893.* Easley, S.C.: Southern Historical Press, 1981.

Gordon, John B. *Reminiscences of the Civil War.* N.Y.: Charles Scribner's sons, 1903.

Hoke, Jacob. *The Great Invasion of 1863.* Dayton, Ohio: W.J. Shuey, 1887.

Howard, McHenry. *Recollections of a Maryland Confederate Soldier and Staff Officer under Johnston, Jackson, and Lee.* Dayton, Ohio: Morningside Bookshop, 1973.

Hubbs, G. Ward, ed. *Voices from Company D: Diaries by the Greensboro Guards, Fifth Alabama Infantry Regiment, Army of Northern Virginia.* Athens. Ga.: The University of Georgia Press, 2003.

Johnson, Robert Underwood, and Clarence C. Buell, eds. *Battles and Leaders of the Civil War,* 4 vols. N.Y.: Century Co., 1887-1888.

Johnston, Hugh Buckner, ed. *The Civil War Letters of George Boardman Battle and of Walter Raleigh Battle, of Wilson, North Carolina.* Wilson, N.C., 1953.

Johnston, Joseph E. *Narrative of Military Operations, Directed, during the Late War between the States, by Joseph E. Johnston, General, C.S.A.* N.Y.: D. Appleton and Co., 1874.

Ledford, Preston L. *Reminiscences of the Civil War, 1861-1865.* Thomasville, N.C.: News Printing House, 1909.

Lee, Laura Elizabeth. *Forget-Me-Nots of the Civil War: A Romance Containing Reminiscences and Original Letters of Two Confederate Soldiers.* St. Louis, 1909.

Leon, Louis. *Diary of a Tar Heel Confederate Soldier.* Charlotte,   N.C.: Stackpole Pub. Co., 1971.

Long, A.L., and Marcus J. Wright. *Memoirs of Robert E. Lee.* N.Y.: J.M. Stoddart and Co., 1886.

Longstreet, James. *From Manassas to Appomattox: Memoirs of the Civil War in America.* Philadelphia: J.B. Lippincott Co., 1896.

McDonald, Archie P., ed. *Make Me a Map of the Valley: The Civil War Journal of Stonewall Jackson's Cartographer.* Dallas: Southern Methodist University Press, 1973.

Maurice, Frederick, ed. *Charles Marshall, An Aide-de-Camp to Lee.* Boston: Little, Brown, 1927.

Monroe, Haskell M., and James T, McIntosh, Lynda Lawell Crist, Mary Seaton Dix, Kenneth H. Williams, eds. *The Papers of Jefferson Davis,* 9 vols. Baton Rouge: Louisiana State University Press, 1971.

Norman, William M. [Lt. Co. A]. *A Portion of My Life.* Winston-Salem, N.C.: John F. Blair, 1959.

North Carolina Civil War Documentary. *Second Annual Report of the President and Directors to the Stockholders of the Western North Carolina Rail Road Company.* Salisbury, N.C.: 1856.

Park, Robert E. *Sketch of the Twelfth Alabama Infantry of Battle's Brigade, Rodes' Division, Early's Corps, of the Army of Northern Virginia.* Richmond: W.E. Jones, 1906.

Pickens, Samuel. *Civil War Diary of Samuel Pickens, Company D   5th Alabama Regiment July 27, 1862—June 17, 1865.* Tuscaloosa, Al.: Alabama Dept. of Archives & History.

Pierce, T.H., ed. *Diary of Captain Henry A. Chambers.* Wendell,   N.C.: Broadfoot, 1983.

Pryor, S.G. *A Post of Honor: The Pryor Letters, 1861-1863; Letters From Capt. S.G. Pryor, Twelfth Georgia Regiment and his Wife, Penelope Tyson Pryor.* Fort Valley, Ga.: Garrett Pub., 1989.

Smith, Gustavus W. *The Battle of Seven Pines.* N.Y.: C.G. Crawford, 1891.

Stiles, Robert. *Four Years Under Marse Robert.* N.Y.: Neale Pub. Co., 1903.

Tapert, Annette, ed. *The Brother's War: Civil War Letters To Their Loved Ones From The Blue and Gray.* N.Y.: Times Books, 1988.

The James E. Taylor Sketchbook. Dayton, OH.: Morningside, 1989.

Taylor, Michael W. *The Letters of Col. Francis Marion Parker and the History of the 30th Regiment North Carolina Troops.* Dayton, OH: 1998.

Thompson, James Monroe, and William S. Hoole, eds. *Reminiscences of the Autauga Rifles (Co. G) Sixth Alabama Volunteer Regiment, C.S.A.* Pratville, Ala.: 1879.

Warren, Edward. *A Doctor's Experiences in Three Continents.* Baltimore: Cushings & Bailey, 1885.

SECONDARY SOURCES

Articles

Albermarle County Historical Society. *Magazine of Albemarle County History,* vol. 5, p. 61.

Boyd, Thomas M. *Southern Bivouac,* vol. 2 (1885-1886), pp. 212-214.

Coleman, Elizabeth Dabney and Hemphill, W. Edwin. "Boats Beyond the Blue Ridge," *Virginia Cavalcade,* vol. iii, no. 4 (Spring 1954), pp. 8-9.

Dooley, Edwin L. "Gilt Buttons and the Collegiate Way: Francis H. Smith as Antebellum Schoolmaster." *Virginia Cavalcade,* 36, (1986).

Gallagher, Gary W. *Civil War History,* vol. 36.

Griffin, Massy. "Rodes On Oak Hill: A Study of Rodes' Division on the First Day of Gettysburg." *Gettysburg Magazine,* no. 4 (Jan. 1991), pp. 33-48.

Haines, Douglas C. "R.S. Ewell's Command, June 29-July 1, 1863." *Gettysburg Magazine,* 9 (July 1993), pp. 17-32.

"The Rodes Family." *The Virginia Magazine of History and Biography,* vol. vii, pp. 82-87, 203-205.

Rodgers, Thomas G. "The 'Bandbox' Soldiers of the 3rd Alabama Infantry Became Combat Hardened Veterans in Virginia. " *America's Civil War* (July 1990), pp. 12, 14, 16.

Samito, Christian G. "Robert Rodes, Warrior in Gray." *America's Civil War* 7 (Jan. 1995), pp. 46-57, 88, 90.

"The 23rd North Carolina Infantry, Organized in 1861, as the 13th Regiment of Volunteers, Historical Sketch." *Southern Historical Society Papers,* vol. 25 (1897), pp. 151-176.

Wert, Jeffery. "Robert E. Rodes." *Civil War Times Illustrated* 16 (Dec. 1977), pp. 4-6, 7-9, 41-45).

Willis, Francis T. "The Twelfth Georgia Infantry." *Southern Historical Society Papers,* 17 (1889), pp. 160-187.

Books and Theses

Abstract of Tax Assessment for Collector-Tuscaloosa County, Alabama, 1894. The Tuscaloosa Genealogical Society, 1989.

Adams, Owen E. *Confederate Major General Robert E. Rodes: A Civil War Biography.* Master's Thesis, University of Southern Mississippi, 1995.

Alexander, Bevin. *Lost Victories: The Military Genius of Stonewall Jackson.* N.Y.: Henry Holt and Co., 1992.

Allen, T. Harrell. *Lee's Last Major General: Bryan Grimes of North Carolina.* Mason City, Iowa: Savas Publishing, 1999.

Asbury, Christian W. *Lynchburg and Its People.* Lynchburg, Va.: J.P. Bell Co., 1900.

Baltz, Louis J. III. *The Battle of Cold Harbor May 27-June 13, 1864.* Lynchburg, Va.: H.E. Howard, Inc., 1990.

Barefield, Marilyn D., comp. *Old Tuscaloosa Land Office and Military Records, 1821-1855.* Easley, S.C.: Southern Historical Press, 1984.

Bean, William B. *Stonewall's Man: Sandie Pendleton.* Chapel Hill, N.C.: University of North Carolina Press, 1959.

Bigelow, John Jr. *The Campaign of Chancellorsville: A Strategic and Tactical Study.* New Haven, CT.: Yale University Press, 1910.

Brewer, Willis. *Alabama, Her History, Resources, War Record, and Public Men.* 1872.

———. *Brief Historical Sketches of Military Organizations Raised in Alabama During the Civil War.* Montgomery, Al.: Alabama Civil War Centennial Commission, 1962.

Bridges, Hal. *Lee's Maverick General: Daniel Harvey Hill.* N.Y.: McGraw-Hill, 1961.

Bushong, Millard K. *Old Jube: A Biography of General Jubal A. Early.* Shippensburg, Pa.: Beidal, 1985.

Cannan, John. *The Wilderness Campaign May 1864.* Conshohocken, Pa.: Combined Books, 1993.

———. *The Spottsylvania Campaign May 7-19, 1864.* Conchohocken, Pa.: Combined Books, 1997.

Carter, James Harold. *History of the North East and South West Alabama Railroad to 1872.* Master's Thesis, University of Alabama, 1949.

Chambers, Allen S. *Lynchburg: An Architectural History.* Charlottesville, Va.: University of Virginia Press, 1981.

Chambers, Lenoir. *Stonewall Jackson.* 2 vols. N.Y.: William Morrow, 1959.

Christian, W. Asbury. *Lynchburg and Its People.* Lynchburg, Va.: J.P. Bell Co., 1900.

Clark, Walter, ed. *Histories of the Several Regiments and Battalions from North Carolina in the Great War, 1861-1865*, 6 vols. Wendell, N.C.: Broadfoot, 1982.

Cline, Wayne. *Alabama Railroads.* Tuscaloosa, Al.: The University of Alabama Press, 1997.

Clinton, Matthew William. *Tuscaloosa, Alabama: Its Early Days, 1816-1865.* Tuscaloosa: The Zonta Club, 1958.

Coddington, Edwin B. *The Gettysburg Campaign: A Study in Command.* N.Y.: Charles Scribner's Sons, 1968.

Coffey, Thomas E. *Battle-Fields of the South.* New York: John Bradburn, 1864.

Coker, William S., ed. *The Mobile Cadets, 1854-1945: A Century of Honor and Fidelity.* Bagdad, Fla.: Patagonia Press, 1993.

Collins, Darrell L. *46th Virginia Infantry.* Lynchburg, Va.: H.E. Howard, Inc., 1992.

Cooke, John Esten. *A Life of Gen. Robert E. Lee.* N.Y.: D. Appleton and Co., 1971.

Cooling, Benjamin F. *Jubal Early's Raid on Washington, 1864.* Baltimore: Nautical and Aviation Pub. Co., 1989.

———. *Monocacy: The Battle That Saved Washington.* Shippensburg, Pa.: White Mane, 1996.

Couper, William. *One Hundred Years at VMI.* 4 vols. Richmond: Garrett & Massie, 1939.

Crute, Joseph J. *Confederate Staff Officers.* Powhatan, Va.: Derwent Books, 1982.

Dannelly, Hermione. *The Life and Times of Robert Jemison, Jr.* Master's Thesis, University of Alabama, 1942.

Davis, Burke. *They Called Him Stonewall.* N.Y.: Wings Books, 1988.

Davis, William C. *Battle at Bull Run: A History of the First Major Campaign of the Civil War.* N.Y.: Doubleday and Co., 1977.

———, ed. *The Confederate General*, 6 vols. The National Historical Society, 1991.

Delauter, Roger U., and Brandon H. Beck. *The Third Battle of Winchester.* Lynchburg, Va.: H.E. Howard, Inc., 1997.

Dowdy, Clifford. *Death of a Nation: The Story of Lee and His Men at Gettysburg.* N.Y.: Alfred A. Knopf, 1958.

———. *Lee's Last Campaign: The Story of Lee and His Men against Grant, 1864.* Boston: Little, Brown and Co., 1960.

———. *The Seven Days: The Emergence of Lee.* Boston: Little, Brown and Co., 1964.

———. *Lee.* Boston: Little, Brown and Co., 1965.

Early, Jubal A., and J. William Jones, Robert A. Brock, James P. Smith, Hamilton J. Eckenrode, Douglas S. Freeman, Frank E. Vandiver, eds. *Southern Historical Society Papers*, 52 vols. 1876-1959.

Early, R.H. *Campbell Chronicles and Family Sketches.* Lynchburg, Va.: J.P. Bell Co., 1927.

Eckert, Ralph Lowell. *John Brown Gordon: Soldier, Southerner, American.* Baton Rouge: Louisiana State University Press, 1989.

Esposito, Vincent J., ed. *The West Point Atlas of the Civil War.* N.Y.: Frederick A. Praeger, 1962.

Farwell, Byron. *Stonewall: A Biography of General Thomas J. Jackson.* N.Y.: W.W. Norton and Co., 1992.

Faust, Patricia, ed. *Historical Times Illustrated Encyclopedia of the Civil War.* N.Y.: Harper & Row, 1987.

Freeman, Douglas S. *R.E. Lee: A Biography.* 4 vols. N.Y.: Charles Scribner's Sons, 1934-35.

———. *Lee's Lieutenants: A Study in Command,* 3 vols. N.Y.: Charles Scribner's Sons, 1942-1944.

Fry, Anna M. *Memories of Old Cahaba.* Nashville, Tenn.: House of the M.E. Church, 1908. [Co. F 5 Ala.].

Furguson, Ernest B. *Chancellorsville, 1863: The Souls of the Brave.* N.Y.: Alfred A. Knopf, 1992.

Gallagher, Gary W. *Stephen Dodson Ramseur: Lee's Gallant General.* Chapel Hill, N.C.: University of North Carolina Press, 1985.

———, ed. *Fighting for the Confederacy: The Personal Recollections of General Edward Porter Alexander.* Chapel Hill, N.C.: University of North Carolina Press, 1989.

———, ed. *Struggle for the Shenandoah: Essays on the 1864 Valley Campaign.* Kent, Ohio: Kent State University Press, 1991.

———, ed. *The First Day at Gettysburg: Essays on Union and Confederate Leadership.* Kent, Ohio: Kent State University Press, 1992.

———, ed. *Lee: The Soldier.* Lincoln, Neb.: University of Nebraska Press, 1996.

———, ed. *Chancellorsville: The Battle and Its Aftermath.* Chapel Hill, N.C.: University of North Carolina Press, 1996.

Genovese, Eugene D. *A Consuming Fire: The Fall of the Confederacy in the Mind of the White Christian South.* Athens, Ga.: University of Georgia Press, 1998.

Govan, Gilbert and James Livingwood. *Gen. Joseph E. Johnston, C.S.A.: A Different Valor.* Indianapolis: Bobbs-Merrill, 1956.

Graham, Martin, and George Skoch. *Mine Run: A Campaign of Lost Opportunities, Oct. 21, 1863-May 1, 1864.* Lynchburg, Va.: H.E. Howard, Inc., 1987.

Hamlin, Augustus Choate. *The Battle of Chancellorsville.* Bangor, Me.: pub. by author, 1896.

Hamlin, Percy Gatling. *"Old Bald Head" (General R.S. Ewell): The Portrait of a Soldier.* Strasburg, Va.: Shenandoah Publishing House, 1940.

Hanson, Joseph Mills. *Bull Run Remembers.* Manassas, Va., 1953.

Hartje, Robert G. *Van Dorn: The Life and Times of a Confederate General.* Nashville: Vanderbilt University Press, 1967.

Hassler, Warren. *Crisis at the Crossroads: The First Day at Gettysburg.* University, Ala.: University of Alabama Press, 1970.

Henderson, G.F.R. *Stonewall Jackson and the American Civil War.* 2 vols. London: Longmans, Green and Co., 1898.

Henderson, William D. *The Road to Bristoe Station: Campaigning With Lee and Meade, August 1-October 20, 1863.* Lynchburg, Va.: H.E. Howard, Inc., 1987.

Hennessey, John. *The First Battle of Manassas: An End to Innocence, July 18-21, 1861.* Lynchburg, Va.: H.E. Howard, Inc., 1989.

Hoole, William Stanley. *History of the Third Alabama Regiment, C.S.A.* Montgomery, Al.: Confederate Pub. Co., 1982. [ADAC]

———. *Historical Sketch of the Fifth Alabama Infantry Regiment, C.S.A. Montgomery, Al.: Confederate Pub. Co., 1985.*

Hubbs, G. Ward. *Tuscaloosa: Portrait of an Alabama County.* Northridge, Ca.: Windsor Publications, 1987.

Krick, Robert E.L. *Staff Officers in Gray: A Biographical Register of the Staff Officers in the Army of Northern Virginia.* Chapel Hill, N.C.: The University of North Carolina Press, 2003.

Krick, Robert K. *Lee's Colonels: A Biographical Register of the Field Officers of the Army of Northern Virginia,* 3rd ed. Dayton, Ohio: Morningside, 1991.

———. *The Smoothbore Volley That Doomed the Confederacy.* Baton Rouge, La.: Louisiana State University Press, 2002.

Laboda, Lawrence R. *From Selma to Appomattox: The History of the Jeff Davis Artillery.* Shippensburg, Pa.: White Mane, 1994.

Lee, Fitzhugh. *General Lee.* N.Y.: D. Appleton and Co., 1894.

Lowry, Don. *No Turning Back: The Beginning of the End of the Civil War: March-June 1864.* N.Y.: Hippocrene Books, 1992.

———. *Fate of the Country: The Civil War from June to September 1864.* N.Y.: Hippocrene Press, 1992.

———. *Dark and Cruel War: The Decisive Months of the Civil War: September-December 1864.* N.Y.: Hippocrene Press, 1993.

[McCabe, James D.]. *The Grayjackets: And How They Lived, Fought and Died.* Richmond: Jones Brothers, 1867.

McWhiney, Grady. *Braxton Bragg and Confederate Defeat.* N.Y.: Columbia University Press, 1969.

Macaluso, Gregory J. *Morris, Orange and King William Artillery.* Lynchburg, Va.: H.E. Howard, Inc., 1991.

Maney, R. Wayne. *Marching to Cold Harbor: Victory and Failure, 1864.* Shippensburg, Pa.: White Mane, 1995.

Marshall, Francis. *The Battle of Gettysburg: The Crest Wave of the American Civil War.* N.Y.: The Neale Pub. Co., 1914.

Martin, David G. *The Peninsula Campaign, March-July, 1862.* Conshohocken, Pa.: Combined Books, 1992.

Martin, Samuel J. *The Road to Glory: Confederate General Richard S. Ewell.* Indianapolis: Guild Press of Indiana, 1991.

Matter, William D. *If It Takes All Summer: The Battle of Spottsylvania.* Chapel Hill, N.C.: University of North Carolina Press, 1988.

Meaney, Peter J. *The Civil War Engagement at Cool Spring July 18, 1864.* Berryville, Va.: Clark County Historical Association, 1980.

Miller, J. Michael. *The North Anna Campaign: "Even to Hell Itself," May 21-26, 1864.* Lynchburg, Va.: H.E. Howard, Inc., 1989.

Montgomery, Walter A. *The Days of Old and the Years that are Past.* Raleigh, N.C.: n.p., n.d.

Moore, John H. *Albemarle: Jefferson's County.* Charlottesville, Va., 1976.

Murfin, James. *The Gleam of Bayonets: The Battle of Antietam and Robert E. Lee's Maryland Campaign, September 1862.* N.Y.: Thomas Yoseloff, 1965.

Newton, Stephen H. *Joseph E. Johnston and the Defense of Richmond.* Lawrence, Kansas: University Press of Kansas,   1998.

Newton, Stephen W. *The Battle of Seven Pines, May 31-June 1, 1862.* Lynchburg, Va.: H.E. Howard, Inc., 1993.

Nye, William Sturtevant. *Here Come the Rebels!* Baton Rouge: Louisiana State University Press, 1965.

Osborne, Charles C. *Jubal: The Life and Times of General Jubal A. Early, C.S.A.* Chapel Hill, N.C.: Algonquin Books, 1992.

Owen, Thomas M. *History of Alabama,* 4 vols. Chicago: S.J. Clarke Pub. Co., 1921.

Pfanz, Donald C. *Richard S. Ewell: A Soldier's Life.* Chapel Hill, N.C.: University of North Carolina Press, 1998.

Pfanz, Harry W. *Gettysburg: The Second Day.* Chapel Hill, N.C.: University of North Carolina Press, 1987.

———. *Gettysburg: Culp's Hill and Cemetery Hill.* Chapel Hill, N.C.: University of North Carolina Press, 1993.

Philpot, William Henry, Jr., son of Capt. William Henry Philpot Co. B 61 Ala. *Unique Bits of History and True Retrospectives.* Pub. by author, 1883.

Pond, George F. *The Shenandoah Valley in 1864.* N.Y.: Scribner's and Sons, 1883.

Potter, Dorothy T. and Potter, Clifton W. *Lynchburg: The Most Interesting Spot.* Lynchburg, Va.: Progress Printing Corp., 1976.

Priest, John M. *Antietam: The Soldiers' Battle.* N.Y.: Oxford University Press, 1994.

———. *Nowhere to Run: The Wilderness, May 4th & 5th, 1864.* Shippensburg, Pa.: White Mane, 1995.

———. *Victory Without Triumph: The Wilderness, May 6th & 7th, 1864.* Shippensburg, Pa.: White Mane, 1996.

———. *Before Antietam: The Battle for South Mountain.* N.Y.: Oxford Univ. Press, 1996.

Reeder, Colonel Red. *The Southern Generals.* N.Y.: Duell, Sloan and Pearce, 1965.

Rhea, Gordon C. *The Battle of the Wilderness, May 5-6, 1864.* Baton Rouge: Louisiana State University Press, 1994.

———. *The Battles for Spottsylvania Court House and the Road to Yellow Tavern, May 7-12, 1864.* Baton Rouge: Louisiana State University Press, 1996.

Rhodes, Howard J., comp. *The Rhodes Family in America.* N.Y.: Greenwich Book Pub., 1959.

Robertson, James I., Jr. *Stonewall Jackson: The Man, the Soldier, the Legend.* N.Y.: Simon & Shuster Macmillan, 1997.

Roman, Alfred. *The Military Operations of General Beauregard in the War Between the States, 1861 to 1865; Including a Brief Personal Sketch of His Services in the War with Mexico,* 2 vols. N.Y.: Harper and Bros., 1883.

Scott, Robert Garth. *Into the Wilderness With the Army of the Potomac.* Bloomington, In.: Indiana University Press, 1985.

Scruggs, Phillip L. *The History of Lynchburg, Virginia, 1786-1946.* Lynchburg, Va.: J.P. Bell, 1972.

Sears, Stephen W. *Landscape Turned Red: The Battle of Antietam.* New Haven: Ticknor and Fields, 1983.

———. *To the Gates of Richmond: The Peninsula Campaign.* N.Y.: Ticknor & Fields, 1992.

———. *Chancellorsville.* Boston: Houghton and Miflin, 1996.

Seitz, Don C. *Braxton Bragg: General of the Confederacy.* Columbia, S.C.: The State Company, 1924.

Sifakis, Stewart. *Who Was Who in the Civil War.* N.Y.: Facts on File, 1988.

———. *Compendium of the Confederate Armies,* 10 vols. N.Y.: Facts on file, 1992-1995.

Smith, Francis H. *History of the Virginia Military Institute.* Lynchburg, Va.: J.P. Bell Co., 1912.

Smith, William A. *The Anson Guards, Company D, Fourteenth Regiment North Carolina Volunteers, 1861-1865.* Wendell, N.C.: Broadfoot, 1978.

Stackpole, Edward. *The Fredericksburg Campaign.* Harrisburg, Pa.: Military Service Publishing Co., 1957.

———. *Chancellorsville: Lee's Greatest Battle.* Harrisburg, Pa.: The Stackpole Co., 1958.

———. *From Cedar Mountain to Antietam: August-September, 1862.* Harrisburg, Pa.: The Stackpole Co., 1959.

———. *Sheridan in the Shenandoah.* Harrisburg, Pa.: The Stackpole Co., 1961.

————. *They Met at Gettysburg.* Mechanicsburg, Pa.: Stackpole, 1995.

Steere, Edward. *The Wilderness Campaign: The Meeting of Grant and Lee.* Harrisburg, Pa.: The Stackpole Co., 1960.

Swisher, James K. *Warrior in Gray: General Robert Rodes of Lee's Army.* Shippensburg, Pa., White Mane, 2000.

Symonds, Craig L. *Joseph E. Johnston: A Civil War Biography.* N.Y.: W.W. Norton and Co., 1992.

Tankersley, Allen P. *John B. Gordon: A Study in Gallantry.* Atlanta: The Whitehall Press, 1955.

Thomas, D.S. *Ready . . . Aim . . . Fire!* Biglerville, Pa.: Osborne Printing Co., 1982.

Thomas, Henry W. *The History of the Doles-Cook Brigade, Army of Northern Virginia, C.S.A.* Atlanta: The Franklin Printing & Pub. Co., 1903.

Trudeau, Noah Andre. *Bloody Roads South: The Wilderness to Cold Harbor, May-June, 1864.* Boston: Little, Brown and Co., 1989.

Tucker, Glenn. *High Tide at Gettysburg.* N.Y.: The Bobbs-Merrill Co., Inc., 1958.

Vandiver, Frank E. *Mighty Stonewall.* N.Y.: McGraw-Hill, 1957.

Wakelon, Jon L. *Biographical Dictionary of the Confederacy.* Westport, N.Y.: Greenwood Press, 1977.

Walker, Charles D. *Memorial, Virginia Military Institute.* Philadelphia: J.B. Lippincott, 1875.

Wall, Henry C. *Historical Sketch of the Pee Dee Guards (Co. D Twenty-third N.C. Regiment) From 1861-1865.* Gaithersburg, Md.: Butternut, 1876.

Wallace, Lee A. Jr. *A Guide to Virginia Military Organizations, 1861-1865.* Lynchburg, Va.: H.E. Howard, Inc., 1986.

Wellman, Manly W. *Rebel Boast: First at Bethel-Last at Appomattox.* N.Y.: Henry Holt, 1956.

Welsh, Jack, M.D. *Medical Histories of Confederate Generals.* Kent, Ohio: Kent State University Press, 1995.

Wert Jeffery D. *From Winchester to Cedar Creek: The Shenandoah Campaign of 1864.* Carlisle, Pa.: South Mountain Press, 1987.

Wiatt, Alex L. *26th Virginia Infantry.* Lynchburg, Va.: H.E. Howard, Inc., 1984.

Williams, T. Hary. *P.G.T. Beauregard: Napoleon in Gray.* Baton Rouge: Louisiana State University Press, 1954.

Wise, Jennings C. *The Military History of the Virginia Military Institute from 1839-1865.* Lynchburg, Va.: 1915.

Wise, John S. *The End of an Era.* Boston, 1899.

Woods, Edgar. *History of Albemarle.* Charlottesville, Va., 1900.

Yancey, Rosa Faulkner. *Lynchburg and Its Neighbors.* Richmond: J.W. Ferguson & Sons, 1935.

A close-up of Maj. Gen. Robert E. Rodes' sword, showing the "proof" stamp.

Mary Rodes Dell, and the Rodes Family

Index